ECONOMICS FOR BUSINESS AND MANAGEMENT

ECONOMICS
FOR
BUSINESS
AND
MANAGEMENT

K. Alec Chrystal and Richard G. Lipsey

Oxford University Press

Oxford University Press, Great Clarendon Street, Oxford OX2 6DP

Oxford New York

Athens Auckland Bangkok Bogotá Buenos Aires Calcutta
Cape Town Chennai Dar es Salaam Delhi Florence Hong Kong Istanbul
Karachi Kuala Lumpur Madrid Melbourne Mexico City Mumbai
Nairobi Paris São Paulo Singapore Taipei Tokyo Toronto Warsaw

and associated companies in
Berlin Ibadan

Oxford is a registered trade mark of Oxford University Press

Published in the United States by
Oxford University Press Inc., New York

British Library Cataloguing in Publication Data
Data available

Library of Congress Cataloging in Publication Data
Data available

ISBN 0-19-877539-3
ISBN 0-19-877538-5 (pbk)

7 9 10 8 6

Printed in Great Britain
on acid-free paper by
The Bath Press, Bath

To Alison

CONTENTS

Preface   xi

PART I. FIRMS AND MARKETS   1

1. Introduction to economics and business   3

Economics and the analysis of business issues   4
The problem of resource allocation   17
Performance of the UK economy   29

Section 1. Markets and Prices   43

2. Demand, supply, and price   45

Demand   46
Supply   60
The determination of market price   65
Demand and supply in action   72

3. Elasticity of demand and supply   84

Demand elasticity   86
Elasticity of supply   101
Measurement of demand and supply   104

Section 2. Optimization of the Firm   117

4. The firm, production, and profit   119

The firm in practice   120
The firm in economic theory   127
Production, costs, and profit   130

5. Costs and output   142

The relationship between output and inputs   143
The short run   146
The long run   158
The very long run: endogenous technical change   173

Contents

6. Profit maximization ... 180

Market structure and firm behaviour ... 181
Profit maximization ... 184
The firm in perfectly competitive markets ... 189
Short-run optimization for the firm ... 193
Long-run optimization for the firm ... 198
The very long run ... 204

Section 3. Firms and Competition ... 211

7. Firms in imperfect markets I: monopoly and monopolistic competition ... 213

A pure monopolist ... 214
Market segmentation: a multi-price monopolist ... 227
Monopolistic competition ... 234

8. Firms in imperfect markets II: oligopoly and business strategy ... 242

Key features of imperfectly competitive markets ... 243
Oligopoly: imperfect competition among the few ... 247
Oligopoly in action: two case studies ... 267

9. Government and the market ... 278

Economic efficiency ... 279
The case for government involvement in markets ... 288
Public policy towards monopoly and competition ... 296

Section 4. Economics of Business ... 311

10. The economics of employment ... 313

The demand for a homogeneous input ... 314
Contracts and performance monitoring ... 324
Internal labour markets ... 335

11. The economics of investment ... 345

Capital and the firm ... 346
Investment appraisal ... 352

12. The economics of business organizations ... 377

Firms as organizations ... 378
Business integration ... 388
The market for corporate control ... 399
Firms and markets ... 404

PART II. THE ECONOMY AS A WHOLE   407

Section 5. National Product and National Income   409

13. Macroeconomic issues and measurement   411

What is macroeconomics?   412
Why macroeconomics?   413
Value added as output   419
GDP, GNP, and national income   421
Interpreting national income and output measures   435

14. A basic model of the determination of GDP   446

Potential GDP and the GDP gap   447
Key assumptions   450
What determines aggregate expenditure?   454
Equilibrium GDP   468
Changes in GDP   473

15. GDP in an open economy with government   484

Government spending and taxes   485
Net exports   488
Equilibrium GDP   492
Changes in aggregate expenditure   499

16. Aggregate demand and aggregate supply   509

Aggregate demand   510
Aggregate supply   520
Changes in GDP and the price level   527

Section 6. Macroeconomic Policy   541

17. GDP, the price level, and fiscal policy   543

Induced changes in input prices   544
The long-run consequences of aggregate demand shocks   549
Real GDP in the short and long runs   557
Fiscal policy and the business cycle   562

18. Money and monetary policy   575

Supply of money and the demand for money   579
Monetary forces and GDP   588
Aggregate demand, the price level, and GDP   602

Contents

Appendix. Schools of thought in macroeconomics   613

19. The balance of payments and exchange rates   619

The balance of payments   620
The market for foreign exchange   627
The determination of exchange rates   632
The exchange rate regime and macroeconomic policy   648

20. Government policy and the business cycle   659

Characteristics of business cycles   660
Theories of the cycle   664
Controversies about the cause of cycles and the role of government   670
Macroeconomics: the unfulfilled promise   681

Glossary   686

Index   706

PREFACE

Economics for Business and Management is designed to meet the needs of students who have to study some economics as part of their business course. It is a book about economics that focuses on those principles and analytic tools developed by economists that are important for an understanding of the business world.

Until recently most business studies students have had to use the same introductory texts as students who wished to go on to be professional economists. These books were written with the latter in mind and so contained much material that was inappropriate or too abstract. This book is an introduction to the key parts of economics that business people need to understand, and wherever possible it uses business examples to illustrate the ideas.

While this is a new book, some of the material in it has been tried and tested as part of our book *An Introduction to Positive Economics* (Oxford University Press, 1995). We believe that this will prove to be a strength of the book, since we have had considerable feedback from teachers and students in the past that has helped us to continue improving the exposition. New material and new emphases have been added to virtually all chapters, but only Chapters 10–12 are entirely new.

Another advantage of this book is that it is shorter than most of the other major introductory economics texts. Our intention is to make it suitable for single-term or single-semester courses. Although such courses will not use the whole book, they may use just the micro (Chapters 2–12) or just the macro (Chapters 13–20) sections. Only a two-term course would be likely to cover all the chapters. We offer some suggested course structures below.

So what's the big idea?

We now set out some of the most important ideas that can be understood by studying economics and that are relevant to those heading for a career in business. Some people may think that, once they have read this list, there is no need to read the rest of the book. This is not so. It is easy to state the messages of economics in simple sentences, but understanding the full implications of economic analysis takes considerably more work. It is a good idea to return to this list at the end of the course to make sure that the lessons have been learned. There are many other important things to learn in this book that are not in this list. Here we emphasize some general ideas from economics that have virtually universal application in business.

Key messages from economics to business

We list these topics in roughly the order in which they are discussed in the book, rather than in any rank order of importance.

RESOURCE CONSTRAINTS AND TRADE-OFFS

Resources are limited and choices have to be made that involve giving up some of one thing in order to have more of another. This is true in different ways for individuals, for firms, and for whole economies. Individuals have a limited income and have to decide to have, for example, either a new car or a holiday. Firms have limited capital and employees and have to decide whether, say, to invest in new computerized equipment or to refurbish their existing hand-controlled machinery, whether to hire more drivers or more accountants, or whether to concentrate on producing more black-and-white or more colour printers. Nations have similar choices, such as whether they should devote more resources to health services or to defence.

COMPARATIVE ADVANTAGE

Scarce resources are most effectively employed when they are allocated to uses in which they are comparatively (relatively) most productive. Accordingly, individuals, firms, and nations are best off concentrating on the production of goods or service in which they have a comparative advantage and then trading with others who have different comparative advantages. This is one of the most important ideas in economics, and although it is simple it is widely misunderstood. One example from business is that it would be a mistake for a manufacturer to try to make all the components of a complex product when some of them could be bought more cheaply from other firms. Rather, the most profitable strategy is to concentrate on doing the parts of the process the firm does relatively more effectively for itself and to buy in those components or services that can be made or done relatively more efficiently by others.

DEMAND AND SUPPLY

Most markets can be understood with the use of the same analytic apparatus of demand and supply. It is pretty obvious that businesses need to understand both their input and output markets. Demand and supply tools are essential in this task. However, the need to understand markets goes much further. Most people in business get to be very good at understanding the market for their own product, but they are less good at understanding other important markets that will affect them from time to time. The capital markets are important for firms that want to raise funds. The money markets affect what interest rate will be charged by the bank, and the foreign exchange markets determine how competitive a product is in foreign markets as well as how expensive the goods of foreign producers are. Economic analysis of demand and supply is a helpful tool for understanding these markets.

INCREMENTAL DECISIONS

Firms face myriad decisions about whether to produce more or less, to hire more or fewer workers, or to buy new machines or not. The economic analysis of firms provides a simple decision rule that managers and entrepreneurs will find useful. This is that any action that adds more to revenue than it adds to cost should be undertaken, while actions that add more to costs than to revenues should not. In the economic theory of the firm this rule is heavily disguised by the assumption that all firms are profit maximizing and thus will be at a point where marginal (incremental) cost is equal to marginal (incremental) revenue. In practice most firms are seeking to take profit-increasing actions, and in this context the incremental decision rule applies.

MARKET STRUCTURE MATTERS

The range of decisions that firms make and the degree of discretion over those decisions varies considerably with the nature of the product involved and the structure of the market in which firms sell. Understanding this market environment is one of the key tasks faced by senior management. In some cases it is technological innovations that give market advantage, in others it may be competitive pricing or brand identity. Economics is not the only tool needed to understand these issues, but economics gives important insights into them.

ASYMMETRIC INFORMATION

In some markets there is uncertainty about the quality of the product or the future behaviour of one of the contracting parties. In labour markets, that fact that potential employees know more about themselves than employers do leads to many subtle issues. Devices to signal quality are often used, and employers have to worry about monitoring and enforcement of contractual obligations. The general problem involved is said to be one of asymmetric information, and recent studies of this problem by economists have led to substantial advances in our understanding of how best to deal with such problems.

PRESENT VALUE

One problem that frequently occurs in business involves choosing between different time paths of cash flow. Should we invest for the long term, or should we distribute as much of today's profit as possible to the shareholders? No one can tell the owner of a business what he or she *must* do. But economic analysis is helpful in showing how to make these intertemporal allocation decisions given simple goals, such as the goal of maximizing the value of the firm. The appraisal of investment decisions can be made manageable by converting cash flows at different times into present value. Where the various choices open to the firm are mutually exclusive, owners or managers can choose the option that maximizes the present value of the firm (otherwise maximizing the value of the firm involves undertaking any option that increases the firm's present value). Again the key idea here is very simple, but applying it in practice requires much greater understanding and experience.

SUNK COSTS

A common mistake is to be influenced by past investment decisions that didn't work: 'We must spend more on our Newtown factory because we have already spent so much on it, and it has to made to work!' Economics makes it clear that such reasoning is always wrong. Bygones are bygones. Future expenditures should be directed to their most productive uses, not to trying to salvage past errors—unless, of course, this offers the highest return available at the margin. Costs that have been incurred in the past but are irreversible are known as sunk costs. The simple rule is that, after they have been incurred, sunk costs should not influence future decisions. However, before such costs have been incurred a value should be assigned to them. This is equivalent to valuing an option. This option to invest should only be exercised (that is, the investment made and the costs sunk) if the value to the firm from proceeding exceeds the value of a wait-and-see strategy.

ORGANIZATIONS MATTER

The traditional economic theory of the firm ignored internal organization. However, much work has been done by economists over the last few decades, especially in US business schools, that has increased our understanding of the importance of internal organization for efficiency. This work also throws light on the issue of why firms exist at all. Some of the theorizing in this area may appear abstract at first sight. However, it is a short step from asking questions such as 'Why do firms exist?' to asking questions such as 'What makes a successful as opposed to an unsuccessful firm?' and 'How can we re-organize this firm to make it perform better?'

BUSINESS CYCLES

All businesses are affected in some way by the general cycles in the economy. Such cycles have been well documented since biblical times, and they are unlikely to disappear any time soon. Understanding the patterns and causes of business cycles is of vital importance to all those who wish to work in industry, commerce, or finance. Hence, an essential input into the training for any business career is an understanding of the economic forces that lead to booms and recessions. It is true that forecasts made by professional economists can be read in the press or bought for a modest sum. However, these forecasts have little informational content beyond about six months ahead, and most businesses need to take a much longer-term view than this. So it would be very dangerous to neglect study of the economy at large. The key message from macroeconomics is that most industrial economies display some positive growth of output and incomes over time (in real terms) but that there is considerable volatility about the long-term trend. Governments have limited power to influence these variations, and there can be little optimism that cycles can ever be eliminated by any single government acting alone, or even in concert with others. Business people need to learn to survive recurrent downturns and to profit from booms.

Course structures

There are several different course structures that could profitably utilize this book. We suggest some of the possibilities below.

- A traditional one-year introduction to economics covering micro and macro:
  Chapters 1–9 and 13–20
- A one-term or one-semester introduction to business economics (micro):
  Chapters 1–12
- A one-term or one-semester introduction to the basics of both micro and macro:
  Chapters 1–8 and 13–17
- A one-term MBA course covering micro and macro:
  Chapters 1–20, with emphasis on Chapters 9–12 and 20
- A one-term course in macroeconomics:
  Chapters 13–20

Please let us know what you think about the book, if you come across errors, have suggestions for improvement, or find some passages unclear. We take such feedback very seriously. This book is our product, and we want to know as much about what you the customers want as possible. We hope for many successful future editions, and your responses are vital in helping us develop this book to fit the needs of as many students and teachers as possible.

Acknowledgements

This book owes a great deal to all those who have contributed over the years to the development of *Positive Economics*. They are too numerous to mention, but both authors remain grateful to all their former colleagues and students who have influenced their evolution as teachers and writers. The current book evolved from discussions between the authors and Tracy Mawson of Oxford University Press. Tracy left OUP just as the final stages of production were under way. Without her, the project would probably never have started. Brendan Lambon also played an important part in bringing the book to fruition, and Andrew Schuller had a central role to play in bringing the 'Lipsey' label to OUP in the first place.

The 1995/6 and 1996/7 MBA classes at City University Business School have acted as guinea-pigs for some of the new material in this book, especially Chapters 10–12. Students on the City University Masters in Health Management have worked through some of the exercises as well as Chapter 11. Several colleagues have commented on earlier drafts of chapters. Two who have had a measurable impact on the content of the book are Charles Baden-Fuller, who alerted us to a new line of literature on the reasons for the existence of firms, and Simon Price, who clarified for us the role of option pricing in the evaluation of irreversible investments. Finally, Debra Durston provided valuable secretarial assistance.

All errors and omissions remain the joint responsibility of the authors.

KAC and RGL

London and Vancouver
April 1997

PART I
FIRMS AND MARKETS

CHAPTER 1

Introduction to Economics and Business

Economics and the analysis of business issues	4	Economics: a working definition	28
Key issues for business	5	**Performance of the UK economy**	29
Markets and prices	5	Living standards	29
The economics of the firm	9	Jobs	29
Concentration and market power	10	Labour productivity	31
Perfect competition	10	Changing technology	34
Monopoly	11	Job structure	34
Imperfect competition	11	Services in manufacturing	34
The economics of organizations	12	Services for final consumption	36
Economics of employment	12	New products	36
Economics of investment	13	Globalization	36
The structure of organizations	13	Conclusion	39
The market for corporate control	14		
Business cycles	15	**Summary**	39
The problem of resource allocation	17	**Topics for review**	40
Resources and scarcity	17		
Kinds of resources	17	**Questions for discussion**	41
Kinds of production	20		
Scarcity	20	**Box 1.1.** The failure of central planning	7
Choice and opportunity cost	21	**Box 1.2.** Company failures and the business cycle	18
Specialization and the principle of comparative advantage	22	**Box 1.3.** The principle of comparative advantage	23
The production-possibility boundary	25		

WHAT has economics got to do with business? Why do students heading for a business career need to study economics? The answer is that economics addresses many questions that help us to understand the environment in which all businesses operate. Economics contains a body of knowledge about how the economy works, and economists are perpetually testing and extending that knowledge. Business leaders are continually asking themselves questions like 'Will the economy pick up next year?', 'What will happen if a new producer enters my market?', 'Will the

Deutschmark appreciate against the dollar?', 'Is the Federal Reserve going to raise interest rates soon, and will European central banks follow suit?', 'How will the North American Free Trade Association affect my exports to Canada and Mexico?', and 'How will the introduction of a European single currency affect the economies of member countries, and of those who stay outside?' These are all questions that an understanding of economics helps to answer. After all, the world of business is the most important part of the economy.

Economics is not the only the subject that is needed in business. Many other subjects—such as accounting, statistics, law, psychology, computer science, languages, not to mention management science—are important. However, economics has to be one of the core subjects relevant to business because economics studies key aspects of the behaviour of business itself, as well as of the environment in which businesses operate.

Being good at economics is neither necessary nor sufficient for being successful in business, but then no course of training provides guarantees of success in later life. However, a good grounding in economics will provide a capacity to analyse business situations with a depth of understanding that is hard to achieve in other ways. Many of the leading thinkers and writers in the business studies field have had a training in economics.

In this chapter, we first review many of the areas in which business studies and economics overlap and outline the approach of economics to these issues. Then we give a broader perspective on what economics is all about before summarizing some important characteristics of the UK economy.

Economics and the analysis of business issues

In this section we outline some of the key topics that are of interest to both economists and those in business. These will be covered in greater depth later in the book. Indeed, the topic areas outlined are essentially a plan of the topics to be discussed in successive chapters. However, before we proceed it is important to note that economics and business studies as academic subjects have fundamentally different goals and, to some extent, different methods.

Economics is a social science that tries to explain the behaviour of the economy by building hypotheses or theories. Specific versions of these theories are sometimes referred to as **economic models.** These models are simplifications of the real world that are potentially useful in illustrating some key feature of how the world works. Theories are tested by their internal consistency, by their conformity with established principles, and against available data. The latter is the ultimate test of how useful economics is to non-economists—does it help explain or predict things that are going on in the real world?

Business studies as a subject has the goal of identifying the knowledge that will help people to make a success of a career in business, either by offering skills that businesses will value or (equivalently) by managing a business successfully. The ultimate test is whether the skills acquired lead to a successful role in running specific businesses. The value of economics to a business person is in providing tools for analysing what may happen in real-world situations and in giving clear indications of what factors need to be considered when developing a scenario of how some business environment may evolve.

> Economics is a social science that builds theories of how the economy works and tests these theories against data. Economics is useful to students of business studies because it incorporates accumulated knowledge of how the economy works, and this is helpful when trying to analyse what is likely to happen in any future business situation.

Key issues for business

Economics as a subject can be divided broadly into two general topic areas—microeconomics and macroeconomics. **Microeconomics** focuses on explaining the behaviour of individual firms, consumers, or product markets. It is concerned with looking at a small part of the economy. It is, for example, a microeconomic question to ask 'Why did the price of coffee go up after there was a frost in Brazil?' or 'Why did the demand for large cars go down after the price of oil went up in the 1970s?'

Macroeconomics, in contrast, looks at the output of the economy as a whole and is concerned with aggregate questions relating to inflation, unemployment, the balance of payments, and business cycles. 'Why did the UK economy (and many other economies in the world) go into recession in 1990–2?' is a macroeconomic question, as is the question 'Should the government increase its spending in order to reduce unemployment?'

Microeconomics is covered in Part I of this book, and macroeconomics is the subject of Part II. We now look at some of the topics to be covered in these two areas in more detail.

MARKETS AND PRICES

Products are bought and sold in **markets.** All markets have two sides to them. Suppliers start off with (or make) the product and offer it for sale in the market. Demanders want to acquire the product and potentially offer to buy it through the market. Hence, each market has a supply side and a demand side. The market is simply the area over which suppliers and demanders interact in order to determine the prices and quantities of the product exchanges that take place.

Some markets have a specific location where buyers and sellers face each other on a trading floor; in other markets traders are connected by telephone around the world; yet others work via showrooms and retail stores, so that producer and consumer are connected only indirectly. There are many different types of market, but they all involve suppliers and demanders ultimately exchanging a product for money. The product does not have to be a physical product, such as a bicycle or a television. It could be a service, such as a haircut or dentistry.

In markets for manufactured consumer goods, firms are the producers of these goods, and so they are the suppliers. Individuals and families (households) are the potential buyers, and so they are the demanders. However, in the job (labour or employment) market, firms are the demanders and individuals are the suppliers. In some markets, such as for machine tools, firms are both the suppliers and demanders.

All firms operate in markets, hence they need to know as much as possible about both their input and their output markets: Could we buy our inputs cheaper by buying from X, and how much more output could we sell if we lowered our price by 10 per cent? In many respects, business studies goes much further in studying markets than does economics. Business strategy involves deciding what product markets a firm should be in and whether to develop new products, but elementary economics tends to assume a given product structure and asks how to do best with what you have got.

Economics has traditionally looked at an economy made up of many interacting markets, the market economy, as only one possible way of organizing the process that takes the economy's natural resources and turns them into the products that people want to consume. One alternative is a centrally planned economy, in which the government directs what gets produced, where and when. Such a centrally planned economy is called a **command economy** because it works by someone at the centre ordering what shall be produced and by whom and is associated with political ideologies, such as communism and socialism. Until recently there were many command economies, such as those of the Soviet Union and Eastern Europe. Some of the reasons why that economic system failed are discussed in Box 1.1.

Even in market economies it is still necessary to ask whether it is desirable to leave uncontrolled market forces to determine how much gets produced and at what price. There are many reasons why markets will not always achieve a socially optimal outcome, and these reasons are used to justify government intervention of various kinds. Students who study economics further will look at these cases of **market failure** in some depth. In this book, we discuss several aspects of government intervention in the market economy in Chapter 9. However, our primary concern is with understanding markets from the perspective of businesses that have to operate in specific markets.

Although a market economy is an alternative to a command economy at the aggregate level, it is important to be aware that a firm is a command economy in so far as its internal organization is concerned. The senior management of firms decide what to produce and whom to hire and fire. They are, in effect, the central planners of the firm. They have power over what goes on within the firm, but they are not as powerful as, say, the Politburo in the old Soviet Union. Managers can be voted out by shareholders, and they can be fired if the firm is taken over. They may also lose their jobs if the firm goes

BOX 1.1.

The failure of central planning

The year 1989 signalled to the world what many economists had long argued: the superiority of a market-oriented price system over central planning as a method of organizing economic activity. The failure of central planning had many causes, but four were particularly significant.

The failure of co-ordination

In centrally planned economies a body of planners tries to co-ordinate all the economic decisions about production, investment, trade, and consumption that are likely to be made by the producers and consumers throughout the country. This proved impossible to do with any reasonable degree of efficiency. Bottlenecks in production, shortages of some goods, and gluts of others plagued the Soviet economy for decades. For example, in 1989 much of a bumper harvest rotted on the farm because of shortages of storage and transportation facilities, and for years there was an ample supply of black-and-white television sets and severe shortages of toilet paper and soap.

Friedrich von Hayek (1899–1992), a persistent critic of central planning, suggested a battle analogy to compare markets to central planning. In one army soldiers can only move exactly in the direction and by the amount they are ordered by some general operating at the centre; in the other army, soldiers are given the general objectives and told to respond as fits the situation as it develops. It is clear who will win the battle.

Failure of quality control

Central planners can monitor the number of units produced by any factory and reward those who over-fulfil their production targets and punish those who fall short. It is much harder, however, for them to monitor quality. A constant Soviet problem, therefore, was the production of poor-quality products. Factory managers were concerned with meeting their quotas by whatever means were available, and once the goods passed out of their factory, what happened to them was someone else's headache. The quality problem was so serious that very few Eastern European-manufactured products were able to stand up to the newly permitted competition from superior goods produced in the advanced market societies.

In market economies, poor quality is punished by low sales, and retailers soon give a signal to factory managers by shifting their purchases to other suppliers. The incentives that obviously flow from such private-sector purchasing discretion are generally absent from command economies, where purchases and sales are planned centrally.

Misplaced incentives

In market economies, relative wages and salaries provide incentives for labour to move from place to place, and the possibility of losing one's job provides an incentive to work

7

BOX 1.1. (*cont.*)

diligently. This is a harsh mechanism that punishes losers with loss of income (although social programmes provide floors to the amount of economic punishment that can be suffered). In planned economies, workers usually have complete job security. Industrial unemployment is rare, and even when it does occur, new jobs are usually found for those who lose theirs. Although the high level of security is attractive to many, it proved impossible to provide sufficient incentives for reasonably hard and efficient work under such conditions. In the words of Oxford historian Timothy Garton Ash, who wrote eyewitness chronicles of the developments in Eastern Europe from 1980 to 1990, the social contract between the workers and the government in the Eastern countries was 'We pretend to work, and you pretend to pay us'.

Because of the absence of a work-oriented incentive system, income inequalities do not provide the normal free-market incentives. Income inequalities were used instead to provide incentives for party members to toe the line. The major gap in income standards was between party members on the one hand and non-party members on the other. The former had access to such privileges as special stores where imported goods were available, special hospitals providing sanitary and efficient medical care, and special resorts where good vacations were available. In contrast, non-members had none of these things.

Environmental degradation

Fulfilling production plans became the all-embracing incentive in planned economies, to the exclusion of most other considerations, including the environment. As a result, environmental degradation occurred in all the countries of Eastern Europe on a scale unknown in advanced Western nations. A particularly disturbing example occurred in central Asia, where high quotas for cotton output led to indiscriminate use of pesticides and irrigation. Birth defects are now found in nearly one child in three, and the vast Aral Sea was half drained, causing incalculable environmental effects.

The failure to protect the environment stemmed from a combination of the pressure to fulfil plans and the lack of a political marketplace. The democratic process allows citizens to express views on the use of scarce resources for environmental protection. Imperfect though the system may be in democratic market economies, their record of environmental protection has been vastly better than that of command economies.

The price system

In contrast to the failures of command economies, the performance of the free-market price system is impressive. One theme of economics is *market success*: how the price system works to co-ordinate with relative efficiency the decentralized decisions made by private consumers and producers, providing the right quantities of relatively high-quality outputs and incentives for efficient work. It is important, however, not to conclude that doing things better means doing things perfectly. Another theme of economics is *market failure*: how and why the unaided price system sometimes fails to produce efficient results and fails to take account of social values that cannot be expressed through the marketplace.

bust. Hence, although managers run a small command economy, they are also disciplined by many incentives, not least of which are external market forces. One of the problems of the old Soviet system was that there was no reliable mechanism for removing incompetent managers.

A key question for managers of firms to be asking all the time is: should we be doing activity X within the firm, or should we buy it in via the market from another firm? Hence, in one sense, activity conducted within a firm is an alternative to a transaction in the market. Thus, while firms operate in markets, they also internalize some transactions, and one of the key economic issues is what transactions should be internal to the firm and what should be left to the market.

In studying how markets work, we focus primarily on the determination of the price and quantity sold of specific products. The theory of the firm will be used to highlight the supply decisions of firms, and consumer demand theory will be used to generate predictions about how demand will change in response to changes in key economic variables, such as the price of the product and the incomes of consumers.

A market is the forum in which suppliers and demanders of any product interact. This interaction determines what gets produced and consumed via the signal of the market price. All successful businesses must have a high level of understanding of the markets in which they operate.

THE ECONOMICS OF THE FIRM

One of the key decision-making units studied in economics is the **firm.** The firm is a business organization that hires workers, buys inputs, and produces some product that it then sells in the market. There are several alternative legal and financial structures available to firms, but, for now, the important point to notice about the firm is that we treat it as an entity in itself that is conceptually separate from its owners and workers. There are other words available that normally mean the same thing as 'firm', such as 'business', 'company', 'corporation', etc. However, we shall use the word 'firm' to refer to all possible categories of such business organization. Other words will be used only when we are referring to specific types of firm.

In economics, *the elementary theory of the firm* refers to a particular conceptual experiment in which we ask questions about a single-product firm.[1] This product is generally assumed to be a manufactured product, but the principles involved can be applied to any firm. In order to manufacture its product a firm typically needs plant and equipment; it hires workers and buys components and raw materials. Plant and machinery (that is, land, factory buildings, machines, tools, and, perhaps, vehicles) is often referred to as **capital** or capital goods. It is important to notice that there are two

---

[1] Economics is well able to deal with multi-product firms. Indeed, these form an important topic in the branch of economics known as Industrial Organization. We discuss the question of which products should be produced within a single firm in Ch. 12.

uses of the word 'capital'. In the theory of the firm it will generally be used to refer to physical capital, such as the plant and equipment just mentioned. However, it can also refer to financial capital, which is the financial resources behind the firm, part of which is invested by the firm's owners. Clearly some of the financial capital is used to buy physical capital, but the two concepts should never be regarded as being the same. The term **working capital,** for example, is often used to refer to financial resources of a firm that are kept in liquid form, such as bank deposits, rather than being invested in physical capital.

In the theory of the firm, we consider how the underlying technology of production, combined with input prices, influences the variation of unit costs as the level of output is changed. We also consider how market conditions influence the demand for the firm's product at various prices. Given the cost structure and the market demand we can then determine what level of output will maximize the firm's profit.

One way to think of the theory of the firm is as a particular form of optimization problem. The mathematics of optimization is about finding the best way of achieving some objective, subject to the constraints that apply on the problem. The optimization problem faced by the firm is to maximize profit given the cost structure of its production process and the market demand for its output. The precise nature of this optimization problem will change as we consider more complicated situations, but it will always be true that the problem faced by the managers of firms is to do the best they can (by some criterion, such as profit maximization) while being constrained both by available resources (capital, technology, the workforce) and by the size of the market for the product. Indeed, later on we shall extend the problem to include wider choices, such as the product range and the organizational structure, but all these choices can still be viewed as optimization problems.

> Firms are decision-making units that hire workers and use capital and raw materials in order to make products for sale. The behaviour of firms is one of the most important topics that economics and business studies have in common.

CONCENTRATION AND MARKET POWER

The choices available to firms in their output markets (and to some extent in the markets for their inputs) are critically influenced by the nature of the competition in those markets. The severity of competition depends upon both the available range of similar, or perhaps superior, products and the number of competing firms. The economic theory of the firm distinguishes three distinct market structures, each with different implications for the choices available to firms.

Perfect competition
Under **perfect competition,** each firm is assumed to produce an identical product to all other firms and to be sufficiently small that it cannot influence the market price. In such

an environment the key question for each firm is simply how much to produce. Each firm can sell as much as it wants at the going market price without having any significant influence over that price. An example is the world wheat market. A single wheat farmer in East Anglia sells wheat at the world market price (ignoring any government intervention policies) and is unable to produce enough to influence that world price. This is not to say that the world price does not change, merely that it cannot be changed by the choices of any one individual producer acting alone.

Monopoly

In extreme contrast to perfect competition is **monopoly.** This is a situation where there is only one producer of a product, and, hence, the single producer faces no competition from other producers. A monopolist will have power to set not just output but also the price of the product. Most firms would like to be monopolists, since any profits being made would not be threatened by other suppliers taking market share. Indeed, most of us as individuals would like to have valuable skills that no one else has so that we could charge a very high price for our services.

Monopoly may be good for the firm involved, but it will generally be bad for consumers, because the monopolist will tend to charge high prices (relative to a competitive industry). This is why most countries have regulations to prohibit monopolies or, where monopoly is unavoidable, regulatory agencies (or perhaps direct government controls) to stop the monopolist setting prices too high. Regulation of monopoly is discussed in Chapter 9.

For a monopoly to survive there have to be some barriers to entry. These can arise if the most efficient scale of production is large relative to the size of the market. So, for example, one firm can sometimes supply the whole market at lower cost than could two or more smaller firms. Entry barriers also arise from patent protection of new inventions. Glaxo, a UK pharmaceuticals company, made billions of pounds from its anti-ulcer drug Zantac in the 1980s and 1990s. Soon after Zantac was first manufactured, rival producers could have sold an identical drug at a fraction of the price. However, they were prevented from doing so by the patent protection afforded to Zantac until 1997.

Imperfect competition

Between the two extremes of perfect competition and monopoly there is a range of different cases known collectively as **imperfect competition.** This is the commonest characterisation of real markets. Imperfectly competitive markets often involve products that are similar but not identical and for which there are a finite number of potential producers, each of which can influence the others by its own behaviour.

There are many sub-cases of imperfect competition. The most common such cases studied in economics are **oligopoly** and **monopolistic competition.** Oligopoly arises where the market is dominated by a small group of competing firms. Here each firm is greatly affected by what its close rivals do in terms of product prices and innovations. Supermarkets in the UK are an oligopoly, with three firms (Sainsbury, Tesco, and

Safeway) dominating the market. Similarly, the UK retail banking market is dominated by NatWest, Barclays, Midland, and Lloyds. It is in oligopolistic markets that business strategy is most important, because success is based not just on having a good product but also on subtle issues of positioning relative to rivals, which are themselves trying to get the upper hand.

'Monopolistic competition' is a term reserved for a market environment in which there are enough potential suppliers that one firm does not have to worry about the reaction of any other single firm, and yet the product of each firm is differentiated from all others in some way, so that each firm can influence its own price. The restaurant market in London, for example, has many suppliers, each having a very small share of the total market, but each having a distinct characteristic and some degree of discretion over prices charged. This contrasts with perfect competition, since in a perfectly competitive market suppliers have no option but to accept the going market price, because their product is exactly the same as those of other suppliers.

We shall discuss these cases in much greater detail in Chapters 7 and 8 of this book.

Firms operate in many different market structures, but the most common structure is imperfect competition, in which there are a finite number of competing suppliers, each selling differentiated products. So most firms have to make decisions about how much to produce and at what price to sell, and they have to worry to varying degrees about what the competition is doing.

THE ECONOMICS OF ORGANIZATIONS

The traditional theory of the firm assumes a very simple structure to the optimization problem that managers of a firm have to solve. This is not because economics cannot deal with more complex problems, but merely because economics has evolved by solving the simple problems first. As a famous First World War General once said, 'What is possible we shall do at once, the impossible will take a little longer.'

Modern firms are typically more complex than the simple unitary firms that we first study. However, the same economic principles apply to more complex firms as apply to our simple conceptual single-product firm. All firms operate in markets; indeed, to operate successfully in many markets simultaneously is far more challenging than to make a success of operating in only one. Also, all firms face the general optimization problem of trying to maximize profit subject to the resources available. The issue is how to direct resources to the activities that offer the greatest rate of return. We shall discuss the economics of more complex firms under the following three headings.

Economics of employment
In the simple theory of the firm, decisions about hiring are straightforward, because workers are assumed to be identical in all respects. The real world of employment is much more complex than this, because individual workers are extremely hetero-

geneous. These differences between workers make the labour market one of the most fascinating areas of modern economics. Not only does each worker differ in terms of personality, education, skills, etc., but even those with similar characteristics may behave differently in different circumstances. Firms face a problem of uncertainty when hiring workers, because they do not know what they are really like in advance. They also face a problem of monitoring their behaviour on the job and creating the right incentives for workers to perform well.

These issues have traditionally been regarded as a problem for personnel managers, or, in more modern terminology, human resource management. However, they have now become the subject of extensive analysis by economists, partly because the latter have been trying to understand observed real features of modern labour markets. Questions addressed by economists go well beyond the simple decision of how many people to hire, and include issues such as optimal reward structures for long-term employees and the incentive effects of paying high salaries to managing directors.

Economics of investment

One level of decision that firms make every day is how to get the best out of an existing stock of physical capital, that is, their existing factories and machinery. An even more difficult decision, made, perhaps, only periodically, is whether to expand the capital stock by building a new factory. The decision to add to the stock of physical capital is known as **investment.** Investment can be a very risky activity, because it involves incurring substantial costs today in order to get a greater stream of revenue in the future. The risk arises because the future revenue stream may not materialize as expected. The world can change, and sometimes very fast.

An important dimension of the investment decision is that it inevitably involves evaluating costs and revenues at different periods. How much revenue in the future would be enough to compensate for costs incurred today? The issues involved are similar to the decisions we all face when we receive some income. Should I spend it now, or should I save it for the future? This is a question of inter-temporal allocation of resources—present consumption versus consumption in the future.

Investment decisions would be moderately easy to take if we knew how much we are giving up today in return for an exactly known sum in the future. In reality, the future is uncertain, so all investment decisions involve some risk. We may have some best guess about the future revenue from the investment, but when the time comes it may be much higher or much lower. This uncertainty has to be taken into account in some way in making investment decisions.

The structure of organizations

The traditional theory of the firm, as studied by economists, concentrated on a single-product firm. It is now clear that virtually all real firms have multiple products. The decision about what that product range should include can be analysed using the tools of economics just as can the decision of how much to produce of a single product.

Once a company produces more than one product, questions of organizational structure inevitably have to be addressed. For example, suppose a company produces three different manufactured products. Should each product be made within a more or less autonomous subsidiary firm, or should all three be made within a single manufacturing division? Should there be a single marketing division for the whole firm, or should there be a separate marketing team for each product? These are economic issues, and they can be viewed as an extension of the general problem for the firm, which is how to maximize its profit subject to the constraints of resources and market demand.

Another question relating to the optimal structure of firms arises from the fact that many products involve inputs that are themselves the product of manufacture or extraction. Each firm has to decide which stages of the production process should be within the firm and which should be done by other firms. A car manufacturer, for example, makes cars out of a vast number of components—steel, tires, engines, electrical equipment, leather, etc. Which of these components, if any, should be made within the car firm and which should be bought in from other firms? This is a question about the level of **vertical integration.** Vertical integration arises when successive stages of a production process are conducted within a single firm.

A contrast is often drawn between vertical integration and **horizontal integration.** The latter arises when firms combine productive activities at the same stage of production. Horizontal integration would occur, for example, if one car manufacturer merged with another, such as when BMW took over the Rover Group; whereas vertical integration would occur if a car manufacture merged with a tyre company, or a car battery manufacturer.

The term **conglomerate integration** refers to combinations of firms that produce unrelated products. An example of a takeover that produced conglomerate integration was that of bread company Rank Hovis MacDougall by engineering company Tomkins. In the 1970s and 1980s, conglomerate integration was very fashionable. In the 1990s, several conglomerates have started to break themselves up. The UK chemicals giant ICI split into two companies, ICI and Zeneca, and Hanson split itself into five independent companies. The economic rationale for these structural changes will be discussed in Chapter 12.

Firms are trying to make the best use of available resources and this is an optimization problem familiar in economics. Issues of optimal employment, investment, and structure are all susceptible to economic analysis.

THE MARKET FOR CORPORATE CONTROL

In many countries, such as the UK and the USA, firms themselves are often bought and sold, through takeovers or mergers.[2] Hence, firms themselves can be thought of as

---

2 In other countries, such as Japan, takeovers are rare. The major countries of continental Europe lie between these extremes. One reason is that there is a complex structure of cross-ownership of shares in Japanese companies, so it is very difficult for potential bidders to buy a majority of the shareholding. Similar obstacles exist to

products that can be demanded and supplied in a market. Clearly, this is a different kind of market from, say, the market for potatoes or the market for toothpaste. None the less, there is an environment in which money is paid to the existing owners for an entire company. This is the market for corporate control.

There is a controversy about whether the threat of takeover is good or bad for the long-term health of firms and the economy. Some argue that the threat of takeover discourages managers from making appropriate long-term investment decisions. This phenomenon is often referred to as 'short-termism'. Others argue that the threat of takeover keeps managers on their toes and makes them perform better, hence improving efficiency.

Firms themselves can be bought and sold, and hence they are the 'product' that changes hands in the market for corporate control. This market can be analysed like any other by focusing on demand and supply. It also has important implications for incentives and the behaviour of managers.

BUSINESS CYCLES

The final general topic area that economics and business have a common interest in understanding relates to the cycles in the economy as a whole. Most economies, certainly those of the main industrial countries, tend to grow over time, in the sense that volume of real output is greater on average as time passes. However, these economies do not generally grow smoothly. Rather, they exhibit cycles about an upward trend. These cycles used to be called **trade cycles** in the UK, but we now use the term **business cycles.** The business cycle is simply the pattern of deviations from the trend level of national output growth.

Figure 1.1 shows the percentage growth rate of output (GDP) of the UK, USA, and Japan since 1965. This figure demonstrates that, although growth is generally positive, it fluctuates significantly from year to year. Periods in which there is a sustained drop in national output are known as **recessions,** while periods of sustained positive growth (especially above average) are known as **booms.**

Understanding the business cycle is vital for the success of all businesses. This is because one of the key characteristics of the business cycle is that demand for all products tends to rise in booms and fall in recessions. The demands for some products are much more cyclical than those for others. People always have to eat, so demand for food does not vary a great deal between booms and recessions. In contrast, if times are hard we do not have to eat out and we can put off buying a new car or a new stereo system, so demand for restaurant meals, particularly in the middle and high price range, and for consumer durable goods, tends to be highly cyclical.

the takeover of many German companies. Other obstacles to takeover arise from government ownership of large stakes in some companies, or from mutual ownership (such as with a savings institution or an insurance company) by members.

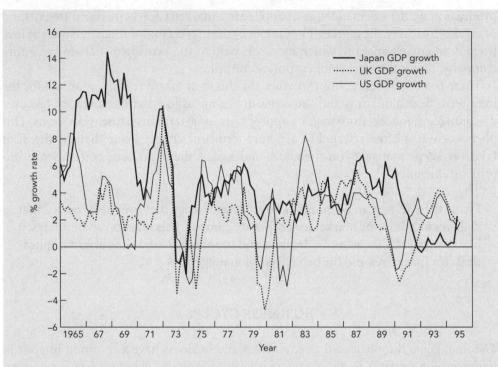

Figure 1.1. Growth rate of GDP of the USA, UK, and Japan, 1965–1995 (quarterly, year on year)

Output growth is generally positive, though it exhibits clear but irregular cycles. The growth rate of Japan was much higher than that of the USA and UK in the 1960s, but since the early 1970s it has been very similar. Not only do the cycles in these three different countries have similar patterns, but they also tend to happen at about the same time. All three had a boom in 1971–3, a recession in 1974–5, a recession in 1980–1, and recession in the early 1990s. All countries have business cycles, and many even have essentially *the same cycle*. This suggests that the business cycle is a worldwide, and not just local, phenomenon.

Source: Datastream.

Businesses worry about how a recession would affect demand for their product, and workers worry about whether they might lose their jobs. Box 1.2 illustrates why economic cycles are important for business from the perspective of company failures. Economists have long worried about whether anything can be done to ameliorate the effects of business cycles—especially to avoid the high unemployment and lost output associated with recessions.

Government policy changes can be used to try to stabilize the business cycle. **Fiscal policy** involves changing the level of taxation and/or government spending in order to affect changes in demand. **Monetary policy** involves using interest rate changes to influence demand. A government that wishes to stimulate demand, for example because the economy is in a recession, might lower taxes or increase its own spending. Alternatively, it might lower interest rates in order to stimulate private sector demand. The logic behind such macroeconomic policies, and the controversies surrounding them, will be discussed in Chapters 13–20 of this book.

All economies exhibit cycles about their trend rate of growth. Demand for most products falls in a recession and rises in a boom. Understanding the business cycle and its links with government policy is vital for anyone hoping to run a successful business.

We now turn to a discussion of the general problem faced by any economy. This is how to satisfy the wants of the residents of a country with the limited resources available.

The problem of resource allocation

Decisions taken by firms are part of a wider process that leads to an allocation of resources within the economy. This means that firms allocate capital, hire workers, and buy raw materials in order to produce certain products. These are the products available to satisfy consumers' wants. Hence, firms are involved in allocating some scarce resources (capital, labour, materials) so that they cannot also be used in any other activity simultaneously. In the previous section we said that the problem faced by firms could be viewed as an optimization problem. The entire economy can also be viewed as an optimization problem. The workings of the economy may not produce what we all consider to be the very best answer to this problem, but they do produce some answer. Indeed, the general problem of economics derives from the fact that all wants cannot possibly be satisfied, and hence some choices have to be made about which wants should be satisfied. It is to this wider resource allocation problem that we now turn our attention.

Resources and scarcity

Kinds of resources
The resources of a society consist not only of the free gifts of nature, such as land, forests, and minerals, but also of human capacity, both mental and physical, and of all sorts of man-made aids to further production, such as tools, machinery, computers, and buildings. It is sometimes useful to divide these resources into three main groups: (1) all those gifts of nature commonly called 'natural resources' and known to economists as land; (2) all human resources, mental and physical, both inherited and acquired, which economists call labour; and (3) all those man-made aids to further production,

BOX 1.2.

Company failures and the business cycle

Cycles in the economy have a significant impact on most businesses. The demand for many products rises in a boom and falls in a recession—only insolvency experts do well in recessions and poorly in booms. These cycles in demand will typically also be reflected in changes in profit, especially in highly cyclical industries.

A very good indicator of the state of the business cycle in the UK economy is the number of companies going into liquidation in each period. Figure (i) in this box shows the absolute number of companies going into liquidation in England and Wales since 1971. These data are per quarter of a year. So, for example, at the peak in 1992 over 6,000 companies failed in a three-month period. This will be an underestimate of the total number of businesses failing, since many people operate in business without forming a company. (The difference between companies and unincorporated businesses is discussed further in Chapter 4.)

Figure (ii) shows the cycle in company failures in a slightly different format. The solid line shows the data from the first chart expressed as a percentage change of the number of failures in the same quarter a year earlier. This indicates a remarkably stable pattern over the three business cycles since 1970. There was about an 80 per cent rise in company failures (as compared to the numbers failing in the same quarter in the previous year) in the recessions of 1974–5, 1980–1, and 1990–2 and a significant fall in failures in the intervening booms.

The amplitude of this cycle in company failures is much greater than that of the index of industrial production, shown as the dotted line. This means that a fairly modest percentage change in aggregate output can be associated with a much larger percentage fluctuation in company failures. However, this large percentage change in failures compared to earlier failure rates would look modest if expressed as a percentage of all companies in existence. At the beginning of 1990, for example, the total number of companies registered in England and Wales was just under 1 million. Ten thousand company failures in any one quarter represents a 1 per cent decline in the total.

The observation of company liquidations is not enough to tell us whether the total number of companies in existence is rising or falling. We need to look also at the rate of new company formation. This also moves with the business cycle. Company formation declines in recessions and increases during booms. During the recession of the early 1990s, the combination of increased liquidations and fewer company formations led to a decline in company numbers—there was a 5.3 per cent decline in 1991–2 and a 2.1 per cent decline in 1992–3. In 1994–5, however, new company formation comfortably exceeded liquidations, so that overall numbers increased by 2.7 per cent.

Since records began in 1862, 3.186 million companies have been registered in Great Britain (England, Wales, and Scotland) but only 1.124 million of these were in existence in March 1995. Not all company disappearances are caused by failure. Many disappear as a result of takeover or merger. However, it is clear that births and deaths of companies are an important part of the dynamics of change in a modern economy, and this process of change does not happen smoothly but, rather, in distinct cycles. This is the business cycle for the economy as a whole, but it is the life-cycle for many of the individual businesses involved.

Sources: Data for the charts are from Datastream. Figures quoted in the text are from DTI, *Companies in 1994–5* (London: HMSO, 1995).

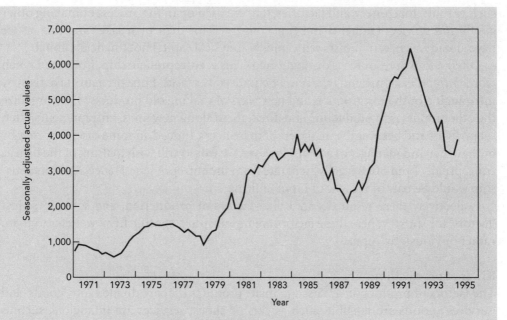

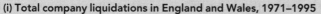

(i) Total company liquidations in England and Wales, 1971–1995

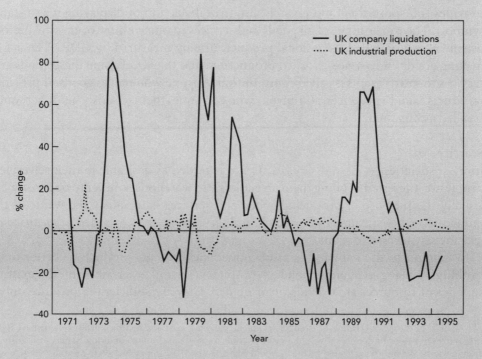

(ii) Growth in industrial production and company liquidations, 1971–1995

such as tools, machinery, and factories, that are used up in the process of making other goods and services (rather than being consumed for their own sake) and that, as we have already seen, economists call 'capital'—physical capital not financial capital.

Often a fourth resource is distinguished. This is **entrepreneurship,** from the French word *entrepreneur,* meaning the one who undertakes tasks. Entrepreneurs take risks by introducing both new products and new ways of making old products. They organize the other inputs into production and direct them along new lines. Entrepreneurs often set up firms and become the managers of these firms. Indeed, in some cases they may be both owner and manager of a firm. However, we would still wish to think of the firm as conceptually (and often legally) separate from the entrepreneur. Hence, entrepreneurship would be part of the labour input of firms.

Collectively these resources are called **factors of production,** and sometimes just 'factors' for short. Where these factors are inputs into a specific firm, we refer to them rather obviously as 'inputs'.

Kinds of production

The factors of production are used to make products that are divided into 'goods' and 'services': **goods** are tangible, such as cars or shoes; **services** are intangible, such as haircuts and education. Economists often refer to 'goods' when they mean goods and services. They also use the terms *products* and *commodities* to mean goods and services.

Goods are themselves valued for the services they provide. A car, for example, provides transportation (and possibly also the satisfaction of displaying it as a status symbol). The total output of all goods and services in one country over some period, usually a year, is called its **national product,** usually measured by **GDP.**[3] The act of making goods and services is called **production,** and the act of using these goods and services to satisfy wants is called **consumption.** Anyone who makes goods or provides services is called a **producer,** and anyone who consumes them to satisfy his or her wants is called a **consumer.**

Scarcity

In most societies goods and services are not regarded as desirable in themselves; few people are interested in piling them up endlessly in warehouses, never to be consumed. Usually the purpose of producing goods and services is to satisfy the wants of the individuals who consume them. Goods and services are thus regarded as *means to an end*, the satisfaction of wants.

In relation to the known desires of individuals for such products as better food, clothing, housing, schooling, holidays, hospital care, and entertainment, the existing supplies of resources are woefully inadequate.[4] They are sufficient to produce only a

---

[3] GDP is short for Gross Domestic Product. Its precise meaning and construction will be explained in Ch. 13.

[4] We do not need to decide if it would ever be possible to produce enough goods and services to satisfy all human wants. We only need to observe that it would take a vast increase in production to raise all the citizens of any country to the standard at present enjoyed by its richer citizens. It is doubtful that, even if this could be done, all citizens would find their wants fully satisfied.

small fraction of the goods and services that people desire. This creates the basic economic problem of **scarcity**.

Most of the problems addressed by economics arise out of this basic fact of life:

> **The production that can be obtained by fully utilizing all of a nation's resources is insufficient to satisfy all the wants of the nation's inhabitants; because resources are scarce, it is necessary to choose among the alternative uses to which they could be put.**

Choice and opportunity cost

Choices are necessary because resources are scarce. Because a country cannot produce everything its citizens would like to consume, there must exist some mechanism to decide what will be done and what left undone; what goods will be produced and what left unproduced; what quantity of each will be produced; and whose wants will be satisfied and whose left unsatisfied. In most societies these choices are influenced by many different people and organizations, such as individual consumers, firms, trade unions, and governments. One of the differences between the economies of the USA, the UK, India, and Taiwan is the amount of influence that various groups have on these choices.

If you choose to have more of one thing, then, where there is an effective choice, you must have less of something else. Think of a man with a certain income who considers buying beer. We could say that the cost of this extra beer is so many pence per pint. A more revealing way of looking at the cost, however, is in terms of what other consumption he must forgo in order to obtain his beer. Say that this person decides to give up some cinema attendances. If the price of a pint of beer is one-quarter of the price of a cinema seat, then the cost of four more pints of beer is one cinema attendance forgone or, put the other way around, the cost of one more cinema attendance is four pints of beer forgone.

Now consider the same problem at the level of a whole society. If the government chooses to build more roads, and finds the required money by building fewer schools, then the cost of the new roads can be expressed as so many schools per mile of road.

The economist's phrase for costs expressed in terms of forgone alternatives is **opportunity cost**.

> **The concept of opportunity cost emphasizes the problem of choice by measuring the cost of obtaining a quantity of one product in terms of the quantity of other products that could have been obtained instead.**

Our discussion may now be summarized briefly. Many of the issues studied in economics are related to the use of scarce resources to satisfy human wants. Resources are employed to produce goods and services, which are used by consumers to satisfy their wants. Choices are necessary because there are insufficient resources to satisfy all human wants.

Specialization and the principle of comparative advantage

Scarcity of resources is not an abstract problem of relevance only at the level of the aggregate economy. It is a problem for each one of us, and it is a problem for firms. Each of us has a limited amount of time and effort available to devote to work, recreation, or sleep. So we have to make choices about how to allocate that time between the various alternatives. Not only do we have to decide how much of our time to devote to work, but also we have to decide what type of work we could do most productively.

The managers of a firm have a similar problem. They have to allocate the time of hired workers and equipment to the activity of producing the firm's output as efficiently as possible. So decisions have to be made about how many employees should be hired and how they can best be used in order to make profit for the firm. Firms also have to decide what component inputs they should buy from other firms and what they could better make for themselves.

An important reason why a modern industrial economy is able to produce so much more output per head than was possible in earlier times is that most workers concentrate on doing a small range of tasks very well, rather than attempting a wide range of tasks that they might be not so good at. There is a very large range of quite different job functions performed within a modern economy, and each one of them is done by someone who is relatively good at doing that function but, perhaps, not so skilled at other functions. Economists call this allocation of different jobs to different people **specialization of labour.** There are two fundamental reasons why specialization is extraordinarily efficient compared to an economy in which self-sufficiency, or doing a wide range of jobs for yourself, is the norm.

First, individual abilities differ, and specialization allows each person to do what he or she can do relatively well, while leaving everything else to be done by other specialists. Even when people's abilities are unaffected by the act of specializing, production is greater with specialization than with self-sufficiency. This, which is one of the most fundamental principles in economics, is called the **principle of comparative advantage.** An example is given in Box 1.3.

The principle of comparative advantage says, for example, that individuals who want to use their time most productively should spend all their working hours doing what they can do *relatively* best, and they should trade with others who are relatively good at doing other things.

BOX 1.3.

The principle of comparative advantage

A simple numerical example is adequate to illustrate the important principle of comparative advantage. This principle is one of the factors generating gains from specialization.

Absolute advantage

Suppose that, working full time on his own, Peter can produce 100 pounds of potatoes *or* 40 sweaters per year, whereas Jane can produce 400 pounds of potatoes *or* 10 sweaters. (This may sound like a silly example, but *any* such example is adequate to illustrate the principles involved. The originator of these ideas, David Ricardo, used two countries, England and Portugal, and the two products were wheat and wine.) These productive abilities are shown in the first pair of columns of Table (i). Jane has an absolute advantage in producing potatoes because she can grow more per year than Peter. However, Peter has an absolute advantage over Jane in producing sweaters for the same reason. If they both spend *half* their time producing each commodity, the results will be as given in the second pair of columns of Table (i).

Table (i).

	Time spent fully producing one product or the other		Time divided equally between producing the two products		Full specialization	
	Potatoes	Sweaters	Potatoes	Sweaters	Potatoes	Sweaters
Peter	either	or				
	100	40	50	20	—	40
Jane	either	or				
	400	10	200	5	400	—
Total			250	25	400	40

Now let Peter specialize in sweaters, producing 40 of them, and Jane specialize in potatoes, producing 400 pounds. The final columns of Table (i), labelled 'Full specialization', show that production of both commodities has risen because each person is better than the other person at his or her specialty. Sweater production rises from 250 to 400, while potato production goes from 25 to 40.

BOX 1.3. (*cont.*)

Comparative advantage

Now make things a little less obvious by giving Jane an absolute advantage over Peter in both commodities. We do this by making Jane more productive in sweaters so that she can produce 48 of them per year, with all other productivities remaining the same. This gives us the new data for productive abilities shown in the first pair of columns of Table (ii). Now compared with Peter, Jane is four times (400 per cent) more efficient at producing potatoes and 20 per cent more efficient at producing sweaters. The second pair of columns of Table (ii) gives the outputs when Peter and Jane each divide their time equally between the two products.

It is possible to increase their combined production of both commodities by having Jane increase her production of potatoes and Peter increase his production of sweaters. The final two columns of Table (ii) give an example in which Peter specializes fully in sweater production and Jane spends 25 per cent of her time on sweaters and 75 per cent on potatoes. (Her outputs of sweaters and potatoes are thus 25 per cent and 75 per cent of what she could produce of these commodities if she worked full time on one or the other.) Total production of potatoes rises from 250 to 300, while total production of sweaters goes from 44 to 52.

Table (ii).

	Time spent fully producing one product or the other		Time divided equally between producing the two products		Peter is fully specialized; Jane divides her time 75% and 25% between potato and sweater production	
	Potatoes	Sweaters	Potatoes	Sweaters	Potatoes	Sweaters
Peter	either 100	or 40	50	20	—	40
Jane	either 400	or 48	200	24	300	12
Total			250	44	300	52

In this latter example, Jane is absolutely more efficient than Peter in both lines of production, but her margin of advantage is greater in potatoes than in sweaters. Economists say that Jane has a **comparative advantage** over Peter in the line of production in which her margin of advantage is greatest (potatoes, in this case) and that Peter has a comparative advantage over Jane in the line of production in which his margin of disadvantage is least

BOX 1.3. (*cont.*)

(sweaters, in this case). This is only an illustration: the principles can be generalized as follows.

- Absolute advantages are not necessary for there to be gains from specialization.
- Gains from specialization occur whenever there are *differences* in the margin of advantage one producer enjoys over another in various lines of production.
- Total production can always be increased when each producer specializes in the production of the commodity in which he or she has a comparative advantage.

The principles set out here apply to individuals, firms, and whole nations. As stated above, the original illustration of these principles used nations. To replicate this example, substitute Portugal for Peter, England for Jane, wheat for potatoes, and barrels of wine for sweaters. It is worth noting that the comparative advantage of individuals, firms, and of whole nations may change. Jane may learn new skills and develop a comparative advantage in sweaters that she does not currently have. Similarly, firms may develop new competencies, and whole nations may develop new abilities and know-how that will change their pattern of comparative advantage, and hence, what they produce and what they trade.

The same idea applies to firms. Firms should concentrate on those activities that reflect their comparative advantage and they should stay out of markets in which they have no such relative superiority. This is perfectly consistent with the modern management literature that values *focus* and an identification of *core competencies*. However, it is not always clear that this is just the application of a very well established principle in economics that has been around for over 150 years.

The second reason why specialization is beneficial concerns changes in people's abilities that occur *because* they specialize. A person who concentrates on one activity becomes better at it than could a jack-of-all-trades. This is called *learning by doing*. It was a factor much stressed by early economists. Modern research into what are called *learning curves* shows that learning by doing is important in many modern industries.

The production-possibility boundary

We now illustrate the choice problem faced by the economy as a whole. There is a maximum that can be produced with the resources available, and society has to decide what combination of different goods should be produced. So that we can show the choice problem in a two-dimensional diagram, we assume that the economy can produce just

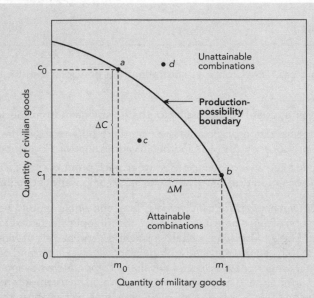

Figure 1.2. A production-possibility boundary

The negatively sloped boundary shows the combinations that are just attainable when all of the society's resources are efficiently employed. The quantity of military goods produced is measured along the horizontal axis, the quantity of civilian goods along the vertical axis. Thus any point on the diagram indicates some amount of each kind of good produced. The production-possibility boundary separates the attainable combinations, such as a, b, and c, from unattainable combinations, such as d. It is negatively sloped because in a fully employed economy more of one good can be produced only if resources are freed by producing less of other goods. For example, moving from point a (whose coordinates are c_0 and m_0) to point b (whose coordinates are c_1 and m_1) implies producing an additional amount of military goods, indicated by the distance between m_0 and m_1 in the figure (or ΔM), at an opportunity cost of a reduction in civilian goods, indicated by the distance between c_0 and c_1 (ΔC). (The Greek letter Delta, Δ, is used to indicate the difference or change in a variable.) Points a and b represent efficient uses of society's resources. Point c represents either an inefficient use of resources or a failure to use all that are available.

two types of goods—civilian goods and military goods. In reality, of course, many thousands of different goods are produced by a modern economy.

The choice between producing military goods or civilian goods ('guns versus butter') is a problem in the allocation of resources, and is illustrated in Figure 1.2. The horizontal axis measures the quantity of military goods produced, while the vertical axis measures the quantity of all other goods, which we call 'civilian goods'. The heavy curve on the figure shows all those combinations of military and civilian goods that can be produced if all resources are fully employed. It is called a **production-possibility boundary** or frontier. Points outside the boundary show combinations that cannot be obtained, because there are not enough resources to produce them. Points on the boundary are just obtainable; they are the combinations that can just be produced using all the available supplies of resources.

> A single production-possibility boundary illustrates three concepts: scarcity, choice, and opportunity cost. Scarcity is implied by the unattainable combinations beyond the boundary; choice, by the need to choose among the attainable points on the boundary; opportunity cost, by the negative slope of the boundary, which shows that obtaining more of one type of output requires having less of the other.

The production-possibility boundary of Figure 1.2 is drawn with a slope that gets steeper as one moves along it from left to right. The increasing slope indicates increasing opportunity cost as more of one product and less of the other is produced. Consider, for example, starting at the vertical axis where all production is of civilian goods with nothing of military goods. As the economy now starts to produce some military goods (moving to the right along the production-possibility boundary), the loss of civilian output is initially small; but as the economy increases military production, the loss of civilian goods per unit of military production gets greater and greater. This reflects the reasonable assumption that some resources are better devoted to military production whereas others are better devoted to civilian production. If all resources were equally suited to the production of either good the production-possibility frontier would be a straight line.

Notice that if an economy is at some point on an unchanging production-possibility boundary, having more of one thing necessarily implies having less of something else. It is, however, possible to have more of everything if: (1) resources previously unemployed are now employed; (2) resources previously used inefficiently are now used efficiently; or (3) economic growth shifts the production-possibility boundary outwards. This latter case is illustrated in Figure 1.3.

The same constrained optimization problem as faces an economy also faces a firm. At a point in time a firm has given resources of land, labour (its workforce), capital (its factories and machinery), and entrepreneurship (its management), and it faces some production-possibility boundary that defines the maximum it can produce of combinations of its outputs. If it produces more of one product it will have to produce less of another—there is an opportunity cost of greater output of one product in terms of lost output of another. The firm can shift its production-possibility boundary by investing in more capital and hiring more workers. It will then face a new, higher-level boundary at which the trade-offs between producing more of one product and less of another will be re-established, but perhaps with a different opportunity cost—the boundary may not shift parallel to itself.

For the economy as a whole, the choices about what gets produced (apart from those goods and services provided by the public sector through non-market channels) are made indirectly by the signals of the market generated by the interaction of millions of consumers and thousands of firms. These market signals mean that firms producing

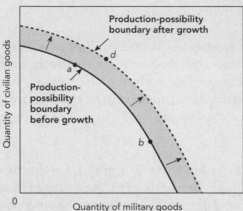

Figure 1.3. The effect of economic growth on the production-possibility boundary

Economic growth shifts the production possibility boundary outward, allowing more of all products to be produced. Before growth in productive capacity, points *a* and *b* were on the production-possibility boundary, and point *d* was an unattainable combination. After growth, point *d* becomes attainable, as do all points within the shaded band.

goods that are in high demand will tend to expand production (in the search for higher profits), while products no longer in demand will tend to disappear. So there is no single individual actually faced with the choice problem 'What should the economy produce?'

Firms and individuals do have a real choice problem, and the way each solves this problem influences what happens in the aggregate economy. These choices will be studied in depth in the following several chapters. Indeed, the choices made by firms and consumers provide the subject material of Sections 1 to 4 below.

Economics: a working definition

Economics today is regarded much more broadly than it was even half a century ago. Earlier definitions stressed only the alternative and competing uses of resources, and focused on choices among alternative points on a stationary production-possibility boundary. Other important problems concern failure to reach the boundary (problems of inefficiency or underemployment of resources) and the outward movement of the boundary over time (problems of growth and development).

Broadly defined, modern economics concerns:

1. the allocation of resources among alternative uses and the distribution of the output at a point in time;

2. the ways in which allocation, distribution, and total output change over time; and
3. the efficiencies and inefficiencies of economic systems.

Performance of the UK economy

Throughout this book we study the functioning of a modern, market-based, economy, such as is found in the UK today. By way of background, this section introduces a few salient features that should be kept in mind from the outset. Casual interpretation of media coverage might give the false impression that the UK economy is doing badly. It may have done badly compared to some other countries, but the true picture is one of real living standards gradually improving over time.

Living standards

The material living standards of any society depend on how much it produces. What there is to consume depends on what is produced. If the productive capacity of a society is small, then the living standards of its typical citizen will be low. Only by raising that productive capacity can average living standards be raised.

No society can generate increased real consumption merely by voting its citizens higher money incomes.

How much a society can produce depends both on how many of its citizens are at work producing things and on their productivity in their work. How well has the UK economy performed in each of these dimensions?

JOBS

The trend in employment in the UK has been positive throughout the twentieth century. However, the rise was rapid in the first half of the century and only gradual in the second half. While employment increased by nearly 50 per cent between 1900 and 1945, it rose by only about 10 per cent between 1946 and 1995. It is clear from Figure 1.4 that the two World Wars each produced a temporary surge in employment, but it is noticeable that employment stayed high after the Second World War. This can largely be attributed to the greater participation of females in the labour force that was encouraged by the war, and only slightly reversed afterwards.

The slow growth in employment since 1945 is broadly in line with the slow growth in

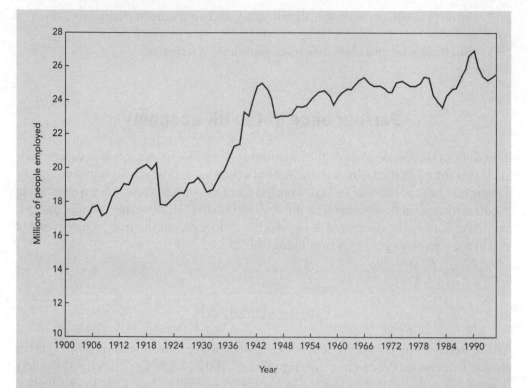

Figure 1.4. The employed labour force in the UK, 1900–1995

Employment behaved differently in the two halves of the century. After rising rapidly up to the mid-1940s, employment rose only slowly thereafter. The First and Second World Wars were both associated with a surge in employment and a subsequent sharp drop. During peacetime, employment fluctuates with the business cycle.

Sources: 100 Years of Economic Statistics (Economist, 1989) and *Economic Trends*.

total population, which increased by only about 16 per cent between 1946 and 1995. Two other factors explain why total employment has grown slightly less than total population in the period since the Second World War. First, there has been a rise in unemployment. This was only 1.7 per cent of the labour force in 1946, whereas it was about 8 per cent in 1995.[5] Second, the proportion of the population over the age of 65 rose from 10 per cent in 1946 to over 15 per cent in 1995.

Another notable feature of UK employment is its cyclical behaviour. Although it is irregular, this cycle seems to be getting more volatile in the sense that the swings in employment in the 1980s and 1990s have been greater than at any time since 1945. The causes of these swings in employment are closely related to the determinants of business cycles and will be discussed in Part II of this book.

[5] Note that the definition of unemployment used in official statistics changed many times over this period, so care should be taken in making historical comparisons using (changing) contemporary definitions.

LABOUR PRODUCTIVITY

Labour productivity refers to the amount produced per hour of work. Rising living standards are closely linked to the rising productivity of the typical worker.

If each worker produces more, then (other things being equal) there will be more production in total, and hence more for each person to consume on average.

In the period from 1750 to 1850, the market economies in Europe and the USA became industrial economies. With industrialization, modern market economies have raised ordinary people out of poverty by raising productivity at rates that appear slow from year to year but have dramatic effects on living standards when sustained over long periods of time.

> Over a year, or even over a decade, the economic gains [of the late eighteenth and the nineteenth centuries], after allowing for the growth of population, were so little noticeable that it was widely believed that the gains were experienced only by the rich, and not by the poor. Only as the West's compounded growth continued through the twentieth century did its breadth become clear. It became obvious that Western working classes were increasingly well off and that the Western middle classes were prospering and growing as a proportion of the whole population. Not that poverty disappeared. The West's achievement was not the abolition of poverty but the reduction of its incidence from 90 per cent of the population to 30 per cent, 20 per cent, or less, depending on the country and one's definition of poverty.[6]

Figure 1.5 shows the rise in labour productivity from 1920 to 1995. For the economy as a whole, labour productivity doubled between 1920 and 1970, and then increased by a further 90 per cent by 1995. Even more spectacular has been the increase in productivity in the manufacturing sector. This doubled between 1920 and 1960 and then doubled again between 1960 and 1980. It increased a further 90 per cent in the fifteen years from 1980 to 1995.

The growth in labour productivity is especially important as a determinant of real output growth in the UK, because, as we have seen, both population and employment have grown very slowly since the Second World War. So increases in production must be associated with greater output per worker. During the postwar period, output per worker for the whole UK economy has grown at an annual rate of 2.1 per cent. Although this may seem rather slow when viewed from one year to the next, it leads to a *doubling* of output in about thirty-four years.[7]

In fact, a productivity growth of 2.1 per cent is high by the standards of Britain's own history. Even during the 'Industrial Revolution' between 1760 and 1860, labour productivity is now thought to have grown at an annual average rate of under 0.7 per cent.

---

6 N. Rosenberg and L. E. Birdzell, Jr., *How the West Grew Rich* (New York: Basic Books, 1986, p. 6).

7 A helpful device is the rule of 72: Divide 72 by the annual growth rate, and the result is approximately the number of years required for output to double.

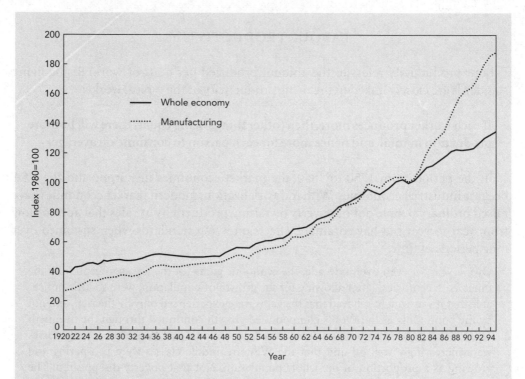

Figure 1.5. Output per person employed in the UK, 1920–1995

Productivity rose steadily throughout the twentieth century. The two lines show the course of output per worker in the whole economy, and in the manufacturing sector, since the end of the First World War. Each line represents an index of real per capita output with 1980 set at 100. Particularly noticeable is the increase in productivity growth in manufacturing after 1980.

Note: Data do not exist for the period of the Second World War, so figures are interpolated.

Sources: *100 Years of Economic Statistics* (Economist, 1989) and *Economic Trends*.

With a growth rate of 0.7 per cent, it takes 100 years to double output. However, even this 'slow' rate causes dramatic changes in life-styles. It means that the average citizen has twice the material living standards of his counterpart a mere 100 years previously.

The long period of sustained productivity growth in the twentieth century, and especially since the Second World War, has caused British citizens to expect to be substantially better off than their parents and grandparents. Indeed, if output per person continues to double every thirty-four years or so, the average citizen will be nearly twice as well off as his or her parents. Figure 1.6 shows average weekly wages since 1940 in real terms (at 1992 prices). It shows that real wages doubled between 1940 and 1973, exactly in line with the increase implied by productivity growth. However, real wages rose by only about 25 per cent between 1974 and 1995, indicating a much slower rate of increase during that period.

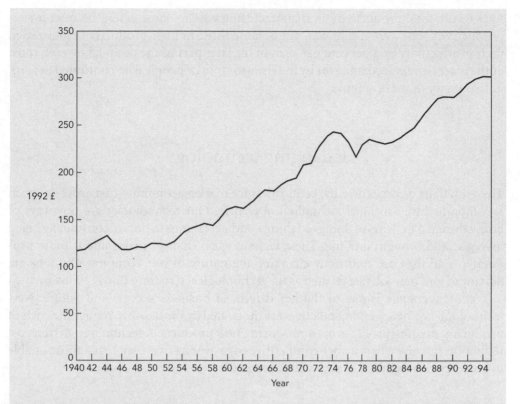

Figure 1.6. Average weekly real wages in the UK, 1940–1995 (at constant 1992 prices)

The trend of average real wages has been upwards since the end of the 1940s. In the early 1950s average weekly wages were sufficient to buy what £120 would buy in 1992, while in 1995 they were sufficient to buy just over £300 worth of goods and services. Although the overall trend has been upwards, real wages fell significantly during three periods, 1944–6, 1974–7, and 1979–81. Notice that real wages doubled (from £150 to £300 at 1992 prices) in the thirty-five years from 1960 to 1995.

Sources: 100 Years of Economic Statistics (Economist, 1989) and *Economic Trends.*

Between 1970 and 1980, productivity in the UK grew by only 1.4 per cent per annum. At this diminished rate, the time taken to double output increased from thirty-four years to over fifty. Fortunately, this slow-down does not appear to have been permanent. The economy returned to its trend productivity growth in the 1980s. Indeed, one important sector of the British economy had a spectacular increase in productivity in the 1980s. This was the manufacturing sector. Productivity growth in this sector was 4.6 per cent per annum from 1980 to 1995, which was well above its postwar average of 2.9 per cent. Productivity increases at the rate of 4.6 per cent will double output every sixteen years! Unfortunately, not all of this increase was accounted for by increased output of each person who remained in a job. Instead, a large number of firms closed down in the 1980s and the ones that closed tended to have lower than average productivity.

As a result, total productivity in manufacturing rose to some extent because lower-productivity jobs were eliminated, not because those in high-productivity jobs raised their productivity by 4 per cent per year. In the later part of the period, however, most of the increase was accounted for by the rising output of people who continued to work in that sector of the economy.

Changing technology

The growth in incomes over the centuries since market economies first arose has been accompanied by continual technological change. Our technologies are our ways of doing things. New ways of doing old things, and new things to do, are continually being invented and brought into use. These technological changes make labour more productive, and they are constantly changing the nature of our economy. Old jobs are destroyed and new jobs are created as the technological structure slowly evolves.

Technical change is one of the key drivers of business success and failure. New technologies or new working practices are motivated by the desire to reduce the costs of producing existing products or of producing new products. A technology-driven cost reduction can give a firm a huge competitive edge over its rivals, such that those unable to keep up with technical change will fade and die.

JOB STRUCTURE

Not only has output per worker changed over time; the pattern of work has also changed. In traditional economies, a high proportion of employment tends to be in agriculture. Britain, as the first industrial nation, was also the first to exhibit a sharp decline in agricultural employment. In 1840, only 25 per cent of its employment was in agriculture, and this had declined to 13.3 per cent by 1901 and 1.0 per cent by 1995. As recently as 1900, the USA had 40 per cent of its population in agriculture. This figure has now fallen to under 3 per cent.

The other clear structural change in employment has been the shift from manufacturing to services. Manufacturing employment peaked in Britain in the mid-1950s, at around 38 per cent of total employment. This declined steadily thereafter, but the fall accelerated sharply in the early 1980s. Employment in services displayed a contrasting pattern. Only 15.5 per cent of employment was in services in 1955, but by the late 1980s this proportion had more than doubled, to over 35 per cent. The trends for this century are shown in more detail in Table 1.1.

Services in manufacturing
The enormous growth in what are recorded as service jobs overstates the decline in the importance of the manufacturing of goods in our economy. This is because many of the

Table 1.1. Percentage of UK employment in major sectors, 1901–1995

	Agriculture, forestry, and fishing	Manu-facturing	Construction	Transportation and communication	Distribution	Services	Public administration and defence	Other
1901	13.3	33.1	6.0	8.0	11.0	19.8	4.9	3.9
1938	5.9	32.5	5.9	7.9	14.4	21.9	3.7	7.8
1955	2.8	38.0	5.7	7.0	9.8	15.5	5.5	15.7
1970	1.9	33.7	5.4	6.4	10.8	23.4	6.0	12.4
1987	1.3	20.3	4.0	5.3	12.1	35.8	6.5	14.7
1995	1.1	15.0	3.2	4.9	13.8	38.9	5.1	18.0

The distribution of employment among the various sectors has changed dramatically over the century. The figures give the percentage of total employment accounted for by each sector in each year. Notice among other things the following changes over time: the dramatic fall in agriculture, forestry, and fishing; the peaking of manufacturing employment in the mid-1950s, followed by a steady fall; the dramatic rise in services and the 'other' sector. 'Services' here includes hotels and restaurants, financial services, other business services, and education, as well as health and other social services. The 'other' category includes mining and quarrying, electricity, gas and water supply, but the largest component, 13 out of 18 percentage points, is self-employment.

Source: Monthly Digest of Statistics.

jobs recorded as service jobs are an integral part of the production of manufactured goods.

First, some of the growth has occurred because services that used to be provided within the manufacturing firms have now been contracted out to specialist firms. These often include design, quality control, accounting, legal services, marketing, and even cleaning. Indeed, among the most significant of the new developments in manufacturing are the breakdown of the old hierarchical organization of firms (sometimes called 'delayering') and the development of a flexible core team of employees who run the business but buy in many of its labour and material inputs from other independent firms or contractors ('outsourcing').

A quaint example of this point concerns shepherds and oil wells! In the 1970s Esso Petroleum had as an employee a full-time shepherd. This was because one of their oil-storage facilities had a significant area of grass, so the company decided to put sheep on it. To look after the sheep they hired a shepherd. This shepherd would have been classified as a worker in the petrochemical industry. In the 1980s Esso decided to contract out the maintenance of their facilities to another company—a company specializing in facilities management. This other company is classified as providing services.

Second, as a result of the rapid growth of international trade, production and sales have required growing quantities of service inputs for such things as transportation, insurance, banking, and marketing.

Third, as more and more products become high-tech, increasing amounts are spent on product design at one end and customer liaison at the other end. These activities, which are all related to the production and sale of goods, are often recorded as service activities.

Services for final consumption

As personal incomes have risen over the decades, consumers have spent a rising proportion of their incomes on services rather than manufactured goods. Today, for example, eating out is common; for our grandparents, it was a luxury. This does not mean, however, that we spend more on food. The extra expenditure goes to pay for the services of those who prepare and serve in restaurants the same ingredients that our grandparents prepared for themselves at home. Young people spend far more on attending live concerts than they used to, and all of us spend vastly more on travel. In 1890 the salesman in a small town was likely to be *the* well-travelled citizen because he had travelled 50 miles by train to the county town. Nowadays, many people commute greater distances to work every day.

NEW PRODUCTS

When we talk of each generation having more real income than previous generations, we must not think of just having more of the same set of products that our parents or grandparents consumed. In fact, we consume very few of the products that were the mainstays of expenditure for our great-grandparents.

One of the most important aspects of the change that permeates market economies is the continual introduction of new products. Most of the myriad instruments and tools in a modern dentist's office, doctor's office, and hospital did not exist fifty years ago. Penicillin, painkillers, bypass operations, films, stereos, television videocassettes and recorders, pocket calculators, computers, ballpoint pens, compact discs, satellite dishes, mobile phones, and fast, safe travel by jet aircraft have all been introduced within living memory. So also have the products that have eliminated much of the drudgery formerly associated with housework. Dishwashers, detergents, disposable nappies, washing machines, vacuum cleaners, microwave ovens, food blenders, refrigerators, deep-freezes, and their complement, the supermarket with its array of ready-made meals, were not there to help your great-grandparents when they first set up house.

The search for new products is, of course, an important part of the dynamics of a modern economy. Products that 'take off' are a source of great profit for the firms that become leading providers. So the perpetual hunt for the next winning product is what successful modern firms are all about.

GLOBALIZATION

The term **globalization** describes the trend towards greater integration of markets around the world that has been noticeable over the last three decades.

At least three forces have contributed to globalization. First, there has been a gradual reduction of protectionism in the form of tariff barriers and other trade obstacles associated with successive rounds of negotiations under the General Agreement on Tariffs and Trade (GATT). The GATT has now been superseded by the World Trade Organization (WTO). Second, communication and transport costs have fallen in real terms, and this has reduced the costs of doing business with far-flung parts of the world. More dramatically, our ability to transmit and to analyse data has been *increasing* dramatically, while the costs of doing so have been *decreasing* equally dramatically. For example, today £1,000 buys a computer that fits into a suitcase and has the same computing power as one that in 1970 cost £5 million and filled a large room. Third, governments have generally abandoned attempts to isolate their domestic financial systems and have abolished exchange controls and capital restrictions that limited domestic residents' investments overseas.

Many *markets* are globalizing; for example, as some tastes become universal among young people, we can see the same designer jeans and leather jackets in virtually all big cities. Many *firms* are globalizing, as they increasingly become what are called *transnational corporations*. These are massive firms with a physical presence in many countries. MacDonald's restaurants are as visible in Moscow or Beijing as in London or New York. Many other brands are also virtually universal, such as Coca Cola, Kelloggs, Heinz, Nestlé, Guinness, Shell, Mercedes Benz, Ford, Rolls-Royce, Sony, and Hoover. Many *labour markets* are globalizing, as the revolutions in communications and transportation allow the various components of any one product to be produced all over the world. A typical compact disc player, TV set, or car will contain components made in literally dozens of different countries. We still know where a product is assembled, but it is becoming increasingly difficult to say where it is *made*.

The growing internationalization of economic activity is illustrated by Figure 1.7, which shows the growing proportion of exports relative to total domestic product in both the UK and the OECD countries as a whole since the early 1960s.[8]

On the investment side, the most important result of globalization is that large firms are seeking a physical presence in many major countries. In the 1950s and 1960s most foreign investment was made by US firms investing abroad to establish a presence in foreign markets. Today, most developed countries see major flows of investment in *both directions*—inward as foreign firms invest in their markets, and outward as their own firms invest abroad.

In the mid-1960s, 50 per cent of all outward-bound foreign investment came from the USA and went to many foreign countries. In the early 1990s, according to United Nations figures, the USA accounted for just under 25 per cent of all outward-bound foreign investment. Japan was the largest single foreign investor, with just over 25 per

8 OECD stands for Organization for Economic Cooperation and Development. It has its head office in Paris and its member countries in 1996 were: Australia, Austria, Belgium, Canada, Denmark, France, Finland, Germany, Greece, Iceland, Ireland, Italy, Japan, Luxembourg, Mexico, the Netherlands, New Zealand, Norway, Portugal, Spain, Sweden, Switzerland, Turkey, the UK, and the USA. 'The OECD countries' is often used as shorthand for 'the countries of the developed world' or 'the industrial countries'.

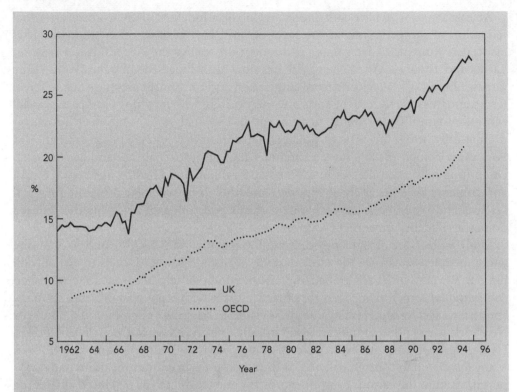

Figure 1.7. Globalization of the economy

The importance of trade in most developed economies has increased significantly since the early 1960s. The chart shows exports as a percentage of GDP for the UK (1962–95) and for the OECD countries as a whole (1963–95). UK exports rose from around 14 per cent of GDP in 1962 to nearly 30 per cent in 1995. For OECD countries as a whole the percentage has risen from about 9 per cent in 1963 to over 20 per cent today.

Note: Data are the ratios (×100) of the volume measures of GDP and exports, seasonally adjusted.

Source: Datastream.

cent of the total, while other major investors were France with 19 per cent, Germany with 17 per cent, and the UK with 15 per cent of the total amount of new foreign investment.

On the inward-bound side, the change is even more dramatic. In mid-1960s, the USA attracted only 9 per cent of all foreign investment. By the late 1980s, however, the USA attracted close to 30 per cent.

Although these flows are volatile from year to year, the total stock of foreign investment remains large. Not only do US firms hold massive investments in foreign countries, but foreign firms now hold massive investments in the USA. As a result, many US citizens work for British, Japanese, German, Dutch, and French firms—and just as many of the citizens of these other countries work for US firms. The same can be said of most other countries, particularly the UK, Germany, France, and Japan.

An important push to the globalization of investment flows was given by the freeing of investment flows from government regulation. Significant regulations on funds flowing abroad were never present in the USA—which is a major reason why it was the world's leading foreign investor from 1945 until the 1980s. In the UK and Europe, however, there were severe restrictions on individuals and firms wishing to invest abroad. These controls came off in 1979 in the UK, and they were eliminated in the 1980s and early 1990s in Japan and most of Europe. In the EU, this liberalization was enforced on the laggards by the EU Capital Liberalization Directive. This required all Member States to abolish exchange and capital controls by June 1990. Greece, Spain, Ireland, and Portugal had until 1992, and all have now complied. France and Italy were also forced down this road by the directive. Without this liberalization of capital flows, the pattern of globalization would have been significantly different and much more dominated by US foreign investment.

It is also interesting to note that globalization of investment has had big effects on what 'national interest' means. The pension funds and personal savings of most UK citizens are now internationally diversified, making them less dependent upon the future success of the UK. Instead, the citizens of most advanced industrialized countries are accumulating shares in the world economy.

The world is truly globalizing in both its trade and investment flows.

Today no country can take an isolationist economic stance and hope to take part in the global economy, where an increasing share of jobs and incomes is created.

Conclusion

In this last part of the chapter, we have briefly discussed how people's living standards are affected by the availability of jobs, the productivity of labour in those jobs, and the distribution of the income produced by those jobs. The discussion reveals an economy characterized by ongoing change in the structure of jobs, in the production techniques used by the workers, and in the kinds of goods and services produced. The issues discussed here arise again at many places throughout this book. Because most of them are interrelated, it helps to know the basic outlines of all of them before studying any one in more depth.

Summary

1. Economics is one of the subjects relevant to understanding the environment in which business operates. Economics is a social science. Economists study data that it is also vital for businesses to understand.

Firms and markets

2. Key topics that are of interest to both economists and students of business include: the behaviour of firms, the operation of markets, the nature of competition, optimal organization of firms, and the causes and control of business cycles.

3. Scarcity is a fundamental problem faced by all economies, because not enough resources—land, labour, capital and entrepreneurship—are available to produce all the goods and services that people would like to consume. Scarcity makes it necessary to choose among alternative possibilities: what products will be produced and in what quantities?

4. The concept of opportunity cost emphasizes scarcity and choice by measuring the cost of obtaining a unit of one product in terms of the number of units of other products that could have been obtained instead.

5. The principle of comparative advantage states that individuals, firms, and economies should concentrate on doing what they are relatively good at and trade with others who are relatively good at different things.

6. A production-possibility boundary shows all of the combinations of goods that can be produced by an economy whose resources are fully employed. Movement from one point to another on the boundary shows a shift in the amounts of goods being produced, which requires a reallocation of resources.

7. Modern market economies have generated sustained growth, which, over long periods, has raised material living standards massively.

8. Modern market economies are characterized by constant change in such things as the structure of jobs, the structure of production, the technologies in use, and the types of products produced.

9. Driven by the revolution in transportation and communications, the world economy is rapidly globalizing. National and regional boundaries are becoming less important as transnational corporations locate the production of each component part of a product in the country that can produce it at the best quality and the least cost.

Topics for review

- Economics as a social science
- Common interests of economics and business studies
- Factors of production

- Goods and services
- Scarcity, choice, and opportunity cost
- Comparative advantage
- Production-possibility boundary
- Resource allocation
- Growth in productive capacity
- Globalization

Questions for discussion

1. Discuss the skills that are required for a successful career in business. Why might an understanding of the economy be helpful?

2. Identify some activities that take place in firms and others that take place through markets. Why do firms buy many components from other firms rather than making them themselves?

3. What criteria should be used to decide if a business is working well? How should a firm decide to go into new activities?

4. Explain how an economy deals with the problem of deciding what products get produced. Why cannot we produce more of everything?

5. Explain the principle of comparative advantage. Why is specialization beneficial?

6. What is opportunity cost? What is the opportunity cost of three years spent doing a degree?

7. What criteria should be used to determine if an economy is performing well? Is the economy performing better now than it was, say, fifty years ago?

8. What is meant by globalization? Which industries are most affected by this?

Section 1
Markets and Prices

CHAPTER 2

Demand, Supply, and Price

Demand	46	Movements along supply curves versus	
Consumers	46	shifts	65
Consumer motivation	47		
The nature of demand	47	**The determination of market price**	65
The determinants of quantity demanded: the		The concept of a market	66
demand function	48	The graphical analysis of a market	67
Demand and price	49	Quantity supplied and quantity demanded	
The demand schedule and the demand curve	50	at various prices	67
An individual's demand	50	Changes in price when quantity demanded	
The market demand curve	51	does not equal quantity supplied	68
Another influence on demand	52	The equilibrium price	68
Market demand: a recapitulation	53	The laws of demand and supply	69
Shifts in the demand curve	54	Prices and inflation	71
Changes in other prices	55		
Changes in total income	56	**Demand and supply in action**	72
The distribution of income	56	The Channel Tunnel	72
Environmental variables	56	Analysis of the impact of the tunnel	72
Changes in tastes	57	What happened?	76
Movements along demand curves versus		Assessment	77
shifts	57	The market for computer chips	77
Supply	60	**Summary**	81
Firms	60		
The determinants of quantity supplied: the		**Topics for review**	82
supply function	60		
Supply and price	61	**Questions for discussion**	82
Shifts in the supply curve	63		
Prices of inputs	64	**Box 2.1.** Do-it-yourself demand and supply	73
Goals of the firm	64	**Box 2.2.** Road pricing and congestion: the	
Technology	65	demand and supply of road space	78

U NDERSTANDING the markets in which they operate is essential for all successful businesses. In this chapter we study the interaction of demand and supply forces and how these forces lead to the determination of the market price. Firms buy their inputs in many markets and sell their output in other markets. Firms are thus demanders in their input markets and suppliers in their output markets.

Markets and prices

For the purposes of developing the tools of demand and supply analysis we focus on markets for products that are demanded by individuals or households and supplied by firms. These tools are easily transferable to other markets, as we shall see later when we study input markets.

We start by discussing the economic behaviour of consumers—individuals or households whose spending decisions create demand for consumer goods—and studying the influences on consumer demand. We then make some simple assumptions about firms' supply curves; these will be discussed in more detail in Chapter 6. Once we put demand and supply together, we can then proceed to analyse the determination of market prices and outline what are known as the *laws of demand and supply*.

Demand

Consumers

Much that we observe in the world's markets can be traced back to decisions taken by millions of individuals. Any person who makes decisions relevant to our analysis is called an **agent**. Firms are one set of agents. Individuals in their capacity as purchasers of consumer goods and services are another. The third major agent in the economy is the government. We shall discuss the role of government in the economy in Chapter 9.

Individuals play two major roles in the economy. First, those who are employed sell their services to employers and receive incomes in return, so they are *suppliers* of labour. Others, such as spouses and children who do not work, share in the incomes of those members of their household who do work. Yet others receive income transfers from the government in such forms as unemployment benefits, student grants, and old age pensions. Second, individuals spend their incomes purchasing goods and services. In this capacity they are often referred to as **consumers,** and they are the *demanders* in consumer goods markets.

In our analysis of markets we assume a world that is inhabited by adult individuals who earn income by selling their labour services to firms (and perhaps get some income from their investments in firms) and spend this income purchasing goods and services. When one looks at real-world data, however, the spending unit that is studied is often not the individual but the household.

A **household** is defined as all the people who live under one roof and who make joint financial decisions or are subject to others who make such decisions for them. Some economists have studied resource allocation within households. For purposes of developing the analysis of market behaviour, however, we stick to individuals who obtain income through their own work, or the work of others, and who spend that income purchasing goods and services for consumption.

CONSUMER MOTIVATION

Economists assume that each individual consumer seeks maximum *satisfaction*, or *well-being*, or *utility*, as the concept is variously called. The consumer does this within the limits set by his or her available resources. Thus, just as the firm has to solve a maximization problem, so the individual has to solve one too. The consumer's problem is to achieve maximum satisfaction from the goods and services purchased, subject to the *budget constraint* that no more than the consumer's income can be spent.[1]

None of us has infinite income, so we all have to make choices about how we allocate our scarce resources (available funds) in order to maximize our satisfaction, or utility. For the student it might be: should I buy this economics text book or should I go out for a meal with my friends? For the young married couple it might be: should we buy a sofa or a stereo system? For the executive it might be: should we take a family holiday in Italy or buy a new car?

Of course, we cannot measure the level of individual satisfaction in the same way as we can measure profit, though we can go a long way in developing a theory of demand without needing such measurement.[2] All we need to assume is that individuals are able to judge their own level of satisfaction and that they behave consistently.

What we wish to explain is the (partly) observable behaviour of consumers with respect to their pattern of spending on goods and services. It is to this that we now turn.

The nature of demand

The amount of a product that consumers wish to purchase is called the **quantity demanded.** Notice two important things about this concept. First, quantity demanded is a *desired* quantity. It is how much consumers *wish* to purchase, not necessarily how much they actually succeed in purchasing. We use phrases such as **quantity actually purchased,** or **quantity actually bought and sold,** to distinguish actual purchases from quantity demanded. Second, note that quantity demanded is a *flow*, that is, a quantity per period. We are concerned not with a single isolated purchase, but with a continuous flow of purchases, and we must, therefore, express demand as so much per period of time—e.g. one million oranges *per day*, or seven million oranges *per week*, or 365 million oranges *per year*.

---

[1] Of course, some current spending can be financed by borrowing. However, the borrowing has to be repaid with interest, so there is still ultimately a constraint on how much can be spent. Other spending can be financed out of savings, so wealth is also relevant. What matters is that each consumer operates under *some* budget constraint.

[2] In the 19th century, a group of economists led by Jeremy Bentham did think that utility could be measurable, and they built theories on this basis. Hence they were known as 'utilitarians'. Not only was utility measurable to them, it was also comparable between people. Modern economists accept neither measurability nor comparability of utility.

The concept of demand as a flow appears to raise difficulties when we deal with the purchases of durable consumer goods (often called *consumer durables*). It makes obvious sense to talk about a person consuming oranges at the rate of thirty per month, but what can we say of a consumer who buys a new television set every five years? This apparent difficulty disappears if we measure the demand for the *services* provided by the consumer durable. Thus, at the rate of a new set every five years, the television purchaser is using the service (viewing TV programmes) at the rate of 1/60 of a set per month.

The determinants of quantity demanded: the demand function

Five main variables influence the quantity of each product that is demanded by each individual consumer:

1. the price of the product,

2. the prices of other products,

3. the consumer's income and wealth,

4. various environmental characteristics, and

5. the consumer's tastes.

The above list is conveniently summarized using mathematical notation in what is called a **demand function:**

$$q_n^d = D(p_n, p_1, \ldots, p_{n-1}, Y, E).$$

In the above expression, q_n^d stands for the quantity that the consumer demands of some product, which we call product n; p_n stands for the price of this product, where $p_1, \ldots, p_{n-1}$ is a shorthand notation for the prices of all other products; Y is the consumer's income; E stands for a host of environmental and, perhaps, sociological factors, such as number of children and place of residence (e.g. big city, small town, country) and the state of the weather;[3] and the form of the function, D, is determined by the tastes of consumers. The demand function is just a shorthand way of saying that quantity demanded depends on the variables listed on the right-hand side, while the form of the function determines the sign and the magnitude of that dependence.

We will not be able to understand the separate influences of each of the above variables if we ask what happens when everything changes at once. To avoid this difficulty,

---

[3] Where these other factors are important, they are often included explicitly in empirical measurements. For example, equations predicting the monthly demand for heating oil usually contain a term for the state of the weather. The same would be true for the demand for ice cream and cold lager. In other cases, they will be included in the error term, which covers 'all other unmeasured influences'. In practice, we concentrate on prices and incomes as determinants of demand. But it is worth remembering that other factors will be important in specific cases.

we consider the influence of the variables one at a time. To do this, we use a device that is frequently employed in economics. We assume that all except one of the variables in the right-hand side of the above expression are held constant; we then allow this one variable, say p_n, to change, and we consider how the quantity demanded (q_n^d) changes. This means we study the effect of changes in one influence on quantity demanded *assuming that all other influences remain unchanged*, or, as economists are fond of putting it, *ceteris paribus* (which in Latin means 'other things being equal').

We can do the same for each of the other variables in turn, and in this way we can come to understand the effect of each variable. Once this is done, we can add up the separate influences of each variable to discover what will happen when several variables change at the same time—as they usually do in practice.

Demand and price

We are interested in developing a theory of how products get priced. To do this, we need to study the relation between the quantity demanded of each product and that product's own price. This requires that we hold all other influences constant and ask: how will the quantity of a product demanded vary as its own price varies?

A basic economic hypothesis is that the lower the price of a product, the greater the quantity that will be demanded, other things being equal.

Why might this be so? A major reason is that there is usually more than one product that will satisfy any given desire or need. Hunger may be satisfied by meat or vegetables; a desire for green vegetables may be satisfied by broccoli or spinach. The need to keep warm at night may be satisfied by several woollen blankets, or one electric blanket, or a sheet and a lot of fuel burned in the boiler. The desire for a vacation may be satisfied by a trip to the Scottish Highlands or to the Swiss Alps; the need to get there by an aeroplane, a bus, a car or a train; and so on. Name any general desire or need, and there will usually be several products that will satisfy it.

Now consider what happens to the quantity demanded of some product if we hold income, tastes, the environment, population, and the prices of all other products constant and vary the price of only that one product.

First, let the price of the product rise. The product then becomes a more expensive way of satisfying a want. Some consumers will stop buying it altogether; others will buy smaller amounts; still others may continue to buy the same amount, but no rational consumer will buy more of it. Because many consumers will switch wholly, or partially, to other products to satisfy the same want, less will be bought of the product whose price has risen. For example, as meat becomes more expensive, consumers may switch some of their expenditure to meat substitutes; they may also forgo meat at some meals and eat less meat at others.

Second, let the price of a product fall. This makes the product a cheaper method of satisfying any given want. Some consumers will buy it who did not buy it before, and others will buy more than they did previously. Some will buy the same amount as before, but none will buy less because the price has fallen. Consumers as a whole will thus buy more of it. Consequently, they will buy less of similar products whose prices have not fallen and which, as a result, have become expensive *relative to* the product in question. When a bumper tomato harvest drives prices down, shoppers buy more tomatoes and fewer alternative vegetables, which are now relatively more expensive.

THE DEMAND SCHEDULE AND THE DEMAND CURVE

An individual's demand

A **demand schedule** is one way of showing the relationship between quantity demanded and price. It is a numerical tabulation that lists some selected prices and shows the quantity that will be demanded at each.

Table 2.1 is an individual's hypothetical demand schedule for carrots, showing the quantity of carrots that the individual would demand at six selected prices. For example, at a price of £0.40 per kilogram, the quantity demanded is 10.25 kg per month. Each of the price–quantity combinations in the table is given a letter for easy reference. We can now plot the data from Table 2.1 in Figure 2.1, with price on the vertical axis and quantity on the horizontal axis.[4]

Next, we draw a smooth curve through these points. This curve, also shown in Figure 2.1, is called the **demand curve;** in this case it is for carrots. It shows the quantity of carrots that the consumer would like to buy at every possible price; its *negative slope* indicates that the quantity demanded increases as the price falls.[5]

A single point on the demand curve indicates a single price–quantity combination. *The whole demand curve shows the complete set of possible combinations of quantity demanded and price.* Economists often speak of the conditions of demand in a particular market as being 'given' or as 'known'. When they do so they are not referring just to the particular quantity that is being demanded at the moment (i.e. not just to a particular point on the demand curve); they are referring rather to the whole demand curve, to the complete functional relation whereby desired purchases are related to all possible alternative prices of the product.

---

4 Readers trained in other disciplines will notice that economists plot demand curves with the axes the 'wrong way round'. The normal convention, which puts the independent variable (the variable that does the explaining) on the horizontal axis and the dependent variable (the variable that is explained) on the vertical axis, calls for price to be plotted on the horizontal axis and quantity on the vertical axis. The reasons for this date back nearly a century to the origins of the subject. Once a convention is adopted it tends to stick. This in itself is an important economic lesson.

5 Mathematicians refer to the slopes of curves as *positive* if both variables change in the same direction along the curve (i.e. either they both increase or they both decrease) and as *negative* if the variables change in opposite directions along the curve (i.e. one increases while the other decreases). Economists often read curves from left to right calling negatively sloped curves 'downward sloping' and positively sloped curves 'upward sloping'. We stick mainly to the unambiguous terminology of positive and negative slopes.

Table 2.1. An individual consumer's demand
schedule for carrots

Reference letter	Price (£ per kg)	Quantity demanded (kg per month)
a	0.20	14.00
b	0.40	10.25
c	0.60	7.50
d	0.80	5.25
e	1.00	3.50
f	1.20	2.50

The table shows the quantity of carrots that one consumer would demand at each selected price, *ceteris paribus*. For example, at a price of £0.20 per kilogram the consumer demands 14 kg per month, while at a price of £1.20 per kilogram he only demands 2.5 kg.

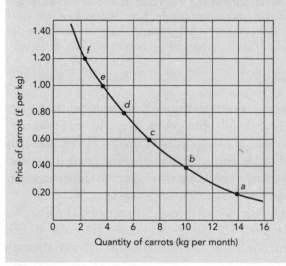

Figure 2.1. An individual consumer's demand curve

An individual consumer's demand curve relates the price of a product to the amount that the consumer wishes to purchase. The curve is drawn from the data in Table 2.1, each point on the figure relating to a row on the table. For example, when price is £1.00, just under 1 kg is bought per month (point *e*), while when the price is £0.40, 10.25 kg are bought each month (point *b*).

The market demand curve

So far we have discussed how the quantity of a product demanded by one consumer depends on the product's price, other things being equal. To explain market behaviour, we need to know the total demand of all consumers. To obtain a market demand relationship, we sum the quantities demanded by each consumer at a particular price to obtain the total quantity demanded at that price. We repeat the process for each price to obtain a schedule of total, or market, demand at all possible prices. A graph of this schedule is called the *market demand curve*. Figure 2.2 shows the summation geometrically. It illustrates the proposition that the market demand curve is the horizontal sum of the demand curves of all the individual consumers in the market.[6]

6 When summing curves, it is possible to become confused between vertical and horizontal summation. Such a confusion can only result from the attempted application of memory rather than common sense. What is going on in Figure 2.2 is that at, say, £0.40 per kilogram, individual A buys 2.5 kg per month and individual B also buys 2.5 kg. So the total market demand at a price of £0.40 is 5 kg per month. The logic is to sum the quantity bought by each individual at each price to get the total market demand at each price.

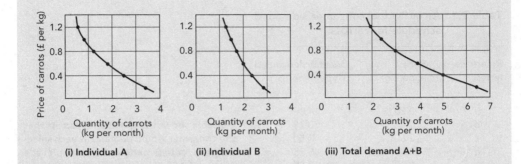

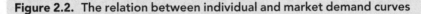

Figure 2.2. The relation between individual and market demand curves

The market demand curve is the horizontal sum of the individual demand curves of all consumers in the market. The figure illustrates aggregation over two individuals. For example, at a price of £0.80 per kilogram, consumer A purchases 1.2 kg and consumer B purchases 1.8 kg. Thus, together they purchase 3 kg. No matter how many individuals are involved, the process is the same.

We have illustrated the market demand curve by summing the demands for only two consumers. An actual market demand curve will represent the demands of all the consumers who buy in that market. In practice, our knowledge of market curves is usually derived by observing total quantities directly. The derivation of market demand curves by summing individual curves is a theoretical operation. We do it to understand the relation between curves for individual consumers and market curves.

In Table 2.2 we assume we have data for the market demand for carrots. The schedule tells us the total quantity that will be demanded by all buyers in that market at a selected set of market prices. The data are plotted in Figure 2.3, and the curve drawn through these points is the market demand curve.

ANOTHER INFLUENCE ON DEMAND

When we go from the individual consumer's demand curve to the market demand curve, we must reconsider item (3) in our list of the determinants of demand. 'Consumer's income' now refers to *the total income of all consumers.* If, for example, the population increases as a result of immigration and each new immigrant has an income, the demands for most products will rise even though existing consumers have unchanged incomes and face unchanged prices. When we take total income of all consumers as our income variable, we must add another factor to the major determinants of demand. This factor is the *income distribution* among individuals.

Consider two societies with the same total income. In one society there are some rich people, many poor people, but only a few in the middle-income range. In the second society, most of the people have incomes that do not differ much from the average in-

Table 2.2. A market demand schedule for carrots

Reference letter	Price (£ per kg)	Quantity demanded ('000 kg per month)
U	0.20	110.0
V	0.40	90.0
W	0.60	77.5
X	0.80	67.5
Y	1.00	62.5
Z	1.20	60.0

The table shows the quantity of carrots that would be demanded by all consumers at various prices, *ceteris paribus*. For example, row *W* indicates that if the price of carrots were £0.60 per kilogram, consumers would desire to purchase 77,500 kg of carrots per month, given the values of the other variables that affect quantity demanded, including average consumers' income.

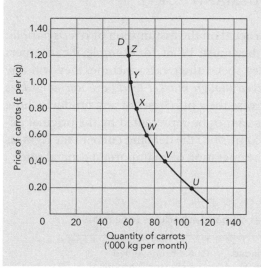

Figure 2.3. A market demand curve for carrots

This demand curve relates quantity of carrots demanded to their price; its negative slope indicates that quantity demanded increases as price falls. The six points correspond to the price–quantity combinations shown in Table 2.2. Each row in the table defines a point on the demand curve. The smooth curve drawn through all of the points and labelled *D* is the demand curve.

come for all consumers. Even if all other variables that influence demand are the same, the two societies will have quite different patterns of demand. In the first there will be a large demand for Mercedes-Benz and Rolls-Royce cars and also for baked beans, bread, and chips. In the second, there will be a smaller demand for these products, but a large demand for ski holidays, medium-sized cars and other middle-income consumption goods. Clearly, the distribution of income is a major determinant of market demand.

MARKET DEMAND: A RECAPITULATION

The total quantity demanded in any market depends on the price of the product being sold, on the prices of all other products, on the income of the individuals buying in that market, on the distribution of that income among the individuals, and on tastes.

Markets and prices

This is not to say that *no other factors* influence demand for specific products, merely that these are the economic variables common to *all of the products* that consumers demand.

To obtain the market demand curve, we hold constant all the factors that influence demand, other than the product's own price.

> The market demand curve relates the total quantity demanded of a product to its own price on the assumption that all other prices, total income, its distribution among individuals, tastes, and all other influencing factors are held constant.

SHIFTS IN THE DEMAND CURVE

The market demand curve has been constructed on the assumption of *ceteris paribus*. But what if other things change, as surely they must? What, for example, if consumers find themselves with more income? If they spend their extra income, they will buy additional quantities of many products *even though market prices are unchanged*, as shown in Table 2.3. But if consumers increase their purchases of any product whose price has not changed, the new purchases cannot be represented by the original demand curve. Thus the rise in consumer income *shifts* the demand curve to the right, as shown in Figure 2.4. This shift illustrates the operation of an important general rule.

Table 2.3.   Two alternative market demand schedules for carrots

(1)	Price (£ per kg) (2)	Quantity demanded at original level of personal income ('000 kg per month) (3)	Quantity demanded when personal income rises to new level ('000 kg per month) (4)	(5)
U	0.20	110.0	140.0	U'
V	0.40	90.0	116.0	V'
W	0.60	77.5	100.8	W'
X	0.80	67.5	90.0	X'
Y	1.00	62.5	81.3	Y'
Z	1.20	60.0	78.0	Z'

An increase in total consumers' income increases the quantity demanded at each price. When income rises, quantity demanded at a price of £0.60 per kilogram rises from 77,500 kg per month to 100,800 kg per month. A similar rise occurs at every other price. Thus the demand schedule relating columns (2) and (3) is replaced by the one relating columns (2) and (4). The graphical representations of these two schedules are labelled D_0 and D_1 in Figure 2.4.

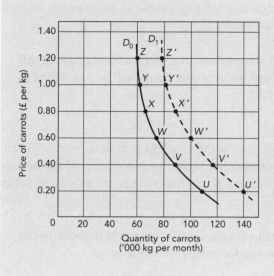

Figure 2.4. Two demand curves for carrots

The rightward shift in the demand curve from D_0 to D_1 indicates an increase in the quantity demanded at each price. The lettered points correspond to those in Table 2.3. A rightward shift in the demand curve indicates an increase in demand in the sense that more is demanded at each price and that a higher price would be paid for each quantity. For example at price £0.60, quantity demanded rises from 77,500 kg (point W) to 100,800 kg (point W'); while the quantity of 90,000 kg, which was formerly bought at a price of £0.40 (point V), will be bought at a price of £0.80 after the shift (point X').

A demand curve shifts to a new position in response to a change in any of the variables that were held constant when the original curve was drawn.

Any change that increases the amount consumers wish to buy at each price will shift the demand curve to the right, and any change that decreases the amount consumers wish to buy at each price will shift the demand curve to the left.

Changes in other prices

We saw that demand curves have a negative slope because the lower a product's price, the cheaper it becomes relative to other products that can satisfy the same needs. Those other products are called **substitutes**. A product becomes cheaper relative to its substitutes if its own price *falls*. This also happens if the substitute's price rises. For example, carrots can become cheap relative to cabbage either because the price of carrots falls or because the price of cabbage rises. Either change will increase the amount of carrots consumers are prepared to buy.

A rise in the price of a product's substitute shifts the demand curve for the product to the right. More will be purchased at each price.

For example, a rise in the price of cabbage could shift the demand curve for carrots from D_0 to D_1 in Figure 2.4, just as did a rise in income.

Products that tend to be used jointly with each other are called **complements**. Cars and petrol are complements; so are golf clubs and golf balls, electric cookers and electricity, an aeroplane trip to Austria and lift tickets at St Anton. Since complements tend to be consumed together, a fall in the price of either will increase the demand for both. For example, a fall in the price of cars that causes more people to become car owners will, *ceteris paribus*, increase the demand for petrol.

> **A fall in the price of one product that is complementary to a second product will shift the second product's demand curve to the right. More will be purchased at each price.**

Changes in total income

If consumers receive more income, they can be expected to purchase more of most products even though product prices remain the same. Such a shift is illustrated in Table 2.3 and Figure 2.4. A product whose demand increases when income increases is called a **normal good.**

> **A rise in consumers' incomes shifts the demand curve for normal goods to the right, indicating that more will be demanded at each possible price.**

For a few products, called **inferior goods,** a rise in income leads consumers to reduce their purchases (because they can now afford to switch to a more expensive, but superior, substitute).

> **A rise in income will shift the demand for inferior goods to the left, indicating that less will be demanded at each price.**

The distribution of income

If total income and all other determinants of demand are held constant while the distribution of income changes, the demands for normal goods will rise for consumers gaining income and fall for consumers losing income. If both gainers and losers buy the good in similar proportions, these changes will tend to cancel out. This will not, however, always be the case.

> **When the distribution of income changes, demands will rise for those goods favoured by those gaining income and fall for those goods favoured by those losing income.**

Environmental variables

Changes in the many 'other' variables that influence demand will cause demand curves to shift. For example, a reduction in the typical number of children per consumer, as has happened in this century, will reduce the demands for many of the things used by children. If the typical age of retirement falls significantly, there will be a rise in the demands for goods consumed during leisure times and a fall in the demands for goods required while working. An unusually hot summer in the UK might raise demand for ice cream and cold beer but reduce the demand for holidays in Spain.

Changes in tastes

If there is a change in tastes in favour of a product, more will be demanded at each price, causing the demand curve to shift to the right. In contrast, if there is a change in tastes away from a product, less will be demanded at each price, causing the entire demand curve to shift left.

One of the interesting questions for businesses is the extent to which tastes can be changed by advertising. We shall discuss this in later chapters of this book when we study markets for differentiated products, that is, imperfectly competitive markets.

Figure 2.5 summarizes our discussion of the causes of shifts in the demand curve. Notice that since we are generalizing beyond our example of carrots, we have relabelled our axes 'price' and 'quantity', dropping the qualification 'of carrots'. The term *quantity* should be understood to mean quantity per period in whatever units the goods are measured. The term *price* should be understood to mean the price measured as £ per unit of quantity for the same product.

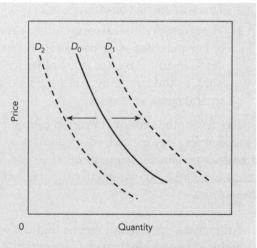

Figure 2.5. Shifts in the demand curve

A shift in the demand curve from D_0 to D_1 indicates an increase in demand; a shift from D_0 to D_2 indicates a decrease in demand. An increase in demand means that more is demanded at each price. Such a rightward shift can be caused by a rise in the price of a substitute, a fall in the price of a complement, a rise in income, a redistribution of income towards groups who favour the product, or a change in tastes that favours the product.

A decrease in demand means that less is demanded at each price. Such a leftward shift can be caused by a fall in the price of a substitute, a rise in the price of a complement, a fall in income, a redistribution of income away from groups who favour the product, or a change in tastes that disfavours the product.

MOVEMENTS ALONG DEMAND CURVES VERSUS SHIFTS

Suppose you read in today's newspaper that carrot prices have soared because more carrots are being demanded. Then tomorrow you read that the rising price of carrots is greatly reducing the typical consumer's demand for carrots as shoppers switch to potatoes, courgettes, and peas. The two statements appear to contradict each other. The first associates a rising price with a rising demand; the second associates a rising price with a declining demand. Can both statements be true? The answer is that they can be, because they refer to different things. The first refers to a shift in the demand curve; the second refers to a movement along a demand curve in response to a change in price.

Consider first the statement that the increase in the price of carrots has been caused by an increased demand for carrots. This statement refers to a shift in the demand curve for carrots. In this case, the demand curve must have shifted to the right, indicating more carrots demanded at each price. This shift will, as we shall see later in this chapter, increase the price of carrots.

Now consider the statement that fewer carrots are being bought because carrots have become more expensive. This refers to a movement along a given demand curve and reflects a change between two specific quantities being bought, one before the price rose and one afterwards.

So what lay behind the two stories might have been something like the following.

1. A TV report about the health-giving properties of carrots shifts the demand curve for carrots to the right as more are demanded at each price. This in turn is raising the price of carrots, since greater supply will only be forthcoming at a higher price. This was the first newspaper story.

2. The rising price of carrots is causing each individual consumer to cut back on his or her purchase of carrots—relative to what they would have bought with their new demand curve but at the old price. This higher price causes a movement upward to the left along any particular demand curve for carrots. This was the second newspaper story.

To prevent the type of confusion caused by our two newspaper stories, economists have developed a specialized vocabulary to distinguish shifts of curves from movements along curves. **Demand** refers to one *whole* demand curve. **Change in demand** refers to a *shift* in the whole curve, that is, a change in the amount that will be bought at *every* price.

> **An increase in demand means that the whole demand curve has shifted to the right; a decrease in demand means that the whole demand curve has shifted to the left.**

Any one point on a demand curve represents a specific amount being bought at a specified price. It represents, therefore, a particular quantity demanded. A movement along a demand curve is referred to as a **change in the quantity demanded**.

> **A movement down a demand curve is called an increase (or a rise) in the quantity demanded; a movement up the demand curve is called a decrease (or a fall) in the quantity demanded.**

To illustrate this terminology, look again at Table 2.3. First, at the original level of income, a decrease in price from £0.80 to £0.60 increases *the quantity demanded* from 67.5 to 77.5 thousand kg a month. Second, the increase in average consumer income *in-*

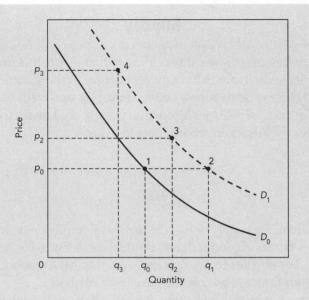

Figure 2.6. Shifts of and movements along the demand curve

A rise in demand means that more will be bought at each price, but it does not mean that more will be bought under all circumstances. The demand curve is originally D_0 and price is p_0 at which q_0 is bought (point 1). Demand then increases to D_1. At the old price of p_0, the quantity demanded is now q_1 (point 2). Next assume that the price rises above p_0. This causes quantity demanded to be reduced below q_1. The net effect of these two shifts can be either an increase or a decrease in the quantity demanded. If price rises to p_2, the quantity demanded of q_2 still exceeds the original quantity q_0 (point 3); whereas a rise in price to p_3 leaves the final quantity of q_3 (point 4) below the original quantity of q_0.

creases demand from what is shown by column (3) to what is shown by column (4). The same contrast is shown in Figure 2.4, where a fall in price from £0.80 to £0.60 increases the quantity demanded from the quantity shown by point X to the quantity shown by point W. An increase in total consumers' income increases demand from curve D_0 to curve D_1.

Figure 2.6 illustrates the combined effect of (1) a rise in demand, and (2) a fall in the quantity demanded. The first of these is shown by a rightward shift in the whole demand curve. The second is shown by a movement upward, along a given demand curve.

The key to determining whether the demand curve has shifted or whether we should be analysing a movement along a given demand curve is to ask what it is that has changed to create the move. If the price of the product itself has changed, perhaps as a result of a change in supply conditions, then we are talking about a movement along a given demand curve, that is, a change in quantity demanded. However, if what has changed is one of the variables that we were holding constant when we first drew the demand curve, such as consumers' income, the price of a substitute, and consumer tastes, then we are talking about a shift of the demand curve.

Supply

The demand curve tells us the quantity of the product that consumers wish to buy at each price. In order to determine what actually happens in the market we need to combine the demand curve with the supply curve. The supply curve tells us how much firms desire to supply at each price. As with demand, we first need to discuss the agents that are responsible for the behaviour we are going to study.

Firms

A **firm** is the agent on the supply side of the theory of market price. It is defined as the unit that employs factors of production to produce products that it sells to other firms or to consumers. For obvious reasons, a firm is often called a *producer*. In our analysis of supply behaviour firms are assumed to have three attributes.

First, each firm is assumed to make consistent decisions, as though it were composed of a single, individual decision maker. This strand of theory ignores the internal problems of how particular decisions are reached by assuming that the firm's internal organization is irrelevant to its decisions. This allows the firm to be treated, at least in basic demand and supply theory, as the individual unit of behaviour on the supply side of product markets, just as the consumer is treated as the individual unit of behaviour on the demand side.[7] Second, in their role as producers, firms are the principal employers of labour and capital. In labour markets the roles of firms and consumers are the reverse of what they are in consumer goods markets: in labour markets, firms do the buying and individuals do the selling. Third, we assume that most firms make their decisions with a single goal in mind: to make as much profit as possible. This goal of *profit maximization* is analogous to the consumer's goal of utility maximization. Later, in Chapter 11, where we discuss evaluation of income streams at different points in time, we shall reinterpret the goal of profit maximization as being to maximize the *present value of the firm*. The assumption of profit maximization is discussed further in Chapter 4.

The determinants of quantity supplied: the supply function

The amount of a product that firms are able and willing to offer for sale is called the **quantity supplied.** Supply is a desired flow: how much firms are willing to sell per period of time, not how much they actually sell.

---

[7] In Ch. 12 we look within the firm to ask questions about its internal organization.

We make a brief study of supply in this chapter, establishing only what is necessary for understanding the supply side of a market. In Chapters 5 and 6 we study the determinants of supply in some detail. In those chapters we first study the behaviour of individual firms, and then aggregate individual behaviour to obtain the market supply curve. For present purposes, however, it is sufficient to go directly to the market supply function, which reflects the collective behaviour of all the firms in a particular market.

Four major determinants of the quantity supplied in a particular market are:

1. the price of the product,
2. the prices of inputs into production,
3. the goals of producing firms, and
4. the state of technology.

This list can be summarized in a **supply function**:

$$q_n^s = S(p_n, F_1, \ldots, F_m),$$

where q_n^s is the quantity supplied of product n; p_n is the price of that product; $F_1, \ldots, F_m$ is shorthand for the prices of all factors of production (inputs); and where the goals of producers and the state of technology determine the form of the function S. (Recall, once again, that the form of the function refers to the precise quantitative relation between the variable on the left-hand side and the variables on the right-hand side.)

Supply and price

For a simple theory of price we need to know how quantity supplied varies with a product's own price, all other things being held constant. We are only concerned, therefore, with the *ceteris paribus* relation, $q_n^s = S(p_n)$. We will look more closely in Chapter 6 at the relationship between price and quantity supplied. For the moment, it is sufficient to state the hypothesis that, *ceteris paribus, the quantity of any product that firms will produce and offer for sale is positively related to the product's own price, rising when price rises and falling when price falls.* The reason is that, *ceteris paribus,* the higher the price of the product, the greater the profits that can be earned, and thus the greater the incentive to produce the product and offer it for sale. Also, the costs of increasing output by another unit tend to be higher, the higher is the existing level of output. The firm will not find it profitable to increase output if it cannot at least cover the additional costs that are incurred. The result is a positively sloped supply schedule, which will be derived explicitly in Chapter 6; for the moment it is necessary to take this on trust.

We now extend the numerical example of the carrot market to include the quantity of carrots supplied. The **supply schedule** given in Table 2.4 is analogous to the demand schedule in Table 2.2, but it records the quantities all producers wish to

Table 2.4. A market supply schedule for carrots

Reference letter	Price (£ per kg)	Quantity supplied ('000 kg per month)
u	0.20	5.0
v	0.40	46.0
w	0.60	77.5
x	0.80	100.0
y	1.00	115.0
z	1.20	122.5

The table shows the quantities that producers wish to sell at various prices, *ceteris paribus*. For example, row *y* indicates that if the price were £1.00 per kilogram producers would wish to sell 115,000 kg of carrots per month.

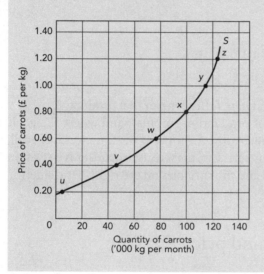

Figure 2.7. A supply curve for carrots

This supply curve relates quantity of carrots supplied to the price of carrots; its positive slope indicates that quantity supplied increases as price increases. The six points correspond to the price–quantity combinations shown in Table 2.4. Each row in the table defines a point on the supply curve. The smooth curve drawn through all of the points, and labelled *S*, is the supply curve.

produce and sell at a number of alternative prices, rather than the quantities consumers wish to buy.

Next, the six points corresponding to the six price–quantity combinations shown in the table are plotted in Figure 2.7. When we draw a smooth curve through the six points, we obtain a **supply curve** for carrots. The curve shows the quantity produced and offered for sale at each price. Since we are not considering individual firms here, all supply curves in this chapter are market curves showing the aggregate behaviour of all firms in the market. Where that is obvious from the context, the adjective 'market' is usually omitted.

The supply curve in Figure 2.7 has a positive slope. This is a graphical expression of the outcome of the following proposition (which we shall derive from firms' profit-maximizing behaviour in Chapter 6):

The quantity supplied is positively related to the market price.

Table 2.5. Two alternative market supply schedules for carrots

(1)	Price (£ per kg) (2)	Original quantity supplied ('000 kg per month) (3)	New quantity supplied ('000 kg per month) (4)	(5)
u	0.20	5.0	28	u'
v	0.40	46.0	76	v'
w	0.60	77.5	102	w'
x	0.80	100.0	120	x'
y	1.00	115.0	132	y'
z	1.20	122.5	140	z'

An increase in supply means a larger quantity is supplied at each price. For example, the quantity that is supplied at £1.00 per kilogram rises from 115,000 kg to 132,000 kg per month. A similar rise occurs at every price. Thus, the supply schedule relating columns (2) and (3) is replaced by one relating columns (2) and (4).

SHIFTS IN THE SUPPLY CURVE

A shift in the supply curve, brought about by a change in something that we have been holding constant (such as input prices or technology), means that, at each price, a different quantity will be supplied. An increase in the quantity supplied at each price is illustrated in Table 2.5 and plotted in Figure 2.8. This change appears as a rightward shift in the supply curve. A decrease in the quantity supplied at each price appears as a leftward shift.

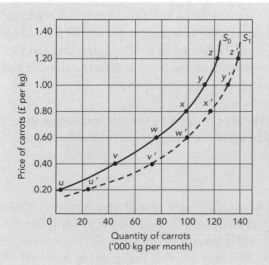

Figure 2.8. Two supply curves for carrots

The rightward shift in the supply curve from S_0 to S_1 indicates an increase in the quantity supplied at each price. The lettered points correspond to those in Table 2.5. A rightward shift in the supply curve indicates an increase in supply in the sense that more carrots are supplied at each price.

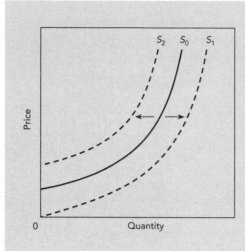

Figure 2.9. Shifts in the supply curve

A shift in the supply curve from S_0 to S_1 indicates an increase in supply; a shift from S_0 to S_2 indicates a decrease in supply. An increase in supply means that more is supplied at each price. Such a rightward shift can be caused by some changes in producers' goals, improvements in technology, or decreases in the costs of inputs that are important in producing the product.

A decrease in supply means that less is supplied at each price. Such a leftward shift can be caused by some changes in producers' goals, or increases in costs of inputs that are important in producing the product.

For supply-curve shifts, there is an important general rule similar to the one stated earlier for demand curves:

When there is a change in any of the variables (other than the product's own price) that affect the amount of a product that firms are willing to produce and sell, the whole supply curve for that product will shift.

The major possible causes of such shifts are summarized in the caption of Figure 2.9 and are considered briefly below.

Prices of inputs

All the things that firms use to produce their outputs—such as materials, labour, and machines—are called the firms' *inputs*. Other things being equal, the higher the price of any input used to make a product, the less will be the profit from making that product. Thus, the higher the price of any input used by firms, the lower will be the amount that firms will produce and offer for sale at any given price of the product.

A rise in the price of any input shifts the supply curve to the left, indicating that less will be supplied at any given price; a fall in the cost of inputs shifts the supply curve to the right.

Goals of the firm

For the most part we assume that firms have a single goal: profit maximization. Firms could, in reality, have other goals, either in addition to, or as substitutes for, profit maximization. If firms worry about risk, they will pursue safer lines of activity even though these lines promise lower probable profits. If firms value size, they may produce and sell more than the profit-maximizing quantities. If they worry about their image in society, they may forsake highly profitable activities when there is major public disapproval.

As long as firms prefer higher to lower profits, they will respond to changes in the profitabilities of alternative lines of action, and supply curves will have positive slopes. But if the importance that firms give to other goals changes, the supply curve will shift, indicating a changed willingness to supply the quantity at each given price.

In Chapter 7 of this book we shall explain that unique supply curves only exist for price-taking firms. For example, some firms have to take a strategic decision about what price to set in anticipation of what they think their rivals will do. For such firms there is not a unique, one-to-one, relationship between the price of the product and the quantity supplied. However, it is still most likely to be true that an industry supply curve is positively sloped, as the potential for higher profits encourages greater production, and, in the long term, attracts new entrants into the industry.

Technology

At any time, what is produced and how it is produced depend on the technologies in use. Over time, knowledge and production technologies change; so do the quantities of individual products supplied.

A technological change that decreases costs will increase the profits earned at any given price of the product. Since increased profitability leads to increased production, this change shifts the supply curve to the right, indicating an increased willingness to produce the product and offer it for sale at each possible price.

MOVEMENTS ALONG SUPPLY CURVES VERSUS SHIFTS

As with demand, it is essential to distinguish between a movement along the supply curve (caused by a change in the product's own price) and a shift of the whole curve (caused by a change in something other than the product's own price). We adopt the same terminology as with demand: **supply** refers to the whole relation between price and quantity supplied, and **quantity supplied** refers to a particular quantity actually supplied at a particular price of the product. Thus, when we speak of an *increase* or a *decrease in supply*, we are referring to shifts in the supply curve such as the ones illustrated in Figures 2.8 and 2.9. When we speak of a *change in the quantity supplied*, we mean a movement from one point on the supply curve to another point on the same curve.

The determination of market price

So far, demand and supply have been considered separately. We now come to a key question: how do the two forces of demand and supply interact to determine price in a competitive market?

The concept of a market

Markets are one of the most important elements of a modern economy, but their precise structure varies from product to product and place to place. Originally the term designated a physical location where products were bought and sold, such as the Smithfield meat market in London. Once developed, however, theories of market behaviour were easily extended to cover products such as wheat, which can be purchased anywhere in the world at a price that tends to be uniform the world over. Thus, the concept of 'the wheat market' extends our viewpoint well beyond the idea of a single place to which the consumer goes to buy something.

It is common now to talk about areas of trade, such as the foreign exchange market or the car market, which have neither a single location nor a single product involved. Such usage is helpful in distinguishing, say, the stock market from the aircraft market, but here we are concerned with markets in which a specific price is determined for a single identifiable product.

For present purposes a **market** may be defined as an area over which buyers and sellers negotiate the exchange of some specific product. It must be possible, therefore, for buyers and sellers to communicate with each other and to make meaningful deals over the whole market.

Individual markets differ in the degree of competition among the various buyers and sellers. For the time being we continue to confine ourselves to markets in which the number of buyers and sellers is sufficiently large that no one of them has any appreciable influence on price, that is, a perfectly competitive market environment. From Chapter 7 on we will consider the behaviour of markets that are not perfectly competitive.

Table 2.6. Demand and supply schedules for carrots and equilibrium price

Price (£ per kg)	Quantity demanded ('000 kg per month)	Quantity supplied ('000 kg per month)	Excess demand (quantity demanded minus quantity supplied) ('000 kg per month)
0.20	110.0	5.0	105.0
0.40	90.0	46.0	44.0
0.60	**77.5**	**77.5**	**0.0**
0.80	67.5	100.0	−32.5
1.00	62.5	115.0	−52.5
1.20	60.0	122.5	−62.5

Equilibrium occurs where quantity demanded equals quantity supplied so that there is neither excess demand nor excess supply. These schedules are repeated from Tables 2.2 and 2.4. The equilibrium price is £0.60. For lower prices, there is excess demand; for higher prices, there is excess supply, which is shown as negative excess demand.

The graphical analysis of a market

Table 2.6 brings together the demand and supply schedules from Tables 2.2 and 2.4. Figure 2.10 shows both the demand and the supply curves on a single graph; the six points on the demand curve are labelled with upper-case letters, while the six points on the supply curve are labelled with lower-case letters, each letter referring to a common price on both curves.

QUANTITY SUPPLIED AND QUANTITY DEMANDED AT VARIOUS PRICES

Consider first the point at which the two curves in Figure 2.10 intersect. Both the figure and Table 2.6 show that the market price is £0.60, the quantity demanded is 77.5 thousand kg, and the quantity supplied is the same. At that price consumers wish to buy exactly the same amount as producers wish to sell. Provided that the demand curve is negatively sloped and the supply curve positively sloped throughout their entire ranges, there will be no other price at which the quantity demanded equals the quantity supplied.

Now, consider prices below £0.60. At these prices, consumers' desired purchases exceed producers' desired sales. It is easily seen that at all prices below £0.60, the quantity demanded exceeds the quantity supplied. Furthermore, the lower the price, the larger the excess of the one over the other. The amount by which the quantity demanded exceeds the quantity supplied is called the **excess demand,** which is defined as quantity demanded *minus* quantity supplied ($q^d - q^s$). This is shown in the last column of Table 2.6.

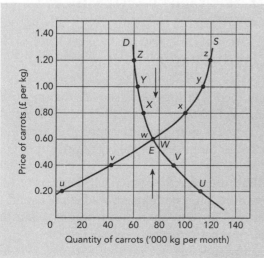

Figure 2.10. Determination of the equilibrium price of carrots

The equilibrium price corresponds to the intersection of the demand and supply curves. Point *E* indicates the equilibrium. At a price of £0.60 quantity demanded (point *W*) equals quantity supplied (point *w*). At prices above equilibrium there is excess supply and downward pressure on price. At prices below equilibrium there is excess demand and upward pressure on price. The pressures on price are represented by the vertical arrows.

Finally, consider prices higher than £0.60. At these prices consumers wish to buy less than producers wish to sell. Thus quantity supplied exceeds quantity demanded. It is easily seen that for any price above £0.60, quantity supplied exceeds quantity demanded. Furthermore, the higher the price, the larger the excess of the one over the other. In this case there is negative excess demand ($q^d - q^s < 0$). This is also shown in the last column of Table 2.6.

Note that negative excess demand is usually referred to as **excess supply,** which measures the amount by which supply exceeds demand ($q^s - q^d$).

CHANGES IN PRICE WHEN QUANTITY DEMANDED DOES NOT EQUAL QUANTITY SUPPLIED

Where there is excess demand, consumers will be unable to buy all they wish to buy; when there is excess supply, firms will be unable to sell all they wish to sell. In both cases some people will not be able to do what they would like to do, and we might expect some action to be taken as a result.

To develop a theory about how the market does behave in the face of excess demand or excess supply, we now make two further assumptions. First we assume that *when there is excess supply, the market price will fall.* Producers, unable to sell some of their goods, may begin to offer to sell at lower prices; purchasers, observing the glut of unsold output, may begin to offer lower prices. For either or both of these reasons, the price will fall.

Second, we assume that *when there is excess demand, market price will rise.* Individual consumers, unable to buy as much as they would like to buy, may offer higher prices in an effort to get more of the available goods for themselves; suppliers, who could sell more than their total production, may begin to ask higher prices for the quantities that they have produced. For either or both of these reasons, prices will rise.

THE EQUILIBRIUM PRICE

For any price above £0.60, according to our theory, the price tends to fall; for any price below £0.60, the price tends to rise. At a price of £0.60, there is neither excess demand creating a shortage, nor excess supply creating a glut; quantity supplied is equal to quantity demanded, and there is no tendency for the price to change. The price of £0.60, where the supply and demand curves intersect, is the price towards which the actual market price will tend. It is called the **equilibrium price:** the price at which quantity demanded equals quantity supplied. The amount that is bought and sold at the equilibrium price is called the **equilibrium quantity.** The term 'equilibrium' means a state of balance; it occurs when desired purchases equal desired sales.

When quantity demanded equals quantity supplied, we say that the market is in

equilibrium. When quantity demanded does not equal quantity supplied we say that the market is in **disequilibrium.** We may now summarize our analysis so far.

Assumptions concerning a competitive market:

1. All demand curves have negative slopes throughout their entire range.

2. All supply curves have positive slopes throughout their entire range.

3. Prices change if, and only if, there is excess demand; rising if excess demand is positive and falling if excess demand is negative.

Implications:

1. There is no more than one price at which quantity demanded equals quantity supplied: equilibrium is unique.

2. Only at the equilibrium price will the market price be constant.

3. If either the demand or the supply curve shifts, the equilibrium price and quantity will change.

The laws of demand and supply

Earlier in this chapter, we studied shifts in demand and supply curves. Recall that a rightward shift in the relevant curve means that more is demanded or supplied *at each price*, while a leftward shift means that less is demanded or supplied *at each price*. How does a shift in either curve affect price and quantity?

The answers to this question are referred to as the 'laws' of supply and demand. Each of these laws summarizes what happens when an initial position of equilibrium is upset by some shift in either the demand or the supply curve, and a new equilibrium position is then established.[8]

To discover the effects of each of the curve shifts that we wish to study, we use the method known as **comparative statics.**[9] We start from a position of equilibrium and then introduce the change to be studied. The new equilibrium position is determined and compared with the original one. The differences between the two positions of equilibrium must result from the change that was introduced, for everything else has been held constant.

The four laws of demand and supply are derived in Figure 2.11, the caption of which must be carefully studied. The analysis of that figure generalizes our specific discussion

---

[8] Some readers may doubt the existence of economic relationships of sufficient stability to be called 'laws'. It is adequate to regard them as the predictions of the theory of demand and supply that we have just developed. Of course, to be useful these predictions have to be consistent with empirical evidence. We do claim that they are consistent with a wide range of experience. However, formal testing of these relationships is beyond the scope of this book.

[9] The term 'static' is used because we are not concerned about the actual path by which the market goes from the first equilibrium position to the second. Analysis of that path would be described as *dynamic analysis*.

Markets and prices

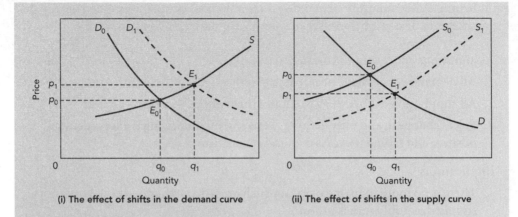

(i) The effect of shifts in the demand curve

(ii) The effect of shifts in the supply curve

Figure 2.11. The 'laws' of demand and supply

The effects on equilibrium price and quantity of shifts in either demand or supply are called the laws of demand and supply.

An increase in demand. In part (i) assume that the original demand and supply curves are D_0 and S, which intersect to produce equilibrium at E_0, with a price of p_0 and a quantity of q_0. An increase in demand shifts the demand curve to D_1, taking the new equilibrium to E_1. Price rises to p_1 and quantity rises to q_1.

A decrease in demand. In part (i) assume that the original demand and supply curves are D_1 and S, which intersect to produce equilibrium at E_1, with a price of p_1 and a quantity of q_1. A decrease in demand shifts the demand curve to D_0, taking the new equilibrium to E_0. Price falls to p_0 and quantity falls to q_0.

An increase in supply. In part (ii) assume that the original demand and supply curves are D and S_0, which intersect to produce an equilibrium at E_0, with a price of p_0 and a quantity of q_0. An increase in supply shifts the supply curve to S_1, taking the new equilibrium to E_1. Price falls to p_1 and quantity rises to q_1.

A decrease in supply. In part (ii) assume that the original demand and supply curves are D and S_1, which intersect to produce an equilibrium at E_1, with a price of p_1 and a quantity of q_1. A decrease in supply shifts the supply curve to S_0, taking the new equilibrium to E_0. Price rises to p_0, and quantity falls to q_0.

about carrots. Because it is intended to apply to any product, the horizontal axis is simply labelled 'quantity' and the vertical axis 'price'.

The laws of supply and demand are:

1. A rise in the demand for a product (a rightward shift of the demand curve) causes an increase in both the equilibrium price and the equilibrium quantity bought and sold.

2. A fall in the demand for a product (a leftward shift of the demand curve) causes a decrease in both the equilibrium price and the equilibrium quantity bought and sold.

3. A rise in the supply of a product (a rightward shift of the supply curve) causes

a decrease in the equilibrium price and an increase in the equilibrium quantity bought and sold.

4. A fall in the supply of a product (a leftward shift of the supply curve) causes an increase in the equilibrium price and a decrease in the equilibrium quantity bought and sold.

In Figures 2.5 and 2.9 we summarized the many events that cause demand and supply curves to shift. Using the four 'laws' derived in Figure 2.11, we can understand the link between these events and changes in market prices and quantities. To take one example, a rise in the price of butter will lead to an increase in both the price of margarine and the quantity bought (because a rise in the price of one product causes a rightward shift in the demand curves for its substitutes, and 'law' 1 tells us that such a shift causes price and quantity to increase).

We shall see below and in subsequent chapters that the theory of the determination of price by demand and supply is beautiful in its simplicity and yet powerful in its range of applications.

Prices and inflation

Up to now we have developed the theory of the prices of individual products under the assumption that all other prices remained constant. Does this mean that the theory is inapplicable during an inflationary period when almost all prices are rising? Fortunately, the answer is no.

We have mentioned several times that what matters for demand and supply is the price of the product in question relative to the prices of other products. The price of the product expressed in money terms is called its **money price** or its **absolute price;** the price of a product expressed as a relation to other prices is called a **relative price.**

In an inflationary world, a product's relative price can be measured by changes in the product's own price relative to changes in the average of all other prices, which is called the *general price level,* usually measured in the UK by the retail price index (RPI). If, during a period when the general price level rose by 40 per cent, the price of oranges rose by 60 per cent, then the price of oranges rose relative to the price level as a whole. Oranges became *relatively* expensive. However, if the price of oranges had risen by only 30 per cent when the general price level rose by 40 per cent, then the relative price of oranges would have fallen. Although the money price of oranges rose substantially, oranges became *relatively* cheap.

In Lewis Carroll's famous story *Through the Looking Glass,* Alice finds a country where everyone has to run in order to stay still. So it is with inflation. A product's price must rise as fast as the general level of prices just to keep its relative price constant.

It has been convenient in this chapter to analyse a change in a particular price in the context of a constant price level. The analysis is easily extended, however, to an inflationary period by remembering that any force that raises the price of one product when other prices remain constant will, given general inflation, raise the price of that product relative to the average of all other prices. Consider the example of a change in tastes in favour of carrots that would raise their price by 20 per cent when other prices were constant. If, however, the general price level goes up by 10 per cent, then the price of carrots will rise by 32 per cent.[10] In each case the price of carrots rises 20 per cent *relative to the average of all prices.*

> **In the analysis of markets, whenever we talk of a change in the price of one product, we mean a change relative to the prices of other goods.**

We now use the tools of demand and supply to help us understand some real-world markets.

Demand and supply in action

So far our discussion of demand and supply has related to hypothetical cases. In the final section of this chapter, and in the next chapter, we discuss some specific cases where the tools we have developed help us to understand what is happening.

The Channel Tunnel

The first example is that of the Channel Tunnel running between Folkestone in England and Calais in France. The opening of this tunnel had a very big impact on the cross-Channel travel market because it involved a massive increase in capacity, that is, an increase in supply.[11] Some other examples of the real-world relevance of demand and supply analysis are presented in Box 2.1.

ANALYSIS OF THE IMPACT OF THE TUNNEL

For simplicity, we confine ourselves to the market in cross-Channel journeys, though there will undoubtedly be other economic effects—such as on the location of industry and on property values in Kent and north-west France—and there is also the market for

---

[10] Let the price level be 100 in the first case and 110 in the second. Let the price of carrots be 120 in the first case and x in the second. To preserve the same relative price, we need x such that $120/100 = x/110$, which makes $x = 132$.

[11] Readers who think that we might be being wise after the event in this section should consult *An Introduction to Positive Economics*, 8th edn. (Oxford: Oxford University Press, 1995), pp. 108–10, in which we set out essentially the same analysis, written a year before the Channel Tunnel opened.

BOX 2.1.

Do-it-yourself demand and supply

This box has two functions. The first is to give some more examples of how the laws of demand and supply really do operate in the real world. All of the quotes below are verbatim extracts from newspaper articles in the recent past. The second function is to give the reader who is new to demand and supply analysis the chance to think about and practise using demand and supply curves. We suggest that those who want to use it in this way should get a pencil and paper. For each quote start with an initial intersection of a demand and supply curve, and then ask: what is it that has changed? Translate this change into a shift of demand or supply and then see if what happened in the news item is consistent with the laws of demand and supply as we have outlined them.

> Coffee prices at the London Commodity Exchange staged another spectacular rise, putting them above their level at the start of the year. . . . Mr Barbosa (President of the Association of Coffee Producing Countries) said that the supply shortages that are underpinning prices would last for quite some time.

> How deep is the art market's recession? . . . in today's unforgiving economic climate, the sales of contemporary, impressionist and modern works of art took hits at this week's auctions. Sales totalled just under £60 million compared with £500 million just one year ago. Many paintings on offer went unsold, and those that did sell went for well under their predicted price.

> Increased demand for macadamia nuts causes price to rise above competing nuts. A major producer now plans to double the size of its orchards during the next five years.

> OPEC countries once again fail to agree on output quotas. Output soars and prices plummet.

> Fish which was once the poor people's staple in Mediterranean countries is now eaten almost exclusively by rich tourists. Over fishing is blamed [for the decrease in size of the catch].

> The effects of [the first year of] deregulation of US airlines were spectacular: cuts in air fares of up to 70 per cent in some cases, record passenger jam-ups at the airports, and a spectacular increase in the average load factor [the proportion of occupied seats on the average commercial flight].

> Since the release of evidence connecting mad-cow disease (BSE) with the human form of the disease, CJD, the price of beef has fallen sharply. Farmers have been unable to sell their cows without taking a huge loss. The lucky ones have had the compensation of an increase in demand for lamb and pork, but the unlucky ones, with mainly beef herds, may not survive.

freight, which we do not discuss. Even in the market for cross-Channel journeys, it is worth bearing in mind that there are really two sub-markets here. One is the market for personal journeys between London and Paris or Brussels, where the main existing suppliers were the airlines. The other is the cross-Channel car transport market, in which the main existing suppliers were the ferry operators. In our current analysis we treat them as one market. In Chapter 8 we shall discuss the strategic interaction between the tunnel operators and the competitors in these various sub-markets.

Markets and prices

The demand curve, then, is for cross-Channel trips of all sorts. Although things other than price, such as speed and convenience, will affect the division of demand between the various types of travel, we hold these factors constant and focus on the feature that the overall quantity demanded varies negatively with the price. The supply comes from the tunnel, several shipping firms, hovercraft, and airlines. Although firms operating each of these types of travel have power over price, it is safe to assume that the total amount they will all wish to supply will vary positively with the price, that is to say that the supply curve is positively sloped.

Before the tunnel, the main suppliers of cross-Channel journeys were the airlines and ferry operators. The question to be answered is: what happens when a major new source of supply opens up? Figure 2.12 analyses the problem using demand and supply curves. The opening of the tunnel is represented by a rightward shift of the supply curve. Figure 2.12(i) shows the total demand and supply for cross-Channel journeys. Figure 2.12(ii) shows the demand for airline and ferry journeys. Initially, the demand

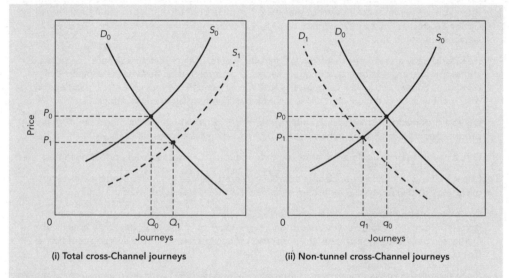

(i) Total cross-Channel journeys　　　**(ii) Non-tunnel cross-Channel journeys**

Figure 2.12. The market for cross-channel journeys

The opening of the tunnel added to total supply but reduced demand for non-tunnel travel. Part (i) shows demand and supply curves for all cross-Channel journeys. The opening of the tunnel shifts the supply curve to the right from S_0 to S_1. With a given demand curve, D_0, this lowers price and increases quantity from P_0 and Q_0 to P_1 and Q_1. Part (ii) shows the demand and supply curves for non-tunnel journeys (air and ferry). The fall in the price of a substitute (tunnel travel has fallen from an infinite price to a finite one) shifts the demand curve for other forms of travel to the left from D_0 to D_1. The price and quantity, accordingly, fall from p_0 and q_0 to p_1 and q_1. Notice that, before the tunnel opened, the original demand and supply curves were the same in both diagrams (so P_0 and Q_0 were equal to p_0 and q_0). Total tunnel journeys after opening will be measured by $Q_0 Q_1$ (the distance between Q_0 and Q_1), which is the extra journeys created by the tunnel, plus $q_1 q_0$, which is those trips that would have gone by air or ferry before, but now shift to the tunnel.

curve facing ferry and airline operators is the same as the total market demand curve. The opening of the tunnel shifts the market supply curve to the right in Figure 2.12(i). However, while the market demand curve remains unchanged after the tunnel opens, the demand curve facing ferry and air companies falls. (One way to think of the effect on demand for air and ferry journeys is that the price of a substitute, tunnel journeys, has fallen from infinity to some positive number.)

Notice that it does not matter for the general analysis whether tunnel journeys are cheaper or more expensive than existing methods of travel, although the quantitative effects will depend on this. All that matters is that they are cheap enough so that some passengers travel by the tunnel who might otherwise have gone by another route—this condition will certainly be met. Notice also that for this purpose we can lump together all forms of transport that are alternatives to the tunnel (and assume an average price). If we wanted to do a more detailed study we could, for example, separate airlines from ferries. Or we could look at each air and ferry route individually. If you were in the airline or ferry business, this might be necessary, but we can draw interesting conclusions even for an aggregate of all suppliers. Also, dealing with suppliers in the aggregate makes the use of a supply curve safer (because, as we shall discuss in Chapter 7, monopolists do not have a unique supply curve).

The first prediction implied by Figure 2.12(i) is that the result of opening the tunnel will be a fall in the average price of cross-Channel journeys and an increase in the quantity purchased. The increase in the total market size results (at least in the short term, when incomes are constant) from the rise in quantity demanded in response to the fall in price. How big this rise will be depends entirely on the size of the price reduction and the sensitivity of quantity demanded to the price fall.

Figure 2.12(ii) shows that the air and ferry operators will experience a fall in demand (price of a substitute falls). Initially, this would have been felt entirely in empty seats and car spaces, because prices are set in advance (though some lower prices may have been set in anticipation of a demand fall). Very soon, however, this would be likely to lead to special cut-price deals, and, eventually, to sustained price cutting even for regular fares. Only if the supply curve of air and ferry services were vertical would there be no fall in air and ferry journeys, but, in that case, there would be a sharp fall in revenue and an even larger fall in price. This could happen in the very short term if the air and ferry operators were determined to keep seats full and followed an aggressive price-cutting strategy. In this event, however, the revenue loss would likely cause airlines to shift some of their aeroplanes to other routes and ferry owners to decommission or sell some of their ferries. Hence, the quantity of air and ferry services supplied falls over time.

In the longer term, one factor that could save the airlines and ferries from the sales decline would be income growth causing a growth in demand for travel. This is likely, since travel typically increases more than in proportion to income. But we cannot say how long it will take.

It was estimated (prior to the tunnel being built) that after the tunnel opened there would be an approximate market size of 70 million journeys per year. Of these, it was thought that the tunnel might take a market share of about 40 per cent, or about 28 million passenger journeys. Up to about half of these 28 million journeys would be diverted from air and ferries, and the rest would be new journeys stimulated by the new, lower prices.

WHAT HAPPENED?

The above predictions, which were based on the application of simple demand and supply analysis, turned out to be remarkably accurate. We demonstrate this, not in our own words, but rather by direct quotes from a series of newspaper reports.

We start with two extracts from articles in the *Financial Times* in September 1995, shortly after the tunnel came into full operation.

> Eurotunnel has grabbed a big slice of the ferry operators' business on the cross-Channel market over the crucial summer months. Stena Sealink, the second largest ferry company on the Dover–Calais route, admitted its passenger volume fell 10 per cent and freight volumes 13 per cent in July compared with the same month last year. These trends have continued during August . . . Eurotunnel's own July traffic figures showed an 11.5 per cent increase over the previous month in the number of cars carried. . . . The price war in the cross-Channel market is growing in intensity, with the ferry companies maintaining discounts of up to 25 per cent on published prices throughout the summer. Eurotunnel has also offered a number of incentives to customers.

> Eurotunnel went on the offensive yesterday against the ferry operators on the cross-Channel route by cutting one-third off the prices of its duty free goods.

The following is an extract from an article in *The Economist* in October 1995, which focused on the impact upon the airlines of the fast train service from London to Paris and Brussels.

> In June . . . the number of passengers flying from London's Heathrow to Paris's Charles de Gaulle—traditionally the world's busiest airline route—was down 35% from the same time last year, according to Britain's Civil Aviation Authority. On the London–Brussels route, the numbers fell by 6% from Heathrow and 22% from Gatwick. . . . Air France has slashed capacity by 38% on its London–Paris routes over the year to July; while British Midland offered 10% fewer seats on its Paris flights compared with the previous year and 18% fewer seats on its Brussels route. . . . Worse still . . . Eurostar has forced down average airline economy fares by 25–30%.

As a follow up to this story, BAA, the company that operates Heathrow and Gatwick airports, reported in May 1996 that it had lost around 1.5 million passengers per annum as a result of the diversion of journeys from air to the Channel Tunnel.

The intense competition between the tunnel and ferry operators continued to rage through the summer of 1996. The following is an extract from an article in the *Financial Times* of 30 May 1996.

> The cut-throat cross-Channel price war intensified yesterday when Eurotunnel, the

Anglo-French operator of the Channel tunnel, announced that it is to halve the standard return fare over the summer to £129. The main ferry companies responded immediately, saying they would match any bargain fares offered by Eurotunnel for comparable trips. . . . Eurotunnel has a market share of Dover–Calais traffic of about 45 per cent. . . . Eurotunnel announced that it would match the best prices on duty free shopping offered by the ferries.

It is to be emphasized that this price war took place in the context of an overall growth in the cross-Channel journey market. However, in the absence of further information we must presume that 'growth' here refers to an increase in quantity demanded as price falls, rather than a rightward shift of the demand curve. The *Investors Chronicle* (12 April 1996, p. 10) estimated this market to have grown by 25 per cent in 1995 and by a further 20 per cent in 1996. Also the *Economist* article referred to above quotes the total seat capacity on the London–Paris/Brussels routes as having been 690,000 in July 1994, rising to 1,297,000 in July 1995. The latter piece of information tells us the scale of the shift in the supply curve.

ASSESSMENT

Let us now compare the simple prediction of our demand and supply analysis with what actually appears to have happened.

First, we predicted a lower price of cross-Channel journeys and a greater quantity demanded. This has clearly been borne out in practice. Indeed the price war continued well into the second year of operation of the tunnel.

Second, we predicted a fall in demand for airline and ferry journeys. This has also clearly happened. Both airlines and ferries have responded with aggressive price cutting. The airlines have also shifted some of their capacity on to other routes. The ferries have not been so quick to cut capacity, but this was clearly on the agenda (in late 1996), since they have had to suffer both lower prices and lower volumes. (See the further discussion of this issue in Chapter 8.)

In short, the tools of demand and supply have given us a very powerful framework for analysing what is likely to happen in real-world market situations. Box 2.2 contains a discussion of another transport area, roads. Since access to roads is generally free, it might be thought that this is not a suitable subject for demand and supply analysis. However, the box discusses why pricing road use may be a sensible solution to the problem created by excess demand for road use at certain times, that is, congestion.

The market for computer chips

We now turn to a completely different market that proves to be just as amenable to demand and supply analysis as the cross-Channel journey market. This time we start

BOX 2.2.

Road pricing and congestion: the demand and supply of road space

Some products are provided free, but this does not mean that everyone can have as much as they like all the time. Demand and supply analysis can give us some insight into the issues involved. Unless provision expands to equal the quantity demanded at zero price, excess demand will develop and will be handled by some other non-price allocation mechanism. Examples include waiting lists for health services and congestion on the roads.

Economists have long argued that efficient road use requires that it be priced. Indeed, in the seventeenth and eighteenth centuries many main roads in the UK were 'turnpikes' and travellers had to pay a fee to travel on a stretch of road. This fee was used to maintain the road surface. Throughout the twentieth century, road provision in the UK has been paid for by the state out of the revenue from general taxation. (Specific taxes on cars, such as the Road Fund Licence, have not been linked directly to expenditure on roads.) Some other countries have charges on some major roads, such as the autostrada of Italy, the autoroutes of France, some turnpikes in the USA, and new motorways in Mexico.

The current problem is that growth of car ownership has been such that demand for road use continually outstrips supply. For example, the orbital motorway around London, the M25, has had frequent jams from the day it opened. Also, most town centres suffer severe traffic congestion during rush hours, and, in some cases, for most of the day.

The economics of demand and supply suggests that the problem of congestion will be common if we let people use roads free. At zero price, the demand for road use exceeds the supply, so congestion will result at busy periods—in effect there will be rationing by queuing. This creates an economic loss for those whose time is valuable. If we introduce a positive price that reduces quantity demanded to the market-clearing price, all users will be able to use road services without congestion. Travellers with essential business will be happy to pay, while those who could easily take another route, use public transport, or post-pone a journey will be encouraged to do so.

Pricing of specific bits of road with limited access presents no technical problem. Hence, for example, there are already tolls on the Severn Bridge, the Dartford Crossing, the Forth Bridge, and the Mersey Tunnel. Although the pricing of road use in, say, Central London presents greater problems, these may soon be solved by the electronic tagging of cars, now in the experimental stage. An electronic meter will soon be able to record the identity of each car passing over city streets and along motorways. Drivers can then be billed for miles travelled, just as householders are now billed for gas or electricity used. This may seem fu-turistic, but the UK government announced in 1993 that it intended to introduce electronic road pricing by 1998. This timetable may not be met, but road pricing seems inevitable at some time in the not-too-distant future.

The price set for road use will be higher in periods of peak demand and lower in off-peak periods. This will tend to even out the flow compared to the zero-price situation in which the road is congested at peak periods but has excess capacity during the off-peak periods. A form of this type of pricing has been operating for some time in Singapore—a country with many people but little space. Licences to drive only at weekends are considerably cheaper

---

BOX 2.2. (*cont.*)

---

than licences to drive at any time, and there is a surcharge for driving in the central area during peak traffic times. Also, the number of licences issued is limited. As a result of this and other supporting measures, such as a first-class public transport system, Singapore has one of the few urban road systems in the whole of South-East Asia that is not heavily congested and polluted. In contrast, Bangkok and Manila are suffering near traffic paralysis from road congestion.

The lesson of this example is that the economics of markets has important applications even in areas where there is not an obvious market structure at present. Free goods can only be consumed without restriction if the supply continues to equal (or exceed) demand at zero price.

with an extract from the *Financial Times*. ('A low point for high-tech' by John Burton, Louise Kehoe, Michio Nakamoto, and Paul Taylor, 28 June 1996, p. 21.)

It is only nine months since the world semiconductor industry was forging ahead. Demand for chips was so great that there was a shortage, analysts were forecasting record growth and manufacturers were unveiling plans for dozens of $1bn chip factories.

The euphoria has been short lived. Disappointing Christmas PC sales in the US slowed demand as the introduction of new production techniques enabled more chips to be produced from each silicon wafer. The shortage rapidly turned into surplus, and the price of dynamic random access memory (D-Ram) chips—the basic memory chips for PCs—has plunged.

'D-Ram prices have dropped by about 65 per cent over the past six or seven months' says Mr Ulrich Schumacher, general manager of the standard integrated circuit division at Siemens, the German electronics group.

Commodity chip prices normally fall by 20 per cent to 30 per cent a year as manufacturing costs fall. But with manufacturers scrambling to protect market share, international spot market prices for 16Mb D-Rams have fallen from $25 to a low of $10—below the break even point of some Asian manufacturers.

While the price falls have been good news for PC buyers, they have sent shockwaves through the semi-conductor industry forcing many chip manufacturers to scale back planned production increases and reassess their investment plans.

There are signs that the collapse in D-Ram prices may have finally reached an end. . . . Prices have fallen below the cost of manufacturing [for some producers]. This has put a floor under any further price reductions. . . . However, a sustained recovery in D-Ram prices will depend on how fast PC buyers move from wanting 8Mb of memory to the 16Mb many believe is ideal for running Windows 95.

There are two key elements to the developments in this market. First, there is the rapidly evolving technology in the production of computer chips. This can be thought of as shifting the supply curve of each producer rightwards year by year. Accordingly, the market supply curve is continually shifting rightwards. The second element is the

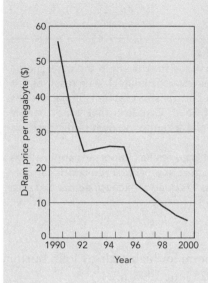

Figure 2.13. The price of computer chips

The price of computer chips tends to fall over time as a result of advances in technology; however, a surge in demand, in the early 1990s, held up prices temporarily. The chart shows the price of D-Ram chips falling between 1990 and the year 2000. Data from 1996 onwards are projected. The interaction of supply and demand forces is illustrated by two features. First, advances in technology lead to a steady decline in the supply price. Second, an excess of demand over supply between 1992 and 1995 forced the market-clearing price to rise. This created high profits in the chip industry and encouraged investment in new capacity, while the price falls of 1996 brought chip prices back to their long-term trend.

Source: Financial Times 28 June 1996, p. 21.

downward sloping demand curve, which is itself shifting in some periods. It is not exactly clear from the above extracts what has caused the demand curve to shift, but a reasonable guess can be made.

Figure 2.13 shows the price of D-Rams over time. This shows actual prices up to mid-1996 and then estimated prices to the year 2000. The trend decline in price of '20 per cent to 30 per cent a year' is clearly shown in the chart. There is an abnormal period between 1992 and 1995 when chip prices actually rose slightly before falling back sharply in 1996, as discussed above. A plausible explanation of this is as follows.

In normal times, the primary influence is that falling chip prices lead to an increase in quantity demanded, as the shifting supply curve moves to the right along a static (or near static) demand curve. In the period 1992–5, the demand curve shifted sharply to the right. This increase in demand was probably the result of increased availability and reduced price of software products, which are complements to computer hardware, such as multimedia games and educational programs. By 1996 the demand curve had stopped shifting to the right, but the supply curve had not. Hence the market clearing price fell sharply.

Notice that the temporary boom in demand between 1992 and 1995, by holding the market price above the minimum average total cost of production, would have increased the quantity supplied on the rightward-shifting supply curve as the high profitability of chip production encouraged higher production at each level of capacity. The fall in price in 1996, no doubt, would have reduced the quantity supplied along the supply curve that existed at that time. However, despite the fall in price, the supply curve continued to shift to the right in successive periods as technical progress continued.

In this chapter we have moved from the hypothetical market for carrots to the real market for computer chips, via the Channel Tunnel. It is hard to think of three more diverse 'products'. Yet these markets, and most other markets, do have an important common feature. This is that they are all amenable to analysis based upon the simple laws of demand and supply that we have developed in this chapter. Each market has some special features, but all have the common characteristic that supply forces and demand forces interact to determine how much of the product gets bought and sold and at what price.

In the following chapter we refine our understanding of markets by developing the important concept of elasticity, before applying it to yet more real-world market situations.

Summary

1. Consumers choose the goods they want to buy in order to maximize their overall levels of satisfaction, or utility, subject to the constraint imposed by their income.

2. An individual consumer's demand curve shows the relation between the price of a product and the quantity of that product the consumer wishes to purchase per period of time. It is drawn on the assumption that all other prices, income, and tastes remain constant. Its negative slope indicates that the lower the price of the product, the more the consumer wishes to purchase.

3. The market demand curve shows the sum of the quantities demanded by all the individual consumers at each price. The demand curve for a normal good shifts right when the price of a substitute rises, or the price of a complement falls, total income rises, the distribution of income changes in favour of those with large demands for the product, or tastes change in favour of the product. It shifts left with the opposite changes.

4. A movement along a demand curve indicates a change in quantity demanded in response to a change in the product's own price; a shift in a demand curve indicates a change in the quantity demanded at each price in response to a change in one of the conditions held constant along a demand curve.

5. The supply curve for a product shows the relationship between its price and the quantity producers wish to produce and offer for sale per period of time. It is drawn on the assumption that all other forces that influence quantity supplied remain constant, and its positive slope indicates that the higher the price, the more producers wish to sell.

6. A supply curve shifts in response to changes in the prices of the inputs used by producers, and to changes in technology. The shift represents a change in the amount supplied at each price. A movement along a supply curve indicates that a different quantity is being supplied in response to a change in the product's own price.

7. At the *equilibrium price* the quantity demanded equals the quantity supplied. At any price below equilibrium there will be excess demand and price will tend to rise; at any price above equilibrium there will be excess supply and price will tend to fall. Graphic-ally, equilibrium occurs where the demand and supply curves intersect.

8. A rise in demand raises both equilibrium price and quantity; a fall in demand lowers both. A rise in supply raises equilibrium quantity but lowers equilibrium price; a fall in supply lowers equilibrium quantity but raises equilibrium price. These are the so-called laws of supply and demand.

9. Price theory is most simply developed in the context of a constant general price level. Price changes discussed in the theory are changes relative to the average level of all prices. In an inflationary period a rise in the *relative price* of one product means that its price rises by more than the rise in the general price level; a fall in its relative price means that its price rises by less than the rise in the general price level.

Topics for review

- Quantity demanded and the demand function
- The demand schedule and the demand curve for an individual and for the market
- Shifts in the demand curve and movements along the curve
- Substitutes and complements
- Quantity supplied and the supply function
- The supply schedule and the supply curve
- Shifts in the supply curve and movements along the curve
- Excess demand and excess supply
- Equilibrium and disequilibrium prices
- The 'laws' of demand and supply
- Money prices and relative prices

Questions for discussion

1. Using each of the news reports in Box 2.1 on page 73, explain using demand and supply curves how the laws of demand and supply can be applied to explain what was going on in the specific market referred to.

2. Use demand and supply analysis to outline developments in the market for vinyl long-playing records following the launch of CDs.

3. Discuss what will happen to the demand curve for introductory economics text-books in response to the following changes: (i) a reduction in student grants; (ii) an increase in rents in student residences; (iii) an increase in the numbers of students taking economics courses; (iv) a price war among bookshops that offers reductions on book prices; (v) the introduction of a fee for the use of university libraries.

4. Discuss what will happen to the supply curve of blue jeans in response to each of the following changes; (i) a wage rise among textile workers; (ii) a rise in the price of raw cotton caused by a boll weevil attack in major cotton growing areas; (iii) a technical advance in textile machinery; (iv) a rise in consumers' income; (v) a shift of consumers' tastes towards cords.

5. Analyse the impact on the market price and quantity bought and sold in the cosmetics market of each of the following: (i) a change in the age distribution of the population increasing the proportion of very old and very young; (ii) a rise in the number of young adults in employment; (iii) a general inflation in consumer prices; (iv) an increase in income tax rates; (v) an increase in VAT on cosmetics.

6. You observe that the price of beer has risen by 10 per cent between one year and the next and yet sales volume has risen by 8 per cent over the same period. Which of the following on its own could be an explanation of this observation? (i) The demand curve for beer is positively sloped; (ii) productivity improvements in the brewing industry have shifted the supply curve to the right; (iii) there has been an increase in demand for beer as a result of price rises in wine and spirits; (iv) there has been an increase in demand for beer as a result of lower-cost meals being provided in pubs; (v) there have been significant pay rises in the brewing industry.

7. Some universities plan to charge entry fees to UK-resident undergraduates, who have previously had their fees paid by the state. Assuming that some universities introduce fees while others do not, analyse the effect on the demand for places at both the fee-charging and non-fee-charging universities.

8. After reading Box 2.2 on pages 78–9, discuss what would happen to demand for rail and coach services following the introduction of charges to car drivers for road use in town centres and on motorways.

CHAPTER 3

Elasticity of Demand and Supply

Demand elasticity	86	What determines elasticity of supply?	103
Price elasticity of demand	86		
Measuring the responsiveness of		**Measurement of demand and supply**	104
demand to price	86	Problems of demand measurement	104
The sign of the measure	87	Everything is changing at once	104
Interpreting price elasticity	88	Separating the influences of demand and	
Elasticity and total revenue	89	supply	106
Some complications	90	Keeping up with *The Times*	109
A more precise measure	93	The effects of the price cut	110
What determines elasticity of		Demand and supply analysis	111
demand?	95		
Definition of the product	95	**Summary**	113
Long-run and short-run elasticity of			
demand	97	**Topics for review**	114
Other demand elasticities	99		
Income elasticity	99	**Questions for discussion**	115
Cross-elasticity	101		
		Box 3.1. Measuring elasticity over a range	94
Elasticity of supply	101	**Box 3.2.** Elasticity and income	96
A definition	102	**Box 3.3.** Price and income elasticities	105
Interpreting supply elasticity	102	**Box 3.4.** The supply curve for coal	108

IN this chapter we continue to refine our analysis of markets via the tools of demand and supply. Here we explain and apply measures of the responsiveness of the quantity demanded and the quantity supplied to changes in the variables that determine them, particularly prices and incomes. These measures are called *elasticities*, and we need to learn how to calculate and interpret them, not least because the concept of 'elasticity' is now widely used in the business world. Studying elasticity not only helps to clarify the specific term, it also helps develop a deeper understanding of markets themselves. At the end of the chapter we shall present a specific example of elasticity calculations and their relevance to business.

To illustrate why we want to have such a measure, consider the effects of an advance in technology in, say, the computer chip industry (as discussed at the end of the previous chapter). This will shift the supply curve of chips to the right because more will be produced at each price (or equivalently, the costs of producing each quantity will fall). If the demand for chips is as shown in part (i) of Figure 3.1, the effect of the new production technology will be to reduce chip prices slightly, while greatly increasing the quantity produced and purchased. If, however, the demand is as shown in part (ii) of Figure 3.1, the effect of the new technology will be to reduce chip prices greatly but to increase chip production and purchase by only a small amount. Clearly the implications

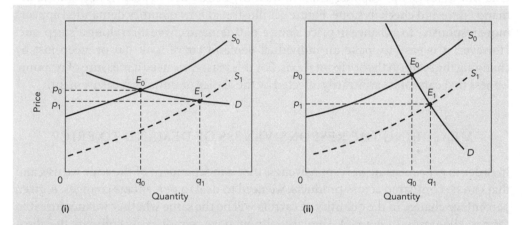

Figure 3.1. The effect of the shape of the demand curve

The flatter the demand curve, *ceteris paribus*, the less the change in price and the greater the change in quantity. Both parts of the figure are drawn on the same scale. Both show the same rightward shift in the supply curve from S_0 to S_1. In each part, the initial equilibrium is at price p_0 and quantity q_0, while the new equilibrium is at p_1 and q_1. In part (i), the effect of the shift in supply is a slight fall in the price and a large increase in quantity. In part (ii), the effect of the identical shift in the supply curve is a large fall in the price and a relatively small increase in quantity.

of these two alternative outcomes for firms in the chip industry are rather different. In one case, the price of chips falls only a little and the size of the market increases considerably, increasing the total revenue of the industry; in the other, market size increases little and price falls a great deal, reducing the total revenue of the industry.

Notice that the supply-curve shift is identical in the two cases illustrated in Figure 3.1. The only difference between the two cases is the slope of the demand curve. This example illustrates that it is often not enough to know that quantity demanded rises in response to a fall in price; it may be important to know by how much. To measure this in a useful way, we use the concept of elasticity.

Demand elasticity

In the first part of this chapter, we deal with quantity demanded along a given demand curve and start by considering its response to changes in the product's own price.

Price elasticity of demand

One way to judge the responsiveness of quantity demanded to price is to draw the demand curve and check its slope. Figure 3.1 illustrated how quantity demanded appears more responsive to a change in price along a 'flat' demand curve than along a 'steep' one. However, it is easy to make an individual demand curve look flat or steep just by changing the scale on the horizontal axis. For this reason we need a measure of responsiveness that cannot be arbitrarily affected by the choice of units of measurement.

MEASURING THE RESPONSIVENESS OF DEMAND TO PRICE

In order to get a measure of responsiveness that is independent of the scale we use, and that can be compared across products, we need to deal in percentage changes. A given percentage change in the quantity of carrots will be the same whether we measure it in tonnes, kilograms, or pounds. Similarly, although we cannot easily compare the absolute changes in tonnes of carrots and barrels of oil, we can compare their two percentage changes.

 These considerations lead us to the concept of the **price elasticity of demand,** which is defined as the percentage change in quantity demanded *divided by* the percentage change in price that brought it about.[1] This elasticity is usually symbolized by the Greek letter eta, η:

$$\eta = \frac{\text{percentage change in quantity demanded}}{\text{percentage change in price}}. \tag{1}$$

Elasticity can be used to measure responsiveness of any single variable to changes in any other. To distinguish η from other elasticities, the full term *price elasticity of demand* is used. Since η is by far the most commonly used elasticity, economists often drop the adjective *price* and refer to it merely as *elasticity of demand*, or sometimes just *elasticity*. When more than one kind of elasticity could be involved, however, η should be given its full title.

---

[1] Elasticity is an example of what mathematicians call a *pure number*, which is a number whose value is independent of the units in which it is calculated. Slope, $\Delta p/\Delta q$, is not a pure number. For example, if price is measured in pence, $\Delta p/\Delta q$ will be 100 times as large as $\Delta p/\Delta q$ along the same demand curve where price is measured in £.

The sign of the measure

Because of the negative slope of the demand curve, the price and the quantity will always change in opposite directions. One change will be positive and the other negative, making the measured elasticity of demand negative. This would pose no problem except for two unfortunate habits of users of elasticity measures. First, sometimes the minus sign is dropped and elasticity is reported as a positive number. Second, it is almost universal practice when comparing two elasticities to compare their absolute, not their algebraic, values. For example, if product X has an elasticity of −2 while product Y has an elasticity of −10, economists will say that Y has a greater elasticity than X (in spite of the fact that −10 is *less than* −2). As long as it is understood that absolute and not algebraic values are being compared, this usage is acceptable.[2] After all, the demand curve with the larger absolute elasticity *is* the one where quantity demanded is more responsive to price changes. For example, an elasticity of −10 indicates greater response of quantity to price than does an elasticity of −2.

This need not cause us trouble as long as we remember the basics:

Demand elasticity is measured by a ratio: the percentage change in quantity demanded divided by the percentage change in price that brought it about; for normal, negatively sloped demand curves, elasticity is negative, but two elasticities are compared by comparing their absolute values.

Table 3.1 shows the calculation of two demand elasticities, one that is quite large and

Table 3.1. Calculation of two demand elasticities

	Original	New	% Change	Elasticity
Good A				
Quantity	100	95	−5%	$\dfrac{-5}{10} = -0.5$
Price	£1.00	£1.10	10%	
Good B				
Quantity	200	140	−30%	$\dfrac{-30}{20} = -1.5$
Price	£5.00	£6.00	20%	

Elasticity is calculated by dividing the percentage change in price by the percentage change in quantity. With good A, a rise in price of 10p on £1, or 10 per cent, causes a fall in quantity of 5 units from 100, or 5 per cent. Dividing the 5 per cent reduction in quantity by the 10 per cent increase in price gives an elasticity of −0.5. With good B, a 30 per cent fall in quantity is caused by a 20 per cent rise in price, making elasticity −1.5.

---

2 The absolute value is the magnitude without the sign. Thus, for example, −2 and +2 have the same absolute value of 2.

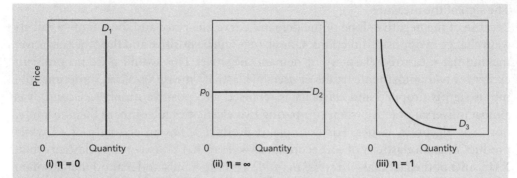

Figure 3.2. Three constant-elasticity demand curves

Each of these demand curves has a constant elasticity. D_1 has *zero elasticity*: the quantity demanded does not change at all when price changes. D_2 has *infinite elasticity at the price* p_0: a small price increase from p_0 decreases quantity demanded from an indefinitely large amount to zero. D_3 has *unit elasticity*: a given percentage increase in price brings an equal percentage decrease in quantity demanded at all points on the curve; it is a rectangular hyperbola for which price *times* quantity is a constant.

one that is quite small. The larger elasticity indicates that quantity demanded is highly responsive to a change in price. The smaller elasticity indicates that the quantity demanded is relatively unresponsive to a change in price.

INTERPRETING PRICE ELASTICITY

The value of price elasticity of demand ranges from zero to minus infinity. In this section, however, we concentrate on absolute values, and so ask by how much the absolute value *exceeds zero*. It is zero if there is no change in quantity demanded when price changes, i.e. when quantity demanded does not respond to a price change. A demand curve of zero elasticity is shown in Figure 3.2(i). It is said to be *perfectly* or *completely* inelastic.

As long as there is some response of quantity demanded to a change in price, the absolute value of elasticity will exceed zero. The more the response, the larger the elasticity. Whenever this value is less than one, however, the percentage change in quantity is less than the percentage change in price and demand is said to be **inelastic.**

When elasticity is equal to one, the two percentage changes are equal to each other. This case, which is called **unit elasticity,** is the boundary between elastic and inelastic demands. A demand curve having unit elasticity over its whole range is shown in Figure 3.2(iii).[3]

[3] The curve is called a rectangular hyperbola. Any rectangular hyperbola has the formula x times y equals a constant. In this case, the two variables are price, p, and quantity, q, so the formula of the unit-elastic demand curve is $pq = C$, where C is a constant.

When the percentage change in quantity demanded exceeds the percentage change in price, the elasticity of demand is greater than one and demand is said to be **elastic.** When elasticity is infinitely large, there exists some small price reduction that will raise demand from zero to infinity. Above the critical price, consumers will buy nothing. At the critical price, they will buy all that they can obtain (an infinite amount, if it were available). The graph of a demand curve having infinite price elasticity is shown in Figure 3.2(ii). Such a demand curve is said to be *perfectly* or *completely elastic.* (This is the demand curve faced by a price-taking firm in a perfectly competitive market environment.)

ELASTICITY AND TOTAL REVENUE

How does consumers' total expenditure react when the price of a product is changed? Notice that the total expenditure of the product's buyers is equal to the revenue of the sellers plus any taxes (such as VAT) levied by the government on the sale. A simple example will show that total expenditure on the product may rise or fall in response to a decrease in price. Suppose 100 units of a product are being sold at a unit price of £1. The price is then cut to £0.90. If the quantity sold rises to 110, the total expenditure falls from £100 to £99; but if quantity sold rises to 120, total expenditure rises from £100 to £108.

The change in total expenditure when price changes is related to the elasticity of demand. If elasticity is less than unity, the percentage change in price will exceed the percentage change in quantity. The price change will then be the dominant one of the two changes, so that total expenditure will change in the same direction as the price changes. If, however, elasticity exceeds unity, the percentage change in quantity will exceed the percentage change in price. The quantity change will then be the more important change, so that total expenditure will change in the same direction as quantity changes (that is, in the opposite direction to the change in price).

1. **If elasticity of demand exceeds unity (demand elastic), a fall in price increases total consumer expenditure and a rise in price reduces it.**

2. **If elasticity is less than unity (demand inelastic), a fall in price reduces total expenditure and a rise in price increases it.**

3. **If elasticity of demand is unity, a rise or a fall in price leaves total expenditure unaffected.**[4]

You should now take the example in Table 3.1 and calculate what happens to total revenue when price falls in each case. When you have done this, you will see that in the case of product A, where the demand is inelastic, a rise in price raises the revenue of

---

[4] Algebraically, total revenue is price *times* quantity. On a demand-curve diagram, price is given by a vertical distance and quantity by a horizontal distance. It follows that on such a diagram total revenue is given by the *area* of a rectangle the lengths of whose sides represent price and quantity.

sellers from £100 [= 100 × £1] to £104.50 [= 95 × £1.10]. In contrast, the rise in the price of good B, whose demand is elastic, lowers revenue from £1,000 [= 200 × £5] to £840 [= 140 × £6].

SOME COMPLICATIONS

We now need to look a little more closely at the elasticity measure. Let us first write out in symbols the definition we have been using, which is percentage change in quantity divided by percentage change in price:

$$\eta = \frac{\dfrac{\Delta q}{q} \cdot 100}{\dfrac{\Delta p}{p} \cdot 100}.$$

We can cancel out the 100s and multiply the numerator and denominator by $p/\Delta p$ to get

$$\eta = \frac{\Delta q}{q} \cdot \frac{p}{\Delta p}.$$

Since it does not matter in which order we do our multiplication (i.e. $q \times \Delta p \equiv \Delta p \times q$), we may reverse the order of the two terms in the denominator and write

$$\eta = \frac{\Delta q}{\Delta p} \cdot \frac{p}{q}. \tag{2}$$

We have now split elasticity into two parts: $\Delta q/\Delta p$, the ratio of the change in quantity to the change in price, which is related to the slope of the demand curve, and p/q, which is related to the place on the curve at which we make our measurement.

Figure 3.3 shows a straight-line demand curve. If we wish to measure the elasticity at a point, we take our p and q at that point and consider a price change, taking us to another point, and measure our Δp and Δq between those two points. The slope of the straight line joining the two points is $\Delta p/\Delta q$. The term in equation (2), however, is $\Delta q/\Delta p$, which is the reciprocal of $\Delta p/\Delta q$. Thus, the first term in the elasticity formula (2) is the reciprocal of the slope of the straight line joining the two price–quantity positions under consideration. The second term is the ratio of price to quantity at the point where elasticity is measured.

Now we can use the expression in (2) to discover a number of things about our elasticity measure.

First, *the elasticity of a downward-sloping straight-line demand curve varies from infinity (∞) at the price axis to zero at the quantity axis.* We first notice that a straight line has a constant slope so that the ratio $\Delta p/\Delta q$ is the same anywhere on the line. Therefore, its reciprocal, $\Delta q/\Delta p$, must also be constant. We can now infer the changes in η by inspecting changes in the ratio p/q as we move along the demand curve. At the price axis,

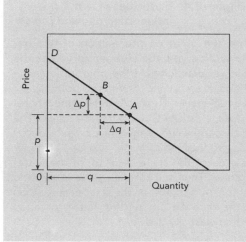

Figure 3.3. Elasticity measured on a linear demand curve

Elasticity depends on the slope of the demand curve and the point at which the measurement is made. Starting at point A and moving to point B, the ratio $\Delta p/\Delta q$ is the slope of the line, while its reciprocal, $\Delta q/\Delta p$, is the first term in the percentage definition of elasticity. The second term is p/q, which is the ratio of the coordinates of point A. Since the slope $\Delta p/\Delta q$ is constant, it is clear that the elasticity along the curve varies with the ratio p/q, which is zero where the curve intersects the quantity axis and 'infinity' where it intersects the price axis.

$q = 0$ and p/q is undefined. However, if we let q *approach* zero, without ever quite reaching it, we see that the ratio p/q increases without limit. Thus, elasticity increases without limit as q approaches zero. Loosely we say elasticity is infinity when q is zero. Now let the point at which elasticity is being measured move down the demand curve. As this happens, p falls and q rises steadily; thus the ratio p/q is falling steadily, so that η is also falling. At the q axis, the price is zero, so the ratio p/q is zero. Thus elasticity is zero.

The second point to make is that *with a straight-line demand curve, the elasticity measured from any point (p, q), according to equation (2) above, is independent of the direction and magnitude of the change in price and quantity.* This follows immediately from the fact that the slope of a straight line is a constant. If we start from some point (p, q) and then change price, the ratio $\Delta q/\Delta p$ will be the same whatever the direction or the size of the change in p.

Our third point takes us back to the beginning of this chapter, where we noted that it is difficult to judge elasticity just by looking at the slope of a demand curve, not least because we can alter the slope by changing the measurement scale. Since we frequently need to compare elasticities on two curves, it is fortunate that there is a way in which this can be done in one key situation: the elasticities of two intersecting straight-line demand curves can be compared *at the point of intersection* merely by comparing slopes, the steeper curve being the less elastic. Figure 3.4 shows two intersecting curves and proves that the steeper curve is less elastic than the flatter curve when elasticity is measured at the point where the two curves intersect. The intuitive reason is that at the point of intersection p and q are common to both curves so all that differs in the elasticity formula is their relative slopes. This is a valuable result that often makes visual elasticity judgements much easier:

> **Measured at the point of intersection of two demand curves, the steeper curve has the lower elasticity.**

Markets and prices

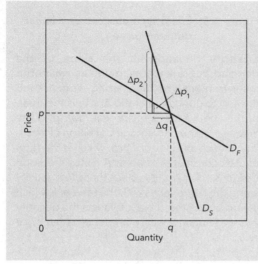

Figure 3.4. Elasticities of two intersecting demand curves

At the point of intersection of two demand curves, the steeper curve has the lower elasticity. At the point of intersection, p and q are common to both curves, and hence the ratio p/q is the same. Therefore, elasticity varies only with $\Delta q/\Delta p$. The absolute value of the slope of the steeper curve, $\Delta p_2/\Delta q$, is larger than the absolute value of the slope, $\Delta p_1/\Delta q$, of the flatter curve. Thus, the absolute value of the ratio $\Delta q/\Delta p_2$ is smaller on the steeper curve than the ratio $\Delta q/\Delta p_1$ on the flatter curve, so that elasticity is lower.

Our final point is that *when equation (2) is applied to a non-linear demand curve, the elasticity measured at any one point varies with the direction and magnitude of the change in price and quantity.* Figure 3.5 shows a non-linear demand curve with elasticity being measured at one point. The figure makes it apparent that the ratio $\Delta q/\Delta p$, and hence the elasticity, will vary according to the size and the direction of the price change. This is very inconvenient. It happens because the ratio $\Delta q/\Delta p$ gives the average reaction of q to a change in p over a section of the demand curve, and, depending on the range that we take, the *average reaction* will be different.

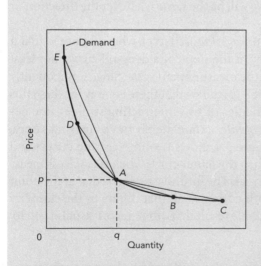

Figure 3.5. Elasticity measured on a non-linear demand curve

Elasticity measured from one point on a non-linear demand curve and using the percentage formula varies with the direction and magnitude of the change being considered. Elasticity is to be measured from point A so the ratio p/q is given. The ratio $\Delta p/\Delta q$ is the slope of the line joining point A to the point reached on the curve after the price has changed. The smallest ratio occurs when the change is to point C and the highest ratio when it is to point E. Since the term in the elasticity formula, $\Delta q/\Delta p$, is the reciprocal of this slope, measured elasticity is largest when the change is to point C and smallest when it is to point E.

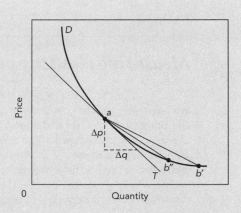

Figure 3.6. Elasticity measured by the exact method

When elasticity is related to the slope of the tangent to the demand curve at some point, there is one and only one measured value of elasticity at that point. In this method, the ratio $\Delta q/\Delta p$ is taken as the reciprocal of the slope of the line that is tangent to the point *a*. Thus, there is only one measured elasticity at the point *a*. It is p/q multiplied by $\Delta q/\Delta p$ measured along the tangent *T*. There is no averaging of changes in *p* and *q* in this measure because only one point on the curve is used.

The percentage formula can be thought of as an approximation to the exact method. Starting from *a*, change the price so that we move to some point *b'*; the ratio $\Delta q/\Delta p$ is the reciprocal of the slope of the straight line joining *a* and *b'*. Next let the price change take us to *b''*. The ratio $\Delta p/\Delta q$ is now the reciprocal of the slope of the line joining *a* and *b''*. The smaller the price change that we make, the closer the point representing the new price–quantity combination comes to point *a*, and the closer the slope of the line joining the two points comes to the slope of the line tangential to the curve at *a*. If the slopes of those two lines get closer together, so also do the reciprocals of the slopes and thus, so do the elasticities as measured by the formula involving $\Delta q/\Delta p$ and the formula dq/dp.

A MORE PRECISE MEASURE

The measure defined in equation (2) gives the elasticity over some range, or *arc*, of the demand curve. This measure is sometimes used in empirical work where elasticity is measured between two discrete observed price–quantity situations. In theoretical work, however, it is normal to use a concept of elasticity that gives a unique measure of the elasticity at each specific point on the demand curve. Instead of using the changes in price (Δp) and quantity (Δq) over some range of the curve, this elasticity measure uses the concept of how quantity is *tending to* change as price changes at each specific point on the curve.

If we wish to measure the elasticity in this way, we need to know the reaction of quantity to a change in price at each point on the curve, not over a whole range on the curve. We use the symbols dq/dp to refer to the reaction of quantity to a change in price at a specific point on the curve. We define this to be *the reciprocal of the slope of the straight line (i.e., $\Delta q/\Delta p$) that is tangent to the demand curve at the point in question.* In Figure 3.6, the elasticity of demand at *a*, calculated according to this measure, is the ratio p/q (as it has been in all previous measures) now multiplied by the ratio of $\Delta q/\Delta p$ measured along the straight line that is tangent to the curve at *a*. This definition may now be written as

$$\eta = \frac{dq}{dp} \cdot \frac{p}{q}. \tag{3}$$

BOX 3.1.

Measuring elasticity over a range

We have seen that the percentage formula gives many different answers for the elasticity at any point on a non-linear demand curve, depending on the size and the direction of the change being considered. Most textbooks just give the percentage elasticity formula without warning the reader of this property. Inquisitive students usually discover this property with a shock the first time they go to calculate some elasticities from numerical data.

One way in which the problem is often discovered is when elasticity on a unit elasticity curve is calculated as not being unity. For example the demand curve

$$p = £100/q \tag{1}$$

is a unit elastic curve because expenditure, pq, remains constant at £100 whatever the price. But if you substitute any two prices into the above equation and calculate the elasticity according to the percentage formula, you will never get an answer of unity, whatever two prices you take. For example, the equation tells us that, if price rises from £2 to £3, quantity falls from 50 to 33.33. If we take the original price as £2, we have a price change of 50 per cent and a quantity change of –33 per cent, making an elasticity of –0.66. If we take the original price as £3, the elasticity comes out to be –1.5.

This is unsatisfactory. The problem can be avoided when measuring elasticity between two separate points on the curve by taking p and q as the average values between the two points on the curve. This measure has two convenient properties. First, it is independent of the direction of the change and, second, it gives a value of unity for any point on a demand curve whose true value is unity.

In the above example, the average p is £2.50 and the average q is 41.666. This makes the percentage change in price 40 per cent ($= [1/2.5] \times 100$) and the percentage change in quantity also 40 per cent ($= [16.667/41.667] \times 100$). So elasticity is correctly measured as one. Whatever two prices you put into equation (1), you will always get a value of unity for the elasticity, provided you use the average of the two prices and of the two quantities when calculating the elasticity. Readers who enjoy algebra can have fun proving this proposition.*

The best approximation to the correct measure when elasticity is measured between two separate points on a demand curve is obtained by defining p and q as the average of the prices and quantities at the two points on the curve.

The above is the best way to measure elasticities given readings from any two points on a curve when that is all that is known. As we have seen in the text, for theoretical purposes, the way out of the problem is to measure the ratio $\Delta q/\Delta p$ as the slope of the tangent to one point on the curve rather than between two points on the curve. To do this we need to know a portion of the demand curve around the point in question.

In practice, economists do not usually estimate elasticity on the basis of only one observation. In such cases, it is common to report an elasticity measure that is valued at the mean of two p and q data points. This is analogous to the averaging we suggest here.

* What you need to prove is that

$$\frac{q_2 - q_1}{p_2 - p_1} \cdot \frac{(p_1 + p_2)/2}{(q_1 + q_2)/2} = 1.$$

The expression dq/dp, as we have defined it, is in fact the differential-calculus concept of the derivative of quantity with respect to price evaluated at the point (p,q).

This elasticity measure is the one normally used in economic theory. Elasticity measured by the percentage formula $(\Delta q/\Delta p)(p/q)$ may be regarded as an approximation to this expression. It is obvious by inspecting Figure 3.6 that the elasticity measured by $(\Delta q/\Delta p)(p/q)$ will come closer and closer to that measured by $(dq/dp)(p/q)$, the smaller the price change used to calculate the value of $\Delta q/\Delta p$. Thus, if we consider the percentage definition of elasticity as an approximation to the precise definition, the approximation improves as the size of Δp diminishes. Box 3.1 further investigates some of the properties of the percentage definition and shows a practical way of avoiding some of their undesirable aspects.

WHAT DETERMINES ELASTICITY OF DEMAND?

The main determinant of elasticity is the availability of substitutes. Some products, such as margarine, cabbage, lamb, and Ford Escorts, have quite close substitutes—butter, other green vegetables, beef, and Vauxhall Astras. A change in the price of any one of these products, *the prices of the substitutes remaining constant*, will lead consumers to substitute one product for another. A fall in price leads consumers to buy more of the product and less of its substitutes; and a rise in price leads consumers to buy less of the product and more of its substitutes. More broadly defined products, such as all foods, all clothing, cigarettes, and petrol, have few if any satisfactory substitutes. A rise in their price can be expected to cause a smaller fall in quantity demanded than would be the case if close substitutes were available.

A product with close substitutes tends to have an elastic demand; one with no close substitutes tends to have an inelastic demand.

Closeness of substitutes—and thus measured elasticity—depends both on how the product is defined and on the time-period under consideration. This is explored in the following sections. One common misconception about demand elasticity is discussed in Box 3.2.

Definition of the product
Food is a necessity of life; there is no substitute for food. Thus, for food taken as a whole, demand is inelastic over a large price range. It does not follow, however, that any one food, such as Weetabix or Heinz tomato soup, is a necessity in the same sense; each of these has close substitutes, such as Kelloggs Cornflakes and Campbells tomato soup. Individual food products can have quite elastic demands, and they frequently do.

Durable goods provide a similar example. Durables as a whole have less elastic demands than do individual kinds of durable goods. For example, when the prices of television sets rise, some consumers may replace their dishwasher or their vacuum

BOX 3.2.

Elasticity and income

It is often argued that the demand for a product will be more inelastic the smaller the proportion of income spent on it. The argument runs as follows. When only a small proportion of income is spent on some product, consumers will hardly notice a price rise. Hence, they will not react strongly to price changes one way or the other. The most commonly quoted example of this alleged phenomenon is salt.

Salt is, however, a poor example for the argument being advanced. Not only does it take up a very small part of consumers' total expenditure, it also has few close substitutes. Consider another product, say one type of mints. These mints no doubt account for only a small portion of the total expenditure of mint-suckers, but there are many close substitutes—other types of mints and other boiled sweets. The makers of Polo mints know, for example, that if they raise Polo prices greatly, mint-suckers will switch to other brands of mints and to other types of sweet. They thus face an elastic demand for their product.

Similar considerations apply to any one brand of baked beans. If Heinz raises its price significantly, people will switch to other brands of baked beans, such as supermarkets' own brands, rather than pay much more than is necessary.

What this discussion shows is that *goods with close substitutes will tend to have elastic demands whether they account for a large or a small part of consumers' incomes.*

There is, however, another aspect of the influence of income. To see this, consider any good that has an inelastic demand. A rise in its price causes more to be spent on it. If consumers spend more on that product, they must spend less on all others taken as a group. But the higher the proportion of income spent on the product, the less likely they are to spend more on it when its price rises. After all, if consumers were to spend all of their income on a single product, demand for that product must have a unit elasticity. As price rises, purchases must fall in proportion since the consumer has only a given income to spend. Thus, *for a good to have a highly inelastic demand it must have few good substitutes, and it must not take up too large a proportion of consumers' total expenditure.*

cleaner instead of buying a new television set. Thus, although their purchases of television sets will fall, their total purchases of durables may stay constant.

Because most specific manufactured goods have close substitutes, they tend to have price-elastic[5] demands. Demand for hats, for example, has been estimated to have an elasticity of −3.0. In contrast, demand for all clothing taken together is estimated to be inelastic, with an elasticity between 0 and −1.

Any one of a group of related products will tend to have an elastic demand, even though the demand for the group as a whole may be inelastic.

[5] Price elastic and elastic so far mean the same thing. However, we shall soon learn that elasticity can be measured with respect to changes in other variables as well, so price elasticity will then need to be distinguished from, say, income elasticity.

Long-run and short-run elasticity of demand

Because it takes time to develop satisfactory substitutes, a demand that is inelastic in the short run may prove elastic when enough time has passed. For example, when cheap electric power was first brought to rural areas of the USA in the 1930s, few houses were wired for electricity. The initial measurements showed demand for electricity to be very inelastic. Gradually, however, houses became electrified and purchased electric appliances, while new industries moved into the area to take advantage of the cheap electric power. Thus, when measured over several years, the response of quantity demanded to the fall in price was quite large, even though, when measured over a short period, the response was quite small.

Petrol provides a similar, more recent, example. Before the first OPEC price shocks of 1973, the demand for petrol was thought to be highly inelastic because of the absence of satisfactory substitutes. But the large price increases over the 1970s led to the development of smaller, more fuel-efficient cars and to less driving. The most recent estimates of elasticity of demand for petrol have risen from around 0.6 to around unity. Given another decade in which to develop substitutes, petrol demand might have proved elastic had the price not fallen back towards its earlier relative level. Each of these measures relates the change in price at one point in time to the change in quantity over time. What is found is that the larger the time-period over which the change in quantity is measured, the larger the elasticity tends to be.

> **The response of quantity demanded to a given price change, and thus the measured price elasticity of demand, will tend to be greater the longer the time-span considered.**

The different quantity responses can be shown by different demand curves. Every demand curve shows the response of consumer demand to a change in price. For such products as cornflakes and ties, the full response occurs quickly and there is little reason to worry about longer-term effects. For these products a single demand curve will suffice. Other products are typically used in connection with highly durable appliances or machines. A change in price of, say, electricity or petrol may not have its major effect until the stock of appliances and machines using these products has been adjusted. This adjustment may take a long time. It is useful to identify two kinds of demand curve for such products. A *short-run demand curve* shows the response of quantity demanded to a change in price, *given* the existing quantities of the durable goods that use the product, and *given* existing supplies of substitute products. A different short-run demand curve will exist for each such structure of durable goods and substitute products.

The *long-run demand curve* shows the response of quantity demanded to a change in price after enough time has passed to allow all adjustments to be made. The relation between long-run and short-run demand curves is shown in Figure 3.7. Assume, for example, that there is a large rise in the price of electricity. The initial response will be along the short-run demand curve. There will be some fall in quantity demanded, but the percentage drop is likely to be less than the percentage rise in price, making

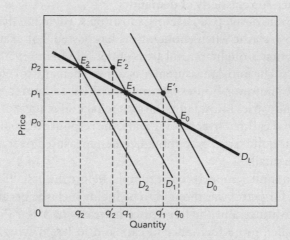

Figure 3.7. Short-run and long-run demand curves

The long-run demand curve is more elastic than the short-run curves. D_L is a long-run demand curve. Suppose consumers are fully adjusted to price p_0. Equilibrium is then at E_0, with quantity demanded q_0. Now suppose price rises to p_1. In the short run, consumers will react along the short-run demand curve D_0 and reduce consumption to q_1'. Once enough time has passed to permit the full range of adjustments to the new price, p_1, a new equilibrium at E_1 will be reached, with quantity at q_1.

Now that all adjustments have been made, there will be a new short-run demand curve, D_1, passing through the point E_1. A further rise in price to p_2 would lead first to a short-run equilibrium at E_2' with quantity q_2', but eventually to a new long-run equilibrium at E_2 with quantity q_2. The long-run demand curve, D_L, is more elastic than the short-run curves.

short-run demand inelastic. Over time, however, many people will replace their existing electric cookers with gas cookers as they wear out. New homes will be equipped with gas rather than electric appliances more often than they would have been before the price rise. Over time, factories will switch to relatively cheaper sources of power. When all these types of long-run adaptation have been made, the demand for electricity will have fallen a great deal. Indeed, over this longer period of time, the percentage reduction in quantity demanded may exceed the percentage increase in price. If so, the long-run demand for electricity will be elastic.

The principal conclusion in the discussion of elasticity is:

The long-run demand curve for a product that is used in conjunction with durable products will tend to be substantially more elastic than any of the short-run demand curves.

The general message is that some thought is required about the nature of the product under consideration. All adjustments to changes in the economic environment take some time, and those that involve some 'lumpy' investment, which itself takes time, will involve longer adjustments than others. Others may take time just because purchases are infrequent; for example, a rise in hotel prices in Spain in October will not have its full impact on demand for Spanish holidays until the following summer. In contrast, a fall in the price of Christmas crackers on 1 December will have its impact within a few weeks or not at all.

Other demand elasticities

So far we have discussed *price elasticity of demand*, the response of the quantity demanded to a change in the product's own price. The concept of demand elasticity can, however, be broadened to measure the response to changes in *any* of the factors that influence demand. How much, for example, do changes in income and the prices of other products affect quantity demanded?

INCOME ELASTICITY

The reaction of demand to changes in income is an important economic variable. In many economies, economic growth has been doubling real national income every twenty or thirty years. This rise in income is shared by most people. As they find their incomes increasing, people increase their demands for many products. In the richer countries the demand for food and basic clothing does not increase with income nearly so much as does the demand for many other, 'luxury' products. In many middle-income countries, the demands that are increasing most rapidly as incomes rise are the demands for durable goods. In an increasing number of the very richest of the Western countries, however, the demand for services is rising more rapidly than the demand for durable goods as income rises.

The responsiveness of demand for a product to changes in income is termed **income elasticity of demand,** and is defined as

$$\eta_y = \frac{\text{percentage change in quantity demanded}}{\text{percentage change in income}}.$$

For most products, increases in income lead to increases in quantity demanded, and income elasticity is therefore positive. For such products, we have the same subdivisions of income elasticity as for price elasticity. If the resulting percentage change in quantity demanded is larger than the percentage increase in income, η_y will exceed unity. The product's demand is then said to be **income elastic.** If the percentage change in quantity demanded is smaller than the percentage change in income, η_y will be less than unity. The product's demand is then said to be **income inelastic.** In the boundary case, the percentage changes in income and quantity demanded are equal, making η_y unity. The product is said to have a *unit income elasticity of demand.*

Markets and prices

Virtually all products have negative price elasticities. Both positive and negative income elasticities are, however, commonly found.

We have already encountered these relations in Chapter 2 (on pages 54–6), where we argued that a change in income would shift the demand curve for a product. If the product is a normal good, a rise in income causes more of it to be demanded, other things being equal, which means a rightward shift in the product's demand curve. If the product is an inferior good, a rise in income causes less of it to be demanded, which means a leftward shift in the product's demand curve. So normal goods have positive income elasticities, while inferior goods have negative income elasticities. Finally, the boundary case between normal and inferior goods occurs when a rise in income leaves quantity demanded unchanged, so that income elasticity is zero.

The important terminology of income elasticity is summarized in Figure 3.8. This figure shows the quantity demanded, for given prices of the product and all other goods (and all other things held constant except consumers' income), as income alone is varied. It shows a product with all types of income elasticity, positive, zero and negative, for different ranges of income. This is to illustrate all of the possible reactions. Specific goods do not usually show all of these. For example, a good may have a positive income elasticity at all levels of income. (You should be able to explain, however, why no good can have a negative income elasticity at *all* levels of income.) A graph that directly relates quantity demanded to income, such as Figure 3.8, is called an *Engel Curve* after

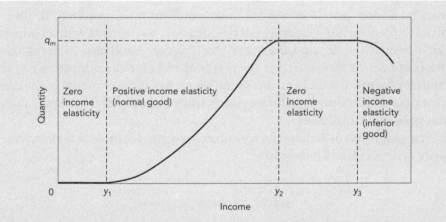

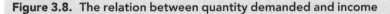

Figure 3.8. The relation between quantity demanded and income

Normal goods have positive income elasticities. Inferior goods have negative elasticities. The graph relates the quantity of some good demanded to income. Nothing is demanded at incomes less than y_1, so for incomes between 0 and y_1 income elasticity is zero. Between incomes of y_1 and y_2, quantity demanded rises as income rises, making income elasticity positive. Between incomes of y_2 and y_3, quantity demanded stays constant at q_m, making income elasticity once again zero. At incomes above y_3, increases in income cause reductions in quantity demanded, making income elasticity negative.

Ernst Engel (1821–96), the German economist who used this device to establish a systematic relationship between household income and expenditure on necessities.

CROSS-ELASTICITY

The responsiveness of quantity demanded of one product to changes in the prices of other products is often of considerable interest. Operators of cross-Channel ferries, for example, found that their demand fell when Le Shuttle lowered its prices for car journeys through the Channel Tunnel (see discussion on pages 76–7). Producers of large cars found their sales falling when the price of petrol rose dramatically after the 1973 and 1979 oil price rises. In the 1990s, software companies, such as Microsoft, have found demand for their programs booming as falling computer chip prices dramatically reduce the price of computing power (see discussion on pages 77–80).

The responsiveness of demand for one product to changes in the price of another product is called **cross-elasticity of demand.** It is defined as

$$\eta_{xy} = \frac{\text{percentage change in quantity demanded of one commodity}}{\text{percentage change in price of another commodity}}.$$

Cross-elasticity can vary from minus infinity to plus infinity. Complementary goods have negative cross-elasticities and substitute goods have positive cross-elasticities.

Bread and butter, for example, are complements: a fall in the price of butter causes an increase in the consumption of both products. Thus changes in the price of butter and in the quantity of bread demanded will have opposite signs. In contrast, butter and margarine are substitutes: a fall in the price of butter increases the quantity of butter demanded but reduces the quantity of margarine demanded. Changes in the price of butter and in the quantity of margarine demanded will, therefore, have the same sign.

Elasticity of supply

We have seen that elasticity of demand measures the response of quantity demanded to changes in any of the factors that influence it. Similarly, elasticity of supply measures the response of quantity supplied to changes in any of the factors that influence it. Because we wish to focus on the product's own price as a factor influencing its supply, we shall be concerned with *price elasticity of supply*. We shall follow the usual practice of dropping the adjective 'price', and will refer simply to 'elasticity of supply' whenever there is no ambiguity in this usage.

Supply elasticities are important in economics. Our treatment is brief for two reasons: first, much of what has been said about demand elasticity carries over to the case of supply elasticity and does not need repeating; second, we shall discuss the factors affecting the supply decisions of firms in more detail in Chapters 5 and 6.

A DEFINITION

The **price elasticity of supply,** which is often shortened to *supply elasticity* is defined as the percentage change in quantity supplied divided by the percentage change in price that brought it about. Letting the Greek letter epsilon, ε, stand for this measure, its formula is

$$\varepsilon = \frac{\text{percentage change in quantity supplied}}{\text{percentage change in price}}.$$

Supply elasticity is a measure of the degree of responsiveness of quantity supplied to changes in the product's own price.

Since supply curves normally have positive slopes, supply elasticity is normally positive.[6]

INTERPRETING SUPPLY ELASTICITY

Figure 3.9 illustrates three cases of supply elasticity. The case of zero elasticity is one in which the quantity supplied does not change as price changes. This would be the case, for example, if suppliers persisted in producing a given quantity and dumping it on the market for whatever it would bring. Infinite elasticity occurs at some price if nothing is supplied at lower prices, but an indefinitely large amount will be supplied at that price. Any straight-line supply curve drawn through the origin, such as the one shown in part (iii) of the figure, has an elasticity of unity. The proof is given in the figure caption. The reason is that for any positively sloped straight-line, the ratio of p/q at any point on the line is equal to the ratio $\Delta p/\Delta q$ that defines the slope of the line. Thus, in the formula $(\Delta q/\Delta p)(p/q)$, the two ratios cancel each other out.

The case of unit supply elasticity illustrates that the warning given earlier for demand applies equally to supply: do not confuse geometric steepness of supply curves with elasticity. Since *any* straight-line supply curve that passes through the origin has an elasticity of unity, it follows that there is no simple correspondence between geometrical steepness and supply elasticity. The reason is that varying steepness (when the scales on both axes are unchanged) reflects varying *absolute* changes, while elasticity

---

6 As with demand elasticity, the unique measure of supply elasticity at any point on a supply curve is given by the formula $(dq/dp)(p/q)$ where dq/dp is the reciprocal of the slope of the tangent to the supply curve at the point (p,q)—which is the same thing as the calculus concept of the *derivative* of quantity supplied with respect to price.

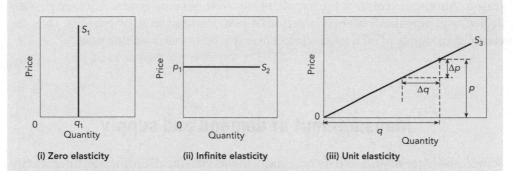

Figure 3.9. Three constant-elasticity supply curves

All three curves have constant elasticity. Curve S_1 has a *zero elasticity* since the same quantity, q_1, is supplied whatever the price. Curve S_2 has an infinite elasticity at the price p_1; nothing at all will be supplied at any price below p_1, while an indefinitely large quantity will be supplied at the price of p_1. Curve S_3, as well as all other straight lines through the origin, has a unit elasticity, indicating that the percentage change in quantity equals the percentage change in price between any two points on the curve.

To prove that a straight-line supply curve through the origin has a unit elasticity, look at the two triangles in part (iii) of the figure. One has sides p, q, and the S curve, while the other has sides Δp, Δq, and the S curve. They are similar triangles. It follows that the ratios of their sides are equal: $p/q = \Delta p/\Delta q$. Elasticity of supply is $\varepsilon = (\Delta q/\Delta p)(p/q)$. Substituting $p/q = \Delta p/\Delta q$ (since, as we have just seen, these two are equal) into the definition of elasticity gives $(\Delta q/\Delta p)(\Delta p/\Delta q)$, which is unity.

depends on *percentage* changes. However, as with demand curves, it is possible to say that, for two supply curves that intersect at positive prices and quantities, the flatter supply curve is more elastic at the point of intersection than the steeper curve.

WHAT DETERMINES ELASTICITY OF SUPPLY?

What determines the response of producers to a change in the price of the product that they supply? We shall see in Chapter 6 that the supply curves of individual firms depend upon the shape of their marginal cost curves. More intuitively, however, the size of the response depends in part on how easily producers can shift from the production of other products to the one whose price has risen. When agricultural land and labour can be readily shifted from one crop to another, the supply of any one crop will be more elastic than when labour cannot easily be shifted. Here also, as with demand, length of time for response is critical. It may be difficult to change quantities supplied in response to a price increase in a matter of weeks or months, but easy to do so over a period of years. One obvious example concerns the planting cycle of crops. Once planting has taken place, supply of one specific crop cannot be greatly changed until next planting season. Another example is the supply of oil. New oilfields can be discovered, wells drilled, and pipelines built over a period of years, but not in a few months. Thus the elasticity of supply of oil is much greater over five years than over one year.

Measurement of demand and supply

Some knowledge of price and income elasticities is vital for all businesses, since it helps them to anticipate both how the market for their product is likely to evolve over time, as incomes increase, and also how demand will respond to specific decisions, such as the price chosen. Demand for a product with a high income elasticity will grow quickly as income increases but may fall sharply in a recession, whereas demand for products with low price elasticities will be little affected by price rises. Before getting into a specific example, however, we have to offer some words of caution as to the difficulties associated with interpreting standard market data.

Problems of demand measurement

Knowledge of demand and supply elasticities has expanded greatly in recent decades as a result of advances in statistical theory and of computing power. A full discussion of these techniques must be left to a course in business statistics or econometrics, but some aspects of the problems involved can easily be understood with the tools of demand and supply curves.

EVERYTHING IS CHANGING AT ONCE

When quantity demanded changes over time, it is often because *all* of the influences that affect demand have been changing at the same time. How, then, can the separate influence of each variable be determined?

What, for example, is to be made of the observation that the quantity of butter consumed per capita rose by 10 per cent over a period in which average consumer income rose by 5 per cent, the price of butter fell by 3 per cent, and the price of margarine rose by 4 per cent? How much of the change is due to income elasticity of demand, how much to price elasticity, and how much to the cross-elasticity between butter and margarine? If this is all we know, the question cannot be answered. If, however, there are many observations showing, say, quantity demanded, income, price of butter, and price of margarine every month for four or five years, it is possible to discover the separate influence of each of the variables. The standard technique for doing so is called multiple

BOX 3.3.

Price and income elasticities

The table in this box presents some official estimates of price and income elasticities for a number of food groups in the UK. Several features of this information are worthy of note.

It is clear that all price elasticities are negative. Some, such as that for bread, are close to zero, but none is positive. This is exactly as we would expect from our theory of demand. Some food groups, however, have an elastic demand while others are inelastic. Of course, specific suppliers within these groups would typically face much higher price elasticities than those for the group as a whole. For example, two bakers in the same high street would find a much higher price elasticity of demand for bread if one raised its prices while the other did not. The elasticity in the table shows what happens to demand when all bread prices rise relative to other goods prices.

Income elasticities of demand for food tend to be less than unity. This means that demand for food rises less than in proportion to the increase in incomes. In other words, the proportion of income spent on food declines as income rises. This result is generally expected to apply to all food groups as well as to food as a whole, though it does not necessarily apply to some specific food brand. In the table, the only income elasticity anywhere close to unity is that for fruit juices, at 0.94. The next highest is 'other fresh vegetables' at 0.35. Four of the food groups have negative income elasticities. This means that they are inferior goods.

Finding bread and potatoes to be inferior goods is not surprising since these are the two products that have been commonly used as examples of inferior goods for over a century in economics textbooks. It is more surprising that 'bacon and ham' are found to be inferior. Carcass meats are also inferior, but very weakly so. Their estimated income elasticity of −0.01 is not significantly different from zero. Before the 1980s, it is likely that 'carcass meats' would have had a positive income elasticity. However, it is possible that demand has been affected by health scares related to red meat, so that people no longer buy more red meat as their income rises. Notice that these data refer to a period prior to the 'mad-cow disease' scare.

Product	Price elasticity	Income elasticity
Carcass meats	−1.37	−0.01*
Cheese	−1.20	0.19
Frozen peas	−1.12	0.15*
Cereals	−0.94	0.03*
Fruit juices	−0.80	0.94
Bacon and ham	−0.70	−0.28
Fresh green vegetables	−0.58	0.13
Other fresh vegetables	−0.27*	0.35
Fresh potatoes	−0.21	−0.48
Bread	−0.09*	−0.25

* Indicates not significantly different from zero at the 5% probability level.
Source: Ministry of Agriculture, Food and Fisheries, *Household Food Consumption and Expenditure* (London: HMSO, 1992).

regression analysis. Some examples of income and price elasticities calculated using this technique are presented in Box 3.3.

SEPARATING THE INFLUENCES OF DEMAND AND SUPPLY

A second, but related, set of problems concerns the separate estimation of demand and supply curves. We do not observe directly what people wish to buy and what producers wish to sell. Rather, we see what they do buy and what they do sell. That is, we observe the quantity and the price, but this price–quantity combination has to be at the intersection of the demand and supply curves. The evolution of these numbers over time does not necessarily trace out a demand curve or a supply curve. Rather, it traces out the shifting intersection of the two. The problem of how to estimate both demand and supply curves from observed market data on prices and quantities actually traded is called the **identification problem.**

To illustrate the problem, we assume in Figure 3.10 that all situations observed in the real world are equilibrium ones, in the sense that they are produced by the intersection of demand and supply curves. The first two parts of the figure show cases where only one curve shifts. Observations made on prices and quantities then trace out the curve that has not shifted. The third part of the figure, however, shows that when both curves are shifting, observations of prices and quantities are not sufficient to identify the slope of either curve.

The key to identifying the demand and supply curves separately is to bring in variables other than price, and then to relate demand to one set and supply to *some other* set. For example, supply of the product might be related not only to the price of the product but also to its cost of production, and demand might be related not only to the price of the product but also to consumers' incomes. Provided that these other variables change sufficiently, it is possible to determine the relation between quantity supplied and price as well as the relation between quantity demanded and price. The details of how this is done are beyond the scope of this book.

Well-trained analysts usually understand the identification problem. Sometimes,

Figure 3.10. The identification problem

Observations on prices and quantities are sufficient to identify the slope of one of the curves only when it is stationary while the other shifts. In each case, the curves in the left-hand column shift randomly from one numbered position to another. All that one sees, however, are the observations indicated by each of the points in the corresponding right-hand column. The problem is to identify the slope of one of the curves in the top row given only the observations in the corresponding bottom row. In case (i) the observations trace out the shape of the demand curve. In case (ii) they trace out the supply curve. In case (iii) neither curve can be identified from the observed prices and quantities.

however, managers who do not have an economics training can make serious mistakes. Whenever you see an argument such as 'We know that the elasticity of demand for our product must be very low because the price rose by 10 per cent last year while sales hardly changed at all', you should ask if the speaker has really identified the demand curve. If the rise in price was the result of a rise in costs that shifted the supply curve to

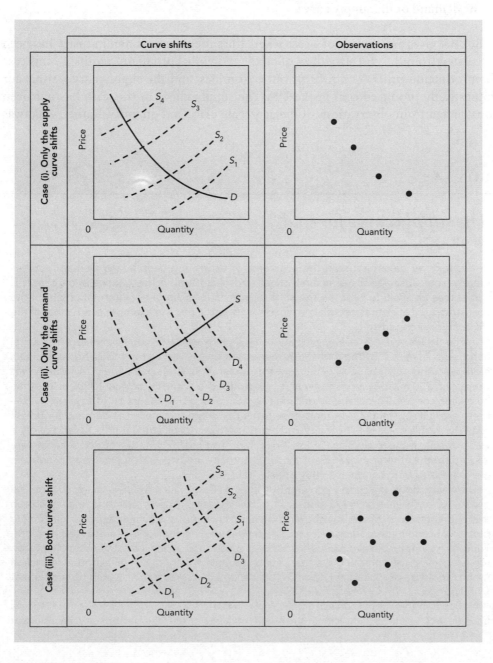

the left, while consumers' incomes rose and shifted the demand curve to the right, the observations would identify neither the demand elasticity nor the supply elasticity. The general proposition to keep in mind is:

> Unless we know that one curve has shifted while the other has not, price and quantity data alone are insufficient to reveal anything about the shape of either the demand or the supply curve.

Box 3.4 gives an example of a case where the supply curve for an industry has been calculated from the cost structures of all the individual production units. In this case the production units are not firms but coal mines, and the supply curve is that for domestically produced coal in the UK. The supply curve in this case has not been constructed from observations of the aggregate price and quantity. Rather, what was

---

BOX 3.4.

The supply curve for coal

In the text we have discussed the problems of estimating supply (and demand) curves merely from observations of market prices and quantities. In this box we show that it is sometimes possible to infer the shape of supply curves from direct information about the cost structures of all the potential producers in the industry. The example used is that of the UK coal-mining industry.

In the 1930s, the UK coal-mining industry employed over 1 million miners in several hundred coal mines. By the mid-1990s there were only less than ten thousand coal miners employed and only a handful of mines were in operation. At its peak, the coal industry was producing 290 million tonnes per year, compared with a figure in the mid-1990s of less than 20 million tonnes. This dramatic decline was not caused by exhaustion of coal reserves—these are still substantial—rather it is the result of a sharp decline in the demand for British coal. Partly this was a result of shifts of energy use towards oil and natural gas, and partly it was a result of the availability of low-price imported coal. The latter effect became very important after the privatization of the UK electricity industry, when electricity producers were released from contracts to buy British coal.

The chart shows the supply curve of British coal. That is, it shows how much coal can be produced each year (at 1992 prices) in mines that are at least covering their long-run average costs. It is derived by showing the industry output accumulated over each mine plotted at each mine's break-even cost of production. Each mine is represented by a dot. Thus, for example, the five most efficient UK mines can produce a total of about 10 million tonnes per year, all operating at a cost of under about £1.30 per GJ. While around 60 million tonnes could be produced at £2 per GJ, only about 25 million tonnes would be supplied at £1.50 per GJ.

Notice that this supply curve is highly elastic in the price range between about £1.40 and £2. This fact is critical in explaining the recent collapse of the UK coal industry. At a market

used is detailed information about the costs of every potential producer in the economy. Hence, the identification problem is avoided in this case.

We now turn to the example of the market for broadsheet newspapers. Here a price cut by one newspaper enables us to illustrate the calculation of price elasticity and cross-price elasticity. We shall also use this example in Chapter 8, where we discuss business strategy.

Keeping up with *The Times*

In September 1993, the owners of *The Times* newspaper launched what was expected to be a price war. They unilaterally lowered the price of *The Times* from 45p to 30p, a price

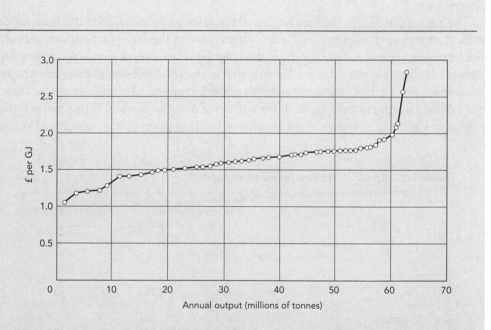

price of £1.30 only about five mines are profitable, whereas at a price of £2 more than forty mines could operate profitably. Unfortunately for many mines and the communities around them, the price of imported coal in 1992 was around £1.33 per GJ. Hence, all but a handful of the most efficient mines were forced to close.

It would be hard to find a more dramatic example of the relevance of the elasticity of supply to events in the real world.

Source: Data for the chart are from House of Commons Trade and Industry Select Committee, *Report on Coal Industry* (London: HMSO, 1993).

reduction of a third. The other broadsheet newspapers responded, not by matching the price cut, as often happens when a price war breaks out, but by doing absolutely nothing. All the major competing newspapers kept their prices constant and carried on as if nothing had happened.

This is an excellent case to analyse precisely because only one price changed. In many real-world situations a lot of variables move together, so it is hard to disentangle the individual effects without using formal statistical analysis. In this case, not only was there just one discrete price change, but it also occurred in a market where there was no reason to believe that total demand for all newspapers changed significantly.

THE EFFECTS OF THE PRICE CUT

Table 3.2 provides price and sale figures for the five major national broadsheet newspapers—*The Times*, the *Guardian*, the *Daily Telegraph*, the *Financial Times*, and the *Independent*.

The sales figures reported are average daily sales on weekdays for the four-month period after the price cut by *The Times*, compared with the same four-month period in the previous year. (Comparing the same months in two years removes any seasonal effects.) Notice that the total market size, that is, the total sales of all these newspapers combined, was virtually constant over this period, at around 2.5 million copies. Hence, the existing suppliers were fighting for a share of a stable market. If one gained more customers, it must be mainly at the expense of rival suppliers. Since consumers' average

Table 3.2. Changes in demand for newspapers

	Price		Average daily sales		Percentage change	
	Before Sept. '93	After Sept. '93	Before Sept. '93	After Sept. '93	Price	Sales
The Times	45p	30p	376,836	448,962	−33.3	+19.4
Guardian	45p	45p	420,154	401,705	0	−4.39
Daily Telegraph	45p	45p	1,037,375	1,017,326	0	−1.93
Independent	50p	50p	362,099	311,046	0	−14.10
Financial Times	65p	65p	289,666	291,119	0	+0.58
			2,486,130	2,470,158		

The Times led but no one followed. The table shows the fall in price of *The Times* and the less-than-proportionate increase in sales. It also shows the constant prices of the other papers, with declining sales (except for the *Financial Times*) as they lost readers to *The Times*.

Source: Audit Bureau of Circulation. The sales figures are average daily circulation for September 1992 to February 1993 and for September 1993 to February 1994.

incomes changed only slightly over the period and newspapers have a low income elasticity, we would expect total sales to be nearly constant, unless there were a major change in tastes over the period in question. The data suggest that tastes did not change significantly.

Table 3.2 shows us that the 33.3 per cent price reduction of *The Times* led to a 19.14 per cent increase in sales of *The Times* itself. This indicates a price elasticity of demand for *The Times* of −0.57 (calculated as percentage change in quantity divided by percentage change in price, or 19.14/−33.3). Hence, although there was a clear sales increase, it was proportionately smaller than the reduction in price. As a result, the total daily sales revenue received by *The Times* fell from £169,576 (376,836 × £0.45) to £134,688 (448,962 × £0.30). Only if the price elasticity had been greater than one would total revenue have increased. We shall enquire shortly why *The Times* might have persisted with its price cut despite the fall in sales revenue. However, let us first look at the effect on other papers.

The *Independent* suffered most, with a 14.1 per cent loss of sales. This would suggest that the *Independent* was the closest substitute for *The Times*. The cross-elasticity of demand implied by these figures was −14.1/−33.3 = 0.42. (This is positive since both the sales and the price changes were negative.) The cross-elasticity for the *Guardian* was −4.39/−33.3 = 0.13, and the cross-elasticity for the *Daily Telegraph* was −1.93/−33.3 = 0.06.

The *Financial Times* had a small increase in sales over this period. Its cross-elasticity was 0.58/−33.3 = −0.017. Taken at face value, this means that the *Financial Times* is (very weakly) complementary to *The Times*. However, the change is very small, and it is more likely that the two papers serve different markets (and hence have a cross-elasticity of zero) while the slight rise in sales of the *Financial Times* was for reasons unrelated to the fall in the price of *The Times*. The demand for the *Financial Times* could, for example, be driven more by the demands of business readers, while the other broadsheets are read by ordinary consumers with no interest in business. Further study of the demand for the Financial Times would be required to settle this issue.

DEMAND AND SUPPLY ANALYSIS

We said earlier in this chapter that it is important in each particular case to think about the special features of each market. The theory of demand and supply developed above assumes that there are many buyers and many sellers, each one of whom must accept the price that is determined by overall demand and supply. Newspapers fit this theory on the demand side since there are tens of thousands of buyers each of whom can do nothing to affect the price. On the supply side, however, there are only a few newspapers each one of which sets the price of its product. When our interest is mainly in the demand side of the market, we can use our demand–supply theory. We fit in the supply side by assuming a perfectly elastic supply of each newspaper: each sets its price and then sells all the copies that are demanded at that price.

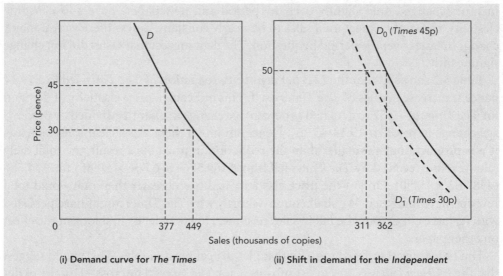

Figure 3.11. Demand for *The Times* and the *Independent*

A cut in the price of *The Times* shifted the *Independent* demand curve to the left. Part (i) shows the demand move for *The Times*. When its price was lowered from 45p to 30p, sales rose from 377,000 to 449,000 copies per day. Part (ii) shows the shift in demand for the *Independent* as a result of the fall in the price of *The Times*. At a constant price of 50p sales fell from 362,000 to 311,000.

Figure 3.11 illustrates the effect of *The Times*'s price cut both on its own quantity demanded and on the demand for the *Independent*. Notice that, since each newspaper is a distinct product there is no industry supply curve for newspapers. Each supplier simply sets a price and lets demand determine the level of its sales.

Our observation that the demand for *The Times* is price inelastic may explain why the rival newspapers did not cut their prices. If their demands were also inelastic, they would have lost more revenue by cutting their prices than they did by leaving them unchanged. As it was, the *Independent* suffered a daily loss of revenue of a little over £25,000 (just over 50,000 sales at 50p each).

The puzzle is why *The Times* persisted with its price drop even though it ended up losing revenue. We can only speculate at the answer since we have no knowledge of what the managers at *The Times* were thinking.

One possibility is that the increased circulation of *The Times*, as a result of its price cut, led to an increase in advertising revenue. Newspapers are able to charge advertisers rates for space that are related to circulation. Hence, revenue from selling the paper on the street is not the only source of income to the publishers. (Many towns in the UK have free newspapers that make all their revenue from advertising.) If *The Times* were able to increase its advertising revenue by more than about £35,000, the price reduction might be understood as a move that increased profit.

A second possibility is that the managers of *The Times* thought that their price cut might force the *Independent* out of business—a strategy sometime referred to as *predatory pricing* (see Chapter 8). The *Independent* was known to be in financial difficulty during the winter of 1993/4, and doubts about its survival persisted until March 1994. At that time, it was taken over by another company (the Mirror Group), which had more financial resources. Hence, if *The Times* was adopting a predatory price, its strategy failed. However, had it succeeded, it is likely that a high proportion of *Independent* readers would have moved over to *The Times* since the sales data suggest that the *Independent* was the closest substitute for *The Times*.

A third possibility is that demand elasticity increases over time, so that eventually the sales increase may have been sufficient to compensate for the price cut. Certainly, *The Times* continued to increase its market share beyond the period studied in Figure 3.11. Indeed, in June 1994, the *Telegraph* reacted to the growing market share of *The Times* by cutting its price, and the *Independent* followed. *The Times* responded to this by cutting its own price still further.

Once many prices are changing simultaneously it becomes more difficult to draw precise conclusions about demand elasticities. However, we shall return to the strategic issues involved in this industry in Chapter 8. At the time of writing (summer of 1996) this price war was continuing—*The Times* started to price its Monday edition at 10p in June 1996, even though its normal daily price was 30p.

The newspaper market clearly exhibits competition, but it is not a perfectly competitive market structure because each firm is able to set its own price and each sells a differentiated product. In Chapters 4–6 we develop an analysis of firms in perfectly competitive markets. In Chapters 7–8 we discuss markets in which imperfect competition and product differentiation are the norm. Perfect competition does apply to some markets and is a helpful case for getting us started on the analysis of firms. However, imperfect competition is the environment in which most firms find themselves, so it is the analysis of firms operating in imperfect markets that is of most general application to business.

Summary

1. *Elasticity of demand* (also called *price elasticity of demand*) is defined as the percentage change in quantity divided by the percentage change in price that brought it about.

2. When the percentage change in quantity is less than the percentage change in price that brought it about, demand is said to be *inelastic* and a fall in price lowers the total amount spent on the product. When the percentage change in quantity is greater than the percentage change in price that brought it about, demand is said to be *elastic* and a fall in price raises total spending on the product.

3. A more precise measure that gives a unique value for elasticity on any point on any demand curve replaces $\Delta q/\Delta p$ measured between two points on the curve with $\Delta q/\Delta p$ measured along the tangent to the curve at the point in question (symbolized by dq/dp).

4. The main determinant of the price elasticity of demand is the availability of substitutes for the product. Any one of a group of close substitutes will have a more elastic demand than the group as a whole.

5. Elasticity of demand tends to be greater the longer the time over which adjustment occurs. Items that have a few substitutes in the short run may develop ample substitutes when consumers and producers have time to adapt.

6. *Income elasticity* is the percentage change in quantity demanded divided by the percentage change in income that brought it about. The income elasticity of demand for a product will usually change as income varies.

7. *Cross-elasticity* is the percentage change in quantity demanded divided by the percentage change in the price of some other product that brought it about. It is used to define products that are substitutes for one another (positive cross-elasticity) and products that complement one another (negative cross-elasticity).

8. *Elasticity of supply* is an important concept in economics. It measures the ratio of the percentage change in the quantity supplied of a product to the percentage change in its price.

9. Measurement of price, income, and cross-elasticities of demand requires the use of statistical techniques to measure the separate influence of each of several variables when all are changing at once. It also requires a solution to the identification problem, which refers to measuring the separate shapes of the demand and the supply curves. This cannot be done from price and quantity data alone.

10. It is important for most businesses to know the size of the price, income, and cross-elasticities of demand for their products. These numbers help managers to anticipate the effects of key changes in the environment in which they operate.

Topics for review

- Price, income, and cross-elasticity of demand
- Zero, inelastic, unitary, elastic, and infinitely elastic demand
- The relation between price elasticity and changes in total expenditure

- Determinants of demand elasticity
- Income elasticities for normal and inferior goods
- Cross-elasticities between substitutes and complements
- Long- and short-run elasticity of demand
- Elasticity of supply and its determinants

Questions for discussion

1. Explain why there is a relationship between price elasticity of demand and the effects on total sales revenue.

2. Which one of each of the following pairs would you expect to have the higher price elasticity: snack foods and Walkers plain crisps; Rolls Royce cars and Ford Escorts; Coca Cola and Sainsbury's own-brand cola; the *Sun* and the *Financial Times*; BP petrol and Shell petrol?

3. If an industry had a perfectly *inelastic* supply curve what would this say about the responsiveness of that industry to changes in demand?

4. If an industry had a perfectly *elastic* supply curve what would this say about the responsiveness of that industry to changes in demand?

5. Read Box 3.1 and then, using the data in Table 3.2, calculate the elasticity of demand for *The Times* at its mean price and quantity. Compare this with the elasticity calculation in the text (which calculated elasticity at the initial price and quantity), and discuss the merits of these alternative methods of calculating elasticity.

6. Analyse what happens to sales and revenue of suppliers when the government imposes a sales tax on cigarettes when: (i) demand is elastic and (ii) demand is inelastic. If the government's goal is merely to raise tax revenue, would it be better to tax goods with elastic or inelastic demand curves?

7. Discuss the significance of the identification problem in interpreting the price and sales figures for a specific product.

8. Why should price elasticities be greater in the long run than the short run? What types of product are likely to show greatest differences?

Section 2
Optimization of the Firm

CHAPTER 4

The Firm, Production, and Profit

The firm in practice	120	The definition of profits	136
Forms of business organization	120	The accounting definition	136
The financing of firms	123	The economist's definition	137
Owners' capital	123	Alternative terminology in economics	137
Debt	126	Clear distinctions, confusing terminology	138
		Profits and resource allocation	139
The firm in economic theory	127	A preview	139
Why are there firms?	127		
Profit maximization	129	**Summary**	140
Production, costs, and profits	130	**Topics for review**	141
Types of input	132		
Evaluating costs	133	**Questions for discussion**	141
Purchased and hired inputs	133		
Imputed costs	133	**Box 4.1.** Anatomy of a public company:	
The firm's own funds	134	Glaxo Wellcome PLC	120
Special advantages	134	**Box 4.2.** Transnational corporations	124
The use of the firm's own capital		**Box 4.3.** Worries about the assumption of	
equipment	134	profit maximization	131

WE now start on our study of the behaviour of the firm. This is the organization of central interest for business and management. In subsequent chapters we shall develop a *model* of a stylized firm. At first we keep the world in which the firm operates very simple, in order to highlight the decision-making problem faced by all firms. In later chapters we shall permit this world to become much more complex. Economists call this model 'the theory of the firm'. It is important not to be put off by the label 'theory', because this exercise will illustrate how all firms make real decisions, such as how much to produce. The range of decisions that firms have to make will increase as we make the environment more complex. Decision making in a complex world is much easier if we can separate problems into a succession of simple ones and solve the easy ones first.

In this chapter we begin by considering the firm as it appears in practice. It is important to know some outlines of the organization and financing of firms in order to know what the subsequent simplifications are abstracting from. Furthermore, many terms that will be used throughout the rest of Part I of this book are introduced. We then go on to compare the treatment of the firm in economics with what we have just studied about the firm in practice. Finally, we introduce the concepts of costs, revenues, and profits and conclude by outlining the key role played by profits in determining the allocation of the nation's resources.

The firm in practice

'Firm' is a word that describes many different types of business. When we discuss the theory of the firm we treat these types as if they were all the same. However, it is important to know what different structures are available.

Forms of business organization

There are five main forms of business organization. A **sole trader** is a business in which there is one owner, who is personally responsible for everything that happens. The firm

---

BOX 4.1.
_____

Anatomy of a public company: Glaxo Wellcome PLC

In this box we show a list of the principal subsidiaries of Glaxo Wellcome PLC, a major UK-registered pharmaceuticals company, in order to illustrate the structure of a major company. As well as the Group, there are thirty-five subsidiary companies listed in twenty-three different countries. Notice that other countries sometimes use different letters instead of Ltd. or PLC.

Companies such as this, which are collections of many subsidiaries, are often referred to as a whole as 'the Group'. Subsidiaries may have special functions within the Group. In this case the functions are indicated as: H = holding company (the PLC that holds all the shares in the subsidiaries, also known as 'the Group'); R = research; D = development; P = production; M = marketing; E = exporting.

In 1995, Glaxo Wellcome PLC had a turnover of £7,630 million, made pre-tax profits of £2,505 million, and had 55,000 employees worldwide. In May 1996, the company had a stock-market value of £30,000 million, making it one of the largest UK companies by value. Glaxo Wellcome reports that it produces thirty-three major pharmaceutical products, with several new drugs in the pipeline.

BOX 4.1. (*cont.*)

Subsidiary	Country	Activity	% owned
Glaxo Group Ltd.	UK	H	100
Glaxo Wellcome Export Ltd.	UK	E	100
Glaxo Research and Development Ltd.	UK	R,D	100
Glaxo Operations UK Ltd.	UK	P	100
Glaxo Wellcome UK Ltd.	UK	M	100
Wellcome PLC	UK	H	100
The Wellcome Foundation Ltd.	UK	R,D,P	100
Laboratoire Glaxo Wellcome SAS	France	R,P,M	100
Glaxo Wellcome GmbH & Co	Germany	P,M	100
Glaxo SpA	Italy	R,P,M	100
Glaxo Wellcome BV	Holland	M	100
Glaxo Wellcome SA	Spain	R,P,M	100
Glaxo Wellcome AG	Switzerland	M	100
The Glaxo Institute for Molecular Biology SA	Switzerland	R	100
Glaxo Wellcome ISAS	Turkey	P,M	100
Glaxo Wellcome SA	Argentina	P,M	100
Glaxo Wellcome SA	Brazil	P,M	100
Glaxo Wellcome Inc.	Canada	R,P,M	100
Glaxo de Mexico SA de CV	Mexico	P,M	100
Glaxo Wellcome Inc.	USA	R,P,M	100
Affymax Research Institute	USA	R	99
Glaxo Wellcome Australia Ltd.	Australia	P,M	100
Chongqing Glaxo Wellcome Pharmaceuticals Ltd.	China	P,M	88
Glaxo Wellcome Egypt SAE	Egypt	P,M	89
Glaxo Wellcome Hong Kong Ltd.	Hong Kong	M	100
Glaxo India Ltd.	India	P,M	100
Burroughs Wellcome (India) Ltd.	India	P,M	32
Nippon Glaxo Ltd.	Japan	P,M	50
Glaxo-Sankyo Ltd.	Japan	M	25
Nippon Wellcome KK	Japan	R,M	55
Glaxo Wellcome New Zealand Ltd.	New Zealand	P,M	100
Glaxo Wellcome Nigeria Ltd.	Nigeria	P,M	100
Evans Medical PLC	Nigeria	P,M	40
Glaxo Wellcome Singapore Pte Ltd.	Singapore	M	100
Glaxo Wellcome Manufacturing Pte Ltd.	Singapore	P	100
Glaxo Wellcome South Africa (Pty) Ltd.	South Africa	P,M	100

Source: Glaxo Wellcome PLC, Annual Report and Accounts 1995.

may or may not have employees, but it has just one owner–manager. In a standard **partnership** there are two or more joint owners, each of whom is personally responsible for all of the partnership debts. A **limited partnership,** which is less common than standard partnerships, provides for two types of partner. *General partners* take part in the running of the business and have *unlimited liability* for the firm's debts. *Limited partners* take no part in the running of the business, and their liability is limited to the amount they actually invest in the enterprise. A **joint-stock company** (called a *corporation* in the USA) is a firm regarded in law as having an identity of its own; its owners are not personally responsible for anything that is done in the name of the firm, though its directors may be. In the UK, joint-stock companies are indicated either by the initials PLC after the firm's name, standing for *public limited company*, or by Ltd. (limited), which indicates a *private* limited liability company. 'Private' in this context means that the firm's shares are not traded on the London Stock Exchange or in any other market, whereas 'public' means that shares are traded on some public exchange. A **public corporation** is set up to run a nationalized industry. It is owned by the state but is usually under the direction of a more or less independent, state-appointed board. Although its ownership differs, the organization and legal status of such a public corporation is similar to that of a joint-stock company.

Notice the important difference between sole traders and partnerships on the one hand and companies and corporations on the other. This is that the latter are legally distinct from their owners, whereas the former are not. If a company goes bust, its owners (the shareholders) are not liable for the debts of the company, although they are likely to find that their shares become worthless. This is the meaning of 'limited liability', and it is one of the features of modern financial systems that encourages people to invest in companies even when they do not know much about what is going on inside the business. In contrast, sole traders and partners are liable for all the debts of their business, however large they might be. Throughout this book we refer to firms as if they were separate legal entities, even though this is not always strictly true. All companies are firms, but not all firms are companies. For example, most large accountancy firms and solicitors are partnerships rather than companies.

At the end of March 1995, there were 981,000 registered companies in Great Britain (England, Wales, and Scotland). Only 11,900 of these were public companies (PLCs). However, most PLCs have many private companies (Ltd.) as wholly owned subsidiaries or as *joint ventures*, which are subsidiaries owned by two or more companies. Box 4.1 contains a list of the principle subsidiaries of the UK company Glaxo Wellcome PLC. This shows how a typical PLC is made up of many subsidiary companies, most of which are wholly owned private (Ltd.) companies.

We do not know how many sole traders and partnerships there are because they do not have to register with Companies House. However, employment data show that there were 3.3 million people classified as self-employed in 1995. Limited partnerships do have to register, and there were 2,183 of these in England and Wales, and 2,500 in Scotland, in March 1995.[1] There used to be many public corporations in the UK; however, most of these were privatized in the 1980s and 1990s. Of those still in public ownership in 1996, the most significant are the Post Office and the BBC.

---

[1] Limited partnerships are mainly used for high-tech start-ups, where the inventor has unlimited liability and the backer limited liability. However, it is in the interest of the general partner (inventor) to convert to Ltd. as quickly as possible, so as to reduce downside risk.

A sixth method of organizing production differs from all the others in that the output is not sold. Instead it is provided to consumers free (or at a nominal price), while costs of production are paid from the tax revenue (in the case of public-sector production) or charitable donations (in the case of private production). Important examples found in all countries are government agencies providing law and order, fire protection, defence, roads, and education, as well as private charities. In the UK, we must also add the National Health Service to this list. (In countries without nationalized medical services, hospitals and doctors behave just as other firms do: they purchase inputs on the open market and gain revenue by selling their services to people who wish, and can afford, to purchase them.)

The first five types of organization make up the market sector of the economy. The sixth type makes up the non-market sector.[2]

Joint-stock companies that have locations in more than one country are often called **multi-national enterprises (MNEs)** or else, as the United Nations officially designates them, **transnational corporations (TNCs)**. Glaxo Wellcome PLC is clearly an example of a TNC, since it has subsidiaries in twenty-three different countries, and no doubt, sells its output in many more. The number and importance of TNCs have increased greatly over the last few decades. They are discussed in more detail in Box 4.2.

The financing of firms

The money a firm raises for carrying on its business is sometimes called its **financial capital** (or its *money capital*). This is distinct from its **real capital** (or *physical capital*), which comprises the firm's physical assets, such as factories, machinery, offices, office equipment, and stocks of material and finished goods.

The use of the term 'capital' to refer to both an amount of money and a quantity of goods can be confusing, but which is being referred to is usually made clear by the context. The two uses are not independent, for much of the financial capital raised by a firm will be used to purchase the capital goods the firm requires for production.

There are two basic types of financial capital used by firms: equity (funds provided by the owners) and debt (funds borrowed from outside the firm).

OWNERS' CAPITAL

The first main source of funds is the firm's owners. For a sole trader and a partnership, one or more owners will put up much of the required funds. A joint-stock company acquires funds from its owners by selling **shares** or **equities** (two names for the same

---

[2] There is a seventh type of organization that does not fit into this category or the previous ones. These are not-for-profit organizations that sell some of their output in the market. We mention these only for completeness. A theatre trust and a business school are examples.

BOX 4.2.

---

*Transnational corporations**

Over the past half century, the concept of a *national* economy has become less precise as a growing portion of production has been undertaken by firms with production facilities in more than one country. Such firms used to be called *multinational corporations*, but they are now officially designated by the United Nations as *transnational corporations* (TNCs). TNCs encourage global competition as well as the transfer of technological know-how among countries.

The number of TNCs has been increasing steadily over the years. In 1969, there were about 7,000 TNCs headquartered in the fourteen major developed countries; in 1990 there were about 24,000. Firms in these developed countries dominate the TNC scene, although in the last decade there has been a rise in TNCs located in Eastern Europe and the developing countries, particularly the NICs. Although large firms still dominate the TNC scene, the role of medium-sized and small TNCs is significant and growing.

The 1980s saw many changes in the behaviour of TNCs. The USA changed from being the leading provider of foreign investment through its TNCs to being the world's leading recipient of investment from foreign TNCs. Japan has become a leading foreign investor through TNCs. The Japanese transnationals have demonstrated a superior ability to innovate in high-tech activities such as the application of microelectronics-based technologies to manufacturing systems and to the handling of information in the service sector. Finally, the less developed countries (LDCs) have suffered large reductions in the amount of foreign capital that they import through foreign TNCs. (As a result, most of the LDCs have ended their anti-foreign-capital rhetoric and instead have adopted policies designed to attract such investment.)

The world is still in the phase of what the United Nations calls the 'continuing trans-nationalization of world economic activity'. TNCs in the USA now seem to have reached a plateau of size after strong expansion in earlier decades. Rapid expansion of TNCs from Japan, Western Europe, Australia, Canada, and Korea suggests, however, that although the location of expanding TNCs may have changed, the overall expansion continues.

At the beginning of the 1990s there were about 37,000 TNCs in the world, and they controlled about 170,000 foreign affiliates. Ninety per cent of these TNCs are headquartered in developed countries. France, Germany, Japan, the USA, and the UK between them are home to over half the developed-country total. About 60 per cent of all parent TNCs are in manufacturing, 37 per cent are in services, and 3 per cent are in primary production, such as mining and forestry.

The TNCs' primary instrument for developing foreign operations has been foreign direct investment (FDI)—acquiring the controlling interest in foreign production facilities either by purchasing existing facilities or by building new ones. During the 1980s, however, FDI fell dramatically, and other instruments have become more common. The most important of these are joint ventures with domestic firms located in countries where the TNCs wish to develop an interest, and licensing arrangements whereby a domestic firm produces a TNC's product locally.

There are many reasons for a company to transfer some of its production beyond its home base (thus becoming a TNC) rather than producing everything at home and then exporting

BOX 4.2. (*cont.*)

the output. First, local conditions matter. As products become more sophisticated and differentiated, locating production in large local markets allows more flexible responses to local needs than can be achieved through centralized production 'back home'. Second, non-tariff barriers to trade make location in large foreign markets, such as the USA and the European Union, less risky than sending exports from the home base. Third, many of the TNCs are now in rapidly developing service industries, such as advertising, marketing, public management, accounting, law, and financial services, where the option of producing everything at home and then exporting the output does not exist: to produce a service in some country, a physical presence is needed in that country. Fourth, the computer and communications revolutions have allowed production to be 'disintegrated' on a global basis. Components of any one product are often manufactured in many countries, each component being made where its production is cheapest. This globalization of production has been a boon to many less developed countries, which have gained increasing employment at wages that are low by world standards but high by their own. In contrast, however, many TNCs that transferred assembly operations abroad in the 1970s have recently been repatriating them to the home country, particularly in North America.

As a result of 'transnationalization', TNCs account for a large proportion of the foreign trade of many developed countries. This has long been so for the USA and is now becoming true for several other countries, particularly Japan. Although all types of TNCs have grown, much of the growth in recent years has been concentrated in small and medium-size TNCs, including some based in less developed countries. As the United Nations puts it, 'This dynamic aspect of the growth of TNCs is one of the major channels by which economic change is spread throughout the world.'

* The material in this box draws on *Transnational Corporations in World Development: Trends and Prospects* (New York: United Nations, 1988) and more recent publications from the UN Centre for the Study of TNCs.

thing) to them. These are basically ownership certificates. The money goes to the company and the purchasers become owners of the firm, risking the loss of their money and gaining the right to share in the firm's profits. Profits that are paid out to shareholders are called **dividends.**

One easy way for an established firm to raise money is to retain current profits rather than paying them out to shareholders. Financing investment from *undistributed profits* has become an important source of funds in modern times. Reinvested profit adds to the value of the firm, and hence raises the market value of existing shares; it is capital provided by owners.

Ownership of a firm changes when its shares are sold on the stock exchange. If one firm wishes to take over another firm, it must obtain control of the majority of the shares that are outstanding and then agree to buy all the rest that it does not own. The majority of US and UK company shares are held by investment institutions, such as insurance companies and pension funds, though such institutions hold them on behalf of their members and policy holders.

DEBT

The firm's creditors are not owners; they have loaned money in return for some form of loan agreement or IOU.

There is a variety of forms of such agreements, which are collectively called **debt instruments.** Each has its own set of characteristics and its own name. The two characteristics that are common to all instruments issued by firms are, first, an obligation to repay the amount borrowed, called the **principal** of the loan, and, second, some form of payment to the lender called **interest.** The time at which the principal is to be repaid is called the **redemption** or **maturity date** of the debt. The amount of time between the issue of the debt and its redemption date is called its **term.**

Most debt instruments can be grouped into three broad classes. First, some debt is in the form of *loans* from financial institutions, such as banks. These are private agreements between the firm and the bank, usually calling for the periodic payment of interest and repayment of the principal, either at a stipulated future date or 'on demand', means whenever the lending bank requests repayment—bank overdrafts are typically repayable on demand.

Second, *bills* and *notes* are commonly used for short-term loans of up to a year. They carry no fixed interest payments, only a principal value and a redemption date. Interest arises because the borrowing firm sells new bills that it issues at a price below their redemption value—at a *discount.* If, for example, a bill promising to pay £1,000 in one year's time is sold to a lender for £950, this gives the lender an interest payment of £50 in one year's time when the bill that he bought for £950 is redeemed for £1,000. This makes an interest rate of 5.26 per cent per year [$= (50/950) \times 100$]. The interest rate that is paid via discounting the face value of a bill is called the **discount rate.** Bills are negotiable, which means they can be bought and sold. So if I buy a ninety-day bill from a firm and want my money back thirty days later, I can sell the bill on the open market to someone else who is prepared to assume the loan to the firm for the sixty days that it still has to run. Many such bills that trade in the London money markets have been guaranteed, or *accepted,*[3] by banks in return for a small percentage of the discount. Such bills, guaranteed by the best banks, are referred to as *prime commercial bills* or *prime bank bills.*

The third type of debt instrument carries a fixed redemption date, as does a bill, and the obligation to make periodic interest payments, as do most loans. These are commonly used for long-term loans—up to twenty or thirty years. A firm that issues a 7 per cent thirty-year instrument of this sort with redemption value of £1,000 is borrowing money now and promising to pay £70 a year for thirty years and then to pay £1,000.[4] These instruments are generally known as **bonds;** but if they carried a variable rather

---

[3] Hence the name *acceptance houses*, which used to refer to what are now called merchant banks in the UK or investment banks in the USA.

[4] Conventionally, bonds issued in sterling each have a redemption value of £100, while dollar bonds have a redemption value of $1,000. A firm typically borrows much larger sums by issuing the appropriate number of bonds to raise the sum required.

than fixed coupon interest rate they would be called *floating rate notes* (FRNs), and if they were secured on the underlying assets of the company they would be called *debentures*. *Eurobonds* are bonds issued in currency other than the local currency. A dollar bond issued in London, for example, would be called a eurobond. Bonds are all negotiable, so that they can be bought and sold on a *secondary* market any time up to maturity. This is important, because few people would be willing to lend money for such long periods of time if there were no way to get their money back before redemption date. The *primary* market for debt instruments is that on which new issues are bought and sold.

Firms' debt falls into three main classes: loans that are non-negotiable agreements to pay interest and repay the principal either at a stated time or on demand; bills that are negotiable promises to pay a stated sum, usually within a year's time; and bonds that are negotiable promises to pay interest periodically and repay the principal sum at some redemption date, usually many years later than the date of issue.

In economics the term **bond** is used as a generic term to refer to any piece of paper that provides evidence of a debt carrying a legal obligation to repay the principal at some stated future time and an actual (as with bonds) or implicit (as with bills) payment of interest (though in reality bonds are long-term debt instruments). Hereafter we refer to all debt instruments as *bonds*, except where we need to distinguish between the various types.

The firm in economic theory

In Chapter 1 we defined the firm as the unit that takes decisions with respect to the production and sale of goods and services. This concept of the firm covers a variety of business organizations, from the sole trader to the joint-stock company, and a variety of business sizes, from the single inventor operating in his garage and financed by whatever he can extract from a reluctant bank manager to vast undertakings with many thousands of shareholders and creditors.

Why are there firms?

In Chapters 2–3 we studied the functioning of markets in allocating goods and services. Markets work through the forces of supply and demand; people with a particular good or service to sell, and people who wish to purchase that good or service, satisfy their mutual desires by exchanging with each other at some price.

Optimization of the firm

However, not all mutually advantageous trades occur through markets; often they occur within institutions, and in particular, within firms. Economists, like most other people, are inclined to take the existence of firms for granted. But in a famous article published in 1937, the British-born economist Ronald Coase, now of the University of Chicago and the recipient of the 1991 Nobel Prize in Economic Science, took up the question of why firms should exist at all.[5]

The key to Coase's analysis is the recognition that there are costs associated with transactions. When a firm purchases some good or service, it must identify the market and then find what different quantities and qualities are available at what prices. This takes time and money, and it usually involves some uncertainty. When the firm decides instead to produce the good or service itself, it uses the *command principle*: it orders the product to be made to its desired specifications. The transactions costs may be lower, but the advantages of buying in a competitive market are lost. Furthermore, as the firm gets larger, the inefficiencies of the command system tend to become large compared with the efficiencies involved in decentralizing through the market system. We discuss these problems of organization in Chapter 12.

The firm must choose when to transact internally and when to transact through the market. For example, a car manufacturer must decide whether to purchase a certain component by contracting with a parts manufacturer to supply it or to *supply the component to itself* by producing it. Coase viewed the firm as an institution that economizes on transactions costs. He argued that the market works best when transactions costs are low, but when transactions costs are high there is an incentive for the firm to use internal mechanisms in place of market transactions.

Coase's insights have stimulated much further research by economists, such as Professor Oliver Williamson of the University of California at Berkeley. This research has contributed to the understanding of the interaction of institutions and markets. Organization theorists have stressed that firms sometimes require less information than markets do for certain types of transactions; for example, transactions within firms do not require that decision makers be fully informed on market prices. Some research even shows that transactions within firms sometimes *generate* information that is useful to the firm. For example, close relationships between the producer of a particular component and the user often lead to improvements in its design and quality. Another consideration is that when firms internalize a production process they use one type of contract (say with their employees) to replace a set of often more complicated contracts with external suppliers.

Coase's analysis has proven remarkably robust over the years, and its influence has spread throughout economics. As economic historian and 1993 Nobel Prize winner Douglass North recently put it, 'Whenever transactions costs are high, institutions become important.'

A new approach to explaining why firms exist is known as the *knowledge-based* or *resources-based* theory of the firm. This sees firms as co-ordinators of the knowledge

5 'The nature of the firm', *Economica* 4 (1937), pp. 386–405.

that is embodied in each of their employees.[6] Successful firms in effect create teams that generate outputs that are greater than the sum of what could be achieved by market transactions (that is, hiring each input independently through the market). These ideas are relatively new and will be not be pursued in depth here. However, reasons why firms exist are important in determining how firms can achieve whatever it is they do better.

> Firms exist as an alternative to a pure market structure of transactions. Inside a firm there is a command economy. Managers of firms have always to be asking: should activity X be done inside the firm or bought in via the market from another supplier?

Profit maximization

We know that the decisions taken by large firms are actually taken by many different individuals. None the less, for many purposes the firm can be regarded as a single, consistent, decision-taking unit because of the assumption that all its decisions are taken in order to maximize its profits. This assumption is critical to what is called the *neoclassical theory of the firm*, and we may state it formally as follows:

> The desire to maximize profits is assumed to motivate all decisions taken within a firm, and such decisions are uninfluenced by who takes them. Thus, the theory abstracts from the peculiarities of the persons taking the decisions and from the organizational structure in which they work.

The assumption of profit maximization allows economists to make predictions about some aspects of firms' behaviour. Economists do this by studying the effect that each of the choices available to the firm would have on its profits. They then predict that the firm will select the alternative that produces the largest profits. For economists, the assumption of profit maximization is a convenient simplification that enables them to find analytic solutions to their models. We shall also use the assumption of profit maximization in much of what follows. However, it is important to be aware that this is an analytic device rather than an exact description of what happens in reality.

Managers of real businesses may have many goals. Even if they thought that they were trying to maximize profit, they would still have many problems to face about how best to do that. In most cases managers would love to know that they are maximizing profit, but they are unsure about how to achieve this outcome. Optimization in such a world, where some of the relevant conditions are unknown, is referred to in modern economics as a problem of **bounded rationality.** This means that managers are indeed trying to

---

6 See Kathleen R. Conner and C. K. Prahalad, 'A resource-based theory of the firm: knowledge versus opportunism', *Organization Science* 7(5) (September–October 1996), pp. 477–501.

maximize the profit of the firm but, given uncertainty and adjustment costs, they can at best get it only approximately right and will hopefully learn from their mistakes. We shall say a great deal more about the implications of bounded rationality later in the book when we discuss more complicated business issues.

Some have argued that making the very highest possible profit is not essential for a good manager. What matters is that there should be a reasonable profit and certainly no great disasters. The strategy of aiming for 'satisfactory' profit which stays above some minimum level is called **satisficing.** One factor that may lead to satisficing is when there is a conflict of interest between the owners of the firm, the shareholders, and the managers. Managers may aim to build empires for themselves or to have unnecessary foreign trips, even though these may not be justifiable in terms of profit, but they will need to make enough profit to keep shareholders happy. Shareholders are in a weak position to monitor managers because they do not have enough information to decide if they are overspending. This problem of monitoring and control is known as a **principal–agent problem.** The shareholder is the principal and the manager is the agent.

Profit maximization or satisficing as goals presume that the interests of the firm's owners or managers are paramount. One popular approach to business suggests that firms should take account of the interests of all of their *stakeholders*. Many different groups—employees, suppliers, pensioners, shareholders, customers—have an interest in the success of a firm, and so they literally have a stake in that firm's future. Return to shareholders is usually the dominant goal in Britain and the USA, but in Japan, for example, employees and suppliers typically have a greater input into decisions and a longer-term mutual commitment with the firm. Of course, a firm that is successful in delivering high returns to its shareholders is likely also to have good relations with its employees, customers, and suppliers. So it is far from clear that profit maximization is inconsistent with a stakeholder orientation. However, this issue is controversial, and it is safer to remain agnostic for the time being. Box 4.3 deals with some other worries about the assumptions of profit maximization.

Production, costs, and profits

A firm's profits are the difference between the revenues it receives from selling its output and its costs of producing that output. This simple-sounding concept turns out to be a tricky one because, as we shall see later in this chapter, costs of production involve some rather subtle notions.

Firms seek profits by producing and selling products. The materials and factor services used in the production process are called **inputs,** and the products that emerge are called **outputs.** One way of looking at the process is to regard the inputs as being combined to produce the output. One might also regard the inputs as being used up, or sacrificed, to gain the output.

BOX 4.3.

Worries about the assumption of profit maximization

Two criticisms are commonly made of the traditional theory of the firm: first, profit maximization is too crude an assumption about motivation and, second, the firm's organizational structure must affect its decisions.

The motivation of the firm

Many critics have argued that it is unrealistic to build an elaborate theory on such a crude assumption as profit maximization. It is well known that some businessmen are not inspired by the desire to make as much money as possible. Some pursue political influence, while others may be influenced by philanthropic urges. Should we not, therefore, say that the assumption that firms seek to maximize profits is refuted by empirical evidence?

The real world is complex. A theory selects certain factors that are assumed to be the most important ones, while those that are ignored are assumed to be relatively unimportant. If it is true that the key factors have been included, then the theory's predictions will be supported by the facts. It follows that it is not an important criticism to point out that a theory ignores some factors known to be present in the world; this tells us nothing more than that we are dealing with a theory rather than a photographic reproduction of reality. If the theory has ignored some really important factors, its predictions will be contradicted by the evidence.

How do these considerations relate to theories based on the assumption of profit maximization? First, such a theory does not require that profit is the only factor that ever influences firms. What it requires is that profits are an important consideration, important enough that assuming profit maximization to be the firm's sole motive will produce predictions that are substantially correct. Thus, pointing out that businessmen are sometimes motivated by considerations other than profits does not constitute a relevant criticism. It may well be that the theory is substantially wrong, but if so, the way to demonstrate this is to show that its predictions are in conflict with the facts. We cannot, of course, even consider such a possibility until we know what the theory does and does not predict. Accordingly, we shall press on to develop the theory. In Chapters 10–12 we incorporate many of the complicating factors, such as uncertainty and incomplete information, that are faced by real businesses.

Organizational structure

In the theory of the firm that we are about to develop, it does not matter whether a decision is taken by a small independent sole trader, a plant manager or the board of directors. As far as the theory is concerned, the decision-taker *is* the firm. This is an assumption of heroic proportions. It amounts to saying that we can treat the farm, the corner greengrocer, the large department store and the giant chemical company, all under the umbrella of a single theory of the behaviour of the firm. Even if this is only partially correct, it represents an enormously valuable simplification. It also illustrates the power of theory in revealing unity of behaviour where to the casual observer there is only a bewildering diversity.

BOX 4.3. (*cont.*)

Do not be surprised, therefore, if the theory seems rather abstract and out of touch with reality at first encounter. Because it does generalize over such a wide variety of behaviour, it must ignore those features with which we are most familiar, and which, in our eyes, distinguish the grocer from Royal Dutch Shell. Any theory that generalizes over a wide variety of apparently diverse behaviour necessarily has this characteristic, because it ignores those factors that are most obvious to us and that create in our minds the appearance of diversity.

While economic models of the firm abstract from organizational structure, this does not imply that issues of organizational structure have no importance—far from it. Indeed, economists have been leaders in the analysis of organizations, and we shall discuss many of their important insights in later chapters of this book. The general principle is that we should try to keep our analytic tools as simple as possible to deal with the problem in hand. This is a far more productive approach than the alternative assumption that large organisations are just so complex that we cannot analyse them at all with simple models and simple assumptions. Organizational structures are discussed in Chapter 12 below.

Types of input

Hundreds of inputs enter into the output of a specific product. Among the inputs entering into car production are, to name only a few, sheet steel, rubber, spark plugs, electricity, the site of the factory, the car park for its employees, machinists, cost accountants, spray-painting machines, forklift trucks, managers, and painters. These inputs can be grouped into four broad classes: (1) those that are inputs to the car firm but outputs from some other firm, such as spark plugs, electricity, and sheet steel; (2) those that are provided directly by nature, such as land; (3) those that are provided directly by people, such as the services of workers and managers; and (4) those that are provided by the factories and machines used for manufacturing cars.

The first class of inputs is made up of goods produced by other firms. They are called *intermediate products*. For example, one firm may mine iron ore and then sell this ore to be used as an input by a second firm that produces steel. Iron ore is thus an intermediate product that is an output of the first firm and an input of the second. Intermediate products thus appear as inputs only because the stages of production are divided among different firms. At any one stage of production, a firm is using as inputs goods produced by other firms at an earlier stage. If these intermediate products are traced back to their sources, all production can be accounted for by the services of the three kinds of inputs that we first discussed in Chapter 1, which are called *factors of production*. These are the gifts of nature, such as soil and raw materials, called *land*; physical and mental efforts provided by people, called *labour*; and factories, machines, and other man-made aids to production, called *capital*.

Evaluating costs

We have said that profit is the difference between revenue and cost. Any rate of output will generate some specific revenue and will have a set of inputs associated with it. To arrive at the cost of producing this output, a value must be put on each of the separate inputs used. The assignment of monetary values to physical quantities of inputs is easy in some cases and difficult in others. All economic costing is, however, governed by a common principle that is sometimes called *user cost* but is more commonly called *opportunity cost*:

> The cost of using something in a particular use is the benefit forgone by (or opportunity cost of) not using it in its best alternative use.

If the firm is a profit maximizer, it must—either explicitly or implicitly—evaluate its costs according to the opportunity-cost principle.

In principle, measuring opportunity cost is easy. The firm must assign to each factor of production it uses a monetary value equal to what it sacrifices in order to have the use of that input.

PURCHASED AND HIRED INPUTS

Assigning costs is straightforward when the firm buys an input on a competitive market and uses up the entire quantity purchased during the period of production. Materials purchased by the firm fall into this category. If the firm pays £10,000 for electricity used by its factory, it has sacrificed its claims to whatever else £10,000 can buy, and thus the purchase price is a reasonable measure of the opportunity cost of using that electricity.

The situation is the same for hired factors of production. Most labour services are hired, but typically the cost is more than the wages paid because employers have to contribute to such things as national insurance and pension funds. The cost of these must be added to the direct wage in determining the opportunity cost of the labour employed.

IMPUTED COSTS

A cost must also be assigned to factors of production that the firm neither purchases nor hires because it already owns them. The costs of using such factors are called **imputed costs.** They are reckoned at values reflecting what the firm could earn if it shifted these factors to their next best use. Important imputed costs arise from the use of owners' money, the use of the firm's own capital equipment, the need to compensate risk taking, and the need to value any special advantages (such as franchises or patents) that the firm may possess. Correct cost imputation is needed if the firm is to discover the most profitable lines of production.

The firm's own funds

What is the opportunity cost to a firm of the financial capital it has tied up in its operations? Say it is £100,000. The answer can best be broken into two parts. First ask what the firm could earn by lending its £100,000 on a riskless loan to someone else—say by purchasing a government bond, which has no significant risk of not being repaid. Say this is 8 per cent per annum. This amount is called the **pure return on capital** or the *risk-free rate of return*. It is clearly a cost to the firm, since the firm could close down operations, lend out its money, and earn an 8 per cent return. Next ask what the firm could earn in addition to this amount by lending its money to another firm where the risk of default was equal to the risk of loss in the firm itself. Say this is an additional 6 per cent. This is called the **risk premium,** and it is clearly also a cost. If the firm does not expect to earn this much in its own operations, it will pay it to close down and lend its money out to some other equally risky use, earning 14 per cent (8 per cent pure return plus 6 per cent risk premium).[7]

Special advantages

Suppose a firm owns a valuable patent or a highly desirable location, or produces a product with a popular brand name, such as Guinness, Chanel, Porsche, or Polo. Each of these involves an opportunity cost to the firm in production (even if it was acquired free) because if the firm did not choose to use the special advantage itself, *it could sell or lease it to others*. The firm must, therefore, charge itself for using the special advantage, if it chooses to do so.

The use of the firm's own capital equipment

The cost of using capital equipment the firm owns, such as buildings, machinery, and office equipment, consists of the loss in the value of the asset, called **depreciation,** caused by its use in production. Accountants use various conventional methods of calculating depreciation based on the price originally paid for the asset. Although such historical costs are often useful approximations, they may, in some cases, seriously differ from the depreciation required by the opportunity-cost principle. Two examples of possible errors are given in the paragraphs that follow.

Example 1. The owner of a firm buys a £12,000 car that she intends to use for six years for business purposes and then discard. She may think this will cost her £2,000 per year. But if after one year the value of her car on the used-car market is £9,000, it has cost her £3,000 to use the car during the first year. Why should she charge herself £3,000 depreciation during the first year? After all, she does not intend to sell the car for six years. The answer is that one of her alternatives is to buy a one-year-old car and operate it for

---

[7] Owner-managed firms must also include an imputed cost for the owner's time.

five years. Indeed, that is the very position she is in after the first year. Whether she likes it or not, she has paid £3,000 for the use of the car during the first year of its life. If the market had valued her car at £11,000 after one year (instead of £9,000), the correct depreciation charge would have been only £1,000.[8]

Example 2. A firm has just purchased a set of machines for £100,000. The machines have an expected life-time of ten years, and the firm's accountant calculates the 'depreciation cost' of these machines at £10,000 per year. The machines can be used to make only one product, and since they are installed in the firm's factory, they can be leased to no one else. They have a negligible second-hand or scrap value. Assume that if the machines are used to produce the firm's product, the cost of all other factors utilized will amount to £25,000 per year. Immediately after purchasing the machines the firm finds that the price of the product in question has unexpectedly fallen, so that the output can now only be sold for £29,000 per year instead of the £35,000 that had originally been expected. What should the firm do?

If in calculating its costs the firm adds in the historically determined depreciation costs of £10,000 a year, the total cost of operation comes to £35,000; with the revenue at £29,000 this makes a loss of £6,000 per year. It appears that the product should not be made. But this is not correct. Since the machines have no alternative use, their opportunity cost to the firm (which is determined by what else the firm could do with them) is zero. The total cost of producing the output is thus only £25,000 per year, and the whole current operation shows a return over cost of £4,000 per year rather than a loss of £6,000. (If the firm did not produce the goods, in order to avoid expected losses, it would earn £4,000 per year less than if it carried on with production.)

Of course, the firm would not have bought the machines had it known that the price of the product was going to fall, but once it has bought them, the cost of using them is zero, and it is profitable to use them as long as they yield any net revenue whatsoever over all other costs. Costs that have been incurred in the past but that should not affect the current production decision are known as **sunk costs**.

The principle illustrated by both of these examples may be stated in terms of an important maxim:

> **Bygones are bygones and should have no influence in deciding what is currently the most profitable thing to do. Bygones in business are known as sunk costs.[9]**

---

[8] Note that we are talking about the economic cost of depreciation and how an economist would measure it. Accounting rules and tax laws may lead to depreciation being treated differently in company accounts or tax returns.

[9] This is an important principle that extends well beyond economics. In many poker games, for example, the cards are dealt a round at a time and betting occurs each time the players have been given an additional card. Players who bet heavily on early rounds because their hands looked promising often stay in through later rounds on indifferent hands because they 'already have such a stake in the pot'. The professional player knows that, after each round of cards has been dealt, a bet should be made on the probability that the hand currently held will turn into a winner when all the cards have been dealt. If the probabilities look poor after the fourth card has been dealt

Table 4.1. Profit and loss account for XYZ Company for the year ending 31 December 1998

	Expenditure (£)	Income (£)
Variable costs		
Wages	200,000	Revenue from sales 1,000,000
Materials	300,000	
Other	100,000	
Total VC	600,000	
Fixed costs		
Rent	50,000	
Managerial salaries	60,000	
Interest on loans	90,000	
Depreciation allowance	50,000	
Total FC	250,000	
Total expenditure	850,000	
Profit		150,000

The profit and loss account shows profits as defined by the firm's accounts. The table gives a simplified version of a real profit and loss statement. The total revenue earned by the firm, minus what it regards as costs, yields profits. Since firms do not count the opportunity cost of capital, this is included in profits as calculated by the firm. (Note that costs are divided into those that vary with output, called variable costs, and those that do not, called fixed costs. This distinction is discussed in detail in Chapter 5.)

The definition of profits

We have earlier defined profits as the difference between the revenue the firm gains from selling its output and the costs of producing that output. Different definitions of profits are in use because of different definitions of costs.

The accounting definition

When firms report their profits, they use the accounting definition of costs, which excludes both the opportunity cost of the firm's own financial capital and any risk premium. According to this definition, the firm's 'profits' are the return on its capital.

The calculation of profits according to the accounting definition is done in a profit

(five usually constitutes a complete hand), the player should abandon the hand whether he or she has put 5p or £5 into the pot already. Amateurs who base their current decisions on what they have put into the pot in earlier rounds of betting will be long-term losers if they play in rational company. In poker, war, and economics, bygones *are* bygones, and to take account of them in current decisions is to court disaster! We discuss sunk costs further in Ch. 11.

Table 4.2. Calculation of pure profits (£)

Profit as reported by the firm	150,000
Opportunity cost of capital:	
(i) Pure return on the firm's capital	−100,000
(ii) Risk premium	−40,000
Pure or economic profit	10,000

The economist's definition of profit excludes the opportunity cost of capital.
To arrive at the economist's definition of profit, the opportunity cost of capital—
the pure return on a riskless investment plus any risk premium—must be
deducted from the firm's definition of profit. What is left is called profit by economists, but the terms 'pure' or 'economic' are sometimes added to distinguish
it from the firm's more inclusive definition of profit.

and loss statement, a simplified version of which is shown in Table 4.1. Notice that this
statement divides the firm's costs between those that vary with output, called variable
costs, and those that do not, called fixed costs. To get from the accountant's definition to
the economist's definition of profits, the opportunity cost of capital must be deducted,
as shown in Table 4.2.

The economist's definition
What economists call profit is the excess of revenue over all opportunity costs including
those of capital. To discover whether profit in the economic sense exists, take the
revenue of the firm and deduct the costs of all inputs other than capital, which gives the
accountant's definition of profits. Then deduct the pure return on capital and any risk
premium necessary to compensate the owners of capital for the risks associated with its
use in this firm and industry. Anything that remains is profit according to the definition
used by economists. It belongs to the owners of the firm and, therefore, may be regarded
as an additional return on their capital, over and above its opportunity cost. Profit in the
sense just defined is variously called **pure profit, economic profit,** or where there is no
room for ambiguity, just **profit.**

Alternative terminology in economics
The opportunity cost of capital is defined by economists as part of total cost. Profits
are thus defined in economics as what is left after deducting this cost from what the
businessman calls profits. An alternative terminology, still used in some elementary
textbooks, but seldom in advanced theory, calls the opportunity cost of capital *normal
profits.* Any excess of revenue over normal profits is then called supernormal profits.
Since you may encounter this alternative terminology, the equivalents are laid out in
Table 4.3.

Table 4.3. Alternative terminology of profits

Accounting definition	Economic definitions		
	Standard usage		Alternative usage
Profits	Opportunity cost of capital	=	Normal profits
	Pure profits	=	Supernormal profits

Economists count the opportunity cost of capital as a cost; accountants include it as part of profits. The distinctions are clear, it is only the words used to describe them that can be confusing.

Clear distinctions, confusing terminology

The distinctions we have been considering are clear enough; the only problem is that the same word, 'profit', is used to describe one thing by firms in their published accounts and another thing by economists. Firms measure how much money they make before paying any return to shareholders, and they call this profit. Economists are interested in the role played in the allocation of resources by the returns that firms made *over and above* the opportunity cost of their capital, and they call this smaller amount profit.

We cannot say that the accountants' definition is wrong and the economists' is right, or vice versa. It is just that they are used for different purposes. Indeed, legally the accountants have to be right, because it is their definition of profit that is used in company accounts and also in the calculation of companies' liability to corporation tax. However, the accountants' definition is problematic in judging firms' performance simply because it does not account for the costs of capital employed. Leading UK business economist Professor John Kay has suggested calling what we call pure or economic profit *added value*,[10] since it is a residual return to shareholders over and above all the opportunity costs of resources:

> Added value is the difference between the (comprehensively accounted) value of a firm's output and the (comprehensively accounted) cost of the firm's inputs. In this specific sense, adding value is both the proper motivation of corporate activity and the measure of its achievement.[11]

In everything that follows, we use the economist's definition of costs and profits, which is the same as Kay's measure of added value, unless we explicitly say otherwise.

[10] Be careful not to confuse 'added value' with 'value added'. The latter is the difference between the revenue of the firm and the value of its inputs bought from other firms. Hence value added is the sum of the return to all factor inputs—wages, salaries, profit, and rent.

[11] John Kay, *Foundations of Corporate Success* (Oxford: Oxford University Press, 1995), p. 19.

Profits and resource allocation

When resources are valued by the opportunity-cost principle, their costs show how much these resources would earn if employed in their best alternative uses. If there is an industry in which all firms' revenues exceed opportunity costs, all the firms in the industry will be earning pure profits. Thus, the owners of factors of production will want to move resources into this industry, because the earnings potentially available to them are greater there than in alternative uses of the resources. If in some other industry firms are incurring losses, some or all of this industry's resources are more highly valued in other uses, and owners of the resources will want to move them to those other uses.

Profits and losses play a crucial signalling role in the workings of a free-market economic system.

Profits in an industry are the signal that resources can profitably be moved into the industry. Losses are the signal that the resources can profitably be moved elsewhere. Only if there are zero economic profits is there no incentive for resources to move into or out of an industry.

A preview

We have seen that firms are assumed to maximize their profits (π), which are the difference between the revenues derived from the sale of their output (R) and the cost of producing that output (C):

$$\pi = R - C.$$

Thus, what happens to profits depends on what happens to revenues and costs.

We have already explained the special meaning that economists give to the concept of costs. In Chapter 5 we develop a theory of how costs vary with output. This theory is common to all firms. We then consider how revenues vary with output and find that it is necessary to deal separately with firms in markets that are competitive (Chapter 6) and monopolistic (Chapter 7). Costs and revenues are then combined to determine the profit-maximizing behaviour for firms in various market situations. The most complicated market environment to analyse is that in which there is a small group of competing firms. This is known as **oligopoly**. The problem here is that the optimal decision of one firm is not independent of what other firms are doing. There is strategic interdependence. This is the subject of Chapter 8.

Summary

1. Production is mainly organized by private-sector firms, which take four main forms —sole traders, with one owner–manager; ordinary partnerships, with several fully liable owners; limited partnerships, with some ordinary partners and some non-active partners who have limited liability; and joint-stock companies, with limited liability for their many owners, who are not usually the firms' managers—or by state-owned enterprises called public corporations.

2. Firms make up the production side of the market sector. The non-market sector consists of organizations that do not seek to cover their costs of production by revenue gained from selling that production.

3. Modern firms finance themselves by obtaining money from their owners by selling them shares or by reinvesting their profits, and by borrowing from both the public and various financial institutions.

4. Much of economic theory treats all types of firm under one umbrella by assuming that all firms make consistent decisions designed to maximize their profits. The theory thus assumes that the organizational structure of firms, and objectives other than profits, do not exert significant influences on the outcomes predicted.

5. Costs in economic theory refer to opportunity costs. These are correctly measured by the price paid for hired inputs, but they must be imputed for the costs of using inputs owned by the firm. The cost of firms' own capital includes the pure return—what could be earned on a riskless investment—and a risk premium—what could be earned over the pure return elsewhere in the economy on an equally risky investment. Profits are the difference between revenues and costs.

6. Accountants do not deduct the cost of the firm's own capital when calculating what they call profit, which thus includes the pure return on capital as well as the risk premium. When these two amounts are also deducted from revenues, the result is the economist's definition of profit, which is sometimes called pure, or economic, profit to distinguish it from what firms call profits.

7. Economic profits play a key role in resource allocation. Positive economic profits attract resources into an industry, negative economic profits induce resources to move elsewhere. Making economic profit is also what should motivate firms' managers and is an appropriate criterion for judging success.

Topics for review

- Forms of business organization
- Methods of financing modern firms
- Loans, bills, and bonds
- Profit maximization
- The definition of costs
- The measurement of opportunity costs for hired and for owned inputs
- Imputed costs
- Sunk costs
- Alternative definitions of profits

Questions for discussion

1. Discuss the factors that will influence which structure is adopted by a firm. Why do you think that large accountancy firms and law firms are still organized as partnerships when most other large firms are Ltd. or PLC?

2. If a firm wants to raise more money to finance an expansion, what factors would influence whether it should increase its debt or raise more equity? If it increases its debt, how should it decide what form of debt to incur?

3. What should be the goal of firms? What objectives can you think of other than profit maximization?

4. Draw up a list of all the inputs into the following types of firm: a brewer, a hairdresser, a farmer, a restaurant, and a garage (car repairer). Which of these input costs are deductible from sales revenue in the calculation of accounting profit, and which are also deducted in the calculation of economic profit?

5. Are there any types of business for which economic profit and accounting profit will be the same?

6. Explain why the existence of economic profit will attract entrants into an industry but the existence of accounting profits alone may not do so.

CHAPTER 5

Costs and Output

The relationship between output and inputs 143
    The short run   144
    The long run   145
    The very long run   145

The short run   146
Short-run variations in output   146
    The law of diminishing returns   148
    The relation between marginal and
    average product curves   150
Short-run variations in cost   151
    Short-run cost curves   152
    How cost varies with output   154
    The definition of capacity   155
    A family of short-run cost curves   155

The long run   158
Profit maximization and cost minimization   158
    Choice of input mix   159
    Long-run equilibrium of the firm   160
The principle of substitution   160
Cost curves in the long run   161
    The shape of the long-run average
    cost curve   161
        Decreasing costs   162
        Increasing costs   162
        Constant costs   163
        Some evidence   163
    Economies of scale and economies of scope 164

Sources of increasing returns to scale   165
    Geometrical relations   165
    One-time costs   165
    The technology of large-scale
    production   166
    Network effects   168
    The learning curve   171
Increasing returns: winner take all?   171
Relationship between long-run and
short-run costs   172
Shifts in cost curves   172

The very long run: endogenous
technical change   173

Summary   177

Topics for review   178

Questions for discussion   179

Box 5.1. Why many firms report that average
costs are constant   156
Box 5.2. Economies of scale in the electricity
industry   167
Box 5.3. The flexible manufacturing
revolution   169
Box 5.4. Endogenous materials design:
a new industrial revolution?   174

P ROFIT is the difference between revenue from sales and the costs of production. In this chapter we focus on costs and, in particular, how costs vary with the volume of production. The following chapter adds revenue to the analysis, and we shall then be able to highlight the conditions necessary for profit to be maximized.

We are now starting on the process of building a model of firms' behaviour. We have already referred to this model as the *theory of the firm*. Recall that we are trying to keep things as simple as possible so that we can get our minds round the key issues. The firm we are going to be talking about is best thought of, at least to start with, as a simple firm that produces a single product in a single factory. Thus, this is a manufacturing firm that takes some material inputs, hires workers, and by use of some machinery makes a physical product that is then sold to consumers. The principles that will be illustrated in this simplified case can easily be generalized to more complex cases, such as multi-product firms or service industries.

This chapter is divided into three main parts. The first part deals with the short run, when a firm can vary only some of its inputs. These variable inputs and outputs are governed by a famous relation called the law of diminishing returns. Having discovered how inputs and outputs are related, we need only to put prices on the inputs and see how the firm's costs vary with its output. We then go on to see how costs vary with output in the long run. Here we pay special attention to economies of scale, where increases in the scale of output result in falling costs per unit of output. In the third and final section we study how firms may seek to alter their costs of production by incorporating new technology. First, however, we define some terms.

The relationship between output and inputs

The relationship between the volume of physical inputs into production and the number of units of output produced is known in economics as the **production function**. It describes the technological relation between what is fed into the productive apparatus by way of materials and the inputs of factor services (labour and capital) and what is turned out by way of product. When using this function, remember that production is a flow: it is so many units *per period of time*. If we speak of raising the level of monthly production from, say, 100 to 101 units, we do not mean producing 100 units this month and one unit next month, but going from a rate of production of 100 units *each month* to a rate of 101 units *each month*.

Using mathematical notation, the production function can be written as:

$$q = g(f_1, \ldots, f_m), \tag{1}$$

where q is the quantity of output of some good or service; $f_1, \ldots, f_m$ are the quantities of m different inputs used in its production; and g summarizes the rate at which conversion of inputs into outputs takes place, everything being expressed as rates per period of time.

An example may help to clarify the meaning of a production function. Suppose a blacksmith can make 10 horseshoes per hour by using his anvil (plus all his other tools,

Optimization of the firm

which are his capital equipment) and 5 kg of iron. Then the blacksmith's production function would be:

10 horseshoes per hour = g(1 blacksmith hour + 1 anvil hour + 5 kg of iron per hour).

In this case the inputs are combined in fixed proportions (1:1:5), but in other cases the relationship may be more complicated and we will want to ask what would happen to output if we changed the combinations of inputs.

For the rest of this chapter we shall assume a simplified production function in which there are only two inputs. We can best focus on essentials in this way. The two inputs are labour, to which we give the symbol L, and capital, to which we give the symbol K. This means that we are ignoring land and other raw materials and all intermediate (manufactured) inputs to deal with the simplified production function:

$$q = g(L,K), \tag{2}$$

where q is quantity of output per period of time, L is labour hours per period employed in production, K is units of capital services (machine hours per period) used, and g stands for the relation that links q to K and L. For example, q might be measured in tonnes per day while L and K were measured in worker days and machine days—i.e. the amount of labour time and machine time used per day. Confining attention to two inputs simplifies without obscuring the essence of the problem.

Suppose that a firm wishes to increase its rate of output. To do so, it must increase the utilization of one or both inputs. But the firm cannot vary all of its inputs with the same degree of ease. It can vary amounts of labour on short notice, but time is needed to install more capital.

To capture the fact that different inputs can be varied with different speeds, we abstract from the more complicated nature of real decisions and think of each firm as making three distinct types of decision: (1) how best to employ its existing plant and equipment; (2) what new plant, equipment, and production processes to select, within the framework of existing technology; and (3) what to do about encouraging the development and implementation of new technology. The first set of decisions is said to be made over the short run; the second, over the long run; the third, over the very long run.

The short run

The **short run** is defined as the period of time over which some inputs, called **fixed inputs,** cannot be varied. The input that is fixed in the short run is usually an element of capital (such as plant and equipment), but it might be land, or the services of management, or even the supply of skilled, salaried labour. What matters is that at least one significant input is fixed.

In the short run, production can be changed only by using more or less of those inputs that can be varied. These inputs are called **variable inputs.** In our example, the variable input is labour services. Thus, in the short run, q is varied by varying L, with K held fixed (see equation (2)).

The short run is not of the same duration in all industries. In the electric-power industry, for example, where it takes three or more years to build new power stations, an unforeseen increase in demand must be served as well as possible with the existing capital equipment for several years. At the other end of the scale, a machine shop can acquire new equipment in a few weeks, and thus the short run is correspondingly short. The length of the short run is influenced by technological considerations such as how quickly equipment can be made and installed. These things may also be influenced to some extent by the price the firm is willing to pay to increase its capacity *quickly*.

The long run

The **long run** is defined as the period long enough for all the inputs to be varied, but not so long that the basic technology of production changes. Again, the long run is not a specific period of time, but varies among industries.

The special importance of the long run for the decision making of the firm is that it corresponds to the situation facing the firm when it is *planning* to go into business, or to expand or contract the scale of its operations. The planning decisions of the firm are made from among fixed technical possibilities but with freedom to choose whatever techniques, and hence combinations of inputs, seem most desirable. Once these planning decisions are carried out—once a plant is built, equipment purchased and installed, and so on—these factors are fixed and the firm makes its operating decisions in the short run, by changing only the variable input.

The very long run

Unlike the short and the long run, the **very long run** is concerned with situations in which the technological possibilities open to the firm are subject to change, leading to new and improved products and new methods of production. In the very long run, the production function itself changes so that *given* inputs of K and L will be associated with *different* amounts of output. The firm may bring about some changes itself, through its own research and development; other changes may come from outside, such as from a new generation of more powerful computer chips.

The *very long run* may not actually be a long period of time in practice. It is just useful to distinguish between output changes that follow from more of the same capital and changes that follow from a new technology. In the theory of the firm, (1) *short run*, (2) *long run*, and (3) *very long run* are equivalent to (1) labour variable but capital and technology fixed, (2) labour and capital variable but technology fixed, and (3) labour, capital, and technology all variable.

These 'runs' are not sequential in the real world. At any moment in time one division of the firm may be deciding how much to produce this month, while another unit is deciding whether to build a new plant, and its R&D laboratories are designing some new process that will, it is hoped, lower future production costs or create a new product. We separate them so that we can understand each of them, not because they are separated in real time. We shall now study the firm's production possibilities, and its costs, under each of these 'runs'.

The short run

In the short run, we are concerned with what happens to output and costs as more, or less, of the variable input is applied to a given quantity of the fixed input. To illustrate, we use the simplified production function of (2) above, and assume that capital is fixed and labour is variable.

Short-run variations in output

Our firm starts with a fixed amount of capital (say 10 units) and contemplates applying various amounts of labour to it. Table 5.1 shows three different ways of looking at how output varies with the quantity of the variable input. As a preliminary step, some terms must be defined.

Table 5.1. Total, average and marginal products in the short run

Quantity of labour (L) (1)	Total product (TP) (2)	Average product (AP) (3)	Marginal product (MP) (4)
1	43	43	43
2	160	80	117
3	351	117	191
4	600	150	249
5	875	175	275
6	1,152	192	277
7	1,372	196	220
8	1,536	192	164
9	1,656	184	120
10	1,750	175	94
11	1,815	165	65
12	1,860	155	45

The relation of output to changes in the quantity of the variable input can be looked at in three different ways. Capital is assumed to be fixed at 10 units. As the quantity of labour increases, the rate of output (the total product) increases, as shown in column (2). The average product in column (3) is found by dividing the total product figure in column (2) by the amount of labour required to produce that product—as shown by the figure in the corresponding row of column (1).

The marginal product is shown between the rows because it refers to the *change* in output from one level of labour input to another. When graphing the schedule, *MP*s of this kind should be plotted at the midpoint of the interval. Thus, graphically, for example, the marginal product of 249 would be plotted to correspond to quantity of labour of 3.5. This is because it refers to the increase in output when labour inputs rise from 3 to 4 units.

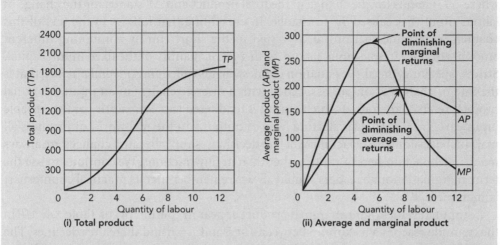

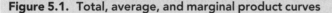

Figure 5.1. Total, average, and marginal product curves

Total product (*TP*), average product (*AP*), and marginal product (*MP*) curves often have the shapes shown here. The curves are plotted from the data in Table 5.1. In (i) the total product curve shows the total product steadily rising, first at an increasing rate, then at a decreasing rate. This causes both the average and the marginal product curves in (ii) to rise at first and then decline. Note that, at the point of maximum average returns (also called the point of diminishing average returns), *MP* = *AP*.

Total product (*TP*) means just what it says: the total amount produced during some period of time by all the inputs that the firm uses. If all inputs but one are held constant, the total product will change as more or less of the variable input is used. This variation is illustrated in column (2) of Table 5.1, which gives a total product schedule. Figure 5.1(i) shows such a schedule graphically. (The shape of the curve will be discussed shortly.)

Average product (*AP*) is merely the total product per unit of the variable input, which is labour in the present illustration:

$$AP = \frac{TP}{L}.$$

Average product is shown in column (3) of Table 5.1. Notice that as more of the variable input is used, average product first rises and then falls. The point where average product reaches a maximum is called the *point of diminishing average productivity*. In the table, average product reaches a maximum when 7 units of labour are employed.

Marginal product (*MP*) is the change in total product resulting from the use of one more (or one less) unit of the variable input:

$$MP = \frac{\Delta TP}{\Delta L},$$

where ΔTP stands for the change in the total product and ΔL stands for the change in labour input that caused TP to change. In everything that follows in the text of this chapter, we assume that output is varied in the short run by combining different amounts of the variable input, labour, with a *given* quantity of the fixed input, capital. Strictly speaking, the above equation defines what is called *incremental product*, that is the rate of change of output associated with a discrete change in an input. Marginal product refers to the rate at which output is tending to vary as quantity of the variable input varies at a particular starting level of output.[1] In the real world of business all marginal decisions are in fact *incremental* decisions, simply because changes are always made in whole numbers of units, rather than in tiny fractions. We continue to use the term 'marginal', though readers should always remember that its practical counterpart is 'incremental'.

Computed values of the marginal product appear in column (4) of Table 5.1. MP in the example reaches a maximum between $L = 5$ and $L = 6$ and thereafter declines. The level of output where marginal product reaches a maximum is called the *point of diminishing marginal returns.*

Figure 5.1(ii) shows the average and marginal product curves plotted from the data in Table 5.1. Notice (1) that MP reaches its maximum at a lower level of L than does AP, and (2) that $MP = AP$ when AP is a maximum. These relations are discussed in more detail below.

Finally, bear in mind that the schedules of Table 5.1, and the curves of Figure 5.1, all assume a specified quantity of the fixed input, capital. If the quantity of capital had been, say, 14 instead of the 10 units that were assumed, there would be a different set of total, average, and marginal product curves. The reason is that, if any specified amount of labour has more capital to work with, it can produce more output: its total, average, and marginal products will be greater.

THE LAW OF DIMINISHING RETURNS

We now consider the variations in output that result from applying different amounts of a variable input to a given quantity of a fixed input. These variations are the subject of a famous hypothesis called the **law of diminishing returns.**

> **The law of diminishing returns** states that if increasing quantities of a variable input are applied to a given quantity of a fixed input, the marginal product, and the average product, of the variable input will eventually decrease.

As illustrated in Figure 5.2, the law of diminishing returns is consistent with mar-

---

[1] Students familiar with elementary calculus will recognize the marginal product as the partial derivative of the total product with respect to the variable input. In symbols: $MP = \partial q / \partial L$. In the text we refer only to finite changes, ΔL and ΔTP, but the phrase 'a change of one unit' should read 'a very small change' when related to the theory of optimization. In real business decisions all changes are in discrete units.

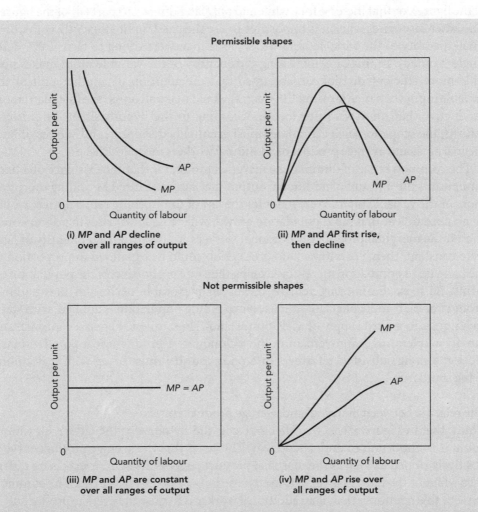

Figure 5.2. Alternative average and marginal product curves

According to the law of diminishing returns, average and marginal product must decline sooner or later as output increases. The law of diminishing returns permits the average and marginal product curves to decline at all positive levels of output, as shown in part (i). The law also allows the average and marginal products to rise over an initial range of output and only then decline, as shown in part (ii). This is the case where the fixed input cannot be efficiently used when combined with very small amounts of the variable input.

The law does not permit average and marginal products that are constant (part (iii)) or rise over the entire range of output (part (iv)). However, constant average and marginal products may well arise in service-type industries, where there is no fixed input, and so the marginal and average product of one worker can be the same as any others.

ginal and average product curves that decline over the whole range of output (part (i) of the figure), or that increase for a while and only later diminish (part (ii) of the figure). The latter case arises when it is impossible to use the fixed input efficiently with only a small quantity of the variable input (if, say, one man were trying to farm 1,000 acres single-handed). In this case, increasing the quantity of the variable input makes possible more efficient division of labour, so that the addition of another unit of the variable input (two men farming 1,000 acres) would make all units (the first man) more productive than they were previously. According to the hypothesis of diminishing returns, the scope for such economies must eventually disappear, and sooner or later the marginal and average product of additional workers must decline.

The common sense of diminishing marginal product is that the existence of a fixed input limits the amount of additional output that can be realized by adding more and more of the variable input. Were it not for the law of diminishing returns, there would be no need to fear that rapid population growth will cause food crises in poorer countries. If the marginal product of additional workers applied to a fixed quantity of land were constant, then a country's food production could be expanded in proportion to the increase in population merely by keeping the same proportion of the population on farms. As it is, diminishing returns means an inexorable decline in the marginal product of each additional labourer as an expanding population is applied, with static techniques, to a fixed supply of agricultural land. Thus, unless there is a continual and rapidly accelerating improvement in the techniques of production, a population explosion among subsistence farmers in a poor country must bring with it declining living standards.[2]

The relation between marginal and average product curves
Notice that in Figure 5.2(ii) the *MP* curve cuts the *AP* curve at the latter's maximum point. It is important to understand why. The key is that the average product curve is positively sloped as long as the marginal product curve is above it; it makes no difference whether the marginal curve is itself negatively or positively sloped. The common sense of this relation is that, if an additional worker is to raise the average product of all workers, the extra output that results from taking on this extra worker must be greater than the average output of all existing workers. It is immaterial whether his contribution to output is greater or less than the contribution of the worker hired immediately before him; all that matters is that his contribution to output exceeds the average output of *all* the workers hired before him. Since *AP* is positively or negatively sloped depending on whether *MP* is above or below *AP*, it follows that *MP* must equal *AP* at the highest point on the *AP* curve.[3]

---

[2] This has not happened throughout the world because rapid technological advances have increased productivity in agriculture faster than population has increased. However, in many poorer countries, farmers subsist mainly on what they themselves grow and use relatively static techniques. For them, rising population in combination with the law of diminishing returns means declining output per person and hence declining living standards.

[3] This is easily proved for those familiar with calculus. Our definitions are: $TP = q(n)$, $AP = q(n)/n$, and $MP = q'(n)$, where the single prime mark indicates the first derivative and n is the quantity of the variable factor

This relationship between average and marginal product is not unique to economics. A good example is cricket scores. Suppose a batsman has had ten innings and he has an average score of 50 runs. In his next innings he scores 100. His marginal score is 100 and his average score will rise above 50 (it will be 54.54, which is 600/11)—so, when the marginal score is above the average, the average must be rising. If instead he had scored a duck (zero), his marginal score would be below the average and the average would be falling (his average would now be 45.45, calculated as 500/11). Only if the marginal score were 50 would the average stay constant and the marginal value would be equal to the average.

We have now learned how, according to economic theory, output varies with variation in the variable input in the short run. However, there are two quite likely cases in which average and marginal products may be constant over a range of output. The first arises when capital is lumpy and production takes place at less than the full capacity of the current capital stock. In this situation additional workers may add to output exactly the same amount as previous workers. Only when the existing capital stock becomes fully utilized will diminishing returns set in. We discuss this case more fully in the context of cost curves below.

The second case could arise where capital goods are not important in the production process. Recall that the firm we have been thinking about is a manufacturing firm. If instead this were a services firm, which had only labour input and no fixed input of capital (say the service of filling in your tax return for you), then diminishing returns would not operate, and both average and marginal products could be constant over a wide range of output, as shown in Figure 5.2(iii). This is because the number of tax returns filled in increases in proportion to the number of tax advisers hired. If one adviser can do 10 tax returns per day, ten advisers can do 100, and one hundred advisers can do 1,000. Of course, if they all had to share the same pen, or were constrained by office space, diminishing returns would again apply at some point.

Short-run variations in cost

We can now discover how a firm's costs of production vary as its output varies. So far we have been talking about the relationships between physical inputs and physical outputs. Now we are about to talk about the *money values* of inputs. Accordingly, we need to have prices for inputs. For the time being, we consider firms that are not in a position to influence the prices of the inputs that they employ. This means that they simply buy their inputs at whatever the going market price happens to be, and they do not influence that market price by their purchases.

employed. A necessary condition for the maximum of the AP curve is that its first derivative, $[nq'(n) - q(n)]/n^2$, be equal to zero. Setting the above expression equal to zero, adding $q(n)/n^2$ to both sides, and multiplying through by n yields: $q'(n) = q(n)/n$, which is to say $MP = AP$.

Optimization of the firm

The following definitions of several cost concepts are closely related to the product concepts defined earlier in this chapter.

Total cost (*TC*) means just what it says: the total cost per period of producing any given rate of output. There are three different types of cost. First, there are some costs that vary with the amount of output produced. These are typically the costs of raw material or component inputs and of certain types of production labour. Second, there are some costs that do not vary with output but can be avoided by producing zero. These may be costs like heating and lighting, or they may be the salaries of some managers or supervisors not directly involved in production. Third, there are some costs that can only be avoided by winding up the business. These are the capital costs, such as interest on debt and rent for the buildings.

For analytic simplicity, in our theory we distinguish only two types of cost, depending on whether or not they vary with output. Hence, total cost is divided into two parts, total fixed costs (*TFC*) and total variable costs (*TVC*). **Fixed costs** are those costs that do not vary with output; they will be the same if output is 1 unit or 1 million units. These costs are also often referred to as 'overhead costs', 'indirect costs', or 'unavoidable costs'. All of those costs that vary positively with output, rising as more is produced and falling as less is produced, are called **variable costs.** In our present example, since labour is the variable input, the wage bill would be a variable cost. Variable costs are often referred to as 'direct costs' or 'avoidable costs'. The latter term is used because the costs can be avoided by not hiring the variable input.

Average total cost (*ATC*) is the total cost of producing any given output divided by the number of units produced, or the cost per unit. This is sometimes called *unit cost*. *ATC* may be divided into **average fixed costs** (*AFC*) and **average variable costs** (*AVC*) in just the same way as total costs were divided.

Marginal cost (*MC*) is the increase in total cost resulting from raising the rate of production by one unit. The marginal cost of the tenth unit, for example, is the change in total cost when the rate of production is increased from nine to ten units per period. The term *incremental cost* can also be used instead of marginal cost, though incremental cost relates to a small change that may be larger than the smallest measurable unit of output.

These three measures of cost are merely different ways of looking at a single phenomenon, and they are mathematically interrelated.[4] Sometimes it is relevant to use one, and sometimes another.

SHORT-RUN COST CURVES

The relations just outlined are most easily understood if we show them as cost curves.

---

[4] Mathematically, average total cost is *total cost* divided by output, while marginal cost is the first derivative of *total cost* with respect to output.

Table 5.2. Variation of costs with capital fixed and labour variable

Inputs		Output	Total cost (£)			Average cost (£)			Marginal cost (£)
Capital (1)	Labour (L) (2)	Output (q) (3)	Fixed (TFC) (4)	Variable (TVC) (5)	Total (TC) (6)	Fixed (AFC)[a] (7)	Variable (AVC)[b] (8)	Total (ATC)[c] (9)	(MC)[d] (10)
10	1	43	100	20	120	2.326	0.465	2.791	0.465
10	2	160	100	40	140	0.625	0.250	0.875	0.171
10	3	351	100	60	160	0.285	0.171	0.456	0.105
10	4	600	100	80	180	0.167	0.133	0.300	0.080
10	5	875	100	100	200	0.114	0.114	0.228	0.073
10	6	1,152	100	120	220	0.087	0.104	0.191	0.072
10	7	1,372	100	140	240	0.073	0.102	0.175	0.091
10	8	1,536	100	160	260	0.065	0.104	0.169	0.122
10	9	1,656	100	180	280	0.060	0.109	0.169	0.167
10	10	1,750	100	200	300	0.057	0.114	0.171	0.213
10	11	1,815	100	220	320	0.055	0.121	0.176	0.308
10	12	1,860	100	240	340	0.054	0.129	0.183	0.444

The relation of cost to the rate of output can be looked at in several different ways. These cost schedules are computed from the product curves of Table 5.1, given the price of capital of £10 per unit and the price of labour of £20 per unit. Marginal cost (in column (10)) is shown between the lines of total cost because it refers to the *change* in cost divided by the *change* in output that brought it about. Marginal cost is calculated by dividing the increase in costs by the increase in output when one additional unit of labour is used. This gives the increase in cost per unit of output over that range of output. For example, the *MC* of £0.08 is the increase in total cost of £20 (from £160 to £180) divided by the 249-unit increase in output (from 351 to 600). This tells us that when output goes from 351 to 600 (because labour inputs go from 3 to 4) the increase in costs is £0.08 per unit of output. In constructing a graph, marginal costs should be plotted midway in the interval over which they are computed. The *MC* of £0.08 would thus be plotted at output 475.5.

a Col. (4) ÷ col. (3).   c Col. (6) ÷ col. (3) = col. (7) + col. (8).
b Col. (5) ÷ col. (3).   d Change in col. (5) from one row to the next ÷ corresponding change in col. (3).

To illustrate how this is done, we take the production relationships in Table 5.1 and assume that the price of labour is £20 per unit and the price of capital is £10 per unit. In Table 5.2, we present the cost schedules computed for these values. (It is important that you see where the numbers come from;[5] if you do not, review Table 5.1 and the defini-

---

5 We have derived the data in Tables 5.1 and 5.2 by letting inputs of labour vary one unit at a time. This gives rise to variation in output of more than one per unit of time. Marginal cost is defined as the change in cost when output varies one unit at a time. To calculate marginal cost, we divide the *increase in costs when labour inputs rise by one unit* by the *increase in output*. This gives us the increase in costs *per unit of output* over that range of output. This, and similar, problems do not arise when all marginal concepts are defined as derivatives. However, real firms can only change inputs by discrete amounts. This emphasizes the point we made above that *incremental cost* is the relevant marginal concept for business.

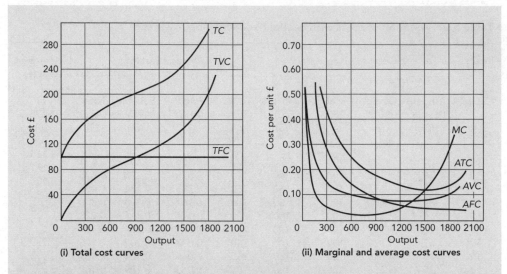

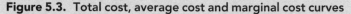

Figure 5.3. Total cost, average cost and marginal cost curves

Total cost (*TC*), average cost (*AC*), and marginal cost (*MC*) curves often have the shapes shown here. These curves are plotted from Table 5.2. Total fixed cost does not vary with output. Total variable cost and the total of all costs (*TC* = *TVC* + *TFC*) rise with output, first at a decreasing rate, then at an increasing rate. The total cost curves in (i) give rise to the average and marginal curves in (ii). Average fixed cost (*AFC*) declines as output increases. Average variable cost (*AVC*) and average total cost (*ATC*) fall and then rise as output increases. Marginal cost (*MC*) does the same, intersecting the *ATC* and *AVC* curves at their minimum points. Capacity output is at the minimum point of the *ATC* curve, which is an output of 1,500 in this example.

tions of cost just given.) Figure 5.3(i) shows the total cost curves; Figure 5.3(ii) plots the marginal and average cost curves.

HOW COST VARIES WITH OUTPUT

Since total fixed costs (*TFC*) do not, by definition, vary with output, average fixed cost (*TFC*/*q*) falls as output increases, while marginal fixed cost is zero (there are no extra fixed costs as additional units of output are made). Variable cost is positively related to output, since to produce more requires more of the variable input, which in turn entails spending more to buy the input. Average variable cost may, however, be negatively or positively related to output. If output rises faster than variable costs, average variable costs will be falling as output rises; if output rises less fast than costs rise, average variable cost will be rising. Marginal variable cost is always positive, indicating that it costs something to increase output, but, as we shall soon see, marginal cost may rise or fall as output rises.

154

Notice that the marginal cost curve cuts the *ATC* and *AVC* curves at their lowest points. This is another example of the relation (discussed above) between a marginal and an average curve. The *ATC* curve, for example, slopes downwards as long as the marginal cost curve is below it; it makes no difference whether the marginal cost curve is itself sloping upwards or downwards.

In Figure 5.3(ii) the average variable cost curve reaches a minimum and then rises. With fixed input prices, when average product per worker is at a maximum, average variable cost is at a minimum. The common sense is that each new worker adds the same amount to cost but a different amount to output, and when output per worker is rising the cost per unit of output must be falling, and vice versa.

> The law of diminishing returns implies eventually increasing marginal and average variable cost.

Short-run *AVC* curves are often drawn U-shaped. This reflects the assumptions that (1) average productivity is increasing when output is low, but that (2) eventually average productivity begins to fall fast enough to cause average total unit costs to increase.[6]

The definition of capacity
The output that corresponds to the minimum short-run average total cost is very often called **capacity**. Capacity in this sense is not an upper limit on what can be produced, as you can see by looking again at Table 5.2. In the example, capacity output is between 1,536 and 1,656 units, but higher outputs can be achieved. A firm producing *below capacity* is producing at a rate of output less than the one for which average total cost is a minimum. A firm producing *above capacity* is producing more than this amount. It is thus incurring costs per unit of output that are higher than the minimum achievable.

In this section we have implicitly assumed that all of the fixed input must be used. However, firms often have the choice of leaving some of their fixed input idle when they reduce output. Indeed, they often plan on the assumption that output will normally vary within some range. The consequences of this deliberate flexibility in capacity utilization are discussed in Box 5.1.

A family of short-run cost curves
A short-run cost curve shows how costs vary with output for a given quantity of the fixed input—say a given size of plant.

---

[6] This point is easily seen if a little algebra is used. (The only new symbol used here is w, which stands for the price of a unit of labour.) By definition $AVC = TVC/q$. But $TVC = L \times w$, and $q = AP \times L$ (since $AP = q/L$). Therefore

$$AVC = (L \times w)/(AP \times L)$$
$$= w/AP.$$

In other words, average variable cost equals the price of the variable factor divided by the average product of the variable factor. Since w is constant, it follows that AVC and AP vary inversely with each other, and when AP is at its maximum value AVC must be at its minimum value.

BOX 5.1.

Why many firms report that average costs are constant

Ever since economists began measuring the cost curves of manufacturing firms more than half a century ago, they have reported flat, short-run variable cost curves, at least over some range of output. The evidence is now clear that in most manufacturing industries, and in some others, cost curves are shaped like the (*AVC*) curve shown in the figure, with a long, flat portion in the middle and sharply rising sections at each end. For such a 'saucer-shaped' curve, there is a large range of output over which average variable costs are constant. Over this range, marginal costs are equal to average variable costs, and thus they, too, are constant per unit of output.

Why are many cost curves saucer-shaped rather than U-shaped? The answer is that firms design plants to have this property so that they can accommodate the inevitable seasonal and cyclical swings in demand for their products.

To see why a firm can choose the shape of its short-run average cost curve, consider again the law of diminishing returns. The U-shaped, short-run cost curve arises when a variable amount of one input, say, labour, is applied to a fixed amount of a second input, say, capital. Imagine starting from zero output and zero use of the variable input and then increasing output. As more of the variable input is used, a more nearly optimal combination with the fixed input is achieved. Once the optimal combination obtains, the use of further units of the variable input leads to too much of that input being used in combination with the fixed input. This causes average variable costs to begin to rise. Only one quantity of labour leads to the least-cost input proportions.

These changing combinations of fixed and variable inputs must occur in the short run whenever all of the fixed input must be used all of the time; in other words, when the fixed input is *indivisible*. This, however, is not usually the case. Even though the firm's plant and equipment may be fixed in the short run, so that *no more* than what exists is available, it is often possible to use *less* than this amount.

Consider, as a simple example, a factory that consists of 10 sewing machines in a shed, each of which has a productive capacity of 20 units per day when operated by 1 operator for 1 shift. If 200 units per day are required, then all 10 machines would be operated by 10 workers on a normal shift. If demand falls to 180, then 1 operator could be laid off. There is no need, however, to have the 9 remaining operators dashing about trying to work 10 machines. Clearly, 1 machine could be 'laid off' as well, leaving constant the ratio of *employed* labour to *employed* machines.

Production could go from 20 all the way to 200 units per day without any change in the proportions in which the employed inputs are used. In this case, we would expect the factory to have constant marginal and average variable costs from 20 to 200 units per day. Only beyond 200 units per day would it begin to encounter rising costs, because production would have to be extended by overtime and other means of combining more labour with the maximum available supply of 10 machines.

In such a case, the fixed input is *divisible*. Because some of it can be left unemployed, there is no need to depart from the most efficient ratio of *labour used* to *capital used* as pro-

BOX 5.1. (*cont.*)

duction is decreased. The *divisibility* of the fixed input means that diminishing returns does not apply, because variations in output below full capacity are accomplished by reducing the input of both labour and capital. Thus, average variable costs can be constant over a large range, up to the point at which all of the fixed input is used.

A similar situation occurs when a firm has many plants. For example, a manufacturer with 10 plants may choose to reduce its output by temporarily closing one or more plants (or operating them on a limited-time basis) while operating the rest at normal-capacity output. Another firm can choose to put its factory on short time, working 6 hours a day or 4 days a week, thus reducing its use of both capital and labour. In such cases the *firm's* short-run variable costs tend to be constant over a large range of output because there is no need to depart from the optimal combination of labour and capital in the plants that are kept in operation.

The figure shows the type of cost curve that is observed when the fixed input is divisible. At outputs between q_1 and q_3, the AVC curve is flat because output is varied by using more or less labour *and* capital in constant proportions. Normal-capacity output is q_2 and full-capacity output is q_3. When output reaches q_3, the fixed stock of capital is fully employed, and further increases in output can only be achieved at rising cost as more labour is applied to a fixed quantity of capital.

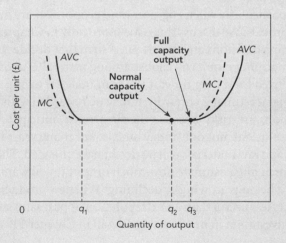

There is a different short-run cost curve for each quantity of the fixed input.

A small plant for manufacturing nuts and bolts will have its own short-run cost curve. A medium-size and a very large-size plant will each have its own short-run cost curve. If a firm expands by replacing its small plant with a medium-size plant, it will move from one short-run cost curve to another. This change from one size of plant to another is a long-run change. We now study how the short-run cost curves of different size plants are related to each other.

The long run

In the short run, with only one variable input, there is only one way to produce a given output: by adjusting the quantity of that input used until the desired rate of output is achieved. Thus, once the firm has decided on a rate of output, there is only one technically possible way of achieving it.

By contrast, in the long run, all inputs are variable. The firm must decide both on a level of output *and* on how to produce that output. Specifically, this means that firms in the long run must choose the nature and amount of plant and equipment, as well as the size of their labour force.

In making this choice, the firm will wish to avoid being technically inefficient, which means using more of *all* inputs than is necessary. Being technically efficient is not enough, however. To be economically efficient, the firm must choose from among the many technically efficient options the one that produces a given level of output at the lowest possible cost. (The distinction between various types of efficiency sometimes causes confusion, particularly when engineers and economists are involved in the same decision-making process. We discuss this issue more fully in Chapter 9.)

Long-run planning decisions are important. A firm that decides to build a new steel mill and invest in machinery for it will choose among many alternatives. Once installed, that equipment is fixed for a long time. If the firm makes a wrong choice, its survival may be threatened; if it estimates shrewdly, it may be rewarded with large earnings.

Long-run decisions are risky because the firm must anticipate what methods of production will be efficient, not only today but also for many years in the future, when the costs of labour and raw materials will no doubt have changed. The decisions are also risky because the firm must estimate how much output it will want to produce. Is the industry to which it belongs growing or declining? Will new products emerge to render its existing products less useful than an extrapolation of past sales suggests? We discuss the evaluation of investment in new capital in detail in Chapter 11.

Profit maximization and cost minimization

Any firm seeking to maximize its profits in the long run must select the economically efficient method, which is the method that produces its output at the lowest possible cost. This implication of the hypothesis of profit maximization is called **cost minimization:** from the alternatives open to it, the profit-maximizing firm will choose the least costly way of producing whatever specific output it chooses.

CHOICE OF INPUT MIX

If it is possible to substitute one input for another to keep output constant while reducing total cost, the firm is not using the least costly combination of inputs. In such a situation, the firm should substitute one input for another, as long as the marginal product of the one input *per pound* expended on it is greater than the marginal product of the other input *per pound* expended on it. The firm cannot minimize its costs as long as these two magnitudes are unequal. For example, if an extra pound spent on labour produces more output than an extra pound spent on capital, the firm can reduce costs by spending less on capital and more on labour.

If we use K to represent capital, L to represent labour, and p to represent the price of a unit of the input, the necessary condition for cost minimization is as follows:

$$\frac{MP_K}{p_K} = \frac{MP_L}{p_L}. \tag{3}$$

Whenever the two sides of equation (3) are not equal, there are possibilities for input substitutions that will reduce costs.

To see why this equation must be satisfied if costs of production are to be minimized, consider a situation where the equation is not satisfied. Suppose, for example, that the marginal product of capital is 20 and its price is £2, making the left side of equation (3) equal to 10. Suppose that the marginal product of labour is 32 and its price is £8, making the right side of equation (3) equal to 4. Thus the last pound spent on capital adds 10 units to output, whereas the last pound spent on labour adds only 4 units to output. In such a case, the firm could maintain its output level and reduce costs by using £2.50 less of labour and spending £1.00 more on capital. Making such a substitution of capital for labour would leave output unchanged and reduce costs by £1.50. Thus the original position was not cost-minimizing.[7]

We can take a different look at cost minimization by multiplying equation (3) by p_K/MP_L:

$$\frac{MP_K}{MP_L} = \frac{p_K}{p_L}. \tag{4}$$

The ratio of the marginal products on the left side of the equation compares the contribution to output of the last unit of capital and the last unit of labour. If the ratio is 4, this means that 1 unit more of capital will add 4 times as much to output as 1 unit more of labour. The right side of the equation shows how the cost of 1 unit more of capital compares to the cost of 1 unit more of labour. If the ratio is also 4, the firm cannot

---

[7] The argument in this paragraph assumes that the marginal products do not change when expenditure changes by a small amount.

reduce costs by substituting capital for labour or vice versa. Now suppose that the ratio on the right side of the equation is 2. Capital, which is four times as productive as labour, is only twice as expensive. It will pay the firm to switch to a method of production that uses more capital and less labour. If, however, the ratio on the right side is 6 (or *any* number more than 4), it will pay to switch to a method of production that uses more labour and less capital.

We have seen that when the ratio MP_K/MP_L exceeds the ratio p_K/p_L, the firm should substitute capital for labour. This substitution is measured by changes in the **capital–labour ratio**—the amount of capital per worker used by the firm.

How far should the firm go in making this substitution? There is a limit, because the law of diminishing returns tells us that as the firm uses more capital, the marginal product of capital falls, and as it uses less labour, the marginal product of labour rises. Thus the ratio MP_K/MP_L falls. When it reaches 2, the firm need substitute no further. The ratio of the marginal products is equal to the ratio of the prices.

> **Profit-maximizing firms will adjust the combination of their inputs until they cannot produce a given level of output any cheaper. At this point the ratio of the marginal products of the inputs will equal the ratio of prices of the inputs. This is true for any number of inputs.**

LONG-RUN EQUILIBRIUM OF THE FIRM

The firm will have achieved its equilibrium capital–labour ratio when there is no opportunity for cost-reducing substitutions. This occurs when the marginal product per pound spent on each input is the same (equation (3)) or, equivalently, when the ratio of the marginal products of inputs is equal to the ratio of their prices (equation (4)).

The principle of substitution

Suppose that a firm is meeting the cost-minimizing conditions shown in equations (3) and (4) and that the cost of labour increases while the cost of capital remains unchanged. The least-cost method of producing any output will now use less labour and more capital than was required to produce the same output before the prices of inputs changed.

> **Methods of production will change if the relative prices of inputs change. Relatively more of the cheaper input and relatively less of the more expensive input will be used.**

This is called the **principle of substitution**, and it follows from the assumption that firms minimize their costs. The principle of substitution plays a central role in resource allocation, because it relates to the way in which individual firms respond to changes in relative input prices that are caused by the changing relative scarcities of various inputs in the economy as a whole. When an input becomes more scarce to the economy as a whole, its price will tend to rise. This motivates individual firms to use less of that input. When some other input becomes more plentiful to the economy as a whole, its price will tend to fall. This motivates individual firms to use more of it. Firms need never know the relative national or global scarcities of the various inputs. As long as relative prices reflect these scarcities, firms will substitute plentiful inputs for scarce ones through their own cost-minimizing responses to the changes in the prices of their inputs.

Cost curves in the long run

When all inputs can be varied, there is a least-cost method of producing each possible level of output. Thus, with given input prices, there is a minimum achievable cost of production for each level of output. If this cost is expressed as a quantity per unit of output, we obtain the long-run average cost of producing each level of output. When this least-cost method of producing each output is plotted on a graph, the result is called a **long-run average cost (*LRAC*) curve.** Figure 5.4 shows one such curve.

This cost curve is determined by the technology of the industry (which is assumed to be fixed for purposes of drawing the graph) and by the prices of inputs. It is a 'boundary' in the sense that points below it are unattainable; points on the curve, however, are attainable if sufficient time elapses for all inputs to be adjusted. To move from one point on the *LRAC* curve to another requires an adjustment in all inputs, which may, for example, require building a larger, more elaborate factory.

> The *LRAC* curve is the boundary between cost levels that are attainable, with known technology and given input prices, and those that are unattainable.

Just as the short-run cost curves discussed earlier in this chapter are derived from the *production function* describing the physical relationship between inputs and output, so is the *LRAC* curve. The difference is that in deriving the *LRAC* curve, there are no fixed inputs, so all inputs are treated as variable. Because all input costs are variable in the long run, we do not need to distinguish between *average variable costs (AVC), average fixed cost (AFC),* and *average total cost (ATC),* as we did in the short run. There is only one long run average cost (*LRAC*) for any given set of input prices.

THE SHAPE OF THE LONG-RUN AVERAGE COST CURVE

The *LRAC* curve shown in Figure 5.4 first falls and then rises. This curve is often

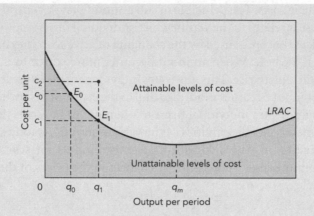

Figure 5.4. A long-run average cost curve

The long-run average cost (_LRAC_) curve provides a boundary between attainable and unattainable levels of cost. If the firm wishes to produce output q_0, the lowest attainable cost level is c_0 per unit. This is point E_0 on the _LRAC_ curve. E_1 represents the least-cost method of producing q_1. Suppose a firm is producing at E_0 and desires to increase output to q_1. In the short run it will not be able to vary all inputs, and thus costs above c_1, say c_2, must be accepted. In the long run, a plant that is the optimal size for producing output q_1 can be built and costs of c_1 can be attained. At output q_m the firm attains its lowest possible per unit cost of production for the given technology and input prices.

described as U-shaped, although 'saucer-shaped' might be a more accurate description of the evidence from many empirical studies.[8]

Decreasing costs

Over the range of output from zero to q_m the firm has falling long-run average costs: an expansion of output permits a reduction of costs per unit of output. Technologies with this property are referred to as exhibiting **economies of scale.** (Of course, when output is increased, such economies of scale will be realized only after enough time has elapsed to allow changes in all inputs.) The prices of inputs are assumed to be constant, and thus the decline in long-run average cost occurs because output is increasing _more than_ in proportion to inputs as the scale of the firm's production expands. Over this range of output, the decreasing-cost firm is often said to enjoy long-run **increasing returns** (or **increasing returns to scale**). This is an extremely important phenomenon and its sources, as well as its implications, are discussed in the section below.

Increasing costs

Over the range of outputs greater than q_m the firm encounters rising long-run costs. An

---

[8] This is because there is often a fairly large range of output, in the middle of the long-run average cost curve, for which costs do not vary.

expansion in production, even after sufficient time has elapsed for all adjustments to be made, will be accompanied by a rise in average costs per unit of output. If costs per unit of input are constant, the firm's output must be increasing *less than* in proportion to the increase in inputs. When this happens, the increasing-cost firm is said to encounter long-run **decreasing returns** (to scale).[9]

Decreasing returns imply that the firm suffers some diseconomy of scale. As its scale of operations increases, diseconomies are encountered that increase its per unit cost of production. These diseconomies may be associated with the difficulties of managing and controlling an enterprise as its size increases. For example, planning problems do not necessarily vary in direct proportion to size. At first, there may be scale economies as the firm grows, but sooner or later planning and co-ordination problems may multiply more than in proportion to the growth in size. If so, management costs per unit of output will rise.

Constant costs
In Figure 5.4 the firm's long-run average costs fall until output reaches q_m and rise thereafter. Another possibility should be noted. The firm's *LRAC* curve might have a flat portion over a range of output around q_m. With such a flat portion, the firm would be encountering constant costs over the relevant range of output. This means that the firm's long-run average costs per unit of output do not change as its output changes. Because input prices are assumed to be fixed, the firm's output must be increasing *exactly in proportion to* the increase in inputs. A firm in this situation is said to be encountering **constant returns** (to scale).

Some evidence
In the real world many shapes of cost curve exist. Below we discuss some of the reasons why economies of scale or increasing returns are common. Where there are increasing returns it is likely that large firms will grow up to benefit from these scale economies. It would not be surprising, therefore, to find economies of scale (or scope) in large firms.

Of equal interest is the shape of cost curves in smaller firms. A recent study by Professor Gavin Reid of the University of St Andrews throws some interesting light on this subject.[10] There were two components to this study, which investigated seventy-three young (under two years old on average) owner-managed firms in a variety of manufacturing and service industries. First, Reid asked the heads of these firms to state their own perceptions of their short-run cost structures. Second, data were obtained for outputs of the firms (sales) and identifiable inputs (capital and labour), which were

[9] Long-run decreasing returns differ from short-run diminishing returns. In the short run, at least one input is fixed, and the law of diminishing returns ensures that returns to the variable input will eventually diminish. In the long run, all inputs are variable, and it is possible that physically diminishing returns would never be encountered—at least as long as it was genuinely possible to increase all inputs.

[10] Gavin C. Reid, 'Scale economies in small entrepreneurial firms', *Scottish Journal of Political Economy* 39(1) (1992), pp. 39–51. Note that his survey was focused on total cost curves, we are converting his results into implications for *SRAVC* curves.

used to estimate whether there were increasing or decreasing returns to scale in the long run (the shape of *LRAC*).

In Reid's sample 55 per cent of firms said that their average variable cost curves (short run) declined throughout the range of potential production. Fifteen per cent said that average variable costs fell for a while but then rose at higher production levels. Fourteen per cent said that average variable cost was constant up to capacity output and then rose sharply (as discussed in Box 5.1). A further 11 per cent thought that their average variable cost was constant throughout all possible ranges of output. Not a single firm said that its average variable cost curve rose throughout its production range. These results add strong support to the contention that the shapes of cost curves we discussed above are realistic, and commonly found in the real world.

An obvious question arising out of the evidence that short-run cost curves are downward sloping in many firms is: why do they not expand further? There are two answers to this. First, many of these firms were expanding at the time the data were collected, and, hence, they have not necessarily arrived yet at the 'equilibrium' analysed above. Second, however, when Reid tested for *long-run* economies or diseconomies of scale, he found that the dominant pattern was one of decreasing returns to scale.

> This suggests that there is some merit in the argument that the ultimate scarce resource in the small entrepreneurial firm is the entrepreneur himself. He is the fixed factor that cannot be made variable, even in the long run, and it is this which ultimately gives rise to decreasing returns. These decreasing returns may be viewed as arising from increasing agency costs as the firm grows larger. Owner-managed firms effectively bypass agency costs when they are small, but as they grow, such costs rise inexorably. Faced with this, the small entrepreneurial firm must either stay small and run the risk of decline predicted by life cycle theories of the firm, or attempt to grow bigger, but with modified organizational form which aims to minimize agency costs. Typically this involves some form of hierarchy, with associated control and monitoring devices, and often some change of capital structure, almost certainly involving outside equity and perhaps a form of market flotation.   (op. cit. p. 47)

We discuss the organizational issues raised in the above extract in Chapter 12.

ECONOMIES OF SCALE AND ECONOMIES OF SCOPE

In this chapter we are discussing only the cost structure of a single-product firm. So when we talk about *scale economies* this refers to the unit costs of production of this single product as increasing numbers of the product are produced, and all inputs can be varied. There is another important concept relating to the economies of size. This is called **economies of scope.**

Economies of scope apply to a multi-product firm. Economies of scope exist if the production of several different products within one firm leads to the unit costs of production of each product being lower than if they had been produced in independent firms. This could result, for example, from shared head-office functions and from a common distribution and marketing function. It may also be that a large firm can raise capital more cheaply than several small firms. The potential existence of economies of scope is very important in deciding what types of diverse activity should be within the same firm. This will be discussed more fully in Chapter 12.

Generally the distinction between economies of scale and scope is clear. However, where the multiple products are all by-products of the same production process the concepts are interrelated.

SOURCES OF INCREASING RETURNS TO SCALE

Whenever a firm finds that, by expanding its output of some product, it can increase its output per unit of input, that product is enjoying economies of large-scale production, and so will the firm that makes the product. These scale economies are important, and wherever they exist they encourage large plants and/or large firms. We mention three important sources of scale economies—geometrical relations, one-time costs, and the technology of large-scale production—before proceeding to outline why increasing returns have very important implications for modern business.

Geometrical relations

One important source of scale economies lies in the geometry of our three-dimensional world. To illustrate how geometry matters, consider a firm that wishes to store a gas or a liquid. The firm is interested in the *volume* of storage space. However, the amount of material required to build the container is related to the *area* of its surface. When the size of a container is increased, the storage capacity, which is determined by its volume, increases faster than its surface area.[11] This is a genuine case of increasing returns—the output, in terms of storage capacity, increases proportionately more than the increase in the costs of the required construction materials.

Here is another of the many other similar effects. The heat loss in a smelter is proportional to its surface area, while the amount of ore smelted depends on its volume. So there is a scale economy in heat needed per tonne of ore smelted as smelters get larger. The size of the smelter is limited, however, by the need to deliver a smooth flow of air to all the molten ore. Thus when improved forced air pumps were invented in the nineteenth century, smelters could be built larger and unit costs fell.

One-time costs

A second source of increasing returns consists of inputs that do not have to be increased

[11] For example, consider a cubic container with metal sides, bottom, and lid, all of which measure 1 foot by 1 foot. To build this container, 6 square feet of metal is required (six sides, each 1 square foot), and it will hold 1 cubic foot of gas or liquid. Now increase all of the lengths of each of the container's sides to 2 feet. Now 24 square feet of metal is required (six sides, each 4 square feet), and the container will hold 8 cubic feet of gas or liquid (2 feet times 2 feet times 2 feet). So increasing the amount of metal in the container's walls fourfold has the effect of increasing its capacity eightfold.

as the output of a product is increased, even in the long run. For example, there are often large fixed costs in developing new products, such as a new generation of aeroplanes, a more powerful computer, a new software package, or a new drug. These research and development (R&D) costs have to be incurred only once for each product, and hence are independent of the scale at which the product is subsequently produced. Even if the product's *production costs* increase in proportion to output in the long run, average total costs, including *product development costs*, will fall as the scale of output rises. The influence of such once-and-for-all costs is that, other things being equal, they cause average total costs to be falling over the entire range of output.[12]

The technology of large-scale production

A third and very important source lies in technology. Large-scale production can use more specialized and highly efficient machinery than smaller-scale production. It can also lead to more specialization of human tasks, with a resulting increase in efficiency.

Even the most casual observation of the differences in production techniques used in large and small plants will show that larger plants use greater specialization. An example from the electricity industry is discussed in Box 5.2.

These differences arise because large, specialized equipment is useful only when the volume of output that the firm can sell justifies employment of that equipment. For example, assembly-line techniques, body-stamping machinery, and multiple-boring engine-block machines in car production are economically efficient only when individual operations are repeated thousands of times. Use of elaborate harvesting equipment (which combines many individual tasks that would otherwise be done by hand and by tractor) provides the least-cost method of production on a big farm but not on a few acres.

Typically, as the level of planned output increases, capital is substituted for labour and complex machines are substituted for simpler machines. Robotics is a contemporary example. Electronic devices can handle huge numbers of operations quickly, but unless the level of production requires such a large volume of operations, robotics or other forms of automation will not provide the least-cost method of production.

Until very recently large-scale production meant mass production, sometimes referred to as 'Fordism', a system that was introduced early in the century. It was based on a very detailed division of jobs, often on a production line, in which each person did one repetitive task in co-operation with very specialized machinery (called dedicated machinery). In this technology, size was very important. Very high rates of output were required in order to reap all the scale economies available to this type of production.

In recent decades, production technology has been revolutionized by what is called *flexible manufacturing*, or *lean production*. This is a somewhat less specialized type of

---

[12] This phenomenon is popularly referred to as 'spreading overhead'. It is similar to what happens in the short run when average fixed costs fall with output. The difference is that fixed short-run production costs are variable long-run production costs. If the firm increases its scale of output for some product, it will incur more capital costs in the long run as a larger plant is built. However, its costs of developing that product are not affected.

BOX 5.2.

Economies of scale in the electricity industry

In the 1940s, 1950s, and 1960s, major economies of scale in electricity generation came from the use of larger and larger generators: from 30MW (= 30,000 kilowatt) generators in 1948 to 100MW in 1956, 200MW in 1959, and 500MW generators in 1966.

Since the 1970s, there has been little increase in the size of generators, but the industry has found a new way of reaping scale economies. It has been reducing the *number* of power stations, each station having several generators. The result has been that the average capacity of each power station has continued to rise significantly, bringing a different type of economy of scale. From 233 power stations with an average capacity of 147MW in March 1965, the Central Electricity Generating Board (which was responsible for the generation of all the electricity supplied to area electricity boards in England and Wales until the industry was privatized in 1989–90) reduced the number of stations to 174 with an average capacity of 324MW by March 1974 and 78 stations with an average capacity of 671MW by March 1987. It is interesting to note that the 'energy crisis' starting in 1973–4 brought a stop to the rapid growth in demand for electricity in Britain, so the overall generating capacity was *smaller* at the end of the 1980s than it had been twenty years earlier. Nevertheless, the adoption of larger generating units and their concentration in larger and larger power stations brought significant scale economies.

The CEGB also benefited from economies of scale in bulk transmission of electricity. As long ago as the mid-1960s, the Board began construction of a 'Supergrid' of 400kV (= 400,000 volts) transmission lines based on the knowledge that such a line could replace three lines operating at 275kV or eighteen lines operating at 132kV, without a corresponding increase in costs.

Economies of scale allowed the industry to cope with rising *real* prices of its main inputs—coal and labour—without raising the real price of electricity. During the 1960s, when the real

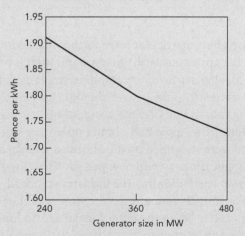

Price per kWh of electricity generated by CCGT generators

BOX 5.2. (*cont.*)

price of the major alternative fuel—oil—was falling (this fall itself being the result of the increasing exploitation of economies of scale in oil tankers delivering crude oil from the Middle East), the UK electricity industry was able to reduce the real price of electricity, which is one of the reasons for electricity being adopted more and more widely in preference to other fuels.

Strictly speaking, scale economies refer to the effects of increasing output *along* a negatively sloped *LRAC* curve as a result of rising output within the confines of known technology, while changes in technological knowledge *shift* the *LRAC* curve. As this example shows, the two forces usually become mixed in most real-world applications.

Privatization did not change the cost structure of the industry immediately, partly because producers were locked into three-year contracts to buy coal. After this period, shifts were made to cheaper, imported coal and, where new capacity was required, to the adoption of the cheaper technology of combined cycle gas turbines (CCGT). The chart shows the cost per kWh in 1996 of electricity generated by CCGT generators of different scale. There are mild economies of scale with current technology as size increases from 240MW to 480MW, but bigger generators do not deliver significant further scale economies.

Competitive forces continue to put pressure on producers to reduce costs, as does the requirement to reduce output prices in real terms imposed by the Office of Electricity Regulation (Offer). Hence the main pressures are on cutting costs through productivity gains, rather than exploiting further economies of even larger-scale production.

production in which workers do many tasks in co-operation with machinery that is also less specialized. One of its most important characteristics is its ability to achieve maximum efficiency with low average costs at much smaller rates of output than is required for mass-production techniques. It is further discussed in Box 5.3.

Network effects

Many high-tech products have particular formats that offer compatibility with related products that also use the same standard. Once a standard has become established in a product group it becomes harder for a new standard to get established, even if the new standard would offer some advantages over the old. Obvious examples include the Microsoft PC operating system that became standard once it was adopted by IBM and was used on all IBM clone PCs. Apple had a better operating system, but they kept it to their own Mac PCs and were swamped by the almost universal adoption of MS-DOS. As most software and applications were developed for IBM clones, it became harder for Apple to compete without itself adopting the industry standard.

Another example of an industry standard is the victory of the VHS video format over Betamax. Video players and tapes in the latter format are no longer produced, though in the mid-1980s they had an even chance of achieving domination.

At the time of writing it seems likely that Sun Microsystems' Java language will emerge as the industry standard for downloadable programs on the Internet. If this is

BOX 5.3.

The flexible manufacturing revolution

Production techniques have recently been revolutionized by the introduction, in many industries and in many countries, of *flexible manufacturing*, or as they are sometimes called, *lean production techniques*. This is the most fundamental change to occur since the introduction of mass production—a technique brought to full development by Henry Ford early in the twentieth century.

To understand the 'lean production revolution' pioneered by the Japanese, one must distinguish the three types of production method used today.

Craft methods employ highly skilled workers to make non-standardized products that are often tailor-made for individual purchasers. The result is usually an expensive product of high quality, made by skilled workers who get considerable job satisfaction.

Mass production methods are based on specialization and division of labour, as first analysed by Adam Smith in the eighteenth century. They use skilled personnel to design products and production methods. They then employ relatively unskilled labour to produce standardized parts and to assemble them using highly specialized, single-purpose machines. The parts are usually manufactured in separate locations, often by distinct companies, and then assembled on a central production facility, often called an *assembly line*. The design of the product is centralized, and suppliers bid competitively to produce parts to the stated specifications. The cost of changing the specialized equipment from the production of one product variant to another is high, and thus specific product types are produced for as long as possible. The result is a standardized product, made in a fairly small number of variants and produced at low cost with moderate quality. The work is repetitive, and workers are regarded as variable costs to be laid off or taken on as the desired rate of production varies.

Flexible manufacturing methods combine the flexibility and high-quality standards of craft production with the low cost of mass-production techniques. They are lean because they use less of all inputs, including time, labour, capital, and inventories, compared with either of the other techniques. They are flexible because the costs of switching from one product line to another are minimized.

In flexible manufacturing, workers are organized as teams; each worker is encouraged to do all of the tasks assigned to the team, using equipment that is less highly specialized than that used in mass-production techniques. This emphasizes individuality and initiative rather than a mind-numbing repetition of one unskilled operation. It also helps workers to identify places where improvements can be made and encourages them to follow up on these. Finally, it reduces the costs of switching equipment from production of one product variant to another.

In mass-production plants, stopping an assembly line to correct a problem at one point stops work at all points. So stopping the line is regarded as a serious matter, and keeping the assembly line running is the sole responsibility of a senior line manager. To reduce stoppages, large stocks of each part are held, and defective parts are discarded. Faults in assembly, which are treated as random events, are left to be corrected after the product has been assembled—often an expensive procedure. Stops are none the less frequent to correct materials-supply and co-ordination problems. In flexible manufacturing, every worker has

BOX 5.3. (*cont.*)

the ability to stop production whenever a fault is discovered. Parts are delivered by the suppliers to the work stations 'just in time'. Defective parts are put aside for their source to be identified, and any defects are treated as events with patterns of causes that need to be understood. When these methods are first introduced, stoppages are frequent as problems are identified and investigated. As the sources are found and removed, work stoppages diminish, and the typical mature flexible production line—where any worker can stop the line—stops much less frequently than the typical mass-production assembly line, where only the line foreman can press the stop button.

The result for labour is more worker identification with the job and more job satisfaction than under mass-production techniques. Employers find that their labour force develops substantial skills, and they try to hold on to workers rather than treating them as strictly variable inputs.

Product design is expensive. Mass-production firms try to reduce the costs by using specialist designers. For example, one person may spend his or her life trying to improve window-opening mechanisms. The specialization creates problems both in co-ordinating the work of various designers and in getting good feedback from parts producers and assembly-line workers to designers. The best theoretical design is of little use if it poses costly production problems. Flexible manufacturers use design teams that are non-specialized and work closely with production engineers and parts producers. This creates more flexibility and better feedback, from the practical problems that arise in production to the basic design of products. It also allows parts producers to be presented with broad specifications of the required parts while they do their own R&D to develop the detailed specifications.

The use of design teams also cuts product development time dramatically. In the specialized design techniques, the designing must be done in a linear manner: the product design must be worked out in detail before the machine makers begin to design the specialized equipment needed to do the work. In the lean design team, everyone is working together. As the new product begins to take shape, the tool designers can begin to work on their outline plans; as the product design becomes better specified, the design of the tools can likewise be more fully developed.

Although flexible production methods still have scale economies—unit costs fall as the volume of output increases—their main effect is to shift the whole long-run cost curve dramatically downward. Flexible methods are also effective in the very long run, especially in developing successful new products that can be produced efficiently and cheaply.

Japanese car firms using these methods have been able to achieve unit costs of production below those of mass-production-based European and North American car factories that have twice their volume of output. They have also been able to lead in international competition to design new products efficiently and rapidly. Flexible production methods have been a major source of the Japanese competitive advantage, both in cars and in a range of other manufactured goods. The ability of firms in other countries to compete successfully with these Japanese firms often depends on the speed with which they can institute such methods in their own production processes.

Source: The material in this box is adapted from J. P. Womack, D. T. Jones, and D. Roos, *The Machine that Changed the World* (New York: Maxwell Macmillan, 1990).

so, computer users will need Java compilers. As this language spreads, more and more applications will use it.

The learning curve

Another reason why established products get locked in, once they are established, is that customers have to make an investment of time and effort to learn how to use them and, once they have made that effort, are reluctant to change to a new product unless the case for such a change becomes overwhelming. This is referred to as a *learning curve* because users get more proficient over time. When the product range is changed to a new standard, the users have to start again on a new learning curve. To make it worth suffering these learning costs, the new product must be very much better. Just a little bit better will not generate a shift.

INCREASING RETURNS: WINNER TAKE ALL?

Increasing returns is such an important phenomenon in a significant part of modern industry, especially the high-technology knowledge-based sector, that it is worth emphasizing some of the implications for firms in the relevant sectors.[13]

Where there are increasing returns, there is a first-mover advantage, and the product that gets established tends to move further ahead over time. This means that, once a product has established market leadership, it is very difficult for a rival product to chip away at that market share. Rather, rivals have to search for the next technology (see the following section). Small cost savings and gradual efficiency improvements do not help much in these industries. Success depends on creating the next industry standard that itself becomes the dominant product.

In such environments, advanced technical knowledge is essential, so research and development expenditures are important. But R&D is not enough on its own. Many products that were technically brilliant have not made it because of an unsuitable business strategy. Managers in such industries require vision and foresight rather than mere administrative competence.

Industries with increasing returns can be highly unstable. A new product that turns out to be a blockbuster, such as Microsoft Windows or Glaxo's Zantac, can grow very fast. But the party can end just as quickly. If a new technology replaces the old, a product can become redundant rapidly, as with non-Windows compatible software. In the case of Zantac (an anti-stomach-ulcer drug) the end of patent protection in 1997 opened the market to cheap generic copies overnight. Glaxo, meanwhile has moved on to look for the next blockbuster.

One effect of increasing returns is to create a high degree of concentration of production in the hands of a small number of dominant producers. Once a product is

---

[13] For further discussion of this issue see W. Brian Arthur, 'Increasing returns and the new world of business', *Harvard Business Review* 74 (July–August 1996), pp. 100–9.

established, because average costs fall over the entire range of production, small competitors are at a substantial cost disadvantage.

It is hard to say how much of the economy is subject to increasing returns. However, what is certain is that the proportion is much more than it used to be. Agriculture, traditional processing industries, and basic manufacture are characterized by diminishing returns. The industries where increasing returns are significant are those that are knowledge-intensive, such as software and pharmaceuticals, where part of the output is more knowledge rather than just a specific physical product. Genuine advances in knowledge are expensive to produce, but they are often cheap to reproduce.

We return temporarily to the more conventional world of a given technology, and traditional manufacture.

RELATIONSHIP BETWEEN LONG-RUN AND SHORT-RUN COSTS

The short-run cost curves and the long-run curve are all derived from the same production function. Each curve assumes given prices for all inputs. In the long run, all inputs can be varied; in the short run, some must remain fixed. The long-run average cost curve shows the lowest cost of producing any output when all inputs are variable. Each short-run average total cost (*SRATC*) curve shows the lowest cost of producing any output when one or more inputs is held constant at some specific level.

No short-run cost curve can fall below the long-run curve, because the *LRAC* curve represents the lowest attainable cost for each possible output. As the level of output is changed, a different-size plant is normally required to achieve the lowest attainable cost. This is shown in Figure 5.5, where the *SRATC* curve lies above the *LRAC* curve at all outputs except q_0.

As we observed earlier in this chapter, a short-run cost curve such as the *SRATC* curve shown in Figure 5.5 is one of many such curves. Each curve shows how costs vary as output is varied from a base output, holding the fixed input at the quantity most appropriate to that output. Each *SRATC* curve is tangent to (touches) the long-run average cost curve at the level of output for which the quantity of the fixed input is optimal, and lies above it for all other levels of output.

Shifts in cost curves

The cost curves derived so far show how cost varies with output, given constant input prices and an unchanging technology. Changes in either technological knowledge or input prices will cause the entire family of short-run and long-run average cost curves to shift. Loss of existing technological knowledge is rare, so technological change normally causes change in only one direction, shifting cost curves downward. Improved ways of producing existing products make lower-cost methods of production available.

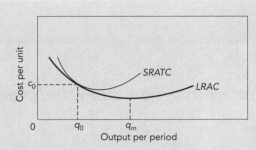

Figure 5.5. Long-run average cost and short-run average cost curves

The short-run average total cost (*SRATC*) curve is tangent to the long-run average cost (*LRAC*) curve at the output for which the quantity of the fixed input is optimal. Assume that output is varied with plant and equipment fixed at the level that is optimal for producing q_0. Costs will then follow the short-run cost curve shown in the figure. The curves *SRATC* and *LRAC* coincide at output q_0, where the fixed plant is optimal for that level of output. For all other outputs there is too little or too much plant and equipment, and *SRATC* lies above *LRAC*. If some output other than q_0 is to be sustained, costs can be reduced to the level of the long-run curve when sufficient time has elapsed to adjust the size of the firm's plant and equipment.

The output q_m is the lowest point on the firm's long-run average cost curve. It is called the firm's *minimum efficient scale* (*MES*). It is the output at which long-run costs are minimized.

Changes in input prices can exert an influence in either direction. If a firm has to pay more for any input it uses, the cost of producing each level of output will rise; if the firm has to pay less for any input it uses, the cost of producing each level of output will fall.

> **A rise in input prices shifts the family of short-run and long-run average cost curves upward. A fall in input prices, or a technological advance, shifts the entire family of average cost curves downward.**

Although input prices usually change gradually, sometimes they change suddenly and drastically. For example, in the mid-1980s oil prices fell dramatically; the effect was to shift downward the cost curves of all users of oil and oil-related products. The reverse happens when the price of some key raw material rises sharply, as happened with oil prices in both 1973 and 1979.

The very long run: endogenous technical change

In the long run, profit-maximizing firms do the best they can to produce known products with the techniques and the resources currently available. This means being *on*, rather than above, their long-run cost curves. In the very long run, production

BOX 5.4.

Endogenous materials design: a new industrial revolution?

Some experts in the science of materials believe that a new industrial revolution has been in progress since the mid-1980s. Many call it the 'Materials Revolution'.

Throughout history, an important element of technical change has been associated with advances in people's understanding of how to produce the physical materials used to make things. Indeed, we label stages of history by the materials that were used to make tools— the stone age, the bronze age, the iron age. Many key twentieth-century advances in manufacturing would not have been possible without materials such as steel and hydrocarbons. Today, important technical progress is built upon silicon chips and fibre optics. The chart shows the changing proportionate use in industry of four types of material: metals, polymers, composites, and ceramics. The invention of steel gave a huge boost to use of metals early in the twentieth century. However, proportionate use of metals has been declining since about 1950.

Economic history used to be taught as though 'inventions' were random events that then had unforeseen implications. The modern view is that these inventions were an endogenous product of economic activity, motivated by solving problems that had already been to some extent defined. For example, the depletion of the supply of wood in the late Middle Ages led to a long sustained drive to find methods of smelting iron with coal.

Previous materials advances were usually the outcome of a process of trial and error— Edison allegedly tried many thousands of different materials and designs before he 'invented' the light bulb. From now on, however, the new materials will themselves be the product of an ongoing process of manufacture. Modern materials science is able to use knowledge of the microstructure of matter, combined with advanced computing power, to design the materials to be used in production simultaneously with the engineering of production itself. This requires close co-operation between suppliers of materials and manufacturers of final products.

An example of this is a long-term co-operative venture between Audi and Alcoa to develop an aluminium-intensive car:

> The result has been a quantum leap in weight reduction technology and automotive structural manufacturing. This revolution is embodied in the development of the aluminium space frame (ASF) and in the ability to integrate the design of the material, the product, and the manufacturing process. The ASF concept breaks away from design and manufacturing mindsets and requirements associated with steel monocoque car body structures. Moreover, the aluminium-intensive vehicle introduced by Audi in 1994 represents a significant first step towards the development of a 'green' car which is cost effective, high-performance, low emission and recyclable. Lower weight facilitates greater fuel efficiency and the reduction of carbon dioxide emissions while at the same time increasing stiffness and passenger safety. . . . Despite a minimum 40% reduction in weight in the spaceframe, it is an extremely strong structure and provides exceptional

safety for the car occupants. Aluminium absorbs more energy, on a weight to weight basis, than steel. The aluminium body structure absorbs more energy in a collision than today's steel mono-coque body structures. Audi claims that the standard of safety and crashworthiness offered by the ASF has not been seen before in conventional cars.*

Another example of new materials technology can be found in sports equipment. When Bjorn Borg won the Wimbledon tennis tournament five times in the late 1970s he played with a wooden racquet. Jimmy Connors won it in 1982 playing with an aluminium alloy racquet. Pete Sampras was the men's champion three times from 1993–5 playing with a graphite composite racquet, a product of the materials revolution.

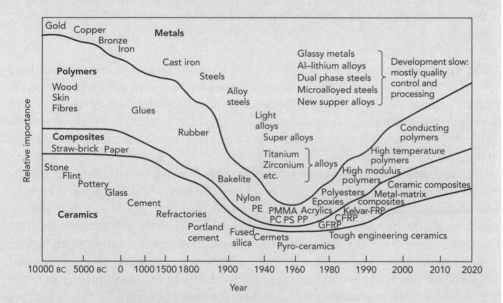

Evolution of engineering materials

The relative importance of four classes of materials—metals, polymers, composites, and ceramics—is shown as a function of time. The diagram is, of course, schematic, and does not describe either tonnage or value. The timescale is non-linear.

* Lakis C. Kaounides, 'New materials and simultaneous engineering in the car industry: the Alcoa-Audi alliance in lightweight aluminium car body structures', Ch. 1 of *Manufacturing Technology* (Institute of Mechanical Engineers, July 1996).

Source: The figure in this box is adapted from M. F. Ashby, *Philosophical Transactions of the Royal Society of London* 322 (July 1987).

techniques change. This means that the production function itself alters so that the same inputs produce more output. This in turn causes long-run cost curves to shift.

The decrease in costs that can be achieved by choosing from among available inputs, known techniques, and alternative levels of output is necessarily limited. Improvements by invention and innovation are potentially limitless, however; hence sustained growth in living standards is critically linked to *technological change.*

Technological change was once thought to be mainly a random process, brought about by inventions made by crackpots and eccentric scientists working in garages and scientific laboratories. As a result of much recent research, we now know better. Many scholars on both sides of the Atlantic have been influential in establishing this key result.[14]

Changes in technology are often *endogenous responses* to changing economic signals; that is, they result from responses by firms to the same things that induce the substitution of one input for another within the confines of a given technology.

The sharp rise in petrol prices in the early 1970s encouraged consumers to substitute fuel-efficient cars for 'gas guzzlers', especially in the USA, where petrol had traditionally been very cheap. Similarly, much of the move to substitute capital for labour in manufacturing, transportation, communications, mining, and agriculture was in response to rising wage rates, and the substitution has taken the form of inventing new labour-saving methods of production.

Until recently, economists analysed only the short- and long-run responses of the firm to various changes that immediately affected incentives faced by firms. Whenever technological change is an endogenous response to economic signals, such an analysis may be seriously misleading. Consider, for example, a rise in the price of an important input in one country. In the short run, firms that use the input will cut back production in response to the rise in costs. In the long run, they will substitute a cheaper input for the one whose price has risen. When all adjustments have been made, however, they will still find themselves at a cost disadvantage compared to competitors in other countries who have not suffered the rise in the price of their inputs. In the very long run, however, the firms may engage in research and development designed to reduce further the quantity required of the costly input. If the firms succeed, they may develop processes that allow them to lower costs to, or even below, those of their competitors.

A rise in input prices that began by conferring a competitive disadvantage may end up by causing a competitive advantage, if it induces research and development that is unexpectedly successful.

---

[14] Probably the most important single book on this issue is N. Rosenberg, *Inside the Black Box: Technology and Economics* (Cambridge: Cambridge University Press, 1982).

Many such instances have been documented by modern researchers into induced technological change. As a result, the response of firms to changes in such economic signals as output price and input costs must be seen in three steps.

1. The short-run response that consists of altering the quantity used of the variable input;

2. The long-run response that consists of adjusting *all* inputs;

3. Induced research and development that seeks to innovate the firm out of difficulties caused by reductions in its product prices and increases in its input prices.

Studies that ignore the third response ignore what are often the most important responses once enough time has been allowed to elapsed.

In this context, it is interesting to note that the techniques of flexible manufacturing (see Box 5.3), which are revolutionizing production all over the advanced countries, were first developed by the Japanese car producers in response to a scale disadvantage. They were unable to reach the efficient scale of production when they were only selling in their small, protected, home market. In response, they innovated their way out of these difficulties. They developed techniques that were efficient at lower levels of output than in the USA and Europe. This allowed them to produce a superior product at lower cost than their American and European competitors and so turned a long-run disadvantage into a very-long-run advantage.

Box 5.4 deals with another revolutionary change, the ability of modern science to design new materials that are appropriate for newly designed products. This links technological change even more closely to economic incentives than it has been in the past.

In the next chapter we proceed to integrate costs with revenues, and we are then able to discover the characteristics associated with the profit-maximizing level of output.

Summary

1. The production function relates physical inputs to physical outputs.

2. In the short run, at least one important input is fixed. In the long run, all inputs can be varied. In the very long run, the production function itself changes so that given amounts of inputs produce an increased amount of output.

3. Short-run variations in a variable input with another input fixed are subject to the law of diminishing returns: equal increments of the variable input sooner or later produce smaller and smaller additions to total output and eventually a reduction in average output per unit of variable input.

4. Short-run average and marginal cost curves are often U-shaped, the rising portion

reflecting diminishing average and marginal returns. They will be flat over a range if all of the fixed factor is not fully utilized.

5. The marginal cost curve intersects the average cost curve at the latter's minimum point, which is called the firm's capacity output.

6. There is a family of short-run average and marginal cost curves, one for each amount of the fixed input.

7. In the long run, the firm will adjust the combinations of inputs in order to minimize the cost of producing any given level of output. This requires that the ratio of marginal product to price be the same for all inputs.

8. The principle of substitution states that, when relative input prices change, firms will substitute relatively cheaper inputs for relatively more expensive ones.

9. Long-run cost curves are often assumed to be U-shaped, indicating decreasing average costs (increasing returns to scale) followed by increasing average costs (decreasing returns to scale).

10. In the very long run, innovations introduce new methods of production that alter the production function. These innovations respond to changes in economic incentives such as variations in the prices of inputs and outputs. They cause cost curves to shift downwards.

Topics for review

- The production function
- The short, long, and very long run
- The law of diminishing returns
- Short-run average, marginal, fixed, and total cost
- Capacity and minimum efficient scale (MES)
- Conditions for cost minimization
- The principle of substitution
- Constant, increasing, and decreasing long-run costs
- Inventions and innovations in the very long run

Questions for discussion

1. What are the inputs into the production function of a student essay? How has this production function changed since the advent of desk-top computers and word-processing packages? Does this production function show increasing or diminishing returns to scale?

2. The industrial revolution, in the late eighteenth and early nineteenth centuries, raised productivity and wages of workers in industry and caused migration from the land to the cities. Why might this have led to the search for new, more capital-intensive production methods in agriculture?

3. Farmer Giles has a 100 acre farm and he works it with one labourer and one tractor. Show what might happen to his output as he hires more and more labourers with the same land and capital. How would this outcome change if he bought an extra tractor?

4. In the situation of question (3), suppose that the farmer had agreed to sell a fixed level of output. How should he decide whether to produce that output by hiring more labourers or by buying one or more tractors?

5. Does the principle of substitution mean that increases in the capital stock must always be associated with the employment of fewer workers?

6. Which of the following industries do you think are most likely to exhibit economies of scale over a significant range of production: publishing, brewing, hotels, car manufacture, hairdressing.

CHAPTER 6

Profit Maximization

Market structure and firm behaviour	181	Short-run profitability of the firm	197
Market structure and behaviour	181		
Competitive market structure	182	**Long-run optimization for the firm**	198
Competitive behaviour	182	The effect of entry and exit	198
Behaviour versus structure	182	An entry-attracting price	199
The significance of market structure	183	An exit-inducing price	200
		The break-even price	202
Profit maximization	184	Marginal and intramarginal firms	202
Revenue and output	184	Comparison of the short-run and long-run	
Rules for all profit-maximizing firms	185	equilibria	203
Should the firm produce at all?	185		
The shut-down price	185	**The very long run**	204
How much should the firm produce?	186	Technical change	204
Maximization not minimization	187	Declining industries	206
The optimum output	187	The response of firms	206
		The response of governments	207
The firm in perfectly competitive			
markets	189	**Summary**	207
Assumptions of perfect competition	189		
An illustration	190	**Topics for review**	208
Revenue for a firm in perfect competition	190		
		Questions for discussion	208
Short-run optimization for the firm	193		
Short-run supply curves	194	**Box 6.1.** Incrementalism as a business	
The supply curve for one firm	195	decision rule	188
The supply curve of an industry	195	**Box 6.2.** 'Rent seeking': the concept of	
Short-run equilibrium price	196	economic rent	200

THIS chapter contains one of the most important ideas in economics. Once you have come to understand it you will carry it with you wherever your career takes you, whether you study more economics or not. The idea relates to the characteristics of a situation in which profits are at a maximum. The conditions for profit maximization are practical and implementable in a wide range of different business situations. Basically, for profit to be at a maximum, there has to be equality between incremental costs and incremental revenues (or, in the terminology of the previous chapter, equality of marginal cost and marginal revenue). Understanding what this means and how it is associated with an optimal production decision for the firm is what this chapter is all about.

In the previous chapter we studied how a firm's costs might vary with its output. To determine profit, we must also have information about how revenue varies with output. (Recall that profit is the difference between total revenue and total cost.) We shall then be able to determine the level of output that maximizes profit.

The way in which revenues vary as the firm changes its output depends on the structure of the market into which the firm is selling. Hence we start with a discussion of market structure. We then set out some general propositions about revenues that are related to the demand conditions faced by the firm. Finally, we develop an explicit analysis of the profit-maximizing output level for firms in the special case where individual firms cannot influence the market price of their product.

Market structure and firm behaviour

Does Shell compete with BP in the sale of petrol? Does NatWest Bank compete with Barclays? Does a wheat farmer from Yorkshire compete with a wheat farmer from Somerset? If we use the ordinary meaning of the word *compete*, the answer to the first two questions is plainly yes, and the answer to the third is no.

Shell and BP both advertise extensively to persuade car drivers to buy *their* products. Gimmicks such as new mileage-stretching additives and free air miles are used to tempt drivers to buy one brand of petrol rather than another. Most town centres in England and Wales have not only Barclays and NatWest banks but also Midland and Lloyds TSB. They all provide similar services but work hard to attract customers from each other. For example, they all offer incentives for students to open bank accounts in the hope that they will stay with that bank for life.

When we shift our attention to firms producing wheat, however, we see that there is nothing that Yorkshire farmers can do to affect either the sales or the profits of Somerset farmers. There would be no point in doing so even if they could, since the sales and profits of the Somerset farmers have no effect on those of Yorkshire farmers.

To sort out the questions of who is competing with whom and in what sense, it is useful to distinguish between the behaviour of individual firms and the *type of market* in which they operate. In everyday use, the word *competition* usually refers to competitive behaviour. However, it is important to understand both the competitive behaviour of individual firms and a quite distinct concept, competitive market structure.

Market structure and behaviour

The term **market structure** refers to all the features that may affect the behaviour and performance of the firms in a market (for example, the number of firms in the market, or the type of product that they sell).

Competitive market structure

The competitiveness of the market refers to the extent to which individual firms have power to influence market prices or the terms on which their product is sold. *The less power an individual firm has to influence the market in which it sells its product, the more competitive that market is.*

The extreme form of competitiveness occurs when each firm has zero market power. In such a case, there are so many firms in the market that each must accept the price set by the forces of market demand and market supply. The firms perceive themselves as being able to sell as much as they choose at the prevailing market price and as having no power to influence that price. If the firm charged a higher price, it would obtain no sales; so many other firms would be selling at the market price that buyers would take their business elsewhere.

This extreme is called a *perfectly competitive market structure*. (Usually the word 'structure' is dropped and economists speak of a *perfectly competitive market.*) In it, there is no need for individual firms to compete actively with one another, since none has any power over the market. One firm's ability to sell its product does not depend on the behaviour of any other firm. For example, the Yorkshire and Somerset wheat farmers operate in a perfectly competitive market (the world wheat market) over which they have no power. Neither can change the market price for their wheat by altering their own behaviour.

Competitive behaviour

In everyday language, the term *competitive behaviour* refers to the degree to which individual firms actively compete with one another. For example, Shell and BP certainly engage in competitive behaviour. It is also true, however, that both companies have some real power over their market. Either firm could raise its prices and still continue to attract customers. Each has the power to decide, within limits set by buyers' tastes and the prices of competing products, the price that people will pay for their petrol and oil. So even though they actively compete with each other, they do so in a market that does not have a perfectly competitive structure.

In contrast, the Yorkshire and Somerset wheat farmers do not engage in *competitive behaviour*, because the only way they can affect their profits is by changing their outputs of (or their costs of producing) wheat.

Behaviour versus structure

The distinction that we have just made explains why firms in perfectly competitive markets (e.g. the Yorkshire and the Somerset wheat producers) do not compete actively with each other, whereas firms that do compete actively with each other (e.g. Shell and BP) do not operate in perfectly competitive markets.

The significance of market structure

Shell and BP are two of several large firms in the oil *industry*. They produce petroleum products and sell them in various *markets*. The terms 'industry' and 'market' are familiar from everyday use. However, economists give them precise definitions that we need to understand.

We noted in Chapter 1 that a *market* consists of an area over which buyers and sellers can negotiate the exchange of some product. The firms that produce a well-defined product, or a closely related set of products, constitute an **industry.**

In Chapter 2 we developed and used market **demand curves.** A demand curve tells us the quantity of a product that consumers wish to buy at each price. The market demand curve for any particular product is the demand curve facing the *industry* that produces the product. We discovered in Chapter 2 that an *industry* demand curve is usually negatively sloped. This means that a greater quantity of the product is demanded at a lower price, and a lower quantity is demanded at a higher price.

When the managers of a firm make their production and sales decisions, they need to know what quantity of a product they can sell at various prices. Their concern is, therefore, not with the *market* demand curve for their industry's product, but rather with the demand curve for their firm's own output of that product. If they know the demand curve that their own firm faces, they know the sales that their firm can make at each possible price, and thus they know its potential revenues. If they also know their firm's costs of producing the product, they can calculate the profits that would be associated with each rate of output. They can, with this information, choose the output that maximizes profits.

In a perfectly competitive market structure, a single firm can sell as much as it wants of its output at the going market price. We shall see that this is equivalent to saying that the individual firm faces a horizontal demand curve. The only problem for the firm to solve under perfect competition is: how much does it want to sell? You might think that the answer is 'as much as possible', but this is not correct, because costs and revenues vary with output.

Most firms are not operating in perfectly competitive markets. Instead they face downward sloping demand curves—they can sell a greater quantity at a lower price, or a lower quantity at a higher price. Hence, they face a trade-off between price and volume of sales. If there is only one producer of a product, this producer is a *monopolist*. A monopolist faces the market demand curve, since the firm and the industry are the same entity. All other market structures in which firms face a downward sloping demand curve for their own output, and in which there are a finite number of competing firms, are referred to as *imperfectly competitive*.

The conditions for profit maximization are quite general and do not depend on market structure. After discussing what these are, we then illustrate how they work out in detail in a perfectly competitive market structure. The behaviour of firms in imperfectly competitive markets is discussed extensively in Section 3 of this book.

Profit maximization

Profit is maximized when the difference between total revenue and total cost is as great as possible. The previous chapter discussed how costs vary with output. We now need to say something about how revenue varies with output. Here we discuss revenues in general terms, and later in the chapter we shall be more specific about how revenue varies with output for the special case of firms in perfectly competitive markets.

Revenue and output

Total revenue from sales of a product is simply the price of the product times the number of units of the product sold. If there were 100 units sold at £5 each, the total revenue would be £500. For a firm that could sell as much as it wants at the going market price, total revenue simply increases in proportion to the numbers sold. In the above example, 1,000 units sold at £5 would yield total revenue of £5,000 and 10,000 units sold would yield total revenue of £50,000.

Only firms operating under perfect competition can increase their sale without lowering their price. All other firms face a negatively sloped demand curve. This means that to sell more they have to lower their price.[1] When a firm lowers its price in order to sell more, does this increase total revenue or does total revenue fall? The answer to this is that it depends on the sensitivity of the quantity demanded to a change in the price. Another word for this sensitivity is *elasticity*. This was discussed in Chapter 3.

If a firm lowers its price and this results in an increase in numbers of the product sold more than in proportion to the price reduction (say a 10 per cent price reduction leads to a 15 per cent increase in numbers sold), then total revenue will increase. However, if a lower price leads to sales increases less than in proportion to the price reduction (such as if a 10 per cent price reduction leads to a 5 per cent increase in units sold), then total revenue will fall.

For most firms that face a negatively sloped demand curve, total revenue will increase over some range of production but then, as output continues to increase, total revenue will start to fall. (We shall examine this relationship in detail in Chapter 7.) However, the important concept that we need immediately is that of *marginal revenue*. In real firms, marginal revenue is approximated by *incremental revenue*. The difference is that marginal revenue is a theoretical construct that refers to the increase in total revenue brought about by an infinitesimally small change in sales. Such tiny changes are unlikely to be observed or measurable in practice. Incremental revenue is the increase in total

---

[1] This is not to say that firms cannot increase sales by measures such as advertising and better marketing. What we are talking about here is the firm's choice in the face of a given demand curve. Even if it does use advertising to shift the demand curve, it then has to determine its new profit-maximizing position with respect to this new demand curve.

revenue that results from a small discrete change in sales. Such changes can be, and frequently are, observed and measured in practice. As with the discussion of costs in Chapter 5, we continue to use the terms 'marginal' and 'incremental' equivalently. Readers should not forget that the latter is an approximation to the former.

Marginal revenue is defined as the change in total revenue brought about by selling one more (small) unit of output. If marginal revenue is positive, total revenue must be rising as output increases. If marginal revenue is negative, however, an increase in output reduces total revenue, so total revenue is falling.

A firm facing a negatively sloped demand curve will also face a negatively sloped marginal revenue curve. This is illustrated in Figure 6.1, which also includes a marginal cost curve. A profit-maximizing firm will never want to produce in a range of output where marginal revenue is negative. It could always increase total revenue by reducing output. The point where marginal revenue becomes negative is the same level of output at which total revenue starts to fall.

The precise point of profit maximization cannot be defined with respect to revenues alone. It depends on the balance between marginal costs and marginal revenues. However, we are now ready to define the conditions for profit maximization and then to illustrate what they mean in detail for a firm under perfect competition.

Rules for all profit-maximizing firms

SHOULD THE FIRM PRODUCE AT ALL?

The firm always has the option of producing nothing. If it exercises this option, the firm will have an operating loss that is equal to its fixed costs—recall that fixed, or indirect, costs are those that still have to be met even if production is zero. If it decides to produce, it will add the variable, or direct, cost of production to its costs and the receipts from the sale of its product to its revenue. Therefore, it will be worthwhile for the firm to produce as long as it can find some level of output for which revenue exceeds variable cost. However, if its revenue is less than its variable cost at *every* level of output, the firm will actually lose more by producing than by not producing.

> *Rule 1*: A firm should not produce at all if, for *all* levels of output, the total variable cost of producing that output exceeds the total revenue derived from selling it or, equivalently, if the average variable cost of producing the output exceeds the price at which it can be sold.

The shut-down price
The price at which the firm can just cover its average variable cost, and that thus leaves it indifferent between producing and not producing, is often called the **shut-down price**. At any price below this price, the firm will shut down. Such a price is shown in

Optimization of the firm

Figure 6.1. Profit maximization: where marginal cost equals marginal revenue

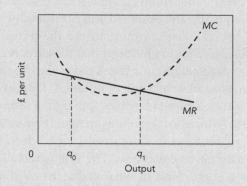

The equality of marginal cost and marginal revenue is necessary, but not sufficient, for profit maximization. The firm is assumed to be able to sell any output at the going market price, so that the market price is the firm's marginal revenue. (If all units can be sold at the prevailing market price then each unit adds that price to the firm's total revenue.)
$MC = MR$ at outputs q_0 and q_1. Output q_0 is a minimum-profit position, because a change of output in either direction would increase profit: for outputs below q_0, marginal cost exceeds marginal revenue and profits can be increased by *reducing* output; while for outputs above q_0, marginal revenue exceeds marginal cost and profits can be increased by *increasing* output. Output q_1 is a maximum-profit position, since at outputs just below it, marginal revenue exceeds marginal cost and profit can be increased by *increasing* output towards q_1; while at outputs just above it, marginal cost exceeds marginal revenue and profit can be increased by *reducing* output towards q_1.

part (i) of Figure 6.5 on page 196. At the price of £2 the firm can just cover its average variable cost by producing q_0 units. Any other output would not produce enough revenue to cover variable costs. For any price below £2 there is no output at which variable costs can be covered. The price £2 in part (i) is thus the shut-down price.

HOW MUCH SHOULD THE FIRM PRODUCE?

If a firm decides that (according to Rule 1) production is worth undertaking, it must decide how much to produce. Common sense dictates that on a unit-by-unit basis, if any unit of production adds more to revenue than it does to cost, producing and selling that unit will increase profits. However, if any unit adds more to cost than it does to revenue, producing and selling that unit will decrease profits. Using the terminology introduced earlier, a unit of production raises profits if the marginal revenue obtained from selling it exceeds the marginal cost of producing it; it lowers profits if the marginal revenue obtained from selling it is less than the marginal cost of producing it.

Now let a firm with some existing rate of output consider increasing or decreasing that output. If a further unit of production will increase the firm's profits, the firm should expand its output. However, if the last unit produced reduced profits, the firm should contract its output. From this it follows that the only time the firm should leave its output unaltered is when the last unit produced adds the same amount to costs as it does to revenue. The results just obtained can be combined in the following rule:

Rule 2: Assuming that it is worthwhile for the firm to produce, the firm should produce the output at which marginal revenue equals marginal cost.

This is the 'Big Idea' of this chapter and, indeed, it is one of the most important things you will learn in economics. It is illustrated in Figure 6.1, and we shall continue to analyse what this rule means throughout the rest of this chapter. Box 6.1 discusses the significance of this rule from the perspective of using it as a decision-making rule in business.

MAXIMIZATION NOT MINIMIZATION

Figure 6.1 shows that it is possible to fulfil Rule 2 and have profits at a minimum rather than a maximum.

In the figure there are two outputs where marginal cost equals marginal revenue. Rule 3 is needed to distinguish minimum-profit positions from maximum-profit positions.

Rule 3: For an output where marginal cost equals marginal revenue to be profit-maximizing rather than profit-minimizing, it is sufficient that marginal cost be less than marginal revenue at slightly lower outputs and that marginal cost exceed marginal revenue at slightly higher outputs.

The geometrical statement of this condition is that, at the profit-maximizing output, the marginal cost curve should intersect the marginal revenue curve from below. This ensures that *MC* is less than *MR* to the left of the profit-maximizing output and greater than *MR* to the right of the profit-maximizing output.

THE OPTIMUM OUTPUT

The above three rules determine the output that will be chosen by any firm that maximizes its profits in the short run. This output is called the firm's **profit-maximizing output,** and sometimes its **optimum output:**

- The firm's optimum output is zero if total revenue is less than total variable cost at all levels of output; the optimum output is positive if there is any output for which total revenue exceeds total variable cost.
- When the firm's optimum output is positive, it is where marginal cost equals marginal revenue.
- If output is reduced slightly from the optimum level, marginal cost must be less than marginal revenue; if output is increased slightly from the optimum level, marginal cost must exceed marginal revenue.

BOX 6.1.

Incrementalism as a business decision rule

Rule 2 in the text is much more than just a 'theoretical' result. It has an important pay-off in a wide range of business decision making. So long as it is safe to assume that the firm prefers more profit to less, then we have discovered a powerful and yet simple guide to decisions. It can be applied to a wide range of production, hiring, and investment decisions.

Once you come to understand this rule fully you will regard it as obvious and common sense. However, it is neither obvious nor common sense to those who do not understand it. Indeed, while the rule is simple in principle, it is not always so simple to apply in practice. The point is that by trying to apply it you are more likely to make the correct decision than by ignoring the rule entirely.

The decision rule is best thought of in terms of incremental costs and incremental revenues. These are only exactly the same as marginal costs and marginal revenues for infinitesimally small changes. Most business decisions involve discrete changes, hence we refer to this rule as 'incrementalism'.

The decision rule is as follows:

For any proposed change in the firm's activity, calculate the addition to costs from the action and the addition to revenues; if the addition to costs exceeds the addition to revenues, don't do it; if the addition to revenues exceeds the addition to costs do it.

For a firm in the short run, that is, with given equipment and technology, the application of this rule is simplest. It requires either not producing at all, if there is no level of output for which additions to revenue exceed additions to cost, or producing up to the output level where additions to costs start to exceed additions to revenue. This optimum is analysed in Figure 6.3 on page 194. The short-run equilibrium of the firm can be thought of as a position where all possible actions, with respect to variable costs and output, that would add more to revenue than to cost have already been taken.

Rule 3 on page 187 means that we should be careful not to close down an operation entirely just because there is *some* range of output for which additions to cost exceed additions to revenue. If the firm is in a range of output where all small changes produce additions to cost greater than additions to revenue, it is important to examine larger changes to see if activity can be shifted to a profitable range of output.

Short-run decisions are those taken on a day-to-day basis within the confines of a given capital stock. The long-run decision is whether or not to add to the capital stock. This can be approached in essentially the same way. The issue is: should we buy another machine or build a new factory? The key question is: will it add more to revenue than it adds to costs?

Complications in investment decisions arise from two main factors. The first is that the addition to costs is normally immediate, whereas the addition to revenue is some time in the future. So we have to have some means of comparing money now with money in the future. How much extra revenue in, say, five years time would compensate for an extra £100 worth of costs today? The second problem is that future revenues are uncertain. We do not know for sure how much extra revenue will be generated by an investment. We devote the whole

BOX 6.1. (*cont.*)

of Chapter 11 to looking at the issues involved in such decisions. Despite complications, it is still important to bear in mind that the key question is whether the investment adds more to revenue than to costs.

A similar approach can be taken to the very-long-run issue of the adoption of new technology, including the introduction of new working practices. Anything that adds more to revenue than it does to costs, or perhaps reduces costs more than it reduces revenues, should be done.

Firms that are not perpetually seeking out and evaluating the latest technical advances to see if they can be implemented will lose out eventually to those who are. Hence, this decision rule is not just a way of checking that the current position is optimal, it is a tool for guaranteeing that managers are always on the look out for ways of innovating so as to increase revenues relative to costs.

The firm in perfectly competitive markets

The above rules apply to *all firms*, so long as they are profit-maximizing, irrespective of what market structure they find themselves in. We now turn to an analysis of how these rules apply to a firm in a *perfectly competitive market structure*. The analysis of firms in monopolistic and imperfectly competitive market structures is postponed until Chapters 7 and 8.

The perfectly competitive market structure—usually referred to simply as *perfect competition*—applies directly to a number of real-world markets, though it is certainly not the dominant market structure for modern business. It also provides an important benchmark for comparison with other market structures, and it is the simplest structure to deal with analytically.

Assumptions of perfect competition

Our analysis of **perfect competition** is built on a number of key assumptions relating to the firm and to the industry. Setting these out explicitly helps us to understand the type of world for which perfect competition is a useful model.

- **Assumption 1:** All the firms in the industry sell an identical product. Economists describe this by saying that the firms sell a **homogeneous product.**
- **Assumption 2:** Customers know the nature of the product being sold and the prices charged by each firm.

Optimization of the firm

- **Assumption 3:** The level of a firm's output at which its long-run average total cost reaches a minimum is small relative to the industry's total output.

- **Assumption 4:** Each *firm* in the industry is a **price taker.** This means that an individual firm can alter its rate of production and sales without significantly affecting the market price of its product. This is why a firm operating in a perfectly competitive market has no power to influence that market through its own individual actions. It must passively accept whatever happens to be the ruling price, but it can sell as much as it wants at that price.[2]

- **Assumption 5:** The *industry* is assumed to be characterized by *freedom of entry and exit*; that is, any new firm is free to enter the industry and start producing if it so wishes, and any existing firm is free to cease production and leave the industry. Existing firms cannot bar the entry of new firms, and there are no legal prohibitions or other artificial barriers to entering or exiting the industry.

An illustration

The Yorkshire and the Somerset wheat farmers that we considered earlier provide us with good illustrations of firms that are operating in a perfectly competitive market.

Because each individual wheat farmer is just one of a very large number of producers who are all growing the same product, one firm's contribution to the industry's total production is only a tiny drop in an extremely large bucket. Each firm will correctly assume that variations in its output have no significant effect on the price at which they sell their wheat. Thus each firm, knowing that it can sell as much or as little as it chooses at that price, adapts its behaviour to a given market price of wheat. Furthermore, anyone who has enough money to buy or rent the necessary land, labour, and equipment can become a wheat farmer.[3] There is nothing that existing farmers can do, and no legal deterrents, to stop another farmer from growing wheat.

The difference between the wheat farmers and Shell or BP is in *degree of market power*. Each firm that is producing wheat is an insignificant part of the whole market and thus has no power to influence the price of wheat. The oil company does have power to influence the price of petrol because its own sales represent a significant part of the total sales of petrol.

Revenue for a firm in perfect competition

We now turn to the question of how revenue varies with output. A firm's revenue is influenced by the shape of its demand curve. As we have already mentioned, a major

---

[2] To emphasize its importance, we identify price taking as a separate assumption, although, strictly speaking, it is implied by the first three assumptions.

[3] Most of the world's wheat growers sell at a price determined in the world wheat market. However, in 1996 farmers in the EU faced a price above the world price because of EU price supports. However, there are so many farmers within the EU that no one of them could affect the EU price even though it is not set on the world market.

distinction between firms operating in perfectly competitive markets and firms operating in any other type of market is in the shape of the firm's own demand curve.

The demand curve facing each firm in perfect competition is horizontal, because variations in the firm's output over the range that it can consider have no noticeable effect on price.

The horizontal demand curve does not mean that the firm could actually sell an infinite amount at the going price. It means, rather, that the variations in production *that it will normally be possible for the firm to make* will leave price virtually unchanged because their effect on total industry output will be negligible. Neither does this mean that the price faced by a firm never changes, merely that this price is not changed by variations in the firm's own output.

To study the revenues that firms receive from the sales of their products, it is helpful to define three concepts called total, average, and marginal revenue, two of which we have already mentioned. These are the revenue counterparts of the categories of total, average, and marginal cost that we discussed in Chapter 5.

Total revenue (*TR*) *is the total amount received by the seller from the sale of a product.* If q units are sold at £p each,[4] $TR = p \times q$.

Average revenue (*AR*) *is the amount of revenue per unit sold.* This is equal to the price at which the product is sold, so long as all units sell for the same price.

Marginal revenue (*MR*) is the change in a firm's total revenue resulting from a change in its rate of sales by one unit. Where discrete changes arise, the term *incremental revenue* is appropriate for practical applications, but we continue to refer to *marginal* revenue in our analysis of the firm, even where discrete changes are involved. Whenever output changes by more than one unit, the change in revenue must be divided by the change in output to calculate marginal revenue. For example, if an increase in output of three units per month is accompanied by an increase in revenue of £1,500, the marginal revenue resulting from the sale of *one extra unit* per month is £1,500/3, or £500. At any existing level of sales, marginal revenue shows what revenue the firm would gain by selling one unit more and what revenue it would lose by selling one unit less.[5]

To illustrate each of these revenue concepts, consider a firm that is selling an agricultural product in a perfectly competitive market at a price of £3 per tonne. Total revenue rises by £3 for every tonne sold. Because every tonne brings in £3, the average revenue per tonne sold will also be £3. Furthermore, because each *additional* tonne sold brings in £3, the marginal revenue of an extra tonne sold is also £3. Table 6.1 shows calculations of these revenue concepts for a range of outputs between 10 and 13 tonnes.

---

4 Four common ways of indicating that any two variables such as p and q are to be multiplied are p × q, p·q, $(p)(q)$, and pq.

5 Total revenue is a function of output. Because we use numerical examples in the text we are, strictly speaking, using the concept of *incremental revenues*, $\Delta TR/\Delta q$. Marginal revenue is defined formally as the first derivative of total revenue with respect to output, dTR/dq. For small changes, incremental revenue may be regarded as an approximation to marginal revenue.

Optimization of the firm

The important point illustrated in Table 6.1 is that as long as the amount of the firm's output does not significantly affect the price at which that output sells, marginal revenue is equal to average revenue (which is *always* equal to price if all customers pay the same price for the product). Graphically, as shown in part (i) of Figure 6.2, average revenue and marginal revenue are the same horizontal line drawn at the level of market price. Because the firm can sell any quantity it chooses at this price, the horizontal line is also the *firm's demand curve*; it shows that any quantity the firm chooses to sell will be associated with this same market price.

> **If the market price is unaffected by variations in the firm's output, then the firm's demand curve, its average revenue curve, and its marginal revenue curve all co-incide in the same horizontal line.**

This result can be stated in a slightly different way:

> **For a firm in perfect competition, price equals marginal revenue, which in turn equals average revenue.**

This means, of course, that total revenue rises in direct proportion to output, as shown in part (ii) of Figure 6.2.

The decision as to what output level maximizes profit will have to be taken in stages. These stages correspond to the three 'runs' of costs that we analysed in Chapter 5. *In the short run* the firm has some fixed inputs and so the decision-making problem is to

Table 6.1. Revenue concepts for a price-taking firm

Quantity sold (q) (units)	Price (p) (£)	$TR = p \cdot q$ (£)	$AR = TR/q$ (£)	$MR = \Delta TR/\Delta q$ (£)
10	3.00	30.00	3.00	
11	3.00	33.00	3.00	3.00
12	3.00	36.00	3.00	3.00
13	3.00	39.00	3.00	3.00

When price is fixed, average revenue, marginal revenue, and price are all equal to each other. The table shows the calculation of total (TR), average (AR), and marginal revenue (MR) when market price is £3.00 and the firm varies its quantity over the range from 10 to 13 units. Marginal revenue is shown between the lines because it represents the change in total revenue in response to a change in quantity. For example, when sales rise from 11 to 12 units, revenue rises from £33 to £36, making marginal revenue (36 − 33)/(12 − 11) = £3 per unit.

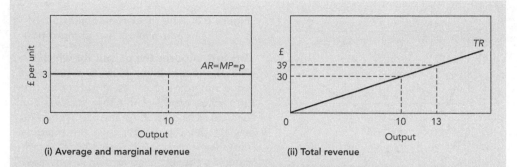

Figure 6.2. Revenue curves for a firm in perfect competition

The demand curve for a perfectly competitive firm is a horizontal straight line. The lines graph the data from Table 6.1. Because price does not change, neither marginal nor average revenue varies with output—both are equal to price. When price is constant, total revenue is a rising straight line from the origin whose slope is given by the price.

choose the quantity of the variable input and the corresponding level of output to maximize profit. *In the long run*, the fixed input can also be varied, and this will lead to a different profit-maximizing output than all but one of the possible short-run profit-maximizing outputs. This is the one at which long-run average cost is minimized. *In the very long run*, of course, changes in technology can shift the long-run cost curves, so this will produce yet another level of profit-maximizing output. Even though the optimal output will vary according to the time horizon, the principles that determine the profit-maximizing output for each 'run' do not.

Short-run optimization for the firm

Rule 2 tells us that any profit-maximizing firm that produces at all will produce at the point where marginal cost equals marginal revenue. However, we have already seen that, for price-taking firms, marginal revenue is the market price. Combining these two results gives us an important conclusion:

> **A firm that is operating in a perfectly competitive market will produce the output that equates its marginal cost of production with the market price of its product (as long as price exceeds average variable cost).**

In a perfectly competitive industry, the market determines the price at which the firm sells its product. The firm then picks the quantity of output that maximizes its profits. We have seen that this is the output for which price equals marginal cost.

When the firm has reached a position where its profits are maximized, it has no

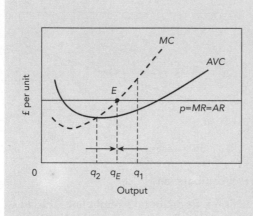

Figure 6.3. The short-run equilibrium of a firm in perfect competition

The firm chooses the output for which $p = MC$ above the level of *AVC*. When price equals marginal cost, as at output q_E, the firm loses profits if it either increases or decreases its output. At any point left of q_E, say q_2, price is greater than the marginal cost, and it pays to increase output (as indicated by the left-hand arrow). At any point to the right of q_E, say q_1, price is less than the marginal cost, and it pays to reduce output (as indicated by the right-hand arrow).

incentive to change its output. Therefore, unless prices or costs change, the firm will continue to produce this output because it is doing as well as it can do, given the market situation. The firm is in *short-run equilibrium*, as illustrated in Figure 6.3. (The long run is considered later in this chapter.)

In a perfectly competitive market, each firm is a price taker and a quantity adjuster. It pursues its goal of profit maximization by increasing or decreasing quantity until it equates its short-run marginal cost with the price of its product that is given to it by the market.

Figure 6.3 shows the equilibrium of the firm using average cost and revenue curves. We can, if we wish, show the same equilibrium using total cost and revenue curves. Figure 6.4 combines the total cost curve first drawn in Figure 5.3 on page 154 with the total revenue curve first shown in Figure 6.2. It shows the profit-maximizing output as the output with the largest positive difference between total revenue and total cost. This must of course be the same output as we located in Figure 6.3 by equating marginal cost and marginal revenue.

Short-run supply curves

In Chapters 2–3 we looked at how the interaction of demand and supply determines the market price of a product. We can now highlight the implications of the above analysis for the **supply curve** of the firm. A supply curve tells us how much will be offered for sale in the market at each price. The supply curve for a firm tells us how much this one firm will supply at each price. The *industry*, or *market*, *supply curve* tells us how much all firms making the same product will supply.

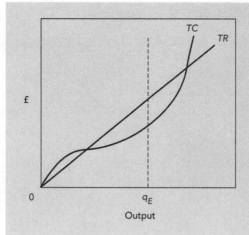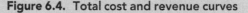

Figure 6.4. Total cost and revenue curves

The firm chooses the output for which the gap between the total revenue and the total cost curves is the largest. At each output, the vertical distance between the *TR* and *TC* curves shows by how much total revenue exceeds total cost. In the figure, the gap is largest at output q_E, which is thus the profit-maximizing output.

The supply curve for one firm

The firm's supply curve is derived in part (i) of Figure 6.5, which shows a firm's marginal cost curve and four alternative prices. The horizontal line at each price is the firm's demand (and marginal revenue) curve when the market price is at that level. The firm's marginal cost curve gives the marginal cost corresponding to each level of output. We require a supply curve that shows the quantity that the firm will supply at each price. For prices below average variable cost, the firm will supply zero units (Rule 1). For prices above average variable cost, the firm will equate price and marginal cost (Rule 2, modified by the proposition that $MR = p$ in perfect competition). This leads to the following conclusion:

> **In perfect competition, the firm's supply curve is its marginal cost curve for those levels of output for which marginal cost is above average variable cost.**

The supply curve of an industry

To illustrate what is involved, Figure 6.6 shows the derivation of an industry supply curve for an industry containing only two firms. The general result is as follows:

> **In perfect competition, the industry supply curve is the horizontal sum of the marginal cost curves (above the level of average variable cost) of all firms in the industry.**

The reason for this is that each firm's marginal cost curve shows how much that firm will supply at each given market price, and the industry supply curve is the sum of what each firm will supply.

This supply curve, based on the short-run marginal cost curves of all the firms in the industry, is the industry's supply curve that was used in Chapter 2. We have now established the profit-maximizing behaviour of individual firms that lies behind that

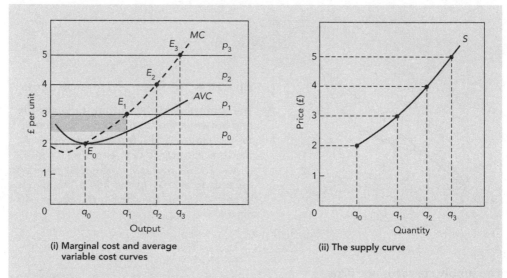

(i) Marginal cost and average variable cost curves

(ii) The supply curve

Figure 6.5. The supply curve for a price-taking firm

For a price-taking firm, the supply curve has the same shape as its *MC* curve above the level of *AVC*. The point E_0, where price p_0 equals *AVC*, is the shut-down point. For prices below £2, optimum output is zero, because the firm is better off if it produces nothing. As prices rise from £2 to £3 to £4 to £5, the firm increases its production from q_0 to q_1 to q_2 to q_3. If, e.g., price were £3, the firm would produce output q_1 rather than zero because it would be earning the contribution to fixed costs shown by the shaded rectangle.

The firm's supply curve is shown in part (ii). It relates market price to the quantity the firm will produce and offer for sale. It has the same shape as the firm's *MC* curve for all prices above *AVC*.

curve. It is sometimes called a **short-run supply curve** because it is based on the short-run, profit-maximizing behaviour of all the firms in the industry. This distinguishes it from a *long-run supply curve*, which relates quantity supplied to the price that rules in long-run equilibrium. In the long run, existing firms can increase their capital and more firms can enter the industry.

Short-run equilibrium price

The price of a product sold in a perfectly competitive market is determined by the interaction of the industry's short-run supply curve and the market demand curve. Although no one firm can influence the market price significantly, the collective actions of all firms in the industry (as shown by the industry supply curve) and the collective actions of consumers (as shown by the market demand curve) together determine the

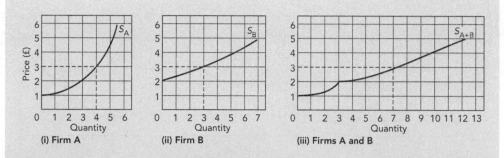

Figure 6.6. The supply curve for a group of firms

The industry supply curve is the horizontal sum of the supply curves of each of the firms in the industry. At a price of £3, firm A would supply 4 units and firm B would supply 3 units. Together, as shown in part (iii), they would supply 7 units. In this example, because firm B does not enter the market at prices below £2, the supply curve S_{A+B} is identical to S_A up to price £2 and is the sum of S_A and S_B above £2.

If there are hundreds of firms, the process is the same: each firm's supply curve (which is derived in the manner shown in Figure 6.5) shows what that firm will produce at each given price. The industry supply curve shows the sum of the quantities produced by all firms at each given price.

equilibrium price. This occurs at the point where the market demand curve and the industry supply curve intersect.

At the equilibrium price, each firm is producing and selling a quantity for which its marginal cost equals price. No firm is motivated to change its output in the short run. Because total quantity demanded equals total quantity supplied, there is no reason for market price to change in the short run; the market and all the firms in the industry are in short-run equilibrium.

Short-run profitability of the firm

We know that when an industry is in short-run equilibrium, each firm is maximizing its profits. However, we do not know *how large* these profits are. It is one thing to know that a firm is doing as well as it can, given its particular circumstances; it is another thing to know how well it is doing.

Figure 6.7 shows three possible positions for a firm in short-run equilibrium. In all cases the firm is maximizing its profits by producing where price equals marginal cost, but in part (i) the firm is suffering losses, in part (ii) it is just covering all of its costs (breaking even), and in part (iii) it is making profits because average revenue exceeds average total cost. In part (i) we could say that the firm is minimizing its losses rather

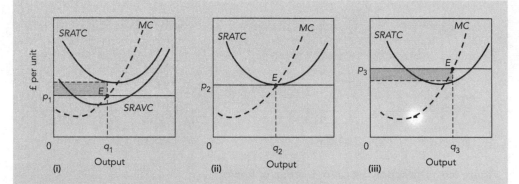

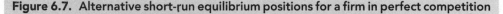

Figure 6.7. Alternative short-run equilibrium positions for a firm in perfect competition

When it is in short-run equilibrium, a competitive firm may be suffering losses, breaking even, or making profits. The diagram shows a firm with given costs faced with three altern-ative prices, p_1, p_2, and p_3. In each part, E is the point at which $MC = MR$ = price. Since in all three cases price exceeds AVC, the firm is in short-run equilibrium.

In part (i), price is p_1. Because price is below average total cost, the firm is suffering losses shown by the shaded area. Because price exceeds average variable cost, the firm continues to produce in the short run. Because price is less than ATC, the firm will not replace its capital as it wears out.

In part (ii), price is p_2 and the firm is just covering its total costs. It will replace its capital as it wears out since its revenue is covering the full opportunity cost of its capital.

In part (iii), price is p_3 and the firm is earning pure profits in excess of all its costs as shown by the shaded area. As in part (ii), the firm will replace its capital as it wears out.

than maximizing its profits, but both statements mean the same thing. In all three cases, the firm is doing as well as it can, given its costs and the market price.

Long-run optimization for the firm

Although Figure 6.7 shows three possible short-run equilibrium positions for the firm in perfect competition, not all of them are possible long-run equilibrium positions.

The effect of entry and exit

The key to long-run equilibrium under perfect competition is entry and exit. We have seen that when firms are in *short-run equilibrium*, they may be making profits, suffering losses, or just breaking even. Because costs include the opportunity cost of capital, firms that are just breaking even are doing as well as they could do by investing their capital elsewhere. Thus, there will be no incentive for such firms to leave the industry. Similarly, if new entrants expect just to break even, there will be no incentive for firms to enter the industry, because capital can earn the same return elsewhere in the economy. If, however, existing firms are earning revenues in excess of all costs, including the opportunity cost of capital, new capital will enter the industry to share in these profits. If existing firms are suffering losses, capital will leave the industry because a better return can be obtained elsewhere in the economy. Let us consider this process in a little more detail.

An entry-attracting price

First, let all firms in the competitive industry be in the position of the firm shown in part (iii) of Figure 6.7. New firms, attracted by the profitability of existing firms, will enter the industry. Suppose that in response to the high profits that the 100 existing firms are making, 20 new firms enter. The market supply curve that formerly added up the outputs of 100 firms must now add up the outputs of 120 firms. At any price, more will be supplied because there are more producers. New entry, in this context, does not have to involve independent firms, the effect would be just the same if existing firms decide to set up new plants producing the same product.

With an unchanged market demand curve, this shift in the short-run industry supply curve means that the previous equilibrium price will no longer prevail. The shift in supply will lower the equilibrium price, and both new and old firms will have to adjust their output to this new price. This is illustrated in Figure 6.8. New firms will continue to enter, and the equilibrium price will continue to fall, until all firms in the industry are just covering their total costs. Firms will then be in the position of the firm shown in part (ii) of Figure 6.7, which is called a *zero-profit equilibrium.*

> **Profits in a competitive industry are a signal for the entry of new firms; the industry will expand, pushing price down until the profits fall to zero.**

The search for new profitable opportunities is, of course, one of the key driving forces

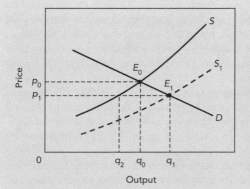

Figure 6.8. The effect of new entrants on the supply curve

New entrants shift the supply curve to the right and lower the equilibrium price. Initial equilibrium is at E_0 with price p_0 and output q_0. The entry of new firms shifts the supply curve to S_1; the equilibrium price falls to p_1 and output rises to q_1. At this price, before entry, only q_2 would have been produced. The extra output is supplied by the new firms.

in a market economy. The perfect-competition model neatly illustrates the dynamics of the profit incentive. High profits attract firms into a particular industry. Negative profits drive them away. The search for economic profit is sometimes referred to as 'rent seeking'. The meaning and origins of this term are set out in Box 6.2.

An exit-inducing price

Now let the firms in the industry be in the position of the firm shown in part (i) of

---

BOX 6.2.

'Rent seeking': the concept of economic rent

'Rent seeking' is a term now commonly used in business studies and it derives from an important concept in economics, that of *economic rent*. Factors of production (land, labour, and capital) must earn a certain return in their present use to prevent them from moving to another use. (This required return is sometimes called the factor's *transfer earnings*.) If there were no non-monetary advantages in alternative uses, the factors would have to earn their opportunity cost (what they could earn elsewhere) to prevent them from moving elsewhere. This is usually true for capital and land. Labour, however, gains important non-monetary advantages in various jobs, and it must earn in one use enough to equate the two jobs' total advantages—monetary and non-monetary.

Any excess that factors earn over the minimum amount needed to keep them in their present use is called **economic rent**. Economic rent is analogous to economic profit as a surplus over the opportunity cost of capital. Hence, firms looking for profitable opportunities (in the sense of making economic profit) can be thought of as 'rent seeking'. The concept of economic rent is crucial in predicting the effects that changes in earnings have on the movement of factors among alternative uses. However, the terminology of rent is confusing because economic rent is often called simply *rent,* which can of course also mean the full price paid to hire something, such as a machine, a piece of land, or a house.

The origins of the term (and the reasons for the confusing terminology) go back to the time of the Napoleonic Wars. In England, the price of wheat soared and so did rents of farm land. Were high wheat prices caused by high land rents, or were high land rents caused by high wheat prices? David Ricardo argued that causation unambiguously ran from wheat prices to land rents. The price of wheat was high, he said, because there was a shortage, which was caused by the Napoleonic Wars. Because wheat was profitable to produce, there was keen competition among farmers to obtain land on which to grow wheat. This competition in turn forced up the rent of wheat land.

The reasoning behind Ricardo's conclusion was as follows. The supply of land was fixed. Land was regarded as having only one use, the growing of wheat. Nothing had to be paid to prevent land from transferring to a use other than growing wheat because it had no other use. No landowner would leave land idle as long as some return could be obtained by renting it out. Therefore, all the payment to land—that is, rent in the ordinary sense of the word—was a surplus over and above what was necessary to keep it in its present use. Given a fixed supply of land, the price of land depended on the demand for land, which depended

Figure 6.7. Although the firms are covering their variable costs, the return on their capital is less than the opportunity cost of capital. They are not covering their total costs. This is a signal for the exit of firms. Old plant and equipment will not be replaced as they wear out. As a result, the industry's short-run supply curve shifts leftward, and the market price rises. Firms will continue to exit, and the market price will continue to rise, until the remaining firms can cover their total costs, that is, until they are all in the zero-profit equilibrium illustrated in part (ii) of Figure 6.7. The exit of firms then ceases.

on the demand for wheat. *Rent*, the term for the payment for the use of land, thus became the term for a surplus payment to a factor over and above what was necessary to keep it in its present use.

The amount of rent in factor payments depends on the shape of the supply curve, as illustrated in the figure. A single demand curve is shown with three different supply curves. In each case the competitive equilibrium price is £600, and 4,000 units of the factor are hired. The total payment (£2.4 million) is represented by the entire shaded area.

When the supply curve is vertical (S_0), the whole payment is economic rent, because a decrease in price would not lead any units of the factor to move elsewhere.

When the supply curve is horizontal (S_1), none of the payment is rent, because even a small decrease in price offered would lead all units of the factor to move elsewhere.

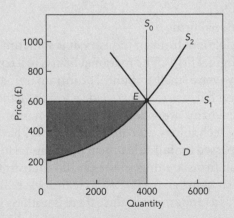

When the supply curve is positively sloped (S_2) part of the payment is rent. As shown by the height of the supply curve, at a price of £600 the 4,000th unit of the factor is receiving just enough to persuade it to offer its services in this market, but the 2,000th unit, for example, is earning well above what it requires to stay in this market. The aggregate of economic rents is shown by the darker shaded area, and the aggregate of what must be paid to keep 4,000 units in this market is shown by the lighter shaded area.

Optimization of the firm

Losses in a competitive industry are a signal for the exit of firms; the industry will contract, driving the market price up until the remaining firms are covering their total costs.

The break-even price
Because firms exit when they are motivated by losses and enter when they are motivated by profits, this conclusion follows:

The long-run equilibrium of a competitive industry occurs when firms are earning zero profits.

The firm in part (ii) of Figure 6.7 is in a zero-profit, long-run equilibrium. For that firm, the price p_0 is sometimes called the **break-even price.** It is the price at which all costs, including the opportunity cost of capital, are being covered. The firm is just willing to stay in the industry. It has no incentive to leave, neither do other firms have an incentive to enter.

Recalling that costs include the opportunity cost of capital, the above conclusion can be restated as follows: the long-run equilibrium of a competitive industry occurs where all firms are just covering the opportunity cost of their capital.

In the preceding analysis, we see profits serving the function of providing signals that guide the allocation of scarce resources among the economy's industries. It is also worth noting that freedom of entry will tend to push profits towards zero in any industry whether or not it is perfectly competitive.

Marginal and intramarginal firms
When considering possible exit from an industry, it is sometimes useful to distinguish marginal from intramarginal firms. The marginal firm is just covering its full costs and would exit if price fell by even a small amount. The intramarginal firm is earning profits and would require a larger fall in price to persuade it to exit. In the pure model of perfect competition, however, all firms are marginal firms in long-run equilibrium. All firms have access to the same technology and all, therefore, will have identical cost curves when enough time has passed for full adjustment of all capital to be made.[6] In long-run industry equilibrium, all firms are thus in the position illustrated in Figure 6.7(ii). If price falls below p_2 in that figure all firms wish to withdraw. Exit must then be by some contrived process, such as a random draw, since there is nothing in the theory to explain who will exit first.

In real-world situations, firms are not identical, since technology changes continually and different firms have different histories. A firm that has recently replaced its capital is likely to have more efficient, lower-cost plant and hence lower cost curves than

---

6 If one firm has some special advantage, such as a patented production process or an unusually good manager, the principle of imputed opportunity cost requires that the extra revenues attributable to such advantages be included as a cost—since the patent or manager could be leased to other firms. This emphasizes once again that all firms have zero economic profit in long-run perfectly competitive equilibrium.

a firm whose capital is ageing. The details of each practical case will then determine the identity of the marginal firm that will exit first when price falls. For one example, assume that all firms have identical costs and differ only in the date at which they entered the industry. In this case, the firm whose capital comes up for replacement first will be the marginal firm. It will exit first because it will be the first to confront the long-run decision about replacing its capital in a situation where no firms are covering long-run opportunity costs.

Comparison of the short-run and long-run equilibria

There is a different short-run equilibrium for the firm for each level of its capital stock. The long-run equilibrium will be the short-run equilibrium associated with the capital stock that minimizes long-run average cost. Figure 6.9 illustrates the situation where one short-run equilibrium is also a long-run equilibrium, but there is another short-run equilibrium that is not a long-run equilibrium.

For a long-run situation that is an equilibrium both for each firm and for the industry, the following three conditions must hold:

1. **No firm will want to vary the output of its existing plants:** short-run marginal cost ($SRMC$) must equal price.

2. **Profits earned by existing plants must be zero:** this implies that short-run ATC

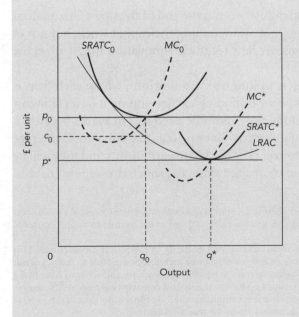

Figure 6.9. Short-run versus long-run equilibrium of a competitive firm

A competitive firm that is not at the minimum point on its *LRAC* curve cannot be in long-run equilibrium. A competitive firm with short-run cost curves $SRATC_0$ and MC_0 faces a market price of p_0. The firm produces q_0 where MC_0 equals price and total costs are just being covered. However, the firm's long-run cost curve lies below its short-run curve at output q_0. The firm could produce output q_0 at cost c_0 by building a larger plant so as to take advantage of economies of scale. Profits would rise because average total costs of c_0 would then be less than price p_0. The firm cannot be in long-run equilibrium at any output below q^* because, with any such output, average total costs can be reduced by building a larger plant. The output q^* is the *minimum efficient scale* of the firm.

must equal price—that is, firms must be in the position of the firm in Figure 6.7(ii).

3. **No firm can earn profits by building a plant of a different size:** this implies that each existing firm must be producing at the lowest point on its long-run average cost curve.

We have already seen why the first two conditions must hold. The reasoning behind the third condition is shown in Figure 6.9. Although the firm shown with average cost curve $SRATC_0$ is in short-run equilibrium, it is not in long-run equilibrium because its *LRAC* curve lies below the market price at some higher levels of output.[7] The firm can, therefore, increase its profits by building a plant of larger size, thereby lowering its average total costs. Since the firm is a price taker, this change will increase its profits.

A price-taking firm is in long-run equilibrium only when it is producing at the minimum point on its LRAC curve.

All three of the conditions listed above are fulfilled when each firm in the industry is in the position shown in Figure 6.9 by the short-run cost curve $SRATC^*$.[8]

The very long run

TECHNICAL CHANGE

The long-run equilibrium of firm and industry is not the end of the story. Our analysis of the long run has assumed the possibility of increasing the capital stock, but not of changing the technology. We now consider how technical innovation might affect the dynamics of the firm and industry.

Suppose that initially the industry is in long-run equilibrium, where each firm is earning zero profits. Now assume that some technological development lowers the cost curves of newly built plants. The technology cannot be used by old plants because it must be *embodied* in new plants and equipment. Since price is just equal to the average total cost for the old plants, new plants will now be able to earn profits and they will be built immediately. But this expansion in capacity shifts the short-run supply curve to

---

[7] Because all costs are variable in the long run, there is no need to distinguish long-run average variable cost from long-run average total cost. They are identical, and we refer to them, as we learned to do in Chapter 5, merely as long-run average costs (*LRAC*).

[8] The text discussion implies that all existing firms and all new entrants face identical *LRAC* curves. This means that all firms face the same set of input prices and have the same technology available to them. Do not forget that we are in the long run *where technological knowledge is given and constant*, and all firms have had a chance to adjust their capital to the best that is available. This is a theoretical construction designed to analyse tendencies. In any industry in which technological change is continuous the long run will never occur and a wide variety of different technologies will be used by different firms (as is typically observed).

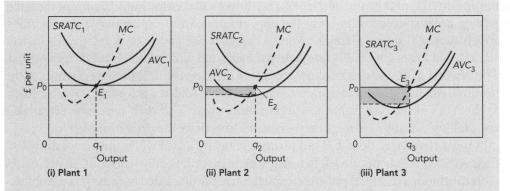

Figure 6.10. Plants of different ages in an industry with continual technical progress

Entry of progressively lower-cost firms forces price down, but older plants with higher costs remain in the industry as long as price covers average variable cost. Plant 3 is the newest plant, with the lowest costs. Long-run equilibrium price will be determined by the average total costs of plants of this type, since entry will continue as long as the owners of the newest plants expect to earn profits from them. Plant 1 is the oldest plant in operation; it is just covering its AVC, and if the price falls any further it will be closed down. Plant 2 is a plant of intermediate age. It is covering its variable costs and earning some contribution toward its fixed costs. In (ii) and (iii), the shaded areas show the excess of revenues over variable costs.

the right and drives price down. The expansion in capacity and the fall in price will continue until price is equal to the *ATC* of the *new* plants. At this price, old plants will not be covering their long-run costs. As long as price exceeds their average variable cost, however, such plants will continue in production. As the outmoded plants wear out, they will gradually disappear. Eventually a new long-run equilibrium will be established in which all plants use the new technology.

What happens in a competitive industry in which this type of technological change occurs, not as a single isolated event, but more or less continuously? Plants built in any one year will tend to have lower costs than plants built in any previous year. Figure 6.10 illustrates such an industry. It will exhibit a number of interesting characteristics.

One is that plants of different ages and different levels of efficiency will exist side by side. This is dramatically illustrated by the variety of types and vintages of generator found in any long-established electricity industry. Critics who observe the continued use of older, less efficient plants and urge that the industry be modernized miss the point of economic efficiency. If the plant is already there, it can be operated profitably as long as it can cover its variable, or direct, costs. If a plant can produce additional output that is valued by the market in excess of the direct costs, then it is creating more value, in the form of output for the economy and profit for the firm, than it would do if it were closed down.

A second characteristic of such an industry is that price will be governed by the

Optimization of the firm

minimum *ATC* of the most efficient plants. Entry will continue until plants of the latest vintage are just expected to cover the opportunity cost of capital over their lifetimes, which they will do by earning profits when they are young with relatively efficient capital, and losses (over full costs) when they are old with relatively inefficient capital. The benefits of the new technology are passed on to consumers because all units of the product, whether produced by new or old plants, are sold at a price that is related solely to the *ATC*s of the new plants. Owners of older plants find their returns over variable costs falling steadily as increasingly efficient plants drive the price down.

A third characteristic is that old plants will be discarded when the price falls below their *AVC*. This may occur well before the plants are physically worn out. In industries with continuous technical progress, capital is usually discarded because it is economically obsolete, not because it has physically worn out. This illustrates the economic meaning of obsolete:

> Old capital is obsolete when its average variable cost exceeds the average total cost of new capital.

DECLINING INDUSTRIES

Technological progress can only lower long-run costs. It cannot increase them, because a cost-increasing technology would simply not be adopted. However, product innovation and changing production technology can lead to a shift of demand away from some kinds of product as they are replaced by something entirely new. The makers of horse-drawn carriages gradually disappeared as the motor industry expanded, and candle makers lost out to electric power supply. Hence decline and contraction is every much a part of a modern economy as is expansion, even though the economy as whole tends to expand over time.

What happens when a competitive industry in long-run equilibrium begins to suffer losses owing to a permanent and continuing decrease in the demand for its products? As market demand declines, market price falls, and firms that were previously covering average total costs are no longer able to do so. They find themselves in the position shown in part (i) of Figure 6.7. Firms suffer losses instead of breaking even; the signal for the exit of capital is given, but exit takes time.

The response of firms
The economically efficient response to a steadily declining demand is to continue to operate with existing equipment as long as its variable costs of production can be covered. As equipment becomes obsolete because it cannot cover even its variable cost, it will not be replaced unless the new equipment can cover its total cost. As a result, the capacity of the industry will shrink. If demand keeps declining, capacity must keep shrinking.

Declining industries typically present a sorry sight to the observer. Revenues are below long-run total costs, and as a result, new equipment is not brought in to replace old equipment as it wears out. The average age of equipment in use thus rises steadily. The untrained observer, seeing the industry's plight, is likely to blame it on the old equipment.

> **The antiquated equipment in a declining industry is often the effect rather than the cause of the industry's decline.**

The response of governments

Governments in the past, and in some other countries today, have been tempted to support declining industries because they are worried about the resulting job losses. Experience suggests, however, that propping up genuinely declining industries only delays their demise—at significant national cost. When the government finally withdraws its support, the decline is usually more abrupt and hence more difficult to adjust to than it would have been had the industry been allowed to decline gradually under the market force of steadily declining demand.

Once governments recognize the decay of certain industries and the collapse of certain firms as an inevitable aspect of economic growth, a more effective response is to provide welfare and retraining schemes that cushion the impacts of change on individuals. These can moderate the effects on the incomes of workers who lose their jobs and make it easier for them to transfer to expanding industries. Intervention that is intended to increase mobility while reducing the social and personal costs of mobility is a viable long-run policy; trying to freeze the existing industrial structure by shoring up an inevitably declining industry is not.

Summary

1. Competitive *behaviour* refers to the extent that individual firms compete with each other to sell their products. Competitive *market structure* refers to the power that individual firms have over the market—perfect competition occurring where firms have no market power and hence no need to react to each other.

2. Any firm maximizes profits by producing the output where the marginal cost curve cuts the marginal revenue from below or by producing nothing if average variable cost exceeds price at all outputs.

3. Perfect competition requires price-taking behaviour and freedom of entry and exit.

4. A perfectly competitive firm is a quantity adjuster, facing a horizontal demand curve at the given market price and maximizing profits by equating its marginal cost to that price.

5. The supply curve of a firm in perfect competition is its marginal cost curve, and the supply curve of a perfectly competitive industry is the sum of the marginal cost curves of all its firms. The intersection of this curve with the market demand curve for the industry's product determines market price.

6. Long-run industry equilibrium requires that each individual firm be producing at the minimum point of its *LRAC* curve and be making zero profits.

7. Technical progress can only shift the *LRAC* curve downwards, leading innovating firms to replace non-innovating firms and the product price to fall.

8. Firms in declining industries should stay in business so long as they are covering average variable costs.

Topics for review

- Competitive behaviour and competitive market structure
- Behavioural rules for the profit-maximizing firm
- Price taking and a horizontal demand curve
- Average revenue, marginal revenue, and price under perfect competition
- Relation of the industry supply curve to its firms' marginal cost curves
- The role of entry and exit in achieving equilibrium
- Short-run and long-run equilibrium of firms and industries

Questions for discussion

1. Which of the following industries would you say were close to being perfectly competitive: brewing, wine making, taxi driving, airlines, copper mining, potato farming, car manufacture?

2. Why would the existence of entry barriers make it unlikely that an industry would be perfectly competitive? What types of entry barrier do you think are important in practice?

3. How can the existence of economies of scale affect the degree of competitiveness in a market?

4. Why might the short-run equilibrium of a firm not be a long-run equilibrium?

5. How does technical progress affect the equilibrium of the firm and of the industry.

6. Why do some industries decline while others grow? At what stage should firms quit an industry?

7. Here are data for total production costs of a manufacturing firm at various levels of output:

Output (units)	Total cost (£)
0	1,000
20	1,200
40	1,300
60	1,380
100	1,600
200	2,300
300	3,200
400	4,300
500	5,650
1,000	13,650

(i) Calculate average variable cost (AVC), average total cost (ATC), and average fixed cost (AFC) (hint: fixed costs have to be incurred even when output is zero and do not vary with the production level in the short run). (ii) Calculate marginal cost (MC) (also known as incremental cost) over each production range for which data are given. (iii) If this firm can sell as much as it wants at a price of £11, what is its profit-maximizing output? (iv) How much profit is made? (v) At output levels either side of the profit-maximizing output (in the table) what level of profit or loss is made.

[Teachers: this numerical example is continued in questions 8 and 9 in the following chapter (page 241). Answers to these three questions are available on request.]

Section 3
Firms and Competition

CHAPTER 7

Firms in Imperfect Markets I: Monopoly and Monopolistic Competition

A pure monopolist	214	When is market segmentation possible?	231
Cost and revenue in the short run	215	Consequences of market segmentation	233
Average and marginal revenue	215		
Marginal revenue and elasticity	218	**Monopolistic competition**	234
Short-run monopoly equilibrium	218	The development of monopolistic	
Competition and monopoly		competition	234
compared	219	Assumptions	235
Monopoly profits	219	Equilibrium for the firm and industry	235
No supply curve for a monopoly	220	Short-run equilibrium	235
Firm and industry	221	Long-run equilibrium	236
A multi-plant monopoly	221	Excess capacity	237
Long-run monopoly equilibrium	222	Is excess capacity wasteful?	237
Entry barriers	222	The empirical relevance of large-group	
Barriers determined by technology	223	monopolistic competition	238
Policy-created barriers	223		
The significance of entry barriers	226	**Summary**	239
'Creative destruction'	226		
		Topics for Review	240
Market segmentation: a multi-price			
monopolist	227	**Questions for discussion**	240
Why market segmentation is profitable	228		
Segmentation among buyers	230	**Box 7.1.** Products and patents	224
Segmentation between markets	230	**Box 7.2.** 'Charge what the traffic will bear'	232

I N Chapter 6 we set out the characteristics associated with profit maximization by firms. We also applied those principles in the case of firms in perfectly competitive markets, that is, where individual firms cannot affect the market price. In this and the following chapter we study the profit-maximizing behaviour of firms that can influence their own product prices. Most modern businesses have at least some discretion over the price they set, and so analysis of this situation is more relevant for them. This influence over price arises because each firm in question is big relative to the total demand for the product, or because the product is different in some way from its closest substitutes.

All markets in which firms have some discretion over their selling prices are said to be *imperfect*. An extreme version of an imperfect market structure is pure monopoly. In theory, a **monopoly** occurs when the output of an entire industry is produced and sold by a single firm, called a **monopolist** or a *monopoly firm*. However, for legal purposes, a monopoly can exist when a firm has some dominant position in the market, which may be much less than 100 per cent market share. The exact legal definition of monopoly varies from country to country.

For the time being we are concerned with the theoretical monopolist, that is, the only supplier to a market. The demand curve facing a monopolist is the market demand curve, since there are no other producers of the product. The optimal price and output decision for a monopolist depends upon whether the market is homogeneous, so that all consumers pay the same price, or whether the monopolist can segment it in some way, charging different prices in different segments.

All forms of market structure that are somewhere in between the extremes of perfect competition and pure monopoly are said to be *imperfectly competitive*, or to be characterized by *imperfect competition*. One form of imperfect competition is known as **monopolistic competition**. This arises when there are many producers each producing branded, or differentiated, goods. Here each producer faces a downward-sloping demand curve, but the existence of profits can attract entry into the industry, which, in turn, shifts the demand curve faced by any one firm; so the outcome is one in which both competitive forces and limited monopoly power have some role.

Another variety of imperfect competition will be discussed in the following chapter. This is known as **oligopoly**. Oligopoly involves a market in which there is competition between a small number of firms. These firms are strategically interrelated in the sense that each firm's profit is directly affected by what its rival firms do. In this market structure an appropriate business strategy becomes essential.

We first discuss the case of a monopoly that sells all its output at a single price, before proceeding to examine what difference it makes if the market can be segmented. Finally, we analyse the profit-maximizing equilibrium of the firm and industry under monopolistic competition.

A pure monopolist

The first part of this chapter deals with the price and output decision of a monopoly firm that charges a single price for its product. The firm's profits, like those of all firms, will depend on the relationship between its production costs and its sales revenues.

Cost and revenue in the short run

We saw in Chapter 5 that U-shaped short-run cost curves are a consequence of the law of diminishing returns. Because this law applies to the conditions under which goods are produced rather than to the market structure in which they are sold, monopoly firms are likely to have U-shaped short-run cost curves just as perfectly competitive firms do.[1]

Because a monopoly firm is the sole producer of the product that it sells, its demand curve is identical to the market demand curve for that product. The market demand curve, which shows the total quantity that buyers will purchase at each price, also shows the quantity that the monopoly firm will be able to sell at each price. Thus the monopoly firm, unlike the perfectly competitive firm, faces a negatively sloped demand curve. This means that it faces a trade-off between the price it charges and the quantity it sells. Sales can be increased only if price is reduced, and price can be increased only if sales are reduced.

AVERAGE AND MARGINAL REVENUE

Starting with the market demand curve, the monopoly firm's average and marginal revenue curves can be readily derived. When the monopoly firm charges the same price for all units sold, average revenue per unit is identical with price. Thus the market demand curve is also the firm's *average revenue curve*.

Now consider the monopoly firm's *marginal revenue* resulting from the sale of an additional (or marginal) unit of production. Because its demand curve is negatively sloped, the monopoly firm must lower the price that it charges on *all* units in order to sell an *extra* unit. It follows that the addition to its revenue resulting from the sale of an extra unit is less than the price that it receives for that unit (less by the amount that it loses as a result of cutting the price on all the units that it was selling already).[2]

The monopoly firm's marginal revenue is less than the price at which it sells its output.

This proposition is illustrated in Figure 7.1.

To clarify these relations, we consider a numerical example of a specific, straight-line demand curve. Some points on this curve are shown in tabular form in Table 7.1, and

---

[1] One reason why monopoly may occur is because long-run average costs continue to fall over a production range that is large relative to the market's size, so that one large firm can produce at lower cost than many small firms. However, this does not necessarily affect the argument that short-run cost curves will be U-shaped—though recall our point that many firms perceive their *SRAC* curve to be flat over some range. This is because they deliberately maintain excess capacity.

[2] Recall also that, when an *average* is falling, the *marginal* value must be below the average. In this case, average revenue falls as output increases, so marginal revenue must be less than average revenue at each level of output.

Firms and competition

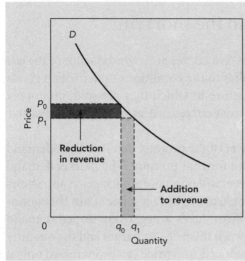

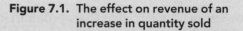

Figure 7.1. The effect on revenue of an increase in quantity sold

Because the demand curve has a negative slope, marginal revenue is less than price. A reduction of price from p_0 to p_1 increases sales by one unit, from q_0 to q_1 units. The revenue from the extra unit sold is shown as the lighter shaded area. But to sell this unit, it is necessary to reduce the price on each of the q_0 units previously sold. The loss in revenue is shown as the darker shaded area. Marginal revenue of the extra unit is equal to the *difference* between the two areas.

the whole curve is shown in Figure 7.2. Notice in the table that the change in total revenue associated with a change of £0.10 in price, and the change in total revenue associated with a change of one unit of output, are both recorded between the rows that refer to specific prices. This is done because the data refer to what happens when the price is changed from the value shown in one row to the value shown in the adjacent row.

Notice also that when price is reduced starting from £10, total revenue rises at first and then falls. The maximum total revenue is reached in this example at a price of £5.

Table 7.1. Total, average, and marginal revenue illustrated

Price $p = AR$ (£)	Quantity (q) (units)	$TR = p \cdot q$ (£)	$MR = \Delta TR / \Delta q$ (£)
9.10	9	81.90	
			8.10
9.00	10	90.00	
			7.90
8.90	11	97.90	

Marginal revenue is less than price because price must be lowered to sell an extra unit. Consider, for example, the marginal revenue of the 11th unit. This is total revenue when 11 units are sold minus total revenue when 10 units are sold. The result is £7.90, which is less than the price of £8.90 at which all 11 units are sold. To see why, notice that to increase sales from 10 to 11 units, the price on all units sold must be reduced from £9.00 to £8.90. The net addition to revenue is the £8.90 gained from selling the extra unit minus £0.10 lost on each of the 10 units already being sold: £8.90 − (£0.10 × 10) = £7.90.

Marginal revenue is shown displaced by half a line to emphasize that it represents the effect on revenue of the *change* in sales.

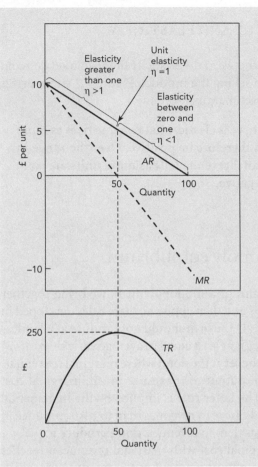

Figure 7.2. Total, average, and marginal revenue curves and elasticity of demand

When *TR* is rising, *MR* is positive and demand is elastic. When *TR* is falling, *MR* is negative and demand is inelastic. In this example, for outputs from 0 to 50, marginal revenue is positive, elasticity is greater than unity, and total revenue is rising. For outputs from 50 to 100, marginal revenue is negative, elasticity is less than unity, and total revenue is falling.

Since marginal revenue measures the change in total revenue from the sale of one more unit of output, marginal revenue is positive whenever total revenue is increased by selling more, but it is negative whenever total revenue is reduced by selling more.[3]

The proposition that marginal revenue is always *less than* average revenue, which has been illustrated numerically in Table 7.1 and graphically in Figure 7.2, provides an important contrast with perfect competition. You will recall that in perfect competition the firm's marginal revenue from selling an extra unit of output is *equal to* the price at which that unit is sold. The reason for the difference is not difficult to understand. The perfectly competitive firm is a price taker; it can sell all it wants at the given market price. The monopoly firm faces a negatively sloped demand curve; it must reduce the market price in order to increase its sales.

---

[3] Notice that the marginal revenue shown in the table is obtained by subtracting the total revenue associated with one price from the total revenue associated with another, lower, price and then apportioning the change in revenue among the extra units sold. In symbols, it is $\Delta TR/\Delta q$. Recall that marginal revenue is really *incremental revenue* where discrete changes are involved.

MARGINAL REVENUE AND ELASTICITY

In Chapter 3 we discussed the relationship between the elasticity of the market demand curve and the total revenue derived from selling the product. Figure 7.2 summarizes this earlier discussion and extends it to cover marginal revenue.[4]

Over the range in which the demand curve is elastic, total revenue rises as more units are sold; marginal revenue must therefore be positive. Over the range in which the demand curve is inelastic, total revenue falls as more units are sold; marginal revenue must therefore be negative.

Short-run monopoly equilibrium

To show the profit-maximizing equilibrium of a monopoly firm, we bring together information about its revenues and its costs and then apply the three rules developed in Chapter 6. Recall that these three rules are (1) the firm should not produce at all unless there is some level of output for which price is at least equal to average variable cost; (2) if the firm does produce, its output should be set at the point where marginal cost equals marginal revenue; and (3) for the chosen output to maximize profit, marginal cost must cut marginal revenue from below. The latter rule is implied by the incremental decision rule: if an extra unit of output adds more to revenues than to costs, produce it; if an extra unit of output adds more to costs than to revenues, don't produce it.

When the monopoly firm equates marginal cost with marginal revenue, it reaches the equilibrium shown in Figure 7.3. The output is found as the quantity for which marginal cost equals marginal revenue. The price is read off the demand curve, which shows the price corresponding to that output.

Notice that, because marginal revenue is always less than price for the monopoly firm, when it equates marginal revenue to marginal cost, both are less than price.

When a monopoly firm is in profit-maximizing equilibrium, its marginal cost is always less than the price it charges for its output.

Notice also that, at the point in Figure 7.3 where marginal cost equals marginal revenue (Rule 2), marginal cost cuts marginal revenue from below (Rule 3). It is also true in this figure that price exceeds average variable cost (Rule 1).

---

[4] It is helpful when you are drawing these curves to remember that if the demand curve is a negatively sloped straight line, the MR curve is also negatively sloped and exactly twice as steep. Its price intercept (where $q = 0$) is the same as that of the demand curve, and its quantity intercept (where $p = 0$) is one-half of that of the demand curve. This is easily established with calculus. A linear demand curve is $p = a - bq$. Total revenue (TR) is $pq = aq - bq^2$. Marginal revenue is $\mathrm{d}TR/\mathrm{d}q = a - 2bq$, which is a straight line of twice the slope of the demand curve.

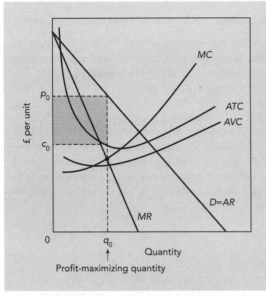

Figure 7.3. The equilibrium of a monopoly

The monopoly maximizes its profits by producing where marginal cost equals marginal revenue. The monopoly produces the output, q_0, for which marginal revenue equals marginal cost (Rule 2), and where marginal cost cuts marginal revenue from below (Rule 3). At this output, the price of p_0—which is determined by the demand curve—exceeds average variable cost (Rule 1). Profits per unit are the difference between the average revenue of p_0 and the average total cost of c_0. Total profits are the profits per unit of $(p_0 - c_0)$ multiplied by the output of q_0, which is the shaded area.

Competition and monopoly compared

The comparison with firms in perfect competition is important. In perfect competition, firms face perfectly elastic demand curves, so that price and marginal revenue are the same. Thus, when they equate marginal cost to marginal revenue, they ensure that marginal cost also equals price. In contrast, a monopoly firm faces a negatively sloped demand curve for which marginal revenue is less than price. Thus, when it equates marginal cost to marginal revenue, it ensures that marginal cost will be less than price.

The relationship between elasticity and revenue discussed above has an interesting implication for the monopoly firm's equilibrium. Because marginal cost is always greater than zero, a profit-maximizing monopoly (which produces where $MR = MC$) will always produce where marginal revenue is positive, that is, where demand is elastic. If the firm were producing where demand was inelastic, it could reduce its output, thereby increasing its total revenue and reducing its total costs. No such restriction applies to firms in perfect competition. Each reacts to its own perfectly elastic demand curve, not to the market demand curve. Thus, the equilibrium can occur where the market demand curve is either elastic or inelastic.

> A profit-maximizing monopoly will never sell in the range where the demand curve is inelastic.

Monopoly profits

The fact that a monopoly firm produces the output that maximizes its profits tells us nothing about how large these profits will be or even whether there will be any profits at all. Figure 7.4 illustrates this by showing three alternative average total cost curves: one where the monopolist can earn pure profits, one where it can just cover its costs and one where it makes losses at any level of output.

219

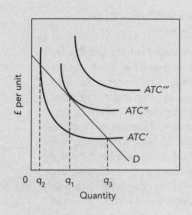

Figure 7.4. Alternative profit possibilities for a monopolist

Profit maximization means that the monopoly is doing as well as it can do, given the cost and demand curves that it faces; it does not mean that profits are being earned. The monopolist faces a demand curve of D. Three alternative cost curves are considered. With the curve ATC''', there is no positive output at which the monopolist can avoid making losses. With the curve ATC'', the monopolist covers all costs at output q_1, where the ATC curve is tangent to the D curve. With the curve ATC', profits can be made by producing at any output between q_2 and q_3. (The profit-maximizing output will be some point between q_2 and q_3, where $MR = MC$, which is not shown on the diagram.)

No supply curve for a monopoly

In describing the monopolist's profit-maximizing behaviour, we did not introduce the concept of a supply curve, as we did in the discussion of perfect competition. In perfect competition the industry short-run supply curve depends only on the marginal cost curves of the individual firms. This is true because, under perfect competition, profit-maximizing firms equate marginal cost with price. Given marginal costs, it is possible to know how much will be produced at each price. This is not the case, however, with a monopoly.

As with all profit-maximizing firms, the monopolist equates marginal cost to marginal revenue; but marginal revenue does not equal price. Hence the monopoly does *not* equate marginal cost to price. In order to know the amount produced at any given price, we need to know the demand curve as well as the marginal cost curve. Under these circumstances, it is possible for different demand conditions to cause the same output to be sold at different prices. This is illustrated in Figure 7.5 by an example in which two

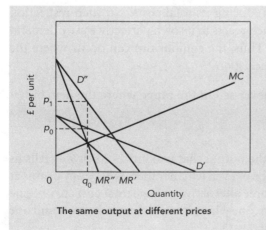

The same output at different prices

Figure 7.5. No supply curve under monopoly

When a firm faces a negatively sloped demand curve, there is no unique relation between the price that it charges and the quantity that it sells. The demand curves D' and D'' both have marginal revenue curves that intersect the marginal cost curve at output q_0. But because the demand curves are different, q_0 is sold at p_0 when the demand curve is D', and at p_1 when the demand curve is D''.

monopolists facing the same marginal cost curves but different demand curves sell identical outputs at different prices.

> **For a monopoly firm, there is no unique relationship between market price and quantity supplied.**

Firm and industry

Because the monopolist is the only producer in an industry, there is no need for separate theories about the firm and the industry, as is necessary with perfect competition. The monopoly firm *is* the industry. Thus the short-run, profit-maximizing position of the firm, as shown in Figure 7.3, is also the short-run equilibrium of the industry.

A multi-plant monopoly

So far we have implicitly assumed that the monopoly firm produces all of its output in a single plant. Fortunately, the analysis easily extends to multi-plant monopolists. Assume, for example, that the firm has two plants. How will it allocate production between them? The answer is that any given output should be allocated between the two plants so as to equate their marginal costs. Assume that plant A was producing 30 units per week at a marginal cost of £20, while plant B was producing 25 units at a marginal cost of £17. Plant A's production could be reduced by one unit, saving £20 in cost, while plant B's production was increased by one unit, adding £17 to cost. Overall output would stay the same while costs were reduced by £3.

The generalization is that, whenever two plants are producing at different marginal costs, the total cost of producing their combined output can be reduced by reallocating production from the plant with the higher marginal cost to the plant with the lower marginal cost.

> **A multi-plant, profit-maximizing monopolist will always operate its plants so that their marginal costs are equal.**

How does the multi-plant monopolist determine its overall marginal cost? Suppose, for example, that both plants are operating at a marginal cost of £10 per unit and one is producing 14 units per week while the other is producing 16. The firm's overall output is 30 units at a marginal cost of £10. This illustrates the following general proposition:

> **The monopoly firm's marginal cost curve is the horizontal sum of the marginal cost curves of its individual plants.**

For each marginal cost, this sum tells us the total output of all the firm's plants *when each plant is operating at that marginal cost.*

It follows that the analysis in this chapter applies to any monopolist, no matter how many plants it operates, so long as these plants are all producing the same product. The marginal cost curve we have used is merely the sum of the marginal cost curves of all the plants. In the special case in which there is only one plant, the *firm's MC* curve is *that plant's MC* curve.

A moment's thought should also make it obvious that the condition that plants within a firm should be operated so that the marginal cost is equal in all of the plants *must apply to any profit-maximizing multi-plant firm, irrespective of the market structure in which it sells its output.* The reason for this is that any total output level could be produced more cheaply by reallocating activity among plants if the marginal costs between plants differ. Hence, there is an important operational lesson here for all business.

Of course, this only applies to plants that are producing *the same product* in different plants within the firm. It would not apply at all to plants that were producing a completely different product even within the same firm. This is because the demand curves, and, therefore, the marginal revenue curves for each product will be different. Here profit maximization implies that marginal cost should equal marginal revenue *for each sub-product* of the firm.

Long-run monopoly equilibrium

In both monopolized and perfectly competitive industries, losses and profits provide incentives for exit and entry.

If the monopoly firm is suffering losses in the short run, it will continue to operate as long as it can cover its variable costs. In the long run, however, it will leave the industry unless it can find a scale of operations at which its full opportunity costs can be covered.

If the monopoly firm is making profits, other firms will wish to enter the industry in order to earn more than the opportunity cost of their capital. If such entry occurs, the equilibrium position shown in Figure 7.3 will change, and the firm will cease to be a monopolist. We discuss this case further below when we talk about monopolistic competition.

Entry barriers

Impediments that prevent entry are called **entry barriers;** they may be either natural or created.

If a monopoly firm's profits are to persist in the long run, the entry of new firms into the industry must be prevented by effective entry barriers.

BARRIERS DETERMINED BY TECHNOLOGY

Natural barriers most commonly arise as a result of economies of scale. When the long-run average cost curve is negatively sloped over a large range of output, big firms have significantly lower average total costs than small firms.

You will recall from Chapter 6 that perfectly competitive firms cannot be in long-run equilibrium on the negatively sloped segment of their long-run average cost curve (see Figure 6.9 on p. 203).

Now suppose that the technology of an industry is such that any firm's minimum achievable average cost is £10, which is reached at an output of 10,000 units per week. Assume too that, at a price of £10, the total quantity demanded is 11,000 units per week. Under these circumstances, only one firm can operate at or near its minimum costs.

A **natural monopoly** occurs when, given the industry's current technology, the demand conditions allow no more than one firm to cover its costs while producing at the minimum point of its long-run cost curve. In a natural monopoly, there is no price at which two firms can both sell enough to cover their total costs.

Another type of technologically determined barrier is *set-up cost*. If a firm could be catapulted fully grown into the market, it might be able to compete effectively with the existing monopolist. However, the cost to the new firm of entering the market, developing its products, and establishing such things as its brand image and its dealer network may be so large that entry would be unprofitable.

POLICY-CREATED BARRIERS

Many entry barriers are created by conscious government action and are, therefore, officially condoned. Patent laws, for instance, may prevent entry by conferring on the patent holder the sole legal right to produce a particular product for a specific period of time. Glaxo PLC, for example, made billions of pounds profit from its anti-ulcer drug Zantac in the 1980s and 1990s. When the main patent on Zantac expired in 1997, many cheaper generic versions of Zantac were expected to appear on the market at a fraction of the price.

Once an invention has been made, it would clearly be better for consumers if all products were produced under competitive conditions, so that the product price would tend to reflect minimum production costs. However, patent protection for a period after an invention is made is thought to be an important way of giving an incentive for research into some new products.[5] Why would a pharmaceuticals company want to

---

[5] We say 'some' because patents do not provide protection against entry into many industries. Pharmaceuticals are unusual in having distinct products without close substitutes. If you vary the chemical structure of aspirin even slightly, you no longer have a substance that will deaden pain. In many other industries, slight variations of product design might not breach a patent, but still give equal satisfaction to end users. For further discussion see Box 7.1.

BOX 7.1.

Products and patents

A patent confers a monopoly right to the exclusive use of an invention. Patent laws differ from one country to another. In the UK, to be patentable an invention must be new, involve an inventive step, be capable of industrial application, and not be 'excluded'. Among exclusions are all discoveries, such as scientific theories or mathematical methods, that have no specific product as an outcome. Also excluded are works of art and literature (such as this book), though these may be covered by copyright laws, and new designs that have no new function other than appearance.

A UK inventor seeking a patent must apply either through the UK Patent Office or through the European Patent Office (EPO). The latter route is growing in popularity since it enables the acquisition of patent protection in other European countries to be obtained simultaneously, though at extra cost—a UK patent can cost as little as £300 while a Europe-wide patent is likely to cost well over £5,000. In practice, the costs will be much greater than this, since expensive legal advice is usually required. In the mid-1990s patent applications were running at nearly 30,000 per year in the UK Patent Office and a further 45,000 per year via the EPO, nearly all of which were UK applicable. Almost a quarter of a million existing UK patents were being renewed annually. (Patents are granted for an initial four-year period, renewable annually after that for up to twenty years.)

There are two important points to be aware of in relation to patents. The first is that, while patent protection potentially enables an inventor to capture the 'rents' associated with a new product (see pp. 200–1 for a discussion of economic rent), the granting of a patent may also hold up the spread of a new technology. One of the most famous examples in history is the patent granted to James Watt for his invention of the steam engine. This patent applied to any process using steam to drive a piston, and no one could infringe the patent until it ran out in 1800. This greatly inhibited the spread of existing engines and held up the development of more effective steam engines—Watt had no faith in the potential of high-pressure engines, but, after Watt's patent ran out, Trevithick and others showed how wrong he was.

The second important point about patents is that patent protection has only proved to be really effective in a narrow range of products—pharmaceuticals being one of the modern industries where patents work best. In many product areas they are less effective, and in some they are of little value in excluding would-be competitors. In many industries it is possible to produce new products that do not breach patents but perform in a very similar manner to the protected product. In all such areas, patent protection creates, at best, very limited barriers to entry of close substitutes. Indeed, the law places the onus on the patent holder to prove that a breach of patent rights has occurred. Obtaining such proof can involve a very expensive legal process with no guarantee of success in the end. Hence, many firms do not even bother to prosecute believed patent violations. Rather they rely on secrecy and a short product-cycle to stay ahead of the field, so that by the time imitations come along some newer product has been developed.

Many firms use their patents as a strategic measure. If they get threatened with a patent infringement suit, they dump a mass of their own patents on the complainant's desk and say 'We don't know if we have infringed some of your patents, but you surely have infringed some of ours. Take a look!' An out-of-court settlement usually follows.

BOX 7.1. (*cont.*)

Many modern products are highly complex in structure. In many of these cases, firms with some innovation do not even bother searching the masses and masses of relevant patents. They just go ahead with the new product or process and see if they get sued. Often those whose patents have been breached don't notice, and even if they do, they may think that legal action is not worth pursuing.

Hence, patent protection has only a limited role in creating monopolies and this is, at best, temporary. Perhaps, a more important product-protection device derives from laws relating to *trade marks* and to *passing-off*. For example, there is no patent protection to stop a soft-drinks manufacturer making a drink identical to Coca Cola. However, this firm would not be allowed to sell this product under the Coca Cola label or to sell it in red cans that might fool customers into believing that they were buying genuine Coca Cola. Here it is the brand label that has commercial value rather than the specific product itself.

invest in years' worth of R&D costs to develop new life-saving drugs if others were free to copy these drugs immediately? The answer is that some protection of 'intellectual property' is necessary and optimal from a social point of view. The role of patents is further discussed in Box 7.1.

A firm may also be granted a charter, or a franchise, that prohibits competition by law. Regulation and licensing of firms, often in service industries, can restrict entry severely. For example, the 1979 Banking Act requires all banks in the UK to be authorized by the Bank of England. The 1986 Financial Services Act requires all sellers of investment products to be authorized by the Securities and Investment Board (SIB) or some other recognized regulatory body. Another example are the franchises awarded to the regional ITV companies, such as Carlton, Central, and Granada, to broadcast terrestrial television signals in specific regions of the country. These franchises, which run for a fixed number of years, were allocated on the basis of a cash bid combined with a quality judgement, but they give one company a monopoly of that service. Yet more examples of UK government-created monopolies include the franchise awarded to Camelot to run the National Lottery and that awarded to BAA PLC as sole operator of UK airports, such as Heathrow, Gatwick, and Stansted.

Other barriers can be created by the firm or firms already in the market. In extreme cases, the threat of force or sabotage can deter entry. The most obvious entry barriers of this type are encountered in the production and sale of illegal goods and services, where operation outside of the law makes available an array of illegal but potent barriers to new entrants. The drug trade is a current example. In contrast, legitimate firms must use legal tactics intended, for example, to increase a new entrant's set-up costs. Examples are the threat of price cutting, designed to impose unsustainable losses on a new entrant, and heavy brand-name advertising. (These and other created entry barriers will be discussed in more detail in Chapter 8.)

THE SIGNIFICANCE OF ENTRY BARRIERS

Because there are no entry barriers in perfect competition, profits cannot persist in the long run.

Profits attract entry, and entry erodes profits.

In monopoly, however, profits can persist in the long run whenever there are effective barriers to entry.

Entry barriers frustrate the adjustment mechanism that would otherwise push profits towards zero in the long run.

'CREATIVE DESTRUCTION'

In the very long run, technology changes. New ways of producing old products are invented, and new products are created to satisfy both familiar and new wants. What has this to do with entry barriers? The answer is that a monopoly that succeeds in preventing the entry of new firms capable of producing its product will sooner or later find its barriers circumvented by innovations. One firm may be able to use new processes that avoid some patent or other barrier that the monopolist relies on to bar entry of competing firms. Another firm may compete by developing a new product that, although somewhat different, still satisfies the same need as the monopoly firm's product. Yet another firm might get around a natural monopoly by inventing a technology that produces the good at a much lower cost than the existing monopoly firm's technology. The new technology may subsequently allow several firms to enter the market and still cover costs.

One distinguished economist, the late Joseph Schumpeter (1883–1950), took the view that entry barriers were not a serious problem in the very long run. He argued that monopoly profits provide one of the major incentives for people who risk their money by financing inventions and innovations. In his view, the large, short-run profits of a monopoly provide a strong incentive for others to try to usurp some of these profits for themselves. If a frontal attack on the monopolist's barriers to entry is not possible, the barriers will be circumvented by such means as the development of similar products against which the monopolist will not have entry protection.

Schumpeter called the replacing of an existing monopoly by one or more new entrants through the invention of new products or new production techniques the *process of creative destruction.* He argued that this process precludes the very-long-run persistence of barriers to entry into industries that earn large profits.

He pushed this further and argued that because creative destruction thrives on innovation, the existence of monopoly profits is a major incentive to economic growth. A key part of his argument can be found in the following passage:

What we have got to accept is that it [monopoly] has come to be the most powerful engine of progress and in particular of the long-run expansion of total output not only in spite of, but to a considerable extent through, this strategy [i.e. creating monopolies], which looks so restrictive when viewed in the individual case and from the individual point of time.

In this respect, perfect competition is not only impossible but inferior, and has no title to being set up as a model. It is hence a mistake to base the theory of government regulation of industry on the principle that big business should be made to work as the respective industry would work in perfect competition.[6]

Schumpeter was writing at a time when the two dominant market structures studied by economists were perfect competition and monopoly. His argument easily extends, however, to any market structure that allows profits to exist in the long run. Today there are few examples of pure monopolies, but there are many industries in which profits can be earned for long periods of time. Such industries, which are called *oligopolies*, are candidates for the operation of the process of creative destruction. We study these industries in detail in Chapter 8.

Market segmentation: a multi-price monopolist

So far in this chapter we have assumed that the monopoly firm charges the same price for every unit of its product, no matter where or to whom it sells that product. A monopoly firm will also, as we shall soon see, find it profitable to sell different units of the same product at different prices whenever it gets the opportunity.[7] Because this is also prevalent in oligopolistic markets, the range of examples quoted covers both types of market structure.

Raw milk is often sold at one price when it is to be used as fluid milk but at a lower price when it is to be used to make ice cream or cheese. Cinemas often have lower admission prices for children than for adults, and different prices again for pensioners. Railways charge different rates per tonne per kilometre for different products. Electricity producers sell electricity at one rate to homes and at a lower rate to firms. Airlines often charge less to people who stay over a Saturday night than to those who come and go within the week.

Economists have traditionally used the term **price discrimination** to apply to what we shall call 'market segmentation'. *Discrimination* is a word that suggests a moral judgement about something we think is bad, such as racial discrimination and sex discrimination. Setting different prices for different market segments is not something that we want to make such moral judgements about, so we use more neutral terminology.

---

6 J. Schumpeter, *Capitalism, Socialism, and Democracy*, 3rd edn. (New York: Harper & Row, 1950), p. 106.

7 Although multiple-price systems are found among many monopolists, such as electricity and water supply firms, they are also found in industries that contain several large firms. Thus we could discuss such practices under monopoly in this chapter or under oligopoly in Ch. 8.

Firms and competition

Market segmentation occurs when a producer charges different prices for different units of the same product for reasons not associated with differences in cost. Not all price *differences* result from market segmentation. Quantity discounts, differences between wholesale and retail prices, and prices that vary with the time of day or the season of the year may not reflect market segmentation, because the same product sold at a different time, in a different place, or in different quantities may have different costs. If an electric power company has unused capacity at certain times of the day, it may be cheaper for the company to provide power at those hours than at peak demand hours. Variations in price that result from cost differences are conceptually different from those that result from segmentation of the demand side of the market.[8] It is the latter that we are talking about here.

It does not cost a cinema operator less to fill seats with children or pensioners than with adults, but it may be worthwhile for the cinema to let the children and pensioners in at different (lower) prices if few of them would attend at the full adult admission price and if they take up seats that otherwise would be empty. In this case, children and pensioners represent different market segments from working-age adults, and it will generally be profitable for cinemas to set a different price for each segment, so long as there is some way to identify who falls into which segment (as there would be here).

Why market segmentation is profitable

Why should a firm want to sell some units of its output at a price that is well below the price that it receives for other units of its output? The simple answer is because it is profitable to do so. Why should it be profitable?

The general answer is: because demand curves have a negative slope, and this means that different units could be sold at different prices. This argument is illustrated in Figure 7.6. In part (i) of this figure we show the situation when all units are sold for the same price. Total revenue to the seller is represented by the lighter shaded area. Notice, however, that some consumers would have been prepared to pay a higher price. The first unit could have been sold at the price just below where the demand curve cuts the vertical axis. So, if the purchaser of this first unit could be asked to pay the maximum that he or she would have been prepared to pay, a higher price could have been obtained.

Another way of looking at this is to note that the darker shaded area in part (i) of the figure represents a net gain to consumers, which is known as **consumer surplus.** This is the gain consumers receive from buying all units of the product at the same market price, while all but the buyer of the last unit bought would have been prepared to pay a higher price. So consumer surplus is the amount of money that consumers would have been prepared to pay in excess of what they actually spent by all paying the same price.

---

[8] In business studies the term 'market segmentation' may also involve the development of different products for each segment. We are only talking here about selling a single product at a different price in each segment.

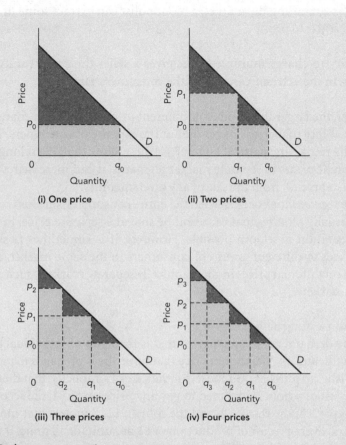

Figure 7.6. Market segmentation

Complete market segmentation turns consumers' surplus into producers' revenue. In each of the four parts a monopolist faces the same demand curve, D, and the total quantity sold is assumed to be q_0. Each firm is assumed to be allowed to do a different amount of market segmentation, and in each case the firm's revenue is shown by the lighter shaded area while consumers' surplus is shown by the darker shaded area.

In part (i), a single price p_0 is charged.

In part (ii), the first q_1 units are sold at p_1 and the next $(q_0 - q_1)$ are sold at p_0.

In part (iii), the first q_2 are sold at p_2; the next $(q_1 - q_2)$ are sold at p_1, and the last $(q_0 - q_1)$ at p_0.

In part (iv), the first q_3 units are sold at p_3; the next $(q_2 - q_3)$ at p_2, the next $(q_1 - q_2)$ at p_1 and the last $(q_0 - q_1)$ at p_0.

As the degree of segmentation increases, consumers' surplus diminishes and producers' revenue increases.

It is equal to the extra expenditure that would have been involved if every consumer had paid the *maximum* that they would have been prepared to pay for each unit of the product. By segmenting the market, a monopolist can extract some of this consumer surplus and add it to profit.

> **The ability to charge multiple prices gives a seller the opportunity to capture some (or, in the extreme case, all) of the consumers' surplus.**

In general, the larger the number of different prices that can be charged, the greater is the firm's ability to increase its revenue at the expense of consumers. This is demonstrated in the remaining parts of Figure 7.6. These show that, if a selling firm is able to charge different prices in separate market segments, it can increase revenues received (and thus also profits) from the sale of any given quantity.

Complete segmentation occurs when the entire consumers' surplus is obtained by the firm. This usually requires that each unit be sold at a separate price. In practice, complete segmentation is seldom possible. However, it is sometimes possible to charge different prices to different groups of consumers in the same market, and even more common to set different prices in geographically separate markets, such as the domestic and export markets.

Segmentation among buyers

Think of the demand curve in a market that is made up of individual buyers, each of whom has indicated the maximum price that he or she is prepared to pay for the single unit each wishes to purchase. Suppose, for the sake of simplicity, that there are only four buyers, the first of whom is prepared to pay any price up to £4, the second of whom is prepared to pay £3, the third, £2, and the fourth, £1. Suppose that the product has a marginal (and average) cost of production of £1 per unit for all units. If the selling firm is limited to a single price, it will maximize its profits by charging £3, sell two units, and earn profits of £4.[9] If the seller can do a different deal with each of the buyers, it could charge the first buyer £4 and the second £3, thus increasing its profits from the first two units to £5. Moreover, it could also sell the third unit for £2, thus increasing its profits to £6. It would be indifferent about selling a fourth unit because the price would just cover marginal cost.

Segmentation between markets

Let the monopoly firm sell in two different markets. For example, it might be the only seller in a tariff-protected home market while in foreign markets it sells in competition with so many other firms that it is a price taker. In this case, the firm would equate its marginal cost to the price in the foreign market but to marginal revenue in the domestic market. As a result, it would charge a higher price on sales in the home market than on sales abroad.

---

[9] Fixed costs are assumed to be zero in this example, so $AVC = ATC$ and both are equal to MC.

A well-known example of such a practice is the price of UK-manufactured cars. These sell at a significantly higher retail price in the UK than they do in, say, Belgium. Some of this difference is the result of tax differences, but it also reflects the pricing decisions of car firms in the face of different demand conditions in the two segments of the market. Closer to home, another example relates to the pricing by Oxford University Press of one of its first-year economics textbooks.[10] Its UK paperback edition (in 1995/6) was priced at £17.95 while its international student edition, which was exactly the same book, printed in the same print run, sold in regions such as South-East Asia for £8.99, or the local currency equivalent. Another example of differential pricing is discussed in Box 7.2.

When is market segmentation possible?

Differential pricing among units of output sold to the same buyer requires that the seller be able to keep track of the units that a buyer consumes in each period. Thus the tenth unit purchased by a given buyer in a given month can be sold at a price that is different from the fifth unit *only* if the seller can keep track of who buys what. This can be done by an electric company through its meter readings or by a magazine publisher by distinguishing between renewals and new subscriptions. It can also be done by distributing certificates or coupons that allow, for example, a car wash at a reduced price on a return visit.

Differentiation between buyers is possible only if the buyers who face the low price cannot resell the goods to the buyers who face the high price. However, even though the local butcher might like to charge the banker twice as much for buying his steak as he charges the taxi driver, he cannot succeed in doing so. The banker can always shop for meat in the supermarket, where her occupation is not known. Even if the butcher and the supermarket agreed to charge her twice as much, she could hire the taxi driver to shop for her. The surgeon, however, may succeed in differentiating (especially if other reputable surgeons do the same) because it will not do the banker much good to hire the taxi driver to have her operation for her.

Differential pricing is possible if the seller can either distinguish individual units bought by a single buyer or separate buyers into classes such that resale among classes is impossible.

The ability to prevent resale tends to be associated with the character of the product or the ability to classify buyers into readily identifiable groups. Services are less easily resold than goods; goods that require installation by the manufacturer (e.g. heavy

---

[10] Richard G. Lipsey and K. Alec Chrystal, *An Introduction to Positive Economics*, 8th edn. (Oxford: Oxford University Press, 1995).

BOX 7.2.

'Charge what the traffic will bear'

The principle of charging different customers different prices has been around for a very long time. The earliest example we have come across is from the Egyptian kingdom of Ramses the Great in the period 1304–1237BC.* In what is now southern Lebanon, there was a toll road maintained by the Egyptians. This was an important route across a range of hills. There were other routes, but they were considerably more tortuous than this one. The servant of the Egyptian ruler sent to administer this toll road found that he had some discretion over pricing. He sent a request back to his employers for guidelines as to what to charge. The reply came back: 'Charge what the traffic will bear.' So famous is this instruction that the phrase has become something of a cliché. However, it is based upon the insight, set out in the text, that setting different prices increases revenue and in practice means that each traveller should be charged the maximum that he or she would be prepared to pay to use the road.

Two more recent examples of price segmentation in the transport area are discussed below. The first is an example where this principle is still applied. The second shows what problems can arise when the principle is ignored.

Air fares

In June 1994, a standard fare on British Airways from London Heathrow to Rome was £445. This fare covered return the same day or within the week. However, if you stayed over Saturday night, the fare was only £176! This difference for the same class of fare on the same planes is meant to discriminate between the business traveller and the tourist. Such discrimination is profitable if the elasticities of demand for these two types of travel are different and lower for business. Indeed, the Minister of Transport has recently quoted figures of −1.25 for the elasticity of demand of leisure travel and −0.3 for business travel. If these are the facts, the only puzzle is why British Airways does not raise business-class fares more since, as we saw in the chapter, no monopolist would ever be in profit-maximizing equilib-

equipment) are less easily resold than movable goods such as household appliances. Transportation costs, tariff barriers, and import quotas separate classes of buyers geographically and may make segmentation possible. The example quoted above of a textbook sold at different prices in UK and Far East markets clearly relies on transport costs to maintain the segmentation. No UK student is going to fly to Taiwan just to save £9 on the cost of an economics book, though, if you happened to be there anyway, it would make sense to take your reading lists with you!

Of course, it is not enough to be able to separate different buyers or units into separate classes. The seller must also be able to control the supply going to each group. There is no point, for example, in asking more than the competitive price from some buyers if they can simply go to other firms who sell the good at the competitive price.

rium with an elasticity of demand less than unity. Presumably, the answer here is that the quoted elasticity is for business travel in general, not for business travel on one airline such as British Airways. If all airlines raised business-class fares, demand elasticity might prove to be only 0.3, but if one airline raises fares on its own, it will lose customers to other airlines and might encounter an elasticity greater than one.

A similar market segmentation applies to trans-Atlantic airfares. In early 1996, a standard economy return fare between London and New York on a reputable airline cost around £900. However, the Apex fare for anyone prepared to book fourteen days in advance and stay at least seven days was around £400, and in the off-peak season even better deals were available. Again, these substantial differences reflect a segmentation of the market between business travellers, who presumably get their fares paid by their companies, and tourists, who are paying out of their own pockets.

British Rail

This example illustrates the problems that may arise when segmentation does not happen even though both producers and consumers could be better off if it did. Some years ago British Rail was not allowed to charge different prices to passengers in different regions. Rather, a fixed fare per passenger mile was laid down by government, and had to be charged on all lines whatever the density of their passenger traffic and whatever the elasticity of demand for their services. In the interests of economy, branch lines that could not cover costs were often closed down. This meant that some lines closed even though the users preferred rail transport to any of the available alternatives and the strength of their preference was such that they would voluntarily have paid a price sufficient for the line to have covered its costs. The lines were none the less closed because it was thought inequitable to charge the passengers on their line more than the passengers on other lines.

In later years, British Rail was allowed to charge prices that took some account of market conditions, and the effect was an increase in revenues, but most lines that had been previously closed under the old pricing regime were never reopened.

*   We are grateful to Professor Arie Melnik of Haifa University for this example.

Consequences of market segmentation

A monopolist who is able to segment two markets will allocate any level of production between those two markets so as to equate the marginal revenues in the two. This is fairly obvious since, if this is not done, total revenue can always be increased by reducing sales by one unit in the market with the lower marginal revenue and raising sales by one unit in the market with the higher marginal revenue. This reallocation of sales raises total revenue by the difference between the two marginal revenues. If the demand curves are different in the two markets, having the same marginal revenues means charging different prices.

Two important consequences of market segmentation follow from this result.

Proposition 1: **For any given level of output, the most profitable system of market segmentation will provide higher total revenue to the firm than the profit-maximizing single price.**

This proposition, which was illustrated in Figure 7.6, requires only that the demand curve has a negative slope. To see that the proposition is plausible, remember that a monopolist with the power to charge multiple prices could produce exactly the same quantity as a single-price monopolist and charge everyone the same price. Therefore, it need never receive *less* revenue, and it can do better if it can raise the price on even one unit sold, as long as the price need not be lowered on any other.

Proposition 2: **Output under differential pricing will generally be larger than under a single-price monopoly.**

Remember that a monopolist that must charge a single price for a product will produce less than would all the firms in a perfectly competitive industry because it knows that selling more depresses its price. Price differentiation allows it to avoid this disincentive. To the extent that the firm can sell its output in separate blocks, it can sell another block without spoiling the market for the block that is already being sold. In the case of complete market segmentation, in which every unit of output is sold at a different price, the profit-maximizing monopolist will produce every unit for which the price charged is greater than or equal to its marginal cost. It will therefore produce the same quantity of output as does the firm in perfect competition.

Monopolistic competition

We now turn to an analysis of a market structure that is somewhere in between perfect competition and monopoly. Each firm faces a downward sloping demand curve for its product and yet there are enough firms in the industry that no firm has to worry too much about any specific rival. Market structures involving strategic interaction between key players, such as the newspaper market and the cross-Channel travel market first introduced in Chapters 2 and 3, are discussed in the following chapter.

The development of monopolistic competition

The analyses of firms under perfect competition and monopoly that we have set out above are adequate to explain many aspects of firms' behaviour. However, they are hard to accept as complete in themselves because most markets do not fit easily into either pattern. Most firms have some discretion over the prices they set and yet there are only a small number of situations in which there is only one supplier. The search for an economic model of the firm somewhere in between the two extremes of perfect competition and monopoly led the American economist Edward Chamberlin (1899–1967) to develop the theory of a market structure called **monopolistic competition.**

ASSUMPTIONS

The model of monopolistic competition is based on four specific assumptions.

1. *Each firm produces one specific variety, or brand, of the industry's differentiated product.* Each firm thus faces a demand curve that, although it is negatively sloped, is highly elastic, because other varieties of the same product that are sold by other firms provide many close substitutes.

2. *The industry contains so many firms that each one ignores the possible reactions of its many competitors when it makes its own price and output decisions.* There are too many firms for it to be possible for any one firm to try to take the other firms' separate reactions into account. In this way, firms in monopolistic competition are similar to firms in perfect competition. They make decisions based on their own demand and cost conditions and do not consider interdependence between their own decisions and those of the other firms in the industry. This is the key aspect that distinguishes the market structure of monopolistic competition from the market structure of oligopoly, which we discuss in the next chapter.

3. *There is freedom of entry and exit in the industry.* If profits are being earned by existing firms, new firms have an incentive to enter. When they do, the demand for the industry's product must be shared among more brands, and this is assumed to take demand equally from all existing firms.

4. *Symmetry.* When a new firm enters the industry selling a new version of the differentiated product, it takes custom equally from all existing firms. For example, a new entrant that captured 5 per cent of the existing market would do so by capturing 5 per cent of the sales of each existing firm.

This theory marked an important step in the development of models of intermediate market structures, and its main predictions are outlined below.

EQUILIBRIUM FOR THE FIRM AND INDUSTRY

Short-run equilibrium

Because each firm has a monopoly over its own product, each firm faces a negatively sloped demand curve. But the curve is rather elastic because similar products sold by

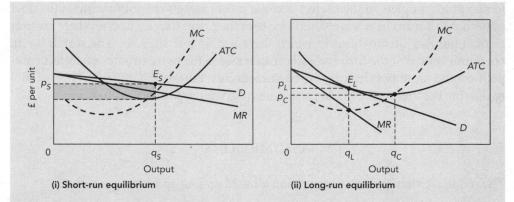

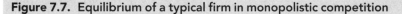

(i) Short-run equilibrium   **(ii) Long-run equilibrium**

Figure 7.7. Equilibrium of a typical firm in monopolistic competition

In the short run, a typical firm may make pure profits, but in the long run it will only cover its costs. In part (i), a typical monopolistically competitive firm is shown in short-run equilibrium at point E_S. Output is q_S, where $MC = MR$, price is p_S, and profits are the shaded area.

In part (ii), the firm is in long-run equilibrium at point E_L. Entry of new firms has pushed the existing firms' demand curve to the left until the curve is tangent to the ATC curve at output q_L. Price is p_L, and total costs are just being covered. Excess capacity is $q_C - q_L$. If the firm did produce at capacity, its costs would fall from p_L per unit of output to p_C.

Note that to make the points q_L and q_C visually distinct, the demand curve in part (ii) has been drawn more steeply sloped than in part (i). The flatter demand curve of part (i) is what is expected in monopolistic competition. If it were drawn on part (i), q_L would more realistically be closer to q_C, but the differences being illustrated by the figure would be harder to see.

other firms provide many close substitutes. The negative slope of the demand curve provides the potential for monopoly profits in the short run, as illustrated in part (i) of Figure 7.7. This is an equilibrium for each firm, but it is not an equilibrium for the industry, since there are profits to be made and no barriers to entry.

Long-run equilibrium

Freedom of entry and exit forces profits to zero in the long run. If profits are being earned by existing firms in the industry, new firms will enter. Their entry will mean that the demand for the product must be shared among more and more brands. Thus the demand curve for each existing firm's brand shifts to the left.[11] Entry continues until profits fall to zero, as shown in part (ii) of Figure 7.7. In this situation, there is an equilibrium for each firm and for the industry.

---

[11] This shift of the demand curve is determined by Chamberlin's critical *symmetry assumption*: a new entrant takes sales in equal proportions from all existing firms. In reality, new entrants will take market share more from some firms than others. However, the general message stands that new entrants, attracted by profitable opportunities, will shift the demand curves faced by existing firms. Even where profits are eliminated, new firms may enter with lower costs (or new varieties of product) than existing firms and drive them out of business. So industry equilibrium may involve a perpetual turnover of firms.

EXCESS CAPACITY

The absence of positive profits requires that each firm's demand curve be nowhere above its long-run average cost curve. The absence of losses, which would cause exit, requires that each firm be able to cover its costs. Thus, for a surviving firm, average revenue must equal average cost at some output. Together these requirements imply that when a monopolistically competitive industry is in long-run equilibrium, each firm will be producing where its demand curve is tangent to (i.e. just touching at one point) its average total cost curve.

Two curves that are tangent at a point have the same slope at that point. If a negatively sloped demand curve is to be tangent to the *LRAC* curve, the latter must also be negatively sloped at the point of tangency. This situation is shown in Figure 7.7(ii): the typical firm is producing an output less than the one for which its *LRAC* reaches its minimum point.

This is the well-known **excess-capacity theorem** of monopolistic competition. Each firm is producing its output at an average cost that is higher than it could achieve by producing its capacity output. In other words, each firm has *unused* or *excess* capacity. So:

The theory of monopolistic competition shows that an industry can be competitive, in the sense of containing numerous competing firms, and yet contain unexploited scale economies, in the sense that each firm is producing on the negatively sloped portion of its average cost curve.

This explanation, however, seems to imply waste and inefficiency. Production is at higher cost than is necessary, and firms typically invest in capacity that is not fully utilized.

Is excess capacity wasteful?

The excess-capacity theorem aroused passionate debate for decades. Was it really true that the free-market system necessarily caused waste and inefficiency whenever an industry produced differentiated products?

The debate was finally resolved with a negative answer by considering the question 'What is the optimal number of differentiated products that should be produced?'

People clearly have different tastes. For example, each brand of breakfast food, hi-fi set, car, word-processing package, and watch has its sincere devotees. Increasing the number of differentiated products has two effects. First, it increases the amount of excess capacity in the production of each product because the total demand must be divided among more products. Second, the increased diversity of available products will better satisfy diverse tastes.

Now consider how to maximize consumers' satisfactions in these circumstances. The correct policy is *not* to reduce the number of differentiated products until each remaining product can be produced at its least-cost output. Instead:

> To maximize consumers' satisfactions, the number of differentiated products should be increased until the marginal gain in consumers' satisfaction from an increase in diversity equals the loss from having to produce each existing product at a higher cost.

For this reason, among others, the charge that large-group monopolistic competition would lead to a waste of resources is no longer accepted as necessarily, or even probably, true.

The empirical relevance of large-group monopolistic competition

A long controversy raged over several decades as to the empirical relevance of monopolistic competition. Of course, product differentiation is an almost universal phenomenon in industries producing consumers' goods and capital goods. None the less, many economists maintained that the monopolistically competitive market structure was almost never found in practice.

To see why, we need to distinguish between products and firms. Single-product firms are extremely rare in manufacturing industries. Typically, a vast array of differentiated products is produced by each of the few firms in the industry. Most of the vast variety of breakfast foods, for example, is produced by a mere three firms. Similar circumstances exist in soap, chemicals, cigarettes, and numerous other industries where many competing products are produced by a few very large firms. These industries are clearly not perfectly competitive and neither are they monopolies. Are they monopolistically competitive? The answer is no, because they contain few enough firms for each to take account of the others' reactions when determining its own behaviour. Furthermore, these firms often earn large profits without attracting new entry. In fact, they operate under a market structure called oligopoly, which we consider in the next chapter.

While accepting that many differentiated products are produced by industries that are not monopolistically competitive, some economists feel that the theory is useful in analysing industries that contain many relatively small firms producing differentiated products.[12] Others agree with the views expounded by the late British economist

---

[12] At first sight, retailing may appear to be closer to the conditions of large-group monopolistic competition than is manufacturing. Every city has many retailers selling any one commodity and differentiated from each other mainly by their geographical location. Each firm, however, tends to have only a few close neighbours and many more distant ones. Thus a model of interlocking oligopolies, with every firm in strong competition with only a few close neighbours, seems to be a better model for retailing than the model of large-group monopolistic competition, in which every firm competes directly, and equally, with all other firms in the industry.

Nicholas Kaldor (1908–86) in his long debate with Chamberlin. Kaldor maintained that, because every variety of a differentiated product was not an equally good substitute for every other variety, even differentiated-product industries with many firms were better studied in a model of overlapping oligopolies.[13]

The 1980s and 1990s have witnessed a great outburst of theorizing concerning all aspects of product differentiation. The newer analyses are consistent with Chamberlin's famous propositions that it pays firms to differentiate their products, to advertise heavily, and to engage in many other forms of competitive behaviour. These are characteristics to be found in the world, but not in perfect competition or monopoly. Most modern industries that sell differentiated products, however, contain only a few firms. This is the market structure of oligopoly that is discussed in the next chapter.

Summary

1. A monopoly is an industry containing a single firm. The monopoly firm maximizes its profits by equating marginal cost to marginal revenue, which is less than price. Production under monopoly is less than it would be under perfect competition, where marginal cost is equated to price.

2. The monopoly can earn positive profits in the long run if there are barriers to entry. These may be man-made, such as patents or exclusive franchises, or natural, such as sufficiently large-scale economies.

3. If a monopolist can segment its market, either among different units or different customers, and charge different prices in each segment, it will always sell more and earn greater profits than if it sets a single price for the whole market.

4. For segmentation to be possible, the seller must be able to distinguish individual units bought by a single buyer or to separate buyers into classes between which resale is impossible.

5. In the theory of large-group monopolistic competition, many firms compete to sell differentiated products. Each may make pure profits in the short run but in the long run freedom of entry shifts its demand curve until it is tangent to the *ATC* curve, leading to excess capacity and production at average costs above the minimum possible level.

---

[13] The symmetry assumption implies, unrealistically, that all differentiated products in an industry are equally good substitutes for each other; if they were not, a new product would not take sales equally from all existing products.

Topics for review

- Relationship between price and marginal revenue for a monopolist
- Relationships among marginal revenue, total revenue, and elasticity for a monopolist
- Short- and long-run monopoly equilibrium
- Natural and created entry barriers
- Market segmentation among different units and different buyers
- The assumptions of monopolistic competition
- Excess capacity under monopolistic competition

Questions for discussion

1. Compare the effects of a tax on the profits of a monopolist with those in a perfectly competitive industry. What effect does this tax have on both a single firm and the industry under perfect competition?

2. Suppose that a monopolist had some product that was acquired with zero marginal cost. What price should the monopolist charge for this product and what quantity should be sold in order to maximize total revenue?

3. Suppose that you are a shop selling cream cakes. There is only an hour before closing time and the cakes will not keep until the next day, so if you do not sell them they will be worthless. What should be the revenue-maximizing strategy: (i) sell just what you can at the list price; (ii) lower the price so that all the cakes are sold; (iii) charge the price at which the (short-run) demand curve is unit elastic? Is there any connection between the answer to this question and the answer to question 2 above?

4. It was argued in the text that a monopolist that produces the same product in two plants must operate these plants so that both produce at the same marginal cost. Under what circumstances should one plant be closed down and production be concentrated in the remaining plant? [Hint: you may want to distinguish the short run from the long run.]

5. Draw up a list of products for which some purchasers pay different prices from others. Try to decide whether these differences are the result of variations in production costs or different demand elasticities. Is it 'unfair' for a firm to charge different prices for the same product?

6. How can it be that a monopolist is maximizing profit if it sells at different prices in separate markets? Surely it should try to sell more where the price is higher?

7. Explain the role of profit in the dynamics of a monopolistically competitive industry. In what ways does this explanation differ from that for a perfectly competitive industry?

8. Using the same cost information as for the firm described in question 7 of Chapter 6 (page 209), you are now given information about the demand this firm faces at each price. This is expressed as the price that would be achieved for the firm to sell all of the quantity at each level of production:

Sales (units)	price (£)
20	19.20
40	18.40
60	17.60
100	16.00
200	12.00
300	8.00
400	4.00
500	0.00
1,000	—

(You might like to know that this is a straight-line demand curve that can be expressed as $p = 20 - 0.04q$, where p is price and q is quantity sold.)

(i) What is the marginal revenue for each level of sales? (ii) What is the approximate profit-maximizing output and at what price will the product sell? (iii) Using total costs and total revenue, show the profit level at each level of production.

9. Suppose now that this firm has constant marginal costs of production of £4.00 per unit (i.e. ignore previous information about costs) and that it faces two segmented markets. One has the demand curve above in question 8, and the other has the following demand curve:

Sales (units)	Price (£)
20	9.60
40	9.20
60	8.80
100	8.00
200	6.00
300	4.00
400	2.00
500	0.00
1,000	—

(If it helps, this demand curve can be written $p = 10 - 0.02q$.)

(i) What quantity will the firm sell in each market (in order to maximize profit)? (ii) What price will be charged in each market?

CHAPTER 8

Firms in Imperfect Markets II: Oligopoly and Business Strategy

Key features of imperfectly competitive markets	243	Set-up costs	261
Firms select their products	244	An application	262
Firms choose their prices	245	Predatory pricing	262
Short-run price stability	245	Contestable markets and potential entry	263
Other aspects of the behaviour of firms	246	The theory	263
Non-price competition	246	Empirical relevance	264
Unexploited scale economies	246	**Oligopoly and the functioning of the economy**	265
Entry prevention	247	The market mechanism under oligopoly	265
		Profits under oligopoly	266
Oligopoly: imperfect competition among the few	247	Very-long-run competition	266
Why bigness?	248		
Natural causes of bigness	248	**Oligopoly in action: two case studies**	267
Economies of scale	248	The UK national newspaper market	268
Economies of scope	249	Demand elasticity	269
Firm-created causes of bigness	249	Non-cooperative equilibrium	269
Is bigness natural or firm-created?	250	The market for cross-Channel travel	272
The basic dilemma of oligopoly	250	Strategic interaction	273
The co-operative solution	251		
The non-cooperative equilibrium	251	**Summary**	276
An example using game theory	251		
Nash equilibrium	252	**Topics for review**	276
Strategic behaviour	253		
Breakdown of co-operation	253	**Questions for discussion**	277
Types of co-operative behaviour	255		
Explicit collusion	255	**Box 8.1.** The prisoner's dilemma	254
Tacit co-operation	255	**Box 8.2.** Strategies and equilibrium concepts in game theory	256
Types of competitive behaviour	258	**Box 8.3.** Brand proliferation in alcoholic drinks	260
Competition for market shares	258		
Covert cheating	258	**Exhibit 8.1.** The market for UK national newspapers	270
Very-long-run competition	258		
Long-run behaviour: the importance of entry barriers	259	**Exhibit 8.2.** Competition in cross-Channel journeys	274
Brand proliferation	259		

MANY firms have to worry about what key competitor firms are doing. Shell cannot ignore the behaviour of BP, and Barclays cannot ignore NatWest, and vice versa. None of the models of firms' behaviour discussed above deals with this interdependence. Indeed, each of them assumes it away by supposing that each firm faces a known demand curve that depends only on the firm's own price. We now wish to make the demand for each firm's product dependent upon what its rivals do as well as on the price that it charges for its output.

In perfectly competitive markets, firms can sell as much as they want at the market price, so they do not need to be bothered by any other specific firm. In a monopolized market, there is only one supplier so, again, other firms do not matter—there are none. Finally, under monopolistic competition, entry of new firms affects all existing producers equally, so there is no direct rivalry between specific firms.

Clearly, an analysis of firms that ignores direct rivalry between major players leaves out a key dimension of the modern business environment. Market structures in which one firm's profit (or demand) is influenced directly by another firm's decisions are known as *oligopoly*. This can be characterized as competition among the few. The markets for most manufactured products in a modern industrial economy are better characterized by oligopoly than by any of the alternative models of market structure. Only in service industries, such as restaurants and hairdressers, is it possible that monopolistic competition may be a better model (although, even here, the geographic location of firms usually leaves each in strong competition with a few close neighbours). Hence, oligopoly is the most generally applicable case of imperfect competition, while monopolistic competition is less common and pure monopoly is positively unusual.

In what follows, we review the key features that contrast imperfectly competitive market structures with competitive markets. We then study some of the special features of firm behaviour in oligopoly. Finally, we discuss some specific examples of the strategic interaction between firms in the real world.

Key features of imperfectly competitive markets

Our earlier studies of simplified, but unrealistic, models of the firm taught us a great deal, especially about the relationships between costs and revenues, as well as the characteristics of a profit-maximizing equilibrium. However, the ultimate goal of our study is to understand real firms and real markets; hence, it is worth highlighting key aspects of the behaviour of most firms in imperfectly competitive markets. Notice that many of these characteristics apply to monopolistically competitive markets (and some even to monopoly), which we discussed in the previous chapter. However, we summarize them here because they also apply in oligopolisic markets and this is the dominant market structure faced by modern business. Hence, this section can be thought of as listing of some key characteristics of the modern business environment (oligopoly), some of which may also apply to other special cases of imperfect markets.

Firms select their products

If a new farmer decides to grow wheat, the full range of products that can be produced is already in existence and is already being produced by many other farmers. In contrast, if a new firm enters the computer software industry, that firm must decide on the characteristics of the new computer programs that it is to produce. It will not produce programs that are identical to those already in production. Rather, it will develop, at substantial cost, one or more new programs, each of which will have its own distinctive characteristics. As a result, firms in this industry sell an array of differentiated products, no two of which are identical. This is true of firms in virtually all consumer and capital goods industries.

The term **differentiated product** refers to a group of products that are similar enough to be called the same product but dissimilar enough that they can be sold at different prices. For example, although one brand of toilet soap is similar to most others, soaps differ from each other in their chemical composition, colour, smell, softness, brand name, reputation, and a host of other characteristics that matter to customers. So all toilet soaps taken together are one product, but each brand is differentiated in some way from each other brand. Developing a product that is 'better' than rival products is a key element of business success.

> **Most firms in imperfectly competitive market structures sell differentiated products. In such industries, the firm itself must decide on the characteristics of the products it will sell.**

For some purposes it is helpful to distinguish two types of differentiation. **Vertical differentiation** arises when products are of different *quality*. Thus, if two vertically differentiated products were offered for sale at the same price, all consumers would buy the product with the higher quality. **Horizontal differentiation** applies when the products are different in some other dimension, such that some consumers would still buy each of the products even at the same price. Characteristics creating horizontal differentiation may be location, such as with a local corner shop, or may be colour, smell, shape, etc., for which tastes of consumers will vary. Vertical differentiation would apply to the differences between a bottle of Chateau Lafitte Rothschild 1953 and a wine box of non-vintage Rioja, or between a Porsche 911 and a Reliant Robin. Horizontal differentiation would apply between a Ford Escort and a Vauxhall Astra; between Weetabix and Shredded Wheat; and between Fosters lager and Castlemaine XXXX.

Firms choose their prices

In perfect competition, firms are price takers and quantity adjusters. In all other market structures, firms face negatively sloped demand curves and thus face a trade-off between the price that they charge and the quantity that they sell.

Because firms' products are not perfect substitutes for each other, each firm must quote a price. Any one manufacturer will typically have several product lines that differ more or less from each other and from the competing product lines of other firms. No market sets a single price for razor blades, television sets, word-processing packages, or any other differentiated product by equating overall demand with overall supply. Instead, each type of the differentiated product has a price that must be set by its maker. Of course, a certain amount of haggling is possible, particularly at the retail level, but this is usually within well-defined limits set by the price charged by the manufacturer.

In such circumstances, economists say that firms *administer* their prices and are **price makers** rather than price takers. An **administered price** is a price set by the conscious decision of an individual firm rather than by impersonal market forces.

Each firm has expectations about the quantity it can sell at each price that it might set for each of its product lines. *Unexpected* market fluctuations then cause unexpected variations in the quantities that are sold at the administered prices.

> **In market structures other than perfect competition, firms set their prices and then let demand determine sales. Changes in market conditions are signalled to the firm by changes in the quantity that the firm sells at its current administered price.**

The changed conditions may or may not then lead firms to change their prices.

Short-run price stability

In perfect competition, prices change continually in response to every change in demand or supply. For example, prices in foreign exchange markets, stock markets, and most commodity markets change minute by minute while the market is open. In markets for differentiated manufactured products, prices usually change much less frequently. Manufacturers' prices for cars, computers, television sets, and dishwashers do not change with anything like the frequency that prices change in markets for basic materials or stocks and shares. (Retail mark-ups are, however, varied more often in response to short-term fluctuations in market conditions.)

Modern firms that sell differentiated products typically have hundreds, or even thousands, of distinct products on their price lists. Changing such a long list of administered prices at the same frequency that competitive market prices change would be physically impossible. Changing them at all involves costs. These include the costs of printing new list prices and notifying all customers, the difficulty of keeping track of frequently changing prices for purposes of accounting and billing, and the loss of customer and retailer goodwill owing to the uncertainty caused by frequent changes in prices. These costs are often a significant consideration to multi-product manufacturing firms.

Because producers of differentiated products must administer their own prices, firms must decide on the *frequency* with which they change these prices. In making this decision, the firm will balance the cost of making price changes against the revenue lost by not making price changes. Clearly, the likelihood that the firm will make costly price changes rises with the size of the disturbance to which it is adjusting and the probability that the disturbance will not be reversed.

Thus, transitory fluctuations in demand may be met by changing output with prices constant, while changes in costs that are thought to be permanent are passed on through price increases.

Other aspects of the behaviour of firms

Several other important aspects of the observed behaviour of firms could not occur under either perfect competition or monopoly.

Non-price competition
Many firms spend large sums of money on advertising. They do so in an attempt both to shift the demand curves for the industry's products and to attract customers from competing firms. Many firms engage in a variety of other forms of non-price competition, such as offering competing standards of quality and product guarantees. Any kind of sales-promotion activity undertaken by a single firm would not happen under perfect competition since each firm can sell any amount at the going market price. Any such scheme directed at competing firms in the same industry is, by definition, inconsistent with monopoly.

Unexploited scale economies
Many firms in industries that contain more than one firm appear to be operating on the downward-sloping portions of the long-run average cost curves for many of the individual product lines that they produce. We have already drawn attention to the importance of these *increasing returns* in Chapter 5. Although increasing returns are possible under monopoly, firms in perfect competition must, in the long run, be at the minimum point of their long-run average cost curves (see Figure 6.9 on page 203).

One set of reasons why many firms operate under increasing returns to scale is found in high development costs and short product lives. Many modern products involve large development costs. For example, roughly US$1 billion was recently spent just to *design the wing* of a new commercial airliner, and hundreds of millions of pounds were spent by Rolls Royce to develop its Trent engine! Today, many products are only sold for a few years before being replaced by a new, superior product. For example, the manager of a large telecommunications firm recently stated that 80 per cent of the products his firm sells today did not exist five years ago! In such cases, firms face steeply falling long-run average total cost curves. The more units that are sold, the less are the fixed development costs per unit. Given perfect competition, these firms would go on increasing outputs and sales until rising marginal costs of production just balanced the falling fixed unit costs, bringing their average total cost to a minimum. As it is, they often face falling average total cost curves all through each product's life-cycle.

Entry prevention

Firms in many industries engage in activities that appear to be designed to hinder the entry of new firms, thereby preventing existing pure profits from being eroded by entry. We will consider these activities in much more detail in the context of our discussion of oligopoly, to which we now turn.

Oligopoly: imperfect competition among the few

An **oligopoly** is an industry that contains only a few competing firms. Each firm has enough market power to prevent its being a price taker, but each firm is subject to enough inter-firm rivalry to prevent its considering the market demand curve as its own. In most modern economies this is the dominant market structure for the production of consumer and capital goods as well as many basic industrial materials, such as steel and aluminium. Services, however, are often produced under somewhat more competitive conditions.

In contrast to a monopoly (which has no competitors) and to a monopolistically competitive firm (which has many competitors), an oligopolistic firm faces a few significant competitors. *The number of competitors is small enough for each firm to realize that its competitors may respond to anything that it does and that it should take such possible responses into account.* In other words, oligopolists are aware of the interdependence among the decisions made by the various firms in the industry, and they engage in the type of rivalrous behaviour first discussed on page 182.

This is the key difference between oligopolists on the one hand and perfect or monopolistic competitors, and monopolies, on the other hand. We say that their behaviour is **strategic,** which means that they take explicit account of the impact of their decisions on competing firms and of the reactions they expect competing firms to make. In contrast, firms in perfect and monopolistic competition engage in **non-strategic** behaviour, which means they make decisions based on their own costs and their own demand curves without considering any possible reactions from their large number of competitors. Monopolists do not engage in strategic behaviour, either; this, however, is because they have no competitors rather than too many.

247

It is worth noting that economists use the word 'strategic' in a more specific sense than is normal in common usage. Firms in non-oligopolistic markets often require what non-economists might call a *business strategy*, involving plans for developing the workforce, customer relations, the quality of the product, etc. We would call this a business plan. We use the term 'strategic' in the narrower sense of the intended course of action for dealing with the potential responses of the main competing firms. This could only apply to the market structure in which such interaction matters. This use of *strategy* derives from military applications, where one army's success clearly depends upon the opposing army's responses. A strategy is, thus, a game plan in a situation where the opposing player also gets to make choices, and, indeed, also has a strategy.

Oligopolistic industries are of many types. In some industries there are only a few firms. In others there are many firms, but only a few dominate the market. Oligopoly is also consistent with a large number of small sellers, called a 'competitive fringe', as long as a 'big few' dominate the industry's production. For example, about 500 banks operate in the UK, but the big four—Barclays, Lloyds, NatWest, and Midland—dominate the commercial banking industry.

In oligopolistic industries, prices are typically administered. Products are usually differentiated. Firms engage in rivalrous behaviour, although its intensity varies greatly across industries and over time. However, for an industry, or a market, to be dominated by only a few firms, the existing firms must be 'big' relative to the size of the market. So it is worth considering some of the sources of this concentration of output in the hands of a few firms.

Why bigness?

Several factors contribute to explaining why so many industries are dominated by a few large firms. Some are 'natural', and some are created by the firms themselves.

NATURAL CAUSES OF BIGNESS

Economies of scale
Much factory production uses specialized division of labour. The manufacture of a product is broken up into hundreds of simple, repetitive tasks. This type of division of labour is the basis of the assembly line, which revolutionized the production of many goods in the early twentieth century, and it still underlies economies of large-scale production in many industries. Such division of labour is, as Adam Smith observed over two hundred years ago (with his famous example of the pin factory), dependent on the size of the market. If only a few units of a product can be sold each day, there is no point in dividing its production into a number of tasks. So big firms with large sales

have an advantage over small firms with small sales whenever there is great scope for economies based on an extensive division of labour.

Economies of scope

Modern industries produce many differentiated products that give rise to a different type of large-scale advantage. To develop a new product is costly, and it may be a matter of only a few years before it is replaced by some superior version of the same basic product. These fixed costs of product development must be recovered in the revenues from sales of the product. The larger the firm's sales, the less the cost that has to be recovered from each unit sold. Consider a product that costs £1 million to develop and to market. If 1 million units are to be sold, £1 of the selling price of each unit must go towards recovering the development costs. If, however, the firm expects to sell 10 million units, each unit need only contribute £0.10 to these costs, and the market price can be lowered accordingly. With the enormous development costs of some of today's high-tech products, firms that can sell a large volume have a distinct pricing advantage over firms that sell a smaller volume.

Other scope economies are related to financing and to marketing. It is costly to enter a market, to establish a sales force, and to make consumers aware of a product. These costs are often nearly as high when a small volume is being marketed as when a large volume is being marketed. Thus the smaller the volume of the firm's sales, the higher the price must be if the firm is to cover all of these costs. Notice that these economies, which are related to the size of the firm, are related neither to the amount the firm produces of any one of its differentiated products, nor to the size of any one of its plants. Economies that depend on the overall size of the *firm* rather than on the size of its *plants* or the volume of production of any one product are called the **economies of scope.**

Where size confers a cost advantage either through economies of scale or of scope, there may be room for only a few firms, even when the total market is quite large. This cost advantage of size will dictate that the industry be an oligopoly, unless government regulation prevents the firms from growing to their efficient size.

FIRM-CREATED CAUSES OF BIGNESS

The number of firms in an industry may be decreased while the average size of the survivors rises, owing to *strategic* behaviour of the firms themselves. Firms may grow by buying out rivals (acquisitions), or merging with them (mergers), or by driving rivals into bankruptcy through predatory practices. This process increases the size and market shares of the survivors and may, by reducing competitive behaviour, allow them to earn larger profit margins. The surviving firms must then be able to create and sustain barriers to entry where natural ones do not exist. The industry will then be dominated by a few large firms only when they are successful in preventing the entry of new firms that would lower the industry's concentration.

We refer to merger and acquisition activity as part of the *market for corporate control*. This is discussed further in Chapter 12.

IS BIGNESS NATURAL OR FIRM-CREATED?

Most observers would agree that the general answer to the question posed in the heading to this section is 'some of both'. Some industries have high concentration of production because the efficient size of the firm is large relative to the overall size of the industry's market. Other industries may have higher concentration ratios than efficiency considerations would dictate because the firms are seeking enhanced market power through large size plus entry restriction. The issue that is debated is the relative importance of these two forces, the one coming from the efficiencies of large scale and scope, and the other coming from the desire of firms to create market power by growing large.

Harvard economist Alfred D. Chandler, Jr is a champion of the view that the major reason for the persistence of oligopolies in the manufacturing sector is the efficiency of large-scale production. His monumental work *Scale and Scope: The Dynamics of Industrial Capitalism*[1] argues this case in great detail for the USA, the UK, and Germany.

The basic dilemma of oligopoly

Oligopoly behaviour is necessarily *strategic* behaviour. In deciding on strategies, oligopolists face a basic dilemma between competing and co-operating.

The firms in an oligopolistic industry will make more profits as a group if they co-operate; any one firm, however, may make more profits for itself if it defects while the others co-operate.

The basic reason is that when only one firm increases its output by 1 per cent the price falls by less than when all firms do the same. Thus, when the point is reached at which profits will be *reduced* if all firms expand output together, it will still pay one firm to expand output *if* the others do not do the same. In a perfectly competitive industry, however, there are so many firms that they cannot reach the co-operative solution unless some central governing body is formed, by either themselves or the government, to force the necessary behaviour on all firms. In contrast, the few firms in an oligopolistic industry will themselves recognize the possibility of co-operating to avoid the loss of profits that will result from competitive behaviour.

[1] A. D. Chandler, Jr, *Scale and Scope: The Dynamics of Industrial Capitalism* (Cambridge, MA: Harvard University Press, 1990).

THE CO-OPERATIVE SOLUTION

If the firms in an oligopolistic industry co-operate—either overtly or tacitly—to pro-duce among themselves the monopoly output, they can maximize their joint profits. If they do this, they will reach what is called a **co-operative solution,** which is the position that a single monopoly firm would reach if it owned all the firms in the in-dustry.

THE NON-COOPERATIVE EQUILIBRIUM

If all the firms in an oligopolistic industry are at the co-operative solution, it will gen-erally be profitable for any one of them to cut its price or to raise its output, as long as the others do not do so. However, if everyone does the same thing, they will be worse off as a group and may all be worse off individually. An equilibrium that is reached by firms when they proceed by calculating only their own gains, without co-operating with others, is called a **non-cooperative equilibrium.**

AN EXAMPLE USING GAME THEORY

The **theory of games** is the study of rational decision making in situations in which a number of players compete, knowing that other players will react to their moves, and taking account of their expected reactions when making moves. For example, firm A asks: shall I raise or lower my price or leave it unchanged? Before arriving at an answer it asks: what will the other firms do in each of these cases, and how will their actions affect the profitability of whatever decision I make?

> When game theory is applied to oligopoly, the players are firms, their game is played in the market, their strategies are their price or output (including product-design) decisions, and the pay-offs are their profits.

A game-theory illustration of the basic dilemma of oligopolists, to co-operate or to compete, is shown in Figure 8.1 for the case of a two-firm oligopoly, sometimes called a **duopoly.** The simplified game, adopted for the purposes of illustration, allows only two strategies for *each firm*: produce an output equal to one-half of the monopoly output or two-thirds of the monopoly output. Even this simple game, however, is sufficient to illustrate several key ideas in the modern theory of oligopoly.

Figure 8.1 presents what is called a *pay-off matrix*. The data in the matrix show that, if both sides co-operate, *each producing* one-half of the monopoly output, they achieve the co-operative solution and jointly earn the monopoly profits by *jointly producing* the output that a monopolist would produce. As a group, they can do no better.

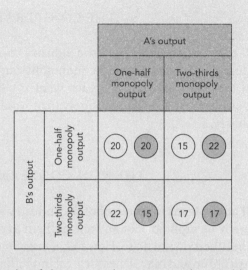

Figure 8.1. The oligopolist's dilemma: to co-operate or to compete

Co-operation to determine the overall level of output can maximize joint profits, but it leaves each firm with an incentive to alter its production. The figure gives what is called a pay-off matrix for a two-firm duopoly game. Only two levels of production are considered in order to illustrate the basic problem. A's production is indicated across the top, and its profits (measured in millions of pounds) are shown in the darker circles within each square. B's production is indicated down the left side, and its profits (in millions of pounds) are shown in the lighter circles within each square. For example, the top right square tells us that if B produces one-half, while A produces two-thirds, of the output that a monopolist would produce, A's profits will be £22 million, while B's will be £15 million.

If A and B co-operate, each produces one-half the monopoly output and earns profits of £20 million, as shown in the upper left box. However, at that position, known as the co-operative solution, each firm can raise its profits by producing two-thirds of the monopoly output, provided that the other firm does not do the same.

Now assume that A and B make their decisions non-co-operatively. A reasons that whether B produces either one-half or two-thirds of the monopoly output, A's best output is two-thirds. B reasons similarly. In this case they reach the non-cooperative equilibrium, where each produces two-thirds of the monopoly output, and each makes less than it would if the two firms co-operated.

Nash equilibrium

The non-cooperative equilibrium shown in Figure 8.1 is called a *Nash equilibrium*, after US mathematician John Nash, who developed the concept in the 1950s. A **Nash equilibrium** is one in which each firm's best strategy is to maintain its present behaviour *given the present behaviour of the other firms.*

With a little thought it can be seen that there is one Nash equilibrium in Figure 8.1. In the bottom-right cell, the best decision for each firm, given that the other firm is producing two-thirds of the monopoly output, is to produce two-thirds of the monopoly output itself. Between them they produce a joint output of one-and-a-third times the monopoly output. Neither firm has an incentive to depart from this position, except through co-operation with the other. In any other cell, each firm has an incentive to alter its output *given the output of the other firm.*

The basis of a Nash equilibrium is rational decision making in the absence of co-operation. Its particular importance in oligopoly theory is that it is the only type of equilibrium that is *self-policing*. It is self-policing in the sense that there is no need for group behaviour to enforce it. Each firm has a self-interest to maintain it because no move that it can make on its own will improve its profits, given what other firms are currently doing.

> If a Nash equilibrium is established—by any means whatsoever—no firm has an incentive to depart from it by altering its own behaviour. It is self policing.

Strategic behaviour

The Nash equilibrium will be attained if each firm behaves strategically by choosing its optimal strategy taking into account what the other firm may do.

Suppose that firm A reasons as follows: B can do one of two things; what is the best thing for me to do in each case? First, what if B produces one-half of the monopoly output? If I do the same, I receive a profit of 20, but if I produce two-thirds of the monopoly output, I receive 22. Second, what if B produces two-thirds of the monopoly output? If I produce one-half of the monopoly output, I receive a profit of 15, whereas if I produce two-thirds, I receive 17. Clearly, my best strategy is to produce two-thirds of the monopoly output in either case. B will reason in the same way, and, in this case, the pay-off is symmetrical. As a result, they end up producing one-and-a-third times the monopoly output between them, and each earns a profit of 17.

This type of game, where the non-cooperative equilibrium makes both players worse off than if they were able to co-operate, is called a Prisoner's Dilemma. The reason for this name, and some further applications, are discussed in Box 8.1.

Breakdown of co-operation

The Nash equilibrium is attained by the strategic reasoning just outlined. It can, however, be used to give an intuitive argument for why oligopolistic co-operation tends to break down.

Assume that the co-operative position has been attained. The data in the figure show that, if A cheats and produces more, its profits will increase. However, B's profits will be reduced: A's behaviour drives the industry's prices down, so B earns less from its unchanged output. Because A's cheating takes the firms away from the joint profit-maximizing monopoly output, their joint profits must fall. This means that B's profits fall by more than A's rise. Figure 8.1 shows that similar considerations also apply to B. It is worthwhile for B to depart from the joint maximizing output, as long as A does not do so. So both A and B have an incentive to depart from the joint profit-maximizing level of output.

Finally, Figure 8.1 shows that when either firm does depart from the joint-maximizing output, the other has an incentive to do so as well. When each follows this 'selfish' strategy, they reach a non-cooperative equilibrium at which they jointly produce one-and-a-third times as much as the monopolist would. Each then has profits that are lower than at the co-operative solution.[2]

---

2 This is why we do not speak of the co-operative *equilibrium*. It is a solution to the problem of finding the best co-operative behaviour. But it is not an equilibrium, since, once achieved, each firm has an incentive to depart from it.

BOX 8.1.

The prisoner's dilemma

The game shown in Figure 8.1 is often known as a prisoner's dilemma game. This is the story that lies behind the name:

> Two men, John and William, are arrested for jointly committing a crime and are interrogated separately. They know that if they both plead innocent they will get only a light sentence. Each is told, however, that if either protests innocence while the other admits guilt, the one who claims innocence will get a severe sentence while the other will be let off. If they both plead guilty, they will both get a medium sentence.

Here is the pay-off matrix for that game:

John's Plea

		Innocent	Guilty
William's plea	Innocent	J light sentence W light sentence	J no sentence W severe sentence
	Guilty	J severe sentence W no sentence	J medium sentence W medium sentence

John reasons as follows: 'William will either plead guilty or innocent. First, assume he pleads innocent. I get a light sentence if I also plead innocent but no sentence at all if I plead guilty, so guilty is my better plea. Second, assume he pleads guilty. I get a severe sentence if I plead innocent and a moderate sentence if I plead guilty. So once again guilty is my preferred plea.' William reasons in the same way and, as a result, they both plead guilty and get a medium sentence, whereas if they had been able to communicate, they could both have agreed to plead innocent and get off with a light sentence.

Another example of a prisoner's dilemma can arise when two firms are making sealed bids on a contract. For simplicity, assume that only two bids are permitted, either a high or a low price. The high price yields a profit of £10m, whereas the low price yields a profit of £7m. If they put in the same price, they share the job and each earns half the profits. If they give different bids, the firm submitting the lower bid gets the job and all the profits. You should have no trouble in drawing up the pay-off matrix and determining the outcomes under strategic and co-operative behaviour.

Game theory is an extremely flexible tool that has led to many advances in the understanding of business behaviour. It also has a direct pay-off for managers in that it helps them to understand in a more systematic way the choices that they have often had to make by luck or intuition. Box 8.2 sets out some more of the basic concepts of this approach to strategy.

TYPES OF CO-OPERATIVE BEHAVIOUR

We have seen that, although oligopolists have an incentive to co-operate, they may be driven, through their own individual decisions, to produce more and earn less than they would if they co-operated. Our next step is to look in more detail at the types of co-operative and competitive behaviour that oligopolists may adopt. We can then go on to study the forces that influence the balance between co-operation and competition in actual situations.

When firms agree to co-operate in order to restrict output and to raise prices, their behaviour is called **explicit collusion**. Collusive behaviour may occur with or without an actual agreement to collude. Where explicit agreement occurs, economists speak of *overt* or *covert collusion*, depending on whether the agreement is open or secret. Where no explicit agreement actually occurs, economists speak of *tacit collusion*.

Explicit collusion

The easiest way for firms to make sure that they will all maintain their joint profit-maximizing output is to make an explicit agreement to do so. Such collusive agreements have occurred in the past, although they have been illegal for a long time in the UK. When they are discovered today, they are prosecuted. We shall see, however, that such agreements are not illegal everywhere in the world, particularly when they are supported by national governments.

When a group of firms gets together to act in this way in international markets, it is called a *cartel*. Cartels show in stark form the basic conflict between co-operation and competition that we just discussed. Full co-operation always allows the industry to achieve the result of monopoly. It also always presents individual firms with the incentive to cheat. The larger the number of firms, the greater the temptation for any one of them to cheat. After all, the cheating of one small firm may not be noticed, because it will have a negligible effect on price. This is why cartels that involve firms in industries that would otherwise be perfectly competitive tend to be unstable.

Cartels may also be formed by a group of firms that would otherwise be in an oligopolistic market. The smaller the group of firms that forms a cartel, the more likely that the firms will let their joint interest in co-operating guide their behaviour. Although cheating may still occur, the few firms in the industry can easily foresee the outcome of an outbreak of rivalry among themselves.

The most famous modern example of a cartel that encourages explicit co-operative behaviour among oligopolists is the Organization of Petroleum Exporting Countries (OPEC).

Tacit co-operation

While collusive behaviour that affects prices is illegal, a small group of firms that recognize the influence that each has on the others may act without any explicit agreement to achieve the co-operative equilibrium. In terms of Figure 8.1, Firm A decides to produce

BOX 8.2.

Strategies and equilibrium concepts in game theory

A *dominant strategy* occurs when there is one best choice for A to make whatever B does, and one best choice for B to make whatever A does. The equilibrium in Figure 8.1 is a dominant strategy since it is always best for each to produce two-thirds of the monopoly output whatever the other produces. The prisoner's dilemma game in Box 8.1 also has a dominant strategy, which is for each to confess no matter what the other does.

All dominant strategies are Nash equilibria, but not all Nash equilibria are dominant strategies. Consider, for example, a hypothetical pay-off matrix that arises when two firms, A and B, are trying to decide which independent R&D laboratory to employ to develop some new technology that they both want to use. (In each cell in Table (i), A's pay-off is written before the comma and B's pay-off after it.) When both firms employ the same laboratory, there is a much bigger pay-off than when the research funds are divided between the two laboratories, neither of which may have enough funding to develop the best new technique.

Table (i).

	Firm A employs	
	Lab. Q	Lab. R
Firm B employs		
Lab. Q	20, 20	5, 8
Lab. R.	8, 5	15, 15

Table (ii).

	Player A chooses	
	U	V
Player B chooses		
S	10, 10	2, 10
T	10, 20	30, 2

If A chooses to employ laboratory Q, the best thing B can do is also to employ Q. But if A chooses to employ laboratory R, B should also employ R. The difference between this game and the one in the text is that the biggest pay-offs come when both make the same choice and the smaller pay-offs when they make different choices. In such cases, each person's best choice depends on the choice made by the other. There are two Nash equilibria, in which both firms make the same choice. Although the choice of laboratory Q is better for both than the choice of R, if either firm chooses R, the best the other can do is also to choose R.

There are two problems with Nash equilibria. First, there are games, including the one just considered, with more than one Nash equilibrium (equilibrium is not unique). Second, there may exist no Nash equilibrium, as in the pay-off matrix in Table (ii). In this game, if A chooses U, B wants to choose T, but if B chooses T, A wants to choose V; but if A does choose V, B wants to choose S, and if B does choose S, A wants to choose U. There is no combination of choices where each will be satisfied with his or her own choice given the other player's choice.

So far, we have implicitly assumed that the game is played only once. In *repeated games* the players play the same game many times, and we need to distinguish between *pure strategies*, which means a strategy that does not change, and *mixed strategies*, which means that each player alternates randomly between each of the available choices with pre-assigned probabilities. In the game of Figure 8.1, one player might choose half the monopoly output with probability 5/6 and two-thirds the monopoly output with probability 1/6. (She could roll a die and choose half the monopoly output if any number from 1 to 5 turned up and two-thirds of the monopoly output if a 6 turned up.) The other might choose either output with a probability of 1/2. It is an interesting theorem in game theory that, whatever the pay-off matrix, there always exists a Nash equilibrium in mixed strategies for a wide class of games. There is some set of probabilities for making choices among the alternatives by each player that leaves *each player* satisfied with his or her choice of strategy, given the other player's current choice of strategy.

The important insight following from prisoner's dilemma games is that individual maximization does not always lead to a Pareto optimum. In the Nash equilibria of the prisoner's dilemma game shown in Box 8.1, both players can be made better off if they co-operate and so move to the top left-hand box. But if they both make individual maximizing decisions, they end up in the bottom right-hand box.

Repeated games give a possibility of avoiding the non-optimal prisoner's dilemma solution. In a game that is repeated for ever, called an *infinite game*, one can establish a reputation by punishing a person who does the 'wrong thing' and rewarding him if he does the 'right thing'. In Figure 8.1, call half the monopoly output the 'right choice'. A can adopt the strategy that if B makes the right choice A will make the right choice the next time the game is played; but if B makes the wrong choice A will punish B by also making the wrong choice on the next round of play. This strategy is called *tit for tat*. In computer experiments, this simple strategy outperforms many other, more complex, strategies. The moral is that both players can learn that co-operation pays if the game is played long enough for them to discover that non-cooperation is followed by a competitive reaction that hurts both players.

Perhaps surprisingly, a repeated game that is played for only a finite number of moves provides no such simple resolution to the prisoner's dilemma. The last move of any finite repeated game is exactly the same as a one-time game, since there are no reputation effects to worry about in a game that will not be played again. Thus, the best strategy for either player on the last play of the game is to sell two-thirds of the monopoly output. But if that is so, then the second-to-last move also carries no penalty for non-cooperation. And so, by what is called backward induction, as long as co-operation cannot be ensured by some binding agreement, there is no incentive to co-operate at any point in a finite repeated game.

Game theory has been used in many contexts in economics. It is rich in its applications and ability to explain phenomena that are observed and seem otherwise inexplicable.

one-half of the monopoly output, hoping that Firm B will do the same. Firm B does what A expects, and they achieve the co-operative equilibrium without ever explicitly co-operating.

In such *tacit* agreements, the two forces that push toward co-operation and competition are still evident. First, firms have a common interest in co-operating to maximize their joint profits at the co-operative solution. Second, each firm is interested in its own profits, and any one of them can usually increase its profits by behaving competitively.

TYPES OF COMPETITIVE BEHAVIOUR

Although the most obvious way for a firm to violate the co-operative solution is to produce more than its share of the joint profit-maximizing output, there are other ways in which rivalrous behaviour can break out.

Competition for market shares
Even if *joint* profits are maximized, there is the problem of market shares. How is the profit-maximizing level of sales to be divided among the competing firms? Competition for market shares may upset the tacit agreement to hold to joint maximizing behaviour. Firms often compete for market shares through various forms of non-price competition, such as advertising and variations in the quality of their product. Such costly competition may reduce industry profits.

Covert cheating
In an industry that has many differentiated products and in which sales are often by contract between buyers and sellers, covert rather than overt cheating may seem attractive. Secret discounts and rebates can allow a firm to increase its sales at the expense of its competitors while appearing to hold to the tacitly agreed monopoly price.

Very-long-run competition
As we first discussed in Chapter 5, very-long-run considerations may also be important. When technology and product characteristics change constantly, there may be advantages to behaving competitively. A firm that behaves competitively may be able to maintain a larger market share and earn larger profits than it would if it co-operated with the other firms in the industry, even though all the firms' joint profits are lower. In our world of constant change, a firm that thinks it can *keep* ahead of its rivals through innovation has an incentive to compete even if that competition lowers the joint profits of the whole industry. Indeed, technological competition is one of the key driving forces in modern business. In some industries, such as pharmaceuticals, it drives the search for new products; in others, such as banking, it drives firms to deliver existing products at lower cost. Such competitive behaviour contributes to the long-run growth of living standards and may provide social benefits over time that outweigh any losses due to the restriction of output at any point in time.

For these and for other reasons, there are often strong incentives for oligopolistic firms to compete rather than to maintain the co-operative solution, even when they understand the inherent risks to their joint profits.

Long-run behaviour: the importance of entry barriers

Suppose that firms in an oligopolistic industry succeed in raising prices above long-run average total costs and earn substantial profits that are not completely eliminated by non-price competition. In the absence of significant barriers to entry, new firms will enter the industry and erode the profits of existing firms, as they do in monopolistic competition. Natural barriers to entry were discussed in Chapter 7. They are an important part of the explanation of the persistence of profits in many oligopolistic industries.

Where such natural barriers do not exist, however, oligopolistic firms can earn profits in the long run only if they can create entry barriers. To the extent to which this is done, existing firms can move towards joint profit maximization without fear that new firms, attracted by the high profits, will enter the industry. We discuss next some types of created barrier.

BRAND PROLIFERATION

By altering the characteristics of a differentiated product, it is possible to produce a vast array of variations on the general theme of that product. Think, for example, of cars with a little more or a little less acceleration, braking power, top speed, cornering ability, petrol mileage, and so on, compared with existing models.

Although the multiplicity of existing brands is no doubt partly a response to consumers' tastes, it can have the effect of discouraging the entry of new firms. To see why, suppose that the product is the type for which there is a substantial amount of brand switching by consumers. In this case, the larger the number of brands sold by existing firms, the smaller the expected sales of a new entrant.

Say, for example, that an industry contains three large firms, each selling one brand of cigarettes, and say that 30 per cent of all smokers change brands in a random fashion each year. If a new firm enters the industry, it can expect to pick up 25 per cent of the smokers who change brands. (The smoker has available one out of the new total of four brands.) This would give the new firm 7.5 per cent (25 per cent of 30 per cent) of the total market in the first year merely as a result of picking up its share of the random switchers, and it would keep increasing its share for some time thereafter. If, however, the existing three firms have five brands each, there would be fifteen brands already available, and a new firm selling one new brand could expect to pick up only

BOX 8.3.

Brand proliferation in alcoholic drinks

Allied–Domecq PLC is one of Britain's largest companies. This is partly because of the diversity of its activities—manufacturing and selling beers and other alcoholic drinks, producing a wide variety of food products, and operating restaurants including Baskin Robins and Dunken Donuts, which are big sellers in North America.

Even within a limited field like alcoholic drinks, the range of apparently competing brands for which the company is responsible is staggering. In addition to the beers produced by the original Ind Coope group and Benskins in the South of England, Allied is responsible for Tetley Bitter, Ansells Bitter, John Bull Bitter, and Draught Burton Ale, all of which originated in the North of England or the Midlands but are increasingly being found in the South. Even if the Scottish brewers in the group—Dryburgh Brewery and Alloa Brewery Company—do not compete much with those further south, there is a wealth of lager brands from which to choose: Lowenbrau, Castlemaine XXXX, Skol, and Oranjeboom. If you want to encourage competition in the cider field, it's no good switching from Gaymer's Olde English to Whiteways: they're both made by Allied. Of course, you could ponder the situation while sipping a whisky: Allied won't mind whether you choose Ballantine's or Teacher's since they own both, while having a 50 per cent share in Grant's Steadfast and Glenfiddich whiskies. Switch to Hiram Walker, Irish Mist, or Laphroaig, and you are still drinking Allied. Try a Lamb's Navy Rum for a change, or Courvoisier brandy, or Kahlua and Tia Maria liqueurs, and you are still buying from Allied. You may prefer fortified wines like Harvey's sherries or Cockburn's ports; your sophisticated friends go for Tico mixer sherry; your less-sophisticated acquaintances for British wines like VP or Rougemont Castle: you are all drinking the products of Allied–Domecq PLC.

Of course, Allied is not the only multi-brand producer. Its main rivals, such as Guinness and Grand Metropolitan, also have a huge portfolio of brands. Guinness, for example, owns: Dimple, Black and White, Vat 69, Gordons, I.W. Harper, Rebel Yell, Tanqueray, Johnnie Walker, Old Parr, White Horse, Harp, Kaliber, Guinness, Hennessy, Moet and Chandon, Hine, Cossack Vodka, Pimm's, Booths, Haig, Dewar's, Bell's, Cardhu, Oban, Talisker, Glen Ord, Glen Elgin, Ushers, Canadian LTD, Mercier, Glenkinchie, and Lagavulin.

The production of such a wide range of differentiated products helps to satisfy consumers' clear demand for diversity. It also has the effect of making it more difficult for a new firm to enter the industry. If the new firm wishes to compete over the whole range of differentiated products it must enter on a massive scale. If it wishes to enter on only a small scale it faces a formidable task of establishing brand images and customer recognition with only a few products over which to spread these expenses of entry.

Note: At the time of writing, Allied was in the process of selling its Carlsberg–Tetley brewing interests to Bass. However, this deal was under investigation by the competition authorities, so it was not clear if it would be allowed to proceed.

one-sixteenth of the brand switchers, giving it less than 2 per cent of the total market the first year, with smaller gains also in subsequent years. This is an extreme case, but it illustrates a general result.

The larger the number of differentiated products that are sold by existing oligopolists, the smaller the market share available to a new firm that is entering with a single new product.

An example of brand proliferation drawn from the alcoholic drinks industry is given in Box 8.3. Similar examples can be found among soap powders, where there are two main producers (Unilever, and Proctor and Gamble) but many brands—Lux, Tide, Dreft, Persil, Ariel, Fairy, etc.—and in the cigarette industry where five firms share 99 per cent of the market, although each has several brands.

SET-UP COSTS

Existing firms can create entry barriers by imposing significant fixed costs on new firms that enter their market. This is particularly important if the industry has only weak natural barriers to entry because the minimum efficient scale occurs at an output that is low relative to the total output of the industry.

Advertising is one means by which existing firms can impose heavy set-up costs on new entrants. Advertising, of course, serves purposes other than that of creating barriers to entry. Among them, it performs the useful function of informing buyers about their alternatives, thereby making markets work more smoothly. Indeed, a new firm may find that advertising is essential, even when existing firms do not advertise at all, simply to call attention to its entry into an industry in which it is unknown.

None the less, advertising can also operate as a potent entry barrier by increasing the set-up costs of new entrants. Where heavy advertising has established strong brand images for existing products, a new firm may have to spend heavily on advertising to create its own brand images in consumers' minds. If the firm's sales are small, advertising costs *per unit sold* will be large, and price will have to be correspondingly high to cover those costs.

Figure 8.2 illustrates how heavy advertising can shift the cost curves of a firm with a low minimum efficient scale (*MES*) to make it one with a high *MES*. In essence, what happens is that a high *MES* of advertising is added to a low *MES* of production, with the result that the overall *MES* is raised.

A new entrant with small sales but large set-up costs finds itself at a substantial cost disadvantage relative to its established rivals.

Any once-and-for-all cost of entering a market has the same effect as a large initial advertising expenditure. For example, with many consumer goods, the cost of developing

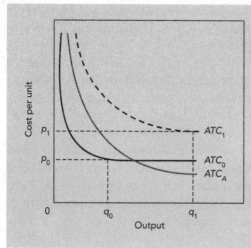

Figure 8.2. Advertising cost as a barrier to entry

Large advertising costs can increase the minimum efficient scale (*MES*) of production and thereby increase entry barriers. The ATC_0 curve shows that the *MES* without advertising is at q_0. The curve ATC_A shows that advertising cost per unit falls as output rises. Advertising increases total cost to ATC_1, which is downward sloping over its entire range. Advertising has given a scale advantage to large sellers and has thus created a barrier to entry.

a new product that is similar, but not identical, to existing products may be quite substantial. Even if there are few economies of scale in the *production* of the product, its large fixed *development cost* can lead to a falling long-run average total cost curve over a wide range of output.

AN APPLICATION

The combined use of brand proliferation and advertising as an entry barrier helps to explain one apparent paradox of everyday life—that one firm often sells multiple brands of the same product, which compete actively against one another as well as against the products of other firms.

The soap and cigarette industries provide classic examples of this behaviour. Because all available scale economies can be realized by quite small plants, both industries have few natural barriers to entry. Both contain a few large firms, each of which produces an array of heavily advertised products. The numerous existing products make it harder for a new entrant to obtain a large market niche with a single new product. The heavy advertising, although it is directed against existing products, creates an entry barrier by increasing the set-up costs of a new product that seeks to gain the attention of consumers and to establish its own brand image.

PREDATORY PRICING

A firm will not enter a market if it expects continued losses after entry. One way in which an existing firm can create such an expectation is to cut prices below costs whenever entry occurs and to keep them there until the entrant goes bankrupt. The existing firm sacrifices profits while doing this, but it sends a discouraging message to potential future rivals, as well as to present ones. Even if this strategy is costly in terms of lost profits in the short run, it may pay for itself in the long run by creating *reputation effects* that deter the entry of new firms at other times or in other markets that the firm controls.

Predatory pricing is controversial. Some economists argue that pricing policies that appear to be predatory can be explained by other motives and that existing firms only hurt themselves when they engage in such practices instead of accommodating new entrants. Others argue that predatory pricing has been observed and that it is in the long-run interests of existing firms to punish the occasional new entrant even when it is costly to do so in the short run. An example of predatory behaviour is reported in Box 9.2 on page 306.

CONTESTABLE MARKETS AND POTENTIAL ENTRY

The theory of contestable markets, developed by the US Professors Baumol, Panzar, and Willig, holds that markets do not have to contain many firms or to experience actual entry for profits to be held near the competitive level. *Potential* entry can do the job just as well as actual entry, as long as (1) entry can be easily accomplished and (2) existing firms take potential entry into account when making price and output decisions.

The theory

Entry is usually costly to the entering firm. It may have to build a plant, it may have to develop new versions of the industry's differentiated product, or it may have to advertise heavily in order to call attention to its product. These and many other initial expenses are often called *sunk costs of entry*. A sunk cost of entry is a cost that a firm must incur to enter the market and that cannot be recovered if the firm subsequently exits. For example, if an entering firm builds a product-specific factory that has no resale value, this is a sunk cost of entry. However, the cost of a factory that is not product-specific and that can be resold for an amount that is close to its original cost is not a sunk cost of entry.

A market in which new firms can enter and leave without incurring any sunk costs of entry is called a perfectly **contestable market.** A market can be perfectly contestable even if the firm must pay some costs of entry, as long as these can be recovered when the firm exits. Because all markets require at least some sunk costs of entry, contestability must be understood as a variable. The lower the sunk costs of entry, the more contestable the market.

> **In a contestable market, the existence of profits, even if they are the result of transitory causes, will attract entry. Firms will enter to gain a share of these profits and will exit when the transitory situation has changed.**

Consider, for example, the market for air travel on the lucrative London–Frankfurt route. This market would be quite contestable if it were not regulated, as are all air routes in the EU[3]—and as long as counter and loading space were available to new entrants at the two cities' airline terminals. An airline that was not currently serving the cities in question could shift some of its existing planes to the market with small sunk costs of entry. Some training of personnel would be needed for them to become familiar with the route and the airport. This is a sunk cost of entry that cannot be recovered if the cities in question are no longer to be served. However, most of the airline's costs are not sunk costs of entry. If it subsequently decides to leave a city, the rental of terminal space will stop, and the aeroplanes and the ground equipment can be shifted to another location. The former head of the American Civil Aeronautics Board, and architect of airline deregulation, captured this point by referring to commercial aircraft as 'marginal cost with wings'.

Sunk costs of entry constitute a barrier to entry, and the larger these are, the larger the profits of existing firms can be without attracting new entrants. The flip side of this coin is that firms operating in markets without large sunk costs of entry will not earn large profits. Strategic considerations will lead them to keep prices near the level that would just cover their total costs. They know that if they charge higher prices, firms will enter to capture the profits while they last and then exit.

Contestability, where it is possible, is a force that can limit the profits of existing oligopolists. Even if entry does not occur, the ease with which it can be accomplished may keep existing oligopolists from charging prices that would maximize their joint profits.

Contestability is just another example, in somewhat more refined form, of the key point that the possibility of entry is the major force preventing the exploitation of market power to restrict output and to raise prices.

Empirical relevance

Most economists take the view that, although contestable markets are an elegant extension of competitive markets in theory, there are at least *some* barriers to entry in almost all real markets—and very large barriers in many markets. Setting up an effective organization to produce or to sell almost anything incurs fixed costs. In the case of airlines, for instance, a new entrant at a given airport must hire and train staff, advertise extensively to let customers know that it is in the market, set up baggage-handling facilities, and overcome whatever loyalties customers have to the pre-existing firms. New firms in almost all industries face entry costs that are analogous to these. Entering a manufacturing industry usually requires a large investment in industry-specific, and sometimes product-specific, plants and equipment.

These considerations suggest that contestability, in practice, is something to be

---

[3] This statement was true up to 1997, though liberalization was planned.

measured, rather than simply asserted. The higher the costs of entry, the less contestable is the market, and the higher the profits that existing firms can earn without inducing entry. Current evidence suggests that, in practice, a high degree of contestability is quite rare in purely domestic markets. However, the threat of potential entry may come from existing foreign firms rather than new domestic ones. They may have lower set-up costs.

Oligopoly and the functioning of the economy

Oligopoly is found in many industries and in all advanced economies. It typically occurs in industries where both perfect and monopolistic competition are made impossible by the existence of major economies of scale or scope (or both). In such industries, there is simply not enough room for a large number of firms all operating at or near their minimum efficient scales. Oligopoly also arises in industries where there are no obvious scale economies but where heavy brand advertising has created a group of dominant products produced by a small number of firms—obvious examples are cigarettes, soap powder, and soft drinks.

Three questions are important for the evaluation of the performance of the oligopolistic market structure. First, do oligopolistic markets allocate resources very differently from perfectly competitive markets? Second, in their short- and long-run price–output behaviour, where do oligopolistic firms typically settle between the extreme outcomes of earning zero profits and earning the profits that would be available to a single monopolist? Third, how much do oligopolists contribute to economic growth by encouraging innovative activity in the very long run? We consider each question in turn.

THE MARKET MECHANISM UNDER OLIGOPOLY

We have seen that under perfect competition, prices are set by the impersonal forces of demand and supply, whereas firms in oligopolistic markets administer their prices. The market signalling system works slightly differently when prices are administered rather than being determined by the market. Changes in the market conditions for both inputs and outputs are signalled to the perfectly competitive firm by changes in the prices of its inputs and its outputs. Changes in the market conditions for inputs are signalled to oligopolistic firms by changes in the prices of their inputs. Changes in the market conditions for the oligopolist's output are typically signalled, however, by changes in the volume of sales at administered prices.

Increases in costs of inputs will shift cost curves upward, and oligopolistic firms will be led to raise prices and lower outputs. Increases in demand will cause the sales of oligopolistic firms to rise. Firms will then respond by increasing output, thereby increasing the quantities of society's resources that are allocated to producing that output. They will then decide whether or not to alter their administered prices.

The market system reallocates resources in response to changes in demands and costs in roughly the same way under oligopoly as it does under perfect competition.

From the perspective of the firm's managers, of course, there are important differences between a perfectly competitive market and oligopoly. In the former, managers can only choose output but not price, while the only way to increase profits is to reduce costs. Under oligopoly, a much wider array of considerations enter, including all the issues of strategy discussed above. In particular, development and marketing of the product itself has to be a central concern.

PROFITS UNDER OLIGOPOLY

Some firms in some oligopolistic industries succeed in coming close to joint profit maximization in the short run. In other oligopolistic industries, firms compete so intensely among themselves that they come close to achieving competitive prices and outputs.

In the long run, those profits that do survive competitive behaviour among existing firms will tend to attract entry. These profits will persist only in so far as entry is restricted either by natural barriers, such as large minimum efficient scales for potential entrants, or by barriers created, and successfully defended, by the existing firms.

VERY-LONG-RUN COMPETITION

Once we allow for the effects of technological change, we need to ask which market structure is most conducive to the sorts of very-long-run changes that we discussed in Chapter 5. These are the driving force of the economic growth that has so greatly raised living standards over the last two centuries. They are intimately related to Schumpeter's concept of creative destruction, which we first encountered in our discussion of entry barriers in Chapter 7 (on pages 226–7).

Examples of creative destruction abound. In the nineteenth century, railways began to compete with wagons and barges for the carriage of freight. In the twentieth century, lorries operating on newly constructed trunk roads, and later motorways, began competing with rail. During the 1950s and 1960s, aeroplanes began to compete seriously with lorries, rail, and ships.

In recent years the development of facsimile transmission and electronic mail eliminated the monopoly of the Post Office in delivering hard-copy (as opposed to oral) communications. In their myriad uses, microcomputers for the home and the office swept away the markets of many once-thriving products and services. For instance, in-store computers answer customer questions, decreasing the need for salespeople. Aided by computers, 'just in time' inventory systems greatly reduce the investment in inventories required of existing firms and new entrants alike. Computer-based flexible manufacturing systems allow firms to switch production easily and inexpensively from one product line to another, thereby reducing the minimum scale at which each can be produced profitably. One day computers may even displace the college textbook, and laser discs may replace the lecture.

An important defence of oligopoly relates to this process of creative destruction. Some economists have adopted Schumpeter's concept of creative destruction to develop theories that intermediate market structures, such as oligopoly, lead to more innovation than would occur in either perfect competition or monopoly. They argue that the oligopolist faces strong competition from existing rivals and cannot afford the more relaxed life of the monopolist. At the same time, however, oligopolistic firms expect to keep a good share of the profits that they earn from their innovative activity.

Everyday observation, and some economic research, provides some confirmation of this finding. Leading North American firms that operate in highly concentrated industries, such as Kodak, Boeing, IBM, Du Pont, Xerox, General Electric, 3M, and Microsoft, have been highly innovative over many years. UK examples include Rolls Royce, Glaxo Wellcome, and GEC.

Oligopoly is an important market structure in modern economies because there are many industries in which the minimum efficient scale is simply too large to support many competing firms. The challenge to public policy is to keep oligopolists competing, rather than colluding, and using their competitive energies to improve products and to lower costs, rather than merely to erect entry barriers. We shall discuss the public-policy issues involved in the next chapter. For the remainder of this chapter we apply the above concepts to two case studies.

Oligopoly in action: two case studies

We now look at two real-world examples of markets in which there is an oligopolistic structure, and, thus, where strategic behaviour is important. The examples chosen are the market for cross-Channel journeys and the newspaper market in the UK. Both of these have been encountered before in this book, and it is worth re-reading pages 72–7 and 109–13. Our earlier analysis of these markets was intended to illustrate the use of demand and supply curves, but was really only appropriate for focusing on demand, since there is no unique supply curve in imperfectly competitive markets. Here we are centrally concerned with the strategic supply (price and output) decisions taken by the main suppliers.

One important caveat to bear in mind in approaching these two cases is that, because they are both real live markets, many things will have happened since this book went to press. This means that readers can add new information to the analysis that was not available at the time of writing. However, the key question to focus on in interpreting any new information, as well as the story so far, is: can we understand the choices of the producers in the market from the perspective of the analysis of strategy set out above?

The central message of these two case studies appears to be that the newspaper market, after a period of tacit collusion (up to September 1993) entered a damaging period of aggressive competition (non-cooperative) that took the industry very close to a non-cooperative equilibrium. At the time of writing it seemed locked into that non-cooperative equilibrium with no obvious way out. In contrast, a similar price war in the cross-Channel travel market had prospects of ending, since the main operators found profits collapsing and some of the main players sought a co-operative solution.

The UK national newspaper market

In Chapter 3 above, we used the price cut by *The Times* in September 1993 to illustrate the concept of elasticity of demand. We could do this because, for some time, no other newspapers reacted. A reaction did come in June 1994, when the *Telegraph* and *Independent* cut their prices and *The Times* made further price cuts. A longer-term view of the aggressive competition is reported in the article reprinted as Exhibit 8.1 (pp. 270–1). This discusses not just the market for the broadsheet newspapers but also the tabloids and the Sunday papers. This exhibit should be read before proceeding further.

We shall concentrate our discussion on the market for weekday newspapers, since most of the same issues apply to the Sundays. Also, the same firms are involved in producing Sunday papers as the dailies. There appear to be three segments[4] to the daily market: the mass-market tabloids (*Sun, Mirror,* and *Star*); the mid-market tabloids (*Mail* and *Express* plus *Today,* which went bust in 1995); and the broadsheets (*The Times, Telegraph, Guardian, Independent,* and *Financial Times*). Notice, however, that each newspaper is not run by an independent firm; for example, Rupert Murdoch's company News International owns *The Times* and the *Sun,* while the Mirror Group owns the *Mirror* and took over the *Independent* in 1995. Notice also that it was the papers owned by News International that initiated the price war in 1993, with price cuts for the *Sun* and *The Times.*

An obvious problem that all newspaper publishers have to live with is that the overall market for newspapers is static. There was virtually no increase in overall newspaper sales as a result of the price cuts in 1993 and 1994. Indeed, the total sales per day in June 1996 were only one-third of one per cent higher than in June 1991. This means that, for one paper to sell more, some other paper has to sell less. Within the three market segments there are obviously some close rivalries between specific titles—the *Sun* competes with the *Mirror* and the *Star;* the *Mail* competes with the *Express;* and *The Times* competes with the *Independent* and, to a lesser extent, with the *Guardian* and the

---

[4] Notice that 'segment' here implies a quality difference, rather than some artificial segmentation of the market, such as was discussed in Chapter 7. The segmentation here is associated with vertical differentiation.

Telegraph. Clearly, the winners from these head-to-head conflicts (at least in terms of sales up to 1996) have been the *Sun,* the *Mail,* and *The Times.*

DEMAND ELASTICITY

It is evident from what we just said above that the overall demand for newspapers has a price elasticity of demand close to zero; that is, it is almost perfectly inelastic. The *relative* price of newspapers was probably about 30 per cent lower in 1996 than in 1991, and yet total sales had increased hardly at all. In Chapter 3 we reported that the demand for *The Times* was inelastic. This was because a price reduction of 33 per cent led to a sales increase of only 19 per cent. However, this was only the short-term response. By 1996, the sales of *The Times* had increased by nearly 100 per cent. This suggests that, in the long run, demand for *The Times* is highly elastic. Indeed, in crude terms, the long run demand elasticity looks to be about −3, while the short run demand elasticity was calculated at −0.57.

In reality, we should be cautious about the precise size of the long-run demand elasticity because other prices have not remained constant, and there have also been quality changes in *The Times* itself, as well as other promotions and advertising—so we have not been holding *other things equal.* However, the fact that other newspapers have cut their prices as well means that we cannot be sure whether we are overestimating or underestimating the long-run demand elasticity. Irrespective of what the true number is, we would have to conclude that the aggressive price cutting by *The Times* looks like a more sensible decision in the longer term than it did from a short-term perspective. The long-run demand elasticity is clearly much higher than the short-run elasticity.

NON-COOPERATIVE EQUILIBRIUM

The problem for *all the newspapers* in 1996 was that the effect of the price war initiated by News International has been virtually to eliminate profit from the entire industry. Indeed, several of the existing titles were losing money. Several had had to lower their prices and lost sales as compared to the pre-1993 situation. For them, the options were few, though it is clear what they would like to happen.

All the newspapers would be jointly better off if they could agree that all would raise their prices. However, any one attempting to do this unilaterally would lose market share and end up even worse off. The alternative strategy would be to be even more aggressive in price cutting. However, a paper that was already in bad financial shape (such as the *Independent*) could not risk such a strategy, because *The Times* would probably follow its price cut, and so losses would mount even higher in the short term.

Thus, in late-1996, the newspaper market seemed to be locked in a non-cooperative equilibrium such that profit margins were thin, or non-existent, and prices were probably close to their perfect-competition level. No one publisher could move the industry

EXHIBIT 8.1.

The market for UK national newspapers*

The fiercest price war in the history of Fleet Street was launched three years ago this month when News International cut the price of The Sun by 5p to 20p. It was a dramatic marketing tactic aimed at reversing years of declining sales of national newspapers and was followed, two months later, by a cut in the price of The Times by 15p to 30p. Within a year almost every newspaper had joined in.

Now, three years on, some newspaper commentators are asking if the tactic really worked and suggesting that millions of pounds have been thrown away in lost profits, advertising on television and ever more desperate reader promotions —all to achieve an overall increase in sales of national daily newspapers of just 38,000 a day.

Even though that 38,000 is at least up instead of down, they have a point. Sales in June were even more depressing for the Editors of the Express and Independent titles than three years ago. Nor was there any real comfort for the Mirror Group titles (apart from The People) or the new Editors of The Observer.

Adding to the grief, all the daily and Sunday tabloids sold fewer copies last month than in January. Month on month, sales of the daily tabloids were down by 157,750 (in spite of Euro 96) and year on year by 76,700. Since January, only five of the 19 national newspapers, all broadsheets, have increased sales.

So, yes, newspaper sales remain in seemingly inexorable decline, despite the price war. Yet the overall trend conceals significant successes which show that even the Editors and owners of the Express or Independent titles should not despair. Victory can still be snatched from the jaws of defeat.

Until the early 1970s, the Daily Mirror was the undisputed—if complacent—king of the mass-market. Once The Sun was bought by Rupert Murdoch and edited by

Larry Lamb, it captured the mood of the times and quickly overtook the Daily Mail. It has remained ahead ever since.

Yet three years ago, sales were beginning to slip. They were down from more than 4 million in the late 1980s to 3.4 million by June 1993. A

Success and failure in Fleet Street, 1991–1996

	1996	+/- on January	+/- June 95	+/- June 91
Sun	3,970,155	−158,330	−16,875	+335,335
Mirror	2,408,455	−151,597	−194,110	−503,447
Star	667,453	−105,764	−58,782	−188,011
Mail	2,038,039	−27,946	+264,786	+335,917
Express	1,219,591	−46,376	−38,160	−340,649
Telegraph	1,054,314	+1,168	−18,121	+2,242
Times	724,839	+36,847	+42,420	+332,321
Guardian	391,062	−17,124	−714	−22,007
Independent	272,928	−19,481	−30,345	−104,334
F.T.	300,889	+5,777	+6,788	
N.O.W.	4,585,807	−131,949	−96,166	−194,293
S. Mirror	2,412,005	−104,108	−215,511	−360,455
People	2,036,302	−58,503	+1,154	−241,484
M.O.S.	2,045,139	−89,806	+80,048	+152,929
S. Express	1,202,354	−84,429	−164,478	−436,163
S. Times	1,296,678	+442	+28,720	+158,405
Observer	443,348	−6,181	−8,193	−126,536
S. Telegraph	683,819	+4,867	−22,030	+128,536
Independent/S	294,923	−14,191	−39,917	−72,802

Source: ABC.

year later, sales were back at 4.1 million and slipped only marginally below 4 million last month for the first time this year. When *The Sun* cut its price, its lead over the *Daily Mirror* was 825,000 a day. Three years later it is 1.5 million a day. On a five-year trend (see table), the *Daily Mirror* has dropped by 500,000 as *The Sun* has risen by 335,000.

The same story has occurred in the middle market, where the *Daily Express* and *Sunday Express*, once the undisputed market leaders, have been overtaken by the *Daily Mail* and *Mail on Sunday*. Over the past five years, the *Daily Mail* is up by 335,000, against a fall of 340,000 for the *Daily Express*. On Sundays, the

Mail is up by 152,000. Meanwhile the *Sunday Express* has plummeted by 436,000 and now sells fewer copies than *The Sunday Times*.

Yet the biggest success story has been *The Times*, which established a new record sale last month—obviously helped by selling at 10p on Mondays for the summer of sport—of 724,839. That meant that sales have now doubled since 1993, repeating the success of *The Daily Telegraph* when it cut its price from twopence to a penny in 1930. Three years ago *The Times* lagged 650,000 behind *The Daily Telegraph*. The gap has now narrowed to 330,000.

It is easy to buy quick circulation fixes in Fleet Street. A serialisation of a sensational book, advertised on

television on a Sunday night, always boosts sales—which quickly fall back once the serial is over. What has been remarkable about *The Times* since 1993 is that readers who were tempted to buy the paper at a cheaper price have obviously enjoyed what they read—a paper radically reorganised four years ago to be more reader-friendly—and carried on buying it. New readers who buy the 10p *Times* on Monday buy the 30p *Times* the rest of the week.

Successful newspapers always have editors with flair and courage and/or owners who love newspapers. That is as true of *The Guardian* or *The Daily Telegraph* and the *Sunday Telegraph*, which

have also been successes in the past five years, as it is of *The Sun*, the *Daily Mail* (which did not cut its price) or *The Times*. Yet editors with flair and courage do not always run successful newspapers. Sometimes their papers are stuck with the wrong image. Sometimes their owners fail to broadcast their merits or to support them through difficult times. There has been no more successful a tactic in helping those editors in this generation than the price war.

* This exhibit reproduces the text of Brian MacArthur, 'Fleet Street sells a cut-price success story', *The Times* 17 July 1996, p. 23. © Times Newspapers Ltd, 1996. Reprinted by permission.

out of this situation on its own, and yet all would certainly prefer a high-price industry in which significant profits could be made. The non-cooperative situation is a Nash equilibrium. Each is doing the best it can given the behaviour of the others.

What could happen to shift the industry away from this non-cooperative equilibrium towards a co-operative solution? The two main possibilities are closure of some titles and mergers or takeovers that increase the power of remaining groups. The latter would be likely to be blocked by the government as creating excessive concentration. However, the demise of, say, the *Independent* is not at all unlikely. If each of the three segments of the market were to become *de facto* duopolies, the remaining publishers might well decide that an all-round price rise was justified, and they could settle down to make money in a less competitive environment.

Of course, once such a co-operative equilibrium were established there would always be a temptation by one of the players to grab market share by aggressive price cutting again, especially in this market, where News International has proved that such a strategy can work, at least in the sense of hurting itself less than its rivals. We would need more information than is currently available to reveal if News International's strategy was one that maximized its own profit. We know for sure that it reduced the joint profits of the newspaper industry.

The market for cross-Channel travel

In Chapter 2 we discussed the impact on the market for cross-Channel journeys of the opening of the Channel Tunnel. We predicted that existing providers would face both a decline in demand and a fall in price—a shift in demand for non-tunnel carriers and a movement down the overall demand curve for journeys. In what follows, we concentrate on the behaviour of the ferries and ignore the impact on the airlines, since the latter were less affected overall by the opening of the tunnel.

It was clear from the evidence reported in Chapter 2 that our analysis was substantially correct. The summer of 1996, which was the first summer of full-scale operation of the tunnel, witnessed an unprecedented price war. The ferry operators appear to have been especially hard hit by this, since they faced both lower volumes and lower prices. Their initial response was to compete aggressively, with low prices and many special promotions. However, by July 1996, it seemed that the ferry operators had admitted that they could not win in a direct price war with the tunnel. The latter had high sunk costs but low marginal costs, while the ferries were in danger of not being able to cover short-run variable costs even in the peak summer months.

Once built, the tunnel could not be moved, and, even if Eurotunnel went bust, the tunnel would still be operated at any prices that more than covered variable costs. A price war with Eurotunnel is one that the ferries could never win. Hence, the ferry operators could only hurt themselves by further pursuit of a non-cooperative strategy. They could not drive the tunnel out of business, but they could drive themselves into bankruptcy. The article presented as Exhibit 8.2 outlines some of the key data in this market, and what follows will assume a reading of that article.

The significant event reported in Exhibit 8.2 that signals a change in strategy by the ferry operators is that P&O had clearly realized that the only way out for it was to seek a co-operative solution. Before the tunnel existed, explicit co-operation between P&O and Stena Sealink, the other main operator, was forbidden by the government. However, in July 1996, P&O was given permission for explicit approaches to other ferry operators to seek either merger of operations or some other form of co-operation.

The goal of P&O was undoubtedly to negotiate a reduction of capacity and thus a rise in price for future years. The tunnel operators would clearly be happy if this happened, and each of the ferry operators would be happier with a co-operative solution than with continued cut-throat competition. The losers from such co-operation would be the consumers, who had benefited from extremely cheap travel and a cross-Channel market that, at least temporarily, approached perfect-competition prices even though there were only a handful of providers.

Given that the ferry operators sought co-operation, there are only three obvious reasons why this might not happen. One is that the government may object to any agreement reached on the grounds that it unfairly restricts competition, even though the government initially gave permission to search for a co-operative solution. Second, if existing operators succeed in raising prices and restricting capacity, one operator may choose to renege on the agreement and cut prices. Third, a new operator may enter the market attracted by the profits that are being made after the co-operative solution has been implemented. The latter scenario seems a long way off, since the next few years are likely to witness significant capacity reductions among existing operators rather than the reverse.

At the time of writing it is far from certain that the co-operative solution will be reached. Indeed, in November 1996, the Secretary of State for Trade and Industry, Ian Lang, referred the merger of ferry operation between P&O and Stena to the Monopolies and Mergers Commission. However, if this co-operative solution is ruled out, at least one of the existing ferry operators may be forced by financial distress to close down capacity. Clearly, each would prefer others to do this first, but the loser in this game of chicken might be the one with the least capital to draw on, and the decision to cease trading could be forced by its bankers rather than by strategy.

Strategic interaction

The two examples developed above make clear that strategic issues can be very important in markets in which there are a few main players. They also make clear that the issues involved can be understood with the help of the game-theoretic framework outlined in this chapter. Indeed, this framework is of more than just academic use for those who want to write case studies in textbooks. It is also helpful for the managers of

EXHIBIT 8.2.

Competition in cross-Channel journeys*

Holidaymakers: this year could be your last cross-Channel summer bonanza. Enjoy it while it lasts.

Ferry leader P&O has effectively ceded defeat in the price war with the Channel Tunnel. The Government last week granted its request to seek co-operation with its seafaring rivals in the Straits of Dover.

That is a recipe for fewer ships and, both on and under the Channel, higher fares.

This summer's unprecedented price war in the Dover/Folkestone to Calais market, which currently sees a family of four with a car buying peak-day returns of £40 and standard returns of £129—by ferry or tunnel—will be the last.

P&O is expected to suggest to its arch-rival Stena Line in the autumn that they collaborate on Channel crossings—which could be anything from joint pricing and sailing to a merging of assets.

The Office of Fair Trading will scrutinise any plans, as will competition authorities in Brussels. But P&O is confident the signals it has been getting from the Department of Trade and Industry indicate it is prepared to consider anything from a merger downwards.

By next summer, the current 11 P&O and Stena ships competing between Dover and Calais could be replaced by six P&O–Stena ferries running joint operations, sales, marketing and pricing. They will have 50 per cent of the cross-Channel drive-on market, compared with Eurotunnel's 40 per cent, with the remainder shared between hovercraft operator Hoverspeed and state-owned Sea France.

Hundreds of ferry jobs are at risk. P&O European Ferries employs 3,000 and Stena 4,500 in the UK.

Mike Stoddart, transport analyst at stockbroker Charterhouse Tilney, said: 'If there is less capacity then that is the end of good deals.

'The ferries are making very good returns, they just want to make more. They have become used to making fantastic profits in the past.'

This is the fifth time in the last 20 years that the Government has been asked to approve either a limited form of co-operation on the fiercely competitive Dover–Calais market or a takeover of Stena by P&O.

P&O and Stena approached the Government jointly in 1993 asking for the ban on collaboration between them and Hoverspeed to be lifted. Each time, on advice from the Monopolies and Mergers Commission, it refused.

The Channel Tunnel is now running its second summer of car-carrying Le Shuttle services between Folkestone and Calais. Passenger and freight traffic has grown but, apart from the peak summer months, there is over-capacity both on and under the water and fares have dropped by 20 per cent on average in the last two years.

All parties claim to be hurting financially, while travellers enjoy value for money.

A source close to one of the operators said: 'The consumer has benefited enormously from the increased Channel competition, but operators are not making a sensible cash return. People are not making the money that is required for future capital investment.

'We are not a charity. We have no interest in ripping off consumers, but we have to make a decent return.'

Capacity to Calais has more than doubled since the tunnel began full operations in 1995. In 1994 there were 20,000 'passenger car units' per day available on the ferries. In 1996 this figure has risen to around 47,000 units, with P&O, Stena, Hoverspeed and Sea France accounting for 30,000 units and the tunnel 17,000, according to stockbrokers Charterhouse Tilney.

When the tunnel opened, the ferry companies were expected to ask the Government to be allowed to pool. They decided instead to go head to head, adding ships. And Stena broke from a pooling agreement it had previously had with SNAT, the predecessor of Sea France.

Ten ferries plied the Dover Strait in 1994. Now there are 13. Stena is replacing one of its vessels next month with the largest ferry ever to sail in this market—capable of carrying 550 cars and 2,300 passengers.

Traffic has grown as well, as travellers have responded to falling fares, the introduction of fast, luxury £50m ferries and the novelty of Le Shuttle's 25-minute tunnel journey.

There have always been 'fares wars' across the Channel, with brochures being reprinted seven or eight times a season and special offers, most eye-catchingly the £1 winter booze cruises, on almost a monthly basis. But the current £129 period return is unheard of.

P&O and Stena do not separate out Dover's contribution to overall ferry profits, but it is substantial—up to 95 per cent in P&O's case, City analysts estimate.

P&O European Ferries' £114m pre-tax profits in 1994 dived to £74.8m last year and are forecast at around £30m for 1996. The P&O Group and its chairman Lord Sterling are under severe pressure in the City for the lacklustre share performance of the last year.

One analyst wondered why P&O had gone back to ask the Government to lift the pooling ban now, when it has been promising shareholders the worst would be over this year.

But this may be the last Tory summer for the foreseeable future and Sterling has always been a Conservative acolyte (and P&O a generous Tory Party benefactor). It was probably felt best to get a request in under the wire.

Meanwhile, Stena Line's total pre-tax ferry profits, including Irish Sea and all Channel services, were only £20m in 1995. The Swedish company has already warned profits will not rise this year, as previously forecast. It said last year that it wanted to operate independently. But now Sterling has acted. Stena has indicated it will listen with interest to whatever he might propose.

Eurotunnel cannot be averse to a virtual duopoly between it and one ferry operation. It is covering operating costs, calculated at around £250m per year, but carrying almost £9bn of debt, with specially postponed interest payments on the debt rolling up at the rate of £2m a day.

It is hoping to agree an outline plan with its leading banks by the end of this month for a massive restructuring of this crippling debt.

If less capacity in the overall market means higher fares, then whoever succeeds Sir Alastair Morton as co-chairman of Eurotunnel will surely not weep. Andrew Fitchie, SBC Warburg analyst, said: 'It is not surprising that the ferries want to cooperate. We need a financially viable ferry industry to compete with the tunnel, which is not going away.

'You cannot have a continuation of what is happening at the moment. Consumers are getting a good deal, but the companies cannot get a sufficient return to invest in the business in the longer term.'

In other words, we've never had it so good.

Channel hopping

- *Traffic across the Channel*

1994	3.22 million passenger cars through Dover	
1995	2.9 million passenger cars by ferry	
	1.22 million passenger cars by tunnel	

- *Capacity in the Strait of Dover (sea and tunnel)*

1994 (pre tunnel)	20,000 passenger car units a day
1996 (post tunnel)	47,000 passenger car units a day

- *The bottom line: Pre-tax profit £m*

	P&O	Stena Line
1994	114	48
1995	74.8	20
1996	30 (estimate)	20 (estimate)

* This exhibit reproduces the text of Joanna Walters, 'Setting sail for happier returns', *Observer* 21 July 1996, p. 2 of Business section.© The Observer, 1996. Reprinted by permission.

businesses themselves in setting out explicitly the choices that they face so that rational decisions can be taken with the maximum of information available. As the newspaper example illustrates, the firm that takes the initiative often has the upper hand, and, as the Channel Tunnel example illustrates, don't play a game you can't win.

Summary

1. Firms in market structures other than perfect competition face negatively sloped demand curves. They must administer their prices and are typically involved in product development.

2. Oligopolistic markets involve strategic interaction between a few major producers. The choices involved in this interaction can be analysed using game theory.

3. Competitive behaviour among oligopolists may lead to a non-cooperative equilibrium that is self-policing in the sense that no one has an incentive to depart from it unilaterally. The prisoner's dilemma example of game theory is a case in point.

4. Oligopolistic profits can persist only if there are entry barriers. Natural barriers include economies of large-scale production and large fixed costs of entering the market. Artificial barriers include brand proliferation and high levels of advertising.

5. In qualitative terms the workings of the allocative system under oligopoly are similar (but not identical) to what they are under perfect competition. Whether oligopoly or perfect competition is more conducive to long-run growth of productivity is an open question.

6. The newspaper market illustrates a case in which the industry has arrived at a non-cooperative (Nash) equilibrium, while the cross-Channel ferries seem to be seeking a co-operative solution.

Topics for review

- Price takers and price setters
- Analysis of strategic interaction using game theory
- The co-operative solution and the non-cooperative equilibrium
- Entry barriers
- Resource allocation under oligopoly

Questions for discussion

1. What are the key differences between perfect and imperfect markets that enable firms in the latter to set their own prices?

2. What kinds of factor would influence firms in imperfect markets to change their prices?

3. Discuss the entry barriers that exist in the following markets: retail banking, supermarkets, electricity distribution, soft drinks, clothing, car manufacture, aero engines.

4. In what ways does advertising create an entry barrier?

5. What role might technical innovation play in the strategy of an oligopolist?

6. Can you think of industries, other than those mentioned in the text, where a few large firms have many different brands? Draw up a list of the main firms in one of your chosen industries and list their brands.

7. 'Creative destruction can work without the entry of new firms; new products developed by existing firms will do just as well.' Explain the reasoning behind this quotation and say whether you agree or disagree.

CHAPTER 9

Government and the Market

Economic efficiency	279	Social obligations	295
Productive efficiency	280		
Allocative efficiency	282	**Public policy towards monopoly and**	
Efficiency and inefficiency in perfect		**competition**	296
competition and monopoly	285	Direct control of natural monopolies	297
Perfect competition	285	Short-run price and output	298
Productive efficiency	285	Marginal cost pricing	298
Allocative efficiency	285	Average cost pricing	298
Monopoly	286	Long-run investment policies	300
Productive efficiency	286	The very long run	300
Allocative efficiency	286	Direct control of oligopolies	301
Efficiency in other market structures	286	Scepticism about direct control	301
		Deregulation and privatization	302
The case for government involvement in		Intervention to keep firms competing	303
markets	288	UK policies	304
Failure to achieve efficiency	288	Restrictive practices	304
Monopoly power	288	Mergers	305
Externalities	289		
Private and social costs	289	**Summary**	308
Common property resources	290		
Public goods	291	**Topics for review**	309
Asymmetric information	292		
Principal–agent problem	293	**Questions for discussion**	310
Failure to achieve other social goals	293		
Income distribution	294	**Box 9.1.** Three concepts of productive	
Protecting individuals from others	295	efficiency	283
Paternalism	295	**Box 9.2.** The MMC in action	306

I N the previous chapters we have studied aspects of the behaviour of firms and consumers. We now discuss the role of the third major agent in the economy, the government. Here we are only concerned with the role of government in specific markets. Part II of this book focuses on the role of government in stabilizing the economy as a whole. Thus, questions like 'Can the government reduce unemployment?' and 'Can the government affect the business cycle?' are dealt with in later chapters. Here our concern is to ask: can the government improve the working of the market mechanism in individual markets?

In the last two decades, there has been a trend towards reducing the role of government in the market economy. The extreme forms of command economies of Eastern Europe collapsed in the late 1980s and were replaced by somewhat more market-oriented economies. Even in the old industrial economies, such as the UK, there have been significant reductions in the direct role of the government. This has been most visible in the form of substantial privatization of formerly state-owned industries.

Some argue that free markets should be left alone to determine the allocation of resources. It is important to understand, however, that this position does not follow from the study of economics. Hence, the purpose of this chapter is to outline the reasons why the market mechanism does not always deliver an optimal outcome. These reasons are collectively described as *market failures*.

Market failures provide a potential case for government intervention. We say 'potential' case because the mere existence of market failure does not prove that government intervention will improve the situation. Government intervention can introduce new distortions, as well as correcting existing ones. Hence, while some ideologues take the view that all government intervention is bad, a safer position is that markets cannot always be relied upon to deliver an optimal outcome. Government intervention can sometimes improve upon market outcomes, but whether or not it does so in practice will vary from case to case.

In what follows, we first focus on the important issue of economic efficiency. This is important because market failure can only be identified relative to some definition of what an efficient outcome would be. We then discuss the main sources of market failure before focusing in more detail on the most important form of government intervention from the perspective of private business, that designed to encourage competition.

Economic efficiency

Economic efficiency requires avoiding any waste of resources. When labour is unemployed and factories lie idle (as occurs in serious recessions), their potential output is lost. If these resources were employed, total output would be increased and hence everyone could be made better off. However, full employment of resources by itself is not enough to prevent the waste of resources. Even when resources are being fully used, they may be used inefficiently. Let us look at three examples of inefficiency in the use of fully employed resources.

1. If firms do not use the least costly method of producing their chosen outputs, they waste resources. For example, a firm that produces 30,000 pairs of shoes at a resource cost of £400,000 when it could have been done at a cost of only £350,000 is using resources inefficiently. The lower-cost method would allow £50,000 worth of resources to be transferred to other productive uses.

2. If, within an industry, the cost of producing its last unit of output is higher for some firms than for others, the industry's overall cost of producing its output is higher than necessary.

3. If too much of one product and too little of another product are produced, resources are being used inefficiently. To take an extreme example, suppose that so many shoes are produced that every consumer has all the shoes he or she could possibly want and so places a zero value on obtaining an additional pair of shoes. Further assume that fewer coats are produced relative to demand, so that each consumer places a positive value on obtaining an additional coat. In these circumstances, each consumer can be made better off if resources are reallocated from shoe production, where the last shoe produced has a low value in the eyes of each consumer, to coat production, where one more coat produced would have a higher value to each consumer.

These examples suggest that we must refine our ideas of the waste of resources beyond the simple notion of ensuring that all resources are employed. The sources of inefficiency just outlined suggest important conditions that must be fulfilled if economic efficiency is to be attained. These conditions are conveniently collected into two categories, called *productive efficiency* and *allocative efficiency*, which were studied long ago by the Italian economist Vilfredo Pareto (1848–1923). Indeed, efficiency in the use of resources is often called Pareto-optimality or Pareto-efficiency in his honour.

PRODUCTIVE EFFICIENCY

Productive efficiency refers to the efficient production of any bundle of products that is being produced. It occurs when it is *impossible* to reallocate resources so as to produce more of some product *without* producing less of some other product. Watch the double negative! An allocation of resources is productively *inefficient* when it is *possible* to produce more of some product without producing less of any other product, and *efficient* when this cannot be done, in other words, when the only way to produce more of one product is to produce less of some other product.

Productive efficiency has two aspects, one concerning production within each firm, and one concerning the allocation of production among the firms in an industry. The first condition for productive efficiency is that each firm should produce any given output at the lowest possible cost. In the short run, with only one variable factor, the firm has no problem of choice of technique: it merely uses enough of the variable input to produce the desired level of output. In the long run, however, more than one method of production is available. Productive efficiency requires that the firm use the least costly of the available methods of producing any given output. This means that firms will be located on, rather than above, their long-run average cost curves.

In Chapter 5 we studied the condition for productive efficiency within the firm.

Productive efficiency requires that each firm produce its given output by combining inputs in such a way that the ratio of the marginal products of each pair of inputs is made equal to the ratio of their prices.

This is the same thing as saying that an extra £1 spent on increments of each of several inputs should yield the same output. If this is not so, the firm can reduce the costs of producing its given output by altering the inputs it uses. It should substitute the input for which an extra £1 of expenditure yields the higher increment of output for the input for which an extra £1 of expenditure yields the lower increment of output.

Any firm that is not being productively efficient is producing at a higher cost than is necessary. This must reduce its profits. It follows that any profit-maximizing firm will normally seek to be productively efficient no matter which market structure—perfect competition, monopoly, oligopoly, or monopolistic competition—it operates within.

There is a second condition for productive efficiency. This ensures that the total output of each industry is allocated among its individual firms in such a way that the total cost of producing the industry's output is minimized.

Productive efficiency requires that the marginal (incremental) cost of producing its last unit of output must be the same for each firm in any industry.

If an industry is productively inefficient for this reason, it is possible to reduce the industry's total cost of producing any given total output by reallocating production among the industry's individual firms. To illustrate, suppose that the Jones Brothers shoe-manufacturing firm has a marginal cost of £70 for the last shoe of some standard type that it produces, while Campbell Ltd. has a marginal cost of only £65 for the same type of shoe. If the Jones plant produces one less pair of shoes while the Campbell plant produces one more, total shoe output is unchanged, but total industry costs are reduced by £5. Thus, £5 worth of resources will be freed to increase the production of other products.

Clearly, this cost saving can go on as long as the two firms have different marginal costs. However, as the Campbell firm produces more shoes, its marginal cost rises, and as the Jones firm produces fewer shoes, its marginal cost falls. (By producing more, the Campbell firm is moving upward to the right along its given MC curve, whereas by producing less, the Jones firm is moving downward to the left along its given MC curve.) Say, for example, that after Campbell Ltd. increases its production by 1,000 shoes per month, its marginal cost *rises* to £67, whereas when Jones Brothers reduces its output by the same amount, its marginal cost *falls* to £67. Now there are no further cost savings to be obtained by reallocating production between the two firms.

Figure 9.1 shows a production-possibility frontier of the sort that was first introduced in Figure 1.2 on page 26. Productive *inefficiency* implies that the economy is at some point inside the frontier. In such a situation it is possible to produce more of some goods without producing less of others.

Firms and competition

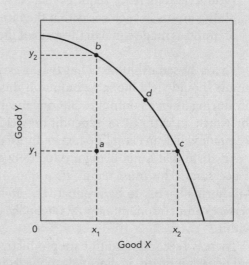
Any point on the production-possibility curve is productively efficient; not all points on this curve are allocatively efficient. The curve shows all combinations of two goods X and Y that can be produced when the economy's resources are fully employed and being used with productive efficiency.

Any point inside the curve, such as *a*, is productively inefficient. If the inefficiency exists in industry X, production could be re-allocated among firms in that industry in such a way as to raise production of X from x_1 to x_2. This would take the economy from point *a* to point *c*, raising production of X without any reduction in production of Y. Similarly, if the inefficiency exists in industry Y, production of Y could be increased from y_1 to y_2, which would take the economy from point *a* to point *b*. If both industries are allocatively inefficient, production can be increased to take the economy to some point on the curve *between b and c*, thus increasing the production of *both* commodities.

Allocative efficiency concerns being at the most efficient point on the production-possibility curve. Assessing allocative efficiency means judging among points on the curve, such as *b*, *c*, and *d*. Usually only one such point will be allocatively efficient, while all others will be inefficient.

Productive efficiency implies being on, rather than inside, the economy's production-possibility frontier.

Box 9.1 deals with two other efficiency concepts that are often confused with the economic concept of productive efficiency.

ALLOCATIVE EFFICIENCY

Allocative efficiency is about choosing between the many productively efficient combinations of outputs.

Allocative efficiency concerns the choice between alternative points on the production-possibility frontier.

For example, it relates to which bundle of outputs should be produced, such as those indicated by points *b*, *c*, and *d* in Figure 9.1.

BOX 9.1.

Three concepts of productive efficiency

In popular discussion, in business decision making, and in government policies, three different types of productive efficiency concept are encountered. These are engineering, technical, and economic efficiency. Each is a valid concept, and each conveys useful information. However, the use of one concept in a situation in which another is appropriate is a potential source of error and confusion.

Engineering efficiency refers to the *physical* amount of some *single key input* that is used in production. It is measured by the ratio of that input to output. For example, the engineering efficiency of an engine refers to the ratio of the amount of energy in the fuel used by the engine to the amount of usable energy produced by the engine. The difference goes in friction, heat loss, and other unavoidable sources of waste. Saying that a steam engine is 60 per cent efficient means that 60 per cent of the energy in the fuel that is burned in the boiler is converted into work that is done by the engine, while the other 40 per cent is lost.

Technical efficiency is related to the *physical* amount of *all factors* used in the process of producing some product. A particular method of producing a given output is technically inefficient if there exist other ways of producing the output that will use less of at least one input while not using more of any others. (Economists often call technical inefficiency *X-inefficiency*.)

We have seen in the text that economic efficiency is related to the *value* of *all inputs* used in producing a given output. The production of a given output is economically efficient if there is no other way of producing the output that will use a smaller total value of inputs.

What is the relationship between economic efficiency and these other two concepts?

We have seen that engineering efficiency measures the efficiency with which a single input is used. Although knowing the efficiency of any given petrol-driven, electric, or diesel engine is interesting, increasing this efficiency is not necessarily economically efficient, because doing so usually requires the use of other valuable resources. For example, the engineering efficiency of a gas turbine engine can be increased by using more and stronger steel in its construction. Raising the energy efficiency of an engine saves on fuel, but at the cost of using more of other inputs. To know whether this is worth doing, the firm must compare the value of the fuel saved with the value of the other inputs used. The optimal level of engineering efficiency is achieved by increasing efficiency where the value of the input saved exceeds the value of the extra resources used, but not into the range where the costs exceed the value of the input saved.

The existence of technical inefficiency means that costs can be cut by reducing some inputs and not increasing any others. If a technically inefficient process is replaced by a technically more efficient process, there is a saving. Avoiding technical inefficiency is therefore a necessary condition for producing any output at the least cost. Avoiding technical inefficiency is not, however, a sufficient condition for producing at lowest possible cost. The firm must still ask which of the many technically efficient methods it should use. This is where the concept of economic efficiency comes in. The appropriate method is the one that uses the smallest value of inputs. This ensures that the firm spends as little as possible to produce any given output.

Firms and competition

Allocative efficiency is defined as a situation in which it is impossible to change the pattern of production of goods in any way so as to make someone better off without making someone else worse off. Changing the pattern of production implies producing more of some goods and less of others, which in turn means moving from one point on the production-possibility frontier to another. This is called changing the *mix* of production.

From an allocative point of view, resources are said to be used *inefficiently* when using them to produce a different bundle of goods makes it possible for at least one person to be better off while making no other person worse off. Conversely, resources are said to be used *efficiently* when it is impossible, by using them to produce a different bundle of goods, to make any one person better off without making at least one other person worse off.

This tells us what is meant by allocative efficiency, but how do we find the efficient point on the production-possibility frontier? For example, how many shoes, dresses, and hats should be produced to achieve allocative efficiency? The answer is as follows:

> The economy's allocation of resources is efficient when, for each good produced, its marginal cost of production is equal to its price.

To understand the reasoning behind this answer, we need to recall a point that was established in our discussion of consumers' surplus in Chapter 7. The price of any commodity indicates the value that each consumer places on the last unit consumed of that commodity. Faced with the market price of some commodity, the consumer goes on buying units until the last one is valued exactly at its price. Consumers' surplus arises because the consumer would be willing to pay more than the market price for all but the last unit that is bought. On the last unit bought (i.e. the marginal unit), however, the consumer only 'breaks even', because the valuation placed on it is just equal to its price.

Now assume that some commodity, say, shoes, sells for £60 per pair but has a marginal cost of £70. If one less pair of shoes were produced, the value that all households would place on the pair of shoes not produced would be £60. Using the concept of opportunity cost, however, we see that the resources that would have been used to produce that last pair of shoes could instead produce another good (say, a coat) valued at £70. If society can give up something that its members value at £60 and get in return something that its members value at £70, the original allocation of resources is inefficient. Someone can be made better off, and no one need be worse off.

This is easy to see when the same household gives up the shoes and gets the coat, but it follows even when different households are involved. In this case, the market value of the gains to the household that gets the coat exceeds the market value of the loss to the household that gives up the shoes. The gaining household *could* afford to compensate the losing household and still come out ahead.

Assume next that shoe production is cut back until the price of a pair of shoes rises from £60 to £65, while its marginal cost falls from £70 to £65. Efficiency is achieved in shoe production because $p = MC = £65$. Now if one less pair of shoes were produced,

£65 worth of shoes would be sacrificed, while, at most, £65 worth of other commodities could be produced with the freed resources.

In this situation the allocation of resources to shoe production is efficient because it is not possible to change it to make someone better off without making someone else worse off. If one consumer were to sacrifice the pair of shoes, he or she would give up goods worth £65 and would then have to obtain for his or herself all of the new production of the alternative commodity produced just to break even. The consumer cannot gain without making another consumer worse off. The same argument can be repeated for every commodity, and it leads to the conclusion that we have stated already: the allocation of resources to production is efficient when each commodity's price equals its marginal cost of production.

Efficiency and inefficiency in perfect competition and monopoly

We now know that, for productive efficiency, marginal cost should be the same for all firms in any one industry and that, for allocative efficiency, marginal cost should be equal to price in each industry. Do the market structures of perfect competition and monopoly lead to productive and allocative efficiency?

PERFECT COMPETITION

Productive efficiency
We saw in Figure 6.9 that in the long run under perfect competition, each firm produces at the lowest point on its long-run average cost curve. Therefore, no one firm could lower its costs by altering its own production.

We also know that in perfect competition, all firms in an industry face the same price of their product and that they equate marginal cost to that price. It follows immediately that marginal cost will be the same for all firms. Because all firms in the industry have the same cost of producing their last unit of production, no reallocation of production among the firms could reduce the total industry cost of producing a given output.

> **Productive efficiency is achieved under perfect competition because all firms in an industry have identical marginal costs and identical minimum unit costs in long-run equilibrium.**

Allocative efficiency
We have seen already that perfectly competitive firms maximize their profits by equating marginal cost to price. Thus, when perfect competition is the market structure for the whole economy, price is equal to marginal cost in each line of production.

the best of the available alternatives when minimum efficient scale is large. The challenge to public policy is to keep oligopolists competing and using their competitive energies to improve products and to lower costs rather than to restrict inter-firm competition and to erect entry barriers. As we shall see later in this chapter, much public policy has just this purpose. What economic policymakers call *restrictive* or *monopolistic practices* include not only output restrictions operated by firms with complete monopoly power, but also anti-competitive behaviour among firms that are operating in oligopolistic market structures.

The case for government involvement in markets

We now return to the general issue of why the market mechanism may fail to deliver desirable outcomes and, thus, potentially provide a role for government intervention in markets.

The term **market failure** describes any market performance that is judged to be less good than the best possible performance. The word *failure* in this context may convey the wrong impression.

> **Market failure means that the *best attainable outcome* has not been achieved; it does not mean that nothing good has happened.**

The phrase 'market failure' is used to apply to two quite different sets of circumstances. One is the failure of the market system to achieve efficiency in the allocation of society's resources. The other is the failure of the market system to serve social goals, such as achieving some desired distribution of income or preserving our value systems. We treat each in turn.

Failure to achieve efficiency

There are five broad types of phenomena that lead to inefficient market outcomes: *monopoly power, externalities, absence of property rights, public goods* (sometimes called *collective consumption goods*), and *information asymmetries*. We consider each of these in a separate section below.

MONOPOLY POWER

As we discussed above, firms that face negatively sloped demand curves will maximize profits at an output where price exceeds marginal cost, leading to allocative inefficiency.

Although some market power is maintained through artificial barriers to entry, such power often arises naturally because in many industries the least costly way to produce a good or a service is to have few producers relative to the size of the market. The standard government remedies are anti-monopoly policy and public-utility regulation. These are discussed in more detail later in this chapter.

EXTERNALITIES

Costs, as economists define them, involve the value of resources used in the process of production. According to the opportunity-cost principle, value is the benefit that resources would produce in their best alternative use. But who decides what resources are used when and what their opportunity cost is?

Consider the case of a selfish student who is thinking of extending a party for one more hour at 1:00 a.m. For this student, the opportunity cost includes the psychological value of getting an extra hour of sleep, as well as the money cost of whatever will be eaten and drunk, the value of repairs to the flat, and so forth. However, there is another resource used when the party runs for an extra hour—the neighbours' sleep—and the student may not consider it when she makes her decision to keep the stereo blasting.

Private and social costs

The difference in the viewpoints of the selfish party thrower and the neighbours illustrates the important distinction between **private cost** and **social cost**. Private cost measures the best alternative use of the resource available to the private decision maker. The party thrower incurs private costs equal to her best alternative use of the resources that go into an extra hour of partying. The party thrower cannot make any use of the neighbours' sleep and so values the sleep at zero. The *social cost* includes the private cost but also includes the best use of *all* resources available to society. In this case, social cost includes the cost imposed on the neighbours by an extra hour of partying.

Discrepancies between social and private cost occur when there are **externalities,** which are the costs or benefits of a transaction that are incurred or received by other members of the society but not taken into account by the parties to the transaction. They are also called *neighbourhood effects* or *third-party effects*, because parties other than the two primary participants in the transaction (the buyer and the seller) are affected. Externalities arise in many different ways, and they may be beneficial or harmful.

A harmful externality occurs, for example, when a factory generates smoke. Individuals who live and work in the neighbourhood bear real costs due to the factory's production: the disutility of enduring the smoke, adverse health effects, and clean-up costs. These effects will not be taken into account by profit-maximizing factory owners when they decide how much to produce. The element of social cost that they ignore is external to their decision-making process. Producers who create harmful externalities will produce more than the socially optimal level of output.

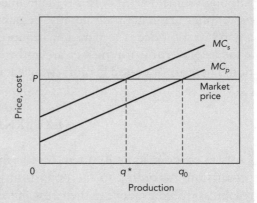

Figure 9.3. Private and social cost

A competitive firm will produce output to the point where its private marginal cost equals the market price. In this case, every unit of output produced imposes *external costs*, equal to the distance between MC_p (private marginal cost—the marginal cost curve that is faced by the firm) and MC_s (social marginal cost).

   The profit-maximizing, competitive firm produces q_0, the output where price equals private marginal cost. If the full social cost of production were taken into account, only q^* would be produced. Notice that for each unit of output between q^* and q_0, the cost borne by all members of society exceeds the value to consumers, which is the market price. Over this range, social cost exceeds private revenue, implying allocative inefficiency.

Beneficial externalities occur, for example, when I paint my house and enhance my neighbours' view and the value of their property, or when an Einstein or a Rembrandt gives the world a discovery or a work of art whose worth is far in excess of what he is paid to produce it. Firms will tend to produce less than the socially optimal level of output whenever their products generate beneficial externalities, because they bear all of the costs while others reap part of the benefits.

> **Externalities, whether harmful or beneficial, cause market failures: marginal private revenue differs from marginal social cost, causing output to diverge from its socially optimal level.**

This is illustrated in Figure 9.3 for the case of a harmful externality.

COMMON PROPERTY RESOURCES

A **common property resource** is a resource that is owned by no one and may be used by anyone. No one owns the ocean's fish until they are caught. The world's international fishing grounds are common property for all fishermen. If, by taking more fish, one fisherman reduces the catch of other fishermen, he does not count this as a cost, although it is a cost to society.

   It is socially optimal to add to a fishing fleet until the last boat increases the *value of the world fleet's total catch* by as much as it costs to operate the boat. This is the size of the fishing fleet that a social planner or a private monopolist (who owned the fish in the sea) would choose.

   The free market, however, will not produce that result. Potential new entrants will judge entry to be profitable if the *value of their own catch* is equal to the costs of operating their boats. But a new entrant's catch is *partly* an addition to total catch, and *partly* a reduction of the catch of other fishermen—because of diminishing stocks, each new boat reduces the catch of all others. Thus, under competitive free entry, there will be too many boats in the fleet.

> **With common property resources, the level of activity will be too high because each new entrant will not take account of the cost that he or she imposes on existing producers.**

Fishing grounds, common pastures, and other common property resources often show a typical pattern of over-exploitation. Most of the world's fishing grounds do so today, except where the catch is effectively regulated by government intervention.

PUBLIC GOODS

A **public good,** which is sometimes called a **collective consumption good,** is one for which the total cost of production does not increase as the number of consumers increases. The classic case is national defence. An army of a given size protects all the nations' citizens whether these number 25 million, 50 million, or 100 million. Another important case is police protection: a visitor would benefit from a city's crime-free streets just as much as its residents would.

Information is also a public good. Suppose a certain food additive causes cancer. The cost of discovering this needs to be borne only once. The information is then of value to everyone who might have used the additive, and the cost of making the information available to one more consumer is essentially zero. Other public goods include lighthouses, weather forecasts (a type of information), the provision of clean air, and outdoor band concerts. Importantly, once a public good is produced, it is available to everyone; its use cannot be restricted to those who are willing to pay for it.

For this reason, the private market will not produce efficient amounts of the public good, because once the good is produced, it is either inefficient or impossible to make people pay for its use. Indeed, markets may fail to produce public goods at all whenever non-payers cannot be made non-users. The obvious remedy in these cases is government provision of the good, paid for by taxes.

There are two key characteristics of a pure public good: it must be non-rivalrous, and it must be non-excludable. By **non-rivalrous** we mean that the amount that one person consumes should not affect the amount that other people can consume. For example, if ten boats enter a channel guided by a lighthouse, this does not reduce the benefit that the eleventh boat can get from the light when entering the channel. In contrast, a normal private good is rivalrous in the sense that, if one person consumes some amount of it, that amount is not available for anyone else to consume. By **non-excludable** we mean that, once produced, there is no way of stopping anyone from consuming it. For example, a national defence system protects everyone in a country whether or not they contribute to the cost, and there is no obvious way of excluding them from that benefit.

In practice, some pure public goods do exist, but in many other cases there is a mixture of public and private characteristics. For example, a good that is subject to congestion may be non-rivalrous up to a point but rivalrous thereafter. A motorway that is operated under capacity has the non-rivalrous characteristics of a public good. One more car on it does not reduce the benefit of existing users. However, once the road starts to get congested, as during a Friday-evening rush hour before a holiday weekend, each additional user reduces the benefit that existing users get, by increasing congestion. At this point, the services of the motorway become rivalrous.

Similar considerations apply to excludability. Exclusion from consumption is easier for some products than for others. It may be impossible to exclude someone from being protected by a defence system, but exclusion from most other products depends upon the technology available. Electronic tagging of cars is, for example, a possible way of charging for road use when up to now roads have been mainly free to all comers.

A pure public good such as defence is completely non-rivalrous and non-excludable. In practice, there is a range of goods that have a mixture of public and private good characteristics.

Public goods cannot be provided by the market, because firms making them could not prevent people from using them without paying. Hence, a producer could not guarantee to receive revenue from consumers and would, therefore, go out of business. This is because, once the good is produced, consumers get the benefit from it whether they pay for it or not. Governments can fund the production of public goods out of general taxes and provide the good to consumers free of direct charge.

ASYMMETRIC INFORMATION

The role of information in the economy has received increasing attention from economists in recent years. Information is, of course, a valuable product, and markets for information and expertise are well developed, as every university student is aware. Although markets for expertise are conceptually identical to markets for any other valuable service, they also pose special problems. We have already discussed one of these: information is often a public good, because once the information is known to anyone it is often easily available to others; this makes it difficult to charge users enough to cover the costs of production and causes the private sector to produce too little.

Even where information is not a public good, markets for expertise are prone to market failure. The reason for this is that one party to a transaction often can take advantage of special knowledge in ways that change the nature of the transaction itself. The two important sources of market failure that arise when privately held information is bought and sold are *moral hazard* and *adverse selection*.

Moral hazard is the name applied to any change of behaviour that occurs after a contract for some service has been signed. The most common examples occur in insurance and labour markets. The purchase of car insurance may make me drive more carelessly, or the insurance of my property may make me less careful about locking up when I go out. Another example would be if an employee on a probationary contract worked very hard but, once given a long-term contract, started to take things easy. We shall discuss this problem, in the context of employment contracts, in more detail in Chapter 10.

Adverse selection also is a common problem in insurance markets. It refers to the tendency of people who are more at risk than average to choose to buy insurance while people who are less at risk are less likely to bother to be insured. It is a problem only because the true characteristics of the customer are not immediately observable. They may be known to the customer but they are not typically known by the insurance provider. This would obviously be a problem for insurance companies because it could make them lose money. Suppose the Metro insurance company priced its car insurance according to the average accident rate in the population and yet it inadvertently sold policies only to people who did not believe in obeying traffic lights. Clearly, it would have sold its policies too cheaply for the risks involved. This, of course, is why insurance companies take great effort to ensure that they really do sell to a typical cross-section of the population and, where identifiable, they set higher rates for higher risks (such as higher rates for property insurance in high-crime areas).

The message for the behaviour of markets is that, first, when insurance leads people to engage in more risky behaviour, social costs are unnecessarily high and, second, when buyers and sellers have unequal knowledge about their transaction, the outcome can be less efficient than if they were equally well informed.

Principal–agent problem

Asymmetric information is involved in many situations of market failure. The *principal–agent* problem, which was first mentioned in Chapter 2, is an example. In its classic form, the firm's managers act as agents for the shareholders, who are the legal principals of the firm. The managers are much better informed than the principals are about what they actually do and what they could do. Indeed, the managers are hired for their special expertise. Given that it is expensive for the shareholders (principals) to monitor what the managers (agents) do, the managers have latitude to pursue goals other than the firm's profits. Hence, some inefficiency may arise.

Failure to achieve other social goals

The great strength of the market system is its ability to generate reasonably efficient outcomes in a great many cases, using a decentralized organization. Markets do this well because, most of the time, the information that they need to perform well is derived from individuals' desires to improve their private circumstances. It should not be surprising that markets do not always perform well in fostering broader social goals such as achieving an 'equitable' distribution of income or promoting shared community values. Markets are not effective in fostering these goals precisely because individuals do not pursue these goals by purchasing goods and services in markets.

INCOME DISTRIBUTION

An important characteristic of a market economy is the *distribution* of income that it determines. People whose services are in heavy demand relative to supply earn large incomes, whereas people whose services are not in heavy demand relative to supply, earn much less.

Differentials in earnings serve the important function of motivating people to adapt. The advantage of such a system is that individuals can make their own decisions about how to alter their behaviour when market conditions change; the disadvantage is that temporary rewards and penalties are dealt out as a result of changes in market conditions that are beyond the control of the affected individuals. The resulting differences in incomes will seem unfair to many—even though they are the incentives that make markets work.

Because the workings of the market may be stern, even cruel, society often chooses to intervene. Should heads of households be forced to bear the full burden of their misfortune if, through no fault of their own, they lose their jobs? Even if they lose their jobs through their own fault, should they and their families have to bear the whole burden, which may include starvation? Should the ill and the aged be thrown on the mercy of their families? What if they have no families? Both private charities and a great many government policies are concerned with modifying the distribution of income that results from such things as where one starts, how able one is, how lucky one is, and how one fares in the labour market.

Problems arise when our measures designed to improve equity seriously inhibit the efficient operation of the price system.

Often the goal of a more equitable distribution conflicts with the goal of a more efficient economy.

Suppose that we were so extreme as to believe that equity demanded that everyone received the same income. All incentives to work hard and to move from job to job would be eliminated. Some command economies came close to these extreme positions, and the results were predictably disastrous. Say that, to be less extreme, we believed that some factor of production's earnings should not reflect short-term fluctuations in demand and supply. The UK controls on rents of living accommodation did just that in the 1960s and 1970s, and current controls in several other countries do that today. The problem then is that the whole incentive system for resource allocation is removed if such intervention is effective. In free markets, a rise in demand creates extra earnings, which attract resources to meet the demand. Remove the price reaction and there is no incentive for the resource reallocation to occur.

PROTECTING INDIVIDUALS FROM OTHERS

People can use and even abuse other people for economic gain in ways that the members of society find offensive. Child labour laws and minimum standards of working conditions are responses to such actions. Yet direct abuse is not the only example of this kind of market failure. In an unhindered free market, the adults in a household would usually decide how much education to buy for their children. Selfish parents might buy no education, while egalitarian parents might buy the same education for all of their children, regardless of their abilities. The members of society may want to interfere in these choices, both to protect the child of the selfish parent and to ensure that some of the scarce educational resources are distributed according to ability rather than the family's wealth. All households are forced to provide a minimum of education for their children, via compulsory but free public schooling, and a number of inducements are offered—through public universities, student grants, low-interest loans, and other means—for talented children to consume more education than they or their parents might choose if they had to pay the entire cost themselves.

PATERNALISM

Members of society, acting through the state, often seek to protect adult (and presumably responsible) individuals, not from others but from themselves. Laws prohibiting the use of heroin, crack, and other drugs and laws prescribing the installation and use of seat belts are intended primarily to protect individuals from their own ignorance or shortsightedness. This kind of interference in the free choices of individuals is called **paternalism.** Whether such actions reflect the wishes of the majority in the society or whether they reflect the actions of overbearing governments, there is no doubt that the market will not provide this kind of protection. Buyers do not buy what they do not want, and sellers have no motive to provide it if there is no demand.

Protection and paternalism are often closely related to **merit goods.** Merit goods are goods that society deems to be especially important and that those in power feel individuals should be required or encouraged to consume. Housing, education, and health care are often cited as merit goods.

SOCIAL OBLIGATIONS

In a free-market system, if you can pay another person to do things for you, you may do so. If you persuade someone else to clean your house in return for £20, presumably both parties to the transaction are better off: you prefer to part with £20 than to clean the house yourself, and the person you hire prefers £20 to not cleaning your house. Normally, society does not interfere with people's ability to negotiate mutually advantageous contracts.

Most people do not feel this way, however, about activities that are regarded as social obligations. For example, during major wars when military service is compulsory, contracts similar to the one between you and a housekeeper could also be negotiated. Some persons, faced with the obligation to do military service, could no doubt pay enough to persuade others to do their tour of service for them. By exactly the same argument as we just used, we can presume that both parties will be better off if they are allowed to negotiate such a trade. Yet such contracts are usually prohibited. They are prohibited because there are values to be considered other than those that can be expressed in a market. In times when it is necessary, military service by all healthy males is usually held to be a duty that is independent of an individual's tastes, wealth, influence, or social position. It is felt that everyone *ought* to do this service, and exchanges between willing traders are prohibited.

Military service is not the only example of a social obligation. Citizens are not allowed to buy their way out of jury duty or to sell their votes, even though in many cases they could find willing trading partners.

> **Even if the price system allocated goods and services with complete efficiency, members of a society might not wish to rely solely on the market since they have other goals that they wish to achieve.**

We now look in more detail at government intervention in response to one source of market failure, deviations from perfect competition.

Public policy towards monopoly and competition

Monopolies, cartels, and price-fixing agreements among oligopolists, whether explicit or tacit, have met with public suspicion and official hostility for over a century. These and other non-competitive practices are collectively referred to as *monopoly practices* or *restrictive practices*. Note that such practices are *not* just what *monopolists* do; they include non-competitive behaviour of firms that are operating in other market structures such as oligopoly. The laws and other instruments that are used to encourage competition and discourage monopoly practices make up **competition policy** and are used to influence both the market structure and the behaviour of individual firms. By and large, UK competition policy has sought to create more competitive market structures where possible, to discourage monopolistic practices, and to encourage competitive behaviour where competitive market structures could not be established.

In addition, the government employs *economic regulations*, which prescribe the rules under which firms can do business, and in some cases determine the prices that businesses can charge for their output.

The goal of economic efficiency provides rationales both for competition policy and for economic regulation. Competition policy is used to promote efficiency by increasing competition in the marketplace. Where effective competition is not possible (as in the case of a natural monopoly, such as a water company), economic regulation of privately owned firms or public ownership can be used as a substitute for competition. The purpose is to protect consumers from the high prices and reduced output that result from the use of monopoly power.[1]

Public policies are indeed used in these ways, but they are also often used in ways that reduce economic efficiency. One reason is that efficiency is not the only thing that policymakers have been concerned with in the design and implementation of competition policy. Most public policies have the potential to redistribute income, and people often use them for private gain, regardless of their original public purpose.

We shall study three aspects of competition policy: first, the direct control of natural monopolies; second, the direct control of oligopolies; and, third, the creation of competitive conditions. The first is a necessary part of any competition policy, the second has been important in the past but is less so now, and the third constitutes the main current thrust of UK competition policy.

Direct control of natural monopolies

The clearest case for public intervention arises with a natural monopoly, an industry in which scale effects are so dominant that there is room for only one firm to operate at the minimum efficient scale. UK policymakers have not wanted to compel the existence of several smaller, less efficient producers whenever a single firm would be much more efficient; neither have they wanted to give a natural monopolist the opportunity to restrict output, raise prices, and reap the profits from large-scale production.

One response to natural monopoly is for government to *assume ownership* of the single firm, setting it up as a nationalized industry. The government appoints managers who are supposed to set prices guided by their understanding of the national interest. Another response has been to allow private ownership but to *regulate* the monopoly firm's behaviour. Earlier in this century, UK policy favoured public ownership. Recently, such industries have been privatized and then, to some extent, regulated. Examples are telecommunications, gas, water, railways, and electricity. Notice, however, that not all privatized industries were natural monopolies, so the cases for their

---

[1] A second kind of regulation, *social regulation*, involves a government's rules that require firms to consider the health, safety, environmental, and other social consequences of their behaviour.

public ownership must have been different. The coal industry, for example, is not a natural monopoly, because many mines could be individually owned and there is a competitive market for imported coal.

SHORT-RUN PRICE AND OUTPUT

Whether the state nationalizes or merely regulates privately owned, natural monopolies, the industry's pricing policy is determined by the government. Usually, the industry is asked to follow some policy other than profit maximization.

Marginal cost pricing
Sometimes the government dictates that the natural monopoly should try to set price equal to short-run marginal cost in an effort to maximize consumers' plus producers' surpluses in that industry. According to economic theory, this policy, which is called **marginal cost pricing,** provides the efficient solution.

Marginal cost pricing does, however, create some problems. The natural monopoly may still have unexploited economies of scale and may hence be operating on the falling portion of its average total cost curve. In this case, marginal cost will be less than average total cost, and pricing at marginal cost will lead to losses. This is shown in part (i) of Figure 9.4.

> **A falling-cost, natural monopoly that sets price equal to marginal cost will suffer losses.**

Demand, however, may be sufficient to allow the firm to produce on the rising portion of its average total cost curve, that is, where output exceeds what is needed to achieve the minimum efficient scale. At any such output, marginal cost exceeds average total cost. If the firm is directed to equate marginal cost to price, it will earn profits. This is shown in part (ii) of the figure.[2]

> **When a rising-cost, natural monopoly sets price equal to marginal cost, it will earn profits.**

Average cost pricing
Sometimes natural monopolies are directed to produce the output that will just cover total costs, thus earning neither profits nor losses. This means that the firm produces to

---

2 Sometimes a natural monopoly is defined as one where long-run costs are falling when price equals marginal cost. This, however, is only *sufficient* for a natural monopoly; it is not *necessary*. Demand may be such that one firm is producing, when price equals marginal cost, on the rising portion of its long-run cost curve, while there is no price at which two firms could both cover their costs. For example, if a firm's minimum efficient scale (*MES*) is 1 million units of output and demand is sufficient to allow the firm to cover costs at 1.2 million units, there may be no price at which two firms, with their combined *MES* of 2 million units, can cover their full costs.

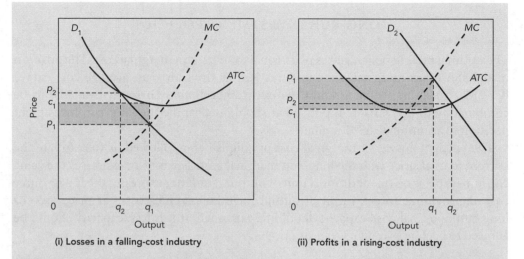

Figure 9.4. Pricing policies for natural monopolies

Marginal cost pricing leads to profit or losses, whereas average cost pricing violates the efficiency condition. In each part, the output at which marginal cost equals price is q_1 and price is p_1.

In part (i), average costs are falling at output q_1, so marginal costs are less than the average cost of c_1. There is a loss of $(c_1 - p_1)$ on each unit, making a total loss equal to the shaded area.

In part (ii), average cost of c_1 is less than price at output q_1. There is a profit of $(p_1 - c_1)$ on each unit sold, making a total profit equal to the shaded area.

In each part of the diagram, the output at which average cost equals price is q_2 and the associated price is p_2. In part (i), marginal cost is less than price at q_2, so output is below its optimal level. In part (ii), marginal cost exceeds price at q_2, so output is greater than its optimal level.

the point where average revenue equals average total cost, which is where the demand curve cuts the average total cost curve. Part (i) of Figure 9.4 shows that, for a falling-cost firm, this pricing policy requires producing at less than the optimal output. The losses that would occur under marginal cost pricing are avoided by producing less than the efficient output.[3] Part (ii) shows that, for a rising-cost firm, the policy requires producing at more than the optimal output. The profits that would occur under marginal cost pricing are dissipated by producing more than the efficient output.

Generally, average cost pricing will not result in allocative efficiency.

[3] Note that the losses are financial losses, not social welfare losses. Every unit produced between the points where AC equals price and MC equals price adds to consumers' surplus but brings private financial loss to the producer.

LONG-RUN INVESTMENT POLICIES

The optimal pricing policy makes price equal to short-run marginal cost. The position of the short-run marginal cost curve (as well as the short-run average cost curve) depends, however, on the amount of fixed capital that is currently available to be combined with the variable input. What should determine the long-run investment decision to accumulate fixed capital?

The efficient answer, if marginal cost pricing is being followed, is to compare the current market price with the long-run marginal cost. The former expresses the value consumers place on one additional unit of output. The latter expresses the full resource cost of providing an extra unit of output including capital costs.[4] If price exceeds long-run marginal cost, capacity should be expanded. If it is less, capacity should be allowed to decline as capital wears out.

> The efficient pricing system rations the output of existing capacity by setting price equal to the short-run resource cost of producing another unit. It also adjusts capacity in the long run until the full marginal cost of producing another unit of output is equal to the price.

THE VERY LONG RUN

Natural monopoly is a long-run concept, meaning that *given existing technology*, there is room for only one firm to operate profitably. In the very long run, however, technology changes. Not only does today's competitive industry sometimes become tomorrow's natural monopoly, but today's natural monopoly sometimes becomes tomorrow's competitive industry.

A striking example is the telecommunications industry. Fifteen years ago, message transmission was a natural monopoly. Now technological developments such as satellite transmission, electronic mail, and fax machines have made this activity highly competitive. In many countries an odd circumstance then arose: nationalized industries, such as the UK Post Office, sought to maintain their profitability by prohibiting entry into what would otherwise become a fluid and competitive industry. Since it has the full force of the legal system behind it, the public firm may be more successful than the privately owned firm in preserving its monopoly long after technological changes have destroyed its 'naturalness'.

> Market economies change continually under the impacts of innovation and growth; to be successful, government policy must also be adapted continually to keep it relevant to the ever-changing existing situation.

4 To make the correct comparison, the cost of capital must be expressed as its current rental price per period (or *user cost*) so that it can be added to such other costs as wages and fuel.

Direct control of oligopolies

Governments have from time to time intervened in industries that were oligopolies, rather than natural monopolies, seeking to enforce the type of price and entry behaviour that was thought to be in the public interest. Such intervention has typically taken two distinct forms. In the UK from 1945 to 1980, it was primarily nationalization of whole oligopolistic industries such as airlines, railways, steel, and coal mining, which were then to be run by government-appointed boards. In the USA, firms in such oligopolistic industries as airlines, railways, and electric power companies were left in private hands, but their decisions were regulated by government-appointed bodies that set prices and regulated entry.

SCEPTICISM ABOUT DIRECT CONTROL

In recent times, policymakers have become increasingly sceptical of their ability to improve the behaviour of oligopolistic industries by having the state control the details of their behaviour either through ownership or regulation. Several experiences have been important in determining this scepticism.

First, oligopolistic market structures have provided much of the economic growth since the Second World War. New products, and new ways of producing old products, have followed each other in rapid succession, all leading to higher living standards and higher productivity. Many of these innovations have been provided by firms in oligopolistic industries such as motor cars, agricultural implements, steel, pharmaceuticals, petroleum refining, chemicals, and telecommunications. As long as governments can keep oligopolists competing with each other, rather than co-operating to produce monopoly profits, most economists see no need to regulate such things as the prices at which oligopolists sell their products and the conditions of entry into oligopolistic industries.

Second, many regulatory bodies have imposed policies that were not related to the cost of each of the services being priced. These prices involved what is called *cross-subsidization*, whereby profits that are earned in the provision of one service are used to subsidize the provision of another at a price below cost. This is allocatively inefficient.

Third, the record of postwar government intervention in regulated industries seemed poorer in practice than its supporters had predicted. After industries were nationalized, antagonism often persisted between management, concerned with financial viability, and workers, concerned with take-home pay. As a result, it was not long before the unexpected became commonplace: strikes against the industries that the British people themselves owned. On the other hand, when industries were *regulated*, as was commonplace in the USA, the results were often less beneficial to consumers than had been expected. Research by economists slowly established that in many industries, regulatory bodies were captured by the very firms that they were supposed to be regulating. As a result, the regulatory bodies that were meant to ensure competition often acted to enforce monopoly practices that would have been illegal if instituted by the firms themselves.

This last point, which entails the use of regulatory policy to protect firms from too much competition rather than to protect consumers from too little, has a long history in North America. Regulation of newly privatized industries in Britain is too recent to tell if UK regulators will fall into the pattern established earlier in North America of protecting sellers rather than buyers.

DEREGULATION AND PRIVATIZATION

The 1980s and 1990s witnessed a movement in virtually all advanced industrial nations and the vast majority of less developed nations to reduce the level of government control over industry.

Figure 9.5 shows the extent of this movement world-wide. The last great wave of nationalizations, mainly in less developed countries, began in the mid-1960s and reached a peak in the early 1970s. It was inspired by the twin beliefs that control over natural resources and key industries was a prerequisite to growth and that such control

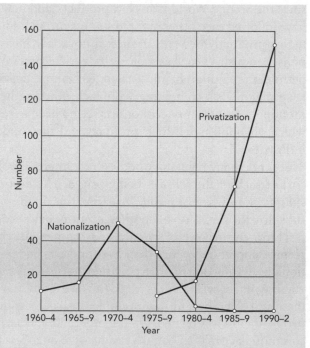

Figure 9.5. Nationalization and privatization, 1960–1992

The last wave of nationalization in the 1960s gave way to a wave of privatization that had not yet crested by 1992. The nationalization data refer to the average number of acts of nationalization in each period. There were earlier peaks not shown in the figure, such as 1945–50, when most UK nationalization occurred. The latest recorded peak occurred in the late 1960s and early 1970s and is shown in the figure. The privatization data refer to the average number of firms privatized during each period. Starting from a low in the 1970s, privatization has been rising dramatically right through the early 1990s.

Source: World Investment Report 1993 (New York: UN, UNCTAD Programme on TNCs), p. 17.

was best exercised through public ownership. By the 1980s these beliefs were fading. As a result, publicly owned activities throughout the world were being transferred to private ownership. This shift of resources from the public to the private sector was still going on in the early 1990s but is likely to tail off at a later date, as the number of industries left to privatize diminishes.

A number of forces had been pushing in the direction of increased privatization: (1) the experience that regulatory bodies often sought to reduce, rather than increase, competition; (2) the dashing of the unreasonable hopes that nationalized industries would work better than private firms in terms of efficiency, productivity growth, and industrial relations; (3) the realization that replacing a private monopoly with a publicly owned one would not greatly change the industry's performance, and that replacing privately owned oligopolists by a publicly owned monopoly often worsens performance; and (4) the awareness that falling transportation costs and revolutions in data processing and communications exposed local industries to much more widespread international competition than they had previously experienced domestically.

More generally, the world-wide movement towards privatization and deregulation is part of the growing belief among policymakers that markets are more efficient allocators of resources than governments. This change of view spreads beyond the advanced industrial nations to most of the poorer developing nations who had tried heavy government intervention for decades and concluded that market determination is on balance superior.

The call is for a diminished role for government in resource allocation—but not for a zero role. All the reasons outlined above continue to suggest that the public interest may call for significant government intervention in the workings of the market system.

> **Privatization and deregulation reflect a new belief in the efficiency of a market-oriented economy, but still leave a major role for government intervention to improve the operation of the market.**

The natural outcome of these revised views was the privatization of nationalized industries and the deregulation of privately owned ones. This latter policy was intended, among other things, to return price determination and entry decisions to market determination. Privatization has gone a long way in the UK. Most of the former nationalized industries have been returned to private ownership.

Intervention to keep firms competing

The least stringent form of government intervention is designed neither to force firms to sell at particular prices nor to regulate the conditions of entry and exit; rather, it is designed to create conditions of competition by preventing firms from merging unnecessarily or from engaging in certain anti-competitive practices such as colluding to set monopoly prices. Here the policy seeks to create the most competitive market structure possible and then to prevent firms from reducing competition by engaging in certain forms of co-operative behaviour.

UK POLICIES

Ultimate responsibility for competition policy in the UK lies with the Secretary of State for Trade and Industry. However, key elements of monitoring and enforcement are delegated to three important institutions: the Restrictive Practices Court (RPC), the Office of Fair Trading (OFT), and the Monopolies and Mergers Commission (MMC).

There is an important difference in the legislation affecting *restrictive practices* from that affecting the potential creation of a monopoly by a *merger*. Restrictive practices must be registered and demonstrated to be in the public interest. The OFT can investigate cases that are not already approved and refer them to the RPC for judgement. By contrast, the onus is entirely on the authorities to prove that a merger is not in the public interest; otherwise it must be permitted to proceed. Here decisions are made by the Secretary of State on the basis of recommendations made by the MMC.

Restrictive practices

Restrictive practices involve, for example, agreements between firms over the prices they will charge or the way in which they will divide up the market (by, perhaps, not competing in specific locations). In the UK, a restrictive practice must pass through one of eight 'gateways', as defined by the 1956 Restrictive Trades Practices Act, to establish that it is in the public interest. (Originally there were seven gateways, but one more was added in 1968; also, the Act was extended to cover services as well as goods.) The gateways for a restrictive practice to be in the public interest are that:

1. It protects the public from physical injury.
2. Consumers gain identifiable benefits from it.
3. Employment is protected as a result of it.
4. It counteracts other restrictions to competition.
5. It is necessary to support other acceptable restrictive practices.
6. Its existence supports greater exports.
7. Its existence enhances a fair market for suppliers of inputs.
8. The restrictive practice does not deter competition.

In the last forty years, over 10,000 restrictive agreements have been registered, but many of these have been ended voluntarily without needing a judgement from the RPC.

The EU Commission can intervene in restrictive agreements affecting trade between EU member states. Article 85 of the Treaty of Rome prohibits anti-competitive agreements, such as market sharing, price fixing, and supply restrictions. The Treaty also prohibits the use of monopoly power to exploit consumers, and distortions to competition resulting from government subsidies.

Mergers

All companies involved in a merger must submit notification to the OFT. The Director-General of Fair Trading must then decide if the creation of a monopoly is involved. In such cases, the OFT will recommend to the Secretary of State that the merger be referred to the MMC. The MMC then has to decide if the merger is against the public interest. The final decision is back with the Secretary of State, who may decide to accept or reject the MMC recommendation.

Under current UK legislation, a merger potentially creates a monopoly if the merging firms together control 25 per cent or more of the market, though a merger involving significant assets may also be referred. Only about one in fifty mergers, over the last thirty years, has been referred to the MMC, and fewer than half of those were ruled against the public interest.

The OFT may recommend an MMC investigation in cases of suspected monopoly behaviour, even where this does not result from merger. Box 9.2 contains a summary of six recent MMC investigations. These cases do not cover all possible types of investigation. The MMC has, for example, recently investigated the monopoly position of British Gas, a natural monopoly privatized in the mid-1980s but regulated by OFGAS. It recommended the splitting off of some of British Gas's activities and the ending of its monopoly supply position within four years. MMC investigations have even been directed at institutions still in public ownership, such as London Underground and the UK Atomic Energy Authority. Privatized utility companies that do not accept the price controls imposed on them by respective regulators have the right of appeal to the MMC, which would then conduct its own inquiry. South West Water made just such an appeal in 1995, as did Northern Ireland Electricity in 1996.

The EU Commission also has a role in monitoring mergers that affect more than one EU country simultaneously, that is, where the companies involved have a significant cross-border presence. There are two criteria, either of which could trigger investigation of a merger by the Commission: (1) the companies involved have a global turnover exceeding 5 billion ECU (European Currency Units); (2) each company involved has an EU-wide turnover of at least 250 million ECU. However, if both merging companies have at least two-thirds of their combined turnover in only one member state, then the merger will be subject to vetting in that member state and not by the Commission. Thus, as UK companies become more international, it is likely that a higher proportion of merger activity will be monitored by the EU Commission rather than by the MMC.

In short, even though governments, on the whole, are no longer in the business of owning industries, they are certainly not indifferent to industry performance. Government has an important role as both rule maker and referee of the market economy. So long as monopoly and restrictive practices continue to be a threat to the efficient working of the economy, governments will correctly regard the behaviour of firms as something that requires appropriate monitoring.

BOX 9.2.

The MMC in action

The Monopolies and Mergers Commission gets into the headline news when a large and controversial takeover bid is referred to it, like the 1992 bid by Lloyds Bank for the Midland Bank (which was abandoned because of the MMC referral, long before the inquiry could be concluded). However, the MMC reports on many specific potential instances of monopoly behaviour, not all resulting from merger proposals. In this box we outline six recent MMC enquiries, out of dozens produced in the last few years. Dates in brackets are the publication dates of the MMC reports.

Allied–Lyons PLC and Carlsberg A/S (July 1992)

Allied–Lyons (as we saw in Box 8.3) is a major force in the UK brewing and pubs business. It concluded an agreement with Danish brewer, Carlsberg, to merge their brewing and whole-saling activities into a new jointly owned company, Carlsberg–Tetley Brewing Ltd. (CTL). Under the agreement, Allied–Lyons would continue to own its pubs but would enter into a seven-year supply contract to buy all of its beer from CTL, up to 15 per cent of which could be third-party brands stocked by CTL.

The MMC recommended (with one member dissenting) that the merger should not proceed unless: (1) CTL undertook not to raise prices charged to Carlsberg's existing customers (regional brewers or independent wholesalers); (2) the supply agreement between CTL and Allied–Lyons was reduced from seven to five years; and (3) Allied–Lyons permitted its tenants (publicans) freedom, after two years, to purchase half their lager from other suppliers.

Notice that tied sales is the key issue here. If publicans have to buy from one distributor, they cannot seek alternative suppliers if prices are raised.

Acquisition of Parker Pen Holdings Ltd. by Gillette (February 1993)

The sole business of Parker is the manufacture of writing instruments. Competition issues arose from the fact that Gillette already owned two suppliers of writing instruments, Paper Mate and Waterman. The MMC concluded that 'any attempt by a merged company to exploit its market position would be held in check by the bargaining strength of retailers and the existence of both actual and potential competitors to which they could turn', so that the proposed merger would not adversely affect competition, price, or choice in the retail market.

Networking arrangements for Channel 3 TV (April 1993)

Following the 1990 Broadcasting Act, new licences were awarded to fifteen regional television companies (such as Carlton, Central, and Anglia). A Network Centre was set up to draw up the network schedule and to acquire and commission programmes from the licensed TV companies and from independent producers. Independent producers were precluded from entering a supply contract with the Network Centre, but, rather, had to do

BOX 9.2. (*cont.*)

so with the TV companies with whom they could be competing to supply programmes. The TV companies, however, could contract directly with the Network Centre.

The OFT concluded that these arrangements failed the competition test under the Broadcasting Act. The issue was referred to the MMC, which proposed a new contracting arrangement involving tripartite agreements between independent producers, the Network Centre, and a TV company (with the latter's role being strictly limited). This was intended to ensure that the TV companies could not unfairly block access to the network for independent programme producers.

Contact lens solutions (May 1993)

Over 2 million people in the UK wear contact lenses, and the market for cleaning solutions (CLS) is about £90 million per annum. Suppliers have to obtain a product licence from the Medicines Control Agency (MCA) of the Department of Health, and CLS may only be sold at retail level by opticians and pharmacists, because the MCA thinks expert advice should be available at the point of sale.

The MMC estimated that opticians have about 60 per cent of the sales (with Dollond and Aitchison PLC (DA) and Boots Opticians Ltd. (BOL) taking 10 and 5 per cent respectively) and pharmacists 40 per cent (with Boots The Chemist Ltd. (BTC) alone having 31 per cent). The leading suppliers are Allergan Ltd., with 38 per cent of the market, and CIBA Vision (UK) Ltd., with 34 per cent.

The MMC concluded that Allergan's pricing policy exploited its monopoly position and that it had made excessive profits. It also concluded that Boots (BTC and BOL together) had enjoyed substantial margins and that its pricing policy was contrary to the public interest. DA and CIBA were not found to be behaving against the public interest.

Notice that this situation was not created by a merger, but, rather, was the outcome of a restrictive regulatory regime. Accordingly, the MMC recommended changes in regulation that would permit entry of new products and permit sales through a wider range of retailers. In the absence of such changes, the MMC recommended direct price controls be placed on Allergan and Boots.

Southdown Motor Services Ltd. (June 1993)

In September 1992, the OFT asked the MMC to investigate the registration, operation, and charging of uneconomic fares by Southdown (a bus company), now called Sussex Coastline Buses Ltd., on routes 262 and 242 in Bognor Regis.

There was a deregulation of the bus industry in the late 1980s. Southdown was the main bus operator in Bognor, but after deregulation a new company, Easy Rider, started up. Southdown started to run a new 262 service just ahead of the buses on one of Easy Rider's routes. This was withdrawn after a while, but then it started the 242 services, again just ahead of an Easy Rider service, and at a revenue that did not even cover the cost of the driver's wage. The 242 made a substantial loss, but caused financial problems for Easy Rider, which eventually sold out to Southdown.

This is an example of *predatory pricing*, which was discussed on pages 262–3. Predatory pricing involves selling goods or services at a loss in order to drive a rival out of business, and

BOX 9.2. (*cont.*)

then resort to monopolistic behaviour. The MMC concluded that the loss of competition could be expected to lead to higher fares and poorer service in the areas previously served by Easy Rider. It recommended that fare increases be limited to the rate of RPI inflation for two years, and that there should be no reduction in the level of service for the same period compared with that existing before the introduction of the 242. Further monitoring by the OFT was also recommended.

National Power bid for Southern Electric, and PowerGen bid for Midlands Electricity (March 1996)

The UK electricity industry was privatized in the early 1990s. National Power (NP) and PowerGen (PG) are the two largest generators of electricity, with 33 per cent and 24 per cent respectively of the market in England and Wales. There are twelve regional distribution companies (RECs) that have a monopoly (until 1998) of supply to customers in their region. Southern Electric (SE) and Midland Electricity (ME) are both RECs. In 1995, NP launched a bid to take over SE and PG bid to take over ME. Both bids were referred to the MMC, and the two MMC reports had the same date and the same conclusion.

The MMC concluded 'that the merger(s) may be expected to operate against the public interest . . . [but] . . . we do not consider that the adverse effects of the merger are sufficiently serious to justify prohibition'. Accordingly, a number of conditions were recommended designed to reduce the threat to competition. However, these conditions turned out to be irrelevant. The Secretary of State for Trade and Industry, Mr Ian Lang, declined to sanction the mergers. He made it clear that he wished to keep the main generation capacity in separate hands from the distributors, thereby closing the door for some time to mergers between electricity-generation companies and RECs.

Summary

1. Resources are said to be used efficiently when it is impossible, by using them differently, to make any one consumer better off without making at least one other consumer worse off. Economists distinguish two main kinds of efficiency: productive and allocative.

2. Productive efficiency exists for given technology when whatever output is being produced is being produced at the lowest attainable cost for that level of output. This requires, first, that firms be on, rather than above, their relevant cost curves and, second, that all firms producing the same product have the same marginal cost.

3. Allocative efficiency is achieved when it is impossible to change the mix of production in such a way as to make someone better off without making someone else worse

off. The allocation of resources will be efficient when each product's price equals its marginal cost.

4. Perfect competition achieves both productive and allocative efficiency. Productive efficiency is achieved because the same forces that lead to long-run equilibrium lead to production at the lowest attainable cost. Allocative efficiency is achieved because in competitive equilibrium, price equals marginal cost for every product. The economic case against monopoly rests on its allocative inefficiency, which arises because price exceeds marginal cost in equilibrium.

5. Very-long-run considerations, such as the effect of market structure on innovation and the incentive effects of monopoly profits, are important in evaluating market structures.

6. Market failure can arise because of externalities creating a divergence between private and social costs, because of absence of property rights, in the production of public goods, because of monopoly power, and where there is asymmetric or incomplete information. Markets, do not, even in principle, achieve certain other social goals such as redistributing income.

7. Efficiency of natural monopolies requires that price be set equal to short-run marginal cost and that investment be undertaken whenever that price exceeds the full long-run marginal cost of providing another unit of output. Average cost pricing results in too much output in the short run and too much investment in the long run in rising-cost industries and too little output and too little investment in falling-cost industries.

8. Government policy is designed to encourage competitive practices and discourage monopolistic ones. It seeks to regulate natural monopolies either by running them as nationalized industries (the UK solution in the past) or putting them in private hands and regulating them (the typical UK solution today). Competition policy has three goals: to permit only those restrictive practices that can satisfy public interest criteria; to prohibit mergers where monopoly power would become excessive; and to regulate firms in industries, such as utilities, where scale economies justify high concentration.

Topics for review

- Productive and allocative efficiency
- Classical preference for competition over monopoly
- Pareto-optimality

Firms and competition

- Sources of market failure
- Effect of cost on market structure
- Effect of market structure on costs
- Marginal and average cost pricing
- Privatization
- Competition policy

Questions for discussion

1. Explain why all firms may be producing efficiently and yet the outcome may not be optimal for society as a whole.

2. Discuss the extent to which each of the following are public goods: street lighting, law and order, education, health services, television programme transmission, commuter rail services, a production by the Royal Shakespeare Company, the M25.

3. Critically assess the argument that perfect competition is the most desirable market structure.

4. Can free markets be left alone to allocate resources in the economy?

5. Why did privatization displace nationalization in the 1980s and 1990s?

6. Why do common property resources tend to be over-exploited?

7. In what ways can information asymmetries lead to market failure?

Section 4
Economics of Business

CHAPTER 10

The Economics of Employment

The demand for a homogeneous input	314	Perverse incentives	333
The quantity of labour demanded	314	Negative effects of monitoring	334
The firm's demand curve for labour	316		
The physical component of *MRP*	316	**Internal labour markets**	335
The value component of *MRP*	316	Pay and promotion	336
From *MRP* to the demand curve	318	Rates of pay attach to jobs	336
The industry's demand curve for the input	318	Tournaments	338
The supply of labour	319	Seniority and *MRP*	341
Population	319	Firms and their employees	342
The labour force	320		
Hours worked	320	**Summary**	342
Supply and demand for labour	321		
Limitations of demand and supply analysis	322	**Topics for review**	343
Contracts and performance monitoring	324	**Questions for discussion**	344
Relational contracts and bounded rationality	324		
Principal–agent theory	325	**Box 10.1.** The paradox of incentive pay	322
Efficiency wages	327	**Box 10.2.** The economics of superstars	328
Signalling	330	**Box 10.3.** Japanese employment	
Incentives and monitoring	331	arrangements	337
Incentive pay	331	**Box 10.4.** CEO pay: fat cats or optimal	
Factors linking effort to pay	332	incentives?	340

S O far in this book we have focused mainly on the price and quantity decisions of firms in the markets for their outputs. Clearly, the product market is of vital importance to firms, because if they do not sell any output they cannot survive. However, there are many other important decisions that firms have to make, connected to the running of a successful business, and these can be the object of economic analysis just as fruitfully as can product markets. Hence, in Section 4 we focus on three key areas affecting the health of businesses. The current chapter examines the employment decision. The following chapter analyses investment decisions, and Chapter 12 discusses the issue of optimal business structure.

We start this chapter with an analysis of the determinants of firms' demand for the input of labour, assuming that the input is entirely homogeneous. Although this approach may be more suited to studying the demand for some input that is indeed homogeneous, such as raw materials, it does give us some important insights into how profit maximization determines input demand. The message of this approach for firms' hiring decisions is twofold. First, any firm's demand for inputs, including labour, is a 'derived demand' that depends upon demand for the final product. Second, to maximize profits, firms should hire an input up to the point where its contribution to additional revenue is just equal to its addition to costs.

Many of the most interesting features of labour markets arise from the fact that labour is not homogeneous. Indeed, not only are workers different when they enter a firm, they respond differently to the incentives they face. Hence, key problems for firms are how to attract the best workers and then how to get the most out of them. These issues have only recently been addressed by economists, but there is no doubt that economics has made important contributions to personnel or human resource management.[1] So the last part of this chapter is devoted to some of these new ideas emerging from the application of economics to the study of employee–firm relationships.

The demand for a homogeneous input

Firms require inputs not for their own sake but as a means to produce goods and services. For example, the demand for computer programmers and technicians is growing as more and more computers are used. The demand for carpenters and building materials rises and falls as the amount of housing construction rises and falls. Thus, demand for any input is derived from the demand for the goods and services that it helps to produce; for this reason, the demand for any input into production is called a **derived demand**.

> **Derived demand provides a link between the markets for output and the markets for inputs.**

We shall concentrate on demand for labour input, but remember that we shall be discussing some of the special and subtle features of labour markets in more detail below.

The quantity of labour demanded

We start by deriving a relationship that holds in equilibrium for every input employed by profit-maximizing firms. In Chapter 6, we established the rules for the maximization

---

[1] Two important recent books in this area are: Edward P. Lazear, *Personnel Economics* (Cambridge, MA: MIT Press, 1995), and Paul Milgrom and John Roberts, *Economics, Organization and Management* (Englewood Cliffs, NJ: Prentice-Hall International, 1992).

of a firm's profits in the short run. When one input, such as capital, is fixed and another input, such as labour, is variable, the profit-maximizing firm increases its output until the last unit produced adds just as much to cost as to revenue, that is, until marginal cost equals marginal revenue. Another way of stating that the firm maximizes profits is to say that *the firm will increase production up to the point at which the last unit of the variable input employed adds just as much to revenue as it does to cost.*

The addition to total cost resulting from employing one more worker hour of labour is its price, the hourly wage rate. (The firm is for now assumed to buy its inputs in competitive markets, so it can buy as much as it wants at the going market price.) So if one more worker is hired at a wage of £15 per hour, the addition to the firm's costs is £15.

The amount that one extra worker hour of the variable input, labour, adds to revenue is the amount that the extra worker hour adds to total output multiplied by the change in revenue caused by selling an extra unit of output. In Chapter 5 we called the variable input's addition to total output its *marginal product.* When dealing with input markets, we use the term **marginal *physical* product** *(MPP)* to avoid confusion with the revenue concepts that we shall also need to use.

The change in revenue caused by selling one extra unit of output is just the price of the output, p (since the firm is for the moment assumed to be a price taker in the market for its output). The resulting amount, which is $MPP \times p$, is called the variable input's **marginal revenue product** and given the symbol *MRP*.

For example, if labour's marginal physical product is two units per hour and the price of a unit of output is £7.50, then labour's marginal revenue product is £15 (£7.50 × 2).

We can now restate the condition for a firm to be maximizing its profits in two ways. First:

$$\frac{\text{The addition to total costs caused by}}{\text{hiring another unit of labour}} = \text{labour's marginal revenue product } (MRP). \tag{1}$$

Because the firm is a price taker in both its input and output markets, we can restate equation (1) by noting that the left-hand side is just the price of a unit of the variable input, labour, which we call w, while the right-hand side is labour's marginal physical product, *MPP*, multiplied by the price at which the output is sold, which we call p. In words, this gives us:

$$\text{Price of a unit of labour} = \frac{\text{Labour's marginal physical product}}{\text{multiplied by its market price.}} \tag{2a}$$

And in symbols:

$$w = MPP \times p. \tag{2b}$$

To check what the two versions of equation (2) mean, consider an example. Suppose that labour is available to the firm at a cost of £10 per worker hour (w = £10 per hour). Suppose also that employing one more worker for one hour adds three units to output ($MPP = 3$). Suppose further that output is sold for £5 a unit (p = £5). Then the additional unit of labour adds £15 to the firm's revenue and £10 to its costs. Hiring one more unit of the factor brings in £5 more than it costs. *The firm will take on more labour whenever its marginal revenue product exceeds its cost.* Now alter the example so that the last unit of labour taken on by the firm has a marginal physical product of one unit of output—it adds only one extra unit to output—and so adds only £5 to revenue. Clearly, the firm can increase profits by cutting back on its use of labour, since laying off one worker by one hour reduces revenues by £5 while reducing costs by £10. *The firm will lay off workers whenever their marginal revenue product is less than their price.* Finally, assume that the marginal worker taken on for an extra hour has an *MPP* of two units, so that he or she increases revenue by £10. Now the firm cannot increase its profits by altering its employment of labour in either direction. *The firm cannot increase its profits by altering employment of labour whenever labour's marginal revenue product equals its price.*

This example illustrates what was said earlier. We are doing nothing new; instead, we are merely looking at the firm's profit-maximizing behaviour from the point of view of its inputs rather than its output. In Chapter 6, we saw the firm varying its output until the marginal cost of producing another unit was equal to the marginal revenue derived from selling that unit. Now we see the same profit-maximizing behaviour in terms of the firm varying its inputs until the marginal cost of another unit of input is just equal to the revenue derived from selling the unit's marginal product.

The firm's demand curve for labour

We now know what determines the quantity of labour a firm will buy when faced with some specific price of labour (the wage rate) and some specific price of its output. Next we wish to derive the firm's whole demand curve, which tells us how much the firm will hire at *each* possible wage rate.

To derive a firm's demand curve for labour, we start by considering the right-hand side of equation (2b), which tells us that the labour's marginal revenue product is composed of a physical component and a value component.

The physical component of *MRP*
As the quantity of labour hired varies, output will vary. The hypothesis of diminishing returns, first discussed in Chapter 5, predicts what will happen: as the firm adds further units of labour to a given quantity of the fixed input, capital, the additions to output will eventually get smaller and smaller. In other words, labour's marginal physical product declines. This is illustrated in part (i) of Figure 10.1, which uses hypothetical data that have the same general characteristics as the data in Table 5.1 on page 146. The negative slope of the *MPP* curve reflects the operation of the law of diminishing returns: each unit of labour adds less to total output than the previous unit.

The value component of *MRP*
To convert the marginal physical product curve of Figure 10.1(i) into a curve showing

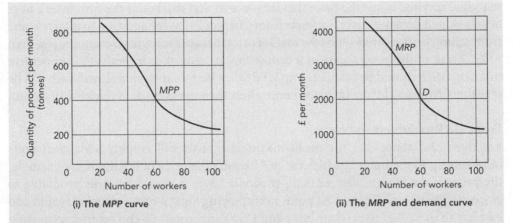

(i) The MPP curve

(ii) The MRP and demand curve

Figure 10.1. From marginal physical product to demand curve

Each additional unit of labour employed adds a certain amount to total product (part (i)) and hence a certain amount to total revenue (part (ii)), and this determines the amount of labour firms will demand at each price. Part (i) assumes data that are consistent with marginal productivity theory; it shows the addition to the firm's *output* produced by additional units of labour hired. The curve is negatively sloped because of the law of diminishing returns.

Part (ii) shows the addition to the firm's *revenue* caused by the employment of each additional unit of labour. It is the marginal physical product from part (i) multiplied by the price at which that product is sold. In this case the price is assumed to be £5. (The multiplication is by market price because the firm is assumed to be a price taker in the market for its output.)

Since the firm equates the price of the variable input, which is labour in this case, to the input's marginal revenue product, it follows that the *MRP* curve, in part (ii), is also the demand curve for labour, showing how much will be employed at each price.

the marginal revenue product of labour, we need to know the value of the extra physical product. As long as the firm sells its output in a competitive market, this value is simply the marginal physical product multiplied by the market price at which the firm sells its product.

This operation is illustrated in part (ii) of Figure 10.1, which shows a marginal revenue product curve for labour on the assumption that the firm sells its product in a competitive market at a price of £5 a unit. This curve shows how much would be added to revenue by employing one more unit of labour *at each level of total employment.*

The basic principle is that firms should equate the addition to cost of buying another unit of a variable input with the addition to revenue caused by selling the output of that unit, which we call the input's marginal revenue product, *MRP*. The *MRP* is always composed of a physical component, which is the input's *MPP*, and a value component, which is the marginal revenue of selling those extra physical units of output. Because, for simplicity, our firms are assumed to be price takers in their output markets, the marginal revenue is just the price that they face in that market. If the firm faces a negatively sloped demand curve, we know from Chapter 7 that the addition to total revenue from selling further units is not the market price, because marginal revenue is less than price. Thus, in the general case of a firm selling its output in imperfectly competitive markets, *MRP* should be calculated as *MPP* times *marginal revenue*. It will then still be true that firms should hire up to the point where the wage is equal to the *MRP* of labour.

From *MRP* to the demand curve

Equation (2a) states that the profit-maximizing firm will employ additional units of labour up to the point at which the *MRP* equals the price of labour. If, for example, the price of the labour were £2,000 per month, then it would be most profitable to employ 60 workers. (There is no point in employing a sixty-first, since that would add just less than £2,000 to revenue but a full £2,000 to costs.) So the profit-maximizing firm hires the quantity of labour that equates the marginal revenue product with the price of labour. Thus, the curve that relates the quantity of labour employed to its *MRP* is also the curve that relates the quantity of labour the firm wishes to employ to its price.

> The *MRP* curve of labour is the same as the demand curve for labour. The same would be true for any other variable input, that is, its *MRP* curve is its demand curve.

The industry's demand curve for the input

So far we have seen how a single firm that takes its market price as given will vary its quantity demanded of labour as the wage rate changes. But when labour's price changes and *all firms* in a competitive industry (or *any firms* in an imperfectly competitive industry) vary the amount of labour that they demand in order to vary their output, the price of the industry's product changes. That change will have repercussions on desired output and the quantity of labour demanded.

For example, a fall in carpenters' wages will reduce the cost of producing houses, thus shifting the supply curve of houses to the right. Price-taking construction firms would plan to increase construction, and hence increase the quantity of carpenters demanded, by some specific amount if the price of houses does not change. Because the demand curve for houses is negatively sloped, however, the increase in output leads to a fall in the market price of houses. As a result, each individual firm will increase its desired output *by less* than it had planned to do before the market price fell.

An increase in carpenters' wages has the opposite effect. The cost of producing houses rises; the supply curve shifts to the left; and the price of houses rises. As a result, the individual firm will cut its planned output and employment of labour by less than it would have done if market price had not changed.

The industry's demand curve for labour, relating the quantity demanded to the input's price, is steeper when the reaction of market price is allowed for than it would be if firms faced an unchanged product price.

It may be useful to summarize the reasoning used so far.

1. The derived demand curve for labour (or any variable input) on the part of a *price-taking* firm will have a negative slope because of the law of diminishing returns. As more labour is employed in response to a fall in its price, its marginal product falls and no further units will be added once its marginal revenue product falls to the new wage rate.

2. An industry's demand curve for labour (or any variable input) is less elastic than suggested by point 1. As the industry expands output in response to a fall in the wage rate, the price of the firm's output will fall (because the industry faces a downward sloping demand curve for the final product), causing the final increase in each firm's output, and hence employment of labour, to be less than would occur if the output price remained unchanged.

As emphasized at the beginning of this chapter, the above analysis would be very easy to apply within the firm if all labour were homogeneous—that is, every hour's worth of work bought from every possible worker had exactly the same effect on output—and if labour were bought in a commodity market in standard bundles, just like potatoes or wheat. Of course, in reality, this is not true, because employers and employees have longer-term relationships, so the employment decision is much more complicated. None the less, the basic point still stands: profit-maximizing firms should aim to hire up to the point where additions to revenue just balance additions to cost.

Now that we have studied the factors affecting the demand for labour we need to say something about supply in order to determine the market-clearing wage rate.

The supply of labour

The number of people willing to work is called the *labour force*; the total number of hours they are willing to work is called the **supply of effort** or, more simply, the **supply of labour.** The supply of effort depends on three influences: the size of the population, the proportion of the population willing to work, and the number of hours worked by each individual. Each of these is partly influenced by economic forces.

Population
Populations vary in size, and these variations are influenced to some extent by economic forces. There is some evidence, for example, that the birth rate and the net immigration rate (immigration minus emigration) is higher in good times than in bad. Much of the variation in population is, however, explained by factors outside economics.

Economics of business

The labour force

The proportion of the total population or of some subgroup such as men, women, or teenagers that is willing to work is called that group's **labour force participation rate**. This rate varies in response to many influences, for example, changes in attitudes and tastes. The enormous rise in female participation rates in the last three decades is a case in point. A force that is endogenous to the economic system is the demand for labour. Generally, a rise in the demand for labour, and an accompanying rise in earnings, will lead to an increase in the proportion of the population willing to work. More married women and elderly people enter the labour force when the demand for labour is high. For the same reasons, the labour force tends to decline when earnings and employment opportunities decline.

Hours worked

Not only does the wage rate influence the number of people in the labour force, it is also a major determinant of hours worked. Workers trade their leisure for incomes. By giving up leisure (in order to work), they obtain income with which to buy goods. They can, therefore, be thought of as trading leisure for goods.

A rise in the wage rate implies a change in the relative price of goods and leisure. Goods become cheaper relative to leisure, since each hour worked buys more goods than before. The other side of the same change is that leisure becomes more expensive, since each hour of leisure consumed is at the cost of more goods forgone.

This change in relative prices has two effects, known as the *income* and the *substitution* effects. The substitution effect leads the individual to consume more of the relatively cheaper goods and *less* of the relatively more expensive leisure—that is, to trade more leisure for goods. The income effect, however, leads the individual to consume more goods and *more* leisure. The rise in the wage rate makes it possible for the individual to have more goods and more leisure. For example, if the wage rate rises by 10 per cent and the individual works 5 per cent fewer hours, more leisure and more goods will be consumed.

Because the income and the substitution effects work in the same direction for the consumption of goods, we can be sure that a rise in the wage rate will lead to a rise in goods consumed. Because, however, the two effects work in the opposite direction for leisure:

A rise in the wage rate leads to less leisure being consumed (more hours worked) when the substitution effect is the dominant force and to more leisure consumed (fewer hours worked) when the income effect is the dominant force.

These conflicting effects are important in providing an answer to the question 'What is the shape of the supply curve of labour?' The supply curve of labour tells us what quantity of labour (worker hours) is offered at each wage rate. If the substitution effect dominates, the labour supply curve will always be positively sloped. Workers will offer to supply more labour at higher wage rates. However, if the income effect dominates, the labour supply curve may be negatively sloped. This means that workers would choose to consume more leisure as their wage per hour increases.

For the purposes of completing the demand and supply analysis of the labour market, we assume that the labour supply curve is positively sloped. Box 10.1 looks more closely at the implications of the possibility that labour supply curves may be backward-bending.

Supply and demand for labour

In Figure 10.1 we derived an individual firm's demand curve for labour and we discussed how the demand curve for each firm can be used to derive an industry demand curve. In order to obtain the market demand curve for labour for the whole economy we simply add the quantities demanded by each industry at every possible wage rate. This is equivalent to the horizontal addition of the demand curve of each industry. The market demand curve shows us the quantity of labour demanded across the whole economy at each wage rate. This is illustrated in Figure 10.2. The supply curve, drawn in the same figure, reflects all the work/leisure choices made by workers, discussed above.

Figure 10.2. Supply and demand for labour

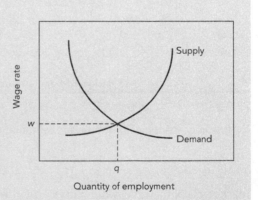

The market-clearing wage and employment level arise where the demand and supply curves intersect. Each firm's demand for labour is derived from its marginal revenue product. The market demand curve for labour is the sum of the demand curves for each firm. The demand curve is downward-sloping because of diminishing returns (and where firms sell in imperfect output markets because of a negatively sloped marginal revenue curve). The labour supply curve depends on the population that wants to work and how many hours they are prepared to work at each wage. Here we assume that the supply curve is positively sloped. The market clearing wage is *w*, and the quantity of employment is *q*.

Where demand and supply curves for labour intersect, the market-clearing wage and equilibrium quantity of employment are determined. Notice that, in the labour market equilibrium, everybody who wants to work *at the market clearing wage* would have a job. In this sense, there would be *full employment*. However, since the supply curve is positively sloped (by assumption), there would be some workers who would be prepared to work more at higher wage rates. Some of these may not be working at all at the

BOX 10.1.

The paradox of incentive pay

The potential for the income effect to dominate the substitution effect in labour-supply decisions has long been understood by economists. It creates the possibility that over some range of wages the labour supply curve may be negatively sloped, or backward bending, as illustrated in the figure. At wage rates below w an increase in wage rates brings forward offers of greater labour supply. However, at wage rages above w, workers choose to work fewer hours, and so take some of their extra real income in leisure.

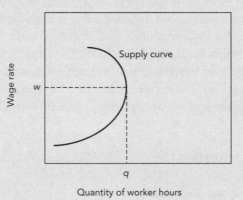

Backward-bending supply curve of labour

It is important for firms to understand that workers will at some times have a backward-

market-clearing wage, while others are in work but would be prepared to work longer hours if paid more. Hence, the market clearing level of employment is not necessarily the maximum level of employment that could be achieved.

LIMITATIONS OF DEMAND AND SUPPLY ANALYSIS

Demand and supply analysis has many uses when applied to labour markets. It helps us see how demand is derived from the needs of firms and how supply reflects the choices of many individual workers. It also offers important insights when discussing the effects of intervention in these markets, such as from minimum wage laws or from trade unions. The broad pattern of relative wages is strongly influenced by demand and

bending supply curve, especially if they intend to use reward structures to stimulate greater effort. Higher pay will not always generate extra effort. Some employers have discovered this lesson by trial and error. In the 1960s, the National Coal Board, which ran Britain's coal mines, increased wages in order to encourage miners to work harder. It had the opposite effect. Many miners decided that they were now well enough off that they only wanted to work four days a week instead of five. Absenteeism increased.

There are ways in which this potential problem can be avoided. The traditional solution is to offer higher wage rates only for overtime work. A worker then has to work the full working week, plus some extra, in order to put in the hours of work that are paid more. In this way, the substitution effect can be guaranteed to dominate the income effect. The extra overtime pay compensates at the margin for the leisure time lost. Harmful effects may arise from paying overtime rates well above normal wage rates if workers deliberately work less hard during normal hours so that they can get extra pay for work that is still to be completed.

For many skilled blue-collar and white-collar workers, the choice is not available to work longer or shorter hours when wage rates change. Rather, the only effective choice is whether or not to have a job at all. We discuss the role of wages in work incentives for such workers in the text under the heading of *efficiency wages*. The key point to note here is that for workers who are highly paid *and* who may lose their job if they perform badly, the income and substitution effects work in the same direction. It is only where workers can choose to work fewer hours *without damaging their future employment prospects* that income and substitution effects work in opposite directions.

The same issues that arise in pay incentives also affect other important questions, such as whether higher income-tax rates are a disincentive to work. In general, the answer again depends on the balance between the income and substitution effects. If the substitution effect dominates, higher income taxes will make people work fewer hours, since they get a lower reward (net of tax) for each extra hour worked. This will make them more inclined to choose extra leisure at the margin in preference to extra work. However, as higher income taxes lower real disposable income, it is possible that people will want to work harder in order to make up for lost income. We cannot say which of these effects will dominate.

supply. Occupations that require much training tend to pay more than occupations that require little—because the supply of trained workers would not be forthcoming without a wage differential sufficient to pay a return on the training. Occupations that require a scarce talent tend to pay more than those that require a minimum of talent. Hazardous and unpleasant jobs tend to pay more than jobs that require the same skill level but are safe and pleasant. And so it goes with major differentials reflecting variations in demand and supply.

In spite of these successes, demand and supply does not successfully explain a number of important characteristics of modern labour markets. For example, there appears to be no obvious tendency for wage rates to adjust to eliminate unemployment (excess supply) in labour markets. Another problem is that labour is not homogeneous. Workers differ in quality and yet those qualities are hard to discern in advance.

and managers of firms. The managers have information and expertise that the shareholders do not have—indeed, that is *why* they are the managers. The shareholders can observe profits, but they cannot directly observe the managers' efforts. To complicate matters further, even when the managers' behaviour can be observed, the shareholders do not generally have the expertise to evaluate whether that behaviour was as good as it might have been. Everyone can see the firm's revenues, but it takes very detailed knowledge of the firm and the industry to know how large those revenues *could* have been. Boards of directors, who represent the firm's shareholders, can acquire some of the relevant expertise and monitor managerial behaviour, but, again, this is costly.

A similar problem arises in any employment situation when the employer (the principal) cannot monitor accurately the performance of an employee (the agent). For example, Tutite PLC, a maker of underwear, may hire a salesman to go around all major retail clothing stores trying to find buyers for its product. When the hoped-for sales do not appear, should it be concluded that the salesman is either no good or has not been trying very hard? Alternatively, it could be that the product is inferior to other well-known brands, is too expensive, or is of the wrong design for current fashions. In order to make sure it is not the salesman's fault, Tutite will either have to monitor his performance in some way or create effective incentives for him to perform well.

These examples illustrate the **principal–agent problem**: the problem of designing mechanisms that will induce *agents* to act in their *principals'* interests. In general, unless there is costly monitoring of the agent's behaviour, the problem cannot be completely solved. Hired managers (like hired gardeners and salespeople) will generally wish to pursue their own goals. They cannot ignore profits, because if they perform badly enough, they will lose their jobs. Just how much latitude they have to pursue their own goals at the expense of profits will depend on many things, including how easy it is to measure performance. We discuss this further below.

> **Principal–agent analysis shows that when ownership and control are separated, or when hired workers have some range of discretion, the self-interest of agents will make profits lower than in a 'perfect', frictionless world in which principals act as their own agents, or agents always do exactly what the principals want.**

Specific models of principal–agent behaviour, developed by economists, have been successful in two ways. First, they have explained why conflicts between principals and agents arise in certain situations, by showing that the incentives induce the agent to do things other than what the principal desires. Second, they have provided a rational explanation of what at first sight seemed to be perverse behaviour, by showing that this behaviour was designed to create incentives for the agent to act in the principal's interest. For example, people put in positions of trust are often paid much more than is needed to induce them to take these jobs. Why should principals pay their agents more than they need to pay to fill the jobs? The explanation is that if the agent is paid much more than he could earn in another job, he has an incentive not to violate the trust placed in him. If he does violate the trust and is caught, he loses the premium attached to the job. The model can then be used to work out the exact premium needed to give the agent a self-interest in doing what the principal requires rather than violating the trust placed in him. We shall return to this issue below both in the context of our discussion of *efficiency wages* and when we discuss the controversial issue of executive pay.

Principal–agent theory predicts co-operation or conflict between principals and agents depending on whether the incentive structure creates a harmony or a conflict between the self-interest of the two types of person. Hence we shall say more below about the related issues of monitoring and incentives.

EFFICIENCY WAGES

One of the puzzles about labour markets has been why those markets do not work in the way suggested by the simple demand and supply analysis set out above. At most points in time, especially in recent years, there have been many people available for work who would be happy to work at the current wage rate, or even less, yet who cannot find jobs. That is, there appears to be an excess supply of labour.

Our market analysis in Chapter 2 suggested that whenever there is an excess supply of something, its price should fall until the quantity demanded just equals the quantity supplied. This does not usually happen in labour markets. Firms do not generally seem keen to cut wages in order to be able to hire more workers at lower wage rates, even though such a move might appear to increase their profits. Another apparent anomaly in labour markets is discussed in Box 10.2.

One possible reason why firms do not lower wages when there is an excess supply of workers is that heterogeneity of the labour force has led to the wage rate having the property of *signalling device*. This means that employers are worried about the quality and performance of workers as well as just their price, so these dimensions have to enter into the employment decision. In this context, the wage that yields the best combination of price and quality of worker is known as the **efficiency wage.**

The idea of the *efficiency wage* forms the core of a strand of thinking about why it may be optimal for firms to set wages (permanently) above the level that would clear the labour market. Efficiency wage theory applies to hiring, to productivity on the job, and to worker turnover.

Workers are not homogeneous. Suppose that there are 'good' workers and 'bad' workers, but there is *asymmetrical information*. Firms do not know the characteristics of specific workers until after they have sunk costs into hiring and training them. Good workers know who they are and are likely to have a higher reservation wage (the wage at which they are prepared to work for a particular firm) than bad workers. By lowering the wage it offers, a firm will significantly lower the average ability of the workers who apply to it for jobs, and so paying lower wages could make it worse off. This tendency for a firm that pays lower wages to attract poor-quality workers is known as *adverse selection*. It is a concept we met in the discussion of market failure in Chapter 9. It is extremely important in insurance markets, but it is also an essential feature of labour markets.

BOX 10.2.

The economics of superstars

A notable feature of modern labour markets is that a small group of people in many professions have come to be paid extraordinarily large salaries. We discuss the case of business leaders in Box 10.4 below. Here we focus on explanations of how this phenomenon arises more widely.

Many examples occur in entertainment and professional sport. Newcastle United are reported to have paid Blackburn Rovers £15 million for the services of Alan Shearer, and Middlesborough are reported to be paying Fabrizio Ravanelli nearly £50,000 per week. Phil Collins the rock star is reputed to have earned £8 million in 1995, and Damon Hill was on a contract worth £7 million even before he became the 1996 Formula 1 world motor racing champion. Similar examples also arise in business and the professions. In October 1996, NatWest Bank bought corporate finance specialist company Hambro Magan. Several of its key employees were tied in to contracts worth in excess of £1 million per year each.

Why are superstars so highly paid? Should not market incentives encourage others to compete for these large rewards, with the end result that the massive rewards for a few would fall and be replaced by more modest rewards for the many? On the contrary, forces in the modern economy appear to be increasing the gap between superstars and the rest. Why is this?

There are three components to the explanation. First, the general increase in real wealth over time has created an increase in demand for output in the sectors in which superstars perform. Second, in the relevant activities, there is a premium to being the very best over what the merely competent can command. For example, if you are wealthy and need a lawyer or a heart surgeon, you are going to pay for the best, and someone who is good but

In labour markets with informational asymmetries, where unobserved characteristics of workers are correlated with the reservation wage, it will not generally be optimal for firms to lower wages, even if other workers can be hired at the lower wage.

Once in employment, workers are likely to give greater effort if they feel they are being well rewarded and the costs of losing their job are high. If wages are so low that workers are just indifferent between staying and leaving, they are likely to please themselves how hard they work and they will not be afraid of losing their jobs. Employers have a problem of monitoring and enforcing efficient work practices—this is another case of the principal–agent problem mentioned above. Paying a high wage reduces the problem, both because workers will expect to be much worse off if they lose their current job and because there will be a queue of good-quality workers prepared to work for the high wage. The high wage improves efficiency—hence the term *efficiency* wages.

Another way in which higher wages may improve productivity is through the direct

not the best will not do. Equally, if you want your team to win the Premier League you need the best striker in the country, coming second is commendable but not good enough. Hence, those who are 'the best' may be only, say, ten per cent better than a bunch behind them, but they may command a substantial wage premium just because there is no one better. (The *MRP* of being the best greatly exceeds the *MRP* of being second.)

Third, modern communications have turned many local competitions to be the best into a single global competition, the winners of which earn huge sums. TV, movie, and pop stars are the obvious examples. Why listen to a local amateur opera company when you can listen to Pavarotti, and why listen to a local band when you can access the latest global music hits?

It is tempting to think that the emergence of superstars is a recent phenomenon. It is not. The great English economist Alfred Marshall noted its existence in the famous book *Principles of Economics* (Macmillan; see 8th edn., 1949 printing, pp. 570–1; but note that the observation appeared in a version written no later than 1920). Indeed, he was the first to point out two of the three elements of the economics of this issue set out above: 'The causes of this change are two; firstly, the general growth in wealth, and secondly, the development of new facilities for communication by which men, who have once attained a commanding position, are enabled to apply their constructive or speculative genius to undertakings vaster and extended over a wider area, than ever before.'

Marshall's economics was sound, but he failed to anticipate just how far communications would advance, for he continued: 'But so long as the number of persons who can be reached by a human voice is strictly limited, it is not very likely that any singer will make an advance on the £10,000 said to have been earned in a season by Mrs Billington at the beginning of the last century'. The sum of £10,000 in 1800 is roughly equivalent to £300,000 in 1997. How much more might she have made if her exceptional voice could have been recorded on CD and enjoyed throughout the world, as it could be today?

effects on worker nutrition and general health. By improving the physical well-being of the worker, the marginal productivity of workers may be increased. This is a very important effect in developing countries, but it may also apply in some sectors of developed economies. However, an effect that clearly does apply in developed countries is that workers who are paid well above their best alternative wage have an incentive to invest in self-education and skill acquisition in order to secure their continued employment prospects.

Finally, firms for which high quit rates would be costly, because they have invested in training, will be reluctant to lower wages for existing workers, even in the face of an excess supply of labour. Thus, workers who are already inside the company and know its work practices are worth retaining, even at premium wages. New workers, though possibly cheaper, may not be as good, and may be costly to train.

Efficiency wage theory says that firms will find it advantageous to pay high enough wages so that working is a clearly superior alternative to being laid off.

329

> This will improve the quality of workers' output without firms having to spend heavily to monitor workers' performance.

The point made in Box 10.1 above, about the apparent paradox of incentive pay, is relevant here. Workers *who can choose how much to work* may choose to work less at higher wage rates. In the analysis of efficiency wages, however, the presumption is that workers have a different choice. This is: work hard for a high reward or don't work at all (or, perhaps, at the much lower average wage). By posing the all-or-nothing choice, employers solve the potential disincentive effects of high incomes. Workers who might choose to work less do not get this option. They would lose all the benefits of high income if they did not work hard enough to retain their jobs. Hence the risk of having a low income forces them to work hard. This *potential-loss-of-income effect* reinforces the substitution effect, and for many workers encourages them to adopt the hard-work/high-pay solution—at least among those who are fortunate enough to have this choice.

SIGNALLING

The notion of the efficiency wage illustrates an important feature of interactions in which asymmetric information is of significance. This is that, where there are some uncertain characteristics involved, market participants will develop informal criteria for signalling information about some of these unseen characteristics.

In the context of the efficiency wage, the wage itself is, in part, a signal. Good workers know they are worth a good wage and, therefore, will only be prepared to work for employers who pay them accordingly. Thus an employer who hires only at low wages will inevitably pick up a high proportion of workers with 'poor' characteristics.

There are, however, many other ways for a potential employee to signal that he or she is high quality. Readers of this book should not find it too hard to think of an example. Most of you are in the process of acquiring an educational qualification—a degree or a diploma. One function of following this course is, hopefully, to accumulate some genuinely useful knowledge and skills. However, another important function of whatever qualification you are pursuing is to convince potential employers that you are ambitious, hard working, intelligent and committed to self-improvement—just the kind of person that every employer is looking for! This is creating a signal about your personal characteristics. In selection situations the signal about who you are may have as important a role as the true underlying characteristics of what you have learned.

Not all aspects of signalling are entirely desirable. Criteria used to 'signal' quality may instead amount to pure prejudice, such as use of 'the old school tie'. However, the point to notice is that the use of some kinds of signalling device is almost inevitable in markets in which uncertain characteristics are important. In labour markets these may include the reservation wage, education, dress, table manners, previous employment, etc. In product markets, one technique for signalling is the franchising of brand labels. Wherever you are in the world, you know what to expect from a MacDonalds restaurant or a Holiday Inn hotel. The employment market has similar brand labels such as a Harvard MBA, an ex-McKinsey consultant, or a Hanson-trained manager.

Incentives and monitoring

In work situations involving relational contracts that are not set out in any great detail, two key factors apply. One is the nature of the *incentives* that are set up to encourage workers to perform in the way that employers desire. The other is the extent to which it is both possible and desirable to *monitor* the performance of employees. As we shall see, the appropriate incentives and the possibilities for monitoring are not independent of each other. There is, for example, no point in setting up an incentive for workers to achieve a certain outcome if that outcome cannot be accurately monitored. You would not want to pay a worker extra for being 'nice to customers' if no objective measure could be determined of what that meant.

INCENTIVE PAY

Incentives are fundamental to economics. Profit is the incentive that drives business. Most people who enter employment do so because they want to earn money to buy food, pay for housing, and spend on holidays, etc.

When we discuss incentives in employment we shall for the most part be talking about financial incentives. However, it is not necessary to assume that people are motivated only by money or that financial motives are the only things that count. Undoubtedly many people are motivated by things other than money, and so important job characteristics include many dimensions other than pay. However, in most business employment situations employees are mainly working for the money, and they will generally work harder at the margin if there is a financial incentive so to do (subject to the provisos discussed above).

Economists tend to assume that individuals are motivated by self-interest. This is a reasonable assumption given that most individuals would prefer higher wages to lower wages, and will work harder if there is some financial incentive to do so. However, this does not mean that individuals will work harder *only* if they get paid extra. Neither does it mean that they will not co-operate in teams, if this is the most suitable format for work to be conducted in. What it does mean is that, if co-operative behaviour is required, whatever incentives exist should reinforce co-operative rather than competitive behaviour. For example, if a sales force is expected to work as a team, then it is better to pay individual bonuses based upon team sales rather than the sales of each individual. This is because individual bonuses may give each salesperson an incentive to conceal information from colleagues and compete with others in the team rather than co-operating.

331

Incentives in employment take many forms, not all of which are tied to current production. At one extreme of the range of possibilities is *piece work*. This involves being paid by how many units of the product each worker produces. Thus, a fruit picker may be paid by the weight of apples picked in a day, a bricklayer by the number of bricks laid, and a car worker by the number of cars produced. At the other extreme, some workers are paid a fixed salary with little or no variation related to current performance. It might be thought that the former types of worker have an incentive to work hard while the latter do not. Certainly, piece workers' incomes are directly related to their output. However, those on a fixed salary also have incentives to perform, but these are of a different nature. Some workers on a fixed salary work hard just to keep their jobs. Others work hard so that they can obtain a promotion in future years.

Although piece rates tie reward directly to output, they do not necessarily provide a 'better' incentive than the alternatives. Similarly, paying a flat salary does not remove all incentives for good performance. In between the two extremes of piece work and flat salary are many alternative incentive pay structures. Most of these involve some basic pay plus some additional incentive, such as a sales commission, a share of the profits, special higher overtime rates, or special responsibility allowances.

Factors linking effort to pay

The extent to which rewards are tied directly to effort varies considerably from context to context. For the moment we shall consider incentives in the form of increases in pay that are directly related to immediate work effort in some way. In general, the optimal incentive structure from the perspective of the firm will vary depending upon three factors.

First, incentives will only be important for a firm if profit is sensitive to the efforts of individuals concerned. This is why incentives are most commonly applied only to workers who can influence output directly. Workers on a production line often receive incentive pay, nightwatchmen and clerical staff rarely do. Equally, there is little role for incentive pay for workers in non-profit organizations, such as teachers in schools, doctors and nurses, civil servants, police, and the military.

Second, incentive pay can only be used effectively if work effort can be reasonably assessed. It would be disruptive of staff morale if some incentive were offered even though it was hard to agree that the effort required had indeed been forthcoming. It is better to avoid incentive pay than to induce arguments and dissatisfaction among workers who believe that their contribution has been inappropriately evaluated relative to some of their work mates. This is why pay tied to output only occurs when individual contributions can easily be measured, as when one trader acts alone so that his profits can be identified accurately, or where each worker acting alone produces a whole unit of a product so that her effort can be measured exactly. Many jobs, of course, are not like this, so tying pay to effort can create more problems than it solves.

Third, the effectiveness of incentives depends upon how sensitive workers' efforts are to the incentives offered. It is obvious that incentives to which workers do not actually respond positively are useless. The actual responsiveness may vary from time to time and from society to society. An incentive structure that works in Britain may not work in Japan. One problem that incentive pay creates for the workers themselves is some degree of income uncertainty. When good workers do not like taking such risks with their income, incentive pay can lead to having a worse workforce than otherwise. Some of the variations in income will result from factors beyond the control of the specific workers, such as from variations in demand for the product, and any such variations are likely to make them more dissatisfied with their working conditions. In short, it is important for firms to be sure that incentives really are creating the outcomes intended, in the form of genuinely greater effort and higher resulting profits. It is rarely a simple matter to ascertain that this is the case.

> **Financial incentives for workers in profit-maximizing firms will only be related directly to performance where that performance can be accurately monitored, where the effort of those monitored contributes directly to profit, and where the workers involved react appropriately to those incentives.**

Perverse incentives

Where incentives are used, it is important that they apply equally to all aspects of performance, or at least all those that are important for the profitability of the firm. The reason is that incentives that apply to only one aspect of a job, while other, perhaps equally important tasks, generate no extra reward at the margin, will encourage a worker to put much effort into the rewarded task and little or no effort into the unrewarded task. Just as all profit-maximizing firms must set marginal costs equal to marginal revenues, marginal costs must be equal in all plants, and marginal revenues must be equal (for the same product) in all markets, so the marginal revenue product of each employee must be equal in all tasks to be performed. For example, if an extra hour of an employee's time generates £15 worth of output in task A but £30 worth of output in task B, then clearly the employee's time should be reallocated away from task A towards task B. However, if the incentive structure is such that the employee gets a commission associated with performing task A while no commission attaches to task B, clearly the employee left alone to choose his or her own time allocation would choose to spend as much time as possible on task A. Indeed, if there were no penalty for under-performance on task B, the rational employee would spend their entire time on task A, because that is how they would get the greatest reward.

Financial incentives may also lead sales staff to seek sales even when the unsuitable nature of the products for customers would hurt the reputation of their firms. A well-known example of this arose in the UK in the market for personal pensions. Personal pensions are savings policies issued by insurance companies that have some tax advantages over other forms of saving, but are often inferior for the individual in employment in comparison to an occupational pension scheme. However, in the late 1980s, when legislation first permitted the sale of such pension policies, the sales people employed by insurance companies were given a substantial commission on every policy sold. As a result, huge effort was put by the sales force into the task of persuading as many people as possible to opt out of perfectly good pension schemes in order to buy these policies. In most cases the purchasers of these policies were made unambiguously worse off (even though they did not understand this at the time). The beneficiaries from these sales were the sales people themselves. In the longer term, the insurance companies whose policies were sold have been forced by the regulators to pay out substantial compensation to those who were 'mis-sold' such inappropriate products.

The problem in this case was that the incentive structure encouraged the sales staff to focus on one thing alone, and that was selling more policies of a specific sort. They had no equal incentive to work for the long-term reputation of the companies whose products they were selling, and so they did not seek to sell the policy that was right for each specific customer. This is a highly unsuitable incentive structure to serve the long-term interests of the insurance companies involved. Indeed, the negative publicity attached to this case has made the public much more suspicious of insurance-related savings products in general, and the companies with the worst reputations for mis-selling have suffered most.

> **Incentives must encourage each productive task equally, otherwise employees will devote too much time to rewarded tasks and insufficient time to unrewarded (but perhaps equally important) tasks. An equilibrium allocation of employee time is achieved where the marginal revenue product from each task is equal.**

NEGATIVE EFFECTS OF MONITORING

Monitoring is costly. It takes up staff time that could be devoted to other productive activities. In general, the marginal cost of monitoring activity should not exceed the marginal revenue product generated by this activity. In an ideal world, resources devoted to monitoring would be minimal because workers could be trusted to work productively. Even in a less than ideal world, direct monitoring will be unproductive where it is costly and difficult to achieve accurately—we do not have a second lecturer in every classroom to make sure that the first lecturer is doing his or her job properly, but we do ask all the students at the end of the course how it went.

Even where monitoring can be performed accurately, and where the activity is important for profitability, there are two reasons why active monitoring may not work. The first is that it creates hostility among the workforce who are being 'watched'. This hostility may be avoided if output is measured, perhaps, by end-of-day accounts or automatic output measures rather than by visible supervisors counting the product.

Modern work practices avoid some aspects of this problem in so far as employees work in teams. It is usually far more acceptable to have members of the same team encouraging each other to greater effort, especially when the incentives are for a team bonus. In effect, members of the same team monitor each other in an informal way, but in a way that may be more effective than being watched by management. Flexible teams also make the work itself less boring, especially where repetitive manual task are concerned, because team members can perform varied tasks rather than repeating a single task continually.

The second problem with monitoring, is what is known as the *ratchet effect*. This arises when targets for performance are raised for the future in response to an increase in output in the past. Suppose, for example, that in the current week workers making bicycles are paid £300 per week for making up to 100 bicycles and then they each get an extra £5 for each bicycle made over 100. Suppose also that in the current week 120 bikes are produced, so each worker takes home an extra £100.

After seeing this increase in output the management then say to the workers: 'OK it is clear that you can make 120 bikes in a week, so this is going to be your target for next week, and we will pay you an extra £5 for bikes over 120 a week.' The effect of this ratchetting-up of targets may be to make the workers work even harder. However, if they had expected this to happen before, they would probably have simply stuck to the lower production target and not bothered to raise their output in the first place.

This problem, which we have called the *ratchet effect*, is also known in economics as the problem of *incentive compatibility*. The firm wants to create incentives for workers to produce more and more. However, by moving the goalposts it may create an incentive for workers to behave perversely and refuse to increase output at all. The solution would be for management to create incentives for greater effort in the current and future periods, so that current good behaviour is not penalized in future. This means that management must agree targets with workers over a longer horizon and, perhaps, only change them when technology changes, or when a change can be agreed by both management and workers as being acceptable.

> **The regime of incentives and monitoring must consider the inter-temporal allocation of effort as well as just the impact in the current period.**

Internal labour markets

The features of labour markets differ greatly between firms, industries, and countries. However, most industrial economies have two broad sectors of employment. The *primary sector* includes many skilled manual workers, most white-collar workers, and virtually all technical, managerial, and professional employment. The *secondary sector* includes most unskilled employment, manual and non-manual, as well as part-time and seasonal workers.[2] Our main focus in this section is on the nature of employment

---

[2] This classification derives from P. Doeringer and M. Piore, *Internal Labor Markets and Manpower Analysis* (Lexington MA: D. C. Heath, 1971). The primary sector is characterized by long-term employment relationships and high-quality workers who have special skills. The secondary sector pays low wages and requires few or no special skills. The latter is the sector in which employees are fairly homogeneous and demand and supply forces most closely apply to wage determination. The primary sector is that where efficiency wage stories are most likely to apply. The categories have some ambiguity but are useful in distinguishing the clear differences between two types of employment relationship.

markets in the primary sector. However, it is worth noting that the analysis of demand for labour at the beginning of this chapter, as if it were a homogeneous commodity, can be applied most directly to the secondary sector.

Most primary-sector workers have a long-term employment relationship that provides a career path within the employing firm or organization. Typically, there are limited entry points into careers with each organization and most senior appointments are made from promotions from within. In contrast, secondary-sector workers have little or no expectation of advancement or even of long-term employment. They are often paid an hourly rate and have little job security.

Primary-sector workers generally find themselves in what is known as an **internal labour market.** This is made up of a firm and its long-term employees. An internal labour market has only limited connections with external labour markets, and its structure reflects the needs and traditions of each specific firm. In effect, an internal labour market offers a *jobs ladder* for the firm's long-term employees, with most employees starting somewhere near the bottom of the ladder and working their way up throughout their career. An extreme form of internal labour market is to be found among large firms in Japan. This is discussed in Box 10.3.

Pay and promotion

RATES OF PAY ATTACH TO JOBS

Employees in internal labour markets do not generally find that firms are trying to assess their marginal productivity and paying them accordingly. Rather, firms have a number of defined job grades and pay rates attached to the job rather than to any individual productivity measure. These pay rates typically have a limited range of possibilities for each grade, and what variations there are will be more likely to depend on seniority than on measured performance.

Individuals within an internal labour market generally improve their pay by moving up the ladder of promotion. Good work in the current job has a potential pay-off more in terms of promotion prospects rather than in terms of dramatically increased current pay. Hence, pay structures within the firm are determined by a firm-wide compensation scheme rather than by immediate calculations of individual performance.

The structure of compensation progression within a firm is something we shall discuss below. However, it is worth pausing to ask: why is it that internal labour markets are an efficient structure for firms? Why do firms not tie pay directly to each individual's marginal revenue product, as discussed at the beginning of this chapter?

There are at least three reasons why internal labour markets may be more efficient. The first is that most primary-sector jobs involve a great deal of learning. A long-term employment relationship, with a potential for promotion, creates an incentive for employees to invest in acquiring skills that will benefit the firm. These firm-specific

BOX 10.3.

Japanese employment arrangements

Traditional Japanese career patterns tend to be very different from those in the anglophone countries, particularly the UK and the USA. While the latter do have long-term employment relationships in many cases, the Japanese worker has to face an employment market in which workers typically commit themselves to one firm for an entire career, with entry only at the lowest level. In return, the company has also traditionally returned the commitment to life-time employment.

This pattern of a one-firm career has a number of important implications for the understanding of incentives among Japanese workers. The fact that there is no effective mid-career entry point into employment means that the internal labour market is the only route available for career progression. The costs of being dismissed are very high, because no other firm will employ a new mid-level manager. High levels of loyalty to the firm result from this fact that failure with one firm is failure for a lifetime. Job turnover is very low, and large firms are more attractive to work for than small firms, because they have more prospects for career advancement.

The positive effects of this restricted career path for the company are that, first, both employees and firms have an incentive to invest in both firm-specific and general training for the workers, because the return to this investment will accrue entirely to the current firm. Second, firms do not have to offer massive pay progression in order for workers to have an incentive to succeed within the firm. Hence, Japanese pay structures are much flatter than those within, say, American companies. Movement up the ladder is based to a considerable degree on seniority, so loyalty to the firm is rewarded, and most workers can expect pay to increase with seniority.

Even for those at the lower levels of the firm, decision making is consensual (rather than orders being transmitted downwards in the organization), so every employee feels able to influence decisions and, in effect, as if they are an important stakeholder in the organization.

The Japanese employment system is one that has proven success in the last fifty years and embodies a complete human resource management system. However, it is hard to replicate in its entirety in other countries. For example, a US firm offering life-time contracts but flat pay structures would find that its star workers quit for better paid jobs with other firms. Only if all firms are behaving as in Japan can the system work, with its implicit threats and long-term rewards. Indeed, some doubt whether the Japanese system can even survive in Japan. This is because rapid technical change and competition from other East Asian economies has forced some Japanese firms to review their commitment to life-time employment contracts, as some of the costs of guaranteed employment start to exceed the benefits, and the double-digit growth rates of the 1960s and 1970s are replaced by the stagnation of the 1990s.

skills[3] will take time to acquire and will take even longer to generate a pay-off for the firm. Hence, to achieve the benefits of this learning effect, firms have to offer the prospect of both long-term employment and of future promotion.

The second reason derives from the *efficiency wage* arguments discussed above. The incentives for good performance built into the efficiency wage require a long-term employment relationship. The 'good' workers are attracted to the firm by high rewards and also by a commitment on the part of the firm to a high degree of employment stability and 'good prospects'. Hence, both employees and employers are likely to generate a more productive relationship via mutual longer-term commitment, rather than via temporary employment contracts and minimal mutual commitment.

The third factor supporting internal labour markets is the fact that a successful firm requires long-term strategic thinking from at least some of its senior staff. The ability to take and implement long-term strategies is not something that shows up or can be tested over a short horizon. Hence, successful firms have significant numbers of senior managers who have been selected as a result of observing their performance within the company, and who have sufficient expectation of continuing employment that they are prepared to take a long-term view. For example, investment in new technologies for producing a firm's product can usually be postponed in the interest of short-term profit, but few things are more likely to damage a firm's long-term prospects than falling behind its rivals in technological capability. A manager who does not expect to stay with a firm very long may postpone important investments, while one who sees his own future as tied to the success of the firm will want to ensure its continued survival. In a sense, the internal labour market increases the convergence of interests between the employee and the firm, thereby reducing principal–agent problems.

> **Many skilled, managerial, and professional employees find themselves in an internal labour market in which pay attaches to jobs and in which there is a long-term career path. The internal labour market in each firm is insulated to some degree from those of other firms.**

TOURNAMENTS

One way to think of an internal labour market is as a *tournament*. Workers enter the tournament when they join a firm on the lower rungs of the ladder. Workers at each level compete with each other to show the senior management that they are most

---

3 Economists distinguish between *firm-specific* skills and *general* skills. The former only have a pay-off within one firm, while general skills can increase productivity in many other firms. In the absence of a long-term employment contract, employees will have an incentive to invest in acquiring general skills because they can sell them to any firm. However, they will not invest in firm-specific skills unless there is some commitment by the firm to reward this investment in due course. Firms will not generally wish to invest in giving their workers general skills, unless they can be locked into the firm in some way, because, if trained workers quit, the return on this investment will accrue to others. However, a firm will have an incentive to invest in giving firm-specific skills to their employees.

worthy of promotion. Periodically, when a more senior job becomes vacant, someone from the grade immediately below the vacant post is chosen to progress up the ladder. As there are fewer senior jobs than junior jobs, not everybody can progress up the ladder at the same pace. The tournament winner is the one who makes chief executive.

Viewing the internal labour market as analogous to a tournament offers an important insight into the issue of senior executive compensation. This is that the pay of the senior executives is as much about motivating everybody in the organization as it is about paying a 'fair' compensation for the incumbent of any specific post. For example, it may be tempting to ask of a highly paid chief executive, 'Did you really add £1m worth of profit to the business to justify your £1m salary?' A better question might be 'Did the fact that the chief executive was paid £1m motivate the entire workforce enough to add more than £1m to profits?' Some other important aspects of the pay of chief executives is discussed in Box 10.4.

Even though those who enter a golf or tennis tournament know that they cannot all win, it remains the case that the tournaments with the greatest prize for winning attract the best players and tend to bring out the best in them.

However, the tournament analogy has some limitations when applied to business organizations. Most importantly, a competition in which there are winners and losers may create an excessively competitive work environment. Too much time may get diverted to activities designed to impress the boss, but not productive in other ways. Such misdirected efforts are known as *influence costs*. Clearly, it is important for a firm to discourage 'internal politics' if such effort does not improve the profit of the firm.

One way to reduce influence costs is to keep the financial steps on the promotion ladder quite small, so that employees do not have an excessive incentive to stab their colleagues in the back in order to gain promotion before they do. Indeed, most organizations will want their employees to work in co-operative teams, and pay structures should do nothing to discourage such co-operation.

Some evidence supports the view that internal labour markets can be fruitfully viewed as tournaments. For example, chief executives in organizations with more employees tend to get larger salaries that those in organizations with fewer employees, and such pay structures do tend to motivate workers to gain promotion.[4] However, the tournament analogy has to be modified in at least two respects to conform with reality. First, a loser in a tournament is out, while workers who fail to get promoted can try again. Indeed, many workers are able to jump over people who were promoted ahead of themselves, at a later date. It is important that this should be possible, otherwise the discouraged losers would be demotivated and would have no further incentive to work hard. Second, real job ladders tend to have frequent small upward steps rather than infrequent large jumps, as suggested by the tournament analogy. This is presumably because workers need to feel that they are continually moving forward. A ladder with many small steps appears to be more efficient than one with a few giant steps.

---

[4] See, for example, B. G. M. Main, C. A. O'Reilly III, and J. Wade, 'Top executive pay: tournament or teamwork?', *Journal of Labor Economics* 11(4) (1993), pp. 606–28.

BOX 10.4.

CEO pay: fat cats or optimal incentives?

One of the most controversial topics of public debate in the USA and the UK in the mid-1990s has been the question of whether the chief executives of large companies could possibly be 'worth' their very large salaries. Multi-million dollar salaries are not uncommon in the USA, and salaries of £1million or more have become observable among UK chief executives and chairmen. To put this in context, the typical Japanese chief executive (CEO) is paid less than twenty times the pay of the average workers, while the typical US equivalent is paid more than one hundred times the pay of the average worker. CEO pay among the largest US companies grew four times faster in the 1980s than the average worker's pay.

There are two alternative explanations of these high US and UK salaries for CEOs. One is that this is an inefficiency caused by the principal–agent problem. CEOs are effectively out of the control of their shareholders, and they are rigging compensation committees with their own friends who have an interest in pleasing the CEO. Hence, high CEO pay is just evidence that shareholders are being ripped off. If this were true, the solution would be to give genuinely independent non-executive directors more power in setting compensation, or to give shareholders a vote on CEO pay rises.

The second possibility is that CEO pay is optimal in respect of the incentives it creates within the company. There are three elements to the incentive issue. One, which we have discussed in the text, relates to the tournament model of internal labour markets. High CEO pay provides an incentive for all the workers in the firm to progress to the top. Hence, it should not be justified solely by the performance of the specific incumbent CEO. Rather, part of the justification is the extra productivity of the entire organization. High CEO pay could, of course, be a disincentive for workers within the firm if it increases their feeling of unfairness. However, for those who have any serious prospects of eventually becoming CEO, high CEO pay may increase loyalty and the ambition to achieve promotion.

The second element is that the CEO does have to be motivated by his rewards, because there is no further promotion available. Hence, while mid-managers may be motivated partly by the prospect of becoming CEO, the CEO has to be motivated by something other than promotion prospects. The third element relates to the incentives in place for the CEO to take risks. It is argued that most individuals are risk averse—they will take the safe option rather than have any chance of being fired for making a bad decision. However, in a modern economy, firms should be risk neutral or risk takers. This means that CEOs may need an incentive to take risks in the interest of the long-term health of the company.

One way to encourage CEOs to take more risk is to offer a reward if risk taking pays off, while they pay no penalty when failures occur. Just such a reward profile is offered by giving CEOs share options. These options become valuable if the company's shares rise in value, but there is no cost to the CEO if the options expire worthless. In this way the gift of share options may provide an optimal incentive structure to encourage senior executives to take risks. A significant proportion of CEO compensation does involve just such incentives.

None of this proves that high CEO salaries are indeed optimal. However, it does suggest that the evidence required to determine whether they are so must cover a wider range of questions than merely whether the profit attributable directly to the efforts of the CEO exceeds the value of his or her salary.

The tournament structure of rewards has three advantages from the perspective of firms. First, selection of a candidate for promotion requires only enough information to make relative judgements between potential candidates; it does not require any absolute or detailed performance measures. Making relative judgements may require less resources devoted to monitoring than any productivity-based reward system. Such relative evaluation may be a better basis for compensation when external factors are important in creating variations in the firm's performance over time. That is to say, if an individual's contribution to output in any period depends in part on his or her own effort and in part on random external influences, then rewards will better mirror individual effort if they are based on relative performance, since the random external influences will be common to all employees.

The second advantage of the tournament employment structure is that pay ranges are set in advance for each job, so time is not wasted on individual pay negotiations with each and every employee. An employee who wants more pay will just have to work for a promotion. So bargaining time may be saved and influence costs are reduced. Equally, there is no incentive for employers to argue about performance in order to avoid having to pay bonuses. In effect, a potential source of moral hazard is avoided.

The third advantage of tournaments is that they reduce the problems of asymmetric information. Employees who are chosen for promotion from within the firm have generally become well known to the senior management, and so there is little uncertainty about their characteristics. Equally, employees who are promoted already know a great deal about the functioning of the company, so they can become effective in their new position more quickly than would be likely with an outsider.

A disadvantage with reliance upon insiders arises when there is rapid change and it is necessary to bring in new skills from outside. This has happened in many firms with the introduction of computers. However, many have dealt with it by creating a special career path for computer specialists that remains largely separate from the main managerial career path. The same is sometimes true for other specialists, such as research chemists in a pharmaceuticals company.

> **The promotion path in an internal labour market can be thought of as a tournament in which higher pay rates in more senior jobs create an incentive for employees to progress up the career ladder.**

SENIORITY AND *MRP*

We argued in the first section of this chapter that firms should aim to hire workers up to the point where the marginal revenue product is just equal to the extra cost. This does not mean that each worker should be paid what they themselves contribute to revenue. For firms to make profits, all but the marginal worker must contribute more to revenues than to costs.

Incentive issues discussed above suggest that, where there is a long-term relationship between firm and workers, firms will find it efficient to reward loyalty and long service. Hence, it will generally be true that longer-serving workers will get higher pay than younger workers. It is common for the rewards for long service to be evident in wage scales. However, even where this is not reflected in current wages it will be implemented via the company pension scheme, which will certainly reward long service with a higher pension. A pension can be thought of as deferred wages.

The need to reward long service means that, on average, there is a cross-subsidy passing from young workers to older workers. However, the young workers have the encouragement of knowing that they themselves will eventually benefit from this cross-subsidy when they become older workers. Thus, expectations of life-time earnings will be the same for both groups.

Firms and their employees

Labour is the most important input into any modern firm. A hundred years ago it was just the manual effort of workers that was being hired. Today, however, the vast majority of workers are not hired for their physical strength. Rather they are hired for their mental skills. It is brain power that drives business success rather than muscle power.

Brain power is a much more complicated input to manage than was muscle power. The mental ability of new potential employees is difficult to assess, and the effort of brain workers is hard to monitor accurately. Yet the success of a firm in the long term depends crucially upon selecting, keeping, and motivating a stock of corporate brain power. Internal labour markets provide the structure within which a company's most talented employees are nurtured, motivated, and developed.

The business world changes quickly, and major firms must adjust rapidly to remain industry leaders. Successful firms will mainly be those that have effective policies for accumulation and utilization of human resources. Economics is likely to play an ever-increasing role in the analysis of what an effective human resource policy looks like.

In the next chapter we discuss another important issue for firms, which is how to decide when to invest in an expansion of the capital stock.

Summary

1. The firm's decisions on how much to produce and how to produce it imply demands for inputs into the production process, which are said to be *derived* from the demand for goods that they help to produce.

2. A profit-maximizing firm will hire units of a variable input until the last unit adds as much to cost as it does to revenue. This means that the marginal cost of the input would

be equated with its marginal revenue product, which is its marginal physical product multiplied by the marginal revenue associated with the sale of another unit of output. When the firm is a price taker in input markets, the marginal cost of the input is its price per unit. When the firm sells its output in a competitive market, the marginal revenue product is the input's marginal physical product multiplied by the output's market price.

3. A price-taking firm's demand curve for an input is negatively sloped because the law of diminishing returns implies that the marginal physical product of an input declines as more of that input is employed (with other inputs held constant). The industry's demand curve is negatively sloped because of diminishing returns, and because the price of the product falls as more is produced under the influence of a fall in the input's price.

4. Real-world employment is complicated by the fact that labour is heterogeneous but the full characteristics of individual workers are hard to discern.

5. Many employment contracts are relational contracts, which do not specify in detail what workers have to do. This creates the potential for principal–agent problems, where the hired employees act, in part, in their own interest rather than that of the employer.

6. Solutions to the principal–agent problem involve some combination of incentives and monitoring.

7. Performance-related incentives are effective only where the activity involved matters for profitability, performance can be accurately measured, and employees respond positively to incentives.

8. Most skilled, managerial, and professional workers now find themselves in an internal labour market. Here the main incentive for lower- and middle-ranking staff is to achieve promotion. Higher pay generally attaches to more senior jobs, and the competition to gain promotion can be thought of as a tournament.

9. Chief executives may need to be encouraged to take risks, and whatever incentives they receive must be built into their own pay packages, since they cannot be promoted any further. However, the appropriate level for chief executive pay must take into account the incentive effect on all those who aspire to the top job.

Topics for review

- Derived demand for inputs
- Marginal physical product

- Marginal revenue product
- Relational contracts
- The principal–agent problem
- Asymmetric information
- Efficiency wages
- Internal labour markets

Questions for discussion

1. What factors set a limit to how much of a variable input a profit-maximizing firm will want to hire?

2. In what ways does the heterogeneity of labour complicate analysis of demand for labour?

3. Under what circumstances should firms use performance-related pay incentives to encourage greater effort from their workers?

4. Discuss the ways in which it would be appropriate to create incentives for each of the following employees: university professors; foreign-exchange dealers; production-line workers; hairdressers; taxi drivers who drive a company cab; the senior management of Glaxo Wellcome PLC; Alan Shearer; research workers in a biotechnology firm.

5. What are the advantages and disadvantages of internal labour markets?

6. What criteria should be used in deciding if a chief executive is overpaid?

7. What incentive might be used to encourage university teachers to give better lectures and do better research? Would you advise your university or college to adopt such an incentive structure?

8. Why does pay tend to rise with age? Is this fair to younger workers?

CHAPTER 11

The Economics of Investment

Capital and the firm	346	Alternative investment criteria	364
Implications of durability	346	Internal rate of return	364
Rental price	348	Payback period	366
Purchase price	348	What firms actually do	367
Present value of future returns	349	Two further applications of *NPV* techniques	368
Present value of a single future payment	349	Lease or buy?	368
One period hence	349	Is an MBA worth it?	371
Several periods hence	350		
Present value of a stream of future payments	350	Summary	374
How much to invest?	351	Topics for review	375
		Questions for discussion	375
Investment appraisal	352		
Application of the net present value criterion	353	Box 11.1. The rental and purchase price of labour	347
An example: gas-fired versus oil-fired electricity generators	353	Box 11.2. The future value of a present sum	352
Choice of discount rate	356	Box 11.3. Real and nominal interest rates	359
Treatment of inflation	357	Box 11.4. The economics of declining industries	362
Risk	360	Box 11.5. The option to invest	364
Sunk costs	361		
In the past	361		
In the future	361		

I N the previous chapter we learned that profit-maximizing firms would hire inputs upto the point where additions to revenue were just equal to additions to cost. The analysis of Chapter 10 was appropriate for purchases of inputs that could be bought in small units and used up immediately, or hired by the hour. However, almost all firms must also purchase some inputs that are 'lumpy' and provide a flow of services over long periods of time. Such inputs are generally referred to as *capital* goods. Examples include buildings, land, machinery, computers, lorries, forklift trucks and office furniture.[1]

---

[1] Another type of capital is *human capital*. This is created by the process of education and training. Human capital usually creates a continuing flow of extra output as a result of the improved skills of the person who has received the training.

The decision to purchase capital goods is called an *investment* decision. Investment decisions differ from other input decisions only in so far as the purchase of a capital good yields inputs over many future time-periods, and this time dimension complicates the calculation of costs and benefits. If all capital goods could simply be hired by the hour, and returned costlessly when no longer needed, there would be no need for special analysis. In practice, most investment decisions are hard to reverse and involve a significant level of *sunk costs* once undertaken.

Successful firms must have made good investment decisions at some point in their history. Unsuccessful firms often have either failed to make good investments or made bad investments.

The central question we address in this chapter is how firms should decide whether to invest in purchasing more capital goods. Here we focus mainly on purchases of physical capital. In the following chapter we shall consider the decision to acquire extra capital via the takeover of other firms. It is worth bearing in mind, however, that the general answer remains unchanged: *firms should buy extra capital goods if the value of the revenue generated exceeds the cost*. We start by discussing how we evaluate the costs of capital and the revenues generated, before discussing some of the practicalities of investment appraisal.

Capital and the firm

It is important to recall the distinction that we first made in Chapter 4 between **financial capital** and **physical capital**. Financial capital usually refers to a sum of money that is available for spending, or perhaps has already been invested in the equity of a company. Physical capital is a quantity of some durable commodity such as machinery or buildings. Throughout most of this chapter we are using the term 'capital' to refer to physical capital and are considering decisions such as those a manufacturing company makes when it decides to build a new factory or a bank makes when it decides to buy a new computer system. We are not concerned here with the alternative ways in which *financial capital* can be raised in order to purchase physical capital. This is a central topic in corporate finance.

Implications of durability

Of central concern is the important complication that arises because physical capital is durable. *It is convenient to think of the life of a particular item of capital equipment as being divided into a number of shorter periods that we refer to as production periods, or*

BOX 11.1.

The rental and purchase price of labour

If you wish to farm a piece of land, you can buy it yourself, or you can rent it for a specific period of time. If you want to set up a small business, you can buy your office and equipment, or you can rent them. The same is true for all capital and all land; a firm often has the option of buying or renting.

Exactly the same would be true for labour if we lived in a slave society. You could buy a slave to be your assistant, or you could rent the services either of someone else's slave or of a free person. Fortunately, slavery is illegal throughout most of today's world. As a result, the labour markets that we know deal only in the rental services of labour; we do not go to a labour market to buy a worker, only to hire his or her services.

You can, however, buy the services of some employees for a long period of time. In professional sports, multi-year contracts are common, and ten-year contracts are not unknown. The late Herbert von Karajan was made conductor for life of the Berlin Philharmonic Orchestra. Publishers sometimes tie up their authors in multi-book contracts, and movie and television production firms often sign up their actors on long-term contracts. In all cases of such *personal services contracts*, the person is not a slave, and his or her personal rights and liberties are protected by law. The purchaser of the long-term contract is none the less buying ownership of the employee's services for an extended period of time. The price of the contract will reflect the person's expected earnings over the contract's life-time. If the contract is transferable, the owner can sell these services for a lump sum (such as in the transfer market for a football player) or rent them out for some period (such as when a worker is contracted out).

As with land and capital goods, the price paid for this *stock* of labour services depends on the present value of the expected rental prices over the contract period. The concept of *present value* is explained in the text below. However, the key idea here is that, if we wanted to replace a wage contract that made regular monthly payments over say two years with a single lump-sum payment at the beginning of the period for the same amount of work, there would be some money sum that could be regarded as equivalent. This would be the (present) capital value of two years' worth of labour services.

rental periods. The present time is the current period. Future time is one, two, three, and so on, periods hence.

The durability of physical capital makes it necessary to distinguish between the item of capital itself and the flow of services that it provides in a given production period. We can, for example, rent the use of a piece of land for some period of time, or we can buy the land outright. This distinction is just a particular instance of the general distinction between flows and stocks.

Although what follows applies to any durable input, applications to capital are of most importance, so we limit the discussion to capital. Box 11.1 discusses some of these issues as they apply to labour inputs.

If a firm hires the use of a piece of capital equipment for some period of time—for example, one lorry for one month—it pays a price for the privilege of using that piece of capital equipment. If the firm buys the lorry outright, it pays a different (and higher) price for the purchase. Consider in turn each of these prices.

RENTAL PRICE

The *rental price of capital* is the amount that a firm pays to obtain the services of a capital good for a given period of time. The rental price of one week's use of a piece of capital is analogous to the weekly wage rate, that is, the price of hiring the services of one worker for a week.

According to the law of diminishing returns, as a firm rents more and more units of capital, with other inputs held constant, the marginal physical product of capital will eventually fall. This means that there will also be a falling marginal *revenue* product of capital. Just as a profit-maximizing firm operating in competitive markets continues to hire labour until its marginal revenue product (*MRP*) equals its wage, so the firm will go on hiring capital until its *MRP* equals its rental price.

If the marginal revenue product of capital exceeds the rental price, then the firm can increase profit by hiring more capital goods. If the marginal revenue product of capital is less than the rental price, then the firm can increase profit by hiring fewer capital goods. This is just another application of the principle that profit-maximizing firms will set marginal cost equal to marginal revenue.

A capital good may also be used by the firm that owns it. In this case the firm does not pay out any rental fee. However, the rental price is the amount that the firm could charge if it leased its capital to another firm. It is thus the *opportunity cost* to the firm of using the capital good itself. This rental price is the *implicit* price that reflects the cost to the firm of using the services of its own capital during the current production period.

PURCHASE PRICE

The price that a firm pays to buy a capital good is called the *purchase price of capital*. When a firm buys, say, a machine outright, it obtains the use of the machine's services over the whole of that machine's life-time. What the machine will contribute to the firm is a flow of extra revenue that is equal to the expected marginal revenue product of the machine's services over its life-time. The price that the firm would be willing to pay for the machine is, naturally enough, related to the total value that it places now on this stream of *expected* extra receipts to be received over future time periods.

The term *expected* emphasizes that the firm is usually uncertain about the prices at which it will be able to sell its outputs in the future. For the sake of simplicity, we temporarily assume that the firm knows the future *MRP*s. We shall discuss the problems created by uncertainty below.

Present value of future returns

Consider the stream of future income that is provided by an item of physical capital. How much is that stream worth *now*? How much would someone be willing to pay now to buy the right to receive that flow of future payments? The answer is called that income stream's *present value*. In general, **present value** *(PV)* refers to the value *now* of one or more payments to be received *in the future*.

PRESENT VALUE OF A SINGLE FUTURE PAYMENT

One period hence

To learn how to find the present value, we start with the simplest possible case. How much would a firm be prepared to pay *now* to purchase a capital good that will produce a single product, valued at £100 (net of all other costs of production), in one year's time, after which time the capital good will be useless? One way to answer this question is to discover how much the firm would have to lend out in order to have £100 a year from now. Suppose for the moment that the interest rate is 5 per cent, which means that £1.00 invested today will be worth £1.05 in one year's time.[2]

If we use *PV* to stand for this unknown amount, we can write PV(1.05) = £100 (the left-hand side of this equation means *PV* multiplied by 1.05). Thus PV = £100/1.05 = £95.24. This tells us that the present value of £100, receivable in one year's time, is £95.24 when the interest rate is 5 per cent. Anyone who lends out £95.24 for one year at 5 per cent interest will receive £95.24 back plus £4.76 in interest, which makes £100 in total. When we calculate this present value, the interest rate is used to *discount* (i.e. reduce to its present value) the £100 to be received one year hence. The maximum price that a firm would be willing to pay for this capital good is £95.24 (assuming that the interest rate relevant to the firm is 5 per cent).

To see why, let us start by assuming that firms are offered the capital good at some other price. Say that the good is offered at £98. If, instead of paying this amount for the capital good, a firm lends its £98 out at 5 per cent interest, it would have at the end of one year more than the £100 that the capital good will produce. (At 5 per cent interest, £98 yields £4.90 in interest, which, together with the principal, makes £102.90.) Clearly, no profit-maximizing firm would pay £98—or, by the same reasoning, any sum in excess of £95.24—for the capital good. It could do better by using its funds in other ways.

Now say that the good is offered for sale at £90. A firm could borrow £90 to buy the capital good and would pay £4.50 in interest on its loan. At the end of the year, the good yields £100. When this is used to repay the £90 loan and the £4.50 in interest, £5.50 is left as profit to the firm. Clearly, it would be worthwhile for a profit-maximizing firm to buy the good at a price of £90 or, by the same argument, at any price less than £95.24.

---

2 The analysis in the rest of this chapter assumes *annual* compounding of interest.

The actual present value that we have calculated depended on our assuming that the interest rate is 5 per cent. What if the interest rate is 7 per cent? At that interest rate, the present value of the £100 receivable in one year's time would be £100/1.07 = £93.46.

These examples are easy to generalize. In both cases we have found the present value by dividing the sum that is receivable in the future by 1 plus the rate of interest.[3] In general, the present value of R pounds one year hence at an interest rate of i per year is

$$PV = \frac{R}{(1+i)}. \tag{1}$$

Several periods hence

Now we know how to calculate the present value of a single sum that is receivable one year hence. The next step is to ask what would happen if the sum were receivable at a later date. What, for example, is the present value of £100 to be received *two* years hence when the interest rate is 5 per cent? This is £100/(1.05)(1.05) = £90.70. We can check this by seeing what would happen if £90.70 were lent out for two years. In the first year the loan would earn an interest of (0.05)(£90.70) = £4.54, and hence after one year the firm would receive £95.24. In the second year the interest would be earned on this entire amount; interest earned in the second year would equal (0.05)(£95.24) = £4.76. Hence, in two years the firm would have £100. (The payment of interest in the second year on the interest income earned in the first year is known as *compound interest*.)

In general, the present value of R pounds after t years at i per cent is

$$PV = \frac{R}{(1+i)^t}. \tag{2}$$

All that this formula does is discount the sum, R, by the interest rate, i, repeatedly, once for each of the t periods that must pass until the sum becomes available. If we look at the formula, we see that the higher i or t is, the higher is the whole term $(1+i)^t$. This term, however, appears in the denominator, so PV is *negatively* related to both i and t.

> The formula $PV = R/(1+i)^t$ shows that the present value of a given sum payable in the future will be smaller the more distant the payment date and the higher the rate of interest.

PRESENT VALUE OF A STREAM OF FUTURE PAYMENTS

Now consider the present value of a stream of receipts that continues indefinitely, as might the *MRP* of a very long-lived piece of capital. At first glance that *PV* might seem very high, because the total amount received grows without reaching any limit as time

---

[3] Notice that in this type of formula, the interest rate, i, is expressed as a decimal fraction; for example, 7 per cent is expressed as 0.07, so $(1+i)$ equals 1.07.

passes. The previous section suggests, however, that potential investors will not value the far-distant money payments very highly.

To find the *PV* of £100 a year, payable forever, we ask: how much would you have to invest now, at an interest rate of *i* per cent per year, to obtain £100 each year? This is simply $iPV = £100$, where *i* is the interest rate and *PV* the sum required. Dividing through by *i* shows the present value of the stream of £100 a year forever:

$$PV = \frac{£100}{i}.$$

For example, if the interest rate is 10 per cent, the present value would be £1,000. This merely says that £1,000 invested at 10 per cent yields £100 per year, forever. Notice that, as in the previous sections, *PV* is negatively related to the rate of interest: the higher the interest rate, the less is the present value of the stream of future payments.

In the text, we have concentrated on finding the present value of amounts available in the future. Box 11.2 reverses the process and discusses the future value of sums available in the present.

HOW MUCH TO INVEST?

From the foregoing discussion we can now state a key proposition that is central to the economic analysis of investment. This proposition is available to us because we have now solved the problem of comparing sums of money in different periods of time. Hence this enables us to handle the fact that capital goods yield flows of benefits into the future. The solution to this problem is to convert all future cash flows into their *present values*. Firms should undertake an investment if the present value of the extra revenue generated exceeds the present value of the extra costs incurred. Another way of stating the same result is in terms of what is known as the **net present value** (*NPV*) criterion:

Firms should undertake investments in projects for which the *NPV* is positive.

Net present value is simply the present value of the sum of the revenues generated *minus* the present value of the sum of the costs. A moment's thought should make it clear that an investment project with a positive *NPV* is adding value to the firm, while a project with a negative *NPV* will subtract value from the firm. Essentially, where the *NPV* of a project is zero, the present value of the marginal cost is just equal to the present value of the marginal revenue.

Economists often assume that firms will always undertake projects that add value so that they will move quickly towards an equilibrium in which all profitable projects have been undertaken. Hence, the equilibrium for firms is characterized by a situation in which the *NPV* of potential investments is zero.

However, firms themselves are operating in a world in which opportunities are continually changing, so they must perpetually be asking questions about where next to

BOX 11.2.

The future value of a present sum

In the text, we have concentrated on the present value of amounts to be received in the future. We can, however, turn the question around and ask what is the future value of an amount of money that is available in the present.

Assume that you have £100 available to you today. What will that sum be worth next year? If you lend it out at 5 per cent, you will have £105 in one year. Letting *PV* stand for the sum you have now and *FV* for the value of the sum in the future, we have $FV = PV(1.05)$ in this case. Writing the interest rate as we have in the text we get:

$$FV = PV(1 + i).$$

If we divide through by $(1 + i)$, we get equation (1) in the text.

Next, if we let the sum build up by reinvesting the interest each year, we get:

$$FV = PV(1 + i)^t.$$

If we divide both sides by $(1 + i)^t$, we get equation (2) in the text.

This tells us that what we did in the text is reversible. If we have an amount of money today, we can figure out what it will be worth if it is invested at compound interest for some number of future periods. Similarly, if we are going to have some amount of money at some future date, we can figure out how much we would need to invest today to get that amount at the specified date in the future.

Our argument tells us that the two sums *PV* and *FV* are linked by the compound interest expression $(1 + i)^t$. To go from the present to the future, we *multiply PV* by the interest expression, and to go from the future to the present we *divide FV* by the interest expression.

The rule of 72 is a convenient way of going from *PV* to *FV* by finding out how long it takes for *FV* to become twice the size of *PV* at any given interest rate. According to that rule, the time it takes for *FV* to become twice *PV* is given approximately by $72/100i$. So, for example, if *i* is 0.1 (an interest rate of 10 per cent) any present sum doubles in value in $72/10 = 7.2$ years.

invest and, indeed, where next to divest. Hence, it is important to look more closely at some of the practicalities of investment appraisal.

Investment appraisal

In the real world of business there are many different ways in which firms make decisions about whether to invest or not. Indeed, most successful business people have had no training in economics and very little in finance or management science. In the case of small businesses, decisions are often based on pure hunches and almost always with no formal explicit analysis. Where these decisions work out, the investor is hailed as a brilliant business person. However, for all those who succeed there are many others who fail. Is the successful investor really excellent at making investment decisions, or is it pure luck when things work out well?

The aim of modern investment appraisal techniques is not to replace the brilliant business tycoon or entrepreneur, or even to eliminate all elements of luck. Rather, it is to quantify all those factors that can be measured in order to provide management with as much information as possible about whether a specific project looks like adding value to the firm. Even the most scientific investment appraisal techniques will occasionally lead to investments that turn out badly, or reject investments that would have turned out well. The reason for this is that the world is always changing and the future is uncertain. That is, all investment is risky.

We first outline how the calculation of *NPV* can be used in a case where the extra revenues from the investment project are known with certainty. We then discuss several practical issues, including the problem of uncertainty.

Application of the net present value criterion

The idea that investment should be decided on the basis of the net present value criterion is simple. But, as with many apparently simple ideas, there turn out to be several factors that complicate the implementation of this approach in practice. We start by outlining a numerical example of how the *NPV* approach is applied in practice before discussing some of the complicating factors. Another common term used to describe the methods we are about to use is **discounted cash flow** (*DCF*), for reasons that should soon be obvious.

AN EXAMPLE: GAS-FIRED VERSUS OIL-FIRED ELECTRICITY GENERATORS

Table 11.1 contains the hypothetical data used to compare two alternative projects for a power company to increase its capacity to generate electricity. One involves the building of a gas-fired plant. The other is an oil-fired plant. Each is designed to add exactly the same total level of generation capacity. With the extra output selling at the same price, both add the same future stream of additional revenues. Each plant has a life of ten years, after which there is no scrap or second-hand value. Capital costs are incurred in period 0, while revenues accrue from period 1 onwards. This reflects the realistic assumption that most of the cost of building a new plant will have to be borne before any revenue is received. The two plants have the same capital cost of £2.5 million.

Although both plants have the same capital cost and generate the same revenue stream, they differ in variable (direct) costs. In this example, the variable costs of running the gas-fired plant are constant throughout the life of the project, while those

Table 11.1. Net present value and investment appraisal (£ million)

	Year										
	0	1	2	3	4	5	6	7	8	9	10
Gas-fired plant											
Revenues	0	1.16	1.21	1.27	1.34	1.40	1.47	1.55	1.63	1.71	1.79
Costs	2.50	1.00	1.00	1.00	1.00	1.00	1.00	1.00	1.00	1.00	1.00
Net	−2.50	0.16	0.21	0.27	0.34	0.40	0.47	0.55	0.63	0.71	0.79
Discount factor at interest rate of 10%	1.00	1.10	1.21	1.33	1.46	1.61	1.77	1.95	2.14	2.36	2.59
PV of Net cash flow (row (3) ÷ row (4))	−2.50	0.15	0.17	0.20	0.23	0.25	0.27	0.28	0.29	0.30	0.30
NPV (summation of row (5)) =−0.06											
IRR= 9.63%											
Payback period = 8 years											
Oil-fired plant											
Revenues	0	1.16	1.21	1.27	1.34	1.40	1.47	1.55	1.63	1.71	1.79
Costs	2.50	0.79	0.82	0.86	0.91	0.95	1.00	1.06	1.11	1.17	1.22
Net	−2.50	0.37	0.39	0.41	0.43	0.45	0.47	0.49	0.52	0.54	0.57
PV	−2.50	0.34	0.32	0.31	0.29	0.28	0.27	0.25	0.24	0.23	0.22
NPV (summation of row (4)) = 0.25											
IRR = 11.97%											
Payback period = 6 years											

Net present value (NPV) is the discounted sum of incremental cash flows. The hypothetical figures in the table show the calculation of the NPV of two alternative projects to generate electricity. Both have the same initial cost and then generate the same additions to revenue. However, the costs of running the two plants vary over their life-times. Row (1) in each case shows the additions to revenues generated in each year and row (2) shows the additions to costs in each year. Row (3) is the net cash flow, calculated simply by subtracting row (2) from row (1). In the case of the gas plant, row (4) shows the discount factor used for calculating the present value. It is $(1.1)^t$, where t is the number of years into the future and it is assumed that the rate of interest is 10 per cent. This same discount factor is applied also to the net cash flows in the oil plant but is not shown again under the oil project. The last line of data in

each case is calculated by dividing the net cash flow (row (3)) by the discount factor (row (4) of the gas example). This gives the present value, at time 0, of the net cash flows in each future period. The net present value of the project is the sum of the discounted cash flows (last line). It is implicitly assumed that the plants are closed down with no scrap value after year 10. The gas plant has a negative present value of −0.06, while the oil plant has a positive NPV of 0.25. Accordingly, the latter will add value to the firm, while the former will not. (IRR and payback period will be explained in the text below.)

Source: Numbers for this example were taken from N. Kulatilaka and A. J. Marcus, 'Project valuation under uncertainty', Journal of Applied Corporate Finance 5(3) (1992), pp. 92–100.

of running the oil-fired plant start low and rise over time. This could reflect anticipated rising oil prices, or it could be that the efficiency of oil-fired stations falls over time.

The result of this difference in time-path of variable costs is summarized in the third line for each project, which shows the *net cash flow* of each plant in every time period. Both have the same capital expenditure of £2.5 million in year 0, represented as a cash flow of –2.5. From year 1 on, the gas-fired plant has a small positive cash flow that rises over time, while the oil-fired plant has a larger initial cash flow but then it falls throughout the life of the project.

From simply eyeballing the figures for the two cash flows, it is not obvious which would be better for the firm. From years 1 to 5 the oil-fired station generates the higher cash flow. In year 6 they are equal. But from then on the gas-fired station generates the higher cash flow. Which should be chosen?

An unambiguous answer can be arrived at using the *NPV* criterion. The final line of numbers in each section of the table shows the actual cash flows in each time-period converted into their present values at time 0. This is done by dividing the net cash flow (line 3) by the discount factor (shown only in the top half of the table, since it is the same for both). The discount factor for each period is calculated assuming an interest rate of 10 per cent. So the discount factor for period 0 is 1. For period 1 it is 1.1 (calculated as $1 + i = 1.1$), and for period 2 it is 1.21 (calculated as $(1 + i)^2$; that is 1.1^2), and so on. Thus, for example, the actual net cash flow in period 10 expected for the gas-fired plant is 0.79. However, this has a present value in period 0 of only 0.3 (calculated as 0.79/2.59, where $2.59 = (1.1)^{10}$).

The *NPV* of each project is then calculated as the sum of the present values of the net cash flows. This is simply the addition of all the numbers in the last line of each part of the table. This tells us the net value at time 0, that is at the beginning of the project, of all the various cash flows from the future time periods.

The answer produced by the example in Table 11.1 is that the gas-fired plant has a net present value of –0.06, while the oil-fired plant has an *NPV* of 0.25. This means that the gas-fired plant does not add value to the firm; rather, it would reduce current value to the tune of £60,000. In contrast, the oil-fired plant adds value to the tune of £250,000. Hence, the *NPV* has given us the unambiguous answer that the company involved should build the oil-fired plant rather than the gas-fired plant.[4]

Notice that an important role in this decision is played by the discount factor. The oil-fired plant has an advantage over gas in its early years of operation. This early cash-flow advantage is important in present value calculations because the weight attached to cash flows in present value calculations declines over time. The higher is the rate of interest used to discount future cash flows, the bigger will be the relative weight attached to early cash flows relative to later cash flows. In contrast, at lower interest rates the relative penalty attached to later cash flows declines. This means that the project that offers the highest *NPV* can change as the discount rate changes, because the project with

---

[4] Do not forget that these numbers are entirely artificial. We have *not* proved that oil-fired power stations are superior to gas-fired stations. The purpose of the example is merely to show how the *NPV* criterion can be used to aid the choice.

the lower *NPV* at one discount rate may have a higher *NPV* at a different discount rate. In particular, projects for which the high positive cash flows are delivered later in time are more likely to be favoured when the discount rate is low, while projects with high cash flow delivered early on are more likely to be favoured when interest rates are high.

> In choosing between projects that offer different time-profiles of cash flows, the calculation of *NPV*s, and, therefore, the ranking of projects, will change over time as the discount rate changes.

We now turn to a discussion of several important factors that need more detailed consideration in the application of *NPV* methods to real investments.

CHOICE OF DISCOUNT RATE

In the above example we used a discount rate of 10 per cent. This may seem like a reasonable round number. However, where does it come from? How should we decide in a real investment appraisal what discount rate to use? The answer is straightforward in principle, but more difficult in practice.

The discount rate appropriate for appraising an investment project is *the true opportunity cost of the financial capital involved as valued by the capital markets*. There are two elements to this. First, there is the pure time value of money. That is usually measured by the market rate of interest on a risk-free investment, such as a government bond. To find this figure it is necessary only to look in the daily financial press. However, even here there is a slight complication. This is that the yield on government bonds varies with the term to maturity (the number of years before principal is paid off) of the bond. Bonds with a long term to maturity usually, though not always, have a higher yield than bonds with a short term to maturity. This means that calculation of the appropriate discount rate should take into account not just current short-term interest rates, but also long-term rates.[5] This is especially true when there are big differences between short rates and long rates, and when the investment project is expected to have a long life.

The second element of the opportunity cost of capital is the return in excess of the risk-free rate that is necessary to compensate for risk. In general, financial markets require a higher expected return to compensate for greater risk.[6] The greater the risk associated with a project the greater should be the *risk premium* attached to the discount rate used in evaluating the project. For example, if the risk-free rate of return

---

[5] The appropriate risk-free rate to use for discounting cash flows at each time horizon is the yield on a single coupon (strip) government bond of matching maturity. This may generate a different discount rate for cash flows in each future time-period. For simplicity, we normally assume that the risk-free rate is the same for each maturity.

[6] The Capital Asset Pricing Model (CAPM) is a standard model for determining the opportunity cost of capital in this context. Details of this are beyond the scope of this book and are covered in finance courses. For present purposes all we need to know is that the (financial) capital markets determine the required return on investments of various degrees of risk.

is 7 per cent, it might be that moderately risky investments require a return of 13 per cent, and high-risk investments require a return of 17 per cent. In this case, the risk premium on the moderate-risk investment would be 6 per cent, while that on high-risk investments would be 10 per cent. In this environment, a project that fell into the moderate-risk category should use a discount rate of 13 per cent, while a high-risk project should use a discount rate of 17 per cent.

It should be stressed that the opportunity cost of capital relevant to these decisions is that set by the capital markets. It is not appropriate for a firm to argue that, for example, since the money used to finance the project is generated internally, the opportunity cost of the capital is lower than it would be if borrowed externally, so a lower discount rate can be used in investment appraisal. But it may be appropriate to use a higher rate if the firm faces credit rationing (as do many small and/or start-up firms).

The reason this would be an error is that the firm has the option of investing its capital in other projects via the capital markets, or of returning the money to shareholders. If it does not use the market valuation of the opportunity cost of capital in valuing its potential project, it will find that it has invested in an internal project that adds less value to the firm than could have been achieved by investing the resources elsewhere via the capital markets. Equivalently, it may accept a project as having a positive *NPV when in fact it has a negative NPV when evaluated at the true opportunity cost of capital.*

In other words, it is the riskiness of the project itself that is relevant for determining the risk premium to incorporate in the rate of discount. This is the most scientific way in which an allowance for risk is incorporated into investment-appraisal techniques.

In practice, many firms use a weighted average cost of capital (*WACC*) as a discount rate for investment-appraisal purposes. This is calculated on the basis of the average yield on all the moneys raised by the firm itself from all its financial sources, such as equity, bonds, and bank loans. Clearly, this is not a correct procedure from the perspective of economic theory, because the *WACC* reflects the average costs of capital to the firm, rather than the riskiness of the project being assessed. However, for an investment project that is about as risky as the existing business this may not be a bad approximation to the true opportunity cost of capital. The danger is that this will also be used in much riskier projects for which it is clearly inappropriate.

In many industries the main risk is how long the capital will be economically useful. In many industries where innovation is high, firms use a high pay-back period. They must get their investment back within some, usually short, time, say two to three years. This is, of course, almost equivalent to the imposition of a high-risk premium. We discuss the pay-back method of appraisal below.

TREATMENT OF INFLATION

Another factor that complicates investment appraisal is inflation. The problem here is that the value of money itself is changing over time, so that care has to be taken to make sure that a project is generating added value *in real terms*.

In fact, net present value methods are ideally suited to judging real added value because the assessment criterion is measured unambiguously in money values at the beginning period of the investment project. In other words, if we are making the decision in 1998, then the calculation is converted into 1998 pounds sterling. However, there are two different ways in which this can be done, and it is important that one or other approach be applied consistently.

The first approach involves using expected current money values for all cash flows—that is, the actual money values that are expected to be recorded at the time the flows accrue. These money values are then discounted back to initial-year present values using a *nominal* discount rate. The nominal discount rate is the actual money value of the interest rate in the markets for the appropriate level of risk.

The second approach measures all future cash flows in terms of, say, 1998 (base-year) money and discounts these back to the present using a *real* discount rate. The real discount rate is approximately equal to the nominal rate minus the rate of inflation.[7] This would mean that all the estimated cash figures are measured in 1998 money values (or whatever the base period is) throughout the exercise. We discuss the important distinction between real and nominal interest rates in Box 11.3.

If applied correctly, both these two methods will come up with exactly the same result. They should give identical results because they are different ways of converting future cash flows into present values: both methods use the same numeraire of base-period money values. Mistakes will only be made if a mixture of real and nominal data slips into the same calculation, such as if nominal cash flows were discounted by the real rate of interest. This would clearly be erroneous.

A simple example should help to clarify this point. Suppose that we want to calculate the present value of an investment that costs £1 million on 1 October 1998 and is expected to generate a single pay-off of £1.3 million on 1 October 1999, where both figures are measured in nominal terms. Suppose also that the appropriate nominal discount rate for this type of investment is 15 per cent and that inflation over this year is expected to be 5 per cent. There are two equivalent ways of working out the *NPV* of this investment opportunity:

1. Work out the *NPV* by using the nominal sum accruing in the future (£1.3 million) and discounting this by the nominal interest rate (15 per cent). Thus, the present value of £1.3 million is 1.3/1.15, which is £1.1304 million. The net present value is thus £130,400 (calculated as £1.1304 million minus £1 million).

2. Value the future revenue from the investment at 1 October 1998 prices. This requires deflating £1.3 million by the ratio of the price level on 1 October 1999 to that on 1 October 1998. Since inflation is expected to be 5 per cent, that ratio is 1.05. So the value of £1.3 million at October 1998 prices is £1.238 million (calculated as 1.3/1.05). The appropriate *real* discount factor is 1.15/1.05 (as explained in Box 11.3), which is 1.095. When £1.238 million is discounted by the real discount rate,

---

[7] The reason why this is approximate is explained in Box 11.3.

BOX 11.3.

Real and nominal interest rates

If today you put £100 into a bank savings deposit and the bank is offering 7 per cent interest, in one year's time you will receive interest of £7. If today's date is 1 January 1999 the money will be received on 31 December 1999. This 7 per cent is referred to as the *nominal rate of interest*. It tells you how much money you will get paid in interest. However, between January 1999 and the end of December 1999 it is likely that the purchasing power of each £1 of money will have changed. This is because of inflation. Inflation is, by definition, a fall in the purchasing power of money—prices of a typical basket of goods, as measured by the retail price index (RPI), are rising.

If there is inflation in 1999, it will mean that the £7 interest you receive at the end of the year will buy fewer goods and services than it would have bought at the beginning of the year. The *real rate of interest* is the number that tells you how much extra goods your money interest will buy you. In order to calculate the real rate of interest *ex post* you need to know what the inflation rate has been over the period in question. *It is approximately true to say that the real rate of interest is the nominal rate of interest minus the rate of inflation.*

We say that this relationship is 'approximate' for two reasons. First, the exact relationship between real interest rates, nominal interest rates, and inflation is $(1 + r) = (1 + i)(1 + p)$, where r is the nominal interest rate, i is the real interest rate, and p is the rate of inflation. If you multiply out the right-hand side of this equation you get: $1 + i + p + ip$. Hence, the nominal rate is not exactly equal to the sum of the real interest rate and the inflation rate, because there is also the term ip. This term will be very small when both i and p are small, but not if they are large, such as when inflation is high. Second, the relationship is often used to apply to 'expected' interest rates. In this context, expectations may be incorrect, so that the relationship holds subject to a random error.

Expected real interest rates are what matter for most investment decisions by firms, because firms are converting a purchase of physical capital today into a stream of extra output of goods in the future. The issue is: how many goods in the future justify giving up some goods today? It is the real return on capital that is central to this decision.

One place where real interest rates can be observed is on the yields offered by government index-linked bonds (gilts). For these instruments, the government guarantees to pay back a nominal sum plus enough to compensate for the rise in the RPI between the issue date and maturity. In December 1996, a UK government index-linked bond with a maturity date of 2020 was yielding a real interest rate of about 3.5 per cent. At the same time, another government bond, which offered only a nominal rate of return (repaying £100 on maturity for each bond held) and had a maturity date of 2021, was offering a yield of 7.8 per cent. This suggests that the financial markets expect an inflation rate of about 4.3 per cent on average over this period.

the result is £1.1304 million. So the net present value is £130,400, just as before. (Note that you will not come up with exactly the same numbers by these two methods if you use rounding of numbers at any stage in the calculation.)

RISK

We have already discussed above the main way in which an allowance for the riskiness of the project should be incorporated into the present value calculation. However, some other points about risk allowances are worthy of notice.

It is quite common in real-world investment appraisals for allowance for risk to be made largely by setting out alternative *scenarios*. For example, in the appraisal of power stations in Table 11.1, there may be doubts about both input prices (oil and gas) and output prices (the market price of electricity), so optimistic, pessimistic, and moderate scenarios may be set out using a range of possibilities for these critical prices. There is nothing wrong in principle with setting out such possible scenarios; however, care must be taken to avoid requiring excessive compensations for risk. For example, the oil-fired station might have a negative present value when the calculation uses both the most pessimistic high oil price, a low electricity price, *and* a discount rate that allowed for the riskiness of similar projects. This would not necessarily mean that the project should be abandoned, merely that the calculation had allowed for risk twice and inevitably come up with an excessively cautious *and possibly wrong* decision.

Two other aspects of risk are worthy of mention. The first is that some value should be attributed to projects that build in flexibility as compared to those that do not. For example, in our gas-fired versus oil-fired power station example, suppose that there was a third possibility, a station capable of using either oil or gas. Such a power station would probably have a greater capital cost than either of the other two, but it would have the huge advantage of reducing the risks from either oil or gas prices rising very high. If no value were to be attributed to such flexibility, the mixed-fuel generator would probably be rejected as too expensive. However, appropriate allowance for the benefits of such flexibility could make it the preferred alternative.[8] In a world in which there is rapid technical change, the benefits of flexibility are reinforced. We shall see below that it is desirable to incorporate a value for this flexibility option in the *NPV* calculations.

Another perspective on risk arises because the choice in investment decisions is not just an either/or decision between mutually exclusive alternatives at a single point in time. Even if we have chosen the best project, the question still arises of when to do it. Should we do it now or should we wait and see how things develop. One of the most important recent theoretical insights into investment behaviour has come from an explicit analysis of the advantages of a wait-and-see policy. This is especially important when there are large and irreversible set-up costs of a project and state-of-the-art technology

---

[8] This point is made by the authors cited in Table 11.1. Their article is the source of this example.

is changing rapidly. Once a project is undertaken it is usually impossible to reverse without significant expenses having been incurred. However, before it is started, a high degree of flexibility can be maintained and a change of direction can be made. The problem is one of what economists call *sunk costs*.

SUNK COSTS

There are two aspects to the problem of sunk costs, depending upon whether these costs have already been incurred or whether the expenditure is yet to be made (and, therefore, is still an object of choice).

In the past

A common error in investment decisions is to give weight to the past and try to rescue past mistakes. It is common to hear statements like: 'We need to spend more money in this factory because otherwise the investment we made last year will be wasted.'

A key element of successful investment appraisal should be that *sunk costs from the past do not enter into the decision about new investments*. Bygones are bygones. What matters is whether incremental expenditures add present value or not. The success or failure of past investments is irrelevant to this decision.

What this means is that decisions about whether to spend more on anything should be forward-looking. The question should always be asked: does the present value of the extra revenue generated exceed the present value of the extra spending incurred? If the answer is yes, then the expenditure will increase the value of the firm; if the answer is no, then the extra expenditure will decrease the value of the firm.

This does not mean that present-value techniques cannot be used to take decisions about whether or not to scrap old plant and machinery; they can. Suppose that we have a factory that is declining in efficiency, and suppose also that it has zero scrap value. The question is whether to keep it going or close it down entirely. The answer will depend solely on the present value of the extra expenditures required to keep it going relative to the extra revenues that will be generated by keeping the plant operating, that is to say, whether revenues can cover average variable costs. The original cost of the factory is irrelevant to the decision, though the scrap or resale value of the factory would not be irrelevant if this were positive (since this would represent a potential future cash flow). An example of how it may sometimes be optimal to let capital slowly decay is provided in Box 11.4.

In the future

Until recently economists assumed (implicitly) that irreversible costs that have not yet been incurred should not be treated in any special way in *NPV* calculations. However, important new insights have been derived from a branch of financial economics known as *option pricing theory*. Box 11.5 explains what 'options' are in this context and illustrates the idea with a numerical example. The detailed mathematical tools required to

BOX 11.4.

The economics of declining industries

The view that public control was needed to save an industry from the dead hand of third-rate, unenterprising private owners was very commonly held about the British coal industry in the period between the First and Second World Wars. It was undoubtedly a factor leading to the nationalization of coal in 1946. The coal industry was returned to private ownership in 1995, after further dramatic decline in public hands.

The question addressed by this box is whether a superficial observation of the state of the capital in any industry is sufficient evidence to determine whether it is being well managed. In the context of the UK coal industry, the late Sir Roy Harrod argued that the run-down state of the industry in South Wales and Yorkshire, and the advanced state of the pits in Notting-hamshire and Derbyshire, represented the correct response of the owners to the signals of the market. He wrote:

> The mines of Derbyshire and Nottinghamshire were rich, and it was worth sinking capital in them. If similar amounts of capital were not sunk in other parts of the country, this may not have been because the managements were inefficient, but simply because it was known that they were not worth these expenditures. Economic efficiency does not consist in always introducing the most up-to-date equipment that an engineer can think of but rather in the correct adaptation of the amount of new capital sunk to the earning capacity of the old asset. In not introducing new equipment, the managements may have been wise, not only from the point of view of their own interest, but from that of national interest, which requires the most profitable application of available capital . . . it is right that as much should be extracted from the inferior mines as can be done by old-fashioned methods (i.e. with equipment already installed), and that they should gradually go out of action.*

Declining industries always present a sorry sight to the observer. Because revenues have fallen below long-run average costs, new equipment is not installed to replace old equipment as it wears out. The average age of equipment in use thus rises steadily. A declining industry will *always* display an old age-structure of capital, and thus 'antiquated' methods. The superficial observer, seeing the industry's very real plight, is likely to blame the antiquated equipment, which is actually the effect, not the cause, of the industry's decline.

To modernize at high capital costs merely makes the plight worse, since output and costs will rise in the face of declining demand and prices. To nationalize a declining industry, as was done with coal, in order to install new plant and equipment that privately owned firms were unwilling to install (at least in some areas) was to use the nation's scarce resources inefficiently. Capital resources are scarce: if investment occurs in mines, there is less for engineering, schools, roads, computer research, and a host of other things. To re-equip a declining industry that cannot cover its capital costs is to use scarce resources where, by the criterion of the market, their product is much less valuable than it would be in other industries. The efficient response to a steadily declining demand is not to replace old equipment, but to continue to operate existing equipment as long as it can cover its variable costs of production. If variable costs cannot be covered, then it is time to close down.

* Roy Harrod, *The British Economy* (New York: McGraw-Hill, 1963), p. 54.

evaluate options are well beyond the scope of this book. However, the idea of applying option theory to this problem is an important one, and it is easy enough to understand the general principles involved.

There are two key features of many real-world investment projects. The first we have already mentioned. This is that some significant chunk of costs is irreversible so that it cannot be recovered if it is later decided to abandon the project. The second feature is that the implementation does not have to be done immediately, since it is usually possible to delay. The advantage of being able to delay is that more information may come along later that would help to avoid making the wrong decision.

The important new idea relating to investment decisions in this context is that some *financial value* should be assigned to the option to wait and see. Once the investment is undertaken, this option is killed and this value is lost. Hence an irreversible investment should only be undertaken if the net present value is sufficiently greater than zero to compensate for the loss in the value of the option.

> **An investment that involves significant sunk costs should only be undertaken if the net present value of proceeding exceeds the value of the wait-and-see option.**

One way to think about why this option must be valuable to a firm is to notice that, if the investment goes ahead, the sunk costs of the project will be incurred with certainty, and there is always some probability that the project itself will lose money (that is, have a negative *NPV*). By postponing the project and perhaps cancelling it later when new information comes along, the firm is *not losing money* with certainty. Hence, by exercising the option to wait and see, the firm could end up creating extra value (by not throwing money down the drain on an unprofitable project). An asset that has some probability of giving the firm some added value and no possibility of losing it value must in itself have a positive value—this is the value of the wait-and-see option that we are discussing.

This idea gives important insights into why it may be that many firms require a substantial estimated *NPV* of a project before they will invest, whereas the theory set out above suggests that *any* positive *NPV* would be adequate.

Another important application of this insight is to the explanation of why it is that many firms stay in business for some time, even when they are not covering their variable costs. Above we have made the clear prediction that such firms would close down, that is, go into liquidation. However, the prediction of immediate close-down ignores the value of the options that this firm may have to invest in valuable investment projects once market conditions improve. If the firm closed down, these options would be lost. Hence, the statement about close-down decisions should be modified to say that firms should close down if the present value of the losses exceeds the present value of the firm's investment options. We have, in effect, been ignoring the irreversibility that is built into a close-down decision. This also explains why other firms are often prepared to pay substantial sums to take over a loss-making business. Essentially, they are buying the investment options that the target firm owns.

BOX 11.5.

The option to invest

Financial options come in two types. A *call option* is the right to buy an underlying asset at a specified price (the exercise price) within some period of time. A *put option* is the right to sell an underlying asset at a specified price within some period of time. These options can be exercised if the buyer so wishes, but there is no obligation so to do. If the buyer is better off not exercising the option then that is OK—hence the term 'option'. The option will just expire worthless. Options have some value so long as they have some time left to run, and so long as there is even a faint possibility that the underlying value of the asset will exceed the exercise price of a call option, or be less than the exercise price of a put option.

Investment by firms that has not yet been implemented is just like the option to buy some underlying assets at some specific price. This is a call option. The value of this call option is conceptually separate from the value of the underlying asset itself. This is because the call option still allows you to back out without any further costs, whereas the investment itself incurs substantial sunk costs.

A simple example may help.* Suppose that a firm has a potential investment project available to it. This project would involve an instant irreversible cost of £800 (you can think of these numbers as millions if you like). The revenue from the project will depend on which of two states of the world emerges in a year's time, affecting whether the output from the project sells for £150 or £50. These alternative states are equally likely to arise, but only next year will it be clear what is going to happen. For simplicity we can assume that the revenue stream established next year will then be perpetual and that the appropriate discount rate is 10 per cent.

Alternative investment criteria

Economic theory is clear that the *NPV* criterion, as modified above, is the best way to evaluate investment decisions. However, there are other methods available, and there is no compulsion attached to economists' recommendations. Indeed, many different approaches are used in practice. We mention here just two of the most common ones, and explain why *NPV* is preferable.

INTERNAL RATE OF RETURN

The internal rate of return (*IRR*) method is related to *NPV* and will often give the same result; but, where it differs, *NPV* is to be preferred.

The *IRR* of any investment is found by taking the same stream of net cash flows as used in calculating *NPV*, but then asking: what rate of interest, when used to discount

Suppose we do the *NPV* calculation relating to an immediate investment. The expected revenue on average will be £100, so the net present value is –£800 plus the present value of £100 for ever. The latter sum is £1,100 (we have £100 produced instantly plus the present value of a perpetuity paying £100 starting next year, which is £1,000). Hence the net present value is £300 (calculated as –£800 + £1,100), and it looks like we should go ahead with the project.

However, suppose we wait and then only go ahead with the project if the revenue received is £150, cancelling the project if it turns out to be £50. (By next year we will know what state of the world has arisen.) The present value today of that alternative is £380 (calculated as half the present value of –£800 ('half' because there is a 0.5 probability of going ahead), plus *half* the present value of £150 in perpetuity, starting next year). Hence, the present value of waiting one year is greater than the present value of investing now. The value of that wait-and-see option today is £80 (calculated as the difference between the present value of waiting, £380, and the present value of investing today, £300). The strategy that maximizes the present value of the firm is to do nothing until next year.

This approach gives important insights into how uncertainty about the environment can inhibit investment. Who will win the next general election? Will there be a single currency in Europe, and if so, will Britain be a member? These are events that can create uncertainty about the future state of the world. If these are perceived to influence future investment returns, then many firms may rationally adopt a wait-and-see attitude before investing.

* The example and much of the argument in this box are drawn from Robert S. Pindyck 'Irreversibility, uncertainty, and investment', *Journal of Economic Literature* 29 (September 1991), pp. 1110–48. See also Avinash K. Dixit and Robert S. Pindyck, 'The options approach to investment', *Harvard Business Review*, 73(3) (May–June 1995), pp. 105–15.

this cash flow stream, would make the *NPV* of this project zero? The idea is to come up with a number that can be considered as a measure of the interest yield of the project. It is equivalent to a concept that is used in stating the return on some financial assets, especially bonds. This concept is the *yield to maturity*. This is the average rate of return you would get from buying a bond at its current market price and holding it until its principal is paid back at some future time.

Two examples of the calculation of the *IRR* of projects are to be found in Table 11.1 on page 354. The net cash flow for the investment in a gas-fired plant generates an *IRR* of 9.63 per cent, while the oil-fired plant generates an *IRR* of 11.97 per cent.[9]

Clearly, a firm would prefer a higher *IRR* to a lower one. Hence, the oil-fired facility would be preferred to the gas-fired plant, just as it was when the *NPV* criterion was used. If the *IRR* and *NPV* criteria give the same result, why should we prefer the latter to

9 *NPV* and *IRR* calculations are easy to do using standard spreadsheet packages such as Microsoft Excel and Lotus 1-2-3. However, notice that such programs typically discount from the first column of data. Hence, if applied to the data in Table 11.1, the discount factor of 1.1 would be applied to column (0) rather than column (1). Users hence need to be careful when using such programs about noting exactly how they do the calculation.

the former? The reason is that they will not always give the same result. This is because the *NPV* of a project varies with the appropriate opportunity cost of capital that is used to discount future cash flows. The *IRR* does not use the opportunity cost of capital in its calculation.

The data in Table 11.1 can be used again to illustrate this important point. Given the cash flows set out for the two power stations, the *IRR* for each of those is a unique number. However, the *NPV of each project will be different for each value of the discount rate*. Hence, there are some discount rates at which the gas-fired plant is preferred to the oil-fired plant. So we would have the *NPV* criterion saying build the gas-fired plant while the *IRR* criterion was saying build the oil-fired plant. Which would be correct? The answer is the *NPV* criterion, because the *IRR* criterion makes no allowance for the current market rate of return on capital of equivalent risk while the *NPV* criterion does. In other words, the *IRR* criterion would be leading to a decision that did not maximize the present value of the firm.

The attraction of *IRR* is that it summarizes the return on an entire project in one number, and this number can be interpreted as an interest rate. It is tempting to assume that a high-yielding project should always be preferred to a lower-yielding one. However, as we have just seen, collapsing the characteristics of a project into one statistic may not always lead to correct decisions. At the very least, *IRR* calculations should be compared with *NPV* calculations to check whether they are giving the same result.

> Internal rate of return (*IRR*) is a measure of the yield on an investment project. It sometimes gives the same ranking of investment projects as *NPV*, but, where it does not, *NPV* is theoretically preferable.

PAYBACK PERIOD

An even simpler investment criterion is one that says that the firm should choose the investment project that pays back the invested capital most quickly. Thus, an investment that pays for itself in five years would be preferred to one that paid for itself in eight.

Again we can use the examples in Table 11.1 to illustrate this criterion. The numbers in line 3 of the top half of the table show the net cash flows associated with the gas-fired plant. In year zero there is a capital cost of £2.5 million. To find the payback period of this project we simply accumulate the cash flows in subsequent years until they add up to £2.5 million. In this case, by the end of year 7 the cash flow has accumulated to £2.4 million. By the end of the eighth year the accumulated cash flow is £3.03 million. This means that the payback is some time in the eighth year.

If we think of the revenue in the eighth year as accruing all at the end, then the payback period is unambiguously eight years. However, it is sometimes assumed that the revenues arrive smoothly throughout the year (even though our discounting procedure assumes that it arrives all together). In this case, since the net cash flow for year eight is £0.63 million, and we only need an additional £0.1 million to achieve the total payback of £2.5 million, we could say that the total payback period is 7.16 years (calculated as 7 plus 0.1/0.63). However, for simplicity, where the payback period occurs in the eighth year, we refer to this as a payback period of eight years. By this method, the payback period for the oil-fired plant in Table 11.1 is six years and for the gas-fired plant it is eight years. Hence, again, we have this criterion giving us the same result as the others. Preference would be given to the oil-fired plant.[10]

It is much easier to see what is inadequate about relying on payback period as an investment criterion. There are two main inadequacies. First, it is possible that, if a firm looked only at the payback period, it would accept a project that had a shorter payback period than alternative projects but not a positive net present value. In such a case, pursuing this project would be lowering the value of the firm.

Second, the payback criterion ignores entirely the value of net cash flows that arise after the payback horizon. Suppose, for example, that the firm had to choose between two projects that both had a payback period of five years. From year six onwards, one of these projects would generate nothing, while the other would double revenues every year for ten years. The payback criterion would leave the firm indifferent between these two, while clearly it should not be. Even more worryingly, it is possible (with slightly different data) that the first project would have a shorter payback and, therefore, would be chosen in preference to the second.

Payback period is, thus, a very crude rule of thumb. It is always reassuring to know that an investment is going to pay off quickly, especially in a world of rapid technical change where an investment in, say, new computers, must pay off before they have to be scrapped. However, no well-trained manager should be using this as the sole criterion for making investment decisions. Its application inevitably involves disregarding significant amounts of additional information that are relevant to the investment decision.

> **The payback period indicates how quickly an investment will pay for itself. This is useful information, but it should not be the sole criterion upon which investment decisions are made because it ignores the value of revenues (or costs) beyond the payback horizon.**

WHAT FIRMS ACTUALLY DO

There have been several studies that have surveyed firms to find out which methods of appraisal they use. The picture we are about to report is based upon a recent survey conducted by Alan Sangster of the University of Aberdeen.[11]

---

[10] A slightly more sophisticated payback method would involve asking: how long is it before the present value of the project becomes positive? This would involve accumulating discounted cash flows rather than undiscounted costs and revenues. Alternatively, the actual revenues could be compared to costs plus *accumulated interest*.

[11] 'Capital investment appraisal techniques: a survey of current usage', *Journal of Business Finance and Accounting* 20(3) (April 1993), pp. 307–32.

Reassuringly, in Sangster's survey, 73 per cent of firms used one or other, or both, of the *NPV* and *IRR* criteria. However, the most popular single criterion appeared to be the payback period. This was used by 78 per cent of firms, though only 14 per cent used this criterion alone—all others who used it used something else as well. Remarkably, 8 per cent of firms reported using no recognizable criteria at all—possibly they made no investment decisions, or possibly they simply made a blind guess.

About half of the firms sampled used the *NPV* criterion, though only a tiny proportion used it alone. However, there are signs, from comparisons with earlier surveys, that the use of the *NPV* technique is growing over time; partly because of the spread of cheap computer power, but also because of the growth of formal business education, such as undergraduate degrees in business and MBAs. Current readers may contribute to this trend.

Two further applications of *NPV* techniques

The approach of calculating net present values is not just applicable to decisions like whether a firm should invest in one capital project or another, and, indeed, whether it should invest at all. We conclude this chapter with two slightly different examples. In the first, the decision facing the firm is whether to lease a piece of equipment or to buy it outright. In the second example, the decision is faced by an individual rather than by a firm. This is the personal decision about whether or not to invest in doing an expensive training course, such as an MBA.

LEASE OR BUY?

Suppose that you are the chief executive of a construction company that builds motorways and other types of road. You have just won a contract to build a direct road between Oxford and Cambridge. In order to carry out this work you need some extra earth-moving equipment. This can either be bought outright from the manufacturer or it can be leased from an equipment hire firm. The issue is simply: which would be the best course of action for the firm? The answer is the one that adds the greatest net present value for the firm. Since the revenue generated will be the same whether the machine is hired or bought, the objective of the firm should be to minimize the present value of costs of acquiring the services of the machine.[12]

Table 11.2 sets out some hypothetical numbers to represent what the two alternative cash flows might look like. Buying an earth mover is assumed to cost the firm £100,000. The machine then has ten years of use, after which it is assumed to have a second-hand

---

[12] In practice one of the attractions of leasing may be that the leased equipment can be updated to incorporate the latest technology, whereas an outright purchase locks the firm into one technology for longer. If this extra flexibility is available then a value should be assigned to it, as in the discussion of sunk costs above.

Table 11.2. The decision to lease or buy

	Expenditure (£) in year:										
	0	1	2	3	4	5	6	7	8	9	10
Buy	−100,000	−1,000	−1,000	−1,000	−1,000	−1,000	−1,000	−1,000	−1,000	−1,000	20,000
Lease	−10,000	−10,000	−10,000	−10,000	−10,000	−10,000	−10,000	−10,000	−10,000	−10,000	−10,000

	NPV @ 5% (£)	NPV @ 10% (£)	NPV @ 15% (£)
Buy	−94,830	−98,048	−99,828
Lease	−87,217	−71,445	−60,188

The decision to lease or buy can be based on the calculation of the present value of two alternative cost streams. The example used here assumes that a firm can buy a machine costing £100,000 or lease the same machine for £10,000 per year over ten years. If the capital purchase is undertaken there are additional costs of maintenance, but the firm will also have the second-hand value of £20,000 after ten years. Using three alternative discount rates, the leasing option is shown to have the lowest net present cost. Hence, in this case the leasing option would almost certainly be chosen, even though leasing would involve the greatest total expenditure over the ten-year period.

value of £20,000. In the intervening years there is assumed to be a maintenance cost of £1,000 per annum for spare parts and servicing. All these numbers are assumed to be in year zero prices, so we need to choose a real discount rate in order to calculate the present value of this cash flow stream. The table reports calculations based upon discount rates of 5, 10, and 15 per cent. The present value of the cost of buying the machine is, for example, calculated at £94,830 for a discount rate of 5 per cent.

The alternative calculation assumes that the firm can hire the earth mover for £10,000 per year and the hiring charge includes servicing and spare parts. Hence, there is no lump sum to be paid out up front, but neither is there any second-hand value after ten years. In this case, the present value of the cost of leasing (calculated in year 0) is £87,217 when future cash flows are discounted at the rate of 5 per cent. Hence, in this case, if 5 per cent is the correct discount rate, it is unambiguously better for the firm to lease the earth mover rather than buy it. The same would also be true if we based the decision on either of the other two discount rates shown in Table 11.2.

Notice, however, that, if we had not learned about why discounting future sums is necessary, we might have come to a different conclusion. Suppose we just add up the total expenditure on buying and leasing. Buying costs £100,000 plus nine years of £1,000 minus £20,000. This comes to £89,000. However, leasing would cost eleven payments of £10,000. This adds up to £110,000. Hence the total expenditure is greatest via the route of leasing. It might be tempting to conclude that buying is the cheaper option.

We now know that this is incorrect, at least for all those discount rates we have tested. The difference, clearly, is that the decision to buy involves a large upfront cash outflow, while leasing spreads payment out evenly over a longer period.

There is one other important point to notice in connection with this example. It looks from these data as if the advantage of leasing over buying increases as the discount rate rises. This will not generally be true. It only follows in this example because we have assumed a constant price of leasing. In reality, the price that a leasing firm would charge would typically rise as market interest rates rise. After all, the leasing company has to make money out of its capital too. It will not set its prices for leasing at a level that will generate a return less than the opportunity cost of its own capital.

Indeed, it might be a very good question to ask: if the leasing company and the road building company both have the same opportunity cost of capital, how can there be any price at which the latter would want to lease from the former and at which both would be better off? One answer may be that the road builder can get a bigger tax deduction for leasing its capital than it could by buying it—leasing is a current expense that can be deducted in total from revenues in calculating profit, whereas capital expenses can be only partly offset against corporation tax.

There may be other advantages available to a leasing company that would possibly make it economically efficient for a leasing arrangement to be attractive to both firms, irrespective of tax advantages. One is that the leasing company may be able to get the equipment more cheaply because of buying in bulk. It may also make better use of the capital over its life-time by keeping it active longer and, perhaps, using it more intensively. One very important point concerns uncertainty. When innovation is rapid, leasing shifts the uncertainty to specialists (the leasers). They are used to dealing with uncertain situations. Also they know the world market better. If companies that need state-of-the-art equipment hand it back after one or two years, the leasing company can usually find other customers that do not need to be at the technological frontier— if not at home, then in poorer countries abroad. In any event, since leasing heavy equipment is very common, there must be some efficiency gain to firms from this course of action.

The important point to take away from this example is that the *NPV* technique can be applied to a wide range of choices relating to either costs or revenues. It is appropriate to use this technique whenever cash flows are being compared at different points in time.

It is worth noting that a very common decision facing individuals has exactly the same structure as the above lease-or-buy decision. This is the decision about whether to rent or buy a house. Here there is no problem of technological obsolescence, but there is uncertainty relating to the capital gains and losses involved in home ownership. The method outlined above can be applied directly to this kind of problem in order to decide which choice is the least expensive in present value terms. Notice that renting is the alternative with the greatest flexibility, since buying a house involves some sunk costs (such as legal fees), though only limited irreversibility, since houses can normally be sold again, if not always immediately.

IS AN MBA WORTH IT?

Our final application of the present-value technique is to the assessment of whether or not it is worth spending a substantial amount of money to do an MBA. This example shows that the calculation of present values has importance for individuals as it does for firms. There are some subtle differences that need to be considered in applying this technique to personal decisions, but we shall outline the example first before discussing these differences. An important message from this example is that *human capital*, in the form of embodied education, is as much a valuable commodity as physical capital. Human capital increases the productivity of the person who has received training, and it is the net present value of this extra output that will determine whether an investment in such training is worthwhile.

Table 11.3 shows a possible scenario in which an individual has two alternative courses of action. One course of action involves staying in the current type of employment, which is assumed to pay an annual salary of £25,000 per year (in year 0 prices) for the next twenty-five years. The alternative course of action involves taking year 0 out of employment and doing a one-year MBA. The cost in year 0 of this course of action is the course fee of £10,000 plus the salary forgone in this year of £25,000. This means that there is total upfront cost of £35,000.

In subsequent years the salary achieved by this individual is presumed to be higher than it otherwise would have been. The top half of the table illustrates one possible case where the post-MBA salary rises to £30,000 in the first year after college, then rises to £35,000 for three years, and to £40,000 for the remainder of the twenty-five-year career. Using discount rates of 5, 10 and 15 per cent produces calculations of the *NPV* of the investment in an MBA as £153,917, £80,761 and £43,339 respectively. For what it is worth, the *IRR* of the net cash flow is calculated as 30.2 per cent. This tells us that the *NPV* of the investment would still be positive up to a discount rate of about 30 per cent.

The bottom half of Table 11.3 uses a much more conservative estimate of the income increase achieved after graduation. This is based on an increase in earnings of only £5,000 for the remainder of a twenty-five-year career. Is an investment of £35,000 worth it for an extra income of only £5,000 per year? Discounting future earnings at either 5 or 10 per cent produces the answer that this is a good investment, since the *NPV* is £35,000 and £10,385 respectively. However, at a discount rate of 15 per cent, the course could not be justified in terms of the pure financial return, given its negative *NPV*. The *IRR* for this investment is 13.7 per cent.

Of course, all these numbers are hypothetical. However, it is clear that a relatively modest expected increase in future salary would be sufficient to justify what is a fairly substantial personal investment, notwithstanding the fact that many MBA students would hope to increase their salaries far more than even our more optimistic example.

Let us now ask: what is the difference between a personal investment decision and the investment decisions of firms? There are two key differences. The first relates to the

Table 11.3. Is it worth doing an MBA?

	0	1	2	3	4	5	6	7	8	9	10	11–25
						Year:						

Optimistic scenario

	0	1	2	3	4	5	6	7	8	9	10	11–25
Cost (£)	−10,000											
New income (£)	0	30,000	35,000	35,000	35,000	40,000	40,000	40,000	40,000	40,000	40,000	40,000
Old income (£)	25,000	25,000	25,000	25,000	25,000	25,000	25,000	25,000	25,000	25,000	25,000	25,000
NCF (£)	−35,000	5,000	10,000	10,000	10,000	15,000	15,000	15,000	15,000	15,000	15,000	15,000

NPV @ 5% = £153,917; NPV @ 10% = £80,761; NPV @ 15% = £43,339
IRR = 30.2%

Conservative scenario

	0	1	2	3	4	5	6	7	8	9	10	11–25
New income (£)	0	30,000	30,000	30,000	30,000	30,000	30,000	30,000	30,000	30,000	30,000	30,000
Old income (£)	25,000	25,000	25,000	25,000	25,000	25,000	25,000	25,000	25,000	25,000	25,000	25,000
NCF (£)	−35,000	5,000	5,000	5,000	5,000	5,000	5,000	5,000	5,000	5,000	5,000	5,000

NPV @ 5% = £35,469; NPV @ 10% = £10,385; NPV @ 15% = −£2,680
IRR = 13.7%

The financial case for doing an MBA can be evaluated using the *NPV* criterion. The data in the table are based on the assumption that the student involved currently has a job that would go on paying £25,000 per annum for the rest of a twenty-five-year career. During the one-year course this income is forgone and there is an additional cost of £10,000 to pay the course fee. Notice that we do not include any allowance for living expenses as these would be incurred whether the course was followed or not. Any extra expenses (positive or negative) should be included in the calculation.

The uncertain element in the calculation is the future gain in earnings. The top half of the table works with an optimistic assumption that earnings are raised by £5,000 in the first year of post-course employment, by £10,000 for the next three years, and then by £15,000 for the remainder of the career. On this scenario, all discount rates up to 30 per cent show a positive net present value to this investment. The bottom half of the table shows a more conservative increase in salary. Here the MBA course adds value at discount rates up to about 14 per cent. Note that the data are presumed to be in year 0 prices, so that the appropriate discount rate is a real rate.

goals of individuals and firms, and the second relates to the opportunity cost of capital and, therefore, to the choice of discount rate.

Firms raise money from shareholders with the explicit objective of increasing the present value of shareholder wealth, that is, of 'adding value' to the firm. Some individuals may have the goal of increasing their wealth, but it is entirely up to them what they choose as goals in life. Accordingly, we cannot say to individuals that they *ought* to take expenditure decisions based upon the *NPV* criterion. Indeed, the decision to take a degree could be justified on the grounds that the course is fun (believe it or not!) irrespective of whether it pays off in extra future income. That is to say, some element of education can be thought of as consumption rather than investment. We do not decide where to go on holiday by reference to an *NPV* calculation, neither need one do so to justify taking a training course if this just happens to be something you would enjoy anyway.

Where the *NPV* calculation would be relevant to individual decision making is when a person cannot decide whether it would be worth taking the MBA course (or whatever) *on purely financial grounds*: 'If I take out this big loan and do this course, will it make me financially better off?' In this narrow context it is sensible to try to set out the costs and benefits in the form of an *NPV* calculation, such as that in Table 11.3.

As noted above, one way of looking at investment in education (or skills acquisition) is to view this as a process of *human capital formation*. Human capital is just like physical capital in so far as it generates a stream of extra outputs into the future. The difference is that human capital is embodied in the people whose productivity has been increased by it. Not only do many individuals want to invest in human capital formation for the return they get themselves, but firms also often choose to invest in the human capital of their workforce because this will increase their productivity. The main problem facing firms in this context relates to whether the return on this investment accrues to the firm or to the employee. It is sometimes argued that a firm will only invest in human capital that is specific to that firm—that is, it only increases productivity of the worker if the worker stays in the firm. Human capital that raises the general market value of an employee will encourage trained workers to move elsewhere unless pay rises to match productivity.

Once we attempt an *NPV* calculation for an individual's investment in human capital, we come across the second difference between firms and individuals. This is that typical firms are regularly trading in capital markets and so it is relatively easy to figure out the appropriate opportunity cost of capital. The risk-adjusted cost of capital faced by firms is clearly not the correct measure to use in discounting the cash flows of individuals.

There are two equally legitimate approaches for an individual to adopt. The first is to discount future cash flows at an interest rate that reflects that individual's own personal rate of time preference. This can be obtained by an honest answer to the following question: 'If we were to take away from you £100 worth of consumption today, how much would you require in one year's time (measured in today's money) to compensate you?' If the answer is £110, then your rate of time preference is 10 per cent.

The alternative approach for an individual is to use as a discount rate the rate of interest at which the individual can borrow to finance the investment in question. In the above example this might be the rate charged by the banks for an MBA loan. This would obviously be the appropriate rate to use for the individual who was only concerned with the narrow financial issue, since the essential element of the calculation is whether the present value of the extra income generated is greater than the present value of the loan repayment (i.e. the capital sum borrowed).

This concludes our discussion of how firms and individuals can make value-maximizing decisions about expenditures for which the costs and benefits may be spread out over time. We shall return to these issues towards the end of the next chapter when we discuss the valuation of entire firms—the value of a firm is essentially the present value of its future profit stream (using economists' definition of profit).

Summary

1. Because capital goods are durable, it is necessary to distinguish between the stock of capital goods and the flow of services provided by them, and thus between their purchase price and their rental price. The linkage between them relies on the ability to assign a present value to future returns. The present value of a future payment will be lower when the payment is more distant and the interest rate is higher.

2. The rental price of capital in each period is the amount that is paid to obtain the flow of services that a capital good provides for a given period. The purchase price is the amount that is paid to acquire ownership of the capital.

3. A profit-maximizing firm should invest in capital goods as long as the present value of the stream of future net receipts that is provided by another unit of capital exceeds its purchase price.

4. A profit-maximizing firm faced with two mutually exclusive investment opportunities should choose the project that offers the highest net present value (*NPV*).

5. To maximize the firm's value, future net cash flows should be discounted using the appropriate opportunity cost of capital taking account of the level of risk involved.

6. Either investment appraisals can be conducted in expected nominal money values and discounted using a nominal interest rate, or they can be set in constant (base-year's) money values and be discounted using a real interest rate.

7. Investment appraisals should include only incremental costs and revenues. They should make no allowance for past investments, which should be considered as sunk costs. The key issue is whether the next expenditure can be justified as adding (present) value to the firm. Past mistakes are irrelevant to this decision. Once an investment has been made, it too is a sunk cost, except in so far as it has second-hand or scrap value.

8. Where an investment that has a significant element of sunk costs has not yet been made, some positive value should be assigned to the option to delay the project. Such projects should only be started when the present value of implementation exceeds the value of the wait-and-see option.

9. Internal rate of return (*IRR*) and payback period are other criteria often used in investment appraisal in addition to *NPV*. Most firms use more than one criterion.

10. The *NPV* technique can be used to evaluate lease-or-buy choices as well as personal investment decisions.

Topics for review

- Rental price and purchase price of capital
- Present value
- Net present value (*NPV*)
- Discounted cash flow (*DCF*)
- Internal rate of return (*IRR*)
- Weighted average cost of capital (*WACC*)
- Payback period
- Real and nominal rates of interest (discount)
- Sunk costs
- Wait-and-see options

Questions for discussion

1. Draw up a list of as many different types of capital goods as you can think of. Are there any types of firm that could operate without some form of physical capital? What type of firm is likely to have need of very large amounts of physical capital?

2. Suppose you work for a firm in the telecommunications industry. How do you think your investment decisions might be affected by the observation that your rival firms were investing heavily? Do you think this observation would make you increase or decrease your own investment?

3. Discuss the arguments as to why the *NPV* criterion is superior to both *IRR* and the payback period. Can you think of any counter-arguments in favour of the latter two approaches?

4. Can investment appraisal ever be a truly scientific procedure when all future cash flows are uncertain anyway and the world is changing faster and faster? Would it be better to make a blind commitment to an investment strategy and then spend whatever is necessary to make it work?

5. You are thinking of buying a house for £80,000, the mortgage interest rate is 10 per cent, and you have an offer of a twenty-five-year loan. Equivalent properties can be rented for £600 per month. What issues arise in deciding whether it is better to rent or buy? Make some explicit assumption about any unknown variables you consider to be important and then set out the present value calculation for these two alternatives. (The calculations can be easily performed within a spreadsheet package such as Excel or Lotus 1-2-3.)

6. Suppose a firm plans to finance an investment out of retained profits rather than borrowing from the financial markets. A non-executive director on the board argues that, since the opportunity cost of internally generated funds is lower than for funds borrowed in the market, the new investment could be evaluated using a discount rate lower than the market rate. Discuss the case for and against this approach.

CHAPTER 12

The Economics of Business Organizations

Firms as organizations	378	Returns to shareholders of target	
Co-ordination by coalition	379	companies	400
Survival of the fittest	380	Returns to stockholders of acquiring	
Multiplication of divisions	381	companies	402
U-form structure	381	Benefits to the economy?	404
M-form structure	383		
P-form structure	384	**Firms and markets**	404
Business integration	388	**Summary**	405
Types of integration	389		
Horizontal integration	389	**Topics for review**	406
Vertical integration	390		
Technological interdependence	390	**Questions for discussion**	406
Market failure	391		
An example	394	**Box 12.1.** Portfolio adjustments	386
Monopoly issues	394	**Box 12.2.** Information technology,	
Conglomerate integration	395	delayering, and firm size	392
		Box 12.3. Hanson: the rise and fall of a	
The market for corporate control	399	conglomerate	396
The effects of takeovers	400	**Box 12.4.** The winner's curse	402

I N this chapter we discuss two important but connected issues. The first relates to the internal organization of firms. Are some forms of organization more efficient than others? The second concerns the factors that influence the proper domain of a single firm. That is to say, what activities are best done within a single firm, and what activities are best done within independent firms that then trade with one another?

In Chapter 4 we noted that firms exist, in part, because they offer an organizational structure that produces outputs at lower transaction costs than those that would arise if every transaction in the production process were conducted via the market. A new perspective on why firms exist is associated with the idea that firms provide an organization that is able to co-ordinate the resources of a diversity of employees, each of whom has specific limited knowledge. This co-ordination of activity is able to add value in ways that would not be possible via market mechanisms. This new approach is known as the *knowledge-based* or *resource-based* theory of the firm.[1]

From the individual firm's point of view, two key questions lie at the heart of the issues we are about to address: 'Is there some internal reorganization that would improve the performance of the firm?' and 'Is there some activity that the firm should be involved in that would add value to the firm, and/or is there some activity that the firm is currently performing that should be sold off or closed down?'

We start by discussing the firm as a complex social organization before proceeding to outline key developments in the structure of modern firms. We then discuss various forms of integration of potentially independent production activities. Finally, we consider the market for buying and selling firms themselves, known as the *market for corporate control*.

Firms as organizations

For most of our earlier discussion of decision making within firms, we have talked as if there is one central decision-making unit for all the firm's output and pricing choices. In Chapter 10, however, we pointed out that employees have their own motivation and that it is not always possible to draw up contracts that specify exactly what every employee is expected to do. In the presence of asymmetric information, firms attempt to have incentive structures that encourage productive behaviour, but these do not necessarily *guarantee* the most productive outcome at all times.

The problem of structuring organizations is partly the same problem as that of ensuring productive behaviour of individual employees in a world where complete monitoring is impossible, but it has an extra dimension. This extra dimension is that, even where all workers are behaving exactly as employers would wish them to behave, their activities must be co-ordinated in such a way as to achieve the overall strategic goals of the organization.

It may seem that if every worker is behaving productively then the overall optimization of output must be guaranteed. However, this is not true, as this simple example illustrates. In the late 1980s a property company called Rosehaugh grew rapidly and was a stock market star. Its early success was partly fortuitous, being based upon the rapid rise in prices of commercial property. It had several groups of developers within the company, each searching out new sites for property development. On at least one occasion, one group within the company was bidding against another group within the company in a land auction, not knowing that the other group was also interested in the property. Each group was behaving appropriately according to its directions, and yet co-ordination was lacking, so that the overall success of the company was diminished. (It should be no great surprise that this company eventually went bust!)

---

[1] For a debate on this new approach see *Organization Science* 7(5) (September–October 1996).

Co-ordination by coalition

One influential study of the internal organization of firms views their decision making as the outcome of a process of bargaining between a set of involved parties whose objectives differ. R. M. Cyert and J. G. March[2] argue that firms contain many individuals each with a different role and each with their own personal agenda and goals. These individuals can be categorized as managers, workers, shareholders, and customers, but there is no particular coherence of interest within groups.

The outcome of the interaction of these different individuals is perceived to be an 'organizational coalition', in which every individual has to make some compromise over objectives, since not all can be simultaneously satisfied. Each individual stays with the firm so long as the outcome is better than could be achieved by leaving, but all find themselves in a sub-optimal position owing to the compromises made.

Internal compromise is not the best way to identify the optimal price, product mix, rate of asset utilization, and rate of innovation. Thus, firms in which political processes (akin to those in a coalition government) determine outcomes will typically exhibit 'organizational slack' in the sense that they will not be maximizing profit or the value of the firm.

The firm's need to survive places bounds on just how sub-optimal these policies can be. The firm cannot behave so sub-optimally that it always loses money. It must do well enough to keep shareholders happy and, perhaps, stave off the threats of takeover or bankruptcy. Doing well enough, without maximizing profit, is widely known as **satisficing.** The outcome of satisficing behaviour is *satisfactory* for all the parties involved, even though it does not maximize the value of the firm.

While the Cyert and March analysis had great plausibility in the 1960s, it is hard to reconcile with the business environment of the 1990s. More than a decade of delayering and various managerial revolutions dedicated to improved 'focus' and value maximization have made the concept of organizational slack far less relevant than it used to be. Indeed, much management theory has been devoted to the issue of how to achieve a structure within which internal conflict is resolved and the overall goals of the firm are served by all of the constituent parts of the organization.

The principal–agent analysis discussed above (especially in Chapter 10) is devoted to this issue. How can incentives be created for all those in an organization to perform in such a way that the overall goals of the organization are achieved? A structure within which motivated individuals have an incentive to perform not only in their own interest but also in the firm's interest is said to be characterized by *incentive compatibility*.

A modern version of the Cyert and March approach is based upon identifying the interests of various groups of *stakeholders*. The stakeholders in a firm are all those, such as employees, suppliers, pensioners, shareholders, and customers, who have a direct economic interest in the firm's behaviour. However, there is no presumption by those

---

2 *A Behavioral Theory of the Firm* (Englewood Cliffs, NJ: Prentice-Hall, 1963).

advocating a stakeholder perspective that firms behave in a sub-optimal way. Rather, successful firms have to build their success on a constructive alliance of all interested parties. No firm can succeed in the long term without a high-quality and motivated management, productive employees, and satisfied customers and suppliers. Bad relations with any of these groups will not serve the value-maximizing objectives of shareholders.

SURVIVAL OF THE FITTEST

An alternative way of thinking about the importance of organization in determining the success of firms relies upon an analogy with Darwinian biology. Hence, this approach is known as the *evolutionary theory*.[3]

The key idea in this approach (as set out by Nelson and Winter) is that individual firms should not be thought of as profit maximizers in the way that we have approached the firm in earlier chapters. Indeed, each firm is not seen to be maximizing anything in particular. Rather firms are structured around standard ways of doing things, or what Nelson and Winter call 'routines'. Some of these routines will be better than others. Some will lead to profit and growth, while some will lead to stagnation and decline. However, successful firms will be those that have organizations that deliver profits and growth, while firms with inferior organizations will die or be taken over and restructured. Hence, over time, successful organizations will tend to dominate, just as natural selection in the biological world is associated with survival of the fittest. In other words, even if no firm deliberately aims to maximize profit, the fact that profitable firms tend to thrive while unprofitable firms wither will mean that profitable firms will be the survivors and their routines will get imitated or replicated.

Of course, much of what a training in business studies aims to achieve is an understanding of 'best practice', that is, the routines that work, so that this can be spread to other organizations. Here the analogy with biological evolution breaks down. Natural selection has limited room for rational decision making and conscious imitation: could the dinosaurs have survived if only they had imitated elephants?

Such alternative approaches are important, but a detailed discussion of them is beyond the scope of this book. For the remainder of this chapter we assume that the dominant goal of firms is and ought to be the maximization of the present value of the firm. This is the dynamic equivalent to the assumption of profit maximization in the traditional static theory of the firm, and it is here considered to be equivalent to the goal of maximizing shareholder wealth. It is none the less worth bearing in mind that this is an *assumption* and not a description of what all firms necessarily do. Certainly, there will be many who want to debate this assumption. However, economic analysis is of most use to business in guiding the application of such clearly defined optimizing

---

[3] The originators of this approach were Richard R. Nelson and Sidney G. Winter, both of Yale University, in their book *An Evolutionary Theory of Economic Change* (Cambridge, MA: Harvard University Press, 1982).

objectives. Firms that want to pursue other objectives have every right to do so, subject to the approval of their shareholders.

Multiplication of divisions

Three basic business structures have categorized firms in the twentieth century. In a *unitary form* (U-form) of business there are several departments that perform different functions, but they all report to the chief executive (or the office of the CEO), who is responsible for the overall running of day-to-day operations. In a *multi-divisional form* (M-form), specific product groups are formed into separate divisions, each with its own functional departments. Every division has its own general manager who is responsible for the day-to-day running of the division. The CEO of the firm is responsible for co-ordination of the activities of the divisions and for providing strategic focus for the business. In a *portfolio form* (P-form), the main company (the Group) is made up of a collection of several wholly, or partly, owned subsidiary companies. Each of the companies within the group has its own chief executive, who is responsible for the day-to-day running of that business, and each of these subsidiary companies may itself be U-form or M-form in structure. The Group has a CEO responsible for deciding the strategy of the entire group, including deciding which businesses should remain in the Group portfolio and which others might be acquired. There is a board of directors for the group, usually referred to as the 'main board', and there is a board for each subsidiary company.

Historically, all companies that started small and grew organically (that is by expanding the existing business rather than taking over other businesses) started out with a U-form structure. Many small businesses today also have such a structure. The M-form structure was first introduced into General Motors in the 1920s by Alfred P. Sloan, Jr, in order to handle the problems of running a large manufacturing concern. Other large US companies, such as Du Pont, Standard Oil, and Sears, also reorganized along these lines in the inter-war years. This structure proved to be a considerable success and was widely imitated. Almost all large public companies today have gone further than the M-form structure, although parts of the business may be in this form. They are collections of many subsidiary companies and hence it is natural to think of them as having a P-form structure. We now outline some of the economic reasons for this evolution of structure.

U-FORM STRUCTURE

The unitary form of structure is the natural place to start for any small business. In a start-up manufacturing business the product might, for example, be produced by its inventor literally in the back of a garage. If the product takes off, production will move

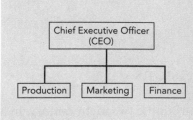

Figure 12.1. The uniform organization

U-form organizations have several functional departments each reporting to the CEO. The functional departments do not have an identifiable product of their own, so measuring their efficiency is difficult. There is a requirement for involvement of the CEO in day-to-day operational decisions. However, there are benefits from functional specialization.

to new premises and additional staff will be hired. Initially, the extra workers may help in production, but soon those involved in production will be unable to handle all aspects of the business. The business has to have accounts, so the services of an accountant will be hired. At first, the accountant might be part time, but if growth continues, there will be a finance department. Similarly, someone will have to take charge of sales, and eventually there may be an entire marketing department. Having taken on all these new staff, the firm will need a personnel department to handle hiring and firing and terms of employment, etc.

Figure 12.1 illustrates what the organizational structure looks like in a U-form business. Each of the departments has a defined function within the business. Each department provides services to the other departments, but the head of each reports to the chief executive (CEO) of the company. The CEO co-ordinates the activities of these departments.

The U-form business structure is adequate for small businesses, or those with a small product range. However, it has two key weaknesses that are likely to show up when the business gets big and the company produces many different products.

The first problem relates to the co-ordination of activities by the CEO. In a multi-product firm, the U-form organization is likely to consume too much of senior-management time in daily operational decisions. If the CEO spends all his time directing the actions of the functional departments, insufficient time will be devoted to the key strategic thinking that only the senior managers can instigate. The business may survive for a while, but it is unlikely to move successfully into new markets or to innovate ahead of the field. It is unlikely ever to become the material for a case study in successful business strategy.

The second problem with the U-form organization arises because it is difficult to measure the productivity of functional departments, many of which have no measurable outputs. This makes monitoring and control difficult, so that it is hard to avoid empire building by department heads, who may get paid according to department size rather than productivity.

Ironically, because the production department is the only one with easily measurable inputs and outputs, early attempts at productivity measurement were targeted at production workers alone (in what used to be called 'time and motion' studies). This created great hostility between the so-called blue-collar and white-collar workers and did nothing to improve white-collar productivity (it probably didn't do much for blue-collar productivity either, but it did make managers feel that they were doing something to improve efficiency).

U-form organizations are not all bad. They are appropriate for small businesses. In larger businesses, they do allow a high degree of task specialization and they do provide clear lines of responsibility and reporting. However, the advantages start to be outweighed by the disadvantages once the organization becomes larger and more complex.

U-form organizations become inefficient once the firm gets large and has many products because the chief executive cannot effectively co-ordinate operational decisions, and because it is difficult to assess productivity in most departments.

M-FORM STRUCTURE

The solution to the control problems first adopted in large firms was to create a multi-divisional structure.[4] Each division was created on an operational rather than functional basis. In a car company, for example, rather than having a finance division and a production division, there would be an engines division, a car division, and a lorries (trucks) division. Each division would be responsible for the production of a major product. Within each division there would be a U-form of organization, so that each function necessary for that division would be available within it. The M-form of organization is illustrated in Figure 12.2.

Some functions in the divisional structure could be retained within head office, such as personnel, but each division can be thought of as having a U-form structure. In effect, each division is a sub-business. It may be producing a product that then is sold in the market, or it may be producing a major component for the final product, which is then assembled in another division.

Divisions have an advantage over functional departments from a management perspective because divisions are structured (deliberately) so that they have measurable inputs and outputs. Their efficiency can be measured in some objective way, and so it is easier to monitor and control performance.

Each division has a manager who is responsible for the day-to-day running of operations. This leaves the CEO of the company devoid of all such operational responsibilities and free to focus on the important strategic issues that only the head of a business can decide. It also means that managers of divisions can be set objectives

---

4 While the M-form structure started to emerge in the 1920s, the most influential analysis of the economics of this structure is found in the work of US economist Oliver Williamson in the 1970s. See especially *Markets and Hierarchies* (New York: Free Press, 1975). The terminology 'U-form' and 'M-form' was, we believe, invented by Williamson; however, 'P-form' has been invented by us to describe the reality of modern firms' structure. Williamson has used 'H-form' to describe a holding company structure; however, holding companies often do not exert the central managerial influence that we perceive to exist in a P-form company.

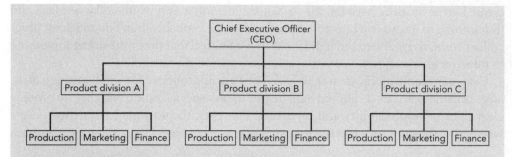

Figure 12.2. The multi-divisional organization

In an M-form organization, each divisional manager is responsible for production and profitability within his or her division. In this structure the CEO is free to work on strategic issues, and productivity of each division is easy to measure.

that are consistent with the overall goals of the organization, so that the possibility of functional departments pursuing their own divergent goals is minimized.

Of course, within a division there are still going to be some functional departments whose output is hard to measure. However, by measuring the productivity of the division as a whole, pressure is maintained to keep down costs all round. So the divisional manager has a strong incentive to incur costs only when they can be justified by extra productivity.

Essentially, the decentralization of operational decisions creates efficiency of managerial effort in a situation where imperfect information and bounded rationality are a reality. Since the CEO cannot keep an eye on everything in a large organization, efficiency can be increased by creating an organizational structure within which the subsets of the whole are all pulling in the same direction.

> The M-form of business creates incentives for good performance at the divisional level and it frees the chief executive to focus on longer-term strategic issues.

P-FORM STRUCTURE

The P-form structure simply takes the multi-divisional structure a step further, and instead of having many divisions within one legal entity it turns some divisions into separate legal entities by giving them Limited Company status, even though in most cases the subsidiary companies are wholly owned by the Group. Often much of the business of the subsidiary companies is done with other parts of the Group, though some subsidiaries do virtually no business with other parts of the group. Figure 12.3 illustrates the structure of a P-form company.

One example of the structure of a modern company, Glaxo Wellcome PLC, was pre-

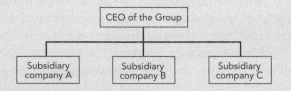

Figure 12.3. The portfolio form of organization

Modern companies are a portfolio of subsidiary companies. The Group CEO is free to focus on the strategy of the Group. Each subsidiary company has its own chief executive, who is responsible for day-to-day management. Subsidiaries have their own capital structure and accounts, so it is easy to assess their profitability. It is also easy to add and subtract subsidiaries to and from the Group.

sented in Box 4.1 on pages 120–1. This is made up of the Group and thirty-five subsidiary companies. Six of these subsidiary companies (as of March 1996) were registered in the UK and the remainder were registered in another twenty-two different countries world-wide. Of these overseas-registered companies, seven were less than 100 per cent owned by the Group. Some companies have a more complicated structure than that of Glaxo Wellcome. Laporte PLC, for example, a UK-listed specialist chemicals company, has fifty-seven subsidiary companies in sixteen different countries. All but nine of these subsidiaries are wholly owned.

The key question for present purposes is: why is it that many modern companies are structuring themselves in this way? The first point to notice is that the arguments for better monitoring and control that were used to justify multi-divisional structures apply even more strongly in the case of wholly owned subsidiaries. A wholly owned subsidiary has to have its own complete set of accounts, and so its performance can be accurately monitored by the group, and appropriate incentives can be given to the chief executive of the subsidiary in order to achieve required performance. Within the divisional structure there may be some doubt about which overhead costs are allocated to each division. For a subsidiary company there are no doubts, since its capital structure is clearly defined. Hence, calculations of returns on capital employed are more easily allocated within the P-form structure. There can be little doubt about which parts of the group are performing well and which badly.

The effect of creating a structure in which, however large the group becomes, individual companies within the group remain at a manageable size is important. It means that a modern corporation need not reach a point at which it becomes too big for managers to retain effective control. Operational control is delegated to the subsidiary level at which it is effective. If subsidiaries become too big they too can be split into more subsidiaries. Thus the P-form structure (potentially) avoids managerial diseconomies of scale that would arise as a uniform organization gets large.

A second reason for moving to a P-form structure from an M-form structure is that it alters the allocation of business risk. In an M-form business, where all divisions operate within the same legal entity, all business risks are borne by the Group. However, when each subsidiary is an independent legal entity incorporated with limited liability, the risk to the Group associated with each business is different. The Group typically owns all the equity in its subsidiaries; however, if a subsidiary goes bust, the group would not have unlimited liability for its debts (unless it had given guarantees of some form). Hence, investment in a subsidiary that is itself a limited company involves less risk than would the same investment in a division of the group.

This is one reason why virtually all overseas subsidiaries have separate legal status, even if they are only distribution companies for the product of another subsidiary in the home country. It also explains why some companies for which finance is tied to specific assets often structure themselves in such a way that the assets and liabilities can be easily matched. Property developers, for example, typically raise funding to finance specific building projects. The loan will be secured on the value of the building involved. Each major building project will often be 'owned' by a limited liability company that is itself owned by the group. If the development ends up losing money,

---

BOX 12.1.

Portfolio adjustments

The following newspaper extracts illustrate the extent to which modern companies have become structured as portfolios of subsidiary businesses. Restructuring such companies often involves changing the mix of businesses in their portfolios. These extracts are all drawn from the *Financial Times* (*FT*) or *Sunday Times* (*ST*) in a single week in November 1996. There were many other similar stories in the same week that we could have chosen, and hundreds more in the course of a year.

> The British construction industry was stunned when George Wimpey and Tarmac, two of its biggest companies, announced plans last November to swap £600m of businesses.
> Wimpey exchanged its building and civil engineering subsidiaries . . . and its quarrying business for Tarmac's UK housebuilding operations. It was a bold decision to unload businesses that had been at the heart of each company's development.   (*FT*, 8 November 1996, p. 21)

> Staveley Industries said yesterday it was considering quitting contracting.
> Mr Roy Hitchens, chief executive, said electrical and mechanical contracting . . . was a business 'we might well want to move out of'. . . .
> Staveley is also building up the non-contracting side of its services division, and yesterday announced the acquisition of Accurate Metallurgical and PCMS, two US-based technical testing businesses, for $4.9m.   (*FT*, 8 November 1996, p. 21)

> NFC, the transport and logistics group, is considering an auction of Lynx, its express parcels business, to a financial buyer who would back a management buy-out.
> NFC is understood to be talking to a number of banks and venture capitalists who might be interested in buying the business, which is considered non-core to the group.   (*FT*, 4 November 1996, p. 26)

the group may be able to walk away from it by allowing the subsidiary to go bust, leaving the residual assets in the hands of the secured lenders.

Another reason for forming separate legal subsidiaries is to enable co-operation between companies with different assets or expertise. Each contributing company then holds some share in the joint venture. For example, Rolls Royce PLC, a UK aero-engine manufacturer, has several joint ventures with other engineering companies, such as BMW, to develop new engines for various types of aircraft. Another example is provided by Cable and Wireless PLC, the UK telecomms firm that, in October 1996, announced the formation of a new joint-venture company to be called Cable and Wireless Communications (CWC). This will be 52.6 per cent owned by Cable and Wireless, 18.5 per cent by Nynex Corp (a US-based cable company), and 14.2 per cent by Bell Canada. CWC will merge the UK telephone operations of Mercury Communications (a wholly owned subsidiary of Cable and Wireless) with the UK cable interests of Nynex and Bell Canada—including the takeover by Bell Canada of a fourth cable company, Videotron. Hence, subsidiary joint ventures provide a channel for technical

Hoechst, the world's largest chemicals company, is to turn itself into a management holding group and split its businesses into independent units. Some of the six units may be quoted separately and the group is seeking partners for three.

The overhaul, to be accompanied by a listing in the US, is one of the most significant attempts by a German company to improve shareholder value.

'We will become more transparent and increase the group's value,' said Mr Jurgen Dormann, chairman.

Hoechst plans to turn its pharmaceuticals, animal health, polyester, basic chemicals, speciality chemicals, and technical polymers units into joint stock companies by the end of the next year. (*FT*, 7 November 1996, p. 29)

Tomkins, the £3 billion industrial combine chaired by Greg Hutchings, is planning a wholesale cull of its smaller subsidiaries.

The clear-out of smaller businesses is needed to free up the time of Hutchings and his finance director, Ian Duncan, and avoid what one insider called 'management indigestion'.

Tomkins' management method involves Hutchings and Duncan engaging in detailed discussions with the managements of individual businesses over their budgets and investment plans. The company now has 74 subsidiaries, including a number owned or acquired when it was a tiny business back in the mid-1980s. . . .

The disposals are likely to be concentrated in Tomkin's 'services to industry' division, although smaller businesses in other divisions may also be sold.   (*ST*, Business Section, 10 November 1996, p. 2)

Notice that the term 'division' is now being used, as in the Staveley and Tomkins reports above, not to refer to a subset of a single legal entity, as we have used it in the text, but rather to refer to collections of Ltd. companies (businesses) within a group that happen to be in the same product area. Thus, in this usage, a division is the part of a group's portfolio of businesses that produces related products and may thus have considerable interaction; so a division is itself a portfolio of businesses.

co-operation between independent companies that clearly assigns property rights to the participants in proportion to their financial or technical contribution.

Another role for joint ventures is in accessing new markets. Many Western companies found joint ventures to be the best way of getting into Eastern Europe after the fall of the Berlin Wall. A joint venture enables the Western company to contribute capital and know-how while the local partner has local contacts and knowledge, which take time to acquire. The locals may also have some advantages over foreigners in allocation of property rights. Such ventures enable the investing company to get a toe hold in new markets while having a clear limitation to the risk involved.

A final important advantage of the P-form structure is that it becomes relatively easy to dispose of a subsidiary if it is not performing well enough within the group. Selling off a division of an existing business would be possible, but it would involve considerable legal work in order to determine what assets and contracts the division owns. All employees would have to be given new contracts. However, a legally separate subsidiary is already a 'nexus of contracts', and hence transference of ownership is relatively straightforward. Some examples of how businesses structure themselves as a portfolio of companies and often restructure that portfolio are presented in Box 12.1.

The P-form of business provides complete information about subsidiaries' performance, thus enabling monitoring and control to be as close as possible. It also changes the risks companies face, especially in new ventures and in new markets.

Once businesses are structured as a portfolio of subsidiary companies, the question is obviously likely to be raised: why that particular portfolio? What should be in the portfolio, and what could be disposed of? The issue of which businesses should fit together is one to which we now turn. In the final section of this chapter we look at business units as commodities that can themselves be bought and sold.

Business integration

A central issue in the study of business organizations is which types of activity belong inside a single firm, or group, and which activities should be in separate organizations. We approach this question not by attempting to define simple criteria of inclusion or exclusion. Rather, we outline the economics of several forms of integration. Some of these justify inclusion of potentially separable activities within one firm because they generate clear efficiency gains—any given output can be produced at lower cost and/or is produced more profitably.

Before proceeding further it is worth recalling that two reasons for merging firms to form a larger business unit are the presence of *economies of scale* and *economies of scope*.

Economies of scale arise when the long-run average cost curve falls over some range of production. If economies of scale have not yet been fully exploited, two firms in the same industry that combine will be able to produce the same combined output at lower cost. Hence there would be advantages from having the two firms working as one rather than independently.

Economies of scope arise when joint production of many products reduces the costs of each as compared with independent production. Again, where economies of scope arise, it improves efficiency to have many such products produced within one firm. Clearing banks, for example, have a big fixed cost represented by their branch network. By selling many different financial products through the same branches, they spread these fixed costs over a wide range of products. In principle, each of the products (loans, deposits, credit cards, insurance policies, travellers cheques, safe deposit boxes, unit trusts, PEPs, etc.) could be provided by separate firms, but there are economies of scope to be derived from one firm selling all to its retail customer base.

Types of integration

There are three main types of interrelatedness that can give rise to integration of business activity within the same firm or group. Two of these involve some direct connection between the parts of the business. First, **horizontal integration** involves joining together two or more businesses that produce the same types of product at the same stage of production. Second, **vertical integration** combines two businesses in the same industry but at different stages of production, as, for example, if a bicycle manufacturer were to combine with a spoke maker and a tyre manufacturer. 'Forward' or 'downstream' integration involves combining a firm with another at a later stage of production, such as a clothes manufacturer with a clothes retailer. 'Backward' or 'upstream' integration arises when a business combines with a provider of some of its inputs, as, for example, if a car manufacturer merged with a steel maker.

The third type of integration we shall discuss is known as **conglomerate integration**. This arises when businesses in unrelated activities are combined within one firm. It is less obvious why this should ever occur, even though it clearly does. Conglomerates are currently out of fashion in the modern business world, so it may be that the truth is that their existence has no justification in terms of long-run efficiency gains, though we return to this issue below.

HORIZONTAL INTEGRATION

Horizontal integration may involve the merger of two previously independent businesses, which then combine to produce a new single product. But it may also involve the continued production of existing brands, but within the new combined company.

As we have already mentioned, one motivation for horizontal integration is to reap economies of scale or scope. Such economies can arise from total integration of new operations. However, economies of scale and scope sometimes arise from the integration of any stage in the production process, such as production of joint components, research and development, or the marketing and distribution of outputs.

Where significant economies of scale or scope do not exist, the motivation for horizontal integration is often to increase market power, since horizontal integration inevitably increases concentration of production into fewer hands. There are two aspects to this. In the market for inputs, a combined firm has more power to force down input prices than do independent smaller firms. In the market for outputs, a combined firm faces less competition than do smaller firms. It thus has more potential influence over its output prices, though how much more depends upon how many other suppliers remain in the industry.

It is precisely because horizontal integration has the potential to reduce competition that any such mergers are looked at closely by the competition authorities in most major countries. In the UK, where there is a *prima facie* case that competition is threatened, there will normally be an inquiry. The focus of this inquiry is usually to discover whether the efficiency gains to consumers (via scale economies) more than to offset the potential costs to consumers resulting from reduced competition.

One recent example of a horizontal merger that was forbidden on competition grounds was in the UK water industry. Both Severn Trent PLC and Wessex Water PLC made takeover bids for South West Water PLC. After an inquiry by the Monopolies and Mergers Commission, the Secretary of State for Trade and Industry, Mr Ian Lang, refused to approve either bid on the grounds 'that the rival bids would harm competition in the industry . . . [and] that the predators could not sustain the sort of price cuts necessary to make up for the harm to public interest'.[5]

> Horizontal integration may add value to the firm either from economies of scale and scope or from greater market power; however, the latter is likely to be affected by intervention from the competition authorities.

VERTICAL INTEGRATION

Vertical integration involves connections between businesses at different stages of producing a particular product. Notice, however, that some degree of vertical integration is involved in all businesses. So the question is how much to integrate. There are three broad approaches to understanding the potential economic benefits from vertical integration.

Technological interdependence
The production of a product in which various stages of processing are more cheaply done closely together will naturally tend to be conducted not only within the same firm,

---

[5] *Financial Times*, 26/27 October 1996, p. 1.

but also within the same plant. For example, blast furnaces making steel and hot-strip mills that shape and cut the steel tend to be adjacent to one another. This enables the hot steel to be rolled, shaped, and cut in the strip mill while it is still hot, thereby saving the energy that would be required to reheat it. There may also be transaction cost reductions resulting from lower handling and/or transport costs involved in locating stages of the manufacture of a product in one place.

Notice that such technological interdependencies will not normally be the motivation behind mergers of existing businesses, because, where such interdependencies exist, integrated production facilities will be built from the start. None the less, such technological linkages will be an important determinant of why several production stages may be within one firm rather than supplied competitively through the market. Technological changes may create a logic for new alliances. An obvious example is the convergence of interests of companies providing voice and visual communication, that is telephone and cable/media companies, resulting from the emergence of new fibre-optic technologies. Box 12.2 discusses another aspect of the impact of technology on business organization.

Market failure

The most general reason for extending the degree of vertical integration is that this often works out cheaper than trading in the market. This is the transaction-cost-minimization explanation due to Ronald Coase.

To clarify the issues involved here let us consider a concrete example. Suppose that you are chief executive of a car-manufacturing company. Cars are made up of many parts, each of which could be manufactured separately—wheels, axles, seats, transmissions (gear boxes), lights, speedometers, engines, etc. What you have to decide is: how many of these components should we manufacture ourselves and how much should we buy in through the market from other, independent parts manufacturers?

A moment's thought will make it clear that there are some inputs that you would not bother to make for yourself. These are inputs that are fairly standardized, have several rival suppliers in competitive market conditions, and for which your firm is likely to be a small part of total market demand. In these conditions you are unlikely to be able to make the inputs more cheaply for yourself, so you might as well buy in from the market. One obvious example of such an input in the car market is tyres. Ford, General Motors, and BMW do not bother to get involved in manufacturing tyres. This is left to such companies as Firestone, Michelin, and Dunlop.[6]

So what type of input might you find that you need to make for yourself? Clearly, it is anything that you can produce more cheaply than you can buy it in the market. The most obvious case is when the component is highly specific to your own production process, and its production requires a significant degree of fixed investment. This means that you would be highly dependent on a single supplier and would, thus, be

---

[6] It is worth noting, however, that, in its early years, Ford not only made its own tyres; it even had a rubber plantation in South America.

BOX 12.2.

Information technology, delayering, and firm size

Over the last two decades there have been two simultaneous revolutions affecting the organization of business. One is the IT revolution that has been associated with the dramatic fall in cost of computing power and information technology. The second has been a managerial revolution that has involved delayering of organizations. Bureaucratic hierarchies have been largely replaced with flatter organizational structures. Flexible teams of skilled operatives with a high degree of discretion have replaced pyramid structures in which orders pass from top to bottom.

To what extent are these two revolutions related? Is it cheaper computer power and better access to information that have enabled organizations to restructure? It is hard to believe that the IT revolution has had no effect on organizational change, but neither does it seem likely that IT is the only important driver of such change. Economics would suggest that there are many other factors driving organizational evolution, including global competition, growing real wage costs (including social security taxes), and the growth of service industries relative to traditional manufacturing.

However, the impact of IT on the organization of firms remains an interesting and important question. At one point in time it was thought that advances in IT would lead to the creation of fewer, larger firms, as better information systems enabled managers successfully to co-ordinate larger vertically integrated firms. However, the evidence, such as it is, now supports the view that IT leads to there being a larger number of smaller enterprises. Let us see why that might be.

The impact of IT on firm size can be thought of as the balance of three distinct effects. First, IT changes production technology in some industries via the introduction of new equipment, such as computer-driven robots. Such technical innovation could increase the output per firm but at the same time reduce the average employment per firm, as capital substitutes for labour. IT also leads to flatter managerial hierarchies as pyramid structures are dismantled, because routine clerical tasks can now be done more efficiently by computers. This also involves lower employment for any given level of output.

The second effect is that IT potentially creates better co-ordination *within* a firm, so that

exposed to the potential for opportunistic attempts to renegotiate the contract and raise the price. If you are going to continue to need this input, the danger of being held to ransom would make it rational to decide that such a supplier should be a wholly owned part of the group so that joint profit maximization could be achieved.

It is for this reason that most car manufacturers have wholly owned subsidiaries making some major components such as engines and car bodies. Indeed, some major US car manufacturers, such as Ford and GM, had a high degree of integration between assembly and components manufacture in their early days, but have now become dependent on a network of competitive suppliers for large numbers of their components. However, the key company-specific components for which alternative competitive suppliers do not exist are still generally manufactured within the firm. The Japanese car

managers are able to control larger firms, and firms find it efficient to do more of the production process for themselves. This would lead to larger firms as measured both by employment and by output.

The third effect is that IT enables better co-ordination of a chain of suppliers *outside* the firm. This would encourage economies of scale within each component supplier, who then supply many separate firms with cheaper components, while the information technology co-ordinates such *outsourcing* and contributes to *lean production* or *just-in-time* methods of organization. (See also Box 5.3 on p. 169 for further discussion of lean production.)

It is possible that each of these three effects will be the most important in different industries and at different points in time. Indeed, there is strong accumulated evidence that the first of these effects is an important reason for the organizational revolution—firms have restructured because computers have enabled them to work more efficiently in new ways.

A recent study of firm size in the USA has found clear evidence of the presence of the third of these effects, leading to smaller firms by all measures of size:

> There is substantial evidence of a relationship between increased levels of IT investment and smaller firm size. The overall relationship is robust to a variety of specifications and at least four measures of firm size. However, our findings should not be interpreted to apply to all industries and all time periods. . . . The decline in firm size is greatest after a lag of one to two years following investment in IT, suggesting that the impacts of the new technology are not fully felt immediately. . . . There is, however, strong reason to believe that most of the growth in IT investment has an exogenous technological basis. Increased investment in IT appears to be almost entirely explained by the rapid drop in its price, and these price declines are directly attributable to improvements in the technology. Although causality can never be proven by statistical regression, the data do support the hypothesis that improvements in technology have enabled a shift towards smaller firms.*

We cannot draw all the connections between information technology and the organization of businesses here, but it is clear that IT and organizational structure are strongly interrelated.

* E. Brynjolfsson, T. W. Malone, V. Gurbaxani, and A. Kambal, 'Does information technology lead to smaller firms?', *Management Science* 40(12) (December 1994), pp. 1628–44.

industry, led by Toyota, developed a different solution. This was to buy in a high proportion of their components but to develop a long-term supply contract with those suppliers for whom a large specific investment was necessary. It appears that the long-term contracts provide sufficient incentive for suppliers to invest in the specific equipment and skills necessary to deliver the required inputs, but the potential threat of moving to another supplier in future is sufficient to avoid opportunistic behaviour by these supply companies.

Both the Japanese and US solutions to providing for specific inputs can be thought of as ways of coping with uncertainty in the input market. This could, clearly, also be extended to apply to output markets. Where the market environment is competitive and stable, firms may be unconcerned about upstream or downstream integration.

However, where product innovation is rapid or the market environment is changing fast for other reasons, firms may feel that integration is a way of increasing control over their input and output markets. However, there are limits to how far this can go. Car firms may integrate both component suppliers and retail outlets into the firm. However, they are unlikely to want to be major producers of steel, and they cannot make consumers buy their cars even if they operate their own showrooms.

It is worth noting, however, that US car manufacturers have moved some way in the direction of the Japanese practice of developing long-term supply relationships with key suppliers. This is partly a response to the globalization of car manufacture and the development of 'world' models such as the Ford Mondeo. Production of standard models in several parts of the world requires standardized components. So, rather than setting up component-making subsidiaries in many countries, car manufacturers find it more efficient to develop supply contracts with multinational component makers who can supply identical parts to a consistent high standard in any location.

An example
In October 1996, UK chemicals company Allied Colloids PLC announced the takeover of one of its main US suppliers, CPS Chemicals, for £234 million. The following is an extract from the report of this takeover in *The Times* (20 November 1996, p. 32):

> David Farrar, Allied's chief executive said the merger would provide the enlarged group with a much stronger command of its core markets and firmer control of raw material costs, which recently forced a decline in profits.
> Mr Farrar said: 'We have been badly hit by price increases in the past, but the combined group will have a huge level of purchasing power, putting us in a much stronger position.'

This is a clear example of a firm merging with one of its suppliers and justifying this on the grounds that it will achieve better control of its input markets. We cannot judge whether these claims are correct without considerably more information.

Monopoly issues
At first sight there would seem to be no monopoly implications associated with vertical integration, since it does not increase concentration in any single market. Hence, firms should obtain no extra monopoly power by vertical integration, and competition authorities need have no concern about any vertical integration. Indeed, this was the conventional view in the past. However, recent work in industrial organization has challenged this view, and it is now generally accepted that enhancing monopoly power may be a motive for vertical integration.[7] Hence, competition authorities, while remaining more concerned about the effects of horizontal integration, cannot ignore vertical integration.

A firm that faces both perfectly competitive input markets and perfectly competitive

---

[7] Much of this literature is technical. Readers with a grasp of mathematics may refer to Jean Tirole, *The Theory of Industrial Organization* (Cambridge, MA: MIT Press, 1988), esp. ch. 4.

output markets will not have any impact on the competitiveness of either set of markets by upstream or downstream integration. It is for this reason that the traditional view was that vertical integration does not affect competition. However, most markets for manufactured goods involve product differentiation, which makes them either monopolistically competitive or oligopolistic.

In any market in which there is a monopoly element, the price charged will be above the marginal cost of production. Suppose that there is a chain of suppliers each with some monopoly power to add a margin to price, above marginal cost. This monopolistic distortion then gets compounded in successive stages of the production chain.[8] The final price of this input will be inflated (away from true marginal cost) by these additive distortions. It can be shown, though we do not attempt a proof, that, if these successive stages of production were inside one firm, the profit of the combined firm would be greater than the sum of the profits of the individual firms. This is because the single owner of the production chain would make only one single optimal pricing decision to maximize profit, and this would generally lead to different product prices from those that would be set by a chain of independent firms with some monopoly power. Hence, vertical integration could be motivated by a desire to increase joint monopoly profit. It is not clear which structure would be preferable for consumers, hence the implications for competition policy are ambiguous.

Also worthy of note in this context is the range of trade relationships that fall short of full integration but have clear anti-competitive implications. These are generally known as **vertical restraints.** Such vertical restraints include tied sales, resale price maintenance, geographical market exclusions, and franchising. Tied sales force a retail outlet to buy a certain amount of its turnover from a single source. For example, many pubs are tied to buying a high proportion of their beer from one brewery. The other types of restraint also restrict the freedom of retail outlets in terms of quantity or price.

Vertical restraints fall short of full vertical integration, but they can lead to an anti-competitive outcome. Hence such restraints are often the subject of inquiries by regulatory authorities.

> **Vertical integration may add value to the firm if it reduces production costs in the production chain. It may also reduce costs of market failure (transaction costs) and in imperfectly competitive markets may increase the joint profits of interrelated producers.**

CONGLOMERATE INTEGRATION

A third form of integration is referred to as *conglomerate integration*. This involves the combination within a single firm (or group) of businesses that are unrelated.

---

8 This is because the price of the input at each stage is a component of marginal cost in the next stage. So each producer is adding a margin to perceived marginal cost, which itself includes its own input supplier's mark-up over its own marginal cost.

BOX 12.3.

Hanson: the rise and fall of a conglomerate

A classic case study in the growth and demise of a conglomerate firm is provided by Hanson PLC. This company grew from virtually nothing in the early 1970s to become one of the UK's top-ten companies, by stock market value, at the end of the 1980s. However, in 1995 it demerged a bundle of its US subsidiaries and in 1996 it announced a four-way split of the remaining business. This four-way split was completed in two stages, in October 1996 and January 1997.

The growth of Hanson was led by two entrepreneurs, Lords Hanson and White. The former was skilled at running businesses, while the latter appeared able to spot hidden value in potential takeover targets. They also learned early on the trick of funding a takeover with borrowed money. Growth was fuelled by a combination of increasing efficiency in the firms that were taken over and selling off parts of purchased firms. The most spectacularly successful example of this was the takeover of Imperial Tobacco in 1986. Sales of other companies within the Imperial Group virtually paid for the entire takeover, so Imperial Tobacco itself was acquired for almost nothing!

As the group got larger, and undervalued companies became scarce, further big deals became harder to find. In the early 1990s Hanson took a stake in ICI in what was regarded as a preliminary to a full bid. However, ICI pre-empted any bid by announcing its own demerger into Zeneca (which contained its pharmaceutical subsidiaries) and ICI (which retained the other chemicals and paints businesses). Zeneca's share price boomed but Hanson stagnated.

In 1995 Hanson demerged a selection of its US subsidiaries, including Jacuzzi the spa bath maker, into a company called US Industries. This company increased its share price by over 50 per cent in its first year of trading. It may have been this evidence that persuaded Hanson of the benefits of demerger. In January 1996 it was announced that the remaining Hanson businesses were to demerge.

Imperial Tobacco became an independently listed company again in October 1996, as did Millennium Chemicals Inc., with a listing in New York. In February 1997 the remaining Hanson business split into the residual Hanson group, which had interests in building materials and bricks, and the Energy Group, which included the UK company Eastern Electricity and the US company Peabody Coal.

Hence, between 1995 and 1997, Hanson demerged into five independent companies. Ironically, one of the reasons given was that better focus would be an advantage for the managements of the new companies. This may be true, but the initial stock-market reaction

'Unrelated' in this context means that they are producing products in entirely different industries. A well-known UK example is Tomkins PLC, which owns several subsidiaries (such as Rank Hovis and British Bakeries) that make bread and cakes in the UK. It also owns Pegler, which makes plumbing fittings; Murray, a US lawnmower manufacturer; and Smith and Wesson, the gun and handcuff maker.[9] Tomkins is made up of

[9] This range of products has earned it the label of the 'guns to buns' conglomerate.

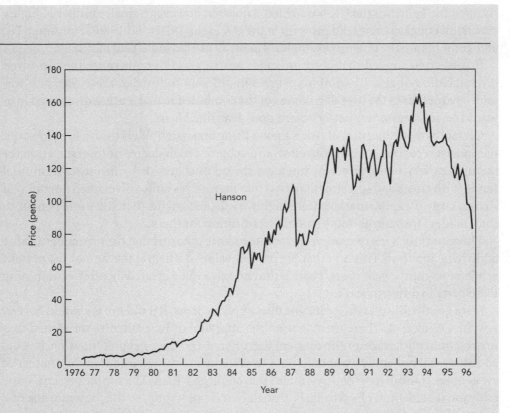

Hanson's share price, 1976–1996

to the Hanson demerger was to cut the value of the shares as shown in the chart. Hence, at the time of demerger, shareholders had lost money from the demerger announcement. However, it is possible that these demerged companies will perform well in future.

This and similar experiences in other conglomerates provide ample evidence that the conglomerate structure does not offer any economic advantages over more coherent business organizations. Some conglomerates have done well in the past, but not because they were conglomerates, merely because of the exceptional talent and opportunism of their senior managers. Such episodes do not provide a long-run justification for the conglomerate structure.

about seventy-five different wholly owned subsidiaries operating in eight different countries.

While it is easy to see why firms in related activities might want to join forces, it is much harder to provide an economic case for combining together totally unrelated activities within the same company. Conglomerate mergers had a boom period in the 1970s and early 1980s, but they have gone out of fashion in the 1990s. In the USA, for example, about half of all mergers in the 1970s were conglomerate mergers. The comparable figure for the UK is more like a quarter; however, a small number of highly successful conglomerates did grow up in the UK in the 1970s and 1980s. Hanson, BTR, and Tomkins are the obvious examples. The story of Hanson is told in Box 12.3.

It used to be argued that conglomerates were a good thing because they involved diversification of risk. By combining firms in different industries, there was, so it was said, a reduction in the overall riskiness of the combined firm. Hence, a diversified firm would be, in some sense, 'better' than a non-diversified firm.

Certainly, diversification of risk is a good thing for shareholders to aim for. However, in modern securities markets, investors can achieve a high degree of diversification for themselves very easily, either by buying a spread of shares or by investing in mutual funds (unit trusts and investment trusts) that themselves hold a diversified portfolio of shares. Only if capital markets were highly inefficient might there be some benefit to shareholders from firms doing some diversification for them.

The consensus view of modern corporate finance theory is that the **principle of value additivity** applies.[10] This says that the present value of a firm is the sum of the present values of its component parts. There is thus no extra value created merely by combining these parts in different ways.

It is a good thing that this principle does apply to firms. If it did not we would have to rewrite Chapter 11. There we discussed the appraisal of investments. We argued that firms should undertake any investment that offered a positive net present value. If value additivity did not apply we should have to evaluate every investment in the context of every other combination of investments that could go with it. The simple present-value criterion would clearly be wrong. Fortunately, it is not wrong, so the present value of a firm is the sum of the present values of its parts.

This does not prove that conglomerate mergers can never add value. Merely it shows that the extra value has to be justified in other ways. The two most plausible ways in which benefits could arise from conglomerate mergers are associated with under-valuation of assets and with superior managerial skills.[11]

The purchase of an unrelated business will add value to a firm if it buys that business for less than its true present value. This could only arise if the managers of the acquiring firm are better able to discern the true potential value of the target firm's assets than the value accorded by the stock market. Such takeovers that release hidden value have happened. The takeover of Imperial Tobacco by Hanson in the 1980s is an example. Hanson subsequently disposed of subsidiaries of Imperial with a value close to the full takeover price, and hence ended up getting Imperial for nothing. However, as stock markets have become more efficient it seems that finding such undervalued targets has

[10] See e.g. Richard A. Brealey and Stewart C. Myers, *Principles of Corporate Finance*, 5th edn. (New York: McGraw-Hill, 1996), pp. 946–7.

[11] Two other arguments we pass over are: (1) conglomerates can allocate capital more efficiently internally than is done via the market, and (2) a large conglomerate may be able to raise capital more cheaply than could each of its subsidiaries alone. Argument (1) may be true in some cases, but even if the market is inefficient there is no reason why the conglomerate structure *per se* offers a better environment than an equally sized focused group of companies. The same argument applies to (2). There is no reason why a focused group of companies would not raise capital just as cheaply. That is, size may give benefits, but these do not arise from diversity.

become much more difficult (though not necessarily impossible). There is no reason today to believe that managers of conglomerates will be any better at valuing potential takeover targets than anybody else, though there certainly was an interval of time in the recent past when the conglomerate structure was a vehicle for business success. This was due in part to the superior ability to identify hidden value in takeover targets and then to manage those companies successfully post-takeover.

The second justification for conglomerate mergers arises, even if the assets are correctly valued, if the new management has superior skills to get a better return out of these assets. No doubt some managers have better skills than others, and there certainly have been many cases in the past where new managements within conglomerates have improved the performance of a target company after a takeover. However, there is no reason why this body of management skills should be uniquely located within conglomerates. Indeed, it is now more widely presumed that some industries require both general management skills and specialist knowledge of the specific industry. Hence, *focus* has become a common recommendation by management experts. Certainly, there is no evidence that businesses perform better within a conglomerate structure than they would without. Indeed, many firms have taken the route of attempting to release shareholder value by demerging a conglomerate into more focused independent businesses. See Box 12.3 above for an example of this.

> The value of a conglomerate is the value of the sum of its parts. There is no added value from diversification. The only potential sources of added value are the ability to purchase undervalued assets and superior management skills. Neither seems likely to give any sustained advantage to the conglomerate structure *per se.*

The market for corporate control

As we have seen, a **takeover** occurs when Company A buys Company B (which then becomes a part of A). A **merger** occurs when Companies A and B join together, often combining even their names. A **buyout** occurs when a group of investors, rather than an existing firm, buys up a firm or one of its subsidiaries. A **management buyout** involves the existing management of a firm buying the firm from its existing owners. A common form of management buyout involves those running a wholly owned subsidiary, within a P-form firm, buying this firm from the group. From then on it becomes an independent firm.

Buyouts, mergers, and takeovers can be interpreted as transactions in a **market for corporate control.** In this market, the product that is bought and sold is the firm itself. This market, like any other, has both buyers (those who would acquire the rights to control a firm) and sellers (the current owners of equity in the firm). As in other markets, the expected outcome is that the assets being bought and sold will wind up in the hands of those who value them most. These will tend to be those who can come closest to maximizing the firm's profits.

A *takeover* begins when the management of the acquiring firm makes a **tender offer** to the stockholders of the target firm. Tender offers are promises to purchase stock at a specified price for a limited period of time, during which the acquiring firm hopes to gain control of the target company. Typically, the prices offered are considerably higher than the prevailing stock-market price. The takeover is called a *hostile takeover* when the current management of the target firm opposes it.

The effects of takeovers

Takeovers, mergers, and buyouts seem to come in waves. Some are driven by technological changes that increase the minimum efficient scale of firms in many industries. They tend to have long-lasting effects. Such was the merger wave at the beginning of this century in the USA. Some are based on experiments that prove to be either outright failures, or far less valuable than originally thought. Such was the wave of conglomerate mergers in the 1970s, which often involved firms selling widely different products in widely different markets. Although some of the conglomerates formed in that period survived, many were dismantled in the wave of buyouts that occurred in the 1980s.

Do takeovers improve economic efficiency? In this section we consider the takeover of one domestic firm by another. The main argument in favour is that, after a takeover, the new management can make more efficient use of the target firm's assets. The acquiring firm should be able to exploit profit opportunities that the target management is not exploiting. This can be done by such means as operating the target firm more efficiently, providing funds that the target firm could not obtain, or providing access to markets that would be too expensive for the target firm to access on its own. If this is true, the value of the target firm will rise in response to a takeover, reflecting the expectation of increased future profits. Further, if the *acquiring* firm's managers are acting in the best interest of *their* stockholders, the value of the acquiring firm should also rise when it is successful in a takeover bid.

RETURNS TO SHAREHOLDERS OF TARGET COMPANIES

Evidence on the effects of takeovers strongly supports the proposition that takeover bids benefit the shareholders of target firms. Estimates of the magnitude of the gains for UK and US shareholders of target firms typically show gains that average about 20 per cent of pre-takeover share price. Some specific cases have produced gains to shareholders well in excess of this level.

Figure 12.4 shows the behaviour over time of the share prices of three UK firms that were recently taken over—Forte, Wellcome, and BET (by Granada, Glaxo, and Rentokil

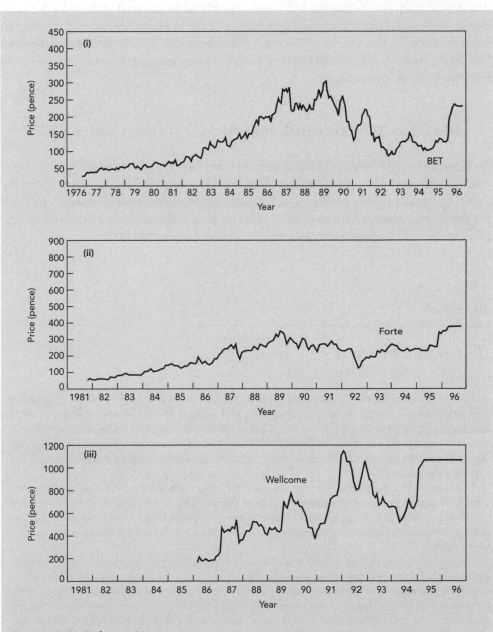

Figure 12.4. Bid premia

Shares typically jump when a takeover bid is announced.

Source: Datastream.

respectively). In each case there was a substantial rise in the price of the shares in the time period from just before the bid being announced to the final victory. In the cases of both Forte and BET there was slight raising of the bid towards the end in order to clinch victory. In the case of Wellcome, the agreement of the largest shareholder (Wellcome Trust) had been obtained prior to the announcement, so raising the bid to clinch victory was unnecessary.

RETURNS TO STOCKHOLDERS OF ACQUIRING COMPANIES

The benefits to shareholders in the acquiring firms vary greatly from takeover to take-over. Sometimes the benefit is large; at other times it is negative (the takeover *lowers* the acquiring firm's profits). However, substantial accumulated evidence seems to show that the *average benefit*, as measured by excess returns, to the acquiring firms in both the USA and the UK has been very close to zero, or possibly slightly negative.

BOX 12.4.

The winner's curse

In any auction market the value of the product for sale is determined by the price that the highest bidder is prepared to pay. In a standard auction the price keeps rising until all bidders but one have dropped out. The highest bidder, who ends up acquiring whatever it was that was for sale, is often described as 'the winner' of the auction. The point of this box is that the winner of an auction, especially in the context of *the winner* of a takeover bid, may not be a winner at all.

The reason why the winner may be the loser is simple. The 'winner' in an auction or take-over bid has had to pay a price so high that both the existing owners are prepared to sell and all other bidders have dropped out at lower prices. In other words, the so-called winner has paid a price for the assets that is higher than the valuation placed on those assets by any other party.

Now, it is possible that the auction winner knows something about the value of the assets involved that nobody else knows. However, the winner *may not know something that all the other interested parties do know*. In other words, it is possible that the winner of the auction has placed a higher value on these assets than their true worth. Indeed, since the winner, by definition, was the highest bidder, it is more likely that the winner overvalued rather than undervalued the assets. Anyone who undervalued the assets would drop out of the bidding long before those who overvalued them.

Accordingly, it might not always add value to a company to be the winner in a takeover bid. Indeed, in a hotly contested bid in which there are rival bidders and the winning bid is well above the initial bid, it may well be that the successful bidder ends up paying more for the target than it is truly worth. This is why this phenomenon is know as **the winner's curse**.

It may seem strange to find evidence that firms taking over other firms do not actually benefit from such actions on average. However, this is what we would expect if the market for corporate control were competitive. A typical takeover starts when an existing firm is perceived to be undervalued. Other firms will want to take the firm over and will bid up the value of its shares to reflect the perceived undervaluation. The result is a large rise in the price of the target firm's shares to the benefit of the owners, whereas the firm that finally makes the successful takeover pays about the price that makes its investment yield a normal return (including a risk premium). Because expectations about the potential profitability of the target firm are subject to a wide margin of error, some takeovers will turn out to be more valuable than expected and the acquiring firm will gain, while others will turn out to be less valuable than expected and the acquirer will lose. If, however, the market judges correctly on average, takeovers will only prove normally profitable on average (no excess returns) for the firm making the takeover. The inevitability that some takeover bids will be a mistake is known as the **winner's curse.** This is discussed in Box 12.4.

The true winners in a takeover battle may be both the shareholders of the target company and the rival bidders who failed to 'win'. The shareholders win because they sell their shares for much more than they are really worth, at least in the opinion of most potential buyers. The other (losing) bidders win because one of their rivals (the bid winner) may be saddled with a capital loss that could weaken its ability to compete in other ways.

A good example of this phenomenon is the takeover of the Crocker Bank of California by UK's Midland Bank. This so weakened Midland that it ended up being taken over itself by HSBC. Another example is the takeover in 1987 of US employment agency Manpower by the much smaller UK employment agency Blue Arrow. This effectively turned Blue Arrow from a fast-growing stock-market star into a basket case overnight. The best example of all is the takeover of RJR Nabisco by Kolberg Kravis and Roberts (KKR) in one of the most famous (and biggest—$25 billion) takeover auctions of all time.* KKR survived, but their ability to raise capital for other activities was severely dented for most of the following decade. It is likely that they would have been a much bigger force on Wall Street in the last decade if they had lost that bid.

The winner's curse applies not just to takeover bids but also to any transaction in which there is competitive bidding, such as for supply contracts. The latter tends to go the lowest bidder. The lowest bidder may have underestimated the true costs and hence may lose on the deal. However, here there is also a downside for those accepting the bid, as the lowest bidder in a supply contract may be unable to deliver at the promised quality, so it may not always be the lowest bid that is accepted. None the less, the same principle applies. It is not always the 'winner' who comes off best.

* For a highly readable account of this takeover see B. Burrough and J. Helyar, *Barbarians at the Gate* (London: Arrow, 1990).

BENEFITS TO THE ECONOMY?

There is considerable controversy about whether the threat of takeover is a good thing. The case against the UK and US practice of hostile takeovers is that it encourages 'short-termism'. Managers cannot take appropriate long-term investment decisions because short-term weakness in the share price may lead to the firm being taken over and the management replaced. In Germany and Japan, hostile takeovers are very unusual, so managers do not have to worry about being deposed in this way.

An alternative view is that takeovers provide a useful discipline that helps to restrain managers from acting in non-maximizing ways. Many also feel that each new bout of takeovers and mergers helps to chart new waters. As technology changes, there are changes in the advantages of scale and scope resulting from changes in production techniques, market demand, and market boundaries. To meet the new circumstances, new forms of organization are often necessary and are sometimes effected through mergers, takeovers, and buyouts (and sometimes through the downsizing of firms). When firms react to rapidly changing circumstances, they must learn by experience. It is not surprising that, even though people generally move in the right direction, some make mistakes. In particular, a merger movement may go too far, so that, among the profit-increasing mergers, takeovers, or buyouts, there are also some profit-reducing ones. Over time, the successful ones will be solidified and unsuccessful ones abandoned.

This is what we would expect in a world of rapidly changing circumstances where people must learn appropriate responses through experience. It makes assessment of any current wave of mergers, buyouts, or takeovers difficult until the whole process is completed. Before then, it is hard to distinguish between some spectacular, attention-getting failures that are an inevitable part of the learning process and a more general failure of the concept behind the wave.

Whatever the case for or against takeovers, they are clearly an important force for change, at least in the UK and USA. The market for corporate control operates as an important influence on the evolving structure of business organizations, though under the watchful eye of the competition authorities.

Firms and markets

This chapter concludes our study of firms and markets. The remainder of this book is about the economy as a whole. It is worth pausing at this stage to review the ground that we have covered.

In Chapters 2 and 3 we set out an analysis of markets based upon demand and supply in which market prices and quantities are determined by the interaction of the decisions of firms and consumers. In Chapters 4, 5, and 6 we looked closely at the costs and production decisions of firms, and we identified the characteristics of the profit-maximizing level of output. We then proceeded (Chapters 6–8) to examine the choices faced by firms in a variety of market structures, such as perfect competition, monopoly, imperfect competition, and oligopoly. Chapter 9 set out several reasons why the free market does not always produce a socially optimal allocation of resources and discussed the role of government in correcting these market failures.

Chapters 4–8 can be thought of as focusing mainly (though not exclusively) on decisions relating to firms' output markets. Chapters 10 and 11 focus on firms' input decisions: labour and capital; while the current chapter discusses decisions about the internal organization of firms, which types of business fit together, and how, in practice, businesses themselves are traded.

All of the issues that we have discussed relating to firms and markets will be viewed again from other perspectives by any student who studies business in greater depth. The economic approach is only one of many approaches to these issues, but it is an influential approach that is itself rapidly evolving. The ultimate test of relevance is the ability of the theory to explain the facts. Readers can test the validity of the economic ideas set out above throughout their future business careers.

Summary

1. Behavioural theories of the firm try to explain firms' behaviour as a compromise between the interests of involved groups. These theories predict that firms will not be true value maximizers since there will be inevitable slack.

2. Firms with a uniform structure have departments organized on functional lines. Such firms benefit from specialization of functions, but they have potential problems of measuring productivity and may involve too much CEO time in day-to-day decision making.

3. Multi-divisional firms are organized around products and have their own day-to-day management. The chief executive of the firm is thereby able to devote time to strategic issues.

4. In the modern portfolio structure of a firm (or Group) each product unit becomes an independent legal entity, albeit usually wholly owned by the Group.

5. Horizontal integration involves the merger of two firms at the same stage of production in the same industry. Such mergers may produce economies of scale or scope and may increase monopoly power.

6. Vertical integration involves mergers between firms at successive stages of production. Such mergers may add value if they reduce transactions costs.

7. Conglomerate mergers cannot be justified on grounds of diversification. Value additivity implies that firms are only as valuable as the sum of the parts.

8. Firms themselves are the product traded in the market for corporate control.

Topics for review

- Firms as complex organizations
- Behavioural theories of the firm
- Uniform (U-form) structure of firms
- Multi-divisional (M-form) structure of firms
- Portfolio (P-form) structure of firms
- Horizontal integration
- Vertical integration
- Conglomerate integration
- Market for corporate control

Questions for discussion

1. In what ways might the conflicting goals of different interest groups within firms lead to sub-optimal outcomes.

2. How could incentives for good performance be implemented in a U-form organization?

3. Why do you think most firms have moved from an M-form to a P-form organizational structure? What are the advantages of the latter over the former? Are there any disadvantages?

4. Rank the three forms of integration (horizontal, vertical, and conglomerate) from the perspective of their likely contribution to (i) cost saving, (ii) greater market power, and (iii) better access to and use of capital. Identify a recent merger or takeover from the press and outline what appear to have been the motives behind it.

5. Why do firms take over other firms if the evidence is that on average takeovers do not add value to the bidding firm?

6. Are conglomerates likely to be a dying phenomenon?

PART II
THE ECONOMY AS A WHOLE

Section 5
National Product and National Income

CHAPTER 13

Macroeconomic Issues and Measurement

What is macroeconomics?   412

Why macroeconomics?   413
Major macroeconomic issues   413
  Business cycles   413
  Overall living standards   416
  Inflation   416
  Unemployment   417
  Government budget deficits   417
  Interest rates   418
  Targets and instruments   418

Value added as output   419

GDP, GNP, and national income   421
GDP expenditure-based   423
  Consumption expenditure   424
  Investment expenditure   424
   Stockbuilding   424
   Fixed-capital formation   425
   Residential investment   425
   Gross and net investment   425
  Government expenditure on goods and
services   425
  Net exports   427
   Imports   427
   Exports   427
  Total expenditures   428
GDP income-based   429
  Factor payments   429
   Income from employment   429
   Income from self-employment   429
   Rent   429
   Profits   430
   GDP at factor cost   430
  Non-factor payments   431

   Indirect taxes   431
   Subsidies   431
   GDP at market prices   431
  Net domestic product   432
   Depreciation   432
  Income produced and income received   432
   Reconciling GDP with GNP   434
  Other income concepts   434

**Interpreting national income and product
measures**   435
Real and nominal measures   435
  The implicit deflator   435
International comparisons of national
income   438
What national income accounts do not
measure   440
  Illegal activities   440
  Unreported activities   440
  Non-marketed activities   441
  Economic bads   441
  Do the omissions matter?   441
Is there a best measure of national income?   442

Summary   442

Topics for review   444

Questions for discussion   444

Box 13.1. The terminology of business
cycles   414
Box 13.2. Value added through stages of
production   420
Box 13.3. Calculation of nominal and real
GDP   436

M ANY people are concerned about such issues as inflation, unemployment, recession, and competitiveness. Firms are concerned about how inflations, recessions, and foreign competition affect their profits and, perhaps, even their survival. Governments worry about how to prevent recessions, reduce inflation, increase competitiveness, and increase employment. Adults of working age are anxious to avoid the unemployment that comes with recessions and to obtain rising real incomes. Pensioners are keen to protect themselves against the hazards of inflation, which can lower the value of their savings.

Each of the concerns just mentioned plays a major role in macroeconomics. In this chapter we explain how macroeconomics differs in approach from the microeconomics of the first part of this book and outline the main issues addressed. We then look in detail at how the activity of the economy as a whole is measured, before discussing the interpretation of these measures. In subsequent chapters we are concerned with explaining how the national product is determined and what government policy can do to influence it.

What is macroeconomics?

Macroeconomics is the study of how the economy behaves in broad outline without dwelling on much of its interesting, but sometimes confusing, detail. Macroeconomics is largely concerned with the behaviour of economic *aggregates*, such as total national product, total investment, and exports for the entire economy. It is also concerned with the average price of all goods and services, rather than with the prices of specific products. These aggregates result from activities in many different markets and from the behaviour of different decision makers, such as consumers, governments, and firms. In contrast, *microeconomics* deals with the behaviour of individual markets, such as those for wheat, computer chips, or strawberries, and with the detailed behaviour of individual agents, such as firms and consumers.

In macroeconomics we add together the value of cornflakes, beer, cars, strawberries, haircuts, and restaurant meals, along with the value of all other goods and services produced, and study the movement of aggregate *national product*. We also average the prices of all goods and services consumed and discuss the *general price level* for the entire economy—usually just called the price level. In Britain, the index that measures the average price of the goods and services bought by the typical consumer is known as the **Retail Price Index** (RPI), while the equivalent in some other countries is called the *consumer price index* (CPI). We know full well that an economy that produces much wheat and few cars differs from one that produces many cars but little wheat. We also know that an economy with cheap wheat and expensive cars differs from one with cheap cars and expensive wheat. Studying aggregates often means missing these important differences; but in return for losing valuable detail, it allows us to view the big picture.

In macroeconomics, we look at the broad range of opportunities and difficulties facing the economy as a whole. When national product rises, the output of most firms, and the incomes of most people, usually rise with it. When interest rates rise, most borrowers, including firms and home owners, have to make bigger payments on their debts, though many savers will get a higher return on their savings. When the price level rises, almost everyone in the economy is forced to make adjustments owing to the lower value of money. When the unemployment rate rises, workers are put at an increased risk of losing their jobs and suffering losses in their incomes. These movements in economic aggregates are strongly associated with the economic well-being of most individuals: the health of the sectors in which they work and the prices of the goods that they purchase. These associations are why macroeconomic aggregates (particularly inflation, unemployment, interest rates, and the balance of payments) are often in the news.

Why macroeconomics?

Economists need a separate subject called macroeconomics because there are forces that affect the economy as a whole that cannot be fully or simply understood by analysing individual markets and individual products. A problem that is affecting all firms, or many workers, in different industries needs to be tackled at the level of the whole economy. Certainly, if circumstances are common across many sectors of the economy, then analysis at the level of the whole economy helps us to understand what is happening.

Business people need to understand macroeconomic issues because the detailed workings of their own businesses, on which they are experts, are affected by the overall working of the economy, in the understanding of which they are not experts. The best-laid business plans can be upset by an unexpected recession, rapid inflation, higher interest rates, or a change in the exchange rate. To take these broad macroeconomic issues into account, business people need to understand the pronouncements made by economists, government statisticians, and others who study them in detail. Big businesses have staff economists who do this for them. Medium and small businesses ignore macroeconomic knowledge and the intelligence generated by others in this field at their peril. Let us look at some of the main issues that are important in macroeconomics.

Major macroeconomic issues

BUSINESS CYCLES

The economy tends to move in a series of ups and downs, called *business cycles*, rather than in a steady pattern. The 1930s saw the greatest world-wide economic depression in the twentieth century, with nearly one-fifth of the UK labour force unemployed for an extended period. In contrast, the twenty-five years following the Second World War marked a period of sustained economic growth, with only minor interruptions caused by modest recessions. Then the business cycle returned in more serious form. There were three major recessions (1974/5, 1980/2, and 1990/2) during the last three decades. (Figure 1.1 on page 16 shows the cycles in GDP growth in the UK, Japan, and the USA since 1965.)

In Chapter 1 we showed why business cycles are important for firms. During recessions many businesses go bust, and even for those that survive, profits fall. In contrast, during booms, demand for most products rises, profits rise, and most businesses find it easy to expand. Understanding the business cycle is, thus, very important for successful

BOX 13.1.

The terminology of business cycles

Although the phases of business fluctuations are described by a series of commonly used terms, no two cycles are the same.

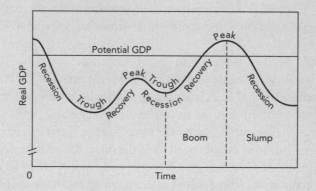

Trough

A **trough** is characterized by high unemployment and a level of demand that is low in relation to the economy's capacity to produce. There is thus a substantial amount of unused productive capacity. Business profits are low; for some individual companies they are negative. Confidence about economic prospects in the immediate future is lacking, and, as a result, many firms are unwilling to risk making new investments.

Recovery

The characteristics of a **recovery,** or expansion, are many—run-down equipment is re-

businesses. Expanding capacity during the onset of a recession could be a recipe for disaster, while having too little capacity during a boom may be a lost opportunity. Most importantly, business cycles are beyond the control of individual firms but all need to understand that the economy moves in cycles. Whatever governments may say, business cycles have been around for a long time, and they are likely to be with us for much longer yet. Box 13.1 outlines some of the terminology associated with a stylized business cycle.

Macroeconomics as a subject was invented to help produce policies that could ameliorate economic fluctuations. Much of what follows is devoted to explanations of why the economy goes through these ups and downs, and what the government can do about them.

placed; employment, income, and consumer spending all begin to rise; and expectations become more favourable as a result of increases in production, sales, and profits. Investments that once seemed risky may be undertaken as the climate of business opinion starts to change from one of pessimism to one of optimism. As demand rises, production can be increased with relative ease merely by re-employing the existing unused capacity and unemployed labour.

Peak

A **peak** is the top of a cycle. At the peak, existing capacity is utilized to a high degree; labour shortages may develop, particularly in categories of key skills; and shortages of essential raw materials are likely. As shortages develop in more and more markets, a situation of general excess demand develops. Costs rise, but since prices rise also, business remains profitable.

Recession

A **recession**, or contraction, is a downturn in economic activity. Common usage defines a recession as a fall in the real GDP for two quarters in succession. Demand falls off, and, as a result, production and employment also fall. As employment falls, so do personal incomes. Profits drop, and some firms encounter financial difficulties. Investments that looked profitable with the expectation of continually rising demand now appear unprofitable. It may not even be worth replacing capital goods as they wear out, because unused capacity is increasing steadily. In historical discussions, a recession that is deep and long-lasting is often called a **depression**.

Booms and slumps

Two non-technical but descriptive terms are often used. The whole falling half of the cycle is often called a **slump,** and the whole rising half is often called a **boom.** These are useful terms to use when we do not wish to be more specific about the economy's position in the cycle.

OVERALL LIVING STANDARDS

Both total and per capita output have risen for many decades in most industrial countries. These long-term trends have meant rising average living standards. Since the early 1970s, however, average living standards have grown much less rapidly than during the preceding decades of the twentieth century. Indeed, in the USA the *real wage* (the quantity of goods and services that can be purchased by the average hourly money wage) was about the same in 1995 as it was in 1973. In the UK (see Figure 1.6 on page 33), the real value of the average wage doubled in the twenty years between 1953 and 1973. It stagnated for a while in the 1970s but then grew rapidly again in the 1980s.

Although long-term growth gets less media attention than does the current inflation rate or unemployment rate, it is the predominant determinant of living standards and the material constraints facing a society from decade to decade and generation to generation. Among the most important issues in macroeconomics is discovering the conditions that would allow world-wide growth to continue without the type of slowdown that happened in the 1970s or the serious recessions of the early 1980s and early 1990s.

INFLATION

The annual inflation rate in Britain was over 25 per cent in 1975. This was the highest level reached in peacetime for at least three centuries. The government of Mrs Thatcher was elected in 1979 on the promise of eliminating inflation from the British economy. Inflation did fall below 5 per cent by 1984, but it rose again to around 10 per cent before the end of the decade. By the mid-1990s inflation had fallen to around 2–3 per cent, the lowest level since the early 1960s.

Accompanying swings in inflation have been swings in economic activity. Generally, attempts by governments to control high inflation have helped to bring about recessions. However, the pattern of booms and recessions has been very similar across many different countries, so it cannot all be attributed to domestic government policy. Also the relationship between inflation and recession seems to change over time. The 1980 recession was accompanied by inflation in the mid-teens, while the 1990–2 recession was accompanied by only single-figure inflation.

The policy problem for governments is how to stimulate economic activity without causing inflation. It is often the pick-up of inflation during boom times that leads governments to tighten their monetary and/or fiscal policies in order to bring inflation under control. When inflation falls after a recession, governments often feel that they have the leeway to stimulate the economy again. Hence, policymakers have to tread carefully to achieve a suitable balance between stimulus and contraction.

Inflation matters to firms because it creates distortions in the price mechanism, most notably by eroding the real value of anything accounted for in money terms. Some firms will make arbitrary gains as a result of inflation, and others will lose. A pick-up in inflation is usually the signal for a tightening of monetary policy that raises interest rates and brings about a slowdown in the economy. Such downturns in the economy have an adverse effect on most firms, except perhaps firms of insolvency experts.

UNEMPLOYMENT

A downturn in economic activity causes an increase in unemployment. Indeed, it was the high unemployment of the 1930s that led to the establishment of the subject now known as macroeconomics, and unemployment is still a central concern of economics. During the Great Depression of the 1930s, unemployment rose to nearly 20 per cent of the labour force. Although in the 1950s and 1960s it was consistently very low, in the 1980s and 1990s high unemployment returned. Accordingly, the analysis of the causes of, and potential cures for, unemployment is very high on the agenda of macroeconomics today.

The solution for temporary bouts of unemployment that economists came up with in the 1930s was for governments to increase their spending or reduce taxes. However, the applicability of this solution is thought to be much more restricted today. We shall discuss why this early promise of macroeconomics has not been fulfilled in Chapter 20.

In times of low unemployment, firms will find it difficult to hire scarce workers, especially those with requisite skills. In periods of high unemployment, firms will often find their employees more interested in bargaining for some measure of job security rather than increased wages.

GOVERNMENT BUDGET DEFICITS

With the exception of two brief periods (1970 and 1988/9) the British government has had a *budget deficit*—it was spending more than it was raising in taxation. In the mid-1970s the budget deficit was around 8 per cent of the national product (GDP), and in the mid-1990s the budget was again in deficit. These deficits have to be financed by government borrowing, which raises the national debt.

At one time it was thought that budget deficits might be good for the economy because government spending creates jobs. But nowadays there is much concern about the potential burden of debt that is created by deficits, the interest on which has to be paid by tax payers, thereby keeping taxes high. This conflict over the role of the government budget is central to macroeconomics. We shall discuss how the budget deficit affects the economy. Deliberate use of government spending and taxes to influence the economy is known as **fiscal policy.**

Firms worry about budget deficits for two main reasons. First, government borrowing competes with firms' borrowing in capital markets and may raise interest rates for firms. Second, governments in deficit may be forced to raise taxes and thereby reduce profits and consumer demand.

INTEREST RATES

In addition to fiscal policy, governments (or the monetary authority where this is independent of government) has available the tools of monetary policy. **Monetary policy** involves using changes in interest rates, or the money supply, to influence the economy.

High interest rates are a symptom of a tight monetary policy. When interest rates are high, firms find it more costly to borrow, and this makes them more reluctant to invest in expanding their business. Also, firms are usually hit by a fall in sales as consumers with mortgages or bank loans reduce their spending in response to high interest rates. Hence, high interest rates tend to reduce demand in the economy—firms invest less and those with mortgages have less to spend. Low interest rates tend to stimulate demand for the opposite reasons.

Another important channel of monetary policy is via the exchange rate, at least for countries whose exchange rate is flexible. Exchange-rate changes can affect the relative prices, and thereby the competitiveness, of domestic and foreign producers. A significant appreciation of the domestic currency can make domestic goods expensive relative to foreign goods. This may lead to a shift of demand away from domestic producers towards foreign goods. Such shifts are a potentially important influence on domestic economic activity.

Firms doing business abroad must be concerned with the exchange rate. If they buy or sell on contracts denominated in foreign currency, they must worry about the sterling values of those amounts at the time when the contract is settled.

TARGETS AND INSTRUMENTS

The issues that we have just discussed can be thought as falling into two types. First there are the things that really matter for their own sake. These are the things that affect living conditions and the state of the economic environment. Living standards, unemployment, business cycles, and inflation are outcomes that matter. We all want growing living standards, high employment and low unemployment, as well as avoidance of recessions and inflation. These things are known as the **targets** of policy. 'Good' values of these variables are what governments would like to achieve.

Fiscal and monetary policies (government spending, taxes, interest rates, and the money supply) are not so much valued for their own sake. Rather, they are the **instruments** of policy and are valued more for the effect they have on the targets than for their own sake. *Instruments* are the variables that the government can change directly, whereas *targets* are the things that they would like to change.

The macroeconomic policy problem is to choose appropriate values of the policy instruments in order to achieve the best possible combination of the outcomes of the targets. This is a continually changing problem because the targets are perpetually being affected by shocks from various parts of the world economy.

We now turn to a discussion of the measurement of aggregate economic activity before returning to explanations of how that activity is determined.

Value added as output

Macroeconomics has as its central goal the explanation of the determinants of national income and output. Indeed, from Chapter 14 onwards we spend a great deal of our time building up an analytic framework that helps us to understand the forces that influence national income and output. First, however, we have to understand what it is we are talking about. What exactly do we mean by national income and the national product? What do people mean when they refer to GDP, and how does it differ from GNP?

We start by discussing the measurement of national output, and find that by summing the *value added* of each industry or sector we arrive at a standard measure of national product. We then discuss how it is that we can arrive at the same measure of national product both from the expenditure side of the economy and from adding up factor (inputs) incomes. An explicit result of this discussion is a demonstration of the equivalence of the concepts of national income and national product.

The national output or the national product is related to the sum of all the outputs produced in the economy by individuals, firms, and governmental organizations. However, we cannot just add up all of the outputs of individual production units to arrive at the total national output.

The reason that getting a total for the nation's output is not quite so straightforward as it may seem at first sight is that one firm's output may be another firm's input. A maker of clothing buys cloth from a textile manufacturer and buttons, zips, thread, pins, hangers, etc. from a range of other producers. Most modern manufactured products have many ready-made inputs. A car or aircraft manufacturer, for example, will have hundreds of component suppliers.

Production occurs in stages: some firms produce outputs that are used as inputs by other firms, and these other firms in turn produce outputs that are used as inputs by yet other firms.

If we merely added up the market values of all outputs of all firms, we would obtain a total that was greatly in excess of the value of the economy's actual output. The errors that would arise in estimating the nation's output by adding all sales of all firms are called **double counting.** 'Multiple counting' would be a better term, since if we added up the values of all sales, the same output would be counted every time that it was sold from one firm to another.

BOX 13.2.

Value added through stages of production

Because the output of one firm often becomes the input of other firms, the total value of goods sold by all firms greatly exceeds the value of the output of final goods. This general principle is illustrated by a simple example in which firm R starts from scratch and produces goods (raw materials) valued at £100; the firm's value added is £100. Firm I purchases these raw materials valued at £100 and produces semi-manufactured goods that it sells for £130. Its value added is £30 because the value of the goods is increased by £30 as a result of the firm's activities. Firm F purchases the semi-manufactured goods for £130 and works them into a finished state, selling them for £180. Firm F's value added is £50. The value of final goods, £180, is found either by counting the sales of firm F or by taking the sum of the values added by each firm. This value is less than the £410 that we obtain by adding up the market value of the commodities sold by each firm. The following table summarizes the example.

Transactions between firms at three different stages of production

	Firm R	Firm I	Firm F		All firms
A Purchases from other firms	£ 0	£100	£130		£230 = Total interfirm sales
B Purchase of factors of production (wages, rent, interest, profits)	£100	£ 30	£ 50		£180 = Value added
Total A + B = value of product	£100	£130	£180 = value of final goods & services		£410 = Total value of sales

The problem of double counting is solved by distinguishing between two types of output. **Intermediate goods and services** are outputs of some firms that are in turn inputs for other firms. **Final goods and services** are goods that are not, in the period of time under consideration, used as inputs by other firms. The term **final demand** refers to the purchase of final goods and services for consumption, for investment (including inventory accumulation), for use by governments, and for export. It does not include goods and services that are purchased by firms and used as inputs for producing other goods and services during the period under consideration.

If the sales of firms could be readily separated into sales for final use and sales for further processing by other firms, measuring total output would still be straightforward. It would equal the value of all *final goods and services* produced by firms, excluding all intermediate goods and services. However, when British Steel sells steel to the Ford Motor Company, it does not care, and usually does not know, whether the steel is for final use (say, construction of a new warehouse) or for use as an intermediate good in the production of cars. The problem of double counting must therefore be resolved in some other manner.

To avoid double counting, statisticians use the important concept of *value added*. Each firm's value added is the value of its output minus the value of the inputs that it purchases from other firms (which were in turn the outputs of those other firms). Thus a steel mill's value added is the value of its output minus the value of the ore that it buys from the mining company, the value of the electricity and fuel oil that it uses, and the values of all other inputs that it buys from other firms. A bakery's value added is the value of the bread and cakes it produces minus the value of the flour and other inputs that it buys from other firms.

The total value of a firm's output is the gross value of its output. The firm's value added is the net value of its output. It is this latter figure that is the firm's contribution to the nation's total output. It is what its own efforts add to the value of what it takes in as inputs.

> **Value added measures each firm's own contribution to total output, the amount of market value that is produced by that firm. Its use avoids the statistical problem of double counting.**

The concept of value added is further illustrated in Box 13.2. In this simple example, as in all more complex cases, the value of total output of final goods is obtained by summing all the individual values added.

> **The sum of all values added in an economy is a measure of the economy's total output. This measure of total output is called gross domestic product (GDP). It is a measure of all final output that is produced by all productive activity in the economy.**

Table 13.1 gives the GDP by major industrial sectors for the UK economy in 1995.

GDP, GNP, and national income

The measures of national income and national product that are used in Britain derive from an accounting system called the National Income Accounts. These accounts have a logical structure, based on the simple yet important idea that whenever national output is produced, it generates an equivalent amount of national income.

Figure 13.1 shows the circular flow of income and expenditure. The right half of the figure focuses on expenditure to purchase the nation's output in product markets, and the left half focuses on factor markets through which the receipts of producers are distributed to factors of production, such as workers and owners of capital and land.

Corresponding to the two halves of the circular flow are two ways of measuring

Table 13.1. Gross domestic product for UK, 1995

Value added by sector	£ million	% of GDP
Agriculture, forestry, and fisheries	11,896	2.0
Mining, oil and gas extraction	14,575	2.4
Manufacturing	131,658	21.8
Electricity, gas, and water supply	15,787	2.6
Construction	31,815	5.3
Wholesale and retail trade	84,706	14.0
Transport and communications	50,835	8.4
Finance and real estate	127,430	21.1
Public administration and defence	39,510	6.5
Education and health	72,972	12.1
Other services	23,255	3.8
Statistical discrepancy	−180	
GDP at factor cost	604,259	100.0

The table shows value added by industrial sector in UK for 1995. The sector values added combine to make GDP at factor cost. As is explained later in the chapter, 'factor cost' means that it is the sum of factor incomes. The values added are calculated from the factor rewards attributable to each sector. Notice that manufacturing is (just) the largest sector, but it only produces about 22 per cent of GDP.

Note: The original publications include a term 'Adjustment for financial services'. This is deducted from total value added to avoid errors in the treatment of interest payments. Here we have deducted this term from the value added of the 'Finance and real estate' sector.

Source: National Income Blue Book, 1996.

national income: by determining the value of what is produced and by determining the value of the income claims generated by production. Both measures yield the same total, which is called **gross domestic product (GDP)**.[1] When it is calculated by adding up the total expenditure for each of the main components of final output, the result is called *GDP expenditure-based*. When it is calculated by adding up all the incomes generated by the act of production, it is called *GDP income-based*.

The conventions of double-entry bookkeeping require that all value produced must be accounted for by a claim that someone has to that value. For example, any expenditure you make must also be received by a supplier in exchange for the product bought. The value of what you spend is the expenditure; the value of the product sold to you is the output. Thus, the two values calculated on income and expenditure bases are identical conceptually and differ in practice only because of errors of measurement. Any discrepancy arising from such errors is then reconciled so that one common total

[1] Each of these totals must also equal the sum of value added in the economy, as discussed in the preceding section.

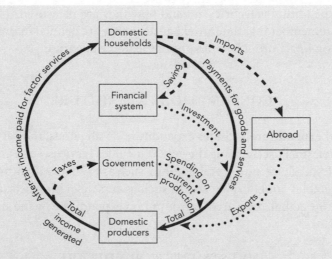

Figure 13.1. The circular flow of income and expenditure

The circular flow of income and expenditure implies that national income is equal to national product. If there were neither leakages (imports, saving, and taxes) nor injections (exports, investment, and government expenditure on goods and services), the flow would be a simple closed circuit, running from domestic households to domestic producers and back to households. Injections (shown as dotted lines) and leakages (also called withdrawals and here shown as dashed lines) complicate the picture but do not change the basic result: domestic production creates a claim on the value of that production; when all of the claims are added up, they must be equal to the value of all of the production.

is given as *the* measure of GDP. Both calculations are of interest, however, because each gives a different and useful breakdown. Also, having two independent ways of measuring the same quantity, in this case the sum of values added in the economy, provides a useful check on statistical procedures and on unavoidable errors in measurement.

GDP expenditure-based

GDP expenditure-based for a given year is calculated by adding up the expenditures going to purchase the final output produced in that year. Total expenditure on final output is the sum of four broad categories of expenditure: consumption, investment, government, and net exports. In the following chapters we will discuss in considerable detail the causes and consequences of movements in each of these four expenditure categories. In Chapter 14, we explain why these particular expenditure categories have received more attention in macroeconomics than have the net sector outputs listed in Table 13.1 and the income categories discussed below (Table 13.3). Here we define what these expenditure categories are and how they are measured. Throughout it is important to remember that they are exhaustive: they are defined in such a way that *all* expenditures on final output fall into one of the four categories.

CONSUMPTION EXPENDITURE

Consumption expenditure includes expenditure on all goods and services produced and sold to their final users during the year. It includes services, such as haircuts, medical care, and legal advice; non-durable goods, such as fresh meat, clothing, cut flowers, and fresh vegetables; and durable goods, such as cars, television sets, and microwave ovens. We denote actual, measured, consumption expenditure by the symbol C^a.

INVESTMENT EXPENDITURE

The next category of total expenditure is called **investment expenditure,** which is defined as expenditure on the production of goods not for present consumption, but rather for future use. The goods that are created by this type of expenditure are called **investment (or capital) goods.** Investment expenditures can be divided into three categories: **stockbuilding, fixed-capital** formation, and the construction of residential housing.

Stockbuilding
Almost all firms hold stocks of their inputs and their own outputs. These stocks are sometimes called *inventories*. Stocks of inputs and unfinished materials allow firms to maintain a steady stream of production in spite of short-term fluctuations in the deliveries of inputs bought from other firms. Stocks of outputs allow firms to meet orders in spite of temporary fluctuations in the rate of output or sales. Modern 'just in time' methods of production pioneered by the Japanese aim to reduce stocks nearly to zero by delivering inputs just as they are needed. Most of the economy, however, does not achieve this level of efficiency and never will. Retailing, for example, would certainly not be improved if shops held no stock.

An accumulation of stock and unfinished goods in the production process counts as current investment because it represents goods produced (even if only half-finished) but not used for current consumption. A drawing down of stocks and work-in-progress, often called *de-stocking*, counts as a fall in investment because it represents a reduction in the stock of finished goods (produced in the current period) that are available for future use. Stocks and work-in-progress are valued at what they will be worth on the market, rather than as what they have cost the firm so far. This is because the expenditure-based measure of national income includes the value of what final expenditures on these goods would be if they were sold, even though they have not been sold yet.

Fixed-capital formation

All production uses capital goods. These are manufactured aids to production, such as machines, computers and factory buildings. The economy's total quantity of capital goods is called the **capital stock.** Creating new capital goods is an act of investment and is called *fixed investment,* or **fixed-capital formation.** Much of the capital stock is in the form of equipment or buildings used by firms or government agencies in the production of goods and services. This would include not just factories and machines, but also hospitals, schools and offices.

Residential investment

A house or a flat is a durable asset that yields its utility (housing services) over a long period of time. This meets the definition of investment that we gave earlier, so housing *construction* is counted as investment expenditure rather than as consumption expenditure. When a family purchases a house from another owner, the ownership of an already-produced asset is transferred, and that transaction is not a part of current national income.

Gross and net investment

The total investment expenditure is called **gross investment** or **gross capital formation.** Gross investment is divided into two parts: replacement investment and net investment. **Replacement investment** is the amount of investment that just maintains the level of existing capital stock; in other words, it replaces the bits that have worn out. Replacement investment is classified as the **capital-consumption allowance** or simply **depreciation.** Gross investment minus replacement investment is **net investment.** Positive net investment increases the economy's total stock of capital, while replacement investment keeps the existing stock intact by replacing what has been used up.

All of gross investment is included in the calculation of national income and national product. This is because all investment goods are part of the nation's total output, and their production creates income (and employment) whether the goods produced are a part of net investment or are merely replacement investment. Actual total investment expenditure is denoted by the symbol I^a.

GOVERNMENT EXPENDITURE ON GOODS AND SERVICES

When governments provide goods and services that their citizens want, such as health care and street lighting, it is obvious that they are adding to the sum total of valuable output in the same way as do private firms that produce cars and video cassettes. With other government activities, the case may not seem so clear. Should expenditures by the government to negotiate over the political situation in Northern Ireland, or to pay a civil servant to help draft legislation, be regarded as contributions to the national product? Some people believe that many (or even most) activities in Whitehall and in town halls are wasteful, if not downright harmful. Others believe that governments produce many of the important things of life, such as education, law and order, and pollution control.

National income statisticians do not speculate about which government expenditures are worthwhile. Instead they include all government purchases of goods and services as part of national income and output. (Government expenditure on investment goods appears as public-sector capital formation, which is a part of total investment expenditure.) Just as the national product includes, without distinction, the outputs of both gin and Bibles, it also includes refuse collection and the upkeep of parks, along with the services of judges, members of Parliament, and even Inland Revenue inspectors. Actual government purchases of goods and services are denoted by the symbol G^a.

Government output typically is valued at cost rather than at the market value. In most cases, there is really no choice. The output of public services is not (generally) sold in the marketplace, so government output is not observed independently of the expenditures that produce it. What, for example, is the market value of the services of a court of law? No one knows. We do know, however, what it costs the government to provide these services, so we value them at their cost of production.

Although valuing at cost is the only possible way to measure many government activities, it does have one curious consequence. If, owing to an increase in productivity, one civil servant now does what two used to do, and the displaced worker shifts to the private sector, the government's measured contribution to national income will register a decline. On the other hand, if two workers now do what one worker used to do, the government's measured contribution will rise. Both changes could occur even though the services the government actually provides have not changed. This is an inevitable but curious consequence of measuring the value of the government's output by the cost of the inputs, mainly labour, that are used to produce it, rather than by outputs.

It is important to recognize that only government expenditures *on currently produced goods and services* are included as part of GDP. A great deal of government expenditure is not a part of GDP. For example, when the Department of Health and Social Security (DHSS) makes a payment to an old-age pensioner, the government is not purchasing any currently produced goods or services from the retired. The payment itself adds neither to employment nor to total output. The same is true of payments for unemployment benefit, income support, student grants, and interest on the national debt (which transfers income from taxpayers to holders of government bonds). All such payments are examples of **transfer payments,** which are government expenditures that are not made in return for currently produced goods and services. They are not a part of expenditure on the nation's total output and, thus, are not included in GDP.[2]

Thus, when we refer to government expenditure as part of national income or use the symbol G^a, we include all government expenditure on currently produced goods and services, and we *exclude* all government transfer payments. (The term *total government*

---

[2] Of course, the recipients of transfer payments spend their money on buying goods and services. Such spending then is measured as consumption expenditure, and thus as part of GDP, in the same way as any other consumption expenditure. We do not want to measure it twice, which is what we would be doing if we included both the government transfer and the spending by the recipient in GDP.

spending is often used to describe all government spending, including transfer payments.)

NET EXPORTS

The fourth category of aggregate expenditure, one that is very important to the UK economy, arises from foreign trade. How do imports and exports influence national income?

Imports

A country's GDP is the total value of final goods and services produced in that country. If you spend £12,000 on a car that was made in Germany, only a small part of that value will represent expenditure on UK production. Some of it represents payment for the services of the UK dealer and for transportation within this country; much of the rest is the output of German firms and expenditure on German products, though there may be component suppliers from several countries. If you take your next vacation in Italy, much of your expenditure will be on goods and services produced in Italy and, thus, will contribute to Italian GDP.

Similarly, when a UK firm makes an investment expenditure on a UK-produced machine tool that was made partly with imported materials, only part of the expenditure is on British production; the rest is expenditure on the production by the countries that are supplying the materials. The same is true for government expenditure on such things as roads and dams; some of the expenditure is for imported materials, and only part of it is for domestically produced goods and services.

Consumption, investment, and government expenditures all have an import content. To arrive at total expenditure on UK output, we need to subtract from total UK residents' expenditure any expenditure on imports of goods and services, which is given the symbol IM^a.

Exports

If UK firms sell goods or services to German consumers, the goods and services are a part of German consumption expenditure but also constitute expenditure on UK output. Indeed, all goods and services that are produced in the UK and sold to foreigners must be counted as part of UK production and income; they are produced in the UK, and they create incomes for the UK residents who produce them. They are not purchased by UK residents, however, so they are not included as part of C^a, I^a, or G^a. Therefore, to arrive at the total value of expenditure on the domestic product, it is necessary to add in the value of UK exports. Actual exports of goods and services are denoted by the symbol X^a.

It is convenient to group actual imports and actual exports together as **net exports.** Net exports are defined as total exports of goods and services minus total imports of goods and services ($X^a - IM^a$), which we will also denote as NX^a. When the value of exports exceeds the value of imports, the net export term is positive. When, as in recent years, the value of imports exceeds the value of exports, the net export term becomes negative.

TOTAL EXPENDITURES

The expenditure based measure of gross domestic product is the sum of the four expenditure categories that we have just discussed, or in symbols:

$$GDP = C^a + I^a + G^a + (X^a - IM^a).$$

The actual expenditure components of GDP for the UK in 1995 are shown in Table 13.2.

Table 13.2. Expenditure-based GDP and its components, 1995

Expenditure category	£ million	% of GDP
Consumption	447,247	63.8
Government expenditure	149,474	21.3
Gross domestic fixed-capital formation	105,385	
Increase in stocks and work-in-progress	3,851	
Gross investment (sum of above 2)	109,236	15.6
Net exports	−5,486	−0.7
Statistical discrepancy	419	
GDP at market prices (money GDP)	**700,890**	100.0
less taxes on expenditures	103,597	
plus subsidies	6,966	
GDP at factor cost	**604,259**	

GDP at market prices	£700,890
plus net property income from abroad	£9,572
= GNP at market prices	**£710,462**

Expenditure-based GDP is made up of consumers' expenditure, government expenditure, investment, and net exports. Consumption is by far the largest expenditure category, equal to just under 64 per cent of GDP. Government accounted for just under 22 per cent, and investment about 15 per cent (note that 'investment' includes residential housing). Whereas exports and imports are both quite large (each over 25 per cent of GDP), net exports are quite small; in 1995 they represented a mere (negative) 0.7 per cent of GDP. GDP at market prices is about 15 per cent bigger than GDP at factor cost. The difference is measured by net indirect taxes and represents output of the economy that does not accrue to factors of production, but is transferred to other individuals. GNP at market prices is GDP at market prices plus net property income from abroad.

Source: National Income Blue Book, 1996.

GDP expenditure-based is the sum of consumption, investment, government, and net export expenditures on currently produced goods and services.

GDP income-based

The production of a nation's output generates income. Labour must be employed, land must be rented, and capital must be used. The calculation of GDP from the income side involves adding up factor incomes and other claims on the value of output until all of that value is accounted for. We have already noted that because all value produced must be owned by someone, the value of production must equal the value of income claims generated by that production.

FACTOR PAYMENTS

National income accountants distinguish four main components of factor incomes: income from employment, income from self-employment, rent, and profits.

Income from employment
This is wages and salaries (which are usually just referred to as *wages*). It is the payment for the services of labour. Wages include take-home pay, taxes withheld, National Insurance contributions, pension fund contributions, and any other fringe benefits. In other words, wages are measured gross. In total, wages represent that part of the value of production that is attributable to hired labour.[3]

Income from self-employment
This category covers those people who are earning a living by selling their services or output but who are not employed by any organization. It includes some consultants and those who work on short contracts but are not formally employees of an incorporated business. The income of the self-employed is little different in principle from employment income, though some of it could be thought of as profit rather than wages.

Rent
Rent is the payment for the services of land and other factors that are rented. A major problem arises with housing. For the purposes of national income accounting, home owners are viewed as renting accommodation from themselves. The amount of rent in GDP thus includes payments for rented housing plus 'imputed rent' for the use of owner-occupied housing.

---

[3] The concepts of wages, rent, and profits that are used in macroeconomics do not correspond to the concepts with the same names that are used in microeconomics, but the details of the differences need not detain us.

Profits

Profits are net business incomes after payment has been made to hired labour and for material inputs. Some profits are paid out as **dividends** to owners of firms; the rest are retained for use by firms. The former are called *distributed profits*, and the latter are called *undistributed profits* or *retained earnings*. Both distributed and undistributed profits are included in the calculation of GDP.

Profits and rent together represent the payment for the use of the nation's capital (including land).

Table 13.3. Components of GDP by income type, 1995

Income type	£ million	% of GDP
Income from employment	377,895	62.5
Gross profits	96,274	15.9
Rent	62,758	10.4
Self-employment	67,685	11.2
Imputed charge for capital consumption	4,729	0.8
less stock appreciation	−4,902	−0.8
statistical discrepancy	−180	
GDP at factor cost	604,259	100.0

The income-based measure of GDP at factor cost is made up of income from employment, profits, rent, and income from self-employment (plus a capital-consumption charge less stock appreciation). By far the largest income category is income from employment, which makes up over 60 per cent of GDP at factor cost.

Source: National Income Blue Book, 1996

The various components of the UK GDP income-based in 1995 are shown in Table 13.3. Note that one of the terms in the table is a 'statistical discrepancy'. This is a small 'fudge factor' (which also appears in Table 13.1 and, with a different value, in Table 13.2). It is there to make sure that the independent measures of income and product come to the same total. The discrepancy is a clear indication that national income and product accounting is not error-free. It should also be noted that the term 'stock appreciation' in Table 13.3 relates to valuation gains that firms receive when the goods they have in stock go up in value. These capital gains add to profit but are not part of current output, so they are deducted from the sum of incomes when we measure GDP.

GDP at factor cost

The sum of the four components of factor incomes—wages, self-employment incomes, rent, and profits—is called **gross domestic product at factor cost**. It represents the share of total production that goes as income to the factors of production, labour, land, and capital. Notice that the measure of GDP arrived at in Table 13.3 is different from what we have labelled 'GDP at market prices' in Table 13.2. This is because we have to take account of what is sometimes called the tax wedge.

NON-FACTOR PAYMENTS

Indirect taxes

Taxes that are levied on transactions in goods and services are known as **indirect taxes.** They are contrasted with **direct taxes,** which are levied on a person's income or wealth independently of how they spend it. When using incomes to calculate GDP, we distinguish between total income valued *at factor cost* and total income valued *at market prices.* The difference between the two is created by two intervening payments: indirect taxes and subsidies.

Suppose you spend £117.50 on a meal in a restaurant—hopefully for more than one person. Only £100 will be kept by the restaurant owner to cover costs of food, wages, etc. The rest will go to the government in the form of value added tax, at the current rate of 17.5 per cent. (In earlier times, the tax might have been purchase tax or what some countries today call sales tax.) A few goods, such as beer and cigarettes, have an additional tax on them known as excise duty. Clearly, whatever the indirect tax is called, its effect is to create a difference between what consumers actually spend and what is received by producers. The market price of a product is greater than the sum received by the factors of production (including in factor rewards all material and labour costs as well as profit).

Subsidies

Some products have a government subsidy. The existence of a subsidy means that the market price may be less than the total rewards to factors. Conceptually, a subsidy is just a negative tax, though the way it is provided may make it hard to express as a tax rate. Suppose that a product costs £120 to make (including all input costs and profit) but sells in the shops for £100, with the other £20 being paid by the government: total factor rewards per unit exceed the market price.

GDP at market prices

Adding indirect taxes to the four components of factor incomes (gross domestic product at factor cost) and subtracting subsidies gives the income-based measure of **gross domestic product at market prices.** Taxes and subsidies are sometimes combined into a single term, called *indirect taxes net of subsidies.*

> **Gross domestic product at market prices equals the sum of wages, income from self-employment, rent, profits, and indirect taxes net of subsidies.**

Arriving at a measure of national output via the expenditure route leads naturally to the concept of GDP at market prices, as ultimate purchasers do pay out indirect taxes. Approaching the measure of GDP from the income or production side leads more naturally to GDP at factor cost, since this is what is received by factors of production. However, the former is the true measure of national output, since the latter excludes some output that is produced but does accrue to factors. This difference is the indirect tax wedge, which is output taken by government and redistributed to individuals, but not on the basis of their factor inputs. Hence, GDP at market prices is the standard measure of the national product and national income. GDP at factor cost is a useful step on the road to measuring GDP at market prices from the data on factor rewards.

The difference between GDP at factor cost and GDP at market prices is reported in Table 13.2. It represents about 15 per cent of GDP (at factor cost).

NET DOMESTIC PRODUCT

Depreciation

The word *gross* is in gross domestic product because no allowance has been made for depreciation. Depreciation, or capital consumption, is the value of capital that has been used up in the process of producing final output. It is part of gross profits, but, being that part needed to replace capital used up in the process of production, it is not part of net profits. Hence, depreciation is not income earned by any factor of production. Instead it is value that must be reinvested just to maintain the existing stock of capital equipment. In the UK, factor incomes are normally reported before making allowance for depreciation.

Subtracting depreciation from gross domestic product gives **net domestic product.**

Net domestic product at factor cost, income-based, is the sum of the factor incomes that are generated in the process of producing final output *minus* **depreciation.**

Income produced and income received

GDP at market prices provides a measure of total output produced in the UK and of the total income generated as a result of that production. However, the total income received by UK residents differs from GDP, for two reasons. First, some domestic production creates factor earnings for non-residents who have previously invested in the UK; on this account, income received by UK residents will be less than UK GDP. Second, many UK residents earn income on overseas investments; on this account, income received by UK residents will be greater than GDP.

While GDP measures the output, and hence the income, that is *produced* in this country, the **gross national product, GNP,** measures the income that is *received* by this country. To convert GDP into GNP it is necessary to add income received by domestic residents from assets owned abroad and to subtract income paid out to non-residents who own assets in this country. The difference between GDP and GNP is *net property income from abroad.*

Total output produced in the economy, measured by GDP, differs from total income received, measured by GNP, owing to net property income from abroad.

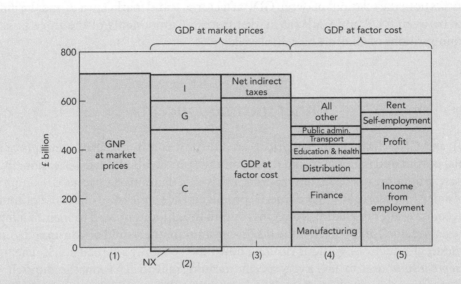

Figure 13.2. UK national income and output measures, 1995

Measurement of national income and output can be approached in three different ways, but they are all related. The figure shows the actual UK aggregates GNP at market prices, GDP at market prices, and GDP at factor cost for 1995. Column (1) is GNP at market prices. Columns (2) and (3) add up to GDP at market prices. Columns (4) and (5) add up to GDP at factor cost.

Column (1) (GNP) exceeds column (2) (GDP) by about 1.4 per cent. This difference is net property income from abroad. In 1995 this was positive but small. Column (2) shows that GDP is made up of the expenditure components: consumption (*C*), investment (*I*), government spending (*G*), and net exports (*NX*). Notice that in 1995 net exports were negative, so *NX* has to be subtracted from the sum of *C* + *I* + *G* to arrive at GDP. Column (3) shows that GDP at factor cost is equal to GDP at market prices minus net indirect taxes (indirect taxes less subsidies).

Column (4) shows that GDP at factor cost is made up of the sum of the values added of each of the production sectors of the economy; manufacturing, for example, produces about 22 per cent of GDP at factor cost. Column (5) shows that GDP at factor cost can also be broken down by income type. Income from employment amounts to over 60 per cent of this.

Source: National Income Blue Book, 1996.

Reconciling GDP with GNP

Table 13.2 shows the reconciliation of GDP with GNP. GNP is greater than GDP, but only by just over 1 per cent. This reflects slightly greater income from foreign assets held by UK residents than is being paid out to foreigners from their assets held in the UK. Clearly, GNP could be smaller than GDP if outward payments were greater than property income from abroad. Broadly speaking, countries that are net debtors are likely to have GNP lower than GDP, while countries that are net creditors are likely to have a GNP that exceeds GDP.

Figure 13.2 provides a visual representation of the information in Tables 13.1–13.3. It shows both the relations between GDP at factor cost and market prices and the difference between GDP and GNP (at market prices). Components of the three possible decompositions of GDP are also displayed.

Other income concepts

GDP and GNP (both at market prices) are the most commonly used concepts of national output and national income. Net domestic product is also used occasionally. As we saw in building up the income approach, this is GDP minus the capital consumption allowance (depreciation). Net domestic product is thus a measure of the net output of the economy after deducting from gross output the amount needed to maintain intact the existing stock of capital. It is the maximum amount that could be consumed (out of domestic production) without running down the economy's capital stock. The term *national income* used to have a very specific meaning in British national accounts. It was the net national product—GNP minus depreciation. However, this usage has gone out of fashion and national income is now loosely used to refer to any of the standard national product measures. We also use national income in this general sense. Once we move on to theory it will be safe to assume that national income or national product are equivalent and refer to GDP at market prices unless told otherwise.

Personal income is income that is earned by or paid to individuals (the personal sector[4]) before allowing for personal income taxes on that income. Some personal income goes for taxes, some goes for savings, and the rest goes for consumption. **Personal disposable income** is the amount of current income that individuals have available for spending and saving; it is personal income minus personal income taxes and national insurance contributions.

> **Personal disposable income is GNP *minus* any part of it that is not actually paid to the personal sector (such as retained profits) minus personal income taxes plus transfer payments received by individuals.**

---

[4] The personal sector in Britain actually contains some unincorporated businesses and non-profit organizations such as charities. So it is not just the behaviour of private individuals that is being measured in practice.

Interpreting national income and product measures

The information provided by national income data is useful, but, unless it is carefully interpreted, it can be misleading. Furthermore, each of the specific measures gives different information. Each may be the best statistic for studying a particular range of problems, but it is important to understand these differences if you are going to use these data for analytic purposes. Here we discuss some of the caveats that should be borne in mind.

Real and nominal measures

It is important to distinguish between *real* and *nominal* measures of national income and output. When we add up money values of outputs, expenditures, or incomes, we end up with what are called *nominal values*. Suppose that we found that a measure of nominal GDP had risen by 70 per cent between 1990 and 1999. If we wanted to compare *real GDP* in 1999 to that in 1990, we would need to determine how much of that 70 per cent nominal increase was the result of increases in the general level of prices and how much was the result of increases in quantities of goods and services produced. Although there are many possible ways of doing this, the basic principle is always the same. It is to compute the value of output, expenditure, and income in each period by using a common set of *base-period prices*. When this is done we speak of real output, expenditure, or income as being measured in *constant pounds* or, say, *1990 prices*.

> **GDP valued at current prices, i.e. money GDP, is a nominal measure. GDP valued at base-period prices is a real measure; in effect, an index number of the volume of national output and national income.**

Any *change* in nominal GDP reflects the combined effects of changes in quantities and changes in prices. However, when real income is measured over different periods by using a common set of base-period prices, changes in real income reflect only changes in real output.

THE IMPLICIT DEFLATOR

If nominal and real GDP change by different amounts over some time-period, this must be because prices have changed over that period. Comparing what has happened to nominal and real GDP over the same period implies the existence of a price index measuring the change in prices over that period. We say 'implies' because no price index was used in calculating real and nominal GDP. However, an index can be inferred by comparing these two values. Such an index is called an *implicit price index* or an *implicit deflator*. It is defined as follows:

$$\text{Implicit deflator} = \frac{\text{GDP at current prices}}{\text{GDP at base-period prices}} \times 100\%.$$

The implicit GDP deflator is the most comprehensive index of the price level because it covers all the goods and services that are produced by the entire economy. Although some other indexes use fixed weights, or weights that change only periodically, implicit deflators are variable-weight indexes. They use the current year's 'bundle' of produc-

---

BOX 13.3.

Calculation of nominal and real GDP

To see what is involved in calculating nominal GDP, real GDP, and the implicit deflator, an example may be helpful. Consider a simple hypothetical economy that produces only two commodities, wheat and steel. Table (i) gives the basic data for output and prices in the economy for two years.

Table (i). Data for a hypothetical economy

	Quantity produced		Prices	
	Wheat (bushels)	Steel (tons)	Wheat (£ per bsl)	Steel (£ per ton)
Year 1	100	20	10	50
Year 2	110	16	12	55

Table (ii) shows nominal GDP, calculated by adding the money values of wheat output and of steel output for each year. In year 1 the value of both wheat and steel production was £1,000, so nominal output was £2,000. In year 2 wheat output rose, and steel output fell; the value of wheat output rose to £1,320, and that of steel fell to £880. Since the rise in value of wheat was greater than the fall in value of steel, nominal output rose by £200.

Table (ii). Calculation of nominal GDP

Year 1	$(100 \times 10) + (20 \times 50) = £2{,}000$
Year 2	$(110 \times 12) + (16 \times 55) = £2{,}200$

tion to compare the current year's prices with those prevailing in the base period. Thus the 1997 deflator uses 1997 output weights, and the 1999 deflator uses 1999 output weights. Box 13.3 illustrates the calculation of real and nominal GDP and an implicit GDP deflator for a simple hypothetical economy that produces only wheat and steel.

A change in any nominal measure of GDP can be split into a change owing to prices and a change owing to quantities. For example, in 1995, UK nominal GDP ('money' GDP) was 4.9 per cent higher than in 1994. This increase was due to a 2.5 per cent increase in prices and a 2.4 per cent increase in real GDP. Table 13.4 gives nominal and real GDP and the implicit deflator for selected years since 1900.

Table (iii) shows real GDP, calculated by valuing output in each year by year 2 prices; that is, year 2 becomes the base year for weighting purposes. In year 2 wheat output rose, but steel output fell. Using year 2 prices, the value of the fall in steel output between years 1 and 2 exceeded the value of the rise in wheat output, and real GDP fell.

Table (iii). Calculation of real GDP using year 2 prices

Year 1	$(100 \times 12) + (20 \times 55) = £2,300$
Year 2	$(110 \times 12) + (16 \times 55) = £2,200$

In Table (iv) the ratio of nominal to real GDP is calculated for each year and multiplied by 100. This ratio implicitly measures the change in prices over the period in question and is called the *implicit GDP deflator* or *implicit GDP price index*. The implicit deflator shows that the price level increased by 15 per cent between year 1 and year 2.

Table (iv). Calculation of implicit deflator

Year 1	$(2,000 / 2,300) \times 100 = 86.96$
Year 2	$(2,200 / 2,200) \times 100 = 100.00$

In Table (iv) we used year 2 as the base year for comparison purposes, but we could have used year 1. The implicit deflator would then have been 100 in year 1 and 115 in year 2, and the increase in price level would still have been 15 per cent. Or, the base year could be some earlier year. No matter what year is picked as the year in which the index had a value of 100, however, the change in the implicit deflator between year 1 and year 2 is 15 per cent.

Table 13.4. Nominal and real GDP at market prices, 1900–1995

Year	Money GDP (£bn)	Real GDP (1990 prices)	Implicit GDP deflator (1990 = 100)
1900	1.9	109.5	1.7
1930	4.7	138.6	3.4
1950	13.1	200.4	6.5
1970	51.6	350.9	14.7
1980	231.2	426.8	54.2
1995	700.9	584.3	118.2

The data in the table are money GDP, real GDP, and the implicit GDP price deflator for selected years. The first column shows that money (nominal) GDP increased 330-fold between 1900 and 1993. However, the second column shows that there was only a 5-fold increase in real GDP over the same period. The difference between the two is accounted for by the final column, which shows that the implicit price deflator for GDP rose 67-fold in this century. Since 1950, real GDP has increased 2.7-fold while the GDP price deflator has increased about 18-fold.

Sources: Economic Trends, and 100 Years of Economic Statistics (Economist, 1989).

International comparisons of national income

One purpose to which national income and product measures are often put is for international comparisons of living standards or real income. It is natural to want to know if people are better off in Britain than in, say, Germany. However, comparisons using measures such as GDP must be conducted with great care. We shall see below that there are many dimensions to living standards that are not measured by GDP or GNP. For some purposes we may want to compare the absolute size of one economy relative to another, but normally we are interested in how well off the average individual is in each country. For this purpose, we want to look at GDP per head or per capita (or perhaps GNP per capita). To get this figure we divide GDP by the total population of the country. This tells us the share of total national income that is available for the average citizen.

GDP in each country is measured in the local currency. So, to make comparisons, we have to convert different countries' nominal GDP into the same currency. To do this, we have to use an exchange rate. This is problematic because exchange rates fluctuate, sometimes dramatically. In September 1992, for example, the exchange rate between US dollars and the UK pound moved from nearly $2 per pound to $1.5 per pound in a short time. Would we be happy to conclude that real incomes in Britain had fallen relative to real incomes in the US by 25 per cent? Even in normal conditions it is not unusual for exchange rates to move by 10 per cent in a few days, but the move could easily be reversed a little later.

To solve the problem of making comparisons using unreliable or untypical exchange rates, economists make comparisons of national income using what they think are equilibrium exchange rates. These are calculated on the basis of what they estimate the exchange rate between two countries ought to be at a point in time if their economies had fully adjusted to their known economic environment. One approximation to the *equilibrium* exchange rate is the *purchasing power parity (PPP)* rate. This is the exchange rate that equates the prices of a representative bundle of goods in two countries. We shall discuss this concept more fully in Chapter 19.

Some comparisons of GDP per capita in thirteen different countries (using PPP exchange rates) are given in Table 13.5. Figures are all expressed in US dollars. Several other indicators of material well-being are included in the table. Broadly speaking they tell the same story as the GDP figures— the inhabitants of the richer countries can purchase more goods and services and tend to have longer life expectancy. However, the rankings would be different for each possible indicator of well-being. The significance

Table 13.5. International comparisons of living standards

	GNP per head (US$ 1994)	Real GNP growth (annual average 1985–94)	Telephones per 100 pop. (1991)	Cars per 1,000 pop. (1990)	Infant mortality per 1,000 live births (1994)	TVs per 1,000 pop. (1991)	Life expectancy at birth (1994)	Doctors per 100,000 pop. (1990)
USA	25,880	1.3	45	589	8	815	77	238
Germany	19,580	2.7*	40	490	6	570	76	270
Japan	21,140	3.2	44	285	4	620	79	164
Canada	19,960	0.3	58	473	6	641	78	222
France	19,670	1.6	50	418	6	406	78	286
Australia	18,120	1.2	47	435	6	486	77	229
UK	17,970	1.3	44	403	6	435	76	164
Spain	13,740	2.8	32	308	7	396	77	357
Mexico	7,040	0.9	6	65	35	139	71	81
Russia	4,610	−4.1	15	50	19	283	64	476
Brazil	5,410	−0.4	6	104	56	213	67	93
China	2,510	7.8	1	2	30	31	69	99
India	1,280	2.9	1	2	70	32	62	41

The table shows eight different indicators of living standards for thirteen countries. Most of the indicators tell the same story—wealthy countries have more goods and better life expectations. However, there are some interesting anomalies. Russia has more doctors per 100,000 people than any other country, yet life expectancy is lower than in China, which has one fifth as many doctors per person.

* The growth rate for Germany is for 1983–92 and is based on West Germany.
Note: Real GNP per capita is calculated using PPP exchange rates.
Source: The Economist, 25 December 1993, and World Development Report (World Bank, 1996).

of this is that GDP per capita contains some useful information but there may be other important indicators that could tell a somewhat different story.

What national income accounts do not measure

National income measures the flow of economic activity in organized markets in a given year. But much economic activity takes place outside of the markets that the national income accountants survey. Although these activities are not typically included in GDP or GNP, they nevertheless use real resources and satisfy real wants and needs.

Illegal activities

GDP does not measure illegal activities, even though many of them are ordinary business activities that produce goods and services sold on the market and that generate incomes for workers and owners of other factors of production. Many forms of illegal gambling, prostitution, and the drug trade come into this category. To gain an accurate measure of the *total* demand for factors of production in the economy, of *total* marketable output, or of incomes generated, we should include these activities, whether or not we as individuals approve of them. The omission of illegal activities is no trivial matter. The drug trade alone is probably a multi-billion-pound business.[5]

Unreported activities

A significant omission from the measured GDP is the so-called underground or black economy. The transactions that occur in the underground economy are perfectly legal in themselves; the only illegality involved is that such transactions are not reported for tax purposes. One example of this is the builder who repairs a leak in your roof and takes payment in cash or in kind in order to avoid taxation. Because such transactions go unreported, they are omitted from GDP.

The growth of the underground economy is encouraged by the rising rates of taxation and is facilitated by the rising importance of services in the nation's total output. The higher the tax rates, the more there is to be gained by 'going underground'. It is also much easier for a carpenter or plumber to pass unnoticed by government authorities than it is for a manufacturing establishment.

Studies of the scale of the underground economy show its importance growing in recent years. Estimates have put the underground economy in Britain at about 7 per cent of GDP. A Canadian study concluded that, in 1992, 15 per cent of Canadian GDP went unreported because it was in the underground economy. In other countries the figures are even higher. The Italian underground economy, for example, has been es-

---

5 Some illegal activities do get included in national income measures, although they are generally misclassified by industry. The income is included because people sometimes report their earnings from illicit activities as part of their earnings from legal activities. They do this to avoid the fate of Al Capone, a famous Chicago gangster in the 1920s and 1930s, who, having avoided conviction on many counts, was finally caught for tax evasion.

timated at about 20 per cent of GDP; for Spain, estimates are close to 25 per cent, and for Greece, 30 per cent!

Non-marketed activities

If home owners hire a firm to do some landscaping, the value of the landscaping enters into GDP; if they do the landscaping themselves, the value of the landscaping is omitted from GDP. Other non-marketed activities include, for example, the services of those who do housework at home, any do-it-yourself activity, and voluntary work, such as canvassing for a political party, helping to run a volunteer day-care centre, or coaching an amateur football team.

One important non-marketed activity is leisure itself. If a lawyer voluntarily chooses to work 2,200 hours a year instead of 2,400 hours, measured national income will fall by the lawyer's hourly wage rate times 200 hours. Yet the value to the lawyer of the 200 hours of new leisure, which is enjoyed outside of the marketplace, must exceed the lost wages (because the leisure has been voluntarily chosen in preference to the extra work), so total economic welfare has risen rather than fallen. Until recently, one of the most important ways in which economic growth benefited people was by permitting increased amounts of time off work. Because the time off is not marketed, its value does not show up in measures of national income.

Economic bads

When a coal-fired electricity generator sends sulphur dioxide into the atmosphere, leading to acid rain and environmental damage, the value of the electricity sold is included as part of GDP, but the value of the damage done by the acid rain is not deducted. Similarly, the petrol that we use in our cars is part of national income, but the damage done by burning that petrol is not deducted. To the extent that economic growth brings with it increases in pollution, congestion, and other disamenities of modern living, national income measures will overstate the value of the growth. They measure the increased economic output and income, but they fail to deduct the increased 'bads', or negative outputs, that generally accompany economic growth.

DO THE OMISSIONS MATTER?

GDP does a reasonable job of measuring the flow of goods and services through the market sector of the economy. Usually, an increase in GDP implies greater opportunities for employment for those households that sell their labour services in the market. Unless the importance of unmeasured economic activity changes rapidly, *changes* in GDP will do an excellent job of measuring *changes* in economic activity and economic opportunities. However, when the task at hand is measurement of the overall flow of goods and services available to satisfy people's wants, regardless of the source of the goods and services, then the omissions that we have discussed above become undesirable and potentially serious. Still, in the relatively short term, changes in GDP will usually be good measures of the direction, if not the exact magnitude, of changes in economic welfare.

The omissions cause serious problems when national income measures are used to compare living standards in structurally different economies, as was discussed above. Generally, the non-market sector of the economy is larger in rural than in urban settings and in less-developed than in more-developed economies. Be cautious, then, when interpreting data from a country with a very different climate and culture. When you hear that the per capita GDP of India is about US$1,150 per year, you should not imagine living in Manchester on that income. The average Indian is undoubtedly poorer than the average Briton, but, perhaps, not fourteen times poorer, as the GDP figures suggest.

Is there a best measure of national income?

To ask which is *the* best income measure is like asking which is *the* best carpenter's tool. The answer depends on the job to be done. The decision concerning which measure to use will depend on the problem at hand, and solving some problems may require information provided by several different measures or information not provided by any conventional measures. If we wish to predict personal consumption behaviour, then personal disposable income may be the measure that we need to use. If we wish to account for changes in employment, then real GDP may be the measure that we want. For an overall measure of economic welfare, we may need to supplement or modify conventional measures of national income, none of which measures *the quality of life*.

Even if economists do develop new measures for some purposes, it is unlikely that GDP (and its relatives) will be discarded. Economists and policymakers who are interested in changes in market activity and in employment opportunities for factors of production will continue to use GDP and other related measures because they are the ones that come closest to telling them what they need to know.

Summary

1. Macroeconomics is about the economy as a whole. It studies aggregate phenomena, such as business cycles, living standards, inflation, unemployment, and the balance of payments. It also asks how governments can use their monetary and fiscal policy instruments to help stabilize the economy.

2. Each firm's contribution to total output is equal to its value added, which is the gross value of the firm's output minus the value of all intermediate goods and services—that

is, the outputs of other firms—that it uses. Goods that count as part of the economy's output are called final goods; all others are called intermediate goods. The sum of all the values added produced in an economy is the economy's total output, which is called gross domestic product (GDP).

3. Gross domestic product (GDP) can be calculated in three different ways: (i) as the sum of all values added by all producers of both intermediate and final goods, (ii) as the expenditure needed to purchase all final goods and services produced during the period, and (iii) as the income claims generated by the total production of goods and services. By standard accounting conventions, these three aggregations define the same total.

4. From the expenditure side of the national accounts, GDP $= C^a + I^a + G^a + (X^a - IM^a)$. C^a comprises consumption expenditures of households. I^a is investment in fixed capital (including residential construction) and stockbuilding. Gross investment can be split into replacement investment (necessary to keep the stock of capital intact) and net investment (net additions to the stock of capital). G^a is government purchases of goods and services. $(X^a - IM^a)$ represents net exports, or exports minus imports; it will be negative if imports exceed exports.

5. GDP income-based adds up all factor rewards in production. Wages, income from self-employment, rent, and profits are the major categories. GDP at factor cost can be converted to GDP at market prices by adding indirect taxes net of subsidies. The deduction of depreciation, or capital consumption, converts gross domestic product into net domestic product.

6. UK GDP measures production that is located in the UK, and UK gross national product (GNP) measures income accruing to UK residents. The difference is net property income from overseas.

7. Real measures of national income and product are calculated to reflect changes in real quantities. Nominal measures of GDP are calculated to reflect changes in both prices and quantities. Any change in nominal GDP can be split into a change in real GDP and a change owing to prices. Appropriate comparisons of nominal and real measures yield implicit deflators.

8. Some related but different income measures are used in addition to GDP. Personal income is income received by individuals before any allowance for personal taxes. Personal disposable income is the amount actually available for the personal sector to spend or to save, that is, income minus taxes.

9. GDP and related measures of national income must be interpreted with their limitations in mind. GDP excludes production resulting from activities that are illegal, take

place in the underground economy, or do not pass through markets. Moreover, GDP does not measure everything that contributes to human welfare.

10. Notwithstanding its limitations, GDP remains a useful measure of the total economic activity that passes through the nation's markets and for explaining changes in the employment opportunities facing citizens who sell their labour services on the market.

Topics for review

- Targets and instruments of macroeconomic policy
- Value added
- GDP as the sum of all values added
- Intermediate and final goods
- Expenditure-based and income-based GDP
- GNP
- Personal disposable income
- Implicit deflator
- The significance of omissions from measured GDP

Questions for discussion

1. Discuss which of the following are microeconomic and which macroeconomic issues: house prices; unemployment in East Anglia; food prices; pensions; the EU single currency; the Common Agricultural Policy; high street spending; income tax rates; mortgage interest rates.

2. Which of the following are instruments of macroeconomic policy and which are targets: the exchange rate; real wages; VAT tax rates; VAT tax revenue; government spending on road building; exports; private gross fixed-capital formation; US dollar interest rates; personal consumption?

3. Using the expenditure-based definition ($C + I + G + NX$), explain where each of the following expenditures appears in the national income accounts measure of GDP, if at all: state pensions; company pensions; student grants; theatre receipts; judges' salaries; unsold cars in showrooms; receipts from beer sales in a students' union bar; receipts from purchases of new copies of this book; receipts from purchases of second-hand copies of this book.

4. Suppose there are only three companies in an economy. Company A grows crops and extracts minerals from its land with no inputs from other companies. Its sales are £100m per year, half of which goes to consumers and half to companies B and C in equal amounts. Company B buys inputs from A and sells its entire output of £200m to company C. Company C buys inputs from A and B and sells its £450m output directly to consumers (though 20 per cent of this is overseas). What is the value of GDP at factor cost? If there is only one indirect tax, value added tax levied at 10 per cent, what is the value of GDP at market prices?

5. Discuss the strengths and weaknesses of using GDP as a measure of national well-being.

6. What would it mean to be told that a country's GNP was greater than its GDP? Is GNP or GDP the more appropriate target for government policy?

7. How could a well-laid plan for a firm's expansion into a new market be affected by each of the following: (i) a severe recession in the home economy; (ii) an unexpected rise in the domestic inflation rate from 3 per cent to 10 per cent; (iii) a sharp rise in interest rates overseas; (iv) an appreciation of sterling from £1 = $1.50 to £1 = $1.80? In each case, would the effect be favourable or unfavourable? Does it matter whether the new market is at home or abroad?

CHAPTER 14

A Basic Model of the Determination of GDP

Potential GDP and the GDP gap   447

Key assumptions   450
Aggregation across industries   451
The government sector   451
Justification   451
Time-scale   452
Short run   452
Long run   452
Temporary assumptions   453
The price level   453
Excess capacity   453
Closed economy   453
No government   453

What determines aggregate expenditure?   454
Some important preliminaries   454
From actual to desired expenditure   454
Autonomous and induced expenditure   455
A simple model   455
Desired consumption expenditure   456
The consumption function   456
Consumption and disposable income   456
Average and marginal propensities to consume   460
The slope of the consumption function   460
The 45° line   460
The saving function   461
Wealth and the consumption function   462
Desired investment expenditure   463
Investment and the real interest rate   464
Stockbuilding   464

Residential housing construction   464
Business fixed-capital formation   465
Expectations and business confidence   465
Investment as autonomous expenditure   466
The aggregate expenditure function   466
The propensity to spend out of national income   467

Equilibrium GDP   468

Changes in GDP   473
Shifts in the aggregate expenditure function   474
Upward shifts   474
Downward shifts   474
The results restated   475
The Multiplier   476
Definition   476
Why the multiplier is greater than unity   476
The simple multiplier defined   477
The size of the simple multiplier   479

Summary   480

Topics for review   482

Questions for discussion   482

Box 14.1. A hydraulic analogue of GDP determination   472
Box 14.2. The multiplier: a numerical example   478

W E now embark on the central task of macroeconomics, building a model of the economy as a whole. In Chapter 13, we encountered a number of important macroeconomic variables. We now turn to a more detailed study of what *causes* these variables to behave as they do, and how they are interrelated. In particular, we study the forces that determine GDP and the price level.

It is important to realize that we are about to discuss *theory*. In this process we will build up a conceptual model of the economy. This model will necessarily be simple. It needs to be simple so that we can understand how it works. In particular, we want to be able to answer questions like 'What happens to GDP when government spending is increased?' or 'Under what conditions do we get inflation?'

We shall proceed by starting from a very simple structure and then adding features to it as we go along. Some clearly stated *assumptions* will define our macroeconomic model. Some of these assumptions will be relaxed as we go along, others will remain throughout. The permanent or temporary nature of individual assumptions will be indicated as they are introduced.

Macroeconomics has been around, as a branch of economics, for over half a century. It has developed and changed a great deal in this time. It is going to take several chapters before we get close to understanding contemporary macroeconomics. Hence, the reader should be patient and not rush to draw policy conclusions too soon.

In this chapter we set out some of the conceptual foundations of macroeconomics. We then build the simplest possible model of national income determination, under some very special assumptions. Later chapters make our model increasingly realistic. The value for business people in this model is that it provides a framework for understanding the important macro issues outlined at the beginning of Chapter 13.

Potential GDP and the GDP gap

In macroeconomics it is useful to distinguish between the long-term trend in GDP and the cycle about the trend. In order to facilitate this separation we use the concepts *actual* and *potential GDP*, and we refer to the difference between them as the *GDP gap*.

Actual GDP represents what the economy does, in fact, produce. An important related concept is **potential GDP,** which measures what the economy could produce if all resources—land, labour, and productive capacity—were fully employed at their normal levels of utilization. This concept is also referred to as 'potential income' and is sometimes called *full-employment income* (or 'high-employment income').[1] We give it

---

[1] In everyday usage the words *real* and *actual* have similar meanings. In national income theory, however, their meanings are quite distinct. *Real* GDP is distinguished from *nominal* GDP, and *actual* GDP is distinguished from *potential* GDP. The latter both refer to real measures, so that the full descriptions are, in fact, 'actual real GDP' and 'potential real GDP'.

the symbol Y^* to distinguish it from actual GDP (or national income), which is indicated by Y.

What is variously called the **output gap** or the **GDP gap** measures the difference between what would have been produced if potential, or full-employment, GDP had been produced and what is actually produced, as measured by the current GDP. The gap is calculated by subtracting actual GDP from potential GDP ($Y^* - Y$).

When potential GDP exceeds actual GDP, the gap measures the market value of goods and services that *could have been produced* if the economy's resources had been fully employed but actually went unproduced. The goods and services that are not produced when the economy is operating below Y^* are permanently lost to the economy. Because these losses occur when employable resources are unused, they are often called the *deadweight loss* of unemployment. When the economy is operating below its potential level of output—that is, when Y is less than Y^*—the output gap is called a **recessionary gap.**

In booms, actual GDP may *exceed* potential GDP, causing the output gap to become negative. Actual output can exceed potential output because potential GDP is defined for a *normal rate of utilization* of factors of production, and these normal rates can be exceeded temporarily. Labour may work longer hours than normal; factories may operate an extra shift or not close for routine repairs and maintenance. Although these expedients are only temporary, they are effective in the short term. When actual GDP exceeds potential GDP there is generally upward pressure on prices. For this reason, when Y exceeds Y^*, the output gap is called an **inflationary gap.**

Figure 14.1(i) shows potential real GDP in the UK for the years 1970–97. The rising trend reflects the growth in productive capacity of the UK economy over this period. The figure also shows actual real GDP, which has kept approximately in step with potential GDP. The distance between the two, which is the GDP gap, is plotted in Figure 14.1(ii). Fluctuations in economic activity are apparent from fluctuations in the size of

Figure 14.1. UK potential GDP and the output gap, 1970–1997 ⟶

Potential and actual GDP have both displayed an upward trend in recent years, but actual GDP fluctuates around its potential level.

(i) Growth in the economy has been such that both potential and actual GDP have increased by about 75 per cent since 1970. Both series are in real terms and are measured in 1990 pounds sterling. Measurement of potential GDP is controversial and there is no official UK series at present. These figures were calculated by the IMF.

(ii) The cycles in the economy are apparent from the behaviour of the output gap. Slumps in economic activity produce large recessionary gaps, and booms produce inflationary gaps. The zero line indicates where actual and potential GDP are the same. The shaded areas below the zero line indicate the deadweight loss that arises from unemployment during periods when there is a recessionary output gap. Notice the large recessionary gaps in the early 1980s and the early 1990s.

Note: Data for 1996 and 1997 are based on forecasts.

Source: International Monetary Fund.

the gap. The deadweight loss from unemployment over any time-span is indicated by the overall amount of the gap over that time-span. It is shown in part (ii) of Figure 14.1 by the shaded area between the curve and the zero line, which represents the level at which actual output equals potential output.

Macroeconomics usually focuses on explaining the GDP gap, while growth theory aims to explain the long-term trend in potential GDP.

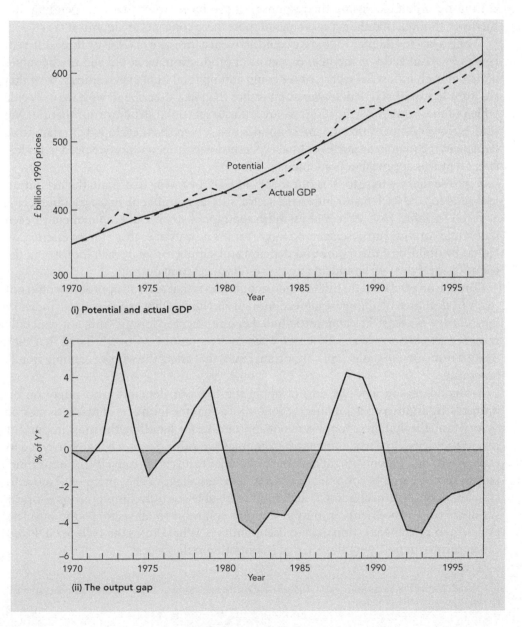

(i) Potential and actual GDP

(ii) The output gap

Key assumptions

In the previous chapter we learned that 'national income' and 'national output' are the same thing, and can be measured by 'GDP'. From now on we shall use these three terms equivalently. However, we refer to national income most frequently when discussing the determinants of domestic spending, since incomes are one of the most important determinants of consumers' expenditure. We refer to national output, or GDP, more commonly when discussing the responses of producers to changes in spending. Remember, though, that the actual values of these three concepts are identical.[2]

We also saw in Chapter 13 that we could arrive at a measure of GDP by three different routes. We could add up incomes of factors of production, we could add up the values added of each industrial sector, or we could add up total final expenditures. Now that we want to *explain* GDP determination rather than just describe it, we have to decide which of these three classifications we are going to rely on to structure our theories. We shall learn very shortly that macroeconomics, as a subject, has developed by attempting to explain the major categories of final expenditure in the economy. We need to understand why this approach was adopted.

Suppose that we were to start our theory of GDP by trying to explain the net output (value added) of each major industrial sector, such as manufacturing, agriculture, etc., as listed in Table 13.1. We could establish the capital stock and employment in each sector and we could analyse demand forces for the output of each sector. In essence, we would be building a theory around demand and supply forces in each industry in the economy, and then we would add up the results to get total output.

One reason we do not do this in macroeconomics is that such an approach would not really be dealing with the aggregate economy at all. Models that explain output industry by industry do exist in economics, but they are microeconomic and not generally regarded as part of macroeconomics. Such models require so much detail that they make it difficult to handle many important issues that affect the whole economy simultaneously.

A second reason why we do not apply the tools of demand and supply on an industry-by-industry basis in macroeconomics is that the founders of macroeconomic theory thought that these tools were not appropriate for handling the most important macro problems. In particular, macroeconomics as a subject was originally invented to explain why an economy might have unemployment and excess capacity for some time. In contrast, the microeconomic analysis of markets suggests that prices will move to clear markets. Macroeconomists also want to be able to study simultaneous (or near simultaneous) movements in output that are common to all sectors—the business cycle. An important question in macroeconomics is 'What causes the cycle in GDP and can government policy stabilize it, that is, smooth out the cycles?'

---

[2] Recall also that we are assuming that GDP and GNP are the same, so there is no difference between 'national' product and 'domestic' product.

AGGREGATION ACROSS INDUSTRIES

In macroeconomics, we take the industrial structure of the economy as fixed. When national output expands or contracts, all sectors expand and contract together. There is no consideration given to relative prices of different goods or services. In this respect the economy is best thought of as being made up of many competitive firms, all producing the same type of product. These firms are all aggregated into a single productive sector. It is the behaviour of this single productive sector that will determine national output and national income.

In macroeconomics, we assume the existence of a single productive sector producing a homogeneous output.

This assumption will remain throughout our study of macroeconomics. We shall also analyse the behaviour of this single sector as if it were a manufacturing industry, though this is only a matter of convenience.

The fact that we assume a single production sector explains why we approach the determination of GDP by focusing on expenditure categories: there are no subdivisions of output by type of product. However, an important implication for final expenditures is that, *in our model*, they are all spent on the same final good—the product of the single industrial sector. This means that, while different categories of expenditures may be differently motivated, they all have the same effect once implemented.

From time to time, we use concrete examples, such as 'Suppose the government increases spending on road building' or 'Suppose firms decide to buy more machines (invest)'. The point to bear in mind is that, once made, all expenditures in the model have the same effect because they are all assumed to be demands for the output of the single-product industrial sector.

The government sector

Confusion can arise out of the assumption of a single sector when we come to discuss the role of government. In reality, part of government activity involves producing goods or services, such as health and education. However, in order to maintain the simplicity of the assumption that there is only one sector, in macroeconomics we ignore the fact that government is a producer and treat government as a purchaser of the output of the private industrial sector.

Justification

The extreme assumption that there is only one output is of course not meant as a description of reality. It is a theoretical abstraction designed to simplify our study without losing the essence of the problem in which we are interested. In this case, the one-product model captures the assumption that, for what we are interested in, the similarities between the effects of £1 spent in each sector of the real-world economy are more important than the differences. Note that it is only similarities with respect to the effects of expenditures that are in question. Causes of expenditures are not assumed to be the same. Indeed, much of our effort is directed to developing consumption, investment, and net export functions that explain the *different* motives that determine the various expenditure flows.

TIME-SCALE

Macroeconomics has traditionally been concerned with the short-run behaviour of an economy, while growth theory has been concerned with long-run trends. It is important to note, however, that the concepts of *short run* and *long run* have a different meaning in macroeconomics from the usage in microeconomics. Indeed, 'long run' itself will be used in two different senses even within macroeconomics.

Short run
In microeconomics 'short run' was used to analyse the behaviour of firms during the period in which their capital stock is taken as given and they can only change their variable inputs (labour and materials). Although in the short run the capital stock is fixed, firms are in equilibrium because they are producing their optimal output given their capital stock. In macroeconomics, the short run is a period during which the economy maintains a deviation of actual from potential output, or a GDP gap. It is associated either with the existence of excess capacity and unemployment, in the case of recession, or unsustainable output and inflation, in the case of a boom. In practice, the short run may be measured in terms of several years, so it is not necessarily short in the commonsense meaning of the term.

In its early days as a discipline, macroeconomics concentrated entirely on the short run, as we have just defined it. Recent developments, however, have restored a role for longer-run considerations.

> **Analysis of the short run in macroeconomics is concerned to explain why national output can deviate from its potential level. It is about the GDP gap and how to close it.**

Long run
The long run is reached in macroeconomics when the economy returns to producing the level of potential (or full-employment) output. This long run may be either static (if potential output is constant) or dynamic (if potential output is growing). For analytic purposes, we shall use the static long run concept in which the level of output is constant and is associated with a fixed capital stock and a fixed level of technical knowledge. We use the static concept of long run, unless we are explicitly discussing growth. This contrasts markedly with the usage of 'long run' in microeconomics, where it relates to a period within which capital stock can vary.

The long run in macroeconomics is the period it takes the economy to return to its potential GDP once it has deviated from it.

TEMPORARY ASSUMPTIONS

In order to get us started in building a theory of macroeconomics, we need to make a few additional assumptions, but these will be relaxed in succeeding chapters.

The price level

At the outset we shall assume that the price level, that is the money price of the output good produced by the economy, is fixed. All input prices are also fixed. Permitting the price level to vary simultaneously with output will be the main task addressed in Chapters 16 and 17. While the price level is held constant, all variables are automatically measured in real terms. But it is important to notice for the future that all expenditures (consumption, investment, government spending, and net exports) will continue to be defined in real terms, even when the price level is permitted to vary.

Excess capacity

Initially we shall think of the economy as having excess capacity; it is not constrained from producing more output by shortage of capital stock or labour. In this context, demand is the single determinant of output. One reason we make this assumption is that we wish to explain how it is that an economy could appear to get stuck (for some time at least) with high unemployment and excess capacity. This is the context in which macroeconomics as a subject got started. When unemployment is approaching 20 per cent and GDP has fallen sharply, as in the early 1930s, this is a sensible assumption to make. It would not be regarded as a reasonable assumption for analysing an economy closer to potential output or full employment.

Another reason we start with the twin assumptions of a fixed price level and excess capacity is that it is a helpful simplification to begin in an environment where all changes in national income are changes in real national income. Explaining the breakdown of increases in money GDP between the price level and real GDP requires a more complicated model, which we come to in Chapter 16.

Closed economy

We shall ignore the fact that the output of our economy could be sold overseas and that domestic consumers could buy foreign-produced goods. We assume an economy with no foreign trade, so domestic expenditure and domestic output are the same thing. This is not an assumption we shall need very long. It will be dropped in the next chapter.

No government

A final simplifying assumption is that there is no government sector either demanding goods or raising money through taxes. Again, we shall drop this assumption in the next chapter. (We have already made clear that government as a producer does not appear at any stage in our macro model, because, like everybody else, it is a purchaser of the single homogeneous product.)

By now the reader may be wondering what is left after we have assumed away so many potentially important things. It is worth summarizing all these assumptions. We have an economy with a single industrial sector, producing a homogeneous output, at a fixed price, in a closed economy, with no government. There is also excess capacity, so there are no resource constraints preventing the expansion of national output. What is left that we have not explicitly assumed away? The answer is final demand or expenditure on the output of the economy. By explaining final expenditure we are going to determine the national product and national income, that is, GDP.

There is a very good reason for starting with an explanation of expenditures. This is that the original inventors of macroeconomics believed that the explanation of recessions was to be found in explaining *demand failure*. Hence they focused on expenditure categories. Their theory was not developed to explain these measures. Rather, the way in which economists now measure these expenditure categories (see Table 13.2) was determined by this early theoretical reasoning.

Accordingly, we now turn to the task of explaining aggregate expenditure.

What determines aggregate expenditure?

Before we can answer the question posed in the heading, we must deal with a few more important preliminaries.

SOME IMPORTANT PRELIMINARIES

From actual to desired expenditure

In Chapter 13 we discussed how national income statisticians divide actual GDP, calculated from the expenditure side, into its components: consumption, investment, government, and net exports.

In this chapter and the next we are concerned with a different concept. It is variously called *desired*, *planned*, or *intended* expenditure. Of course, all people would like to spend virtually unlimited amounts, if only they had the resources. Desired expenditure does not refer, however, to what people would like to do under imaginary circumstances; it refers to what people want to spend out of the resources that are at their command. The *actual* values of the various categories of expenditure are indicated by C^a, I^a, G^a, and $(X^a - IM^a)$. We use the same letters without the superscript a to indicate the *desired* expenditure in the same categories: C, I, G, and $(X - IM)$.

Everyone with income to spend makes expenditure decisions. Fortunately, it is unnecessary for our purposes to look at each of the millions of such individual decisions.

Instead, it is sufficient to consider four main groups of decision makers: individual consumers (or households), firms, governments, and foreign purchasers of domestic output. The actual purchases made by these four groups account for the four main categories of expenditure that we have studied in the previous chapter: consumption, investment, government, and net exports. Their desired expenditures, made up of desired consumption, desired investment, desired government purchases, and desired exports, account for total desired expenditure. (To allow for the fact that many of the commodities desired by each group will have an import content, we subtract expenditure on imports, see Chapter 13, page 427.) The result is total desired expenditure on domestically produced goods and services, called **aggregate expenditure,** *AE*:

$$AE = C + I + G + (X - IM).$$

Desired expenditure need not equal actual expenditure, either in total or in any individual category. For example, firms may not plan to invest in the accumulation of stocks of finished goods this year but may do so unintentionally. If they produce goods to meet estimated sales but demand is unexpectedly low, the unsold goods that pile up on their shelves are undesired, and unintended, inventory accumulation. In this case, actual investment expenditure, I^a, will exceed desired investment expenditure, I.

> **National income accounts measure actual expenditures in each of the four categories: consumption, investment, government, and net exports. The theory of GDP determination deals with desired expenditures in each of these four.**

Recall, however, that these expenditure categories differ because different agents are doing the spending, and have different motivations for that spending. They are not different in the effects of their spending because they all generate spending on the final output of the single productive sector.

Autonomous and induced expenditure
In what follows it will be useful to distinguish between *autonomous* and *induced* expenditure. Components of aggregate expenditure that do *not* depend on national income are called **autonomous expenditures,** or, sometimes, *exogenous* expenditures.[3] Autonomous expenditures can and do change, but such changes do not occur systematically in response to changes in national income. Components of aggregate expenditure that *do* change in response to changes in national income are called **induced expenditures,** or *endogenous* expenditures. As we will see, the induced response of aggregate expenditure to a change in national income plays a key role in the determination of equilibrium GDP.

A simple model
To develop a theory of GDP determination, we need to examine the determinants of

---

[3] 'Autonomous' means self-motivated, or independent. 'Exogenous' means determined outside the model.

each component of desired aggregate expenditure. In this chapter we focus on desired consumption and desired investment. Consumption is the largest single component of aggregate expenditure (over 60 per cent of UK GDP in 1995), and as we will see, it provides the single most important link between desired aggregate expenditure and GDP. Investment is national output that is not used either for current consumption or by governments, and it is motivated by firms' desire to increase the capital stock.

Desired consumption expenditure

People can do one of two things with their disposable income: spend it on consumption or save it. **Saving** is all disposable income that is not consumed.

> By definition there are only two possible uses of disposable income, consumption or saving. So when each individual decides how much to put to one use, he or she has automatically decided how much to put to the other use.

What determines the division between the amount that people decide to spend on goods and services for consumption and the amount that they decide to save? The factors that influence this decision can be summarized in either the consumption function or the saving function.

THE CONSUMPTION FUNCTION

The **consumption function** relates the total desired consumption expenditure of the personal sector to the factors that determine it. It is, as we shall see, one of the central relationships in macroeconomics.

Although we are ultimately interested in the relationship between consumption and *national* income (GDP), the underlying behaviour of consumers depends on the income that they actually have to spend—their disposable income. Under the simplifying assumptions that we have made in this chapter, there are no taxes. All income that is generated is received by individuals.[4] Therefore, disposable income, which we denote by Y_d, is equal to national income, Y. (Later in our discussion, Y and Y_d will diverge, because taxes are a part of national income that is not at the disposal of individuals.)

CONSUMPTION AND DISPOSABLE INCOME

It should not surprise us to hear that a consumer's expenditure is related to the amount

---

[4] We are assuming here that all firms pass on all their profits to the persons who own them, so there is no retained profit.

of income available. There is, however, more than one way in which this relationship could work. To see what is involved, consider two quite different types of individual.

The first behaves like the proverbial prodigal son. He spends everything he receives and puts nothing aside for a rainy day. When overtime results in a large pay cheque, he goes on a binge. When it is hard to find work during periods of slack demand, his pay cheque is small and expenditures have to be cut correspondingly. This person's expenditure each week is thus directly linked to each week's take-home pay, that is, to his current disposable income.

The second individual is a prudent planner. She thinks about the future as much as the present and makes plans that stretch over her life-time. She puts money aside for retirement and for the occasional rainy day when disposable income may fall temporarily—she knows that she must expect some hard times as well as good times. She also knows that she will need to spend extra money while her children are being raised and educated and that her disposable income will probably be highest later in life when the children have left home and she has finally reached the peak of her career. This person may borrow to meet higher expenses earlier in life, paying back out of the higher income that she expects to attain later in life. A temporary, unexpected windfall of income may be saved. A temporary, unexpected shortfall may be cushioned by spending the savings that were put aside for just such a rainy day. In short, this person's current expenditure will be closely related to her expected average *life-time income*. Fluctuations in her *current income* will have little effect on her current expenditure, unless such fluctuations also cause her to change her expectations of life-time income, as would be the case, for example, if an unexpected promotion came along.

John Maynard Keynes (1883–1946), the famous English economist who developed the basic theory of macroeconomics—and, incidentally, gave his name to 'Keynesian economics'—peopled his theory with prodigal sons. For them, current consumption expenditure depended only on current income. To this day, a consumption function based on this assumption is called a *Keynesian consumption function*. Later, two US economists, Franco Modigliani and Milton Friedman, both subsequently awarded the Nobel Prize in economics, analysed the behaviour of prudent consumers who take a longer-term view in determining their consumption. Their theories, which Modigliani called the *life-cycle theory* and Friedman *the permanent-income theory*, explain some observed consumer behaviour that cannot be explained by the Keynesian function.

However, the differences between the theories of Friedman and Modigliani, on the one hand, and Keynes, on the other, are not as great as they might seem at first sight. To see why this is so, let us return to our two imaginary individuals and see why their actual behaviour may not be quite as divergent as we have described it.

Even the prodigal son may be able to do some smoothing of expenditures in the face of income fluctuations. Most people have some money in the bank and some ability to borrow, even if it is just from friends and relatives. As a result, every income fluctuation will not be matched by an equivalent expenditure fluctuation.

In contrast, although the prudent person wants to smooth her pattern of consumption completely, she may not have the borrowing capacity to do so. Her bank may not

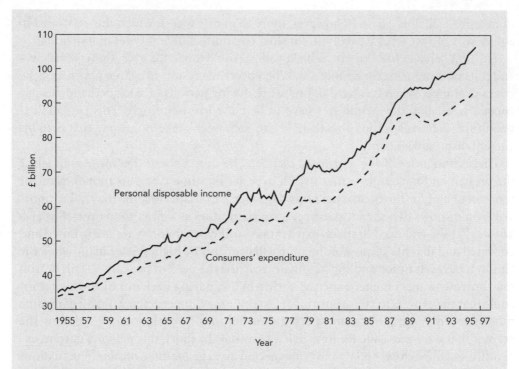

Figure 14.2. Consumers' expenditure and personal disposable income, UK, 1955–1996 (£bn at constant prices, seasonally adjusted)

Consumer spending and income are closely related over time. The chart shows real consumption expenditure and real personal disposable income since 1955. The trend rate of growth of disposable income and consumption in real terms is between 2 and 2.5 per cent.

Source: Datastream.

be willing to lend money for consumption when the security consists of nothing more than the expectation that income will be much higher in later years. This may mean that, in practice, her consumption expenditure fluctuates more with her current income than she would wish.

This suggests that the consumption expenditure of both types of individual will fluctuate to some extent with their current disposable incomes and to some extent with their expectations of future disposable income. Moreover, in any economy there will be some people of both extremes, spendthrifts and planners, and aggregate consumption will be determined by a mix of the two types. As we develop our basic theory, we will often find it useful to make the simplifying assumption that consumption expenditure is primarily determined by current disposable income. That is, we will often use a Keynesian consumption function and then indicate how things change if we consider more sophisticated theories of consumer spending. Figure 14.2 shows personal disposable income and consumers' expenditure in the UK since 1955. It is clear that the two series are closely related.

Table 14.1. The calculation of average propensity to consume (*APC*) and marginal propensity to consume (*MPC*) (£ million)

Disposable income (Y_d) (1)	Desired consumption (C) (2)	$AP = C/Y_d$ (3)	Change in Y_d (ΔY_d) (4)	Change in C (ΔC) (5)	$MPC = \Delta C/\Delta Y_d$ (6)
0	100	—			
			100	80	0.80
100	180	1.800			
			300	240	0.80
400	420	1.050			
			100	80	0.80
500	500	1.000			
			500	400	0.80
1,000	900	0.900			
			500	400	0.80
1,500	1,300	0.867			
			250	200	0.80
1,750	1,500	0.857			
			250	200	0.80
2,000	1,700	0.850			
			1,000	800	0.80
3,000	2,500	0.833			

APC measures the proportion of disposable income that households desire to spend on consumption; *MPC* measures the proportion of any increment to disposable income that households desire to spend on consumption. The data are hypothetical. We call the level of income at which desired consumption equals disposable income the break-even level; in this example it is £500 million. *APC*, calculated in the third column, exceeds unity—that is, consumption exceeds income—below the break-even level; above the break-even level, *APC* is less than unity. It is negatively related to income at all levels of income. The last three columns are set between the lines of the first three columns to indicate that they refer to *changes* in the levels of income and consumption. *MPC*, calculated in the last column, is constant at 0.80 at all levels of Y_d. This indicates that, in this example, £0.80 of every additional £1.00 of disposable income is spent on consumption, and £0.20 is used to increase saving.

The term 'consumption function' describes the relationship between consumption and the variables that influence it; in the simplest theory, consumption is primarily determined by current disposable income.

When income is zero, a typical individual will still (via borrowing or drawing on savings) consume some minimal amount.[5] This level of consumption expenditure is *autonomous* because it persists even when there is no income. The higher a person's income, the more he or she will want to consume. This part of consumption is *induced*: it varies with disposable income and hence, in our simple model, with national income.

Consider the schedule relating disposable income to desired consumption expenditure for a hypothetical economy that appears in the first two columns of Table 14.1.

---

[5] Many individuals have no income but continue to consume, such as dependent children or non-working housewives. In this case there is normally at least one earner in a household, and it is the household income that is relevant. The household would be the decision unit in that context. Such distinctions are important if we want to study the behaviour of individual spending units, but they are not critical in macroeconomics, which studies the aggregate behaviour of all consumers and relates their total spending to their total income.

Here, autonomous consumption expenditure is £100 million, whereas induced consumption expenditure is 80 per cent of disposable income. In what follows we use this hypothetical example to illustrate the various properties of the consumption function.

Average and marginal propensities to consume

To discuss the consumption function concisely, economists use two technical expressions.

The **average propensity to consume** (*APC*) is total consumption expenditure over total disposable income: $APC = C/Y_d$. The third column of Table 14.1 shows the *APC* calculated from the data in the table. Note that *APC* falls as disposable income rises.

The **marginal propensity to consume** (*MPC*) relates the *change* in consumption to the *change* in disposable income that brought it about. *MPC* is the disposable income change divided into the resulting consumption change: $MPC = \Delta C/\Delta Y_d$ (where the Greek letter Δ, delta, means 'a change in'). The last column of Table 14.1 shows the *MPC* corresponding to the data in the table. Note that, by construction, the *MPC* is constant.

The slope of the consumption function

Part (i) of Figure 14.3 shows a graph of the consumption function, derived by plotting consumption against income using data from the first two columns of Table 14.1. The consumption function has a slope of $\Delta C/\Delta Y_d$, which is, by definition, the marginal propensity to consume. The positive slope of the consumption function shows that the *MPC* is positive; increases in income lead to increases in expenditure.

Using the concepts of the average and marginal propensities to consume, we can summarize the assumed properties of the short-term consumption function as follows:

1. There is a break-even level of income at which *APC* equals unity. Below this level, *APC* is greater than unity; above it, *APC* is less than unity. Below the break-even level consumption exceeds income, so consumers run down savings or borrow. Above the break-even level, income exceeds consumption, so there is positive saving.

2. *MPC* is greater than zero but less than unity for all levels of income. This means that, for each additional £1 of income, less than £1 is spent on consumption and the rest is saved. For a straight-line consumption function, the *MPC* is constant at all levels of income.

The 45° line

Figure 14.3(i) contains a line that is constructed by connecting all points where desired consumption (measured on the vertical axis) equals disposable income (measured on the horizontal axis). Because both axes are given in the same units, this line has a positive slope of unity; that is, it forms an angle of 45° with the axes. The line is therefore called the **45° line**.

The 45° line makes a handy reference line. In part (i) of Figure 14.3 it helps to locate the break-even level of income at which consumption expenditure equals disposable

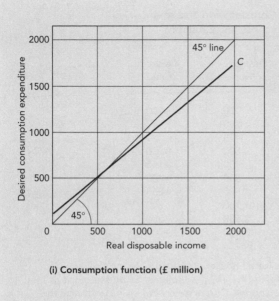

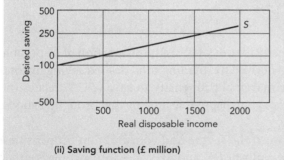

(i) Consumption function (£ million)

(ii) Saving function (£ million)

Figure 14.3. The consumption and saving functions

Both consumption and saving rise as disposable income rises. Line *C* in part (i) relates desired consumption to disposable income by using the hypothetical data from Table 14.1. Its slope, $\Delta C/\Delta Y_d$, is the marginal propensity to consume (*MPC*). The consumption line cuts the 45° line at the break-even level of disposable income, £500 million in this case. Note that the level of autonomous consumption is £100 million.

Saving is all disposable income that is not spent on consumption ($S = Y_d - C$). The relationship between desired saving and disposable income is derived in Table 14.2, and it is shown in part (ii) by line *S*. Its slope, $\Delta S/\Delta Y_d$, is the marginal propensity to save (*MPS*). The saving line cuts the horizontal axis at the break-even level of income. The vertical distance between *C* and the 45° line in part (i) is by definition the height of *S* in part (ii); that is, any given level of disposable income must be accounted for by the amount consumed plus the amount saved. Note that the level of autonomous saving is −£100 million. This means that at zero income consumers will run down existing assets by £100 million a year.

income. The consumption function cuts the 45° line at the break-even level of income, in this instance £500 million. (The 45° line is steeper than the consumption function because the *MPC* is less than unity.)

THE SAVING FUNCTION

Individuals decide how much to consume and how much to save. As we have said, this is a single decision: how to divide disposable income between consumption and saving. It follows that, once we know the dependence of consumption on disposable income, we also automatically know the dependence of saving on disposable income. (This is illustrated in Table 14.2.)

There are two saving concepts that are exactly parallel to the consumption concepts

Table 14.2. Consumption and saving schedules (£ million)

Disposable income	Desired consumption	Desired saving
0	100	−100
100	180	−80
400	420	−20
500	500	0
1,000	900	+100
1,500	1,300	+200
1,750	1,500	+250
2,000	1,700	+300
3,000	2,500	+500
4,000	3,300	+700

Saving and consumption account for all household disposable income. The first two columns repeat the data from Table 14.1. The third column, desired saving, is disposable income minus desired consumption. Consumption and saving both increase steadily as disposable income rises. In this example, the break-even level of income is £500 million. At this level, all income is consumed.

of APC and MPC. The **average propensity to save** (APS) is the proportion of disposable income that households want to save, derived by dividing total desired saving by total disposable income, $APS = S/Y_d$. The **marginal propensity to save** (MPS) relates the change in total desired saving to the *change* in disposable income that brought it about: $MPS = \Delta S/\Delta Y_d$.

There is a simple relationship between the saving and consumption propensities. APC and APS must sum to unity, and so must MPC and MPS. Because income is either spent or saved, it follows that the fractions of incomes consumed and saved must account for all income ($APC + APS = 1$). It also follows that the fractions of any increment to income consumed and saved must account for all of that increment ($MPC + MPS = 1$). Calculations from Table 14.2 will allow you to confirm these relationships in the case of the example given. MPC is 0.80 and MPS is 0.20 at all levels of income, while, for example, at an income of £2,000 million, APC is 0.85 and APS is 0.15.

Figure 14.3(ii) shows the saving schedule given in Table 14.2. At the break-even level of income, where desired consumption equals disposable income, desired saving is zero. The slope of the saving line $\Delta S/\Delta Y_d$ is equal to the MPS.

WEALTH AND THE CONSUMPTION FUNCTION

The Keynesian consumption function that we have been analysing can easily be combined with the 'permanent-income' theory of consumption. According to the

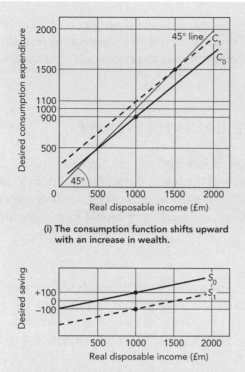

Figure 14.4. Wealth and the consumption function

Changes in wealth shift consumption as a function of disposable income. In part (i) line C_0 reproduces the consumption function from Figure 14.3(i). An increase in the level of wealth raises desired consumption at each level of disposable income, thus shifting the consumption line up to C_1. In the figure, the consumption function shifts up by £200, so with disposable income of £1,000, for example, desired consumption rises from £900 to £1,100. As a result of the rise in wealth, the break-even level of income rises to £1,500.

The saving function in part (ii) shifts down by £200 from S_0 to S_1. Thus, for example, at a disposable income of £1,000, saving *falls* from +£100 to −£100.

permanent-income theory, households save in order to accumulate wealth that they can use during their retirement (or pass on to their heirs[6]). Suppose that there is an unexpected rise in wealth. This will mean that less of current disposable income needs to be saved for the future, and it will tend to cause a larger fraction of disposable income to be spent on consumption and a smaller fraction to be saved. Thus, the consumption function will be shifted upward and the saving function downward, as shown in Figure 14.4. A fall in wealth increases the incentive to save in order to restore wealth. This shifts the consumption function downward and the saving function upward.

Desired investment expenditure

Investment expenditure is the most volatile component of GDP, and changes in investment expenditure are strongly associated with economic fluctuations. For example, the

---

6 Empirical evidence suggests that there is a significant 'bequest motive' for saving. This means that individuals plan even further ahead than their own life-times, because they want to leave money to their children.

Great Depression witnessed a major fall in investment. Total investment fell by nearly a quarter between 1929 and 1932. A little less dramatically, at the trough of the recession of the early 1990s (in 1992), investment expenditure was 13 per cent less than the level two years earlier.

INVESTMENT AND THE REAL INTEREST RATE

Other things being equal, the higher is the real interest rate, the higher is the cost of borrowing money for investment purposes and the less is the amount of desired investment expenditure. This relationship is most easily understood if we disaggregate investment into its major parts: stockbuilding, business fixed-capital formation, and residential house building.[7]

Stockbuilding
Changes in stocks of finished goods, work-in-progress, or raw materials represent only a small percentage of private investment in a typical year, but their average size is not an adequate measure of their importance. They are one of the more volatile elements of total investment and therefore have a major influence on shifts in investment expenditure.

When a firm ties up funds by holding stocks, those same funds cannot be used elsewhere to earn income. As an alternative to investing in stock, the firm could lend the money out at the going rate of interest. Thus, the higher the real rate of interest (see pages 358–60), the higher will be the opportunity cost of holding stocks of a given size; the higher that opportunity cost, the smaller are the stocks that will be desired.

The higher the real rate of interest, the lower is the desired stock of goods and materials. Changes in the rate of interest cause temporary bouts of investment (or disinvestment) in stocks.

Residential housing construction
Expenditure on new houses is also volatile. Between 1970 and 1995 it varied between 3.7 and 6.0 per cent of GDP in the UK and between 20 and 25 per cent of total investment. Because expenditures for housing construction are both large and variable, they exert a major impact on the economy.

Most houses are purchased with money that is borrowed by means of mortgages.

---

[7] These represent different motives for investment, and, in practice, would create demand for different kinds of goods. However, recall that they will all end up creating demand for the output of the single production sector. Thus, the impact, in our model, of £1 worth of stockbuilding, is the same as £1 worth of fixed-capital formation and, indeed, of £1 worth of consumption. The reason we distinguish investment from consumption is that it is affected by different factors, the most important of which will be the interest rate.

Interest on the borrowed money typically accounts for over one-half of the purchaser's annual mortgage payments; the remainder is repayment of the original loan, called the principal. Because interest payments are such a large part of mortgage payments, variations in interest rates exert a substantial effect on the demand for housing. During the mid-1980s interest rates fell sharply, and there was a boom in the demand for housing; that boom persisted until late 1988, when interest rates started to rise again. The housing market collapsed and house prices fell. The lower interest rates that arrived in 1992 and 1993 permitted the beginning of a recovery in the housing market; however, this recovery was very slow and house prices did not pick up until 1996.

Expenditure for residential construction tends to vary negatively with interest rates.

Business fixed-capital formation

Investment in fixed capital (factories, offices, and machines) by firms is the largest component of domestic investment. Over one-half is financed by firms' retained profits (profits that are *not* paid out to their shareholders). This means that current profits are an important determinant of investment.

The rate of interest is also a major determinant of investment. As became abundantly clear, both during the early 1980s and during 1989–92, high interest rates greatly reduce the volume of investment as more and more firms find that their expected profits from investment do not cover the interest on borrowed investment funds. Other firms who have cash on hand find that purchasing interest-earning assets provides a better return than investment in factories and machinery; for them, the increase in real interest rates means that the opportunity cost of investing in fixed capital had risen. Interest rates are determined in the monetary sector, so we do not fully incorporate interest-rate effects until we have studied money in Chapter 18.

EXPECTATIONS AND BUSINESS CONFIDENCE

Investment takes time. When a firm invests, it increases its future capacity to produce output. If the new output can be sold profitably, the investment will prove to be a good one. If the new output does not generate profits, the investment will be a bad one. When the investment is undertaken, the firm does not know if it will turn out well or badly—it is betting on a favourable future that cannot be known with certainty.

When firms see good times ahead, they will want to invest so as to reap future profits. When they see bad times, they will not invest, because, given their expectations, there will be no pay-off from doing so.

Business investment depends in part on firms' forecasts of the future state of the economy.

INVESTMENT AS AUTONOMOUS EXPENDITURE

We have seen that investment is influenced by many things. For the moment we treat investment as autonomous, meaning only that it is uninfluenced by changes in national income. This allows us to study, first, how national income is determined when there is an unchanged amount of desired investment expenditure and, second, how alterations in the amount of desired investment cause changes in equilibrium national income. (In Chapter 18, we will link changes in GDP to changes in investment via induced changes in interest rates.)

The aggregate expenditure function

The aggregate expenditure function relates the level of desired real expenditure to the level of real income. Generally, total desired expenditure on the nation's output is the

Table 14.3. The aggregate expenditure function in a closed economy with no government (£ million)

National income (Y)	Desired consumption expenditure ($C = 100 + 0.8Y$)	Desired investment expenditure ($I = 250$)	Desired aggregate expenditure ($AE = C + I + G + (X - IM)$)
100	180	250	430
400	420	250	670
500	500	250	750
1,000	900	250	1,150
1,500	1,300	250	1,550
1,750	1,500	250	1,750
2,000	1,700	250	1,950
3,000	2,500	250	2,750
4,000	3,300	250	3,550

The aggregate expenditure function is the sum of desired consumption, investment, government, and net export expenditures. In this table, government and net exports are assumed to be zero, investment is assumed to be constant at £250 million, and desired consumption is based on the hypothetical data given in Table 14.2. The autonomous components of desired aggregate expenditure are desired investment and the constant term in the desired consumption expenditure (£100 million). The induced component is the second term in desired consumption expenditure (0.8Y).

The marginal response of consumption to a change in national income is 0.8, the marginal propensity to consume. The marginal response of desired aggregate expenditure to a change in national income, $\Delta AE / \Delta Y$, is also 0.8, because all induced expenditure in the economy is consumption expenditure.

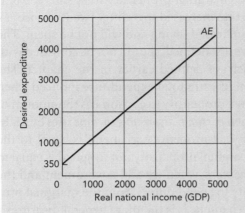

Figure 14.5. An aggregate expenditure function

The aggregate expenditure function re-lates total desired expenditure to national income. The *AE* curve in the figure plots the data from the first and the last columns of Table 14.3, which are repeated in Table 14.4. Its intercept (which in this case is £350) shows autonomous expenditure, which in this case is the sum of autonomous consumption of £100 and investment of £250. Its slope (which in this case is 0.8) shows the marginal propensity to spend.

sum of desired consumption, investment, government, and net export expenditures. In the simplified economy of this chapter, aggregate expenditure is just equal to $C + I$.

$$AE = C + I.$$

Table 14.3 shows how the *AE* function can be calculated given the consumption function of Tables 14.1 and 14.2 and a constant level of desired investment of £250 million. In this specific case, all of investment expenditure is autonomous, as is the £100 million of consumption that would be desired at zero national income (see Table 14.1). Total autonomous expenditure is thus £350 million—induced expenditures are just equal to induced consumption, which is equal to $0.8Y$. Thus, desired aggregate expenditure, whether thought of as $C + I$ or as autonomous plus induced expenditure, can be written as $AE = £350$ million $+ 0.8Y$. This aggregate expenditure function is illustrated in Figure 14.5.

The propensity to spend out of national income

The fraction of any increment to national income that will be spent on purchasing domestic output is called the economy's **marginal propensity to spend.** The marginal propensity to spend is measured by the change in aggregate expenditure divided by the change in income, or $\Delta AE / \Delta Y$, the slope of the aggregate expenditure function. In this book, we will denote the marginal propensity to spend by the symbol z, which will typically be a number greater than zero and less than one.

Similarly, the **marginal propensity not to spend** is the fraction of any increment to national income that does not add to desired aggregate expenditure. This is denoted $(1 - z)$: if z is the part of £1 of incremental income that is spent, $(1 - z)$ is the part that is not spent.[8]

---

[8] More fully, these terms would be called the marginal propensity to spend *on national income* and the marginal propensity not to spend *on national income*. The marginal propensity not to spend, $(1 - z)$, is often referred to as the *marginal propensity to withdraw*. Not spending part of income amounts to a *withdrawal* or a *leakage* from the circular flow of income, as illustrated in Figure 13.1 on page 423.

In the example given in Table 14.3, z, the marginal propensity to spend, is 0.8. If national income increases by £1, 80p will go into increased spending. Twenty pence (£1 times 0.2, the value of $(1 - z)$) will go into increased saving and will not be spent. The marginal propensity to spend, which we have just defined, should not be confused with the marginal propensity to consume, which we defined earlier in the chapter. The marginal propensity to spend is the amount of extra total expenditure induced when *national income* rises by £1, while the marginal propensity to consume is the amount of extra consumption expenditure induced when *personal disposable income* rises by £1. In the simple model of this chapter, the marginal propensity to spend is equal to the marginal propensity to consume, and the marginal propensity not to spend is equal to the marginal propensity to save. In later chapters, when we add government and the international sector, the marginal propensity to spend differs from the marginal propensity to consume. Both here and in later chapters, it is the more general measures z and $(1 - z)$ that are important for determining equilibrium national income (GDP).

Equilibrium GDP

We are now ready to see what determines the *equilibrium* level of national income and output, that is, GDP. When something is in equilibrium, there is no tendency for it to change; forces are acting on it, but they balance out, and the net result is *no change*. Any conditions that are required for something to be in equilibrium are called its *equilibrium conditions*.

Table 14.4 illustrates the determination of equilibrium GDP for our simple hypothetical economy. Suppose that firms are producing a final output of £1,000 million, and thus national income is £1,000 million. According to the table, at this level of income aggregate desired expenditure is £1,150 million. If firms persist in producing a current output of only £1,000 million in the face of an aggregate desired expenditure of £1,150 million, one of two things must happen.[9]

One possibility is that consumers, firms, and governments will be unable to spend the extra £150 million that they would like to spend, so queues or unfulfilled order books will appear. These will send a signal to firms that they can increase their sales if they increase their production. When the firms increase production, national income rises. Of course, the individual firms are interested only in their own sales and profits, but their individual actions have as their inevitable consequence an increase in GDP.

The second possibility is that all spenders will spend everything that they wanted to spend. Then, however, expenditure will exceed current output, which can happen only when some expenditure plans are fulfilled by purchasing stocks of goods that were produced in the past. In our example, the fulfilment of plans to purchase £1,150 million

---

[9] A third possibility, that prices could rise, is ruled out by assumption in this chapter.

Table 14.4. The determination of equilibrium GDP (£ million)

National income (GDP) (Y)	Desired aggregate expenditure (AE = C + I)	
100	430	
400	670	
500	750	Pressure on Y
1,000	1,150	to rise
1,500	1,550	↓
1,750	**1,750**	**Equilibrium Y**
2,000	1,950	↑
3,000	2,750	Pressure on Y
4,000	3,550	to fall

National income (GDP) is in equilibrium where aggregate desired expenditure equals national output. The data are copied from Table 14.3. When GDP is below its equilibrium level, aggregate desired expenditure exceeds the value of current output. This creates an incentive for firms to increase output and hence for GDP to rise. When GDP is above its equilibrium level, aggregate desired expenditure is less than the value of current output. This creates an incentive for firms to reduce output and hence for GDP to fall. Only at the equilibrium level of GDP is aggregate desired expenditure equal to the value of current output.

worth of commodities in the face of a current output of only £1,000 million will reduce stocks by £150 million. As long as stocks last, more goods can be sold than are currently being produced.[10]

Eventually, stocks will run out. But before this happens, firms will increase their output as they see their sales increase. Extra sales can then be made without a further depletion of inventories. Once again, the consequence of each individual firm's behaviour, in search of its own individual profits, is an increase in the national product and income. Thus, the final response to an excess of aggregate desired expenditure over current output is a rise in GDP.

> **At any level of GDP at which aggregate desired expenditure exceeds total output, there will be pressure for GDP to rise.**

Next consider the £4,000 million level of GDP in Table 14.4. At this level desired expenditure on domestically produced goods is only £3,550 million. If firms persist in producing £4,000 million worth of goods, £450 million worth must remain unsold.

[10] Notice that, in this example, actual national income is equal to £1,000 million. Desired consumption is £900 million and desired investment is £250 million, but the reduction of inventories of £150 million is unplanned negative investment; thus, actual investment is only £100 million.

Therefore, stocks of unsold goods must rise. However, firms will not allow unsold goods to accumulate indefinitely; sooner or later they will reduce the level of output to the level of sales. When they do, GDP will fall.

> **At any level of GDP for which aggregate desired expenditure is less than total output, there will be pressure for GDP to fall.**

Finally, look at the GDP level of £1,750 million in Table 14.4. At this level, and only at this level, aggregate desired expenditure is equal to national output (GDP). Purchasers can fulfil their spending plans without causing inventories to change. There is no incentive for firms to alter output. Because everyone wishes to purchase an amount equal to what is being produced, output and income will remain steady; GDP is in equilibrium.

> **The equilibrium level of GDP occurs where aggregate desired expenditure equals total output.**

This conclusion is quite general and does not depend on the numbers that are used in the specific example.

Figure 14.6 shows the determination of the equilibrium level of GDP. In that figure, the line labelled AE graphs the aggregate expenditure function given by the first and last columns of Table 14.3 and also shown in Table 14.4. The line labelled 45° line ($AE = Y$) graphs the equilibrium condition that aggregate desired expenditure equals national output. Since in equilibrium the variables measured on the two axes must be equal, the line showing this equality is a 45° line. Anywhere along that line, the value of desired expenditure, which is measured on the vertical axis, is equal to the value of real national output, which is measured on the horizontal axis.[11]

Graphically, equilibrium occurs at the level of GDP at which the aggregate desired expenditure line intersects the 45° line. This is the level of income where desired expenditure is just equal to total national output and therefore is just sufficient to purchase that output.

Exactly the same equilibrium is illustrated in panel (ii), but in terms of the saving–investment balance. The line labelled S is equal to aggregate saving. In an economy without government and without international trade (the case we are studying here), aggregate saving is just equal to $Y - C$, the difference between national income and

---

[11] Because it turns up in many different guises, the 45° line can cause a bit of confusion until one gets used to it. The main thing about it is that it can be used whenever the variables plotted on the two axes are measured in the same units, such as pounds, and are plotted on the same scale. In that case, equal distances on the two axes measure the same amounts. One centimetre may, for example, correspond to £1,000 on each axis. In such circumstances, the 45° line joins all points where the values of the two variables are the same. In Figures 14.3 and 14.4, the 45° line shows all points where *desired consumption expenditure in real terms* equals *real disposable income* because these are the two variables that are plotted on the two axes. In Figure 14.5 and all those that follow it, the 45° shows all points at which *desired total expenditure in real terms* equals *real national income* because those are the variables that are measured on the two axes of these figures.

Figure 14.6. Equilibrium national income and output

Equilibrium national income occurs at E_0, where the desired aggregate expenditure line intersects the 45° line. If real national income is below Y_0, desired aggregate expenditure will exceed national output, and production will rise. This is shown in part (i) by the arrow to the left of Y_0. If national income is above Y_0, desired aggregate expenditure will be less than national output, and production will fall. This is shown by the arrow to the right of Y_0. Only when real national income is Y_0 will desired aggregate expenditure equal real national output.

When saving is the only withdrawal and investment is the only injection, the equilibrium Y_0 is also the level of national income at which saving equals investment, shown in part (ii). At levels of national income greater than Y_0 saving exceeds investment (withdrawals exceed injections), so aggregate spending is less than output and the economy contracts. At levels of national income below Y_0, investment exceeds saving (injections exceed withdrawals) so spending exceeds output and the level of national income increases. Part (i) and (ii) are just two different ways of looking at the same phenomena.

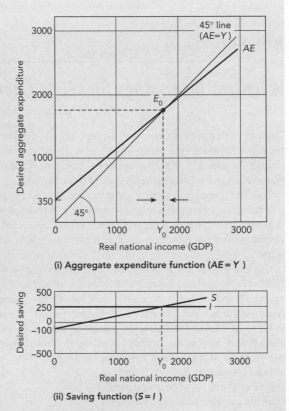

(i) Aggregate expenditure function ($AE = Y$)

(ii) Saving function ($S = I$)

consumption. The line labelled I is investment, in this case assumed to be constant at all levels of income.

Notice that the vertical distance between S and I is just equal to the distance between the 45° line and AE. When desired investment exceeds desired saving, desired aggregate expenditure exceeds national output by the same amount. When desired investment is less than desired saving, desired aggregate expenditure is less than national output by the same amount.

Now we have explained the determinants of the equilibrium level of GDP at a *given price level*. A simple analogy, which will help to understand why it is that equilibrium GDP is associated with equality of desired investment and saving, is set out in Box 14.1. In the next section we shall study the forces that cause equilibrium income to change. We shall see that shifts in autonomous consumption and investment expenditure cause changes in equilibrium GDP.

BOX 14.1.

A hydraulic analogy for GDP determination

The key concept to understand in this chapter is how it is that GDP achieves some static, or equilibrium, level (for given values of autonomous expenditures). This is one of the most important ideas in macroeconomics, because it explains how GDP can be in equilibrium even when there is excess capacity in the economy.

Think of the economy as a water container, say a basin, which has inflows and outflows on a continuous basis—the tap is turned on and there is no plug in the plug hole. So the water is always changing, but there is some condition under which the water in the basin will stay at one level. This is when the volume of the inflow and the volume of the outflow are exactly equal.

Call the inflow 'investment', the outflow 'saving', and the level of water in the bath 'GDP'. GDP will stay at one level so long as the volume of investment just equals the volume of saving. If investment increases, this increases desired expenditure, and so the level of national output will rise until the increased water pressure (national income) is such that the volume of saving (at the higher level of national income) now equals the higher level of investment again. If, on the other hand, investment falls, GDP will fall until the lower pressure of water (lower national income) reduces saving to equal the new lower level of investment. (The same principle can be viewed in terms of the circular flow diagram, Figure 13.1, when there is no foreign trade and no government. Only when $I = S$ will the level of the circular flow be stable.)

What happens if the basin fills up to overflowing? That is the problem of capacity constraints and full employment, which we discuss in later chapters. Hopefully, the basin will never run empty, because that means national income and output fall to zero—though the problem of the water getting undesirably low is exactly what macroeconomics was invented to avoid.

Note also that, in later chapters, we shall see that investment is not the only inflow, or injection (government expenditure and exports will be added), and saving is not the only leakage, or withdrawal (taxes and imports are also leakages).

Changes in GDP

Because the *AE* function plays a central role in our explanation of the equilibrium value of national income and output (GDP), you should not be surprised to learn that shifts in the *AE* function play a central role in the explanation of why GDP changes. (Remember here that we continue to assume that the price level is constant.) To understand this influence, we must recall an important distinction that was first encountered in Chapter 2—the distinction between *shifts* in a curve and *movements along* a curve (see pages 57–9).

Suppose desired aggregate expenditure rises. This may be a response to a change in national income, or it may be the result of an increased desire to spend at each level of national income. A change in national income causes a *movement along* the aggregate expenditure function. An increased desire to spend at each level of national income causes a *shift in* the aggregate expenditure function. Figure 14.7 illustrates this important distinction.

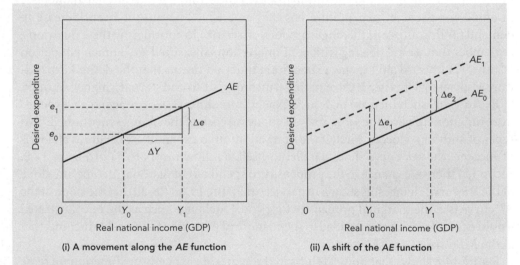

(i) A movement along the *AE* function

(ii) A shift of the *AE* function

Figure 14.7. Movements along and shifts of the *AE* function

A movement along the aggregate expenditure function occurs in response to a change in income; a shift of the *AE* function indicates a different level of desired expenditure at each level of income. In part (i), a change in income of ΔY, from Y_0 to Y_1, changes desired expenditure by Δe, from e_0 to e_1. In part (ii), a shift in the expenditure function from AE_0 to AE_1 raises the amount of expenditure associated with *each level* of income. At Y_0, for example, desired aggregate expenditure is increased by Δe_1; at Y_1 it is increased by Δe_2. (If the aggregate expenditure line shifts parallel to itself, $\Delta e_1 = \Delta e_2$.) (Notice that from here on we drop 'aggregate' from the vertical axis label and write 'Desired expenditure'. The term 'aggregate' is always understood, even when we omit it to save space.)

SHIFTS IN THE AGGREGATE EXPENDITURE FUNCTION

For any specific aggregate expenditure function, there is a unique level of equilibrium GDP. If the aggregate expenditure function shifts, the equilibrium will be disturbed and national output will change. Thus, if we wish to find the causes of changes in GDP, we must understand the causes of shifts in the *AE* function.

The aggregate expenditure function shifts when one of its components shifts, that is, when there is a shift in the consumption function, in desired investment expenditure, in desired government expenditure on goods and services, or in desired net exports. In this chapter we consider only shifts in the consumption function and in desired investment expenditure. Both of these are changes in desired aggregate expenditure at every level of income.

Upward shifts

What happens if households permanently increase their levels of consumption spending at each level of disposable income, or if ICI invests in more fixed capital because of improved confidence about the future health of the economy? (Recall that an increase in any component of expenditure has the same effect, because it is an increase in demand for the output of the single production sector.) In considering these questions, remember that we are dealing with continuous flows measured as so much per period of time. An upward shift in any expenditure function means that the desired expenditure associated with each level of national income rises to and stays at a higher amount.

Because any such increase in desired expenditure shifts the entire aggregate expenditure function upward, the same analysis applies to each of the changes mentioned. Two types of shift in *AE* occur. First, if the same addition to expenditure occurs at all levels of income, the *AE* curve shifts parallel to itself, as shown in part (i) of Figure 14.8. Second, if there is a change in the propensity to spend out of national income, the slope of the *AE* curve changes, as shown in part (ii) of Figure 14.8. (Recall that the slope of the *AE* curve is z, the marginal propensity to spend.) A change such as the one illustrated would occur if consumers decided to spend more of every £1 of disposable income, that is, the *MPC* rose.

Figure 14.8 shows that upward shifts in the aggregate expenditure function increase equilibrium GDP. After the shift in the *AE* curve, output is no longer in equilibrium at its original level because at that level desired expenditure exceeds national output. Equilibrium GDP now occurs at the higher level indicated by the intersection of the new *AE* curve with the 45° line, along which aggregate expenditure equals real national output.

Downward shifts

What happens to GDP if there is a decrease in the amount of consumption or investment expenditure desired at each level of income? These changes shift the aggregate expenditure function downward. A constant reduction in desired expenditure at all levels of income shifts *AE* parallel to itself. A fall in the marginal propensity to spend out of national income reduces the slope of the *AE* function. When we use the saving–investment relation, we must note that a downward shift in the consumption function causes an upward shift in the saving function, reducing the equilibrium level of income at which saving equals investment.

The results restated

We have derived two important general propositions of the theory of GDP determination.

1. **A rise in the amount of desired aggregate expenditure that is associated with each level of national income will increase equilibrium national output.**

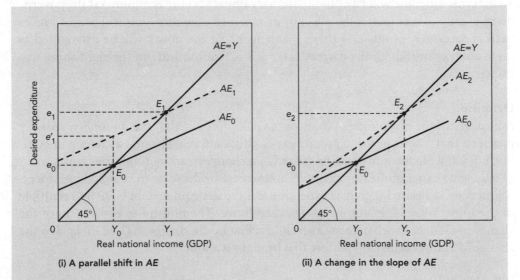

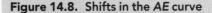

Figure 14.8. Shifts in the *AE* curve

Upward shifts in the *AE* curve increase equilibrium income and output; downward shifts decrease equilibrium income and output. In parts (i) and (ii), the aggregate expenditure curve is initially AE_0 with national income Y_0. In part (i), a parallel upward *shift* in the *AE* curve from AE_0 to AE_1 means that desired expenditure has increased by the same amount at each level of national income. For example, at Y_0 desired expenditure rises from e_0 to e_1' and therefore exceeds national income. Equilibrium is reached at E_1, where income is Y_1 and expenditure is e_1. The increase in desired expenditure from e_1' to e_1, represented by a *movement along* AE_1, is an induced response to the increase in income from Y_0 to Y_1.

In part (ii), a non-parallel upward shift in the *AE* curve, say from AE_0 to AE_2, means that the marginal propensity to spend at each level of national income has increased. This leads to an increase in equilibrium national income. Equilibrium is reached at E_2, where the new level of expenditure e_2 is equal to income Y_2. Again, the initial *shift* in the *AE* curve induces a *movement* along the new *AE* curve. Downward shifts in the *AE* curve, from AE_1 to AE_0 or from AE_2 to AE_0, lead to a fall in equilibrium income to Y_0.

2. A fall in the amount of desired aggregate expenditure that is associated with each level of national income will lower equilibrium national output.

THE MULTIPLIER

We have learned how to predict the direction of the changes in GDP that occur in response to various shifts in the aggregate expenditure function. We would like also to predict the *magnitude* of these changes.

During a recession the government sometimes takes measures to stimulate the economy. If these measures have a larger effect than estimated, demand may rise too much and full employment may be reached with demand still rising. (We will see in Chapter 16 that this outcome will have an inflationary impact on the economy.) If the government greatly overestimates the effect of its measures, the recession will persist longer than is necessary. In this case there is a danger that the policy will be discredited as ineffective, even though the correct diagnosis is that too little of the right thing was done.

Definition

A measure of the magnitude of changes in GDP is provided by the *multiplier*. We have just seen that a shift in the aggregate expenditure curve will cause a change in equilibrium GDP. Such a shift could be caused by a change in any autonomous component of aggregate expenditure, for example, an increase or decrease in desired investment. An increase in desired aggregate expenditure increases equilibrium GDP by a multiple of the initial increase in autonomous expenditure. The **multiplier** is the ratio of the change in GDP to the change in expenditure, that is, the change in GDP *divided by* the change in autonomous expenditure that brought it about.

Why the multiplier is greater than unity

What will happen to GDP if ICI spends £100 million per year on new factories? Initially the construction of the factories will create £100m worth of new demand for the output of the production sector (recall that there is only one type of output) and £100m of new national income, and a corresponding amount of extra wages for workers and profits for firms (the income components of GDP). But this is not the end of the story. The increase in national income of £100m will cause an increase in disposable income, which in turn will cause an induced rise in consumption expenditure.

Workers, who gain new income directly from the building of the factory, will spend some of it on consumer goods. (In reality, they will spend on many different goods, such as beer and cinema visits. In the simplified world of our model, all spending is on the final output of the single industrial sector.) When output and employment expand to meet this demand, further new incomes will then be created for workers and firms. When they then spend their newly earned incomes, output and employment will rise further. More income will be created, and more expenditure will be induced. Indeed, at

Basic model of GDP determination

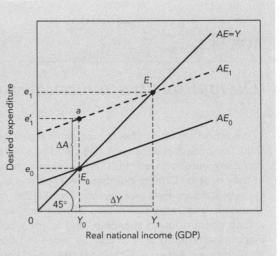

Figure 14.9. The simple multiplier

An increase in the autonomous component of desired aggregate expenditure increases equilibrium national income by a multiple of the initial increase. The initial equilibrium is at E_0, where AE_0 intersects the 45° line. At this point, desired expenditure, e_0, is equal to national income, Y_0. An increase in autonomous expenditure of ΔA then shifts the desired expenditure function upward to AE_1. If national income stays at Y_0, desired expenditure rises to e_1'. (The coordinates of point a are Y_0 and e_1'.) Because this level of desired expenditure is greater than national output, national output will rise.

Equilibrium occurs when GDP rises to Y_1. Here desired expenditure, e_1, equals output, Y_1. The extra expenditure of e_1 represents the induced increases in expenditure. It is the amount by which the final increase in GDP, ΔY, exceeds the initial increase in autonomous expenditure, ΔA. Because ΔY is greater than ΔA, the multiplier is greater than unity.

this stage we might wonder whether the increases in income will ever come to an end. To deal with this concern, we need to consider the multiplier in somewhat more precise terms.

The simple multiplier defined

Consider an increase in autonomous expenditure of ΔA, which might be, say, £100m per year. Remember that ΔA stands for *any* increase in autonomous expenditure; this could be an increase in investment or in the autonomous component of consumption. The new autonomous expenditure shifts the aggregate expenditure function upward by that amount. GDP is no longer in equilibrium at its original level, because desired aggregate expenditure now exceeds output. Equilibrium is restored by a *movement along* the new *AE* curve.

The **simple multiplier** measures the change in equilibrium GDP that occurs in response to a change in autonomous expenditure *at a constant price level.*[12] We refer to it as 'simple' because we have simplified the situation by assuming that the price level is fixed. Figure 14.9 illustrates the simple multiplier and makes clear that it is greater than unity. Box 14.2 provides a numerical example.

[12] It should be remembered also that we have assumed that there is excess capacity in the economy, so an increase in expenditure can lead to extra real activity. The situation is very different when we start out with resources already fully employed. We come to this situation in later chapters.

BOX 14.2.

The multiplier: a numerical example

Consider an economy that has a marginal propensity to spend out of national income of 0.80. Suppose that autonomous expenditure increases by £100m per year because a large company spends an extra £100m per year on new factories. National income (and output) initially rises by £100m, but that is not the end of it. The factors of production involved in factory building that received the first £100m spend £80 million. This second round of spending generates £80 million of new income. This new income, in turn, induces £64 million of third-round spending, and so it continues, with each successive round of new income generating 80 per cent as much in new expenditure. Each additional round of expenditure creates new income (and output) and yet another round of expenditure.

The table carries the process through ten rounds. Students with sufficient patience (and no faith in mathematics) may compute as many rounds in the process as they wish; they will find that the sum of the rounds of expenditures approaches a limit of £500 million, which is five times the initial increase in expenditure.

The graph of the cumulative expenditure increases shows how quickly this limit is approached. The multiplier is thus 5, given that the marginal propensity to spend is 0.8. Had the marginal propensity to spend been lower, say, 0.667, the process would have been similar, but it would have approached a limit of three, instead of five, times the initial increase in expenditure. Notice that, since our model has only a single productive sector, it makes no difference what the initial spending goes on. That and all subsequent spending is on the output of this single industry. In reality, the impact of spending increases may vary slightly depending on the product first demanded.

Round of spending	Increase in expenditure (£m)	Cumulative total (£m)
Initial increase	100	100.0
2	80	180.0
3	64	244.0
4	51.2	295.2
5	41.0	336.2
6	32.8	369.0
7	26.2	395.2
8	21.0	416.2
9	16.8	432.8
10	13.4	446.2
11–20 combined	47.9	494.1
All others	5.8	500.0

THE SIZE OF THE SIMPLE MULTIPLIER

The size of the simple multiplier depends on the slope of the AE function, that is, on the marginal propensity to spend, z. This is illustrated in Figure 14.10.

A high marginal propensity to spend means a steep AE curve. The expenditure induced by any initial increase in income is large, with the result that the final rise in income is correspondingly large. By contrast, a low marginal propensity to spend means a relatively flat AE curve. The expenditure induced by the initial increase in income is small, and the final rise in income is not much larger than the initial rise in autonomous expenditure that brought it about.

The larger the marginal propensity to spend, the steeper is the aggregate expenditure function and the larger is the multiplier.

The precise value of the simple multiplier can be derived by using elementary

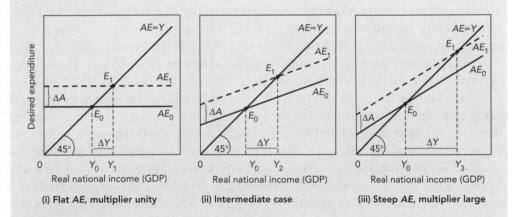

(i) Flat *AE*, multiplier unity   **(ii) Intermediate case**   **(iii) Steep *AE*, multiplier large**

Figure 14.10. The size of the simple multiplier

The larger the marginal propensity to spend out of national income (z), the steeper is the *AE* curve and the larger is the multiplier. In each part of the figure, the initial aggregate expenditure function is AE_0, equilibrium is at E_0, with income Y_0. The AE curve then shifts upward to AE_1 as a result of an increase in autonomous expenditure of ΔA. ΔA is the same in each part. The new equilibrium is at E_1. In part (i), the AE function is horizontal, indicating a marginal propensity to spend of zero ($z = 0$). The change in GDP, ΔY, is only the increase in autonomous expenditure, because there is no induced expenditure by those who receive the initial increase in income. The simple multiplier is then unity, its minimum possible value. In part (ii), the AE curve slopes upward but is still relatively flat (z is low). The increase in GDP to Y_2 is only slightly greater than the increase in autonomous expenditure that brought it about. In part (iii), the AE function is quite steep (z is high). Now the increase in GDP to Y_3 is much larger than the increase in autonomous expenditure that brought it about. The simple multiplier is quite large.

algebra, but we do not show the full derivation here. The result is that the simple multiplier, which we call K, is

$$K = \frac{\Delta Y}{\Delta A} = \frac{1}{1-z},$$

where z is the marginal propensity to spend out of national income. (As we have seen, z is the slope of the aggregate expenditure function.)

As we saw earlier, the term $(1-z)$ stands for the marginal propensity not to spend out of national income. For example, if £0.80 of every £1.00 of new national income is spent ($z = 0.80$), then £0.20 is the amount not spent. The value of the multiplier is then calculated as $K = 1/(0.20) = 5$.

The simple multiplier is the reciprocal of the marginal propensity not to spend.

From this we see that, if $(1-z)$ is small (that is, if z is large), the multiplier will be large (because extra income induces much extra spending). What if $(1-z)$ is large? The largest possible value of $(1-z)$ is unity, which arises when z equals zero, indicating that none of any additional national income is spent. In this case the multiplier itself has a value of unity; the increase in equilibrium GDP is confined to the initial increase in autonomous expenditure. There are no induced additional effects on spending, so GDP only increases by the original increase in autonomous expenditure. The relation between $(1-z)$ and the size of the multiplier is illustrated in Figure 14.10.

To estimate the size of the multiplier in an actual economy, we need to estimate the value of the marginal propensity not to spend out of national income in that economy, that is, $(1-z)$. Evidence suggests that in the UK the value of the marginal propensity not to spend is much larger than 0.2. This is because there are other 'leakages' from the circular flow of income—income taxes and import expenditures (which will be added to our model in the next chapter). Allowing for these extra withdrawals leads to a realistic estimate for $(1-z)$ of something around 0.65 (calculated using a marginal propensity to save of 0.2, a marginal propensity to import of 0.25, and an income tax rate of 0.25 (25p in the pound)). Thus, the simple multiplier for the UK is just over 1.4, rather than of the order of 5 as in the above example.

The simple multiplier is a useful starting point for understanding the effects of expenditure shifts on GDP. However, as we shall see later, many qualifications will arise, so the reader should not place too much policy significance on its value at this stage.

Summary

1. Macroeconomics is concerned to build simple models of the economy as a whole that can explain the determination of real GDP and why actual GDP often deviates from its potential or long-term equilibrium level.

2. The GDP gap is the difference between actual GDP and potential GDP. Macro-economics aims to explain deviations of actual from potential GDP. Growth theory aims to explain the long-term trends in potential GDP.

3. For simplicity, we aggregate all industrial sectors into one, so the economy produces only one type of output good. We approach the explanation of GDP determination through the major expenditure categories—consumption, investment, government spending, and net exports.

4. Desired aggregate expenditure includes desired consumption, desired investment, and desired government expenditures, plus desired net exports. It is the amount that economic agents want to spend on purchasing the national product. In this chapter we consider only consumption and investment.

5. A change in disposable income leads to a change in consumption and saving. The responsiveness of these changes is measured by the marginal propensity to consume (*MPC*) and the marginal propensity to save (*MPS*), which are both positive and sum to one, indicating that all disposable income is either spent on consumption or saved.

6. A change in wealth tends to cause a change in the allocation of disposable income between consumption and saving. The change in consumption is positively related to the change in wealth, while the change in saving is negatively related to this change.

7. Investment depends, among other things, on real interest rates and business confidence. In our simple theory, investment is treated as autonomous.

8. In the simple theory of this chapter, investment expenditures and the constant term in the consumption function (that is the level of consumption when income is zero, shown in Table 14.1) are both autonomous expenditures. The part of consumption that responds to income is called induced expenditure.

9. At the equilibrium level of GDP, purchasers wish to buy an amount of the national output equal to what is being produced. At GDP above equilibrium, desired expenditure falls short of national output, and output will sooner or later be curtailed. At GDP below equilibrium, desired expenditure exceeds national output, and output will sooner or later be increased.

10. In a closed economy with no government, desired saving equals desired investment at equilibrium GDP.

11. Graphically, equilibrium GDP is the point where the aggregate expenditure curve cuts the 45° line, i.e. where total desired expenditure equals total output. This is the same level of national income at which the saving function cuts the investment function.

12. With a constant price level, equilibrium GDP is increased by a rise in the desired consumption, or investment, expenditure that is associated with each level of the national income. Equilibrium GDP is decreased by a fall in these desired expenditures.

13. The magnitude of the effect on GDP of shifts in autonomous expenditure is given by the multiplier. It is defined as $K = \Delta Y / \Delta A$, where ΔA is the change in autonomous expenditure.

14. The simple multiplier is the multiplier when the price level is constant. It is equal to $1/(1 - z)$, where z is the marginal propensity to spend out of national income. Thus, the larger z is, the larger is the multiplier. It is a basic prediction of macroeconomics that the simple multiplier, relating £1 worth of spending on domestic output to the resulting increase in GDP, is greater than unity.

Topics for review

- Aggregation across sectors
- Actual and potential GDP
- The GDP gap
- Desired expenditure
- Consumption function
- Average and marginal propensities to consume and to save
- Aggregate expenditure function
- Marginal propensities to spend and not to spend
- Equilibrium GDP at a given price level
- Saving–investment balance
- Shifts of, and movements along, expenditure curves
- The effect on GDP of changes in desired expenditures
- The simple multiplier
- The size of the multiplier and slope of the AE curve

Questions for discussion

1. What do you understand by the term 'potential GDP'? What evidence would help to decide whether the current level of GDP is above or below its potential level?

2. Recalculate the data in Table 14.1 (after column (1)) assuming that the consumption function is given by: $C = 100 + 0.6Y$.

3. Work out the implications of the changes made in Question 2 for the AE function, and then determine the new equilibrium level of national income.

4. What factors in addition to real interest rates are likely to be important determinants of investment by firms?

5. The consumption function is usually estimated using seasonally adjusted data. What seasonal factors do you think would alter the relationship between disposable income and consumption at different times of year?

6. Table 14.4 shows an equilibrium level of GDP of £1,750 million. Explain why there are no forces tending to move the economy from that level of income even though there is excess capacity in the economy. What could bring about an increase in that equilibrium level of GDP?

7. What would be the value of the multiplier for the following values of the MPC (assuming no government or foreign trade): (i) 0.4, (ii) 0.75, (iii) 0.95?

8. You are running a firm that sells consumer goods. The government has just announced a cut in income tax rates, thereby giving many consumers a boost in their disposable income. What effect would you expect this to have on your sales? Would this effect be different if the marginal propensity to consume were 0.98 instead of 0.6?

CHAPTER 15

GDP in an Open Economy with Government

Government spending and taxes	485	Additional injections and leakages	498
Government spending	485	Graphical exposition	498
Tax revenues	486		
The budget balance	486	**Changes in aggregate expenditure**	499
Tax and expenditure functions	487	The simple multiplier revisited	499
		Net exports and equilibrium GDP	500
Net exports	488	Autonomous net exports	500
The net export function	488	Induced net exports	500
Shifts in the net export function	490	Fiscal policy	500
Foreign income	490	Changes in government spending	502
Relative international prices	491	Changes in tax rates	503
		Tax rates and the multiplier	504
Equilibrium GDP	492	Balanced-budget changes	504
The income–expenditure approach	492	Lessons and limitations of the income–	
Relating desired consumption to national		expenditure approach	505
income	493		
The aggregate expenditure function	494	**Summary**	506
The marginal propensity to spend	495		
Determining equilibrium GDP	496	**Topics for review**	507
Graphical exposition	496		
The augmented saving–investment approach	497	**Questions for discussion**	507

I N this chapter, we continue building a model of national income and output (GDP) determination. So far, we have assumed a highly simplified environment. In building our model in Chapter 14, we maintained four simplifying, but temporary, assumptions—no government, no foreign trade, fixed price level, and excess capacity. This chapter relaxes the first two of these. The following chapter relaxes the last two.

Our task in this chapter, then, is to add a government and a foreign sector to our simple model. Adding the government sector allows us to study *fiscal policy*, the ability of the government to use its taxing and spending powers to affect the level of national income. In an open economy, net foreign demand for domestic output is an important source of final expenditure, so it has to be included in any complete treatment of the expenditure components of national income. We proceed, first, to add the government.

Then we add the foreign trade sector. Finally, we examine how these additions change both the structure of the model and its behaviour in response to changes in autonomous expenditures.

As we proceed, it is important to remember that the key elements of our theory of income determination are unchanged. The most important of these, which will remain true even after incorporating government and the foreign sector, are restated here.

1. Aggregate desired expenditure can be divided into autonomous expenditure and induced expenditure. Induced expenditure is expenditure that depends on the level of national income.

2. The equilibrium level of GDP (national income and output) is the level at which the sum of autonomous and induced desired expenditure is equal to output. Graphically, this is where the aggregate expenditure line intersects the 45° line.

3. The simple multiplier measures the change in equilibrium GDP that takes place in response to a unit change in autonomous domestic expenditure, with the price level held constant.

Recall that the expenditure-based measure of GDP is made up of consumption, investment, government expenditure, and net exports. We have built a model of GDP determination that includes consumption and investment. We are about to extend this model to include government spending and net exports. Recall also that 'national income', 'national output', and 'GDP' are all equivalent terms.

Government spending and taxes

Government spending and taxing policies affect equilibrium GDP in two important ways. First, government expenditure is part of autonomous expenditure. Second, in deriving disposable income, taxes must be subtracted from national income, and government transfer payments must be added. Because disposable income determines consumption expenditure, the relationship between desired consumption and national income becomes more complicated when a government is added. A government's plans for taxes and spending define its *fiscal policy*, which has important effects on the level of GDP in both the short and the long run.

GOVERNMENT SPENDING

In Chapter 13 we distinguished between *government expenditure on goods and services* and government *transfer payments*. The distinction bears repeating here. Government expenditures on goods and services are part of GDP. When the government hires a civil servant, buys a paper clip, or purchases fuel for the navy, it is directly adding to the demands on the economy's current output of goods and services. Thus, desired government purchases, *G*, are part of aggregate expenditure. As explained in Chapter 14, in our model we treat government spending on goods and services as if it were all buying the output from the single industrial sector. This means that the effect of government spending on GDP is exactly the same as the effect of any other component of autonomous expenditures.

The other part of government spending, transfer payments, also affects desired aggregate expenditure, but only indirectly. Consider, for example, state pensions, unemployment benefit, or student grants. These are payments (transfers) made by government to individuals. The recipients may well then spend the money. However, that demand is recorded as personal consumption, so we don't want to count it twice by recording it under *G* as well. Hence, government transfer payments affect aggregate expenditure only through the effect that these payments have on *disposable* income. Transfer payments increase disposable income, and increases in disposable income, via the consumption function, increase desired consumption expenditure.

This distinction (between transfers and government spending on goods and services) is important when it comes to issues such as how much of national income is taken by government. Measuring the size of government to include transfers makes it look as though government's share of national output is much bigger than it really is. However, looking only at *G* makes the government's revenue needs look smaller than they are, since transfers must be financed by taxes or borrowing, just as expenditures on goods and services must be. In what follows, government spending always excludes transfers, unless the contrary is clearly stated.

TAX REVENUES

Tax revenues may be thought of as negative transfer payments in their effect on desired aggregate expenditure. Tax payments reduce disposable income relative to national income; transfers raise disposable income relative to national income. For the purpose of calculating the effect of government policy on desired consumption expenditure, it is the net effect of the two that matters.

We define **net taxes** to be total tax revenues received by the government minus total transfer payments made by the government, and we denote net taxes as *T*. (For convenience, when we use the term 'taxes', we will mean *net* taxes unless we explicitly state otherwise.) Since transfer payments are smaller than total taxes, net taxes are positive, and personal disposable income is less than national income. (It was 72 per cent of GDP at market prices in 1995.)

THE BUDGET BALANCE

The **budget balance** is the difference between total government revenue and total government expenditure, or, equivalently, it equals net taxes minus government spending,

$T - G$. When revenues exceed expenditure, the government is running a **budget surplus.** When expenditures exceed revenues, as they have for most of the postwar period (1988–9 and 1969–70 were the only exceptions in the UK), the government is running a **budget deficit.**[1] When the budget surplus (and deficit) is zero, the government has a **balanced budget.** When the budget is in deficit, the government is adding to the national debt, since it must borrow to cover its deficit. When the budget is in surplus, the government is reducing the national debt, since the surplus funds are used to pay off old debt.

The **Public Sector Borrowing Requirement** (PSBR) is similar to the budget deficit but it differs from the budget deficit by (1) (minus) asset sales and (2) borrowing by parts of the public sector other than central government. The budget deficit is the concept most relevant to macroeconomics because changes in the ownership of assets do not affect current GDP. Since the budget deficit is simply a negative budget surplus, we generally use 'budget surplus' to cover both cases, so bear in mind that the budget surplus can be negative.

TAX AND EXPENDITURE FUNCTIONS

We treat government expenditure as autonomous. The government is assumed to decide on how much it wishes to spend in real terms and to hold to these plans whatever the level of national income. We also treat *tax rates* as autonomous. The government sets its tax rates and does not vary them as national income varies. This, however, implies that *tax revenues* are induced, or endogenous. As national income rises, a tax system with given rates will yield more revenue. For example, when income rises, people will pay more income tax in total even though the income tax rates are unchanged.

Table 15.1 and Figure 15.1 illustrate these assumptions with a specific example. They show size of the government's surplus when its desired purchases (G) are constant at £170 million and its net tax revenues are equal to 10 per cent of national income. Notice that the government budget surplus (or public saving) increases with national income. This relationship occurs because net tax revenues rise with income but, by assumption, government expenditure does not. The slope of the budget surplus function is just equal to the income tax rate. The *position* of the function is determined by fiscal policy, as we discuss later in this chapter.[2]

[1] When the government runs a budget deficit, it must borrow the excess of spending over revenues. It does this by *selling government bonds* (gilts). When the government runs a surplus, it uses the excess revenue to purchase outstanding government bonds. The stock of outstanding bonds is termed the *national* or *public debt* (public debt is the debt of the entire public sector, which includes local authorities and nationalized industries; national debt is the debt of the central government only).

[2] The numerical example used here is designed only to illustrate the principles of income determination developed in this chapter. To avoid the appearance of direct applicability of overly simplified models, we have deliberately chosen not to use 'realistic' numbers. The example produces GDP of £2,000 million, whereas UK money GDP in 1995 was a little over £700,000 million.

Table 15.1. The budget surplus function

GDP (Y) (£m)	Government expenditure (G) (£m)	Net taxes (T = 0.1Y) (£m)	Government surplus (T − G) (£m)
500	170	50	−120
1,000	170	100	−70
1,750	170	175	5
2,000	170	200	30
3,000	170	300	130
4,000	170	400	230

The budget surplus is negative at low levels of GDP and becomes positive at sufficiently high levels of GDP. The table shows that the size of the budget surplus increases with GDP, given constant expenditure and constant tax rates. For example, when GDP rises by £1,000 million, the deficit falls or the surplus rises by £100 million in the case shown here.

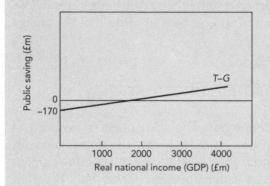

Figure 15.1. Budget surplus function

The budget surplus function increases as GDP increases. The figure plots the $T - G$ column from Table 15.1. Notice that the slope of the surplus function is equal to the income tax rate of 0.1.

The government budget surplus (public saving), for given tax rates, tends to increase as national income rises and fall when national income falls.

Net exports

The foreign trade sector of the UK economy is significant in relation to the size of GDP. Exports of goods and services in 1995 were just over 28 per cent of GDP at market prices. Although the total volume of trade is important for many purposes, such as determining the amount by which a country gains from trade, it is the balance between exports and imports (the current account balance) that is particularly important in the determination of GDP.

THE NET EXPORT FUNCTION

In macroeconomics, we are interested in how the balance of trade responds to changes in national income, the price level, and the exchange rate. Our theory covers trade in goods *and services*. The effects on national income of selling a service to a foreigner are identical to those of selling a physical commodity (recall that we only have one type of product in our economy, and all expenditures are treated as demands for this product).

Exports depend on spending decisions made by foreign consumers or firms that purchase UK goods and services. Typically, therefore, exports will not change as a result of changes in UK GDP (or, at least, this is what we assume). They are autonomous, or exogenous expenditures, from the point of view of UK national income determination.

Imports, however, depend on the spending decisions of domestic residents. Most categories of expenditure have an import content; British-made cars, for example, use large quantities of imported components and raw materials in their manufacture.

Table 15.2. The net exports schedule

GDP (Y) (£m)	Exports (X) (£m)	Imports (IM = 0.25Y) (£m)	Net exports (£m)
0	540	0	540
1,000	540	250	190
2,160	540	540	0
3,000	540	750	−210
4,000	540	1,000	−460
5,000	540	1,250	−710

Net exports fall as GDP rises. The data in the table assume that exports are constant and that imports are 25 per cent of GDP. In this case, net exports are positive at low levels of GDP and negative at high levels of GDP.

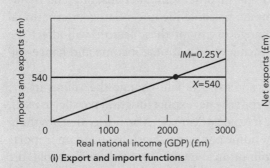

(i) Export and import functions

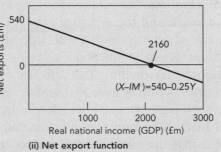

(ii) Net export function

Figure 15.2. The net export function

Net exports, defined as the difference between exports and imports, are inversely related to the level of GDP. In part (i), exports are constant at £540 million, while imports rise with national income. Therefore, net exports, shown in part (ii), decline with national income. The figure is based on hypothetical data in Table 15.2. With national income equal to £2,160 million, imports are equal to exports at £540 million and net exports are zero. For levels of national income below £2,160 million, imports are less than exports, and hence net exports are positive. For levels of national income above £2,160 million, imports are greater than exports, and hence net exports are negative.

Thus, imports rise when the other categories of expenditure rise. As consumption rises with income, imports of foreign-produced consumption goods, and materials that go into domestically produced consumption goods, also rise with income.

> **Desired net exports are negatively related to national income because of the positive relationship between desired imports and national income.**

This negative relationship between net exports and national income is called the *net export function*. Data for a hypothetical economy with constant exports and with imports that are 25 per cent of national income are given in Table 15.2 and illustrated in Figure 15.2. In this example, exports form the autonomous component and imports form the induced component of the desired net export function. The formulation in the table implicitly assumes that all imports are for final consumption. Imports rise when income rises, but imports do not change when *other* categories of autonomous expenditure change, so there is no direct import content of G, I, and X. This simplification will prove useful in our development of the determination of equilibrium income and does not affect the essentials of the theory.

SHIFTS IN THE NET EXPORT FUNCTION

We have seen that the net export function relates net exports, $(X - IM)$, which we also denote NX, to national income. It is drawn on the assumption that everything that affects net exports, except domestic national income, remains constant. The major factors that must be held constant are foreign national income, relative international price levels, and the exchange rate. A change in any of these factors will affect the amount of net exports that will occur at each level of national income and hence will shift the net export function.

Notice that anything that affects domestic exports will change the values in the 'Exports' column in Table 15.2, and so will shift the net export function parallel to itself, upward if exports increase and downward if exports decrease. Also notice that anything that affects the proportion of income that home consumers wish to spend on imports will change the values in the 'Imports' column in the table, and thus will change the slope of the net export function by making imports more or less responsive to changes in domestic income. What factors will cause such shifts?

Foreign income

An increase in foreign income, other things being equal, will lead to an increase in the quantity of UK-produced goods demanded by foreign countries, that is, to an increase in our exports. Because more exports will be sold whatever the level of UK national income, the increase is in the constant, X, of the net export function, causing NX to shift upward, parallel to its original position. A fall in foreign income leads to a parallel downward shift in the net export function.

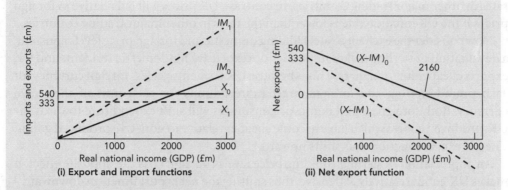

Figure 15.3. Shifts in the net export function

An upward shift in imports and/or a downward shift in exports shifts the net export function downward. A rise in the domestic price level relative to foreign price levels, or a rise in the exchange rate, lowers exports from X_0 to X_1 and raises the import function from IM_0 to IM_1. This shifts the net export function downward from $(X - IM)_0$ to $(X - IM)_1$. (In the figure, imports are 25 per cent of Y along IM_0 and are assumed to rise to a third of Y when domestic goods become more expensive relative to foreign goods, while exports fall from £540 million to £333 million).

Relative international prices

Any change in the prices of home-produced goods relative to those of foreign goods will cause both imports and exports to change. This will shift the net export function.

Consider first a rise in domestic prices relative to prices in foreign countries. On the one hand, foreigners now see UK goods as more expensive relative both to goods produced in their own country and to goods imported from other countries. As a result, UK exports will fall. On the other hand, UK residents will see imports from foreign countries become cheaper relative to the prices of home-made goods. As a result, they will buy more foreign goods, and imports will rise. Both of these shifts cause the net export function to shift downwards and change its slope, as shown in Figure 15.3.

Second, consider the opposite case of a fall in UK prices relative to prices of foreign-made goods. On the one hand, potential UK exports will now look cheaper in foreign markets relative both to their home-produced goods and to goods imported from third countries. As a result, UK exports rise. On the other hand, the same change in relative prices—British-made goods become cheaper relative to foreign-made goods—causes UK imports to fall. Thus, the net export function shifts upwards, in exactly the opposite way to the movement in Figure 15.3.

What kinds of things will cause relative international prices to change? Two important causes of changes in competitiveness, for a country as a whole, are international differences in inflation rates and changes in exchange rates.

Consider inflation rates first. Holding the sterling exchange rate constant, UK prices will rise relative to foreign prices if the UK inflation rate is higher than the inflation rates in other major trading countries. In contrast, UK prices will fall relative to foreign prices if the UK inflation rate is lower than the rates in other major trading countries.

Now consider the exchange rate. Holding domestic and foreign price levels constant, a devaluation of sterling makes imports more expensive for domestic residents and UK exports cheaper for foreigners. This is because UK residents get less foreign currency for each pound sterling and foreigners get more pounds for each unit of their own currency. Both foreigners and domestic consumers will shift expenditure towards the UK-produced goods, which have become cheaper relative to non-UK-produced goods. The net export function thus shifts upward.

An appreciation of sterling (holding price levels constant) has the opposite effect. It makes UK goods relatively expensive, thus shifting the net export function downward.[3]

The results of this important chain of reasoning are summarized below.

1. UK prices rise relative to foreign prices if the UK inflation rate exceeds the rate in other major trading countries (with exchange rates fixed) or if the pound sterling appreciates (with price levels constant). This discourages exports and encourages imports, causing the net export function to shift downwards.

2. UK prices fall relative to foreign prices if the UK inflation rate is less than the rates in competitor countries (with exchange rates fixed) or if the pound sterling depreciates (with price levels constant). This encourages exports and discourages imports, causing the net export function to shift upwards.

Equilibrium GDP

We are now ready to see how equilibrium GDP is determined in our new model that includes a government and a foreign sector. As in Chapter 14, we can determine the equilibrium in two ways, which come to the same thing in the end: by relating income and expenditure, and by relating savings and investment.

The income–expenditure approach

In Chapter 14, we determined equilibrium national income (and output) by finding the

---

[3] A depreciation of sterling that is exactly proportional to the excess of UK inflation over foreign inflation will leave the relative price of UK exports and imports unchanged. This would be referred to as a constant *real exchange rate*, or as preserving purchasing power parity (PPP). The real exchange rate is the relative price of home- and foreign-produced goods. It is also referred to as 'competitiveness' or the 'terms of trade'. A rise in the real exchange rate (fall in competitiveness) shifts the net export function down because it lowers exports and increases imports at each level of national income.

Table 15.3. Consumption as a function of disposable income and national income (GDP)

National income (GDP) (Y) (£m)	Disposable income $(Y_d = 0.9Y)$ (£m)	Desired consumption $(C = 100 + 0.8Y_d)$ (£m)
100	90	172
1,000	900	820
2,000	1,800	1,540
3,000	2,700	2,260
4,000	3,600	2,980

If desired consumption depends on disposable income, which in turn depends on national income, desired consumption can be written as a function of either income concept. The second column shows deductions of 10 per cent of any level of national income to arrive at disposable income. Deductions of 10 per cent of Y imply that the remaining 90 per cent of Y becomes disposable income. The third column shows consumption as £100 million plus 80 per cent of disposable income.

By relating the second and third columns, one sees consumption as a function of disposable income. By relating the first and third columns, one sees the derived relationship between consumption and national income. In this example, the change in consumption in response to a change in disposable income (i.e. the *MPC*) is 0.8, and the change in consumption in response to a change in national income is 0.72.

level of national income where desired aggregate expenditure is equal to national income (and output). The addition of government and the foreign sector changes the calculations that we must make but does not alter the basic principles that are involved. Our first step is to derive a new aggregate expenditure function that incorporates the effects of government and foreign trade.

RELATING DESIRED CONSUMPTION TO NATIONAL INCOME

Our theory of national income determination requires that we relate each of the components of aggregate expenditure to national income, Y. Personal income taxes cause personal disposable income to differ from national income (by the proportion of income taxation net of transfers). We shall simply assume that disposable income is always 90 per cent of national income.[4] Thus, whatever the relationship between C and Y_d, we can always substitute $0.9Y$ for Y_d. For example, if changes in consumption were

---

[4] In this case, T, desired net taxes, would be given by the function $T = 0.1Y$. Recall that, for simplicity, we ignore indirect taxes.

always 80 per cent of changes in Y_d, changes in consumption would always be 72 per cent (80 per cent of 90 per cent) of changes in Y.

Table 15.3 illustrates how we can write desired consumption as a function of Y as well as of Y_d. We can then derive the marginal response of consumption to changes in Y by determining the proportion of any change in *national income* that goes to a change in desired consumption.

> **The marginal response of consumption to changes in national income ($\Delta C/\Delta Y$) is equal to the marginal propensity to consume out of disposable income ($\Delta C/\Delta Y_d$) multiplied by the fraction of national income that becomes personal disposable income ($\Delta Y_d/\Delta Y$).**

We now have an equation that shows how desired consumption expenditure varies as national income varies, including the effects of taxes and transfer payments ($C = 100 + 0.72Y$; arrived at from $C = 100 + 0.8Y_d$ by substituting $0.9Y$ for Y_d). This is part of the aggregate expenditure function.

THE AGGREGATE EXPENDITURE FUNCTION

In order to determine equilibrium national income, we start by defining the aggregate expenditure function,

$$AE = C + I + G + NX.$$

Table 15.4 illustrates the calculation of the aggregate expenditure function. It shows a schedule of desired expenditure for each of the components of aggregate expenditure,

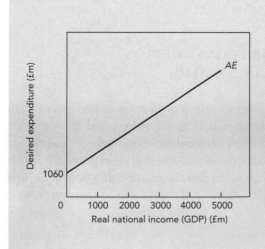

Figure 15.4. An aggregate expenditure curve

The aggregate expenditure curve relates total desired expenditure to national income. The *AE* curve in the figure plots the data from the first and last columns of Table 15.4. Its intercept shows £1,060 million of autonomous expenditure (equal to £100 million autonomous consumption plus £250 million investment plus £170 million government plus £540 million autonomous net exports). Its slope is the marginal propensity to spend (which, following the calculations in Table 15.4, is 0.47 in this case).

Table 15.4. The aggregate expenditure function (£ million)

National income (GDP) Y	Desired consumption expenditure $(C = 100 + 0.72Y)$	Desired investment expenditure $(I = 250)$	Desired government expenditure $(G = 170)$	Desired net export expenditure $(IM = 540 - 0.25Y)$	Desired aggregate expenditure $(AE = C + I + G + (X - IM))$
0	100	250	170	540	1,060
100	172	250	170	515	1,107
500	460	250	170	315	1,195
1,000	820	250	170	290	1,530
2,000	1,540	250	170	40	**2,000**
3,000	2,260	250	170	−210	2,470
4,000	2,980	250	170	−460	2,940
5,000	3,700	250	170	−710	3,410

The aggregate expenditure function is the sum of desired consumption, investment, government, and net export expenditures. The autonomous components of desired aggregate expenditure are desired investment, desired government spending, desired export expenditure, and the constant term in desired consumption (first row). These sum to £1,060 million in the above example. The induced components are the second terms in desired consumption expenditure (0.72Y) and desired imports (0.25Y).

The marginal response of consumption to a change in national income is 0.72, calculated as the product of the marginal propensity to consume (0.8) and the fraction of national income that becomes disposable income (0.9). The marginal response of desired aggregate expenditure to a change in national income, $\Delta AE/\Delta Y$, is 0.47.

and it shows total desired *aggregate* expenditure at each level of national income. Figure 15.4 shows this aggregate expenditure function in graphical form.

THE MARGINAL PROPENSITY TO SPEND

The slope of the aggregate expenditure function is the *marginal propensity to spend* on national income (z). With the addition of taxes and net exports, however, the marginal propensity to spend is no longer equal to the marginal propensity to consume.

Suppose that the economy produces £1.00 of extra income and that the response to this is governed by the relationships in Tables 15.1 and 15.2, as summarized in Table 15.4. Since £0.10 is collected by the government as net taxes, £0.90 is converted into disposable income, and 80 per cent of this amount (£0.72) becomes consumption expenditure. However, import expenditure also rises by £0.25, so expenditure on domestic goods, that is, aggregate expenditure, rises by only £0.47. Thus, z, the marginal propensity to spend out of national income, is 0.47. What is not spent on domestic output includes the £0.10 in taxes, the £0.18 of disposable income that is saved, and the

£0.25 of import expenditure, for a total of £0.53. Hence, the marginal propensity not to spend, $(1 - z)$, is $1 - 0.47 = 0.53$.

DETERMINING EQUILIBRIUM GDP

The logic of GDP determination in our (now more complicated) hypothetical economy is exactly the same as in the closed economy without government discussed in Chapter 14. We have added two new components of aggregate expenditure, G and $(X - IM)$. We have also made the calculation of desired consumption expenditure more complicated; taxes must be subtracted from national income in order to determine disposable income. However, *equilibrium national income (GDP) is still the level of national income at which desired aggregate expenditure equals national income (and output)*.

The aggregate expenditure function can be used directly to determine equilibrium national income. In Table 15.4, the equilibrium is £2,000 million. When national income is equal to £2,000 million, it is also equal to desired aggregate expenditure.

Suppose that national income is less than its equilibrium amount. The forces leading back to equilibrium are exactly the same as those described on pages 468–80 of Chapter 14. When domestic consumers, firms, foreign consumers, and governments try to spend at their desired amounts, they will try to purchase more goods and services than the economy is currently producing. Thus, some of the desired expenditure must either be frustrated or take the form of purchases of inventories of goods that were produced in the past. As firms see that they are (or could be) selling more than they are producing, they will increase production, thus increasing the level of national income and output.

The opposite sequence of events occurs when national output is greater than the level of aggregate expenditure desired at that income. Now the total of personal consumption, investment, government spending, and net foreign demand for the economy's output is less than the national product. Firms will notice that they are unable to sell all of their output. Their unsold stocks will be rising, and they will not let this happen indefinitely. They will seek to reduce the level of output until it equals the level of sales, and national income will fall.

Finally, when national output is equal to desired aggregate expenditure (£2 billion in Table 15.4), there is no pressure for output to change. Firms are producing exactly the quantity of goods and services that purchasers want to use, given the level of income.

> **Equilibrium GDP is determined where desired aggregate expenditure equals national output. In our extended model, aggregate expenditure includes consumption, investment, government spending, and net exports.**

Graphical exposition

Figure 15.5 illustrates the determination of equilibrium GDP and the behaviour of the economy when it is not in equilibrium. The line labelled '*AE*' is simply the aggregate expenditure function shown in Figure 15.4. The slope of *AE* is the marginal propensity

Figure 15.6. National saving and national asset formation

The economy is in equilibrium at Y_0, where desired national saving, $S + (T - G)$, equals desired national asset formation, $I + (X - IM)$. To the left of Y_0, desired national asset formation exceeds desired national saving. This implies that desired aggregate expenditure exceeds national output. Firms will respond to the imbalance by producing more, moving the economy towards equilibrium. To the right of Y_0, desired national asset formation is less than desired national saving, and aggregate expenditure is less than national output. Firms will cut back on output in order to avoid accumulating excess inventories, and the economy will move towards equilibrium.

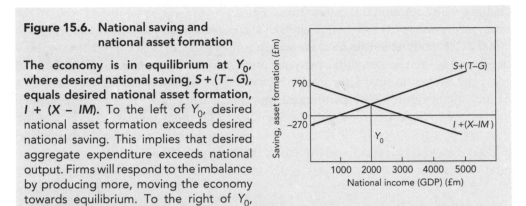

GDP are equal (as was approximately true in the UK in 1995), net exports equal the rate of accumulation of claims on foreigners. This is because if we sell to foreigners more than we buy from them we must acquire a financial claim against them. (This claim could be foreign money, but it could also be shares in foreign companies, foreign government bonds, etc.) Hence, net exports represent the net acquisition of foreign assets or overseas investment (but only in the special case where GNP = GDP). I is domestic investment, so $I + (X - IM)$ is domestic plus overseas investment, or national asset formation. Thus, the equation $S + (T - G) = I + (X - IM)$ can be interpreted as a generalization of the condition that saving equals investment, since it says that national saving equals national asset formation.

Figure 15.6 illustrates how GDP is determined where the national saving and national asset formation schedules intersect. Notice that this is exactly the same level of national income at which $AE = Y$.

Changes in aggregate expenditure

Changes in any of the autonomous components of planned aggregate expenditure will cause changes in equilibrium GDP. In Chapter 14 we investigated the consequences of shifts in the consumption function and in the investment function. Here we discuss fiscal policy—the effects of government spending and taxes. We also consider shifts in the net export function. First, we take account of the fact that the simple multiplier is reduced by the presence of taxes and the marginal propensity to import.

The simple multiplier revisited

In Chapter 14 we saw that the *simple multiplier*, the amount by which equilibrium GDP

Figure 15.5. Equilibrium GDP

Equilibrium GDP occurs at E_0, where the desired aggregate expenditure line intersects the 45° line. Here the aggregate expenditure line is taken from Table 15.4; autonomous expenditure is £1,060 million, and the slope of AE is 0.47. If real national income is below £2,000 million, desired aggregate expenditure will exceed national output, and production will rise. This is shown by the arrow to the left of $Y = £2,000$ million. If national income is above £2,000 million, desired aggregate expenditure will be less than national output, and production will fall. This is shown by the arrow to the right of $Y = £2,000$ million. Only when real GDP is £2,000 million will desired aggregate expenditure equal real national output.

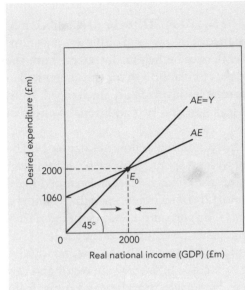

to spend out of national income (0.47 in our example). Recall that AE plots the behaviour of desired purchases in the economy. It shows demand for the domestic product at each level of national income. (The AE curve is sometimes referred to as the 'aggregate demand curve' in this context. However, we reserve this term for another, related construct that we use in the next chapter, once we have permitted the price level to be variable.)

The line labelled $AE = Y$ (the 45° line) depicts the equilibrium condition that desired aggregate expenditure is equal to actual national income (and output). Any point on this line *could* be an equilibrium, but only one is. Equilibrium occurs where behaviour (as depicted by the AE function) is consistent with equilibrium (as depicted by $AE = Y$). At the equilibrium level of GDP, desired expenditure is just equal to national income and is therefore just sufficient to purchase the total domestic product.

The augmented saving–investment approach

An equivalent way of determining equilibrium national income is analogous to finding the point where desired saving equals desired investment. Finding the level of income where $S = I$ was appropriate in Chapter 14, where we were dealing with a closed economy with no government. Now we have to take account of the facts that there is government saving as well as private saving, and that net exports provide an injection of spending which plays a similar role to investment.

Additional injections and leakages

The reason why saving and investment had to be equal for GDP to be in equilibrium is that this is the only point at which there is a balance of inflows and outflows (injections and leakages) in the circular flow of income. It may be helpful to review both the hydraulic analogy in Box 14.1 on page 472 and the circular flow of income illustrated in Figure 13.1 on page 423, at this stage. The principles involved are unchanged. Now, however, we have two additional sources of leakages and two additional sources of injections.

Saving was our only leakage of expenditure from the circular flow in Chapter 14. The marginal propensity to save told us how much was not spent out of each additional £1 of income received. Now we add personal income taxes. These are levied on individuals' gross incomes, and so they also represent a proportion of income earned that cannot be spent. The second additional leakage is imports. Imports are a leakage because they create demand for foreign output. This does not generate domestic income.

Investment was the only injection in our model in Chapter 14. In this chapter we have added government spending. This is received as income by the private sector and this extra income leads to further spending as before. Similarly, export demand comes from other countries, but it generates domestic incomes. Hence, export demand is our second new injection.

The condition for GDP to be in equilibrium is now that the sum of desired injections should equal the sum of desired leakages. We can write this condition as an equation, with the sum of all leakages (saving, S, plus taxes, T, plus imports, IM) equal to the sum of all injections (investment, I, plus government spending, G, plus exports, X):

$$S + T + IM = I + G + X.$$

An equilibrium condition for the determination of equilibrium national income equivalent to $AE = Y$ is that injections (investment plus government spending plus exports) must equal leakages (saving plus income taxes plus imports).

Graphical exposition

In order to illustrate the determination of national income via the equality of injections and leakages, it is convenient to rearrange the above equation slightly. The convenience is partly the creation of graphical simplicity, but also there is an advantage in terms of economic intuition.

Subtracting G and IM from both sides of the above equation gives:

$$S + (T - G) = I + (X - IM).$$

The brackets do not change the meaning of anything, but they do identify two terms we are already familiar with. $(T - G)$ is the government budget surplus. In this context it can be thought of as public sector (government) saving. Since S is private saving, $S + (T - G)$ is total domestic saving, or national saving. $(X - IM)$ is our old friend net exports. When there is no net property income from abroad, that is, when GNP and

498

changes when autonomous expenditure changes by £1, was equal to $1/(1 - z)$. In the example considered throughout Chapter 14, z, the marginal propensity to spend, was equal to 0.8, and the multiplier was equal to 5, or $1/(0.2)$. In the example that we have developed in this chapter, with a marginal propensity to import of 0.25 and a marginal (net) income tax rate of 0.1, the marginal propensity to spend is 0.47. (Ten per cent of a £1 increase in autonomous spending goes to taxes, leaving £0.90 of disposable income. With a marginal propensity to consume of 0.8, £0.72 is spent. Of this, £0.25 is spent on imports, leaving a total of £0.47 to be spent on domestically produced consumption goods.) Thus, $(1 - z)$ is 0.53, and the simple multiplier is $1/(0.53) = 1.89$.

Net exports and equilibrium GDP

As with the other elements of desired aggregate expenditure, if the net export function shifts upward, equilibrium GDP will rise; if the net export function shifts downward, equilibrium GDP will fall.

Autonomous net exports

Net exports have both an autonomous component and an induced component. Generally, exports themselves are autonomous with respect to domestic national income. Foreign demand for UK goods and services depends on foreign income, on foreign and UK prices, and on the exchange rate, but it does not depend on UK domestic income. Export demand could also change because of a change in tastes. Suppose that foreign consumers develop a taste for British-made goods (perhaps, in reality, Jaguars or Land Rovers, but in the model it is for the output of the single sector) and desire to purchase £500 million more per year of such goods than they had in the past. The net export function (and the aggregate expenditure function) will shift up by £500 million, and equilibrium GDP will increase by £500 million times the multiplier.

Induced net exports

The domestic demand for imports depends, in part, on domestic income. The greater is domestic income, the greater will be UK residents' demand for goods and services in general, including those produced abroad. Because imports are subtracted to obtain net exports (net exports equal $X - IM$), the greater is the marginal propensity to import, the lower will be the marginal propensity to spend on the domestic product, and the lower will be the multiplier $1/(1 - z)$.

Fiscal policy

Fiscal Policy involves the use of government spending and tax policies to influence total

500

desired expenditure in order to dampen fluctuations in the economy. In practical terms, this means trying to avoid unsustainable booms and recessions.

Since government expenditure increases aggregate desired expenditure and taxation decreases it, the *directions* of the required changes in spending and taxation are generally easy to determine once we know the direction of the desired change in GDP. But the *timing, magnitude,* and *mixture* of the changes pose more difficult issues.

Any policy that attempts to stabilize GDP at or near any desired level (usually potential GDP) is called **stabilization policy.** Here we deal only with the basic ideas of stabilization through fiscal policy. The main alternative to fiscal policy, monetary policy, will be discussed in Chapter 18, after we have added a monetary sector to our model of GDP determination.

The basic idea of stabilization policy follows from what we have already learned. A reduction in tax rates or an increase in government expenditure shifts the *AE* curve upward, causing an increase in equilibrium GDP. An increase in tax rates or a decrease in government expenditure shifts the *AE* curve downward, causing a decrease in equilibrium GDP.

If the government has some target level of GDP, it can use its tax and expenditures as instruments to push the economy towards that target. First, suppose the economy is in a serious recession. The government would like to increase GDP. The appropriate fiscal tools are to raise expenditures and/or to lower tax rates. Second, suppose the economy is 'overheated'. In the next two chapters we will study what this means in detail. In the meantime, we observe that an 'overheated' economy has such a high level of GDP (relative to potential) that shortages are pushing up prices and causing inflation. Without worrying too much about the details, just assume that the current level of GDP is higher than the target level that the government judges to be appropriate. What should the government do? The fiscal tools at its command are to lower government expenditure and to raise tax rates, both of which have a depressing effect on GDP.

The proposition that governments can avoid recessions by deliberately stimulating aggregate demand created a major revolution in economic thought. This is still known as the Keynesian Revolution. We have already done enough macroeconomics to understand what this was all about. The idea was that an economy could reach an equilibrium level of GDP that was well below the full employment or potential level. The way out of this was for the government to use its fiscal policy to increase aggregate expenditure by increasing government spending or reducing taxes (or both).

The expenditure model of national income and output determination predicts that GDP can get stuck at a level below its full potential. It also suggests how fiscal policy might be used to return the economy to its potential level of GDP.

Now let us look in a little more detail at how this might work out. However, bear in mind that we are still dealing with a special case in which prices are fixed and there is excess capacity, so we are just looking at how our model, as developed so far, works, not at how the real world works.

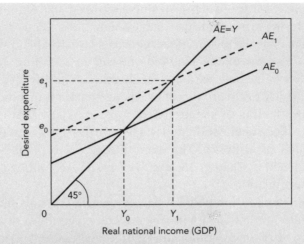

Figure 15.7. The effect of a change in government spending

A change in government spending changes GDP by shifting the *AE* line parallel to its initial position. The figure shows the effect of an increase in government spending. The initial level of aggregate expenditure is AE_0, and the equilibrium level of GDP is Y_0, with desired expenditures e_0. An increase in government spending shifts aggregate expenditure upwards to AE_1. As a result, GDP rises to Y_1, at which level desired expenditures are e_1. The increase in GDP from Y_0 to Y_1 is equal to the increase in government spending times the multiplier.

A reduction in government spending can be analysed in the same figure if we start with aggregate expenditure function AE_1 and GDP Y_1. A reduction in government spending shifts the *AE* function downwards from AE_1 to AE_0 and, as a result, equilibrium GDP falls from Y_1 to Y_0. The fall is equal to the change in government spending times the multiplier.

CHANGES IN GOVERNMENT SPENDING

Suppose the government decides to increase its road-building programme by £10 million a year.[5] Desired government spending (*G*) would rise by £10 million at every level of income, shifting *AE* upwards by the same amount. How much would equilibrium income change? This can be calculated, in our simple model, using the multiplier. Government purchases are part of autonomous expenditure, so a *change* in government purchases of ΔG will lead to a *change* in equilibrium GDP of the multiplier times ΔG. In this example, equilibrium GDP would rise by £10 million times the simple multiplier, or £18.9 million. Figure 15.7 shows the effect on GDP of an increase in government spending. It shows an upward parallel shift of the aggregate expenditure function, and a resulting increase in national income and output. The same analysis

[5] It does not matter what we assume the extra expenditure goes on. In our model it is always spent on the output of the single homogeneous industrial sector. Notice also that the value of the multiplier used in this section is hypothetical and based on the numerical example in Table 15.4.

could be applied equally to an increase in any other autonomous expenditure, such as investment or exports.

Reducing government expenditure has the opposite effect of shifting the *AE* function downwards, parallel to itself, and reducing equilibrium GDP. For example, if the government were to spend £2 million less on new roads, equilibrium GDP would fall by £2 million times the simple multiplier, or £3.78 million.

> **A change in government spending, in this model, changes the equilibrium level of GDP by the size of the spending change times the simple multiplier.**

CHANGES IN TAX RATES

If tax rates change, the relationship between disposable income and national income changes. As a result, the relationship between desired consumption expenditure and national income also changes. For any given level of national income there will be a different level of disposable income and thus a different level of consumption. Consequently, a change in tax rates will also cause a change in z, the marginal propensity to spend out of national income.

Consider a decrease in tax rates. If the government decreases its rate of income tax so that it collects 5p less out of every £1 of national income, then disposable income rises in relation to national income. Thus, consumption also rises at every level of national income. This results in a non-parallel upward shift of the *AE* curve, that is, an increase in the slope of the curve, as shown in Figure 15.8. The result of this shift will be a rise in equilibrium GDP.

A rise in taxes has the opposite effect. A rise in tax rates causes a decrease in disposable

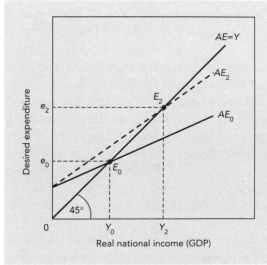

Figure 15.8. The effect of changing the tax rate

Changing the tax rate changes equilibrium GDP by changing the slope of the *AE* curve. A reduction in the tax rate pivots the *AE* curve from AE_0 to AE_2. The new curve has a steeper slope, because the lower tax rate withdraws a smaller amount of national income from the desired consumption flow. Equilibrium GDP rises from Y_0 to Y_2, because at every level of national income desired consumption, and hence aggregate expenditure, is higher. If we take AE_2 and Y_2 to be the initial equilibrium, an increase in tax rates will reduce the slope of the *AE* curve, thereby reducing equilibrium GDP, as shown by AE_0 and Y_0.

income, and hence consumption expenditure, at each level of national income. This results in a (non-parallel) downward shift of the *AE* curve and thus decreases the level of equilibrium GDP.

Tax rates and the multiplier

We have seen that the *simple multiplier* is equal to the reciprocal of one minus the marginal propensity to spend. That is, the multiplier equals $1/(1-z)$, where z is the marginal propensity to spend out of national income. The simple multiplier tells us how much equilibrium national income changes when autonomous expenditure changes by £1 and there is no change in prices.

When tax rates change, the multiplier also changes. Suppose that the *MPC* is 0.8 and the tax rate *falls* by 5p per pound of national income. This would increase the marginal propensity to spend by 4p per pound of national income. (Disposable income would rise by 5p per pound at each level of national income, and consumption would rise by the marginal propensity to consume, 0.8 times 5p, which is 4p.) The increase in the value of z, the marginal propensity to spend, would cause the multiplier to rise, making equilibrium income more responsive to changes in autonomous expenditure from any source. In our example, the multiplier has gone up from 1.89 to 1.96, ($(1-z)$ has fallen from 0.53 to 0.51).

> **The lower is the income tax rate, the larger is the simple multiplier.**

GDP may change as a result of a shift in any of the other exogenous components of expenditure—net exports, investment, and autonomous consumption. An increase in any of these would increase GDP by the shift times the multiplier, as illustrated (for the case of a government spending increase) in Figure 15.7. An increase in any exogenous expenditure shifts the *AE* line vertically upwards by the amount of the expenditure increase. The new intersection with the 45° line determines the new level of GDP, and its increase is measured relative to the original position on the horizontal axis. A reduction in any of these exogenous expenditures would shift the *AE* line downwards by the amount of the fall in spending.

Changes that would alter the slope of the *AE* line are a shift in the marginal propensity to consume, a shift in the rate of income tax, or a shift in the propensity to import. A fall in the marginal propensity to save (hence a rise in *MPC*, the marginal propensity to consume), a fall in the income tax rate, and a fall in the propensity to import all make the *AE* line steeper, and increase the multiplier, as illustrated in Figure 15.8. A rise in any of these three has the opposite effect.

BALANCED-BUDGET CHANGES

Another policy available to the government is to make a balanced-budget change by altering spending and taxes equally. Say the government increases tax rates enough to raise an extra £100 million that it then uses to purchase goods and services. Aggregate expenditure would remain unchanged if, and only if, the £100 million that the government takes from the private sector would otherwise have been spent on that sector. If so, the government's policy would reduce private expenditure by £100 million and raise its own spending by £100 million. Aggregate demand, and hence national income and employment, would remain unchanged.

But this is not the case in our model. When an extra £100 million in taxes is taken away from households, they reduce their spending on domestically produced goods by less than £100 million. If the marginal propensity to consume out of disposable income is, say, 0.75, consumption expenditure will fall by only £75 million. If the government spends the entire £100 million on domestically produced goods, aggregate expenditure will increase by £25 million. In this case the balanced-budget increase in government expenditure has an expansionary effect because it shifts the aggregate expenditure function upwards, and thus increases GDP.

> A balanced-budget increase in government expenditure will have a mild expansionary effect on GDP, and a balanced-budget decrease will have a mild contractionary effect.

The **balanced-budget multiplier** measures these effects. It is the change in income divided by the balanced-budget change in government expenditure that brought it about. Thus, if the extra £100 million of expenditure (combined with the tax increases to finance it) causes GDP to rise by £50 million, the balanced-budget multiplier is 0.5; if GDP rises by £100 million, it is 1.0.

When government expenditure is increased with no corresponding increase in tax rates, we say it is deficit-financed. With a deficit-financed increase in government expenditure, there is no increase in tax rates, and hence no consequent decrease in consumption to offset the increase in government spending. With a balanced-budget increase in expenditure, however, the offsetting increase in tax rates and decrease in consumption does occur. Thus, the balanced-budget multiplier is much lower than the multiplier that relates the change in GDP to a deficit-financed increase in government expenditure (with tax rates constant).

Lessons and limitations of the income–expenditure approach

In this and the preceding chapter, we have discussed the determination of the four categories of aggregate expenditure and seen how they simultaneously determine equilibrium national income and output (GDP). The basic approach, which is the same no matter how many categories are considered, was first presented in Chapter 14 and has been restated and extended in this chapter.

Any factor that shifts one or more of the components of desired aggregate expenditure will change equilibrium GDP, *at a given price level.*

In the following chapters we augment the income–expenditure model by allowing the price level to change, in both the short run and the long run. When prices change, real GDP will change by amounts different from those predicted by the simple multiplier. We shall see that changes in desired aggregate expenditure generally change both prices *and* real GDP. This is why the simple multiplier, derived under the assumption that prices do not change, is too simple.

However, there are three ways in which the simple income–aggregate expenditure model developed here remains useful, even when prices are incorporated. First, the simple multiplier will continue to be a valuable starting place in calculating actual changes in GDP in response to changes in autonomous expenditure. Second, no matter what the price level, the components of aggregate expenditure add up to GDP in equilibrium. Third, no matter what the price level, equilibrium requires that desired aggregate expenditure must equal output (GDP) in equilibrium, or equivalently, that injections equal leakages.

Summary

1. Government spending is part of autonomous aggregate expenditure. Taxes minus transfer payments are called net taxes and affect aggregate expenditure indirectly. Taxes reduce disposable income, whereas transfers increase disposable income. Disposable income, in turn, determines desired consumption, according to the consumption function.

2. The budget balance is defined as government revenues minus government expenditures. When the result is positive, the budget is in surplus; when it is negative, the budget is in deficit.

3. When the budget is in surplus, there is positive public saving because the government is using less national product than the amount of income that it is withdrawing from the circular flow of income and product. When the government budget is in deficit, public saving is negative.

4. Since desired imports increase as national income increases, desired net exports decrease as national income increases, other things being equal. Hence, the net export function is negatively sloped.

5. National income (GDP) is in equilibrium when desired aggregate expenditure, $C + I + G + (X - IM)$, equals national output.

6. The sum of investment and net exports is called national asset formation because investment is the increase in the domestic capital stock and net exports represent investment in foreign assets. At the equilibrium level of GDP, desired national saving, $S + T - G$, is just equal to national asset formation, $I + X - IM$.

7. Equilibrium GDP is negatively related to the amount of tax revenue that is associated with each level of national income. The size of the multiplier is negatively associated with the income tax rate.

8. Shifts in exogenous expenditures change GDP by the value of the shift times the simple multiplier.

Topics for review

- Taxes and net taxes
- The budget balance
- Public saving
- The net export function
- The marginal propensity to spend
- National asset formation
- National saving
- Calculation of the simple multiplier
- Fiscal policy and equilibrium GDP

Questions for discussion

1. Which of the following categories of expenditure are part of government spending, G, in the macro model: pensioners' cold-weather payments; state subsidies to loss-making public enterprises; the costs of the BBC world service; the salaries of the Guards Regiment at Buckingham Palace; drugs distributed to those entitled to free prescriptions; expenditure on new road building?

2. Explain why an increase of tax revenue accompanied by an equal increase in government spending will not leave GDP unchanged.

3. If there is an autonomous rise of both imports and exports of the same amount, what effect does this have on equilibrium GDP?

4. Compare and contrast the results in questions 2 and 3. What do these results say about the differences between the 'balanced-budget multiplier' and the 'balanced-trade multiplier'?

5. Explain how governments can use their fiscal policy instruments to end a recession. What practical difficulties might be encountered in implementing such a policy?

6. Calculate the multiplier for a model in which the marginal (net) tax rate is 0.2, the propensity to import is 0.28, and the marginal propensity to consume is 0.9.

CHAPTER 16

Aggregate Demand and Aggregate Supply

Aggregate demand	510		Increases in productivity	525
Shifts in the *AE* curve	510		Macroeconomic equilibrium	525
Changes in consumption	510			
Inside assets	511		**Changes in GDP and the price level**	527
Outside assets	511		Aggregate demand shocks	527
Changes in net exports	512		The multiplier when the price level	
Changes in equilibrium GDP	513		varies	529
The aggregate demand curve	514		The importance of the shape of the	
The slope of the *AD* curve	517		*SRAS* curve	532
Points off the *AD* curve	517		Aggregate supply shocks	535
Shifts in the *AD* curve	518			
The simple multiplier and the *AD* curve	519		**Summary**	537
Aggregate supply	520		**Topics for review**	538
The aggregate supply curve	521			
The slope of the short-run aggregate			**Questions for discussion**	538
supply curve	521			
Costs and output	521		**Box 16.1.** The shape of the aggregate	
Prices and output	521		demand curve	516
Real and nominal wages	522		**Box 16.2.** The Keynesian *SRAS* curve	528
Shifts in the *SRAS* curve	524		**Box 16.3.** More on the shape of the *SRAS*	
Changes in input prices	524		curve	532

I N this chapter we abandon the assumption that the price level is constant. Virtually all shocks to the economy affect *both* real GDP *and* the price level; that is, they have both real and nominal effects, at least initially. To understand these effects, we need to develop some further tools, called the *aggregate demand curve* and *aggregate supply curve*.

In the process of making the price level endogenous, we are also going to need an explicit description of the supply side of our macroeconomic model. No longer will we maintain the assumption that national output is purely demand-determined. As a result, we shall be able to analyse more realistic situations where an economy operates close to potential GDP, or full employment.

We make the transition to a variable price level in two steps. First, we study the consequences for GDP of *exogenous* changes in the price level—changes that happen for reasons that are not explained by our model of the economy as developed in Chapters 14 and 15. This gives us what we call the 'aggregate demand curve'. Then we develop a model of aggregate supply that, when combined with aggregate demand, *explains* simultaneous movements in both GDP *and* the price level.

Aggregate demand

What happens to equilibrium GDP when the price level changes for some exogenous reason, such as a rise in the price of imported TV sets? To find out, we need to understand how the change affects desired aggregate expenditure.

Shifts in the *AE* curve

There is one key result that we need to establish: a rise in the price level *shifts* the aggregate expenditure curve downward, while a fall in the price level *shifts* it upward. In other words, the price level and desired aggregate expenditure are negatively related to each other. A major part of the explanation lies with how the change in the price level affects desired consumption expenditure and desired net exports.[1]

CHANGES IN CONSUMPTION

The link between a change in the price level and changes in desired consumption is provided by wealth. This link is in two parts.

The first part is provided by the effect of changes in the price level on the wealth of the private sector. Much of the private sector's total wealth is held in the form of assets with a fixed nominal money value. One obvious example is money itself—cash and bank deposits. Other examples include many kinds of financial instruments, such as government bonds (gilts) and bills. When a bill or a bond matures, the owner is repaid a stated sum of money. What that money can buy—its real value—depends on the price level. The higher the price level, the less the given sum of money can purchase. For this reason, a rise in the domestic price level lowers the real value of all assets that are denominated in money units.

---

[1] The effect on investment expenditure is also important, and it works in the same direction as the change in consumption and net exports. This is discussed in Ch. 18.

How does this affect individuals? An individual who holds a bond has loaned money to the person (or institution) that issued it. When the real value of the asset falls the individual who holds it has her wealth reduced. However, the individual that issued the bond has his real wealth increased. This is because the face value of the bond represents less purchasing power as a result of the rise in the price level. So the individual who has to repay the bond will part with less purchasing power to do so, and so has more wealth.

> **A change in the price level affects the wealth of holders of assets denominated in money terms in exactly the opposite way to how it affects the wealth of those who issued the asset.**

Inside assets

An *inside asset* is one that is issued by someone (an individual or a firm) in the private sector and held by someone else in the private sector. It follows that for inside assets, a rise in the price level lowers the real wealth of a bond holder but raises the real wealth of the bond issuer, who will have to part with less purchasing power when the bond is redeemed. With inside assets, therefore, the wealth changes are exactly offsetting. A rise in the price level lowers the real wealth of the person who owns any asset that is denominated in money, but it raises the real wealth of the person who must redeem the asset.

Outside assets

Outside assets are those held by someone in the domestic private sector but issued by some agent outside of that sector. In practice this usually means the government or any foreign issuer. In this case the only private-sector wealth holders to experience wealth changes when the price level changes are the holders of the outside assets. There are no offsetting private-sector wealth changes for the issuers of the assets since they are not in the domestic private sector. It follows that a change in the price level does cause a change in net private wealth held in outside assets denominated in nominal money units. A rise in the price level lowers the real wealth of holders of these assets.[2]

> **A change in the price level causes no net change in the wealth of the private sector with respect to inside assets, but it does cause a change with respect to outside assets since the issuers are not in the domestic private sector.**

The second link in the chain running from changes in the price level to changes in desired consumption is provided by the relationship between wealth and consumption that we stressed in Chapter 14 (see Figure 14.1 on pages 448–9). Whenever households suffer a decrease in their wealth, they increase their saving so as to restore their wealth to the level that they desire for such purposes as retirement. At any level of income, of

---

[2] We are assuming that tax payers do not include in their wealth calculations the real value of future tax liabilities. Tax payers must pay taxes to service the national debt, and when a rise in the price level lowers its real value, it also lowers the real value of future tax liabilities by exactly the same amount. We ignore this possible offsetting change.

course, an increase in desired saving implies a reduction in desired consumption. Conversely, whenever households get an increase in their wealth they reduce their saving and consume more, causing an upward shift in the function that relates desired consumption expenditure and national income.

> A rise in the domestic price level lowers the real value of total private-sector wealth by lowering the real value of outside assets denominated in money units; this leads to a fall in desired consumption; this, in turn, implies a downward shift in the aggregate expenditure curve. A fall in the domestic price level leads to a rise in wealth and desired consumption, and thus to an upward shift in the aggregate expenditure curve, *AE*.

We have concentrated here on the direct effect of the change in wealth on desired consumption expenditure. There is also an indirect effect that operates through the interest rate. Although this effect is potentially very powerful, we cannot study it until we have studied the macroeconomic role of money and interest rates. Further discussion of this point must therefore be postponed until Chapter 18.[3]

CHANGES IN NET EXPORTS

When the domestic price level rises, domestically produced goods become more expensive relative to foreign goods. As we saw in Chapter 15, this change in relative prices causes UK consumers to reduce their purchases of domestically produced goods, which have now become relatively more expensive, and to increase their purchases of foreign goods, which have now become relatively less expensive. At the same time, consumers in other countries reduce their purchases of the now relatively expensive UK goods. We saw in Chapter 15 that these changes can be summarized as a downward shift in the net export function.

> A rise in the domestic price level shifts the net export function downward, which means a downward shift in the aggregate expenditure curve. A fall in the domestic price level shifts the net export function and the aggregate expenditure curves upward.

In simple language, if home-produced goods and services become more expensive,

---

[3] Here is a brief summary of what is involved. When the price level rises, firms and households need to cover their increased money expenses between one payday and the next. This means that they need to hold more money on average. The increased demand for money bids up the price that must be paid to borrow money (the interest rate). Firms that borrow money to build factories and to purchase equipment, and households that borrow money to buy consumer goods and housing, respond to rising interest rates by choosing to spend less on a host of items such as capital goods, housing, motor cars, and many other durable goods. This means that there is a decrease in the aggregate desired expenditure on the nation's output.

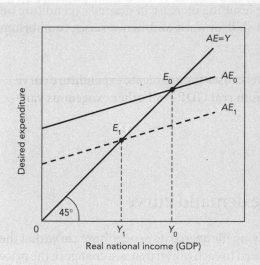

Figure 16.1. Aggregate expenditure and the price level

Changes in the price level cause the AE curve to shift and thus cause equilibrium GDP to change. At the initial price level, the AE curve is given by the solid line AE_0, and hence equilibrium GDP is Y_0. An increase in the price level reduces desired aggregate expenditure and this causes the AE curve to shift downwards to the dashed line AE_1. As a result, equilibrium GDP falls to Y_1. Starting with the dashed line, AE_1, a fall in the price level increases desired aggregate expenditure, shifting the AE curve up to AE_0 and raising equilibrium GDP to Y_0.

less of them will be bought, so total desired expenditure on UK output will fall; if home-produced goods and services become cheaper, more will be bought, and total desired expenditure on them will rise.[4]

Changes in equilibrium GDP

Because it causes downward shifts in both the net export function and the consumption function, a rise in the price level causes a downward shift in the aggregate desired expenditure curve, as shown in Figure 16.1. This figure also allows us to reconfirm what we already know from Chapter 15: when the AE curve shifts downward, the equilibrium level of GDP falls.

> **Because a rise in the domestic price level causes the aggregate expenditure curve to shift downward, it reduces equilibrium GDP—all other exogenous variables being held constant.**

Now suppose that there is a fall in the domestic price level. Because this is the opposite of the case that we have just studied, we can summarize the two key effects briefly. First, UK goods become relatively cheaper internationally, so net exports rise. Second, the purchasing power of some existing assets that are denominated in money terms

[4] This assumes that the price elasticity of demand for traded goods exceeds unity. This standard assumption in the study of international trade is discussed further in Ch. 19.

increases, so consumers spend more. The resulting increase in desired expenditure on domestic output causes the *AE* curve to shift upward and hence raises equilibrium GDP. This is also shown in Figure 16.1.

> Because a fall in the domestic price level causes the aggregate expenditure curve to shift upwards, it increases equilibrium real GDP—all other exogenous variables being held constant.

The aggregate demand curve

We now know from the behaviour underlying the aggregate expenditure curve that the price level and real GDP are negatively related to each other; that is, a change in the price level changes equilibrium GDP in the opposite direction, holding all other exogenous variables (like government spending, tax rates and investment) constant. This negative relationship can be shown in an important new construct, called the *aggregate demand curve*.

Recall that the *AE* curve relates national income (GDP) to desired expenditure for a given price level, plotting income on the horizontal axis. The **aggregate demand (*AD*) curve** relates equilibrium GDP to the price level, again plotting GDP (national income) on the horizontal axis. Because the horizontal axes of both the *AE* and the *AD* curves measure real GDP (national income), the two curves can be placed one above the other so that the level of GDP on each can be compared directly. This is shown in Figure 16.2.

Now let us see how the *AD* curve is derived. Given a value of the price level, equilibrium GDP is determined in part (i) of Figure 16.2 at the point where the *AE* curve crosses the 45° line. In part (ii) of Figure 16.2, the combination of the equilibrium level of GDP and the corresponding value of the price level is plotted, giving one point on the *AD* curve.

When the price level changes, the *AE* curve shifts, for the reasons just seen. The new position of the *AE* curve gives rise to a new equilibrium level of GDP that is associated with the new price level. This determines a second point on the *AD* curve, as shown in Figure 16.2(ii).

> Any change in the price level leads to a new *AE* curve and hence to a new level of equilibrium GDP. Each combination of equilibrium GDP and its associated price level becomes a particular point on the *AD* curve.

Note that, because the *AD* curve relates equilibrium GDP to the price level, changes in the price level that cause *shifts in* the *AE* curve cause *movements along* the *AD* curve. A movement along the *AD* curve thus traces out the response of equilibrium GDP to a change in the price level. Notice also that the only exogenous change we are permitting

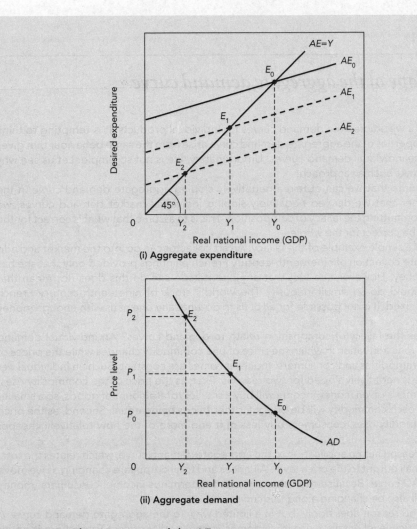

Figure 16.2. The *AD* curve and the *AE* curve

Equilibrium GDP is determined by the *AE* curve for each given price level; the level of GDP and its associated price level are then plotted to yield a point on the *AD* curve. When the price level is P_0, the *AE* curve is AE_0, and hence equilibrium GDP is Y_0, as shown in part (i). (This reproduces the initial equilibrium from Figure 16.1.) Plotting Y_0 against P_0 yields the point E_0 on the *AD* curve in part (ii).

An increase in the price level to P_1 causes AE_0 in part (i) to shift downwards to AE_1 and thus causes equilibrium national income to fall to Y_1. Plotting this new, lower level of national income, Y_1, against the higher price level, P_1, yields a second point, E_1, on the *AD* curve in part (ii). A further increase in the price level to P_2 causes the *AE* curve in part (i) to shift downwards further, to AE_2, and thus causes equilibrium GDP to fall further, to Y_2. Plotting Y_2 against P_2 yields a third point, E_2, on the *AD* curve in part (ii).

Thus, a change in the price level causes a shift in the *AE* curve in part (i) and a movement along the *AD* curve in part (ii).

BOX 16.1.

The shape of the aggregate demand curve

In Chapter 2 we studied the demand curves for individual products. It is tempting to think that the properties of the aggregate demand curve arise from the same behaviour that gives rise to those individual demand curves. Unfortunately, life is not so simple. Let us see why we cannot take such an approach.

If we assume that we can obtain a negatively sloping aggregate demand curve in the same manner that we derived negatively sloping individual market demand curves, we would be committing the fallacy of composition. This is to assume that what is correct for the parts must be correct for the whole.

Consider a simple example of the fallacy. An art collector can go into the market and add to her private collection of nineteenth-century French paintings provided only that she has enough money. However, the fact that any one person can do this does not mean that everyone could do so simultaneously. The world's stock of nineteenth-century French paintings is fixed. It is not possible for *all* of us to do what any *one* of us with enough money can do.

How does the fallacy of composition relate to demand curves? An individual demand curve describes a situation in which the price of one commodity changes while the prices of all other commodities and consumers' money incomes are constant. Such an individual demand curve is negatively sloped for two reasons. First, as the price of the commodity rises, each consumer's given money income will buy a smaller *total* amount of goods, so a smaller quantity of each commodity will be bought, other things being equal. Second, as the price of the commodity rises, consumers buy less of it and more of the now relatively cheaper substitutes.

The first reason has no application to the aggregate demand curve, which relates the total demand for all output to the price level. All prices and total output are changing as we move along the *AD* curve. Because the value of output determines income, consumers' money incomes will also be changing along this curve.

The second reason does apply, but in a limited way, to the aggregate demand curve. A rise in the price level entails a rise in *all* domestic commodity prices. Thus, there is no incentive to substitute among domestic commodities whose prices do not change relative to each other. However, it does give rise, as we saw earlier in this chapter, to some substitution between domestic and foreign goods and services. Domestic goods and services rise in price relative to imported goods and services, and the switch in expenditure will lower desired aggregate expenditure on domestic output and hence will lower equilibrium GDP.

at present is a change in the price level. All other exogenous expenditures are, therefore, held constant along a given *AD* curve.

> The aggregate demand curve shows for each price level the associated level of equilibrium GDP for which aggregate desired expenditure equals total output.

In Chapter 15, we showed that points for which aggregate desired expenditure is equal to output are equivalent to points for which injections equal leakages (or in the model of Chapter 14, for which investment equals saving). This equivalence carries through to the *AD* curve. Hence, points on the *AD* curve can be thought of as combinations of real GDP and the price level (for given values of all exogenous expenditures) for which injections equal leakages, that is, for which $I + G + X = T + S + IM$. Recall that this equation can be rearranged to make clear the further equivalence to the condition that national saving is equal to national asset formation: $S + (T - G) = I + (X - IM)$.

THE SLOPE OF THE *AD* CURVE

Figure 16.2 shows that the *AD* curve is negatively sloped.

1. A rise in the price level causes the aggregate expenditure curve, *AE*, to shift downward and hence leads to a movement upward and to the left along the *AD* curve, reflecting a fall in the equilibrium level of GDP.

2. A fall in the price level causes the aggregate expenditure curve, *AE*, to shift upward and hence leads to a movement downward and to the right along the *AD* curve, reflecting a rise in the equilibrium level of GDP.

In Chapter 2 we saw that demand curves for individual goods such as carrots and cars are negatively sloped. However, the reasons for the negative slope of the *AD* curve are different from the reasons for the negative slope of individual demand curves that are used in microeconomics; this important point is discussed further in Box 16.1.

POINTS OFF THE *AD* CURVE

The *AD* curve depicts combinations of GDP and the price level that give equilibrium between aggregate desired expenditure and actual output. These points are said to be *consistent* with expenditure decisions.

The level of GDP given by any point on the aggregate demand curve is such that, *if* that level of output is produced, aggregate desired expenditure at the *given price level* will exactly equal the output.

Points to the left of the *AD* curve show combinations of GDP and the price level that cause aggregate desired expenditure to exceed output. There is thus pressure for output to rise because firms could sell more than current output. Points to the right of the *AD* curve show combinations of GDP and the price level for which aggregate desired expenditure is less than current output. There is thus pressure for output to fall because firms will not be able to sell all of their current output. These relationships are illustrated in Figure 16.3.

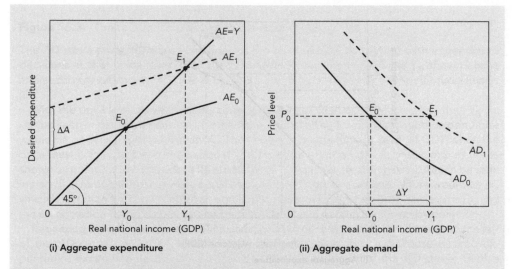

Figure 16.4. The simple multiplier and shifts in the *AD* curve.

A change in autonomous expenditure changes equilibrium GDP for any given price level, and the simple multiplier measures the resulting horizontal shift in the aggregate demand curve. The original desired expenditure curve is AE_0 in part (i). Equilibrium is at E_0, with GDP Y_0 at price level P_0. This yields point E_0 on the curve AD_0 in part (ii).

The *AE* curve in part (i) then shifts upwards from AE_0 to AE_1 because of an increase in autonomous expenditure of ΔA. Equilibrium output now rises to Y_1, with the price level still constant at P_0. Thus, the *AD* curve in part (ii) shifts to the right to point E_1, indicating the higher equilibrium GDP Y_1, associated with the same price level P_0. The magnitude of the shift, ΔY, is given by the simple multiplier.

A fall in autonomous expenditure can be analysed by shifting the *AE* curve from AE_1 to AE_0, which shifts the *AD* curve from AD_1 to AD_0 at the price level of P_0. The equilibrium value of GDP falls from Y_1 to Y_0.

that was demanded at that price level, the simple multiplier would still show the change in equilibrium GDP that would occur in response to a change in autonomous expenditure.

Aggregate supply

So far we have explained how the equilibrium level of GDP is determined *when the price level is taken as given* and how that equilibrium changes as the price level is changed exogenously. We are now ready to take an important further step: to take account of the supply decisions of producers. Once we have done this we shall be able to combine aggregate demand and supply in order to provide an *explanation* for the simultaneous determination of the price level and real GDP.

The aggregate supply curve

Aggregate supply refers to the total output of goods and services that firms wish to produce, assuming that they can sell all that they wish to sell. Aggregate supply thus depends on the decisions of firms to hire workers and buy other inputs in order to produce goods and services to sell to consumers, governments, and other firms, as well as for export.

An *aggregate supply curve* relates aggregate supply to the price level. It is necessary to define two types of such curve. The **short-run aggregate supply (*SRAS*) curve** relates the price level to the quantity that firms would like to produce and to sell *on the assumption that the prices of all factors of production (inputs) remain constant*. The **long-run aggregate supply (*LRAS*) curve,** which we will define more fully in the next chapter, relates the price level to desired sales after the economy has fully adjusted to that price level. For the remainder of this chapter we confine our attention to the *SRAS* curve.

THE SLOPE OF THE SHORT-RUN AGGREGATE SUPPLY CURVE

To study the slope of the *SRAS* curve, we need to see how costs are related to output and then how prices and outputs are related.

Costs and output
Suppose that firms wish to increase their outputs above current levels. What will this do to their costs per unit of output—often called their **unit costs?** *The short-run aggregate supply curve is drawn on the assumption that the prices of all factors of production that firms use, such as labour, remain constant.* This does not, however, mean that unit costs will be constant. As output increases, less efficient standby machinery may have to be used, and less efficient workers may have to be hired, while existing workers may have to be paid overtime rates for additional work. For these and other similar reasons unit costs will tend to rise as output rises, even when input prices are constant.[5]

Unit costs and output are positively related.

Prices and output
To consider the relationship between price and output, we need to consider firms that sell in two distinct types of markets: those in which firms are price takers and those in which firms are price setters. Some industries contain many individual firms. In these cases each one is too small to influence the market price, which is set by the overall

---

[5] Readers should recognize the law of diminishing returns (see Ch. 3) as one reason why costs rise in the short run, as firms try to squeeze more output out of a fixed stock of capital equipment.

forces of demand and supply; each firm must accept whatever price is set on the open market and adjust its output to that price. The firms are said to be *price takers* and *quantity adjusters*. When the market price changes, these firms will react by altering their production.

> **Because their unit costs rise with output, price-taking firms will produce more if price rises and will produce less if price falls.**

Many other industries, including most of those that produce manufactured products, contain few enough firms that each can influence market prices. Most such firms sell products that differ from one another, although all are similar enough to be thought of as the single commodity produced by one industry. For example, no two kinds of car are the same, but all cars are sufficiently alike so that we have no trouble talking about the car industry and the commodity 'cars'. In such cases each firm must quote a price at which it is prepared to sell each of its products; that is, the firm is a *price setter*. If the demand for the output of price-setting firms increases sufficiently to take their outputs into the range in which their unit costs rise (e.g. because overtime is worked and stand-by equipment is brought into production), these firms will not increase their outputs unless they can pass at least some of these extra costs on through higher prices. When the demand falls, they will reduce output, and competition among them will tend to cause a reduction in prices whenever their unit costs fall.

> **Price-setting firms will increase their prices when they expand output into the range in which unit costs are rising.**

This is the basic behaviour of firms in response to the changes in demand and prices when factor prices are constant, and it explains the slope of the *SRAS* curve, such as the one shown in Figure 16.5.[6]

> **The actions of both price-taking and price-setting firms cause the price level and total output to be positively associated with each other; the graphical expression of this relationship is the positively sloped, short-run aggregate supply curve.**

Real and nominal wages

Another way of looking at why the *SRAS* curve is likely to be positively sloped involves focusing on the behaviour of real wages. Let us think in terms of the behaviour of firms that are price takers, so that they are selling in competitive markets for their output. With given money prices of their inputs—we will concentrate on the labour input—and a given price at which they can sell their output, each firm will produce

---

[6] Notice that our argument here relating to two different types of firm is not really consistent with our assumption of a homogeneous production sector. However, since both price takers and price setters generate a positively sloped supply curve, for most purposes this does not cause any difficulties. Only if we wished to study price and output dynamics in more detail would these differences be important.

Figure 16.5. A short-run aggregate supply curve

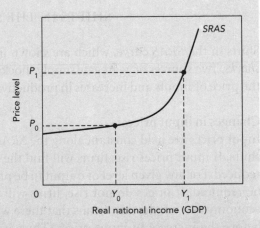

The *SRAS* curve is positively sloped. The positive slope of the *SRAS* curve shows that, with the prices of labour and other inputs given, total desired output and the price level will be positively associated. Thus, a rise in the price level from P_0 to P_1 will be associated with a rise in the quantity of total output supplied, from Y_0 to Y_1.

Notice that the slope of the *SRAS* curve is fairly flat at low levels of GDP and very steep at higher levels. Box 16.3 provides a detailed explanation of this characteristic shape. Briefly, at low levels of GDP, where there is excess capacity in the economy, output can be increased with little change in cost. As the economy approaches potential GDP (somewhere between Y_0 and Y_1 in the figure), it becomes very difficult to increase real output in response to demand changes, and increased demand will mainly generate higher prices.

its output at the level where its marginal cost is equal to its marginal revenue (and average revenue, which is also equal to the market price of its output, as shown in Chapter 4).

Now what happens if an increase in total demand for final output leads to a rise in the output price? Each firm will find that its marginal revenue curve (and average revenue) has shifted upwards. They will increase profits by expanding output up to the point where their new marginal revenue curve cuts their marginal cost curve. In the process, they will also increase employment. Thus, as the price level rises, output increases. This is the positively sloped *SRAS* curve.

Notice, however, what is happening to the real wage rate. Money wages are fixed (by assumption, in the short run) in money terms. As the price of final output goes up, workers will become worse off because their money wages will buy fewer goods. The *real wage* has fallen. This is why firms are happy to hire more labour and expand output. The relative price of their inputs has fallen in comparison with the price of their output.

Of course, this will not be the end of the story. Workers will not accept a permanent fall in their real wage. Money wages will eventually start to rise and, as they do, the relative input and output prices faced by firms will tend to return to their initial level. So firms' output and employment will return to their original level. But this is the long-run story, to which we return in Chapter 17.

As we move upwards along a given *SRAS* curve, the rise in the price level and output is associated with a fall in the real wage—that is, with a rise in the price of output relative to input prices.

SHIFTS IN THE *SRAS* CURVE

Shifts in the *SRAS* curve, which are shown in Figure 16.6, are called *aggregate supply shocks*. Two sources of aggregate supply shocks are of particular importance: changes in the price of inputs and increases in productivity.

Changes in input prices

Input prices are held constant along the *SRAS* curve, and when they change the curve shifts. If input prices rise, firms will find the profitability of their current production reduced. For any given level of output to be produced, an increase in the price level will be required. If prices do not rise, firms will react by decreasing production. For the economy as a whole, this means that there will be less output at each price level than before the increase in input prices. Thus, if input prices rise, the *SRAS* curve shifts upwards. (Notice that when a positively sloped curve shifts upward, indicating that any given quantity is associated with a higher price level, it also shifts to the left, indicating that any given price level is associated with a lower quantity.)

Similarly, a fall in input prices causes the *SRAS* curve to shift downwards (and to the right). This increase in supply means that more will be produced and offered for sale at each price level.[7]

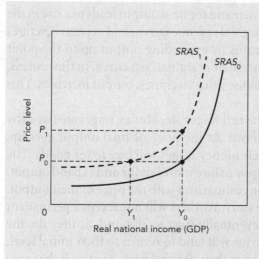

Figure 16.6. Shifts in the *SRAS* curve

A shift to the left of the *SRAS* curve reflects a decrease in supply; a shift to the right reflects an increase in supply. Starting from (P_0, Y_0) on $SRAS_0$, suppose there is an increase in input prices. At price level P_0 only Y_1 would be produced. Alternatively, to get output Y_0 would require a rise to price level P_1. The new supply curve is $SRAS_1$, which may be viewed as being above and to the left of $SRAS_0$. An increase in supply, caused, say, by a decrease in input prices, would shift the *SRAS* curve downwards and to the right, from $SRAS_1$ to $SRAS_0$.

[7] Note that, for either the *AD* or the *SRAS* curve, a shift to the right means an increase, and a shift to the left means a decrease. Upward and downward shifts, however, have different meanings for the two curves. An upward shift of the *AD* curve reflects an increase in aggregate demand, but an upward shift in the *SRAS* curve reflects a decrease in aggregate supply.

Increases in productivity

If labour productivity rises, meaning that each worker can produce more, the unit costs of production will fall as long as wage rates do not rise sufficiently to offset the productivity rise fully. Lower costs generally lead to lower prices. Competing firms cut prices in an attempt to raise their market shares, and the net result of such competition is that the fall in production costs is accompanied by a fall in prices.

Because the same output is sold at a lower price, this causes a downward shift in the *SRAS* curve. This shift is an increase in supply, as illustrated in Figure 16.6.

A rightward shift in the *SRAS* curve, brought about, for example, by an increase in productivity with no increase in input prices, means that firms will be willing to produce more output with no increase in the price level. This result has been the object of many government policies that have sought to encourage increases in productivity.

> A change in either input prices or productivity will shift the *SRAS* curve, because any given output will be supplied at a different price level than previously. An increase in input prices or a decrease in productivity shifts the *SRAS* curve to the left; an increase in productivity or a decrease in input prices shifts it to the right.

Macroeconomic equilibrium

We have now reached our objective: we are ready to see how both real GDP and the price level are simultaneously determined by the interaction of aggregate demand and aggregate supply.

The equilibrium values of national output and the price level occur at the intersection of the *AD* and *SRAS* curves, as shown by the pair Y_0 and P_0 that arise at point E_0 in Figure 16.7. We describe the combination of real GDP and price level that is on both the *AD* and the *SRAS* curves as a *macroeconomic equilibrium* and its determination in Figure 16.7 should be studied carefully at this point.

To see why the pair of points (Y_0, P_0) is the only macroeconomic equilibrium, first consider what Figure 16.7 shows would happen if the price level were below P_0. At this lower price level, the desired output of firms, as given by the *SRAS* curve, is less than desired aggregate expenditure at that level of national income (GDP). The excess desired aggregate expenditure will cause prices to be bid up, and output will increase along the *SRAS* curve. Hence, there can be no macroeconomic *equilibrium* when the price level is below P_0.

Similarly, Figure 16.7 shows that, when the price level is above P_0, the behaviour underlying the *SRAS* and *AD* curves is not consistent. In this case producers will wish to supply more than the level of output that is demanded at that price level. If firms were to produce their desired levels of output, desired expenditure would not be large enough to purchase everything that would be produced.

BOX 16.2.

The Keynesian SRAS curve

Here we consider an extreme version of the *SRAS* curve, which is horizontal over some range of GDP. It is called the Keynesian short-run aggregate supply curve, after John Maynard Keynes, who in his famous book *The General Theory of Employment, Interest and Money* (1936) pioneered the study of the behaviour of economies under conditions of high unemployment.

The behaviour that gives rise to the Keynesian *SRAS* curve can be described as follows. When real GDP is below potential GDP, individual firms are operating at less than their normal-capacity output, and they hold their prices constant at the level that would maximize profits if production were at normal capacity. They then respond to demand variations below that capacity by altering output. In other words, they will supply whatever they can sell at their existing prices as long as they are producing below their normal capacity. This means that the firms have horizontal supply curves and that their output is *demand-determined.**

Under these circumstances, the economy has a horizontal aggregate supply curve, indicating that any output up to potential output will be supplied at the going price level. The amount that is actually produced is then determined by the position of the aggregate demand curve, as shown in the figure. Thus, we say that real GDP is demand-determined. If demand rises enough so that firms are trying to squeeze more than normal output out of their plants, their costs will rise, and so will their prices. Thus, the horizontal Keynesian *SRAS* curve applies only to situations below potential GDP.

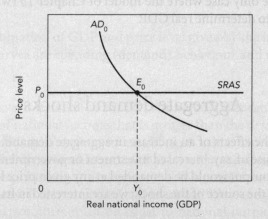

* The evidence is strong that firms, particularly in the manufacturing sector, do behave like this in the short run. One possible explanation for this is that changing prices frequently is too costly, so firms set the best possible (profit-maximizing) prices when output is at normal capacity and then do not change prices in the face of short-term fluctuations in demand.

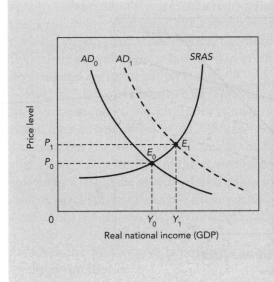

Figure 16.8. Aggregate demand shocks

Shifts in aggregate demand cause the price level and real GDP to move in the same direction. An increase in aggregate demand shifts the *AD* curve to the right—say, from AD_0 to AD_1. Macroeconomic equilibrium moves from E_0 to E_1. The price level rises from P_0 to P_1 and real GDP rises from Y_0 to Y_1, reflecting a movement along the *SRAS* curve.

A decrease in aggregate demand shifts the *AD* curve to the left—say, from AD_1 to AD_0. Equilibrium moves from E_1 to E_0. Prices fall from P_1 to P_0, and real GDP falls from Y_1 to Y_0, again reflecting a movement along the *SRAS* curve.

price level and real GDP. As is shown in the figure, following an increase in aggregate demand, both the price level and real GDP rise.

Figure 16.8 also shows that both the price level and real GDP fall as the result of a decrease in demand.

> **Aggregate demand shocks cause the price level and real GDP to change in the same direction; both rise with an increase in aggregate demand, and both fall with a decrease in aggregate demand.**

An aggregate demand shock means that there is a shift in the *AD* curve (for example, from AD_0 to AD_1 in Figure 16.8). Adjustment to the new equilibrium following an aggregate demand shock involves a movement along the *SRAS* curve (for example, from point E_0 to point E_1).

THE MULTIPLIER WHEN THE PRICE LEVEL VARIES

We saw earlier in this chapter that the simple multiplier gives the extent of the horizontal shift in the *AD* curve in response to a change in autonomous expenditure. If the price level remains constant and *if* firms are willing to supply all that is demanded at the existing price level (that is, the aggregate supply curve is horizontal), then the simple multiplier gives the increase in equilibrium GDP.

Now that we can use aggregate demand and aggregate supply curves, we can answer a more interesting question: what happens in the more usual case in which the aggregate supply curve is positively sloped? In this case a rise in GDP caused by an increase in

529

BOX 16.3.

More on the shape of the SRAS curve

The *SRAS* curve relates the price level to the quantity of output that producers are willing to sell. Notice two things about the shape of the *SRAS* curve that is reproduced in Figure 16.8: it has a positive slope, and the slope increases as output rises.

Positive slope

The most obvious feature of the *SRAS* curve is its positive slope, indicating that a higher price level is associated with a higher volume of real output, other things being equal. Because the prices of all of the inputs to production are being held constant along the *SRAS* curve, why is the curve not horizontal, indicating that firms would be willing to supply as much output as might be demanded with no increase in the price level?

The answer is that, even though *input prices* are constant, *unit costs of production* eventually rise as output increases. Thus, a higher price level for increasing output—rising short-run aggregate supply—is necessary to compensate firms for rising costs.

The preceding paragraph addresses this question 'What has to happen to the price level if national output increases, with the price of inputs remaining constant? Alternatively, one could ask 'What will happen to firms' willingness to supply output if product prices rise with no increase in input prices?' Production becomes more profitable, and since firms are interested in making profits, they will usually produce more.* Thus, when the price level of final output rises while input prices are held constant, firms are motivated to increase their outputs. This is true for the individual firm and also for firms in the aggregate. This increase in the amount produced leads to an upward slope of the *SRAS* curve.

---

curve in part (ii). The horizontal shift in the *AD* curve is measured by the simple multiplier, but this cannot be the final equilibrium position because firms are unwilling to produce enough to satisfy the extra demand at the existing price level.

Second, we take account of the rise in the price level that occurs owing to the positive slope of the *SRAS* curve. As we have seen, a rise in the price level, via its effect on net exports and on wealth, leads to a downward shift in the *AE* curve. This second shift of the *AE* curve partially counteracts the initial rise in GDP and so reduces the size of the multiplier. The second stage shows up as a downward shift of the *AE* curve in part (i) of Figure 16.9 and a movement upward and to the left along the *AD* curve in part (ii).

THE IMPORTANCE OF THE SHAPE OF THE *SRAS* CURVE

We now have seen that the shape of the *SRAS* curve has important implications for how the effects of an aggregate demand shock are divided between changes in real GDP and

Thus, whether we look at how the price level responds in the short run to increases in output or how the level of output responds to an increase in the price level with input prices being held constant, we find that the *SRAS* curve has a positive slope.

Increasing slope

A less obvious, but in many ways more important, property of a typical *SRAS* curve is that its slope *increases* as output rises. It is rather flat to the left of potential output and rather steep to the right. Why? Below potential output, firms typically have unused capacity—some plant and equipment are idle. When firms are faced with unused capacity, only a small increase in the price of their output may be needed to induce them to expand production—at least up to normal capacity.

Once output is pushed far beyond normal capacity, however, unit costs tend to rise quite rapidly. Many higher-cost expedients may have to be adopted. Standby capacity, overtime, and extra shifts may have to be used. Such expedients raise the cost of producing a unit of output. These higher-cost methods will not be used unless the selling price of the output has risen enough to cover them. The further output is expanded beyond normal capacity, the more rapidly unit costs rise, and hence the larger is the rise in price that is needed to induce firms to increase output even further.

This increasing slope is sometimes called the *first important asymmetry* in the behaviour of aggregate supply. (The second, 'sticky wages', will be discussed in the next chapter.)

---

* The analysis of Ch. 6 shows how a firm, in a perfectly competitive market, when faced with a higher output price, expands output *along* its marginal cost curve until marginal cost is once again equal to price.

changes in the price level. Figure 16.10 highlights this by considering *AD* shocks in the presence of an *SRAS* curve that exhibits three distinct ranges. Box 16.3 explores some possible reasons for such an increasing slope of the *SRAS* curve.

Over the *flat* range, from 0 to Y_0, any change in aggregate demand leads to no change in prices and, as seen earlier, a response of output equal to that predicted by the simple multiplier.

Over the *intermediate* range, along which the *SRAS* curve is positively sloped, from Y_1 to Y_4, a shift in the *AD* curve gives rise to appreciable changes in both real GDP and the price level. As we saw above, the change in the price level means that real GDP will change by less in response to a change in autonomous expenditure than it would if the price level were constant.

Over the *steep* range, for GDP above Y_4, very little more can be produced, however large the demand is. This range deals with an economy near its capacity constraints. Any change in aggregate demand leads to a sharp change in the price level and to little change in real GDP. The multiplier in this case is nearly zero.

How do we reconcile what we have just discovered with the analysis of Chapters 14

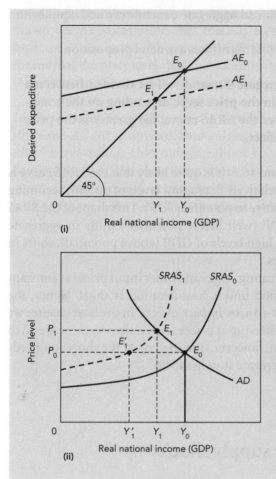

Figure 16.12. Aggregate supply shocks

Shifts in aggregate supply cause the price level and real GDP to move in opposite directions. The original equilibrium is at E_0, with GDP of Y_0 appearing in both parts of the figure. The price level is P_0 in part (ii), and at that price level the desired aggregate expenditure curve is AE_0 in part (i).

An aggregate supply shock now shifts the SRAS curve in part (ii) to $SRAS_1$. At the original price level of P_0, firms are now willing to supply only Y_1'. The fall in supply, with no corresponding fall in demand, causes a shortage that leads to a rise in the price level along $SRAS_1$. The new equilibrium is reached at E_1, where the AD curve intersects $SRAS_1$. At the new, and higher, equilibrium price level of P_1, the AE curve has fallen to AE_1, as shown in part (i), which is consistent with equilibrium GDP of Y_1.

An aggregate supply shock means that there is a shift in the SRAS curve (for example, from $SRAS_0$ to $SRAS_1$ in Figure 16.12). Adjustment to the new equilibrium following the shock involves a movement along the AD curve (for example, from E_0 to E_1).

Oil prices have provided three major examples of aggregate supply shocks in recent decades. The economy is especially responsive to changes in the market for oil, because, in addition to being used to produce energy, oil is an input into plastics and many other materials that are widely used in the economy. Massive increases in oil prices during 1973–4 and 1979–80 caused leftward shifts in the SRAS curve. GDP fell while the price level rose, causing stagflation. During the mid-1980s oil prices fell substantially. This shifted the SRAS curve to the right, increasing GDP and putting downward pressure on the price level.

We can see now how a rightward shift in the SRAS curve, which is brought about by an increase in productivity or a fall in input prices, raises real national income and lowers the price level.

Summary

1. The *AE* curve shows desired aggregate expenditure for each level of income at a particular price level. Its intersection with the 45° line determines equilibrium GDP for that price level, on the assumption that firms will produce everything that they can sell at the going price level. Equilibrium income then occurs where desired aggregate expenditure equals national output. A change in the price level leads to a *shift* in the *AE* curve: upward when the price level falls and downward when the price level rises. This leads to a new equilibrium level of GDP.

2. The *AD* curve plots the equilibrium level of GDP that corresponds to each possible price level. A change in equilibrium GDP following a change in the price level is shown by a *movement along* the *AD* curve.

3. A rise in the price level lowers exports and lowers consumers' spending (because it decreases consumers' wealth). Both of these changes lower equilibrium GDP and cause the aggregate demand curve to have a negative slope.

4. The *AD* curve shifts when any element of autonomous expenditure changes, and the simple multiplier measures the magnitude of the shift. This multiplier also measures the size of the change in real equilibrium GDP when the price level remains constant *and* firms produce everything that is demanded at that price level.

5. The short-run aggregate supply (*SRAS*) curve, drawn for given input prices, is positively sloped because unit costs rise with increasing output and because rising product prices make it profitable to increase output. An increase in productivity or a decrease in input prices shifts the curve to the right. A decrease in productivity or an increase in input prices has the opposite effect.

6. Macroeconomic equilibrium refers to equilibrium values of real GDP and the price level, as determined by the intersection of the *AD* and *SRAS* curves. Shifts in the *AD* and *SRAS* curves, called aggregate demand shocks and aggregate supply shocks, change the equilibrium values of real GDP and the price level.

7. When the *SRAS* curve is positively sloped, an aggregate demand shock causes the price level and real GDP to move in the same direction. The division of the effects between a change in output and a change in the price level depends on the shape of the *SRAS* curve. When the *SRAS* curve is flat, shifts in the *AD* curve primarily affect real GDP. When the *SRAS* curve is steep, shifts in the *AD* curve primarily affect the price level.

8. An aggregate supply shock moves equilibrium real GDP along the *AD* curve, causing

the price level and output to move in opposite directions. A leftward shift in the *SRAS* curve causes a stagflation—rising prices and falling output (GDP). A rightward shift causes an increase in real GDP and a fall in the price level. The division of the effects of a shift in *SRAS* between a change in real GDP and a change in the price level depends on the shape of the *AD* curve.

Topics for review

- Effects of a change in the price level
- Relationship between the *AE* and *AD* curves
- Negative slope of the *AD* curve
- Positive slope of the *SRAS* curve
- Macroeconomic equilibrium
- Aggregate demand shocks
- The multiplier when the price level varies
- Aggregate supply shocks
- Stagflation

Questions for discussion

1. Explain why it is that changes in the price level lead to changes in desired aggregate expenditure for each level of national income.

2. Explain what happens to the *AD* curve in response to each of the following exogenous changes: a rise in optimism leads to higher investment; the government decides to build some new schools; there is a recession in the USA; consumers become cautious about the future and decide to lower their marginal propensity to consume; GDP in France and Germany rises.

3. Show what would happen to the *SRAS* curve if: there is technical innovation in manufacturing industry; oil prices rise; workers agree to work for lower wages; there is an increase in export demand.

4. Outline how the interaction of *AD* and *SRAS* curves determines the course of GDP and the price level in response to: a rise in wage rates; an increase in investment; a reduction in government spending.

5. Explain why the change in GDP in response to an increase in export demand is smaller than suggested by the simple multiplier in Chapter 15. What happens to the size of this effect as GDP gets above its potential level?

6. Explain how it is that the shifts in *AD* set out in Question 2 are consistent with the condition that injections equal leakages.

Section 6
Macroeconomic Policy

CHAPTER 17

GDP, the Price Level, and Fiscal Policy

Induced changes in input prices	544	Cyclical fluctuations	560
Another look at potential output and the GDP gap	544		
		Fiscal policy and the business cycle	562
Input prices and the output gap	544	The basic theory of fiscal stabilization	563
Upward and downward wage pressures	546	A recessionary gap	564
		An inflationary gap	564
Actual GDP exceeds potential GDP	547	A key proposition	564
Potential GDP exceeds actual GDP	547	The paradox of thrift	564
Adjustment asymmetry	547	Limitations	566
Inflationary and recessionary gaps	549	Automatic stabilizers	567
		Limitations of discretionary fiscal policy	568
The long-run consequences of aggregate demand shocks	549	Lags	569
Expansionary shocks	549	The role of discretionary fiscal policy	569
Contractionary shocks	550	Economic policy, economic stability, and economic growth	570
Flexible wages	551		
Sticky wages	553	**Summary**	571
The asymmetry	553		
The long-run aggregate supply (*LRAS*) curve	554	**Topics for review**	573
Shape of the *LRAS* curve	554		
Long-run equilibrium	555	**Questions for discussion**	573
Real GDP in the short and long runs	557	**Box 17.1.** Anticipated demand shocks	552
Increases in aggregate demand	557	**Box 17.2.** Demand shocks and business cycles	
Increases in aggregate supply	557		559
Economic growth	559	**Box 17.3.** The paradox of thrift in action	566

EMPLOYEES of firms know that the best time to ask for a pay rise is during a boom, when the demand for labour is high. They also know that it is difficult to get significant wage increases during a recession, when high unemployment signals a low demand for labour. Every manager in industry knows that the cost of many materials tends to rise rapidly during business expansions and to fall—often dramatically—during recessions. In short, input prices change with economic conditions, and we need to allow for these effects.

It is necessary, therefore, to go beyond the assumption of fixed input prices that we used to study the initial effects of aggregate demand and aggregate supply shocks in Chapter 16. To do this we need to see what happens in a longer-term setting, when changes in GDP *induce* changes in input prices. Once we have completed this task, we can use our model of the macroeconomy to investigate the causes and consequences of business cycles and further our analysis of fiscal policy.

Induced changes in input prices

We begin by revising two key concepts that we first encountered in Chapter 14: potential output and the GDP gap.

ANOTHER LOOK AT POTENTIAL OUTPUT AND THE GDP GAP

Recall that potential output is the total output that can be produced when all productive resources—labour and capital equipment in particular—are being used at their *normal rates of utilization*. When a nation's actual output diverges from its potential output, the difference is called the GDP gap or output gap. (See Figure 14.1 on pages 448–9.)

Although growth in potential output has powerful effects from one decade to the next, its change from one year to the next is small enough to be ignored when studying the year-to-year behaviour of GDP and the price level. Therefore, in this discussion we will continue with the convention, first adopted in Chapter 14, of ignoring the small changes in potential income caused by year-to-year changes in productivity. This means that variations in the output gap are determined solely by variations in actual GDP around a given potential GDP.

Figure 17.1 shows actual GDP being determined by the intersection of the *AD* and *SRAS* curves. Potential GDP is constant, and it is shown by identical vertical lines in the two parts of the figure. In part (i), the *AD* and *SRAS* curves intersect to produce an equilibrium GDP that falls short of potential GDP. The result is called a *recessionary gap* because recessions often begin when actual output falls below potential output. In part (ii) the *AD* and *SRAS* curves intersect to produce an equilibrium GDP that exceeds potential output, resulting in an *inflationary gap*. The way in which an inflationary output gap puts upward pressure on prices will become clear in the following discussion.

INPUT PRICES AND THE OUTPUT GAP

The output gap provides a convenient measure of the pressure of demand on input prices. When GDP is high relative to potential output, demand for inputs will also be

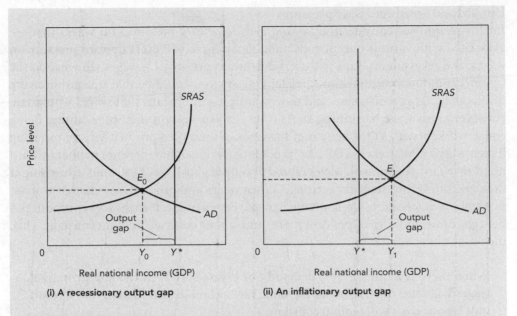

Figure 17.1. Actual GDP, potential GDP, and the output gap

The output gap is the difference between potential GDP, Y^*, and the actual GDP, Y. Potential GDP is shown by a vertical line because it refers to a given, constant level of real GDP. Actual GDP is determined by the intersection of the aggregate demand (AD) and short-run aggregate supply ($SRAS$) curves.

In part (i), the positions of the AD and $SRAS$ curves result in a recessionary gap: equilibrium is at E_0, so actual GDP is given by Y_0, which is less than potential GDP. The output gap is thus $Y^* - Y_0$. In part (ii), the positions of the AD and $SRAS$ curves result in an inflationary gap. Although potential GDP is unchanged at Y^*, equilibrium is now at E_1, so actual GDP is given by Y_1, which is greater than potential GDP. The output gap is $Y_1 - Y^*$.

high. When GDP is low relative to potential output, demand for inputs will be relatively low. This relationship is true of all inputs. The discussion that follows is simplified, however, by focusing on one key input, labour, and on its price, the wage rate.

> When there is an inflationary gap, actual output exceeds potential, and the de-
> mand for labour services will be relatively high. When there is a recessionary
> gap, actual output is below potential and the demand for labour services will be
> relatively low.

Each of these situations has implications for wages. Before turning to a detailed analysis, we first consider a benchmark for the behaviour of wages. Earlier we referred to average costs per unit of output as *unit costs*; to focus on labour costs, we now use average wage costs per unit of output, which we refer to as *unit labour costs*.

Upward and downward wage pressures

In this section we consider the *upward* and *downward* pressures on wages that are associated with various output gaps. Inflationary gaps will exert upward pressure on wages, and recessionary gaps will exert downward pressure on wages. To what do the upward and downward pressures relate? One answer would be that upward pressure means that wages would rise, and downward pressure means that wages would fall. However, most wage bargaining starts from the assumption that, other things being equal, workers will get the benefit of increases in their own productivity by receiving higher wages. Thus, when GDP is at its potential level, so that there are neither upward nor downward pressures on wages caused by output gaps, wages will tend to be rising at the same rate as productivity is rising.[1] When wages and productivity change proportionately, *unit labour costs* remain unchanged. For example, if each worker produces 4 per cent more and earns 4 per cent more, unit labour costs will remain constant. This, then, is the benchmark:

> **When there is neither excess demand nor excess supply in the labour market, wages will tend to be rising at the same rate as labour productivity; as a result, unit labour costs will remain constant.**

Note that, with unit labour costs remaining constant, there is no pressure coming from the labour market for the *SRAS* curve to shift and hence no pressure for the price level to rise or to fall. Notice also that we are assuming a correspondence between a position where GDP is at its potential level and a situation where there is no excess demand or supply in labour markets. Indeed, a key characteristic of the definition of 'potential' GDP is that it is a situation in which there is no pressure for unit labour costs to rise or fall, hence the state of the labour market and the level of potential GDP are inextricably connected.

In comparison with this benchmark, upward pressure on wages means that there is pressure for wages to rise faster than productivity is rising. Thus, unit labour costs will also be rising. For example, if money wages rise by 8 per cent while productivity rises by only 4 per cent, labour costs per unit of output will be rising by about 4 per cent. In this case, the *SRAS* curve will be shifting to the left, reflecting upward pressure on wages coming from the labour market.

Downward pressure on wages means that there is pressure for wages to rise slower than productivity is rising. When this occurs, unit labour costs will be falling. For example, if productivity rises by 4 per cent while money wages rise by only 2 per cent, labour costs per unit of output will be falling by about 2 per cent. In this case, the *SRAS*

---

[1] Ongoing inflation would also influence the normal pattern of wage changes. Wage contracts often allow for changes in prices that are expected to occur during the life of the contract. (Of course, if wages merely rise to keep pace with product prices, there is no effect on unit labour costs; labour cost per £1 worth of output will be constant.) For now we make the simplifying assumption that the price level is expected to be constant; hence, changes in money wages also are expected to be changes in real wages. The distinction between changes in money wages and real wages, and the important role played by expectations of price-level changes, will be discussed later.

curve will be shifting to the right, reflecting downward pressure on wages coming from the labour market.

Actual GDP exceeds potential GDP

Sometimes the *AD* and *SRAS* curves intersect where actual output exceeds potential, as illustrated in part (ii) of Figure 17.1. Firms are producing beyond their normal capacity output, so there is an unusually large demand for all inputs, including labour. Labour shortages will emerge in some industries and among many groups of workers, particularly skilled workers. Firms will try to bid workers away from other firms in order to maintain the high levels of output and sales made possible by the boom conditions.

As a result of these tight labour market conditions, workers will find that they have considerable bargaining power with their employers, and they will put upward pressure on wages relative to productivity. Firms, recognizing that demand for their goods is strong, will be anxious to maintain a high level of output. Thus, to prevent their workers from either striking or quitting and moving to other employers, firms will be willing to accede to some of these upward pressures.

> **The boom that is associated with an inflationary gap generates a set of conditions—high profits for firms and unusually large demand for labour—that exerts upward pressure on wages.**

Potential GDP exceeds actual GDP

Sometimes the *AD* and *SRAS* curves intersect where actual output is less than potential, as illustrated in part (i) of Figure 17.1. In this situation firms are producing below their normal capacity output, so there is an unusually low demand for all inputs, including labour. The general conditions in the market for labour will be the opposite of those that occur when actual output exceeds potential. There will be labour surpluses in some industries and among some groups of workers. Firms will have below-normal sales, and will not only resist upward pressures on wages, but also tend to offer wage increases below productivity increases, and may even seek reductions in money wages.

> **The slump that is associated with a recessionary gap generates a set of conditions —low profits for firms, unusually low demand for labour, and a desire on the part of firms to resist wage demands and even to push for wage concessions— that exerts downward pressure on wages and unit labour costs.**

Adjustment asymmetry

At this stage we encounter an important asymmetry in the economy's aggregate supply behaviour. Boom conditions, along with severe labour shortages, cause wages, unit labour costs, and the price level to rise rapidly. When there is a large excess demand for labour, wage (and price) increases often run well ahead of productivity increases. Money wages might be rising by 10 or 15 per cent, while productivity might be rising at only 2 or 3 per cent. Under such conditions, unit labour costs will be rising rapidly.

Macroeconomic policy

The experience of many developed economies suggests, however, that the downward pressures on wages during slumps often do not operate as quickly as do the upward pressures during booms. Even in quite severe recessions, when the price level is fairly stable, money wages may continue to rise, although their rate of increase tends to fall below that of productivity. For example, productivity might be rising at, say, 1.5 per cent per year while money wages are rising at 0.5 per cent. In this case, unit labour costs are falling, but only at about 1 per cent per year, so the rightward shift in the *SRAS* curve and the downward pressure on the price level are correspondingly slight. Money wages may actually fall, reducing unit wage costs even more, but the reduction in unit labour costs in times of the deepest recession has never been as fast as the increases that have occurred during several of the strongest booms.

Both upward and downward adjustments to unit labour costs do occur, but there is a difference in the speed at which they typically operate. Excess demand can

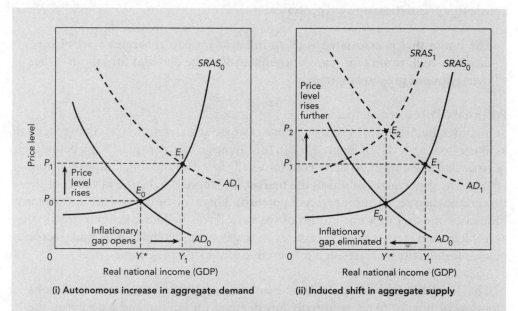

(i) Autonomous increase in aggregate demand   **(ii) Induced shift in aggregate supply**

Figure 17.2. Demand-shock inflation

A rightward shift of the *AD* curve first raises prices and output along the *SRAS* curve. It then induces a shift of the *SRAS* curve that further raises prices but lowers output along the *AD* curve. In part (i), the economy is in equilibrium at E_0, at its level of potential GDP Y^* and price level P_0. The *AD* curve then shifts to AD_1. This moves equilibrium to E_1, with GDP Y_1 and price level P_1, and opens up an inflationary gap of $Y^* - Y_1$.

In part (ii), the inflationary gap results in an increase in wages and other input costs, shifting the *SRAS* curve leftwards. As this happens, GDP falls and the price level rises along AD_1. Eventually, when the *SRAS* curve has shifted to $SRAS_1$, GDP is back to Y^* and the inflationary gap has been eliminated. However, the price level has risen to P_2.

cause unit labour costs to rise very rapidly; excess supply often causes unit labour costs to fall only slowly.[2]

Inflationary and recessionary gaps

Now it should be clear why the output gaps are named as they are. When actual GDP exceeds potential GDP, there will normally be rising unit costs, and the *SRAS* curve will be shifting upward. This, in turn, will push the price level up. Indeed, the most obvious event accompanying these conditions is likely to be a significant inflation. The larger is the excess of actual output over potential output, the greater will be the inflationary pressure. The term 'inflationary gap' emphasizes this salient feature, when output exceeds potential output.

When actual output is less than potential output, as we have seen, there will be unemployment of labour and other productive resources. Unit labour costs will fall only slowly, leading to a slow downward shift in the *SRAS* curve. Hence, the price level will be falling only slowly, so that *unemployment* will be the output gap's most obvious result. The term 'recessionary gap' emphasizes this salient feature, that high rates of unemployment occur when actual output falls short of potential output.

The induced effects of output gaps on unit labour costs and the consequent shifts in the *SRAS* curve play an important role in our analysis of the long-run consequences of aggregate demand shocks, to which we now turn.

The long-run consequences of aggregate demand shocks

We can now extend our study to cover the longer-run consequences of aggregate demand shocks, when incorporating changes in input prices. We need to examine separately the effect of aggregate demand shocks on input prices for expansionary and for contractionary shocks, since the behaviour of unit costs is not symmetrical for the two cases.

Expansionary shocks

Suppose that the economy starts with a stable price level at full employment, so actual GDP equals potential GDP, as shown by the initial equilibrium in part (i) of Figure 17.2.

Now suppose that this happy situation is disturbed by an increase in autonomous

---

[2] This is the second asymmetry in aggregate supply that we have encountered. The first refers to the variable slope of the *SRAS* curve, as discussed in Box 16.3.

expenditure, perhaps caused by a sudden boom in investment spending. Figure 17.2(i) shows the effects of this aggregate demand shock in raising both the price level and GDP. Now actual GDP exceeds potential GDP, and there is an inflationary gap.

We have seen that an inflationary gap leads wages to rise faster than productivity, which causes unit costs to rise. The *SRAS* curve shifts to the left as firms seek to pass on their increases in input costs by increasing their output prices. For this reason, the initial increases in the price level and in real GDP shown in part (i) Figure 17.2 are *not* the final effects of the demand shock. As seen in part (ii) of the figure, the upward shift of the *SRAS* curve causes a further rise in the price level, but this time the price rise is associated with a fall in output.

The cost increases (and the consequent upward shifts of the *SRAS* curve) continue until the inflationary gap has been removed, that is, until output returns to Y^*, its potential level. Only then is there no abnormal demand for labour, and only then do wages and unit costs, and hence the *SRAS* curve, stabilize.

This important expansionary demand-shock sequence can be summarized as follows:

1. Starting from full employment, a rise in aggregate demand raises the price level and raises output above its potential level as the economy expands along a given *SRAS* curve.

2. The expansion of output beyond its normal-capacity level puts pressure on input (especially labour) markets; input prices begin to increase faster than productivity, shifting the *SRAS* curve upward, such that prices are higher at every level of output.

3. The shift of the *SRAS* curve causes GDP to fall along the *AD* curve. This process continues *as long as* actual output exceeds potential output. Therefore, actual output eventually falls back to its potential level. The price level is, however, now higher than it was after the initial impact of the increased aggregate demand, but inflation will have come to a halt.

The ability to wring more output (and income) from the economy than its underlying potential output (as in point 2) is only a short-term possibility. GDP greater than Y^* sets into motion inflationary pressures that tend to push GDP back to Y^*.

There is an adjustment mechanism that eventually eliminates any inflation caused by a one-time demand shock by returning output to its potential level and thus removing the inflationary gap.

Contractionary shocks

Let us return to that fortunate economy that has full employment and stable prices. It appears again in part (i) of Figure 17.3, which is similar to part (i) of Figure 17.2.

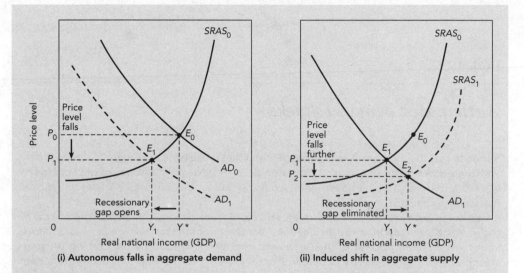

Figure 17.3. Demand-shock deflation with flexible wages

A leftward shift of the *AD* curve first lowers prices and output along the *SRAS* curve and then induces a (slow) shift of the *SRAS* curve that further lowers prices but raises output along the *AD* curve. In part (i), the economy is in equilibrium at E_0, at its level of potential GDP Y^* and price level P_0. The *AD* curve then shifts to AD_1, moving equilibrium to E_1, with GDP Y_1 and price level P_1, and opens up a recessionary gap of $Y^* - Y_1$.

Part (ii) shows the adjustment back to full employment that occurs from the supply side of the economy. The fall in wages shifts the *SRAS* curve to the right. Real GDP rises, and the price level falls further along the *AD* curve. Eventually, the *SRAS* curve reaches $SRAS_1$, with equilibrium at E_2. The price level stabilizes at P_2 when GDP returns to Y^*, eliminating the recessionary gap.

Now assume that there is a *decline* in aggregate demand, perhaps owing to a major reduction in investment expenditure, or to a fall in exports resulting from a fall in GDP overseas.

The first effects of the decline are a fall in output and some downward adjustment of prices, as shown in part (i) of the figure. As output falls, unemployment rises. The difference between potential output and actual output is the recessionary gap that is shown in the figure.

Flexible wages

What would happen if severe unemployment caused wage rates to fall rapidly relative to productivity? For example, with productivity rising by 1 per cent per year, say that money wages fell by 4 per cent. Unit costs would then *fall* by 5 per cent. Falling wage rates would lower unit costs, causing a rightward shift of the *SRAS* curve. As shown in part (ii) of Figure 17.3, the economy would move along its fixed *AD* curve, with falling prices and rising output, until full employment was restored at potential GDP, Y^*. We

BOX 17.1.

Anticipated demand shocks

Suppose that the increase in aggregate demand that is illustrated in Figure 17.2 was widely anticipated well before it occurred. For example, an approaching election might lead to the widespread belief that the government would stimulate the economy in order to improve its electoral chances.

Further, suppose that most employers and employees believe that one of the effects of the demand stimulation will be an inflation. Workers might press for wage increases to prevent the purchasing power of their earnings from being eroded by the coming price increases. Firms might believe that demand for their products was likely to rise, enabling them to raise their selling prices; they might therefore be persuaded to grant wage increases now and pass these on to consumers in terms of higher prices.

A demand stimulus that was widely expected to occur and whose inflationary effects were widely understood could lead to upward pressure on wages, even without the opening of any inflationary gap.

If this were to occur, the leftward shift in the *SRAS* curve that is depicted in part (ii) of Figure 17.2 could occur quickly, perhaps accompanying, or even preceding, the rightward shift in the *AD* curve in part (i). Given *perfect* anticipation of the effects of the demand stimulus, and *full* adjustment to it in advance, the equilibrium would go straight from E_0 to E_2. The intermediate position, E_1, with its accompanying inflationary gap (with GDP in excess of potential), would be completely bypassed.

A similar story might be told for an anticipated fall in aggregate demand. The effects of an unanticipated fall are shown in the two parts of Figure 17.3. However, if the fall is widely anticipated and its effects are generally understood, firms might reduce their wage offers, and workers might accept the decreases because they expect prices to fall as well. In this case, it is conceivable that the economy could bypass the recessionary stage and go straight to a lower price level at an unchanged level of real GDP.

This possibility that anticipated demand shocks might have no real effects on real GDP, and hence on unemployment, plays a key role in some important controversies concerning the effectiveness of government policies. We shall discuss these in Chapter 20.

In the meantime, we may notice that, for the complete absence of real effects in the transitionary period, with the only change being in the price level, everyone must have full knowledge both of the exact amount of the stimulus that the government will induce and of the new equilibrium values of the relevant prices and wages. In other words, everyone knows what the new equilibrium will be and goes directly to it. Generally, people do not have such perfect knowledge and foresight, so there is some groping towards the equilibrium, and hence some real effects, until the final equilibrium set of wages and prices is reached.

conclude that, if wages were to fall rapidly whenever there was unemployment, the resulting fall in the *SRAS* curve would restore full employment.

> Flexible wages that fell rapidly during periods of unemployment would provide an automatic adjustment mechanism that would push the economy back towards full employment whenever output fell below potential.

Box 17.1 takes up the interesting case of how the adjustment mechanism might work if the aggregate demand shock were anticipated in advance.

Sticky wages

Boom conditions, along with severe labour shortages, do cause wages to rise rapidly, shifting the *SRAS* curve upwards. However, as we noted earlier, the experience of many economies suggests that wages typically do not fall rapidly in response to recessionary gaps and their accompanying unemployment. It is sometimes said that wages are 'sticky' in a downward direction. This does not mean that wages never fall. In recession money wages often rise more slowly than productivity and some money wages even fall. But the gap between money-wage changes and productivity changes is typically quite small during recessions. This means that unit labour costs will fall only slowly. This, in turn, means that the downward shifts in the *SRAS* curve occur slowly, and the adjustment mechanism that depends on these shifts will act sluggishly.

One reason why wages rates do not adjust quickly to clear labour markets was discussed in Chapter 10. This explanation is associated with the idea of *efficiency wages*. Where labour is heterogeneous and employers face the problem of moral hazard (creating the need for monitoring and incentives), wages have an important signalling role. Employers are reluctant to lower wages, even when there is an excess supply, because of quality and motivational problems that such action may generate.

The weakness of the adjustment mechanism does not mean that slumps must always be prolonged. Rather, this weakness means that speedy recovery back to full employment must be generated mainly from the demand side. If the economy is to avoid a lengthy period of recession or stagnation, the force leading to recovery usually must be a rightward shift of the *AD* curve rather than a downward drift of the *SRAS* curve. The possibility that government *stabilization policy* might assist this adjustment is one of the more important and contentious issues in macroeconomics, one that we will return to later in this book.

> The SRAS curve shifts to the left fairly rapidly when GDP exceeds Y^*, but it shifts to the right only slowly when GDP is less than Y^*.

The asymmetry

This difference in speed of adjustment is a consequence of the important asymmetry in the behaviour of aggregate supply that was noted earlier in this chapter. This asymmetry helps to explain two key facts about our economy. First, unemployment can persist for quite long periods without causing decreases in unit costs and prices of sufficient magnitude to remove the unemployment. Second, booms, along with labour shortages and production beyond normal capacity, do not persist for long periods without causing increases in unit costs and the price level.

The long-run aggregate supply (*LRAS*) curve

The adjustment mechanism leads us to an important construct: the **long-run aggregate supply (*LRAS*) curve.** This curve relates the price level to real GDP after wage rates and all other input costs have been fully adjusted to eliminate any unemployment or overall labour shortages.[3]

Shape of the *LRAS* curve

Once all the adjustments that are required have occurred, the economy will have eliminated any excess demand or excess supply of labour. In other words, full employment will prevail, and output will necessarily be at its potential level, Y^*. It follows that the aggregate supply curve becomes a vertical line at Y^*, as shown in Figure 17.4. The *LRAS*

Figure 17.4. The long-run aggregate supply (*LRAS*) curve

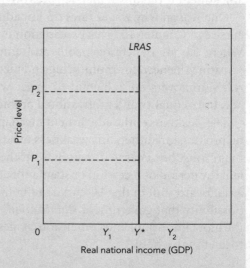

The long-run aggregate supply curve is a vertical line drawn at the level of GDP that is equal to potential GDP, Y^*. It is a vertical line because the total amount of goods that the economy produces when all factors are efficiently used at their normal rate of utilization does not vary with the price level. If the price level were to rise from P_1 to P_2 and wages and all other factor prices were to rise by the same proportion, the total desired output of firms would remain at Y^*.

If GDP were Y_1, which is less than Y^*, wages would be falling and the *SRAS* curve would be shifting rightwards; hence the economy would not be on its *LRAS* curve. If GDP were Y_2, which is greater than Y^*, wages would be rising and the *SRAS* curve would be shifting leftwards; hence, again, the economy would not be on its *LRAS* curve.

---

[3] Notice that this use of the term 'long run' is different from its meaning in microeconomics, as we pointed out in Ch. 14. Note, however, the key similarity that in the long run more adjustment is completed than in the short run.

curve is sometimes called the classical aggregate supply curve because the classical economists were concerned mainly with the behaviour of the economy in long-run equilibrium.

Notice that the vertical *LRAS* curve does not represent the same thing as the vertical portion of the *SRAS* curve (see Figure 16.10 on page 531). Over the vertical range of the *SRAS* curve, the economy is at its utmost limit of productive capacity, when no more can be squeezed out, as might occur in an all-out war effort. The vertical shape of the *LRAS* curve results from the workings of an adjustment mechanism that brings the economy back to its potential output, even though output may differ from potential for considerable periods of time. It is called the long-run aggregate supply curve because it arises as a result of adjustments that take a significant amount of time.

Along the *LRAS* curve all the prices of all outputs and all inputs have been fully adjusted to eliminate any excess demands or supplies. Proportionate changes in money wages and the price level (which, by definition, will leave real wages unaltered) will also leave equilibrium employment and total output unchanged. In the next section, we will ask what changes when we move from one point on the *LRAS* curve to another.

Long-run equilibrium

Figure 17.5 shows the equilibrium output and the price level as they are determined by the intersection of the *AD* curve and the vertical *LRAS* curve. Because the *LRAS* curve is vertical, shifts in aggregate demand change the price level but not the level of equilibrium output, as shown in part (i). By contrast, a shift in aggregate supply changes both output and the price level, as shown in part (ii). For example, a rightward shift of the *LRAS* curve increases real GDP and leads to a fall in the price level.

> With a vertical *LRAS* curve, total output is determined in the long run solely by conditions of supply, and the role of aggregate demand is simply to determine the price level.

What does change when the economy moves from one point on the LRAS curve, such as E_0 in part (i) of Figure 17.5, to another point, such as E_1? Although total output and total desired expenditure do not change, their *compositions* do change. The higher the price level, the lower is personal wealth (for a given nominal stock of assets), and hence the lower is consumption. (Recall from Chapter 14 that, the lower is wealth, the higher is saving, and hence the lower is consumption.) Also the higher the price level, the lower are exports and the higher are imports, and hence the lower are net exports.

Say the economy starts at a point on the *SRAS* curve and an increase in government expenditure then creates an inflationary gap. Money wages and the price level rise until the gap is removed. At the new long-run equilibrium, the higher level of government spending is exactly offset by lower consumption and net exports, leaving total output

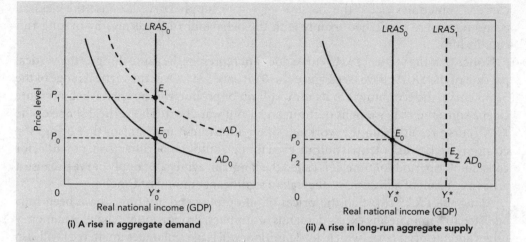

Figure 17.5. Long-run equilibrium and aggregate supply

When the *LRAS* curve is vertical, aggregate supply determines the long-run equilibrium value of GDP at Y*. Given Y*, aggregate demand determines the long run equilibrium value of the price level. In both parts of the figure, the initial long-run equilibrium is at E_0, so the price level is P_0 and GDP is Y_0^*.

In part (i), a shift in the *AD* curve from AD_0 to AD_1, with the *LRAS* curve remaining unchanged, moves the long-run equilibrium from E_0 to E_1. This raises the price level from P_0 to P_1 but leaves GDP unchanged at Y_0^* in the long run.

In part (ii), a shift in the *LRAS* curve from $LRAS_0$ to $LRAS_1$, with the aggregate demand curve remaining constant at AD_1, moves the long-run equilibrium from E_0 to E_2. This raises GDP from Y_0^* to Y_1^* but lowers the price level from P_0 to P_2.

unchanged. A similar analysis holds for an increase in investment. In the new long-run equilibrium the higher level of investment spending will be exactly offset by lower consumption spending and net exports.[4]

> The vertical *LRAS* curve shows that, given full adjustment of input prices, potential GDP, Y^*, is compatible with any price level, although its composition among consumption, investment, government, and net exports may be different at different price levels.

In Chapter 18 we will discover circumstances under which a rise in the price level has *no real effects*, so that not only are real GDP and total expenditure the same at all points on the *LRAS* curve, but the composition among C, I, G, and (X − IM) is also the same. We shall also learn, once we have added a monetary sector, that interest-rate changes resulting from *AD* shocks have important effects on the composition of expenditure.

---

[4] Once we have studied the effect of interest rates on investment, in Ch. 18, we will see that an increase in government spending can also 'crowd out' investment via increases in interest rates.

Real GDP in the short and long runs

We have now identified two distinct equilibrium conditions for the economy.

1. In the short run, the economy is in equilibrium at the level of GDP and the price level where the *SRAS* curve intersects the *AD* curve.

2. In the long run, the economy is in equilibrium at potential GDP, the position of the vertical *LRAS* curve. The price level is that at which the *AD* curve intersects the *LRAS* curve.

When the economy is in long-run equilibrium, it is also in short-run equilibrium.

The *position* of the *LRAS* curve is at Y^*, which is determined by past economic growth. Deviations of actual output from potential output—GDP gaps—are generally associated with business cycles. Changes in total real output (and hence in employment, unemployment, and living standards) may take place as a result of either growth or the business cycle.

This discussion suggests a need to distinguish three ways in which GDP can be increased. These are illustrated in Figure 17.6.

Increases in aggregate demand

As shown in part (i) of Figure 17.6, an increase in aggregate demand will yield a one-time increase in real GDP. If that increase occurs when there is a recessionary gap, it pushes GDP toward its potential level and thus short-circuits the working of the automatic adjustment mechanism that eventually would have achieved the same outcome by depressing unit costs, as discussed earlier in this chapter.

If the demand shock pushes GDP beyond its potential level, the rise in GDP above potential will only be temporary; the inflationary gap will cause wages and other costs to rise, shifting the *SRAS* curve to the left. This drives GDP back towards its potential level, so that the only lasting effect is on the price level. Box 17.2 gives a number of reasons why we might expect the effect of demand shocks on GDP to be cyclical, that is, to cause GDP to move first one way, then the other.

Increases in aggregate supply

Increases in aggregate supply will also lead to an increase in GDP. Here it is useful to distinguish between two possible kinds of increases that might occur—those that leave the *LRAS* curve unchanged and those that shift it.

Part (ii) of Figure 17.6 shows the effects of a temporary increase in aggregate supply. This will shift the *SRAS* curve to the right but will have no effect on the *LRAS* curve and, therefore, none on potential income. The shock will thus cause GDP to rise relative to potential, but the increase will eventually be reversed.

In any given year, the position of the *LRAS* curve is at potential GDP, Y^*. The 'long run' to which the *LRAS* curve refers is thus one in which the resources available to the economy do not change, but in which all markets reach equilibrium. Economic growth moves the *LRAS* curve to the right, year by year. Here, there is no 'long run' in which everything settles down, because growth is a continuing process. Rather, the movement in *LRAS* is a continuing movement in Y^*.

Determinants of the long-run shifts in potential national income, or economic growth, used to be regarded as beyond the scope of macroeconomics. However, it is clearly one of the most important factors in determining living standards. There is now a much stronger case for treating growth as an integral part of macroeconomics. This is that the forces of growth may be endogenous; that is, apparently short-term policies may have implications for long-term growth. No longer is it safe to assume that the determinants of growth are independent of the determinants of the short-term cycle, though the integration of explanations of growth and the cycle is beyond the scope of this book.

CYCLICAL FLUCTUATIONS

Figure 17.6 allows us to distinguish the causes of trend growth in potential GDP, which is the gradual rightward shifting of the *LRAS* curve, from the causes of cyclical fluctuations, which are deviations from that trend.

> Cyclical fluctuations in GDP are caused by shifts in the *AD* and *SRAS* curves that cause actual GDP to deviate temporarily from potential GDP.

These shifts, in turn, are caused by changes in a variety of factors, including interest rates, exchange rates, consumer and business confidence, and government policy.

Figure 17.7. UK real GDP and growth rate, 1885–1997

Real GDP, which measures the total production of goods and services for the whole economy over a year, has grown steadily over the last century.

(i) Long-term growth is reflected in the upward trend of real GDP. There were significant declines in real GDP after each of the world wars, there was a recession in the 1930s, and there have been three noticeable recessions since 1970. Otherwise, the trend dominates the cycle in the long term.

(ii) Real growth is measured by the annual rate of change of GDP. This has fluctuated sharply, but has generally been positive. The biggest swings in activity were the booms in output and subsequent slowdowns associated with the two world wars. However, the 1930s recession and the three recent recessions are clearly evident. Notice that the 1950s and 1960s were unusual in that, although there were cycles, annual GDP never fell.

Source: 100 Years of Economic Statistics (Economist, 1989) and *Economic Trends.*

Although the resulting deviations of actual from potential GDP are described as 'temporary,' recall from the discussion above that the automatic adjustment mechanism may work slowly enough that the deviations can persist for some time, perhaps several years.

Figure 17.7(i) shows the level of real GDP in the UK since 1885. The dominant

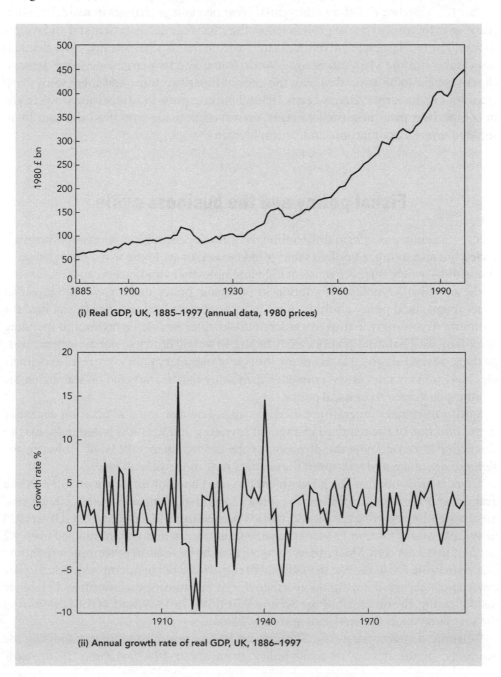

(i) Real GDP, UK, 1885–1997 (annual data, 1980 prices)

(ii) Annual growth rate of real GDP, UK, 1886–1997

feature of this graph is the continued upward trend that has led to a more than trebling of real GDP in just over 100 years. The average year-to-year increase is only about 2.25 per cent, but the cumulative effect of this slow but steady growth has been spectacular. This long-term trend reflects the steady rightward shift in the *LRAS* curve associated with sustained increases in potential GDP.

Part (ii) of Figure 17.7 shows the year-to-year percentage changes in real GDP. Fluctuations in the annual rate of growth reflect the effects of aggregate demand and supply shocks. The two largest positive shocks derive from the increases in aggregate demand associated with the First and Second World Wars. The two largest negative demand shocks appear to be associated with the ends of those two wars, and there were sharp recessions in the early 1920s and early 1930s. The three post-1970 recessions look trivial in comparison with these earlier events, even though many who lived through them suffered severe loss of income and/or employment.

Fiscal policy and the business cycle

Macroeconomics, as a formal discipline, was developed not just to explain business cycles, but also to suggest policies that could be used to avoid the worst occurrences of recessions—where there is persistent high unemployment and excess capacity. Central to the so-called Keynesian Revolution in economic policy making was the idea that government fiscal policy could be used in a counter-cyclical manner to stabilize the economy. Accordingly, in the remainder of this chapter we discuss taxing and spending as tools of fiscal stabilization policy. In Chapter 18 we will return to the subject, because, by then, we shall also be able to discuss the role of monetary policy. We refer to deliberate changes in tax rates or government expenditure that are targeted on stabilizing the economy as *discretionary* fiscal policy.

Since government expenditure increases aggregate demand and taxation decreases it, the *direction* of the required changes in spending and taxation is generally easy to determine once we know the direction of the desired change in GDP. However, the *timing*, *magnitude*, and *mixture* of the changes pose more difficult issues.

There is no doubt that the government can exert a major influence on GDP. Prime examples are the massive increases in military spending during major wars. UK government expenditure during the Second World War rose from 13.4 per cent of GDP in 1938 to 49.2 per cent of GDP in 1944. At the same time, the unemployment rate fell from 9.2 per cent to 0.3 per cent. Most observers agree that the increase in government spending helped to bring about the rise in GDP and the associated fall in unemployment. Similar experiences occurred during the rearmament of most European countries before, or just following, the outbreak of the Second World War in 1939, and in the USA during the Vietnam War in the late 1960s and early 1970s.

When used appropriately, fiscal policy can be an important tool for stabilizing the economy. In the heyday of fiscal policy, from about 1945 to about 1970, many economists were convinced that the economy could be stabilized adequately just by varying the size of the government's taxes and expenditures. That day is past. Today most economists are aware of the many limitations of fiscal policy.

The basic theory of fiscal stabilization

A reduction in tax rates or an increase in government expenditure will shift the AD curve to the right, causing an increase in GDP. An increase in tax rates or a cut in government expenditure will shift the AD curve to the left, causing a decrease in GDP.

A more detailed look at how fiscal stabilization works will provide a useful review. It will also help to show some of the complications that arise in making fiscal policy.

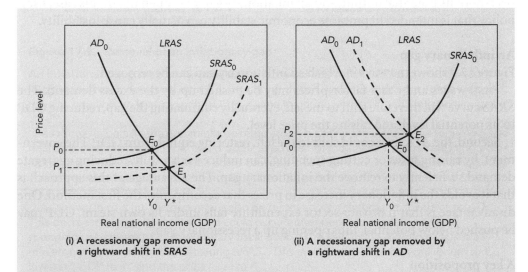

Figure 17.8. Removal of a recessionary gap

A recessionary gap may be removed by a (slow) rightward shift of the SRAS curve, a natural revival of private-sector demand, or a fiscal-policy-induced increase in aggregate demand. Initially, equilibrium is at E_0, with GDP at Y_0 and the price level at P_0. The recessionary gap is $Y^* - Y_0$.

As shown in part (i), the gap might be removed by a shift in the $SRAS$ curve to $SRAS_1$. The increase in aggregate supply could occur as a result of reductions in wage rates and other input prices. The shift in the $SRAS$ curve causes a movement down and to the right along AD_0. This movement establishes a new equilibrium at E_1, achieving potential GDP, Y^*, and lowering the price level to P_1.

As shown in part (ii), the gap might also be removed by a shift of the AD curve to AD_1. This increase in aggregate demand could occur either because of a natural revival of private-sector expenditure or because of a fiscal-policy-induced increase in expenditure. The shift in the AD curve causes a movement up and to the right along $SRAS_0$. This movement shifts the equilibrium to E_2, raising GDP to Y^* and the price level to P_2.

belief that success is based on hard work and frugality and not on prodigality; as a result, the idea often arouses great hostility.

This significance of the paradox of thrift for understanding the severity of the 1990–2 recession in the UK is discussed in Box 17.3.

Limitations

The paradox of thrift concentrates on shifts in aggregate demand caused by changes in saving (and hence spending) behaviour. Thus, it applies only in the short run, when the *AD* curve plays an important role in GDP determination. In the long run, when the economy is on its *LRAS* curve, and so aggregate demand is not important for the determination of real GDP (see Figure 17.5), the paradox of thrift does not apply. The more people and governments save, the larger the supply of funds available for investment.

The more people invest, the greater is the growth of potential GDP. Increased potential output causes the *LRAS* curve to shift to the right. These longer-term effects were discussed briefly earlier in this chapter and are illustrated in Figure 17.6. Here, we concentrate on the short-run demand effects of saving and spending.

BOX 17.3.

The paradox of thrift in action

The contemporary relevance of the paradox of thrift is clearly illustrated by the behaviour of UK personal savings in the 1988 boom and the 1990–2 recession. The figure shows the personal savings ratio (personal savings as a percentage of personal disposable income) and unemployment (as a percentage of the workforce).

In the mid-1980s the personal savings ratio fell to around 4 per cent, from a high of around 13 per cent in 1984. The fall in saving was associated with a consumer boom, a positive shift in *AD*, and an accompanying fall in unemployment. This boom peaked in 1988, which coincided with the trough in the savings ratio. A key element in the decline in the savings ratio was a sharp increase in personal borrowing—gross saving (acquisition of financial and real assets) did not fall at all. Rather, it was the increase in expenditures funded by borrowing that caused the overall savings ratio to fall. Borrowing was encouraged by low interest rates and rising house prices, so that people rushed to buy housing before prices rose even further.

In 1988 the government raised interest rates and reduced the tax incentives on mortgages. The savings ratio recovered sharply. This represented a downward shift of *AD*. In the 1990 Budget the government (in the person of the then Chancellor, John Major) introduced further incentives for saving, in the form of Tax Exempt Special Savings Accounts (TESSAs). As a result of higher saving and lower spending, the economy slid into recession and unemployment rose sharply. A fall in house prices lowered personal wealth and this lowered consumer spending still further.

This recession continued right through until the end of 1992. Other factors contributed to the severity of the 1990–2 recession, including low world demand and a high exchange rate.

The paradox of thrift is based on the short-run effects of changes in saving and investment on aggregate demand.

AUTOMATIC STABILIZERS

The government budget surplus increases as GDP increases because tax revenues rise, and some transfer payments, especially unemployment-related benefits, fall. Thus, net taxes move in the same direction as GDP. (Unless there are changes in policy, government expenditure on goods and services is generally unaffected by cyclical movements in the economy.) With pro-cyclical net tax revenues, disposable income moves in the same direction as national income (GDP) but does not move by as much. The government keeps a share of the increased GDP when it rises. When GDP falls, the fall in net taxes makes disposable income fall by less.

In Chapter 15, for example, we assumed that the net income tax rate was 10 per cent

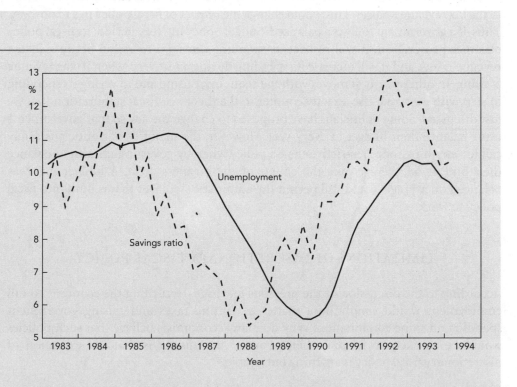

However, there is no doubt that swings in saving behaviour contributed importantly to a major boom and to the subsequent severe recession, exactly as predicted by the paradox of thrift.

of national income. This implies that a £1 rise in autonomous spending would increase disposable income by only £0.90, dampening the multiplier effect of the initial increase. Generally, the wedge that income taxes place between national income and disposable income reduces the marginal propensity to spend out of national income, thereby reducing the size of the multiplier. The lower the multiplier, the less will equilibrium GDP tend to change for a given change in autonomous expenditure. The effect is to stabilize the economy, reducing the fluctuations in GDP that are caused by changes in autonomous expenditure. Because no policies need to be changed in order to achieve this result, the properties of the government budget that cause the multiplier to be reduced are called **automatic fiscal stabilizers.**

> **Even when the government does not undertake to stabilize the economy via discretionary fiscal policy, the fact that net tax revenues rise with GDP means that there are fiscal effects that cause the budget to act as an *automatic stabilizer* for the economy.**

Of course, it is possible that a government might try to tie its spending in each period to the tax revenue it raises. This would change the impact of fiscal policy in a major way. Thus, if a government follows a balanced-budget policy in every period, its fiscal policy becomes **pro-cyclical.** It will restrict its spending during a recession because its tax revenue is low, and it will increase its spending during a recovery, when its tax revenue is rising. In other words, it moves with the economy, raising and lowering its spending in step with everyone else, exactly counter to the theory of fiscal stabilization that we just discussed. Some politicians have proposed to change the law so that governments must balance their budget in every year. However, the majority of politicians rarely call for anything more restrictive than a policy whereby governments aim to balance their budget on average over the course of the business cycle. A budget that was balanced on average would still permit the automatic stabilizer that is built into fiscal policy to work.

LIMITATIONS OF DISCRETIONARY FISCAL POLICY

According to the discussion of the previous few pages, returning the economy to full employment would simply be a matter of cutting taxes and raising government spending, in some combination. Why do many economists believe that such policies would be as likely to harm as help? Part of the answer is that the execution of discretionary fiscal policy is anything but simple.[6]

---

[6] Another part of the answer has to do with the long-term consequences of budget deficits. Governments that run deficits for long periods build up substantial debts. These debts require significant tax revenues just to pay the interest, and this limits the ability of governments to spend on other programmes. Also, depending on the exchange rate regime, international considerations may reduce (but not eliminate) fiscal policy's effectiveness as a stabilization tool.

Lags

To change fiscal policy, changes have to be made in taxes and government expenditures. In the UK, the changes must be agreed upon by the Cabinet and passed by Parliament. Major changes are normally announced only once a year, in the November Budget Statement, although 'mini-budgets' are possible if crisis measures need to be taken at other times of the year.

The political stakes in such changes are generally very large; taxes and spending are called 'bread and butter issues' precisely because they affect the economic well-being of almost everyone. Thus, even if experts agreed that the economy would be helped by, say, a tax cut, politicians may spend a good deal of time debating *whose* taxes should be cut by *how much*. The delay between the initial recognition of a recession or inflation and the enactment of legislation to change fiscal policy is called a **decision lag.** Even prior to this lag there is an inevitable delay because statistics take time to collect and process; this is known as an **information lag.**

Once policy changes are agreed upon, there is still an **execution lag,** adding time between the enactment and the implementation of the change. Furthermore, once policies are in place, it will usually take still more time for their economic consequences to be felt. Because of these lags, it is quite possible that by the time a given policy decision has any impact on the economy, circumstances will have changed such that the policy is no longer appropriate. Figure 17.10 illustrates the problems that can arise in these circumstances.

To make matters even more frustrating, tax measures that are known to be temporary are generally less effective than measures that are expected to be permanent. If consumers know that a given tax cut will only last for a year, they may recognize that the effect on their long-run consumption possibilities is small and may adjust their short-run consumption relatively little.

> **The more closely household consumption expenditure is related to life-time (or 'permanent') income rather than to current income, the smaller will be the effects on current consumption of tax changes that are known to be of short duration.**

The role of discretionary fiscal policy

All of the above-mentioned difficulties suggest that attempts to use discretionary fiscal policy to fine-tune the economy are fraught with difficulties. **Fine-tuning** refers to the use of fiscal and monetary policy to offset virtually all fluctuations in private-sector spending and so hold GDP at, or very near, its potential level at all times. However, neither economic nor political science has yet advanced far enough to allow policymakers to undo the consequences of every aggregate demand shock. On the other hand, many economists would still argue that when a recessionary gap is large enough and persists for long enough, gross-tuning may be appropriate. **Gross-tuning** refers to the occasional use of fiscal and monetary policy to remove large and persistent GDP gaps. Advocates of gross-tuning hold that fiscal policy can and should be used to help the

Figure 17.10. Effects of fiscal policies that are not reversed

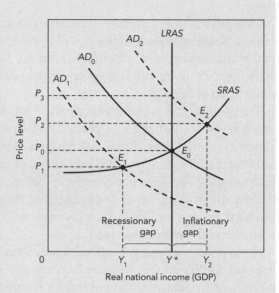

Fiscal policies that are initially appropriate may become inappropriate when private expenditure shifts. The normal level of the aggregate demand function is assumed to be AD_0, leaving GDP normally at $Y*$ and the price level at P_0. Suppose a slump in private investment shifts aggregate demand to AD_1, lowering GDP to Y_1 and causing a recessionary gap of $Y* - Y_1$.

The government now introduces fiscal expansion to restore aggregate demand to AD_0 and GDP to $Y*$. Suppose that private investment then recovers, raising aggregate demand to AD_2. If fiscal policy can be quickly reversed, aggregate demand can be returned to AD_0 and GDP stabilized at $Y*$. If the policy is not quickly reversed, equilibrium will be at E_2 and an inflationary gap, $Y* - Y_2$, will open up. This gap will cause wages to rise and thus will shift the SRAS curve leftward and eventually restore $Y*$ at price level P_3.

Now suppose that, starting from equilibrium E_0, a persistent investment boom takes AD_0 to AD_2. In order to stop the price level from rising in the face of the newly opened inflationary gap, the government introduces fiscal restraint, thereby shifting aggregate demand back to AD_0. Further assume, however, that the investment boom then comes to a halt, so that the aggregate demand curve shifts downward to AD_1. Unless the fiscal policy can be rapidly reversed, a recessionary gap will open up and equilibrium GDP will fall to Y_1.

economy return to full employment when a GDP gap is large and has persisted for a long time. Other economists believe that fiscal policy should not be used for economic stabilization under any circumstances. Rather, they would argue, tax and spending behaviour should be the outcome of public choices regarding the long-term size and financing of the public sector and should not be altered for short-term considerations.

Economic policy, economic stability, and economic growth

The desirability of using fiscal policy to stabilize the economy depends a great deal on the speed with which the adjustment mechanism returns the economy to potential GDP. If the adjustment mechanism works quickly, there is no role for discretionary fiscal policy. If the adjustment mechanism works slowly, there may well be a role for policies that can be used to shift aggregate demand. Fiscal policy is one such policy.

Monetary policy, which we take up in the next chapter, is another. Only when we have completed our study of the way in which money fits into the overall macroeconomy can we fully outline the choices available to governments wishing to stabilize their economies.

Stabilization policy will generally have consequences for economic growth—for the movement of the *LRAS* curve over time. Given that an economy is at or near potential GDP, the more expansive is its fiscal policy, the lower will be national saving and national asset formation. Thus, the lower will be economic growth. Of course, if the economy would otherwise stay in recession for a period of years, the gain in output in the near term could easily outweigh the longer-term consequences of a smaller stock of assets at full employment. (After all, and this was part of Keynes's message, the state of the world at full employment is not very interesting to members of a society who are a long way from it.)

Business cycles, and the effects of economic policy on them, are among the key subjects of this book. With the tools that we have developed thus far, we have been able to begin to see how they fit together. Once we add a better understanding of money and monetary policy we will be able to complete the story of stabilization policy.

Summary

1. In this chapter potential GDP is treated as given and is represented by a vertical line at Y^*. The output gap is equal to the horizontal distance between Y^* and the actual level of GDP, as determined by the intersection of the *AD* and *SRAS* curves.

2. An inflationary gap means that actual GDP, Y, is greater than Y^*, and hence demand in the labour market is relatively high. As a result, wages rise faster than productivity, causing unit costs to rise. The *SRAS* curve shifts leftwards, and the price level rises.

3. A recessionary gap means that Y is less than Y^*, and hence demand in the labour market is relatively low. Although there is some resulting tendency for wages to fall relative to productivity, asymmetrical behaviour means that the strength of this force will be much weaker than that indicated in point 2 above. Unit costs will fall only slowly, so the output gap will shrink only slowly.

4. An expansionary demand shock creates the inflationary gap discussed in point 2. It causes wages to rise faster than productivity. Unit costs rise, shifting the *SRAS* curve to the left and resulting in a higher level of prices, with output eventually falling back to its potential level.

5. A contractionary demand shock works in the opposite direction by creating the

5. Is a high level of saving a good thing for the economy?

6. Explain what is meant by 'automatic stabilizers'. How do these help to reduce the amplitude of the business cycle?

CHAPTER 18

Money and Monetary Policy

Financial assets	576	The *IS* curve	598
The rate of interest and present value	576	The *LM* curve	599
A single payment one year hence	576	*IS/LM* and aggregate demand	600
A perpetuity	577		
Present value and market price	577	**Aggregate demand, the price level, and**	
The rate of interest and market price	578	**GDP**	602
		The slope of the *AD* curve revisited	603
Supply of money and the demand for		The effect of a monetary policy change	
money	579	in the short run	603
The supply of money	579	The effect of a monetary policy change	
The demand for money	580	in the long run	605
The transactions motive	582	The effect of a change in fiscal policy in	
The precautionary motive	583	the short run	607
The speculative motive	584	The effect of a change in fiscal policy in	
Real and nominal money balances	585	the long run	609
Total demand for money	588		
		Summary	610
Monetary forces and GDP	588		
Monetary equilibrium and aggregate demand	588	**Topics for review**	612
Determination of the interest rate	588		
Interest rates as a policy instrument	590	**Questions for discussion**	612
The transmission mechanism	592		
From monetary disturbances to		**Box 18.1.** Definitions of UK monetary	
changes in the interest rate	592	aggregates	580
From changes in the interest rate to		**Box 18.2.** The quantity theory of money	586
shifts in aggregate expenditure	592	**Box 18.3.** The transmission mechanism in	
From shifts in aggregate expenditure		an open economy	596
to shifts in aggregate demand	593		
An alternative derivation of the *AD* curve:		**Appendix. Schools of thought in**	
IS/LM	594	**macroeconomics**	613

I N this chapter we continue the task of building up our understanding of the determinants of GDP and the price level. In particular, we now focus on how monetary forces affect economic activity. We approach this issue via a number of separate steps. First, we discuss the factors that influence the demand and supply of money balances in the economy. Second, we ask how disequilibrium (excess demand or supply) in the monetary sector spills over into real activity. Having resolved that question, we shall then be able to accomplish the final task of integrating money and monetary policy into the aggregate demand and aggregate supply framework that we built up in Chapters 14–17. We start with some background material on financial assets and interest rates.

Financial assets

At any given moment, people have a stock of wealth that they hold in many forms. Some of it may be money in the bank or building society; some may be cash in hand or under the mattress; some may be in shares; and some of it may be in property, such as a house.

To simplify our discussion, we will group wealth into just two categories, which we will call *money* and *bonds*. By 'money' we mean the assets that serve as a medium of exchange, that is, paper money, coins, and deposits on which cheques may be drawn.[1] By 'bonds' we mean all other forms of financial wealth; these include interest-earning financial assets *plus* claims on real capital.[2]

Money and bonds have different characteristics as assets. Bonds are risky because their price can rise or fall. The price of bonds is related to market interest rates, so our first task is to understand this relationship.

THE RATE OF INTEREST AND PRESENT VALUE

A bond is a financial asset that promises to make one or more interest payments and to repay a capital sum at a specified date in the future. The **present value** (*PV*) of a bond, or of any asset, refers to the value now of the future payment or payments to which the asset represents a claim. The concept of present value was discussed in more detail in Chapter 11 on pages 349–52.

Present value depends on the rate of interest, because when we calculate present value the interest rate is used to *discount* the future payments. This relationship between the rate of interest and present value can be seen by considering two extreme examples.

A single payment one year hence
We start with the simplest case. How much would someone be prepared to pay *now* to purchase a bond that will produce a single payment of £100 in one year's time?

---

[1] The precise definition of money is problematic and has changed frequently in the UK as a result of financial innovation. However, our analysis can be applied to any of the standard definitions of money. We do not have space in this book to discuss institutional detail, though the main definitions of money in current use in the UK are discussed in Box 18.1 on p. 580. The principles we are discussing can be applied, *mutatis mutandis*, to most economies, so long as they have an independent currency.

[2] This simplification can take us quite a long way and is necessary in order to keep our model simple.

Suppose that the interest rate is 5 per cent, which means that £1.00 invested today will be worth £1.05 in one year's time. Now ask how much someone would have to lend out in order to have £100 a year from now. If we use PV to stand for this unknown amount, we can write $PV(1.05)$ (which means PV *multiplied by* 1.05) = £100. Thus, PV = £100/1.05 = £95.24.[3] This tells us that the present value of £100 receivable in one year's time is £95.24; anyone who lends out £95.24 for one year at 5 per cent interest will get back the £95.24 plus £4.76 in interest, which makes £100.

What if the interest rate had been 7 per cent? At that interest rate, the present value of the £100 receivable in one year's time would be £100/1.07 = £93.46, which is less than the present value when the interest rate was 5 per cent.

A perpetuity

Now consider another extreme case—a perpetuity that promises to pay £100 per year to its holder *for ever*. The *present value* of the perpetuity depends on how much £100 per year is worth, and this again depends on the rate of interest.

A bond that will produce a stream of income of £100 per year forever is worth £1,000 at 10 per cent interest because £1,000 invested at 10 per cent per year will yield £100 interest per year forever. However, the same bond is worth £2,000 when the interest rate is 5 per cent per year, because it takes £2,000 invested at 5 per cent per year to yield £100 interest per year. The lower the rate of interest obtainable on the market, the more valuable is a bond paying a fixed amount of interest.

Similar relations apply to bonds that are more complicated than single payments but are not perpetuities. Although the calculation of present value is more complicated, the same negative relationship between the interest rate and present value still holds.

> **The present value of any asset that yields a given stream of money over time is negatively related to the interest rate.**

PRESENT VALUE AND MARKET PRICE

Present value is important because it establishes the market price for an asset.

> **The present value of an asset is the amount that someone would be willing to pay now to secure the right to the future stream of payments conferred by ownership of the asset.**

To see this, return to our example of a bond that promises to pay £100 one year hence. When the interest rate is 5 per cent, the present value is £95.24. To see why this is the maximum that anyone would pay for this bond, suppose that some sellers offer to sell

---

[3] Notice that in this type of formula the interest rate is expressed as a decimal fraction; thus, for example, 5 per cent is expressed as 0.05, so $(1 + i)$ equals 1.05.

the bond at some other price, say, £98. If, instead of paying this amount for the bond, a potential buyer lends her £98 out at 5 per cent interest, she would have at the end of one year more than the £100 that the bond will produce: at 5 per cent interest, £98 yields £4.90 in interest, which when added to the principal makes £102.90. Clearly, no well-informed individual would pay £98—or by the same reasoning any sum in excess of £95.24—for the bond.

Now suppose that the bond is offered for sale at a price less than £95.24, say, £90. A potential buyer could borrow £90 to buy the bond and would pay £4.50 in interest on the loan. At the end of the year, the bond yields £100. When this is used to repay the £90 loan and the £4.50 in interest, £5.50 is left as profit. Clearly, it would be worthwhile for someone to buy the bond at the price of £90 or, by the same argument, at any price less than £95.24.

This discussion should make clear that the present value of an asset determines its market price. If the market price of any asset is greater than the present value of the income stream that it produces, no one will want to buy it, and the market price will fall. If the market value is below its present value, there will be a rush to buy it, and the market price will rise. These facts lead to the following conclusion:

> In a free market, the equilibrium price of any asset will be the present value of the income stream that it produces.

THE RATE OF INTEREST AND MARKET PRICE

The discussion above leads us to three important propositions. The first two stress the negative relationship between interest rates and asset prices:

1. **If the rate of interest falls, the value of an asset producing a given income stream will rise.**

2. **A rise in the market price of an asset producing a given income stream is equivalent to a decrease in the rate of interest earned by the asset.**

Thus, a promise to pay £100 one year from now is worth £92.59 when the interest rate is 8 per cent and only £89.29 when the interest rate is 12 per cent: £92.59 at 8 per cent interest (£92.59 × 1.08) and £89.29 at 12 per cent interest (£89.29 × 1.12) are both worth £100 in one year's time.

The third proposition focuses on the term to maturity of the bond:

3. **The sooner the maturity date of a bond, the less the bond's value will change with a change in the rate of interest.**

To see this, consider an extreme case. The present value of a bond that is redeemable for £1,000 in one week's time will be very close to £1,000 no matter what the interest rate is. Thus, its value will not change much, even if the rate of interest leaps from 5 per cent to 10 per cent during that week. Note that the interest-earning assets included in our definition of money are so short-term that their values remain unchanged when the interest rate changes.

As a second example, consider two assets, one that promises to pay £100 next year and one that promises to pay £100 in ten years. A rise in the interest rate from 8 to 12 per cent will lower the value of £100 payable in one year's time by 3.6 per cent, but it will lower the value of £100 payable in ten years' time by 37.9 per cent.[4]

We now use what we have learned about the relationship between bond prices and interest rates to understand the factors affecting the choice between money and bonds.

Supply of money and the demand for money

The supply of money

The money supply is a *stock* (it is so many billions of pounds), not a *flow* of so many pounds per unit of time. There are several different ways of measuring the money stock: the main categories currently used in the UK are set out in Box 18.1. For simplicity of analysis, we do not enter into debates about which measure of money is the 'best'. Rather, we proceed as if there were a single accepted definition of money, which can be thought of as M2, though nothing much changes if M4 is chosen. For the purposes of incorporating money into our macro model, it is convenient to assume that the monetary authorities control the money stock directly, or, in other words, that the money stock is exogenously fixed by policymakers.[5]

Once we have the necessary analytic tools we shall see that it is easy to switch the analysis to situations in which the authorities are setting interest rates rather than the money stock. In any event the demand-for-money relationship is the one that has the most important effects on the behaviour of the economy. Our analysis therefore concentrates on the factors influencing money demand.

---

[4] The example assumes annual compounding. The first case is calculated from the numbers of the previous example: $(92.58 - 89.29)/92.58$. The ten-year case uses the formula

$$\text{Present value} = \text{principal}/(1 + i)^n,$$

which gives £46.30 at 8 per cent and £28.75 at 12 per cent. The percentage fall in value is thus $(46.30 - 28.75)/46.30 = 0.379$, or 37.9 per cent.

[5] This is not correct for two reasons. First, the monetary authorities could, if they wished to operate this way, control the monetary base, M0. However, in most countries, including the UK, they do not choose to do so. Rather, the authorities implement monetary policy by setting a key short-term interest rate, and then providing as much base money, M0, as the markets wish to hold at that interest rate. Thus, in practice M0 is demand-determined. Second, even if the authorities did set the stock of M0, the interaction of the banking system and the rest of the economy would then determine all broader monetary aggregates, such as M2 and M4. So in all events, monetary aggregates broader than M0 would be demand-determined.

BOX 18.1.

Definitions of UK monetary aggregates

The way in which 'money' is defined has changed a great deal over time and is likely to change again in future. In 1750, money would almost certainly have been defined as the stock of gold in circulation (specie). By 1850, it would probably have been defined as gold in the hands of the non-bank public plus bank notes in circulation. In 1950, the most likely definition would have been currency held by the public plus current account bank deposits. In 1997, money is usually defined to include currency held by the public plus all deposits (current and savings) in banks and building societies. By 2050, who knows?

There have been several changes in the definitions of money even in the last few years. Many of these are the result of financial innovations of the 1980s. We cannot expect this to be the end of the story. Money measures such as M1 and £M3 (sterling M3), which were at the centre of monetary policy debates into the first half of the 1980s, have disappeared. These had to be dropped when, in 1989, the Abbey National Building Society converted into a bank. Thereafter, any monetary aggregate that contained bank deposits but not building society deposits became distorted. M0 contains neither; M2 and M4 contain both.

The money measures current in 1997 were as follows:

- **M0** (the monetary base). This measure refers to all the currency in circulation outside the Bank of England plus bankers' deposits with the Bank of England.

- **M2.** This measure encompasses UK non-bank and non-building society holdings of notes and coins, plus sterling retail deposits with UK banks and building societies. ('Retail' effectively means 'held by individuals rather than companies'.) The definition of M2 was changed in 1992 to make it a subset of M4.

- **M4.** M4 is made up of M2 plus all other private-sector sterling interest-bearing deposits at bank and building societies, plus sterling certificates of deposit (and other paper issued by banks and building societies of not more than five years' original maturity). (£M3 was effectively M4 minus building society deposits.)

The demand for money

The amount of wealth that everyone in the economy wishes to hold in the form of money balances is called the **demand for money.** Because in our theory people are choosing how to divide their given stock of wealth between money and bonds, it follows that if we know the demand for money, we also know the demand for bonds. With a *given level of wealth*, a rise in the demand for money necessarily implies a fall in the demand for bonds; if people wish to hold £1 billion more money, they must wish to hold £1 billion less of bonds. It also follows that if households are in equilibrium with respect to their money holdings, they are in equilibrium with respect to their bond holdings.

When we say that on 30 September 1996 the quantity of money demanded was £454 billion (the approximate value of M2 at that time), we mean that on that date the public

The table presents data for these monetary aggregates for October 1996.

UK money supply, October 1996 (£ million, not seasonally adjusted)

Notes and coin outside Bank of England	24,302
Bankers' deposits at Bank of England	139
M0	**24,441**
Notes and coin with public (*part of* M0)	19,767
Non-interest-bearing bank deposits	35,202
Other retail bank deposits	192,486
Building society retail shares and deposits	206,171
M2	**453,626**
Wholesale bank deposits + CDs	202,156
Wholesale building society deposits + CDs	14,651
M4	**670,432**

Note: M0 is not a subset of M2 and M4 because it includes notes and coin held by banks, which are excluded from M2 and M4. If notes and coin held by banks were included in the latter, there would be double counting because notes and coins held by banks are assets. The deposits (liabilities) that are counterparts to those assets are included in M2 and M4 already.

Source: Financial Statistics.

wished to hold money balances that totalled £454 billion. But why do firms and individuals wish to hold money balances at all? There is a cost to holding any money balance. The money could have been used to purchase bonds, which earn higher interest than does money.[6] For the present, we assume no ongoing inflation, so there is no difference between real and nominal interest rates.

[6] Many of the bank and building society deposits that are included in 'money' now yield interest. This complicates, but does not fundamentally alter, the analysis of the demand for money. In particular, it means that the opportunity cost of holding those interest-bearing components of money is not the *level* of interest rates paid on bonds but the *difference* between that rate and the rate paid on money. Because the interest earned on deposits tends to fluctuate less than rates on marketable securities, the difference tends to move with the level of interest rates in the economy, rising when rates rise and falling when rates fall. For simplicity, we talk of the demand for money responding to the *level* of interest rates, although in reality it is the *difference* that is the opportunity cost of money.

The opportunity cost of holding any money balance is the extra interest that could have been earned if the money had been used instead to purchase bonds.

Clearly, money will be held only when it provides services that are valued at least as highly as the opportunity cost of holding it. Three important services that are provided by money balances give rise to three motives for holding money: the transactions, precautionary, and speculative motives. We examine each of these in detail.

THE TRANSACTIONS MOTIVE

Most transactions require money. Money passes from consumers to firms to pay for the goods and services produced by firms; money passes from firms to employees to pay for the labour services supplied by workers to firms. Money balances that are held to finance such flows are called **transactions balances.**

In an imaginary world in which the receipts and disbursements of consumers and firms were perfectly synchronized, it would be unnecessary to hold transactions balances. If every time a consumer spent £10 she received £10 as part payment of her wages, no transactions balances would be needed. In the real world, however, receipts and payments are not perfectly synchronized.

Consider the balances that are held because of wage payments. Suppose, for purposes of illustration, that firms pay wages every Friday and that employees spend all their wages on the purchase of goods and services, with the expenditure spread out evenly over the week. Thus, on Friday morning firms must hold balances equal to the weekly wage bill; on Friday afternoon the employees will hold these balances.

Over the week, workers' balances will be drawn down as a result of purchasing goods and services. Over the same period, the balances held by firms will build up as a result of selling goods and services until, on the following Friday morning, firms will again have amassed balances equal to the wage bill that must be met on that day.

The transactions motive arises because payments and receipts are not synchronized.

What determines the size of the transactions balances to be held? It is clear that in our example total transactions balances vary with the value of the wage bill. If the wage bill doubles for any reason, the transactions balances held by firms and households for this purpose will also double, on average. As it is with wages, so it is with all other transactions: the size of the balances held is positively related to the value of the transactions. It is the average value of money balances that people choose to hold over a particular period that is relevant for macroeconomics, but we need to know how money demand relates to GDP rather than to total transactions. In fact, the value of all transactions exceeds the value of the economy's final output. When the miller buys wheat from the farmer and when the baker buys flour from the miller, both are transactions against which money balances must be held, although only the value added at each stage is part of GDP.

Generally, there will be a stable, positive relationship between transactions and GDP. A rise in GDP also leads to a rise in the total value of all transactions and hence to an associated rise in the demand for transactions balances. This allows us to relate transactions balances to GDP.

The larger the value of GDP, the larger is the value of transactions balances that will be held.

THE PRECAUTIONARY MOTIVE

Many expenditures arise unexpectedly, such as when your car breaks down, or when you have to make an unplanned journey to visit a sick relative. As a precaution against cash crises, when receipts are abnormally low or disbursements are abnormally high, firms and individuals carry money balances. **Precautionary balances** provide a cushion against uncertainty about the timing of cash flows. The larger such balances are, the greater is the protection against running out of money because of temporary fluctuations in cash flows.

The seriousness of the risk of a cash crisis depends on the penalties that are inflicted for being caught without sufficient money balances. A firm is unlikely to be pushed into insolvency, but it may incur considerable costs if it is forced to borrow money at high interest rates in order to meet a temporary cash crisis. Indeed, most firms have an over-draft facility with their bank precisely for this reason; this gives them the right to borrow money quickly when they are short of cash. (Of course, they still have to pay interest on what they borrow.)

The precautionary motive arises because individuals and firms are uncertain about the degree to which payments and receipts will be synchronized.

The protection provided by a given quantity of precautionary balances depends on the volume of payments and receipts. A £100 precautionary balance provides a large cushion for a person whose volume of payments per month is £800 and a small cushion for a firm whose monthly volume is £250,000. Fluctuations of the sort that create the need for precautionary balances tend to vary directly with the size of the firm's cash flow. To provide the same degree of protection as the value of transactions rises, more money is necessary.[7]

---

[7] Institutional arrangements affect precautionary demands. In the past, for example, a traveller would have carried a substantial precautionary balance in cash, but today a credit card covers most unforeseen expenses that may arise during travelling.

The precautionary motive, like the transactions motive, causes the demand for money to vary positively with the money value of GDP.

For most purposes the transactions and precautionary motives can be merged, since they both involve desired money holdings being positively related to GDP (national income and output). Indeed, they both involve money being held in relation to planned or potential transactions.

THE SPECULATIVE MOTIVE

Money can be held for its characteristics as an asset. Firms and individuals may hold some money in order to provide a hedge against the uncertainty inherent in fluctuating prices of other financial assets. Money balances held for this purpose are called **speculative balances.** This motive was first analysed by Keynes, and the classic modern analysis was developed by Professor James Tobin, the 1981 Nobel Laureate in economics.

Any holder of money balances forgoes the extra interest income that could be earned if bonds were held instead.[8] However, market interest rates fluctuate, and so do the market prices of existing bonds (their present values depend on the interest rate). Because their prices fluctuate, bonds are a risky asset. Many individuals and firms do not like risk; they are said to be *risk-averse*.[9]

In choosing between holding money or holding bonds, wealth holders must balance the extra interest income that they could earn by holding bonds against the risk that bonds carry. At one extreme, if individuals hold all their wealth in the form of bonds, they earn extra interest on their entire wealth, but they also expose their entire wealth to the risk of changes in the price of bonds. At the other extreme, if people hold all their wealth in the form of money, they earn less interest income, but they do not face the risk of unexpected changes in the price of bonds. Wealth holders usually do not take either extreme position. They hold part of their wealth as money and part of it as bonds; that is, they *diversify* their holdings. The fact that some proportion of wealth is held in money and some in bonds suggests that, as wealth rises, so will desired money holding.

The speculative motive implies that the demand for money varies positively with wealth.

Although one individual's wealth may rise or fall rapidly, the total wealth of a society changes only slowly. For the analysis of short-term fluctuations in GDP, the effects of

---

[8] In Keynes's speculative motive money can be expected to have a higher return than bonds. This arises if interest rates are low and *expected to rise*, so bond prices are expected to fall, creating a capital loss on bond holdings. In our analysis, which follows Tobin, interest rates are just as likely to rise or fall, irrespective of their current level. However, it is Keynes's analysis that gives rise to the term 'speculative' since it involves interest rate expectations.

[9] A person is risk-averse when he or she prefers a certain sum of money to an uncertain outcome for which the expected value is the same.

changes in wealth are fairly small, and we ignore them for the present. Over the long term, however, variations in wealth can have a major effect on the demand for money.

Wealth that is held in cash or deposits earns less interest than could be earned by holding bonds; hence, the reduction in risk involved in holding money carries an opportunity cost in terms of forgone interest earnings. The speculative motive leads individuals and firms to add to their money holdings until the reduction in risk obtained by the last pound added is just balanced (in each wealth holder's view) by the cost in terms of the interest forgone on that pound. A fall in the rate of return on bonds for the same level of risk will encourage people to hold more of their wealth as money and less in bonds. A rise in their rate of return for a given level of risk will cause people to hold more bonds and less money.

The speculative motive implies that the demand for money will be negatively related to the rate of interest.

The precautionary and transactions motives may also be negatively related to interest rates at the margin, because higher returns on bonds encourage people to economize on their money holding. However, in practice we only observe total money holdings, so we cannot distinguish the components held for different motives. Hence, demand for money as a whole is positively related to GDP and wealth, and negatively related to the interest rate.

REAL AND NOMINAL MONEY BALANCES

It is important to distinguish demand for real money balances from nominal money demand. Real money demand is the number of units of purchasing power that the public wishes to hold in the form of money balances. For example, in an imaginary one-product (wheat) economy, this would be measured by the number of bushels of wheat that could be purchased with the money balances held. In a more complex economy, it could be measured in terms of the number of 'baskets of goods', represented by a price index such as the RPI, that could be purchased with the money balances held. When we speak of the demand for money in real terms, we speak of the amount demanded in constant pounds (that is, with a constant price level):

The real demand for money (or the demand for real money balances) is the nominal quantity demanded divided by the price level.

In the ten years from the end of 1985 to the end of 1995, the nominal quantity of money balances held in the UK nearly trebled, from just over £225 billion to £622 billion.[10] Over the same period, however, the price level, as measured by the RPI, rose

10 This is the M4 definition of money, which is given in Box 18.1.

BOX 18.2.

The quantity theory of money

The quantity theory of money can be set out in terms of four equations. Equation (i) states that the demand for money balances depends on the value of transactions as measured by nominal GDP, which is real GDP multiplied by the price level:

$$M^D = kPY. \tag{i}$$

Equation (ii) states that the supply of money, M, is set by the central bank:

$$M^S = M. \tag{ii}$$

Equation (iii) states the equilibrium condition that the demand for money must equal the supply:

$$M^D = M^S. \tag{iii}$$

Substitution from (i) and (ii) into Equation (iii) yields:

$$M = kPY. \tag{iv}$$

The original classical quantity theory assumes that k is a constant given by the transactions demand for money and that Y is constant because full employment (equilibrium GDP) is maintained. Thus, increases or decreases in the money supply lead to proportional increases or decreases in prices.

Often the quantity theory is presented by using the *equation of exchange*:

$$MV = PY, \tag{v}$$

where V is the **velocity of circulation,** defined as nominal GDP divided by the quantity of money:

$$V = PY/M. \tag{vi}$$

Velocity may be interpreted as showing the average amount of 'work' done by a unit of money. If annual money GDP is £600 billion and the stock of money is £200 billion, on average, each pound's worth of money is used three times to create the values added that compose GDP.

There is a simple relationship between k and V. One is the reciprocal of the other, as may be seen immediately by comparing (iv) and (vi). Thus, it makes no difference whether we choose to work with k or V. Further, if k is assumed to be constant, this implies that V must also be treated as being constant.

An example may help to illustrate the interpretation of each. Suppose the stock of money that people wish to hold equals one-fifth of the value of total transactions. Thus, k is 0.2 and V, the reciprocal of k, is 5. If the money supply is to be one-fifth of the value of annual transactions, each pound must be 'used' on average five times.

The modern version of the quantity theory does not assume that k and V are exogenously fixed. However, it does argue that they will not change in response to a change in the quantity of money.

by about 58 per cent. This tells us that the real quantity of money less than doubled, from £225 billion to about £394 billion, measured in constant 1985 prices.

So far we have held the price level constant, identifying the determinants of demand for real money balances as real GDP, real wealth, and the interest rate. Suppose that with the interest rate, real wealth, and real GDP being held constant, the price level doubles. Since the demand for real money balances will be unchanged, the demand for nominal balances must double. If the public demanded £300 billion in nominal money balances before, it will now demand £600 billion. This keeps the real demand unchanged at £600/2 = £300 billion. The money balances of £600 billion at the new, higher price level represent exactly the same purchasing power as £300 billion at the old price level.

> **Other things being equal, the nominal demand for money balances varies in proportion to the price level; when the price level doubles, desired nominal money balances also double.**

This is a central proposition of the quantity theory of money, which is discussed further in Box 18.2.

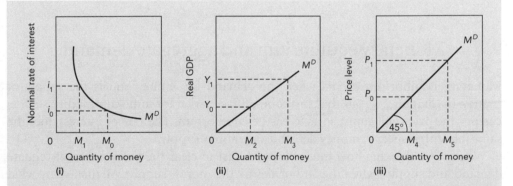

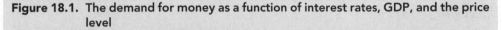

Figure 18.1. The demand for money as a function of interest rates, GDP, and the price level

The quantity of money demanded varies negatively with the nominal rate of interest and positively with both real GDP and the price level. In part (i) the demand for money is shown varying negatively with the interest rate along the money demand function. When the interest rate rises from i_0 to i_1, individuals and firms reduce the quantity of money demanded from M_0 to M_1.

In part (ii) the demand for money varies positively with real GDP. When GDP rises from Y_0 to Y_1, individuals and firms increase the quantity of money demanded from M_2 to M_3.

In part (iii) the demand for money varies in proportion to the price level. When the price level doubles from P_0 to P_1, individuals and firms double the quantity of money demanded from M_4 to M_5.

In the text we refer to the M^D curve in (i) as the money demand function. It is drawn for given values of real GDP, wealth, and the price level.

Figure 18.1 summarizes the influences of real GDP, the nominal rate of interest, and the price level, the three variables that account for most of the short-term variations in the nominal quantity of money demanded. The function relating money demanded to the rate of interest is often called the **demand for money function**, even though the demand for nominal money depends also on GDP, wealth, and prices.

Monetary forces and GDP

We are now in a position to examine the relationship between monetary forces, on the one hand, and the equilibrium values of GDP and the price level, on the other. The first step in explaining this relationship is a new one: the link between monetary equilibrium and aggregate demand. The second is familiar from earlier chapters: the effects of shifts in aggregate demand on equilibrium values of GDP and the price level.

Monetary equilibrium and aggregate demand

Monetary equilibrium occurs when the demand for money equals the supply of money. In Chapter 2 we saw that, in a competitive market for some commodity, such as carrots, the price will adjust so as to ensure equilibrium. The rate of interest does the same job with respect to money demand and money supply.

We start by showing how interest rates adjust to clear the money market (equate demand and supply) when the authorities fix the money supply. We then show what changes under the more realistic assumption that the authorities set the interest rate directly.

Figure 18.2 shows supply and demand curves for money. The supply of money is assumed to be fixed by the monetary authorities so it is shown as a vertical line, indicating that the money supply does not change as interest rates change. The money demand curve is based upon the speculative demand illustrated in Figure 18.1(i). It is negatively sloped because people desire to hold less money as interest rates rise. The money demand curve is drawn for given levels of real GDP, the price level, and wealth, and will shift to the right if any of these variables increase.

Figure 18.2 also shows how the interest rate will move in order to equate the demand

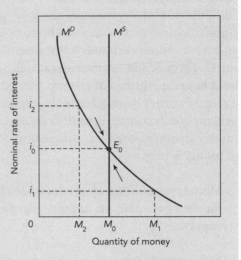

Figure 18.2. Determination of the interest rate

The interest rate rises when there is an excess demand for money and falls when there is an excess supply of money. The fixed quantity of money, M_0, is shown by the completely inelastic supply curve, M^S. The demand for money is M^D; its negative slope indicates that a fall in the rate of interest causes the quantity of money demanded to increase. Equilibrium is at E_0, with a rate of interest i_0.

If the interest rate is i_1, there will be an excess demand for money of M_0M_1. Bonds will be offered for sale in an attempt to increase money holdings. This will force the rate of interest up to i_0 (the price of bonds falls), at which point the quantity of money demanded is equal to the fixed available quantity, M_0. If the interest rate is i_2, there will be an excess supply of money M_2M_0. Bonds will be demanded in return for excess money balances. This will force the rate of interest down to i_0 (the price of bonds rises), at which point the quantity of money demanded has risen to equal the fixed money supply, M_0.

for money with its supply. When a few people find that they have less money than they wish to hold, they can sell some bonds and add the proceeds to their money holdings. This transaction simply redistributes given supplies of bonds and money among individuals; it does not change the total supply of either money or bonds.

Now suppose that all of the firms and households in the economy have excess demands for money balances. They all try to sell bonds to add to their money balances, but what one person can do, all cannot necessarily do. At any moment the economy's total supply of money and bonds is fixed; there is just so much money and there are just so many bonds in existence. If everyone tries to sell bonds, there will be no one to buy them, and the price of bonds will fall.

We saw earlier in this chapter that a fall in the price of bonds means a rise in the rate of interest. As the interest rate rises, people economize on money balances, because the opportunity cost of holding such balances is rising. This is what we saw in Figure 18.1(i), where the quantity of money demanded falls along the demand curve in response to a rise in the rate of interest. Eventually, the interest rate will rise enough that people will no longer be trying to add to their money balances by selling bonds. At that point there is no longer an excess supply of bonds, and the interest rate will stop rising. The demand for money again equals the supply.

Suppose now that all firms and households hold larger money balances than they would like. A single household or firm would purchase bonds with its excess balances, achieving monetary equilibrium by reducing its money holdings and by increasing its bond holdings. However, just as in the previous example, what one individual can do, all cannot do. At any moment the total quantity of bonds is fixed, so everyone cannot simultaneously add to personal bond holdings. When all actors enter the bond market and try to purchase bonds with unwanted money balances, they bid up the price of existing bonds, and the interest rate falls. Individuals and firms then become willing to hold larger quantities of money; that is, the quantity of money demanded increases along the money demand curve in response to a fall in the rate of interest. The rise in the price of bonds continues until firms and households stop trying to convert bonds into money. In other words, it continues until everyone is content to hold the existing supply of money and bonds.

> **Monetary equilibrium occurs when the rate of interest is such that the demand for money equals its supply, and hence the demand for bonds equals their supply.**

The determination of the interest rate, depicted in Figure 18.2, is often called the *liquidity preference theory* of interest and sometimes the *portfolio balance theory*.

As we shall see, a monetary disturbance—a change in either the demand for money or the supply of money—will lead to a change in the interest rate. However, as we saw in Chapter 16, desired aggregate expenditure is sensitive to changes in the interest rate. Here, then, is a link between monetary factors and real expenditure flows.

INTEREST RATES AS A POLICY INSTRUMENT

In most industrial countries, the assumption that the monetary authorities fix the level of the money supply is not a realistic one. In practice, policymakers almost universally set the interest rate and then let the money supply adjust to whatever rate is set.

Figure 18.3(i) illustrates what difference this makes. Suppose the economy were to start at E_0 with interest rate i_0 and money supply M_0. If the authorities wished to relax monetary policy they could do so by increasing the money supply to, say, M_1. If they did this there would initially be an excess supply of money. Holders of this money would demand more bonds, and via the process discussed above this would raise the price of bonds and lower the interest rate to i_1.

However, in reality, this is not what happens. The final situation could have been the same, but it would have been achieved in a different way. Rather than setting a level of the money supply the authorities would have set the level of the interest rate i_0. In order to make this stick, they would have had to supply whatever money was demanded at that interest rate.[11] In Figure 18.3(i), the initial level of the money supply that would have been provided is M_0.

---

[11] In practice, it is M0 that the authorities supply in order to maintain interest rates. Broader aggregates are then determined by demand at whatever level the set interest rates determine (as a result of interaction between the banks and the rest of the economy). This complication does not change the principles involved.

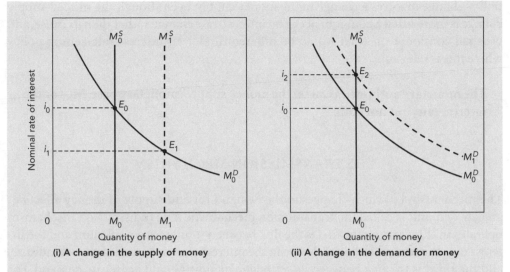

Figure 18.3. Monetary disturbances and interest rate changes

Shifts in the money supply or in the demand for money cause the equilibrium interest rate to change. In both parts of the figure the money supply is shown by the vertical curve M_0^S, and the demand for money is shown by the negatively sloped curve M_0^D. The initial equilibrium is at E_0, with corresponding interest rate i_0.

In part (i) an increase in the money supply causes the money supply curve to shift to the right, from M_0^S to M_1^S. The new equilibrium is at E_1, where the interest rate is i_1, less than i_0. Starting at E_1, with M_1^S and i_1, it can be seen that a decrease in the money supply to M_0^S leads to an increase in the interest rate from i_1 to i_0.

In part (ii) an increase in the demand for money causes the M^D curve to shift to the right from M_0^D to M_1^D. The new equilibrium occurs at E_2, and the new equilibrium interest rate is i_2, greater than i_0. Starting at E_2, we see that a decrease in the demand for money from M_1^D to M_0^D leads to a decrease in the interest rate from i_2 to i_0.

Now suppose that the authorities decide to relax monetary policy: what happens? The authorities simply announce to the money markets that the rate at which they will provide money has fallen from i_0 to i_1. At this lower interest rate, there is now an excess demand for money, and the authorities have to provide exactly that extra money demanded by permitting the money supply to increase. In practice they do it by buying all the bonds (with new money) that people want to sell at the lower interest rate.

Notice that the outcome in Figure 18.3(i) is exactly the same when the authorities fix interest rates and let the money supply adjust as it is when they set the money supply and let interest rates adjust. It is not generally true, when analysing the impact of exogenous shocks on the economy, that a policy of fixing interest rates leads to identical adjustment paths to a policy of setting the money stock (or the monetary base). However, it is true that it makes no difference to the equilibrium structure of our macro model which way it is done. Accordingly, we shall continue to talk as if a monetary-policy change involves a change in the money supply, even though the money-supply change is more often a consequence of an interest-rate change rather than its cause, and we shall comment on what would be different under an interest-rate-setting policy where this is relevant.

> **The monetary authorities can set the money supply (monetary base, M0) or the interest rate, but not both.**

THE TRANSMISSION MECHANISM

The mechanism by which changes in the demand for and supply of money affect aggregate demand is called the **transmission mechanism.** The transmission mechanism operates in three stages: the first is the link between monetary equilibrium and the interest rate, the second is the link between the interest rate and investment expenditure, and the third is the link between investment expenditure and aggregate demand. For this discussion we assume an exogenously determined money supply, rather than a fixed interest rate.

From monetary disturbances to changes in the interest rate
The interest rate will change if the equilibrium depicted in Figure 18.2 is disturbed by a change in either the supply of money or the demand for money. Thus, as shown in Figure 18.3(i), an increase in the supply of money, with an unchanged money demand function, will give rise to an excess supply of money at the original interest rate. As we have seen, an excess supply of money will cause the interest rate to fall. As also shown in Figure 18.3(i), a decrease in the supply of money will cause the interest rate to rise.

As shown in Figure 18.3(ii), an increase in the demand for money, with an unchanged supply of money, will give rise to an excess demand for money at the original interest rate and will cause the interest rate to rise. As also shown in part (ii) of Figure 18.3, a decrease in the demand for money will cause the interest rate to fall.

> **Monetary disturbances, which can arise from changes in either the demand for or the supply of money, cause changes in the interest rate.**

From changes in the interest rate to shifts in aggregate expenditure
The second link in the transmission mechanism relates interest rates to expenditure. We saw in Chapter 14 that investment, which includes expenditure on inventory accumulation, residential construction, and business fixed investment, responds to changes in the real rate of interest. Other things being equal, a decrease in the real rate of interest makes borrowing cheaper and generates new investment expenditure.[12]

---

[12] In Ch. 14 we saw that purchases of durable consumer goods also respond to changes in the real interest rate. In this chapter we concentrate on investment expenditure, which may be taken to stand for *all* interest-sensitive

This negative relationship between investment and the rate of interest is called the **investment demand function.**

The first two links in the transmission mechanism are shown in Figure 18.4. We concentrate for the moment on changes in the money supply, although, as we have seen already, the process can also be set in motion by changes in the demand for money. In part (i) we see that a change in the money supply causes the rate of interest to change in the opposite direction. In part (ii) we see that a change in the interest rate causes the level of investment expenditure to change in the opposite direction.[13] Therefore, changes in the money supply cause investment expenditure to change in the same direction.

> **An increase in the money supply leads to a fall in the interest rate and an increase in investment expenditure. A decrease in the money supply leads to a rise in the interest rate and a decrease in investment expenditure.**

The change in investment expenditure shifts the aggregate expenditure curve, *AE*, as shown in Chapters 14 and 15.

Notice that, when the authorities are setting interest rates rather than the money stock, the transmission mechanism is even more direct. Policy-determined changes in interest rates lead directly to changes in investment expenditure. The money supply also adjusts, as discussed above, but the key macroeconomic effect is that of interest-rate changes on real desired expenditures.

From shifts in aggregate expenditure to shifts in aggregate demand

Now we are back on familiar ground. In Chapter 16 we saw that a shift in the aggregate expenditure curve leads to a shift in the *AD* curve. This is shown again in Figure 18.5.

A change in the money supply, by causing a change in desired investment expenditure (which earlier was assumed to be exogenous) and hence a shift in the *AE* curve, causes the *AD* curve to shift. An increase in the money supply causes an increase in investment expenditure and hence an increase in aggregate demand. A decrease in the money supply causes a decrease in investment expenditure and therefore a decrease in aggregate demand.

> **The transmission mechanism connects monetary forces and real expenditure flows. It works from a change in the demand for or the supply of money to a change in bond prices and interest rates, to changes in investment expenditure, and to a shift in the aggregate demand curve.**

---

expenditure, and we maintain our simplifying assumption that expected inflation is zero so that the real and nominal interest rates are equal.

[13] Recall that we have assumed that real and nominal interest rates are the same. Generally, as long as inflation expectations are constant, the change in the nominal interest rate determined in part (i) of Figure 18.4 is equal to the change in the real interest rate in part (ii).

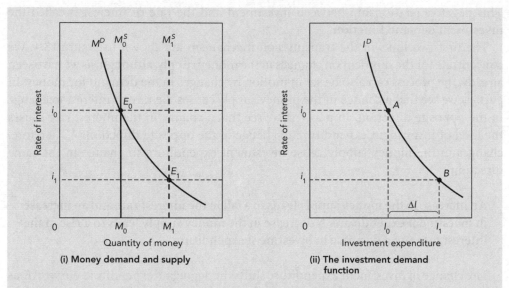

Figure 18.4. The effects of changes in the money supply on investment expenditure

Increases in the money supply reduce the rate of interest and increase desired invest-
ment expenditure. Initial equilibrium is at E_0, with a quantity of money M_0 (shown by the
inelastic money supply curve M_0^S), an interest rate of i_0, and an investment expenditure of I_0
(point A). The monetary authorities then increase the money supply to M_1 (shown by the
money supply curve M_1^S). This lowers the rate of interest to i_1 and increases investment expenditure by ΔI to I_1 (point B). A reduction in the money supply from M_1 to M_0 raises the
interest rate from i_1 to i_0 and lowers investment expenditure by ΔI from I_1 to I_0.

A similar analysis applies when the authorities are setting interest rates and change
them deliberately in order to influence the economy. A lowering of the interest rate
increases investment and this shifts the *AD* curve to the right. A raising of interest rates
lowers investment and this shifts *AD* to the left. A preliminary discussion of how the
openness of the economy affects the transmission mechanism is presented in Box 18.3.
This discussion is extended in the following chapter.

An alternative derivation of the *AD* curve: *IS/LM*

We now set out a well-known derivation of aggregate demand. There are no new economic relationships or even different assumptions involved here compared with our
earlier discussions of aggregate demand. This particular diagrammatic exposition was
devised by Nobel Laureate Sir John Hicks (1904–89). It is so familiar to economists who
have trained since the Second World War that it is frequently quoted. Students who have

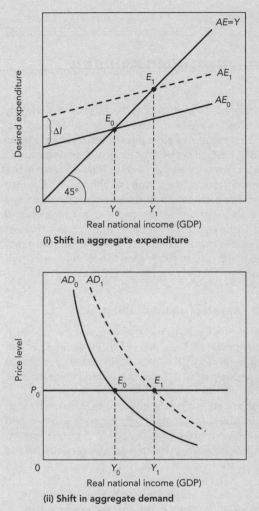

(i) Shift in aggregate expenditure

Figure 18.5. The effects of changes in the money supply on aggregate demand

Changes in the money supply cause shifts in the aggregate expenditure and aggregate demand functions. In Figure 18.4 an increase in the money supply increased desired investment expenditure by ΔI. Here, in part (i) the aggregate expenditure function shifts up by ΔI (which is the same as ΔI in Figure 18.4), from AE_0 to AE_1. At the fixed price level P_0, equilibrium GDP rises from Y_0 to Y_1, as shown by the horizontal shift in the aggregate demand curve from AD_0 to AD_1 in part (ii).

When the supply of money falls (from M_1^S to M_0^S in Figure 18.4), investment falls by ΔI, thereby shifting aggregate expenditure from AE_1 to AE_0. At the fixed price level P_0, this reduces equilibrium income from Y_1 to Y_0.

(ii) Shift in aggregate demand

followed the macroeconomics chapters this far already know the economics behind the *IS/LM* model, but it is also helpful to know what specific bit of analysis '*IS/LM*' refers to. The diagrammatic apparatus does, however, have one important pay-off, in that it helps to make clear differences in the transmission mechanism between monetary and fiscal policy. We shall use it in that context later in this chapter. It is also helpful in understanding some different approaches in macroeconomics, which are discussed in the appendix to this chapter.

For purposes of the present analysis, we assume that real wealth is constant and that there are no relative price changes between domestic and foreign goods—these were the factors that gave us a negatively sloped aggregate demand curve in Chapters 16 and 17. In the above discussion we have, in effect, demonstrated that interest-rate linkages

BOX 18.3.

The transmission mechanism in an open economy

The text focuses on the interest rate as the channel through which the effects of monetary policy are transmitted to the economy. However, as we have observed in earlier chapters, the 'openness' of the economy to international trade and to capital flows means that two additional complications must be allowed for.* First, the effects of monetary contraction or expansion are weakened because UK interest rates are closely linked to interest rates in the rest of the world; this restricts the scope for domestic interest rates to change in response to monetary policy. (The strength of this restriction varies with the exchange rate regime— it is weakest under floating exchange rates, stronger under pegged exchange rates, and would be overwhelming under a single EU currency.) Second, there is an added channel through which the effects of monetary policy are transmitted to real aggregate demand. This is through changes in the external value of the pound sterling on the foreign exchange market. (This effect applies almost exclusively to a floating exchange rate regime.)

The link between interest rates and the external value of the pound

If UK interest rates rise relative to those in other countries, the demand for sterling-denominated assets will also rise. UK residents will be less inclined to invest in assets of other countries, and foreign demand for high-yielding UK assets will increase. In order to invest in these assets, foreigners need to buy pounds, and their demand for these pounds on the foreign exchange market will cause the pound to appreciate.

Low UK interest rates have the opposite effect. UK residents will want to invest in foreign assets, and foreigners will be less anxious to invest in UK assets. Foreigners will demand fewer pounds, and people in the UK will be selling more pounds in order to obtain foreign currencies to invest in higher-yielding foreign assets. This will cause a depreciation of the pound on the foreign exchange market.

> Other things being equal, the higher UK interest rates are, the higher will be the external value of the pound, and the lower UK interest rates are, the lower will be the external value of the pound.

The impact of changes in the money supply

Suppose that in order to stimulate the economy, the monetary authorities increase the money supply. The initial effects will be exactly the same as in the (financially) closed economy analysed in the text. Holders of money now find that they have excess money balances at the current level of GDP, prices, and interest rates. Hence, they increase their demand for bonds. This drives up the price of bonds and lowers the interest rate. (Equivalently, we could just start with a policy-imposed fall in interest rates.)

It is at this point that open-economy forces come into play. As UK interest rates fall, foreigners and UK residents will start to sell UK assets in order to purchase foreign assets that now earn interest rates higher than those prevailing in the UK.

Because people are selling sterling assets, the fall in UK interest rates is mitigated. In this way, UK interest rates are constrained by those abroad; the availability of interest-earning assets in foreign currencies that investors think are substitutes for UK securities implies that UK interest rates do not move as much in response to changes in the money supply as they would in a closed economy.

People who have sold their sterling-denominated assets will now wish to sell pounds in order to buy foreign exchange that they will use to purchase foreign assets. This causes a depreciation of the pound on the foreign exchange market.[†]

> A relaxation of UK monetary policy will lead to a fall in domestic interest rates and a depreciation of sterling. A tightening of UK monetary policy will have the opposite effects, resulting in an increase in interest rates and an appreciation of sterling.

The transmission mechanism

How are impacts on the interest rate and the external value of the pound transmitted into changes in the level of economic activity? The reduced response of interest rates to monetary policy implies less effect, for a given change in the money supply, on interest-sensitive expenditures. However, the induced changes in the value of the pound add a new channel by which monetary policy is transmitted to the economy, though clearly this only applies when the exchange rate is floating. A depreciation of the pound, other things being equal, makes UK-produced goods more competitive on world markets and thus increases exports and decreases imports.

> Because a relaxation of monetary policy leads to a depreciation of the pound sterling, it stimulates net exports and thereby raises aggregate demand. Similarly, a tightening of monetary policy will lower aggregate demand because it leads to an appreciation of the pound and hence to a fall in net exports.

The operation of this channel of the transmission mechanism can be seen in terms of the definition of aggregate demand:

$$AD = C + I + G + (X - IM).$$

In a closed economy, monetary policy operates through changes in the interest rate influencing investment expenditure (I) as well as any interest-sensitive consumption expenditures (C); in the open economy, that channel is weakened, but the effects on aggregate demand are reinforced through the effects of changes in the exchange rate on net exports ($X - IM$).

Although the channels are different, the ability of monetary policy to affect GDP remains. In the rest of this chapter, we maintain the (financially) closed-economy analysis for simplicity; we return to the open economy issues in Chapter 19.

* These issues are discussed further in Ch. 19.
[†] Equilibrium will occur when the pound has depreciated so much that people expect it to appreciate later (i.e. the exchange rate 'overshoots' its long-run value), and that expected appreciation compensates investors for the lower nominal interest rate on UK bonds.

(the transmission mechanism) also imply a negatively sloped aggregate demand curve. What follows amounts to an explicit derivation of that negatively sloped *AD* curve using the interest-rate linkages.

THE *IS* CURVE

We saw above that investment expenditures were assumed to be related to the rate of interest. Figure 18.4(ii) plots the negative relationship between interest rates and investment, called the investment demand function. We have also seen (in Figure 18.5) that an increase in investment shifts the *AE* curve upwards and that this is associated with an increase in equilibrium GDP (a rightward shift of *AD*).

The *IS* curve plots the relationship between the interest rate and the equilibrium level of GDP, via the aggregate expenditure line *AE*. It is telling us what the level of final expenditures, and therefore the equilibrium level of GDP, will be for each rate of interest. The relationship is negative, because higher interest rates cause investment to fall, which shifts *AE* down and lowers equilibrium *Y*. Lower interest rates cause investment to rise, which shifts *AE* up and raises equilibrium *Y*. This relationship is plotted in Figure 18.6.

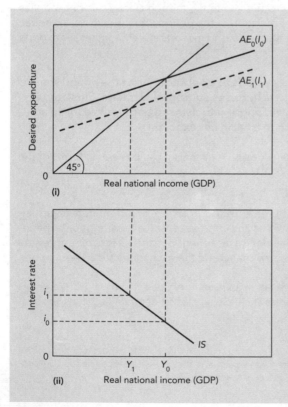

Figure 18.6. The *IS* curve

The *IS* curve shows the equilibrium level of GDP associated with each given rate of interest. It shows combinations of the interest rate and GDP for which desired expenditures equal actual national income and output, and for which injections equal withdrawals. Part (i) shows a fall in *AE* resulting from a fall in investment from I_0 to I_1. This fall in *I* is caused by a rise in the interest rate from i_0 to i_1. The fall in investment produces a fall in GDP from Y_0 to Y_1.

Part (ii) shows the resulting combinations of the interest rate and real GDP. For given values of exogenous expenditures, i_0 leads to level of GDP Y_0, and i_1 leads to level of GDP Y_1. Choosing any other level of the interest rate and following through its effect on GDP via investment produces all the other points on the *IS* curve.

In a closed economy with no government, the *IS* curve would plot the combinations of the interest rate and GDP for which saving and investment were equal. However, in an open economy with a government, it is the combinations of the interest rate and GDP for which desired expenditure (*AE*) equals output, or for which injections equal withdrawals ($S + T + IM = I + G + X$).

> The *IS* curve is the locus of interest rates and equilibrium levels of GDP that are consistent with equilibrium between desired expenditures and output. It is drawn for given values of all other exogenous expenditures, such as *G* and *X*, and for a given price level.

An increase in exogenous expenditures shifts the *IS* curve to the right (by the initial increase in expenditure times the multiplier), while a fall in exogenous expenditures shifts the *IS* curve to the left.

THE *LM* CURVE

Figure 18.2 illustrates equilibrium in the money market at the point where the money demand curve intersects the (exogenously determined) money supply curve. The money demand curve is plotted for given levels of real GDP, the price level, and wealth. We continue to assume that wealth and the price level are constant, but what happens in that figure if real GDP were to increase? The answer is shown in figure 18.7(i). As GDP increases, transactions and precautionary demands for money both increase, and so the money demand curve shifts to the right. At higher GDP levels, and with a given money supply, the equilibrium interest rate will rise. This is because, while the actual money supply is fixed, higher GDP has increased money demand. People will try to sell bonds (to get more money) until the price of bonds falls and interest rates, therefore, rise. The required rise in the interest rate is the amount that is just sufficient to cause a fall in speculative demand that exactly offsets the rise in transactions demand.

> The *LM* curve plots combinations of GDP and the interest rate, for a given money supply and given price level, that are consistent with the equality of money demand and money supply.

The *LM* curve is shown in Figure 18.7(ii). It shows a positive locus of combinations of GDP and the interest rate consistent with money market equilibrium. An increase in the money supply shifts the *LM* curve to the right, while a decrease in the money supply shifts the *LM* curve to the left. To see this, shift the vertical money supply curve in part (i) of the figure. An increase in the money supply produces a lower equilibrium interest rate for each level of Y (and therefore for each M^D curve), whereas a decrease in the money supply produces a higher equilibrium interest rate for each level of Y.

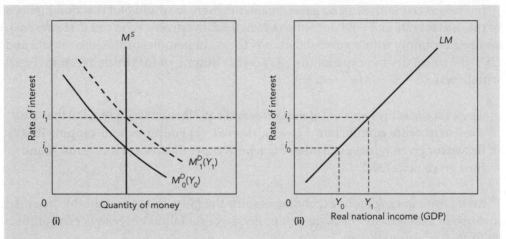

Figure 18.7. The *LM* curve

The *LM* curve shows the combinations of real GDP and the interest rate that are consistent with the equality of money demand and supply, for a given nominal money supply and given price level. Part (i) shows equilibrium in the money market with a fixed money supply and an M^D function that is negatively sloped. At an initial level of GDP, Y_0, the demand for money is given by M_0^D and the equilibrium interest rate is i_0. At higher levels of GDP the M^D curve shifts to the right (higher levels of GDP cause higher transactions demand for money). When GDP increases to Y_1, money demand shifts to M_1^D and the associated equilibrium interest rate rises to i_1.

In part (ii) the *LM* curve plots out the equilibrium interest rate associated with each possible Y. This is a positively sloped curve. An increase in the nominal money supply shifts the *LM* curve parallel to the right and a decrease in the nominal money supply shifts the *LM* curve to the left.

IS/LM AND AGGREGATE DEMAND

The *IS* and *LM* curves each tell part of the story of the determination of aggregate demand. The *IS* curve determines GDP for given interest rates; the *LM* curve determines the interest rate for given levels of GDP. In effect, they are two simultaneous equations in GDP and the interest rate. One (*IS*) represents the set of equilibrium points for which desired expenditures equal national output. The other (*LM*) represents the set of equilibrium points for which money demand equals money supply. Equilibrium for the whole economy (but still excluding the aggregate supply side) must be on both the *IS* and *LM* curves. This will be where they intersect. This is shown in Figure 18.8.

In the past, the *IS/LM* model was widely used to analyse the effects of either changes in the monetary policy (shifts in *LM*) or changes in fiscal policy (shifts in IS) on GDP. However, this framework has the limitation that it can only be used (on its own) for cases where either the price level is fixed and real GDP is variable, or where real GDP is fixed and the price level is variable. When output and prices are simultaneously variable we need to move to the *AD/AS* framework to handle the analysis.

600

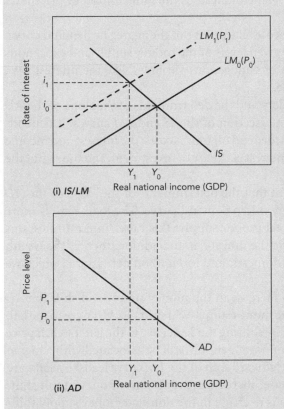

Figure 18.8. *IS/LM* and aggregate demand

The *AD* curve plots the *IS/LM* equilibrium level of GDP for each given price level, holding all exogenous expenditures and the nominal money supply constant. Part (i) has the initial position as the intersection of LM_0 (which is drawn with price level P_0) with the *IS* curve. This gives the overall equilibrium levels of real GDP and the interest rate as Y_0 and i_0. At higher price levels the *LM* curve shifts to the left (because the real money supply falls). At price level P_1 the *LM* curve is given by LM_1, and this leads to equilibrium GDP and the interest rate of Y_1 and i_1. Part (ii) plots out the resulting combinations of the price level and GDP. This is the aggregate demand curve, *AD*. An increase in the money supply or exogenous expenditures will shift the *AD* curve to the right. A decrease in the money supply or of exogenous expenditures will shift the *AD* curve to the left.

There is nothing wrong in the *IS/LM* model; it is just incomplete. Indeed, it can be used to derive the *AD* curve (thereby illustrating that the *IS/LM* model is consistent with our approach to *AD*). The *AD* curve implied by our *IS/LM* model is derived in Figure 18.8(ii).

To derive the *AD* curve we take given *IS* and *LM* curves and ask what happens to the level of GDP (determined by their intersection) as the price level rises. The answer is that a higher price level shifts the *LM* curve to the left and, for a given nominal money supply and given all exogenous expenditures, leads to a lower level of equilibrium GDP.

The reason why an increase in the price level shifts the *LM* curve to the left is that the fixed money supply is *nominal* but money is demanded in relation to its *real* purchasing power. This means that, as the price level rises, there will be an increase in the nominal quantity of money demanded to finance a given volume of real transactions. This would lead to an upward shift in the M^D curves in Figure 18.7(i) and so would lead to a higher equilibrium interest rate for each level of real GDP. This shifts the *LM* curve (upwards) to the left. An alternative way of making the same point (that a higher price level shifts the *LM* curve to the left) would be to draw Figure 18.7(i) with the *real* money stock on the horizontal axis. Then, an increase in the price level would simply reduce the real money supply and shift the money supply curve to the left. These two different ways of expressing the point are equivalent and lead to the same impact of price level changes on the *LM* curve.

By taking different values for the price level we plot out the aggregate demand curve. Notice that the *AD* curve is drawn for given levels of the money supply and exogenous expenditures, but *not* for given levels of endogenous variables, like the interest rate, consumption, investment, and income.

This derivation also helps us to understand the determinants of the slope of the *AD* curve. Since it is determined by the intersection of the *IS* and *LM* curves, it depends upon the slopes of both. These, in turn, depend on four factors: the interest and income elasticities of demand for money, the interest elasticity of investment, and the size of the multiplier.

This reinforces our earlier argument that the determinants of the slope of the *AD* curve are not logically the same as any micro demand curve. The logic here is more tortuous—higher price level lowers real money supply; this raises interest rates; this lowers investment; this lowers GDP via the multiplier. In addition, there is the wealth effect and the effect of relative prices (domestic and foreign) on net exports, which we studied in Chapter 16.

All that remains is to show that an increase in the money supply will shift the *AD* curve to the right while a decrease in the money supply will shift the *AD* curve to the left. This can be done in Figure 18.8 simply by shifting the *LM* curve to the left for each price level. With a given *IS* curve, each higher money supply will be associated with a higher equilibrium level of GDP. Therefore, a leftward shift of the *LM* curve leads to a leftward shift of the *AD* curve. Hence, an exogenous increase in the nominal money supply shifts the *AD* curve to the right. An exogenous decrease in the nominal money supply shifts the *AD* curve to the left.

Changes of monetary policy can be interpreted as shifts of the *LM* curve irrespective of whether the authorities are fixing the interest rate or the money supply. Hence, once we are in the *IS/LM* framework, we have an analytic tool that is just as suitable for either policy environment. The reason that this is true is that the *LM* curve represents equilibrium states in the money market: it does not matter whether that equilibrium is achieved by the interest rate adjusting to the money stock or by the money stock adjusting to the interest rate—the outcome is the same either way. A relaxation of monetary policy involves the *LM* curve shifting to the right, while a tightening of monetary policy involves the *LM* curve shifting to the left.

Aggregate demand, the price level, and GDP

We have now completed a major task in macroeconomics, the addition of a monetary sector to our model of the macroeconomy. As a result, we are now able to analyse *monetary* influences on GDP determination as well as all those we discussed in Chapters 14–17. However, by adding a monetary sector we have also added to the economic linkages that affect the transmission of exogenous expenditure shocks (including fiscal policy). In particular, we have added a feedback mechanism involving interest rates. Accordingly, for the remainder of this chapter we must first see how monetary shocks feed through the economy in the *AD/AS* framework, and then re-examine how other shocks now influence GDP in the presence of monetary feedbacks.

THE SLOPE OF THE *AD* CURVE REVISITED

Let us now review how the monetary transmission mechanism adds to the explanation (given in Chapter 16) of the negative slope of the *AD* curve; that is, we need to explain why equilibrium GDP is negatively related to the price level (other things being held constant—including all exogenous expenditures and the money supply). In Chapter 16, when explaining the negative slope of the *AD* curve, we mentioned three reasons: the wealth effect, the substitution of domestic for foreign goods, and the effect operating through interest rates. Now that we have developed a theory of money and interest rates, we are able to understand in more detail the effect that works through the monetary sector. This effect is significant because, empirically, the interest rate is a very important link between monetary factors and real expenditure flows.

The essential feature of this effect is that a rise in the price level raises the money value of transactions. This leads to an increased nominal demand for money, which brings the transmission mechanism into play. People try to sell bonds to add to their nominal money balances, but, collectively, all they succeed in doing is forcing up the interest rate. The rise in the interest rate reduces investment expenditure and so reduces equilibrium GDP.[14]

We now turn to an analysis of how the effects of monetary and expenditure shocks work their way through the economy. For simplicity we consider the monetary shock to be a policy-induced change in the money supply: this is equivalent to a policy decision to change interest rates. The expenditure shock is considered to be a fiscal policy change through a change in government spending.

THE EFFECT OF A MONETARY POLICY CHANGE
IN THE SHORT RUN

In order to consider the effects of a change in the money supply in our complete macroeconomic model we need to put the *AD* curve together with the *AS* curve. To start with, we will consider the short-run *AS* curve as shown in Figure 18.9.

Let us take the case of a relaxation of monetary policy that involves an increase in the nominal money supply (or, equivalently, a cut in the interest rate). This is represented

---

14 Even when interest rates are pegged by the authorities, this link remains important, not least because they fix only short-term interest rates, whereas investment depends partly on long-term rates, which continue to be market-determined.

Macroeconomic policy

An increase in the money supply shifts the *AD* curve to the right and leads to an increase in GDP and the price level. The initial point is at the intersection of AD_0 and the short-run aggregate supply curve *SRAS*, with associated GDP and price level of Y_0 and P_0. After an increase in the money supply the *AD* curve shifts to AD_1. The resulting increase in expenditures (resulting from lower interest rates and associated with higher investment) would, through the multiplier effect, tend to lead to GDP of Y_1, indicated by point *C*. This would only be the outcome if the price level stayed constant and all the extra output demanded were forthcoming. However, excess demand for final output will lead to some increase in goods prices. As prices rise the real money supply falls and interest rates rise (there are also wealth effects and effects resulting from a rise in relative price of domestic goods). The combination of the stimulation to output caused by the initial expenditure increase combined with the negative feedback induced by a rising price level takes the economy from *B* to *D*, though the process can be analysed in two steps: *B* to *C* and *C* to *D*. So, in the short run, the economy moves to Y_2P_1. Clearly, the proportions in which real GDP and the price level rise are determined by the slope of *SRAS*. With a flat *SRAS* most of the impact falls on *Y*. With a steep *SRAS*, most of the impact falls on *P*.

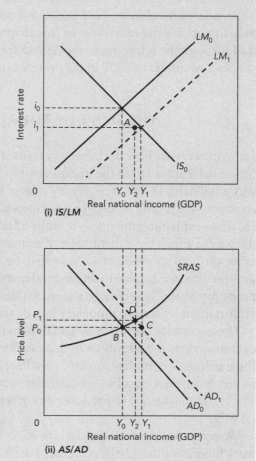

(i) *IS/LM*

(ii) *AS/AD*

by a rightward shift of the *LM* curve in part (i) and a rightward shift in the *AD* curve in part (ii). The economy moves to the intersection of the new *AD* curve with the *SRAS* curve. In the figure this looks very simple, but in reality there are several steps in the economic process that moves the economy between these two points.

1. The increase in the money supply means that people find that they have excess money balances, so they all attempt to shift from money into bonds. This is shown in Figure 18.9(i) by a rightward shift of the *LM* curve. This raises the price of bonds and lowers the rate of interest.

2. The lower interest rate causes an increase in investment, which, via the multiplier effect, causes a further increase in desired expenditures (shown as a movement

along IS_0). This increase in desired expenditures is represented by the horizontal shift in AD in part (ii) of the figure. Notice that the size of the horizontal shift in AD is equal to the horizontal distance between the original intersection of LM_0 and IS_0 and the new intersection between LM_1 and IS_0.

3. Because desired expenditure exceeds actual output, there is an inflationary gap. The economy is trying to move to P_0Y_1 in part (ii). Excess demand for final output causes the price level to rise. In the short run, input prices (wages and raw materials) are fixed in nominal terms, so firms expand output.

4. The rise in the price level chokes off some of the increase in desired expenditures through the three effects that give a negative slope to AD: the decline in real wealth, the rise in the relative price of domestic goods, and the reduction in the real money supply. These effects shift both LM_1 and IS_0 leftwards slightly so that, after the rise in the price level from P_0 to P_1, the IS and LM curves intersect at point A (consistent with the level of GDP Y_2).

Steps 1 and 2 try to take the economy from B to C in Figure 18.9(ii). Steps 3 and 4 conceptually take the economy from C to D. The actual path may not go exactly from B to C to D, but neither will it necessarily go straight from B to D. The actual path followed depends upon the speeds of adjustment of all the bits of the process. Our analysis is powerful enough to tell us where we end up, but not the precise path when the economy is out of equilibrium. The overall effect, however, has been an increase in output from Y_0 to Y_2 and a rise in the price level from P_0 to P_1. Notice that whether this stimulus to aggregate demand affects mainly output or mainly prices depends entirely upon the slope of the short-run aggregate supply curve.

A tightening of monetary policy could be analysed in exactly the same way, except that we would have a leftward shift of the LM curve and a leftward shift of the AD curve rather than a rightward shift. In this case, we would get a rise in the interest rate, leading to a fall in investment and a fall in desired expenditures. The fall in final demand would in turn lead to a fall in GDP and prices.

THE EFFECT OF A MONETARY POLICY CHANGE IN THE LONG RUN

Steps 1–4 above are not the end of the story. If real GDP at the initial point in Figure 18.9 was at its potential level, the short-run outcome at point D is at a point where current GDP exceeds potential GDP. This means that there is still an inflationary gap. What happens next is shown in Figure 18.10.

The adjustment that occurs in the long run involves a leftward shift in the aggregate supply curve. This is step 5.

5. While actual output is above potential output, the upward pressure on final goods prices persists. However, what shifts the $SRAS$ curve to the left is the upward

adjustment of input prices, especially wages. In steps 3 and 4 above, workers suffer a fall in real wages, because the price of final goods has risen but money wages have been held constant. This is despite the fact that output has increased and firms' profits have risen. Wage rates will start to rise, both because demand for labour has temporarily risen and because employees (or their unions) will start to

Figure 18.10. The effects of an increase in the money supply in the long run

Starting from full equilibrium, an increase in the money stock leads to no increase in national income in the long term but it does increase the price level. The initial increase in the money stock shifts the LM curve to the right, just as in Figure 18.9. Here we show LM_1, in part (i), as the LM curve after both the initial increase in the money stock and the resulting short-run increase in the price level from P_0 to P_1. (We neglect the possible shift in IS_0 that could also result from this initial rise in the price level.) The resulting rightward shift in the AD curve from AD_0 to AD_1 is shown in part (ii). The economy is initially in equilibrium at point B with price level P_0 and national income Y^*. The shift in AD moves the economy up the $SRAS$ curve $SRAS_0$, so that in the short run the economy goes from point B to point D. However, the inflationary gap Y^*Y_2 drives up wage rates, causing the $SRAS$ curve to move up and to the left from $SRAS_0$ to $SRAS_1$. The price level rises to P_2, and this rise in the price level reduces the real money supply, so the LM curve shifts leftwards in part (i). Wealth effects and the rising relative price of domestic goods also shift the IS curve leftwards. If there were no wealth effects or relative price effects, then the IS and LM curves in part (i) would be back in their initial positions in full equilibrium, IS_0 and LM_0. The real money supply would have returned to its original level, and nothing else real (including the interest rate) would have changed. However, where these effects are present, the interest rate will go to a level like that at point F, which may be higher or lower than its initial position.

The process comes to a halt when national income has returned to its potential level, Y^*, with price level P_2. The economy, which started at point B in part (ii), ends up at point E via point D.

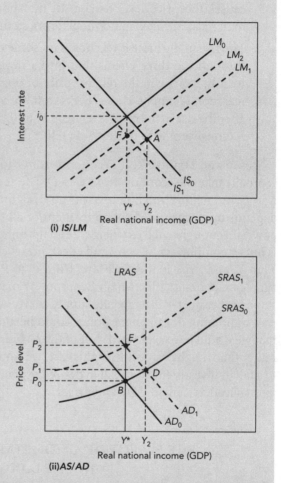

negotiate for a restoration of their real wage (or even a real-wage increase). Competitive firms will have to concede at least the restoration of real wages by granting money-wage increases. Accordingly, as the *SRAS* curve shifts to the left, the price level rises further and real GDP falls back to its potential level.

This latter adjustment does not all take place in the supply side of the economy. As the *SRAS* curve moves to the left, the economy is moving back up the *AD* curve. This movement involves a leftward shift of the *IS* curve owing to wealth effects, higher prices of domestic relative to foreign goods, and a rise in the interest rate, the latter having a further negative effect on investment. Indeed, it is possible that the long-run outcome will involve all real variables being restored to their original level and all nominal variables, including the price level, increasing in proportion to the initial increase in the money supply. We say 'possible' because this depends partly on the long-run wealth effect and on the effect of the higher price of domestic goods relative to foreign goods. These two effects can be regarded as negligible in the long term because they will be reduced by price adjustments, so the critical determinant of the outcome is what happens in the monetary sector. The general presumption, following from the quantity theory of money, is that, following a nominal increase in the money supply, the price level will rise in the same proportion, so that the real money supply returns to its original level at LM_0. All nominal prices have accordingly risen, but all *relative* prices remain unchanged, so the real economy is returned exactly to its original point, with the *IS* curve at IS_0 and the economy at point *E* in Figure 18.10(ii).

This argument cannot be totally correct, since we have seen that, during the expansion that resulted from the nominal money supply increase, there was an increase in investment. This in turn will have increased the capital stock above the previous level. This will have some effect on potential GDP. Macroeconomics has traditionally neglected these effects. Also note that we started with the economy in equilibrium at Y^*. If we had started with a recessionary gap, the increase in the money supply could have had the beneficial effect of returning the economy to Y^* more quickly than will occur eventually through downward pressure on prices and wages.

THE EFFECT OF A CHANGE IN FISCAL POLICY IN THE SHORT RUN

Let us now consider the effect of a fiscal policy expansion, which could come from an increase in government spending or a reduction in taxes. Just as with an increase in the money supply, an expansionary fiscal policy shifts the *AD* curve to the right. As a result, the effect on the economy will be the same as in Figure 18.9. However, the steps, at least initially, are not quite the same, so it is helpful to go through them. We shall find in Chapter 19 that the impacts of monetary and fiscal policy can be quite different under different exchange-rate regimes, but we focus here mainly on the internal adjustment mechanism. The impact of fiscal policy is shown in Figure 18.11.

Figure 18.11. The short-run and long-run effects of an expansionary fiscal policy

An expansionary fiscal policy, starting from equilibrium, has the same short- and long-run effects on national income and prices as an expansionary monetary policy, but it has different effects on the composition of expenditures. The economy starts in full equilibrium at point X in part (i) and point B in part (ii). An increase in government spending shifts the IS curve to the right in part (i) and the AD curve to the right in part (ii). The shift in AD with a given price level creates an inflationary gap, which means that the economy is trying to get to point C. However, this inflationary gap generates a short-term rise in the price level from P_0 to P_1. The new IS and LM curves, IS_1 and LM_1, are drawn to incorporate the effects of this initial rise in the price level. (Immediately after the rise in G but before the increase in P, the relevant IS curve would be to the right of IS_1 and the relevant LM curve would be LM_0.)

The result that the effect on the price level and output is the same as for monetary policy in both the short and the long run is illustrated in part (ii) by the path of the economy from point B to E (in the long run) via D (in the short run). However, what is differ-

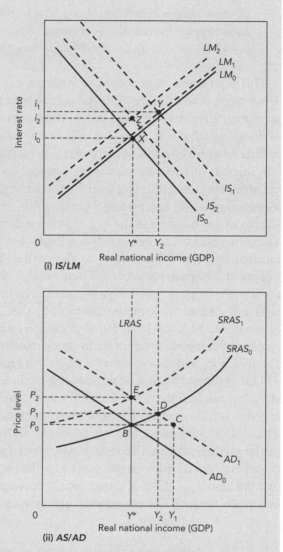

(i) IS/LM

(ii) AS/AD

ent about the effects of fiscal policy can be seen in part (i). The increase in government expenditure increases the interest rate, initially from i_0 to i_1. This rise in the interest rate reduces investment, so government spending crowds out investment. Initially, the combination of national income and the interest rate moves from point X to point Y (as the price level rises from P_0 to P_1). In the long run, as the price level rises to P_2 and national income returns to Y^*, wealth effects and higher domestic prices shift the IS curve to IS_2 and the fall in the real money supply shifts the LM curve to LM_2. Thus, the long-run effect of a fiscal expansion is a permanently higher interest rate (like i_2 at point Z), which crowds out investment, and a higher price level, which could crowd out consumption (via wealth effects) and net exports (via a rise in domestic prices relative to foreign prices).

Let us suppose that there has been an increase in government spending. What happens next?

1. The increase in *G* shifts the *IS* curve to the right by a horizontal distance equal to the increase in *G* times the multiplier. This is the multiplier that includes the effects of income taxes and import propensities (see pages 499–500). The *AD* curve shifts rightwards by the horizontal distance between the original and new intersections of the *IS* and *LM* curves.

2. The excess demand for final output in the economy (inflationary gap) causes the price level to rise and output to increase. This creates an excess demand for money, for two reasons. First, as prices rise, the real money supply falls with the nominal money supply held constant. Second, as output increases, the transactions demand for real money balances increases. This excess demand for money causes people to try to sell bonds, which lowers their price and raises interest rates, shown as a move from *X* to *Y* in Figure 18.11(i).

3. The higher interest rate lowers investment, which offsets some of the initial increase in aggregate demand. The rise in the price level also leads to wealth effects and relative price effects between domestic and foreign goods.

4. The economy in the short run moves to a point like *D* in Figure 18.11(ii). This is the same effect on GDP and the price level as for a money supply increase, but important underlying differences are concealed. In particular, at point *D*, after a fiscal-policy expansion the interest rate is higher and investment is lower than at *B*. With a monetary expansion the reverse is true—interest rates at *D* are lower and investment is higher than at *B*.

Thus, while fiscal- and monetary-policy expansions have the same analytic effect on the price level and real GDP, they have very different effects on the composition of total expenditure. Part (i) of Figure 18.11 makes clear that a monetary-policy expansion shifts the *LM* curve to the right, which lowers the equilibrium interest rate, while a fiscal-policy expansion shifts the *IS* curve to the right, which raises the equilibrium interest rate. The remaining differences result from the fact that the former increases investment while the latter lowers it.

THE EFFECT OF A CHANGE IN FISCAL POLICY
IN THE LONG RUN

The remaining adjustment from the short- to long-run case is the same for fiscal-policy changes as for monetary policy, since it involves a leftward shift in the *SRAS* curve, which results from increases in input prices, especially wages, as in step 5 above. There may be long-run implications of the fact that the government is now running a budget deficit when it was not before. However, there is more to be said about comparisons between the effects of monetary and fiscal policy in the context of Figures 18.10 and 18.11.

For the case of a monetary-policy expansion, we argued that the economy will return to the same real equilibrium level with all real variables unchanged, subject to some minor qualifications. However, we cannot make the same claim for the outcome of a fiscal-policy expansion. It is true, subject to the same qualifications as above, that real GDP will return to its initial (potential) level. However, our fiscal-policy expansion involved a permanent increase in real government spending. If G has risen but Y is unchanged some other component of final expenditure must have fallen. It is largely investment. Consumption could have fallen because higher prices reduce wealth, but wealth effects of modest price-level changes are unlikely to be large. Exports can have fallen only if there has been a permanent rise in the relative price of domestic goods, which is possible in the short run but unlikely in the long run, as the following chapter explains. So, in the long term, the most likely outcome is that the expansion of government spending replaces, or *crowds out*, investment expenditure via an increase in interest rates. In order to bring these higher interest rates about, the real money supply must be lower than in the initial position.

Thus fiscal and monetary policies, while acting in similar ways via the shift in AD and having similar consequences for real GDP and the price level, have quite different consequences for the composition of final expenditures. We shall learn in Chapter 19 that these effects are sensitive to the exchange-rate regime and to the degree of mobility of financial capital.

Summary

1. For simplicity, we divide all forms in which wealth is held into money, which is a medium of exchange, and bonds, which earn a higher interest return than money and can be turned into money by being sold at a price that is determined on the open market.

2. The price of existing bonds varies negatively with the rate of interest. A rise in the interest rate lowers the prices of all outstanding bonds. The longer its term to maturity, the greater the change in the price of a bond will be for a given change in the interest rate.

3. The value of money balances that the public wishes to hold is called the *demand for money*. It is a stock (not a flow), measured in the UK as so many billions of pounds.

4. Money balances are held, despite the opportunity cost of bond interest forgone, because of the transactions, precautionary, and speculative motives. These have the effect of making the demand for money vary positively with real GDP, the price level,

and wealth, and negatively with the nominal rate of interest. The nominal demand for money varies proportionally with the price level.

5. When there is an excess demand for money balances, people try to sell bonds. This pushes the price of bonds down and the interest rate up. When there is an excess supply of money balances, people try to buy bonds. This pushes the price of bonds up and the rate of interest down. Monetary equilibrium is established when people are willing to hold the existing stocks of money and bonds at the current rate of interest.

6. With given inflationary expectations, changes in the nominal interest rate translate into changes in the real interest rate. A change in the real interest rate causes desired investment to change along the investment demand function. This shifts the aggregate desired expenditure function and causes equilibrium GDP to change. This means that the aggregate demand curve shifts.

7. Points 5 and 6 together describe the transmission mechanism that links money to GDP. A decrease in the supply of money (or a rise in interest rates) reduces aggregate demand. An increase in the supply of money (or a cut in interest rates) increases aggregate demand.

8. The negatively sloped aggregate demand curve indicates that the higher the price level, the lower the equilibrium GDP. The explanation lies in part with the effect of money on the adjustment mechanism: other things being equal, the higher the price level, the higher the demand for nominal money and the rate of interest, the lower the level of investment and therefore the lower the aggregate expenditure function, and thus the lower the equilibrium level of GDP.

9. Combinations of the interest rate and equilibrium GDP for which desired expenditure equals actual real national output can be represented by the *IS* curve, which is negatively sloped. Combinations of real GDP and the equilibrium interest rate for which money demand equals money supply can be represented by the *LM* curve, which is positively sloped.

10. The *AD* curve can be derived from the *IS/LM* model, holding all exogenous expenditures and the nominal money supply constant. A rise in the price level lowers the real money supply, leading to higher interest rates and lower GDP. A fall in the price level leads to an increase in the real money supply, which lowers interest rates and increases GDP. Hence the *AD* curve is negatively sloped. This reinforces our earlier discussion of why *AD* has a negative slope.

11. Changes in the money supply affect GDP via shifts in the *AD* curve; therefore, they have a positive relationship with GDP in the short run but no effect on GDP in the long run.

12. Fiscal policy has a similar effect to monetary policy so far as GDP and the price level are concerned, but it has different effects on the composition of expenditures.

Topics for review

- Interest rates and bond prices
- Transactions, precautionary, and speculative motives for holding money
- Negative relationship between the quantity of money demanded and the interest rate
- Monetary equilibrium
- Transmission mechanism
- Investment demand function
- Money and the adjustment mechanism
- The *IS* and *LM* curves
- The slope of the *AD* curve
- The effects of monetary and fiscal policy in the short run and the long run.

Questions for discussion

1. Under what conditions will individuals be happy to hold the existing stock of money and bonds? Since bonds yield more interest than money does, what compensates money holders at the margin for the loss of interest on the last £1 of money they choose to hold?

2. Explain what happens to the equilibrium interest rates if: the introduction of electronic money reduces demand for traditional forms of money; better bank service increases demand for money; the authorities relax monetary policy?

3. Explain what happens in the complete macro model if: there is a technical change that improves labour productivity; there is an increase in export demand; there is an autonomous increase in investment.

4. Discuss the role of monetary and fiscal policies in trying to remove a recessionary gap that has been caused by a recession in world GDP.

5. Compare and contrast the long-run effects of expansionary monetary and fiscal policies.

6. Are there any circumstances in which it might be desirable to implement simultaneously an expansionary fiscal policy and a contractionary monetary policy; or an expansionary monetary policy and a contractionary fiscal policy?

Appendix:
Schools of thought in macroeconomics

The model we have built up since Chapter 14, and now extended to include a monetary sector, has been set out as if its relationships were generally accepted. In reality there have been many fierce controversies about the appropriate model with which to describe the economy. In this appendix we outline some of the disagreements between different participants in macroeconomic debates. It is helpful to identify broad schools of thought within macroeconomics, even though no one may subscribe to these precise collections of views today.

Early Keynesians

Early, and more extreme, Keynesian models placed all their emphasis on explaining the expenditure categories ($C + I + G + NX$) and had no place for monetary influences. They used perfectly elastic (horizontal) LM and $SRAS$ curves. The perfectly elastic LM curve arose because the demand for money was assumed to be highly sensitive (in the limit, infinitely sensitive) to changes in the interest rate;[1] as a consequence, the expansionary effects of rightward shifts in the IS curve were not in the least crowded out through interest-rate changes. The perfectly elastic $SRAS$ curve arose because wages and prices were assumed to be inflexible downwards and the economy was at less than full employment; as a consequence, there was no crowding out of the effects of expenditure changes through changes in the price level.

This early Keynesian model has several characteristics, illustrated in Figure 18A.1. First, changes in aggregate desired expenditure caused large changes in income and employment, changes that were not damped by variations in either the interest rate or the price level. Second, changes in monetary aggregates did not affect GDP because the perfectly elastic LM curve was unaffected by changes in the quantity of money. (Recall that a change in the quantity of money shifts the LM curve to the left or to the right; which means that the perfectly elastic curve 'shifts into itself' and thus undergoes no visible change.) In an alternative version, investment was insensitive to the interest rate, so that, even if changes in the money supply changed the interest rate, they would not affect real expenditures. Third, there was no automatic adjustment mechanism to restore full employment, since the downward rigidity of wages and prices prevented the $SRAS$ curve from shifting downwards. In brief, both short- and long-run aggregate

---

[1] This horizontal LM curve was known as the *liquidity trap*, because, when it occurred, it meant that money and bonds were perfect substitutes, so an excess supply of money would not lead people to bid up the price of bonds and thereby lower the interest rate. Hence increases in the money supply would not be transmitted into increases in expenditure. This was only expected to happen in deep recessions when interest rates were very low—so low that it was not worth the effort to switch into bonds.

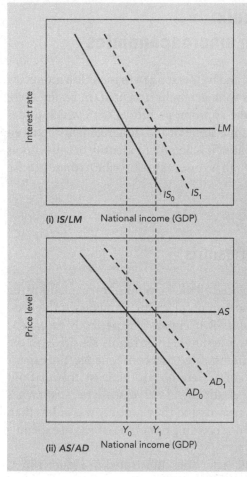

Figure 18A.1. The early or extreme Keynesian model

The early Keynesian model had a horizontal *LM* curve and a horizontal aggregate supply curve. This meant that any shift in autonomous expenditures would have an effect on GDP equal to the change in expenditure times the simple multiplier. This is illustrated in part (i) by a shift in the *IS* curve from IS_0 to IS_1, which leads in part (ii) to a shift in the *AD* curve of an equal amount from AD_0 to AD_1. GDP increases from Y_0 to Y_1. Notice that early Keynesians did not use an *AD* curve (they used *AE* or *IS*), but according to their assumptions it would have been vertical, because they had no linkages from changes in the real money supply to interest rates, no relative price effects, and no wealth effects. *AD* is drawn negatively sloped here for familiarity; with a horizontal and fixed aggregate supply curve, it makes no difference.

supply curves were considered to be horizontal, and only changes in autonomous expenditures (not the money supply) would shift the aggregate demand curve.

The main policy implication of the early Keynesian model is that government fiscal policy is needed to restore full employment whenever the economy shows signs of settling down into equilibrium with substantial unemployment.

Early monetarists

Early monetarists disputed these conclusions while accepting the underlying model. For example, when challenged to outline his model, Milton Friedman, the leader of the monetarist school, used an *IS/LM* model in which the *LM* curve was steep, rather than flat, and the *SRAS* curve was flexible downwards because prices and wages were flexible downwards. The early versions of the extreme monetarist model, illustrated in Figure

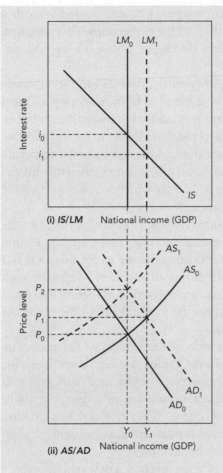

(i) **IS/LM**   National income (GDP)

(ii) **AS/AD**   National income (GDP)

Figure 18A.2. The early monetarist model

The early monetarist model had a vertical LM curve, which came from the assumption of a constant velocity of circulation. With a vertical LM curve, shifts in the IS curve (fiscal policy) would have no effect on AD since they would be exactly crowded out by interest rate rises. An increase in the money supply would shift the LM curve from LM_0 to LM_1, and the AD curve from AD_0 to AD_1. GDP would increase in the short run from Y_0 to Y_1, and the price level would increase from P_0 to P_1. However, inflationary pressure would eventually pass through into wages, and the aggregate supply curve would shift from AS_0 to AS_1. The rise in the price level would return the LM curve to LM_0. Thus, in the long run, prices would rise in proportion to the increase in the money stock and all real variables would be left unchanged. The monetarist rule of thumb was that it took about one year for a change in the money supply to influence real output and a further year before it affected the price level.

18A.2, had a vertical LM curve because the demand for money depended only on GDP and not on the interest rate. The consequence of this was 100 per cent crowding out of any fiscal stimulus. Monetary policy, however, had powerful effects on the economy because any shift in the LM curve had a large effect on the AD curve. The early monetarist model also had an easily shifted $SRAS$ curve because prices and wages were assumed to be quite flexible. This meant that any deviation from full employment (potential GDP) would be corrected relatively quickly by adjustments in wages and prices that would shift the $SRAS$ curve back to intersect the AD curve at full employment.

Modern moderate monetarists and Keynesians

A great debate, accompanied by a vast amount of empirical work, raged between the two camps in the 1950s, 1960s, and 1970s. One by one, as evidence accumulated,

Macroeconomic policy

Keynesians and monetarists abandoned their extreme positions and moved towards a common ground, until finally little but rhetoric divided the two groups. This common ground is largely reflected in the model we have developed above, so we will not illustrate it again here.

Eventually, both sides had come to agree on a downward-sloping *IS* and an upward-sloping *LM* curve, which allowed the economy to respond to both monetary and real expenditure shocks. Keynesians agreed that there was some downward flexibility in wages and prices; they argued, however, that it acted too slowly to be an effective mechanism for restoring full employment quickly after a downward shift in aggregate desired expenditure. Monetarists agreed that wages and prices were sufficiently inflexible downwards to cause serious deviations from full employment when the economy was hit by either a monetary or an expenditure shock.

Early monetarists also argued against fine-tuning, saying that the lags in the economy's response to monetary shocks were long and variable, and that fine-tuning would be more likely to do harm than good. Keynesians came to accept this view but continued to hold that the system often settled into slumps that were prolonged enough for there to be plenty of time to diagnose the situation; corrective monetary and fiscal policies could then be applied at leisure, without having to worry about the pitfalls of fine-tuning against sharp, transitory fluctuations.

In 1980 the US Nobel Laureate James Tobin, one of the leaders of the moderate Keynesians, debated with the British economist David Laidler, a moderate monetarist, in the pages of the *Economic Journal*. Neutral observers could find little real gulf between them. They disagreed, as one might expect, on matters of judgement about speeds of reactions and the precise slopes of some curves. They revealed, however, no discernible differences of underlying models or of fundamental assessment of what were the key relations that governed the economy's behaviour.

Just as that apparently satisfactory situation was being reached, a new school became prominent. This was the *New Classical school*, whose intellectual leaders were the US economists Robert Lucas, Thomas Sargent, and Neil Wallace.

THE NEW CLASSICAL SCHOOL

Keynesians and monetarists had, all along, shared the presumption that macroeconomics was about explaining periods of *disequilibrium* (unemployment and excess capacity on the one hand, and inflationary gaps on the other). They certainly disagreed about adjustment speeds and appropriate policy responses, but they shared an assumption that recessions involved, at least temporary, market failure.

The New Classical school, in contrast, picked up the agenda of the *Austrian school*, which was to explain business cycles in an equilibrium model.[2] Thus, they assume that

---

[2] The Austrian School was founded by Carl Menger (1840–1921) and Eugen von Böhm-Bawerk (1851–1914). Its most influential disciples were Ludwig von Mises (1881–1973) and Friedrich von Hayek (1899–1991). The British economist Lionel (later Lord) Robbins (1898–1984) was also influenced by their ideas.

markets clear continuously, *as if* they were perfectly competitive. This makes full employment (no involuntary unemployment) the equilibrium position that would normally be achieved. The economy deviates from full employment either when mistakes are made or when rational agents (decision takers are called 'agents') voluntarily decide to work less than the full-employment amount of work.

New Classical economics uses the theory of **rational expectations.** This means that agents form expectations based upon all available information about the future at the time they take decisions. So agents make only random errors in foreseeing the future course of market variables. Since markets always clear, and since agents do not make systematic errors, full-employment equilibrium is the normal state of the economy. Prices will always adjust to ensure that there are neither unsatisfied buyers nor unsatisfied sellers in any market, including the labour market. We will consider how this approach can be reconciled (if at all) with the observation of sustained periods of unemployment when we discuss business cycles in Chapter 20. An alternative 'equilibrium' approach to business cycles, known as 'real business cycles', is also discussed in Chapter 20.

The critics of New Classical economics argue that markets do not always clear. They believe that, even when a shock is foreseen so that no one misperceives what is happening, output will be affected because agents could not anticipate all of the economy's reactions in advance. Agents cannot, therefore, establish the new equilibrium set of prices by anticipating what these will be. Instead, it is argued, agents' reactions would have to be worked out slowly, and only as the price and quantity adjustments are observed to evolve over time.

Market clearing

There are many subtle differences between different schools. The two most fundamental differences concern market clearing and expectations formation. New Classical theorists assume that markets always clear; moderate monetarists assume that markets do not clear instantaneously, especially when downward adjustments are required. This sluggishness is sufficient to cause significant excess supplies to persist in goods and factor markets for some time. In the longer run, however, markets do tend to clear and full-employment equilibrium is the point to which the economy gravitates.

Moderate Keynesians agree with the moderate monetarists, but think that the adjustment takes a little longer than the monetarists think. As a result, they are inclined to give a place to demand-management policies that will stabilize the economy against persistent recessionary and inflationary gaps—even if smaller, more transient, gaps must be accepted as unavoidable. Some extreme Keynesians believe that markets do not clear even in the long term and, thus, that government demand management must be used more or less continually to stabilize the economy at or near full employment. Modern, or *New*, Keynesians, believe that unemployment (or a big chunk of it that cannot be removed by stimulating aggregate demand) is caused by rigidities in labour markets, and they seek solutions through structural reforms and supply-side intervention (in addition, perhaps, to aggregate demand policies).

Macroeconomic policy

Expectations formation

On expectations, the New Classical theorists believe in fully rational expectations, in which prediction errors are 'pure white noise'. Loosely, this means that systematic errors of prediction are not made. Since prices always clear all markets and systematic mistakes are not made, deviations from full employment cannot be reduced by government intervention. Other economists believe that expectations are formed by some mixture of rational calculation, extrapolation from the past, and adaptive learning behaviour. Different economists vary on how they believe the typical mix combines the rational, the extrapolative, and the adaptive.[3] Those economists who believe that the economy is too complicated for contemporary economists to understand fully are inclined to believe that private decision makers can make major, often systematic, mistakes. They ask: if economists disagree as much as they clearly do over how the economy behaves, how can private agents be expected to get this behaviour right on average?

It is important to be aware that the dividing lines in macroeconomic debates are perpetually shifting. Many modern Keynesians would not subscribe to many of the views we have attributed to the Keynesian school above. Indeed, much of the attention of what is now called New Keynesian economics is directed not at cyclical (demand-deficient) unemployment, but rather at what used to be called 'Classical' unemployment. And the Keynesian policy solution for unemployment (fiscal stimulus) has shifted to supply-side measures (training, benefits structure, and wage-bargaining institutions).

[3] *Rational expectations* assumes that the expected value of a variable is equal to the mean of its statistical probability distribution, while the actual outcome will deviate from that expectation by a white-noise random error. *Extrapolative expectations* assumes that next period's expectation of the value of the variable will be equal to last period's value or the extrapolation of some existing trend. *Adaptive expectations* assumes that agents adjust their expectations in proportion to the size and direction of the error in expectations (deviation between the expectation and the out-turn) they made last time.

CHAPTER 19

The Balance of Payments and Exchange Rates

The balance of payments 620
Balance of payments accounts 620
  Current account 621
  Capital account 622
    Short-term and long-term capital flows 623
    Portfolio investment and direct investment 623
The meaning of payments balances and imbalances 624
  The balance of payments must balance overall 624
  Does the balance of payments matter? 625
    Actual and desired transactions 627

The market for foreign exchange 627
The demand for and supply of pounds 628
  The demand for pounds 629
    UK exports 629
    Capital inflows 629
    Reserve currency 630
  The total demand for pounds 630
  The shape of the demand curve for pounds 630
  The supply of pounds 631
  The shape of the supply curve of pounds 632

The determination of exchange rates 632
Flexible exchange rates 633
Fixed exchange rates 634
Changes in exchange rates 636
  A rise in the domestic price of exports 636
  A rise in the foreign price of imports 637
  Changes in price levels 638
  Capital movements 638

  Short-term capital movements 639
  Long-term capital movements 639
  Structural changes 639
The behaviour of exchange rates 640
  Purchasing power parity 640
  Exchange rate overshooting 642
    Implications of overshooting 647

The exchange rate regime and macroeconomic policy 648
Mobile financial capital 649
  Interest rates under fixed exchange rates 650
  Interest rates with floating exchange rates 650
Monetary policy and the exchange rate regime 651
  Fixed exchange rate 651
  Floating exchange rate 652
Fiscal policy and the exchange rate regime 654
  Fixed exchange rate 654
  Floating exchange rate 655

Summary 656

Topics for review 657

Questions for discussion 657

Box 19.1. The volume of trade, the balance of trade, and the new mercantilism 626
Box 19.2. Exchange rates and the quantity theory 641
Box 19.3. Why exchange rate changes are unpredictable 644

T HIS chapter focuses on the linkages between the macroeconomy and the rest of the world. We have mentioned these linkages many times before, but here they become the main concern. There are financial (or monetary) linkages, through the international money and capital markets, and there are 'real' dimensions, through international trade and travel. The real and the monetary factors are not independent of each other. Real transactions cannot take place without money and finance, and are influenced by monetary forces; equally, money markets are influenced by the fundamentals of the real economy.

We have had the exchange rate and the balance of payments (net exports of goods and services, *NX*) explicitly in our macroeconomic model since Chapter 15. Also we have seen in Box 18.3 that external linkages can have a critical effect on the transmission mechanism of macro policy. We now look at these issues in greater detail.

In the first part of this chapter we discuss the balance of payments. This is an important concept concerned with net transactions between one country and the rest of the world. We ask what the 'balance of payments' means, how it is measured, and whether it matters. In the second part we discuss the exchange rate—what role does it play in connecting the domestic economy with foreign economies, and what economic forces determine its value? Finally, we outline the significance of various possible exchange rate regimes for the impact of monetary and fiscal policies.

The balance of payments

The balance of payments position of the UK economy has had a high profile in political arguments over economic policy since at least the Second World War, and probably longer. We shall first explain how the balance of payments is recorded in the UK, and we shall then ask in what ways the balance of payments matters.

Balance of payments accounts

In order to know what is happening to the course of international trade, governments keep track of the transactions between countries. The record of such transactions is made in the *balance of payments accounts*. Each transaction, such as a shipment of exports or the arrival of imported goods, is classified according to the payments or receipts that would typically arise from it.

Transactions that lead to a receipt of payment from foreigners, such as a commodity export or a sale of an asset abroad, are recorded in the balance of payments accounts as a credit item with a positive sign. In terms of our later objective of analysing the market for foreign exchange, these transactions represent the supply of foreign exchange and the demand for sterling on the foreign exchange market, because foreigners have to buy our currency in order to pay us in sterling for the goods they have bought. Transactions that lead to a payment to foreigners, such as a commodity import or the purchase of a foreign asset, are recorded as a debit item with a negative sign. These transactions represent the demand for foreign exchange and the supply of sterling on the foreign exchange market, because we have to buy foreign currency with sterling in order to pay for our overseas purchases.

Balance of payments accounts are normally divided into two broad parts. One part deals with payments for goods and services, interest, and transfers. This is known as the **current account.** The other part records transactions in assets and is, accordingly, known as the **capital account.** A summary of the balance of payments accounts of the UK for 1995 appears in Table 19.1.

Table 19.1. UK balance of payments, 1995 (£ million)

Visible trade balance	−11,628
Exports	152,346
Imports	−163,974
Invisibles balance	8,736
Services	6,142
Investment income	9,572
Transfers	−6,978
Current account balance	−2,892
Transactions in assets	−124,045
Transactions in liabilities	124,491
Net transactions (capital flows)	446
Balancing item	2,446

The balance of payments accounts record transactions between the domestic economy and the rest of the world that cross the foreign exchanges. The trade balance is the difference in value between imports and exports. The current account includes also the balance of payments in invisibles. The capital account records net purchases and sales of assets and liabilities. If records were accurate, the current account balance and the capital account balance must be equal and of opposite sign. The balancing item is the measurement error in this set of accounts. Its presence is what makes the accounts balance in practice.

CURRENT ACCOUNT

The current account records transactions arising from trade in goods and services, from income accruing to capital owned by one country and invested in another, or from transfers by residents of one country to residents of another. The current account is divided into two main sections.

The first of these, variously called the **visible account,** the **trade account,** and the **merchandise account,** records payments and receipts arising from the import and export of tangible goods, such as computers, cars, wheat, and shoes. UK imports require payments to be made to foreign residents in foreign exchange, and hence are entered as debit items on the visible account. In 1995, UK residents spent almost £164 billion on buying goods imported from overseas. UK exports earn payments from foreign residents in foreign exchange (though the foreign exchange will be converted into sterling through the foreign exchange market), and hence are recorded as credit items. In 1995, UK exports amounted to just over £152 billion. Exports represent goods leaving the country, but payment for those goods passes in the opposite direction. With imports, goods enter the country and payment has to be made to the foreign manufacturers. We can see that in 1995 there was a visible trade deficit of about £11.6 billion, which is the difference between the value of imports and exports.

The second part of Table 19.1, the **invisibles account,** records payments arising out of trade in services, payments for the use of capital, and transfers to persons. There are three components to invisibles: trade in such services as insurance, banking, shipping, and tourism; payments of interest, dividends, and profits that are made for capital used in one country but owned by residents of another country; and transfer payments, such as might arise when an Italian waiter in London sends money home to his mother in Turin, or when a UK pensioner receives her pension in the Costa del Sol.[1] The figures for invisibles in Table 19.1 are reported net. This means that, while for each category there are payments in both directions, it is only the balance that appears. So in 1995 the UK was a net recipient of payments for services (+£6.1 billion) and investment incomes (+£9.6 billion), but made net transfers overseas (−£7 billion). Invisibles as a whole were in surplus to the value of £8.7 billion (calculated as £6.1 billion + £9.6 billion − £7 billion).

The UK trade account deficit in 1995, therefore, was £11.6 billion, while the invisibles surplus was £8.7 billion. The combination of this negative trade balance and positive invisibles balance gave an overall *current account balance* that was in deficit to the tune of about £2.9 billion.[2]

CAPITAL ACCOUNT

The other major component in the balance of payments is the **capital account,** which records transactions related to international movements of ownership of financial assets. It is important to notice right away that the capital account does not relate to imports and exports of physical capital: trade in such things as machine tools or construction equipment is part of the *visible trade account*. Rather, the capital account of the balance of payments relates only to cross-border movements in financial

---

[1] The symbols *X* and *IM* as used in this book refer to exports and imports of both tangible goods *and* services, but do not include payments of interest, dividends, and profits, or transfers.

[2] It is possible that there will be revisions to these figures in later years. Later revisions are possible in all national income statistics. These revisions often have a significant effect on balance of payments figures. This is because the balance of payments records the difference between two large numbers. A small percentage revision on either side of the accounts can lead to a large percentage revision in the balance. For example, a 1 per cent rise in the value of exports would reduce the trade deficit by nearly 10 per cent.

instruments, such as ownership of company shares, bank loans, or government securities.

UK purchases of foreign investments (which then become assets to the UK) are called a *capital outflow*. They use foreign exchange to buy the foreign investment, and so they are entered as a debit (negative) item in the UK payments accounts.[3] Foreign investment in the UK (which, thereby, increases UK liabilities to foreigners) is called a *capital inflow*. It earns foreign exchange and so is entered as a credit (positive) item.

As shown in Table 19.1, in 1995 UK residents increased their investments abroad by about £124 billion, while foreigners increased their investments in the UK by a similar amount. These may seem like very large amounts, and, indeed, they are. However, a high proportion of this activity is the international borrowing and lending of the financial institutions in the City of London, which is a major centre of international financial intermediation. The net capital inflow resulted in a surplus in the capital account of only about £0.4 billion. This means that there was a net increase in foreign liabilities of £0.4 billion.[4]

Short-term and long-term capital flows

The capital account is often divided into two categories that distinguish between movements of short-term and long-term capital. Short-term capital is money that is held in the form of highly liquid assets, such as bank accounts and short-term Treasury bills. Long-term capital represents funds coming into the UK (a credit item) or leaving the UK (a debit item) to be invested in less liquid assets, such as long-term bonds, or in physical capital, such as a new car assembly plant.

Portfolio investment and direct investment

The two major subdivisions of the long-term part of the capital account are *direct investment* and *portfolio investment*. **Direct investment** relates to changes in non-resident ownership of domestic firms and resident ownership of foreign firms. One form of direct investment, called greenfield investment, is the building of a factory in the UK by a foreign firm—for example, the Toyota car factory near Derby. Another form of direct investment, called brownfield investment, is a takeover, in which a controlling interest in a firm, previously controlled by residents, is acquired by foreigners—such as when BMW acquired a majority interest in the Rover Group from British Aerospace. **Portfolio investment,** on the other hand, is investment in bonds or a minority holding of shares that does not involve legal control.

---

[3] Capital outflows are sometimes also referred to as *capital exports*. It may seem odd that, whereas a merchandise export is a credit item on current account, a capital export is a debit item on capital account. To understand this terminology, consider the export of UK funds for investment in a German bond. The capital transaction involves the purchase, and hence the *import*, of a German bond, and this has the same effect on the balance of payments as the purchase, and hence the import, of a German good. Both items involve payments to foreigners, and both use foreign exchange. Both are thus debit items in UK balance of payments accounts.

[4] Note that this figure only relates to transactions in assets. It does not account for capital gains or losses resulting from valuation changes of existing asset holdings. Thus, the capital account balance is **not** a measure of the total change in indebtedness between the UK and the rest of the world.

The meaning of payments balances and imbalances

We have seen that the payments accounts show the total of receipts of foreign exchange (credit items) and payments of foreign exchange (debit items) on account of each category of payment. It is also common to calculate the *balance* on separate items or groups of items. The concept of the balance of payments is used in a number of different ways, so we must approach this issue in a series of steps.

THE BALANCE OF PAYMENTS MUST BALANCE OVERALL

The notion that the balance of payments accounts must balance should be no great mystery. They are constructed so that it has to be true. The idea behind this proposition is quite general. Take your own personal income and expenditures. Suppose you earn £100 by selling your services (labour) and you buy £90 worth of clothing. You have exports (of services/labour) worth £100 and imports (of clothing) worth £90. Your current account surplus is £10. However, that £10 surplus must be invested in holding a financial claim on someone else—if you hold cash it is a claim on the Bank of England; if you deposit the money in the building society, it becomes a claim on the building society; and so on.

Whichever way you look at it, the £10 you have acquired is the acquisition of an asset. It represents a capital outflow from your personal economy that is the inevitable consequence of your current account surplus. So, you have a current account surplus of £10 and a capital account deficit (outflow) of £10. The only difference between your accounts and those for the economy as a whole is that with the latter, payments across the foreign exchange markets are involved. A country with a current account surplus in its balance of payments must, at the same time, have acquired net claims on foreigners to the same value.

The current and capital accounts of the balance of payments are necessarily of equal and opposite size. When added together, they equal zero.

There is one important caveat to the above statement with regard to actual official accounts. This is that, while conceptually the current and capital account are defined to be equal and opposite, in practice the national income statisticians are not able to keep accurate records of all transactions, and hence there are always errors in measurement. This means that a 'balancing item' is included in the balance of payments table. The balancing item stands for all unrecorded transactions and is defined to be equal to the difference between the measured current account and the measured capital account. The sum of the current account, the capital account, and the balancing item is always zero by construction.

DOES THE BALANCE OF PAYMENTS MATTER?

The *balance of payments on current account* is the sum of the balances on the visible and invisible accounts. As a carry-over from a long-discredited eighteenth-century economic doctrine called *mercantilism*, a credit balance on current account (where receipts exceed payments) is often called a **favourable balance,** and a debit balance (where payments exceed receipts) is often called an **unfavourable balance.** Mercantilists, both ancient and modern, hold that the gains from trade arise only from having a favourable balance of trade. This misses the point of the doctrine of *comparative advantage*, which states that countries can gain from a balanced increase in trade because it allows each country to specialize on doing what it is *relatively* good at. The modern resurgence of mercantilism is discussed in Box 19.1.

It would be tempting to refer to a deficit on capital account as an unfavourable balance as well. However, by now it should be clear that this would be a nonsense, because a current account surplus is the same thing as a capital account deficit. Hence it is impossible for one to be 'good' and the other 'bad'. However, this discussion does have one important implication.

> The terms 'a balance-of-payments *deficit*' and 'a balance-of-payments *surplus*' must refer to the balance on some part of the payments accounts. In the UK these terms almost always apply to the current account.

A current account deficit is just as likely to be the product of a healthy growing economy as it is of an unhealthy economy. Suppose, for example, that an economy has rapidly growing domestic industries that offer a high rate of return on domestic investment. Such an economy would be attracting investment from the rest of the world, and as a result it would have a capital account surplus (capital inflows) and a current account deficit. Far from being a sign of weakness, the current account deficit would indicate economic health. True, the economy is acquiring external debts; but if this debt is being used to finance rapid real growth, it can be repaid out of higher future output.[5]

In contrast, another economy may, indeed, have inefficient and unproductive domestic industry, and may be in a situation where domestic spending exceeds domestic output. (Recall from Chapter 15 that the current account balance is equal to the difference between total domestic expenditure and total domestic production.) Therefore, it will have a current account deficit and is borrowing from abroad to finance extra consumption.

> The existence of a current account balance of payments deficit tells us only that an economy's total spending exceeds its total output and that it has a capital

---

[5] 'Debt' is used here in its general sense rather than in the context of debt versus equity. These external debts could be in any specific form, including equity, bonds, or bank loans.

BOX 19.1.

The volume of trade, the balance of trade, and the new mercantilism

Media commentators, political figures, and much of the general public often judge the national balance of payments as they would the accounts of a single firm. Just as a firm is supposed to show a profit, the nation is supposed to secure a balance of payments surplus on current account, with the benefits derived from international trade measured by the size of that surplus.

This view is related to the exploitation doctrine of international trade: one country's surplus is another country's deficit. Thus, one country's gain, judged by its surplus, must be another country's loss, judged by its deficit.

People who hold such views today are echoing an ancient economic doctrine called *mercantilism*. The mercantilists were a group of economists who preceded Adam Smith. They judged the success of trade by the size of the trade balance. In many cases, this doctrine made sense in terms of their objective, which was to use international trade as a means of building up the political and military power of the state, rather than as a means of raising the living standards of its citizens. A balance of payments surplus allowed the nation (then and now) to acquire foreign exchange reserves. (In those days the reserves took the form of gold. Today, they are a mixture of gold and assets in the currencies of other countries.) These reserves could then be used to pay armies, to purchase weapons from abroad, and generally to finance colonial expansions.

People who advocate this view in modern times are called *neo-mercantilists*. In so far as their object is to increase the military power of the state, they are choosing means that could achieve their ends. In so far as they are drawing an analogy between what is a sensible objective for a business, interested in its own material welfare, and what is a sensible objective for a society, interested in the material welfare of its citizens, their views are erroneous, because their analogy is false.

If the object of economic activity is to promote the welfare and living standards of ordinary citizens, rather than the power of governments, then the mercantilist focus on the balance of trade makes no sense. The principle of comparative advantage (discussed in Chapter 1) shows that average living standards are maximized by having individuals, regions, and countries specialize in the things that they can produce comparatively best and then trade to obtain the things that they can produce comparatively worst. The more specialization there is, the more trade occurs.

On this view, the gains from trade are to be judged by the volume of trade. A situation in which there is a *large volume* of trade but in which each country has a *zero balance* of trade can thus be regarded as quite satisfactory. Furthermore, a change in commercial policy that results in a balanced increase in trade between two countries will bring gain, because it allows for specialization according to comparative advantage, even though it causes no change in either country's trade balance.

To the business interested in private profit and to the government interested in the power of the state, it is the balance of trade that matters. To the person interested in the welfare of ordinary citizens, it is the volume of trade that matters.

inflow. The existence of such a deficit is consistent with both healthy, growing economies and unhealthy, inefficient economies.

Actual and desired transactions

The discussion in this section has focused on *actual* transactions as measured in the balance of payments accounts. It is the actual capital inflow that must equal the actual current account deficit. There is no reason at all, however, why *desired* (or planned) current account transactions should add up to desired capital account transactions. In practice, it is movements in the exchange rate that play a key role in reconciling actual and desired transactions. We now turn to a discussion of the exchange rate and how it is determined.

The market for foreign exchange

The foreign exchange markets are the markets in which one currency can be converted into another. We are used to thinking about markets in which goods are exchanged for money. In a foreign exchange market it is one country's money that is exchanged for another country's money. As with all markets, the foreign exchange market can be analysed with the tools of demand and supply developed earlier in this book. Before proceeding with this exercise, it is helpful to remind ourselves why we need such markets.

Money is central to the efficient working of any modern economy that relies on specialization and exchange. Yet money as we know it is a *national* matter, one that is closely controlled by national governments. Each nation-state has its own currency: if you live in Sweden, you earn kronor and spend kronor; if you run a business in Austria, you borrow schillings and meet your wage bill with schillings. The currency of a country is acceptable within the bounds of that country, but usually it will not be accepted by people and firms in another country. The Stockholm bus company will accept kronor for a fare but not Austrian schillings; the Austrian worker will not take Swedish kronor for wages, but expects to be paid in schillings.

UK producers require payment in pounds sterling for their products. They need pounds to meet their wage bills, to pay for their raw materials, and to reinvest or to distribute their profits. There is no problem when they sell to UK-based purchasers. However, if they sell their goods to, say, Indian importers, either the Indians must exchange their rupees to acquire pounds to pay for the goods, or the UK producers must accept rupees;[6] and they will accept rupees only if they know that they can exchange the rupees for pounds. The same holds true for producers in all countries; they must eventually receive payment in the currency of their own country.

---

6 Some trade, especially in primary commodities such as wheat and oil, is conducted in US dollars, even when US residents are not involved. In this respect, the US dollar has a special role as an international medium of exchange or unit of account.

Trade between nations typically requires the exchange of one nation's currency for that of another.

International payments involve the exchange of currencies between people who have one currency and require another. Suppose that a UK firm wishes to acquire ¥3 million for some purpose. (¥ is the currency symbol for the Japanese yen.) The firm can go to its bank and buy a cheque, or money order, that will be accepted in Japan as ¥3 million. How many *pounds* the firm must pay to purchase this cheque will depend on the value of the pound in terms of yen.

The exchange of one currency for another is a *foreign exchange transaction*. The term 'foreign exchange' refers to the actual foreign currency or various claims on it, such as bank deposits or promises to pay, that are traded for each other. The *exchange rate* is the value of the pound in terms of foreign currency; it is the amount of foreign currency that can be obtained with one unit of the domestic currency. For example, if one can obtain ¥150 for £1, the yen–pound exchange rate is 150.

A rise in the external value of the pound (that is, a rise in the exchange rate) is an **appreciation** of the pound; for example, if one can now obtain ¥175 for £1, the pound has *appreciated*. A fall in the external value of the pound (that is, a fall in the exchange rate) is a **depreciation** of the pound; for example, if one can now obtain only ¥125 for £1, the pound has *depreciated*.[7]

Because the exchange rate expresses the value of one currency in terms of another, when one currency appreciates, the other must depreciate.

The demand for and supply of pounds

The exchange rate is just a price, albeit a very important price for the economy concerned. As with other prices, we shall approach the explanation of exchange rates from the perspective of demand and supply analysis. However, the exchange rate is potentially influenced by (and influences) all payments into and out of the national economy from abroad. Hence we need to be clear about what those payments are before proceeding to discuss the determinants of the exchange rate.

For the sake of simplicity, we use an example involving trade between the UK and the USA and the determination of the exchange rate between their two currencies, the pound sterling[8] and the dollar. The two-country example simplifies things, but the

[7] When the external value of the currency changes as a result of explicit policy of the central bank, it is often said to have been *devalued* when it falls and *revalued* when it rises.

[8] We use the words 'pounds', 'sterling', and 'pounds sterling' to refer to the UK currency. In the foreign exchange markets it is usually classified as GBP or GBX, while the dollar is USD. The foreign exchange market between the GBP and USD is referred to in the market as 'cable', because it grew to its present structure by use of one of the first transatlantic telephone cables.

principles apply to all foreign transactions. Thus, 'dollar' stands for foreign exchange in general, and the value of the pound in terms of dollars stands for the foreign exchange rate in general.

When £1 = $1.50, a US importer who offers to buy £1 million with dollars must be offering to sell $1.5 million. Similarly, a UK importer who offers to sell £1 million for dollars must be offering to buy $1.5 million.

> **Because one currency is traded for another in the foreign exchange market, it follows that a demand for foreign exchange implies a supply of pounds sterling, while a supply of foreign exchange implies a demand for pounds.**

For this reason, a theory of the exchange rate between sterling and the dollar can deal either with the demand for and the supply of pounds or with the demand for and the supply of dollars: both need not be considered. We will concentrate on the demand, supply, and price of the pound (quoted in dollars).

We develop our example in terms of the demand-and-supply analysis first encountered in Chapter 2. To do so, we need only to recall that, *in the market for foreign exchange*, transactions that generate a receipt of foreign exchange represent a demand for pounds, and transactions that require a payment of foreign exchange represent a supply of pounds. We focus on the demand and supply of pounds arising from both the current and capital accounts. Later we turn to the important role of official intervention by the Bank of England (acting as agent for the Treasury through the Exchange Equalization Account).

THE DEMAND FOR POUNDS

The demand for pounds arises from all international transactions that generate a receipt of foreign exchange.

UK exports

One important source of demand for pounds in foreign exchange markets includes foreigners who do not currently hold pounds but who wish to buy UK-made goods and services. A German importer of Scotch whisky is such a purchaser; an Austrian couple planning to vacation in Cornwall is another; the Chinese national airline seeking to buy Rolls Royce engines for its passenger aircraft is yet another. All are sources of demand for pounds, arising out of international trade. Each potential buyer wants to sell their own currency and buy pounds for the purpose of purchasing UK exports.

Capital inflows

A second source of a demand for pounds comes from foreigners who wish to purchase UK assets. In order to buy UK assets, holders of foreign currencies must first buy pounds

Who wants to sell pounds? UK residents seeking to purchase foreign goods and services or assets will be supplying pounds and purchasing foreign exchange for this purpose. In addition, holders of UK assets may decide to sell their UK holdings and shift them into foreign assets, and if they do they will sell pounds; that is, they will be supplying pounds to the foreign exchange market. Similarly, a country with some sterling reserves of foreign exchange may decide that the sterling assets offer a poor return and sell pounds in order to buy another currency.

THE SHAPE OF THE SUPPLY CURVE OF POUNDS

When the pound depreciates, the sterling price of US exports to the UK rises. It takes more pounds to buy the same US goods, so UK residents will buy fewer of the now more expensive US goods. The amount of pounds being offered in exchange for dollars in order to pay for US exports to the UK (UK imports) will therefore fall.[10]

In the opposite case, when the pound appreciates, US exports to the UK become cheaper, more are sold, and more pounds are spent on them. Thus more pounds will be offered in exchange for dollars to obtain the foreign exchange needed to pay for the extra imports. The argument also applies to purchases and sales of assets.

The supply curve of pounds in the foreign exchange market is positively sloped when it is plotted against the dollar price of pounds.

This too is illustrated in Figure 19.1.

The determination of exchange rates

The demand and supply curves in Figure 19.1 do not include official foreign exchange market intervention by the Bank of England, though they do include any transactions in sterling by foreign monetary authorities. In order to complete our analysis, we need to incorporate the role of domestic official intervention.[11] Three important cases need to be considered.

---

10 As long as the demand for imports is elastic (price elasticity greater than −1 (in absolute terms)), the fall in the volume of imports will swamp the rise in price and hence fewer pounds will be spent on imports. If the elasticity of demand for imports is less than −1 (in absolute terms), the volume of imports will fall but the amount of domestic money spent on them will rise. In what follows, we adopt the case of elastic demand, which is usual in this area. In a more general form, it is called the *Marshall–Lerner condition*, after two famous British economists who first studied the problem.

11 Official intervention is included in the balance of payments accounts in Table 19.1 under 'Transactions in assets'. Official intervention used to be reported in the aggregate balance of payments figures under a separate category called 'Balance for official financing'. This practice is still followed in many other countries, where it is sometimes called the 'official settlements balance'.

1. When there is no official intervention by the Bank of England, the exchange rate is determined by the equality between the supply and demand for pounds arising from the capital and current accounts. This is called a *flexible*, or *floating*, *exchange rate*.

2. When official intervention is used to maintain the exchange rate at (or close to) a particular value, there is said to be a *fixed*, or *pegged*, *exchange rate*.

3. Between these two 'pure' systems are a variety of possible intermediate cases, including the *adjustable peg* and the *managed float*. In the adjustable peg system, governments set and attempt to maintain par values for their exchange rates, but they explicitly recognize that circumstances may arise in which they will change the par value. In a managed float, the central bank seeks to have some stabilizing influence on the exchange rate but does not try to fix it at some publicly announced par value.

Flexible exchange rates

Consider an exchange rate that is set in a freely competitive market, with no intervention by the central bank. Like any competitive price, this rate fluctuates according to the conditions of demand and supply.

Suppose that the current price of pounds is so low (say, e_1 in Figure 19.1) that the quantity of pounds demanded exceeds the quantity supplied. Pounds will be in scarce supply in the foreign exchange market; some people who require pounds to make payments to the UK will be unable to obtain them; and the price of pounds will be bid up. The value of the pound *vis-à-vis* the dollar will appreciate. As the price of sterling rises, the dollar price of UK exports to the USA rises and the quantity of pounds demanded to buy UK goods decreases. However, as the pound price of imports from the USA falls, a larger quantity will be purchased and the quantity of pounds supplied will rise. Thus, a rise in the price of the pound reduces the quantity demanded and increases the quantity supplied. Where the two curves intersect, quantity demanded equals quantity supplied, and the exchange rate is in equilibrium.

What happens when the price of the pound is above its equilibrium value? The quantity of pounds demanded will be less than the quantity supplied. With the pound in excess supply, some people who wish to convert pounds into dollars will be unable to do so.[12] The price of pounds will fall, fewer pounds will be supplied, more will be demanded, and an equilibrium will be re-established.

A foreign exchange market is like other competitive markets in that the forces of

---

12 Equivalently, we could say that there is an excess demand for foreign exchange.

demand and supply lead to an equilibrium price in which quantity demanded equals quantity supplied.

In a floating exchange rate system, it is exchange rate adjustment that determines the actual current and capital account transactions, even though planned, or desired, trade and investment decisions may have been inconsistent. Suppose that, at the beginning of some period, importers and exporters had plans that would have created a current account deficit, and domestic investors had plans to buy foreign securities (while foreigners had no such plans). The attempt to implement these plans would create a massive excess supply of sterling (demand for foreign exchange). This would force a sterling depreciation, which would continue until it moved far enough to force changes in plans. Indeed, it would depreciate just far enough so that any supply of sterling generated by a current account deficit was just balanced by a capital inflow (or any current account surplus was just balanced by a capital outflow).

Fixed exchange rates

When there is official intervention in the foreign exchange market to maintain a particular exchange rate, this stops some movement in the exchange rate that would otherwise have happened. In this way, it may prevent the exchange rate from adjusting sufficiently to guarantee that the current account balance and the (private-sector) capital account balance are equal and opposite. In this situation, any desired excess demand or supply of sterling by the private sector must be met by the Bank of England. In the process of intervention the Bank will be building up or running down its foreign exchange reserves.

The official foreign exchange reserves are the stock of foreign-currency-denominated assets that the monetary authorities hold in order to be able to intervene in the foreign exchange markets.

When central banks peg their exchange rates, they do not do so at one specific rate, but, rather, within some range. In the postwar exchange regime that existed until 1972 (in the UK case) exchange rates were pegged within plus or minus 1 per cent of a central (or 'par') rate. This is known as the Bretton Woods regime, after the town in the USA where, in 1944, the agreement was drawn up. In the European Exchange Rate Mechanism (ERM) of the 1980s and early 1990s, the range of permitted fluctuation was plus or minus 2.25 per cent for some countries and 6 per cent for others (including the UK from October 1990 to September 1992).[13]

---

[13] In 1993 the wider band of fluctuation within the ERM was broadened to 15 per cent.

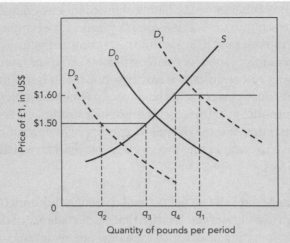

Figure 19.2. Managing fixed exchange rates

Under a fixed exchange rate regime the central bank intervenes in the foreign exchange market to ensure that the exchange rate of the home currency stays within specified bands. The figure shows three possible outcomes when there is a given supply curve and the bands within which the exchange rate is pegged are given by the range $1.50–$1.60. If the demand curve is given by D_0, the equilibrium exchange rate is within the bands so no intervention by the central bank is required. With demand curve D_1, the equilibrium exchange rate would be above $1.60. To stop the exchange rate rising above $1.60, the central bank has to sell q_4q_1 pounds per period and buy dollars of equivalent value. (For every £100 it sells it will acquire $160.) If the demand curve were D_2, the exchange rate would fall below $1.50 in a free market, so the central bank has to buy q_2q_3 pounds per period with dollars. The dollars come out of official reserves. This is the case that causes most problems because these reserve losses cannot be allowed to go on indefinitely. At some time they will run out. Here there has to be either a change of economic policy that shifts the D and S curves back to an intersection within the band or a shift in the band (devaluation) such that it encompasses the current equilibrium price.

Let us consider a simplified analysis of how such pegged exchange rate regimes operate. Assume for simplicity that the Bank of England fixed the UK exchange rate between, say, $1.50 and $1.60. This case is illustrated in Figure 19.2. The Bank would then enter the market to prevent the rate from going outside this range. At the price of $1.50, the Bank offers to buy pounds (in exchange for dollars) in unlimited amounts. At the price $1.60, the Bank offers to sell pounds (in exchange for dollars) in unlimited amounts. When the bank buys foreign exchange (sells pounds) its exchange reserves rise, but when it sells foreign exchange (buys pounds) its foreign exchange reserves fall.

If, on average, the demand and supply curves intersect in the range $1.50–$1.60, then exchange reserves will be relatively stable. However, if demand for pounds intersected the supply curve below $1.50, the Bank would find itself losing reserves each period, and such a situation cannot be sustained indefinitely (because the Bank will run out of reserves). It must then either move the bands of fluctuation (devalue) or take action to shift the demand or supply curves. This could be done, for example, by trade restrictions, or by raising interest rates to attract short-term capital inflows.

In the remainder of this chapter we focus on flexible exchange rates. However, before leaving fixed exchange rate regimes, it is worth noting that it is in a fixed exchange rate regime with an overvalued currency that balance of payments problems are directly felt by the monetary authorities. In this case, it is not necessarily a current account deficit that is the problem; rather, it is the overall excess supply of domestic currency (excess demand for foreign currency) in the foreign exchange market, which could arise from any of the components.

With fixed exchange rates and an overvalued currency, the monetary authorities will be suffering a loss of reserves. It is this that causes balance of payments crises for governments operating under such exchange rate regimes.

Changes in exchange rates

What causes exchange rates to move? The simplest answer to this question is: changes in demand or supply in the foreign exchange market. Anything that shifts the demand curve for pounds to the right or the supply curve for pounds to the left leads to an appreciation of the pound; anything that shifts the demand curve for pounds to the left or the supply curve for pounds to the right leads to a depreciation of the pound. This is nothing more than a restatement of the laws of supply and demand, applied now to the market for foreign currencies; it is illustrated in Figure 19.3.

What causes the shifts in demand and supply that lead to changes in exchange rates? There are many causes, some of which are transitory and some of which are persistent; we will discuss some of the most important ones.

A RISE IN THE DOMESTIC PRICE OF EXPORTS

Suppose that the sterling price of UK-produced telephone equipment rises. The effect on the demand for pounds depends on the price elasticity of foreign demand for the UK products.

If the demand is inelastic (say, because the UK is uniquely able to supply a product for which there are no close substitutes), then more will be spent; the demand for pounds to pay the bigger bill will shift the demand curve to the right, and the pound will appreciate. This is also illustrated in Figure 19.3(i).

If the demand is elastic, perhaps because other countries supply the same product to competitive world markets, the total amount spent will decrease and thus fewer pounds

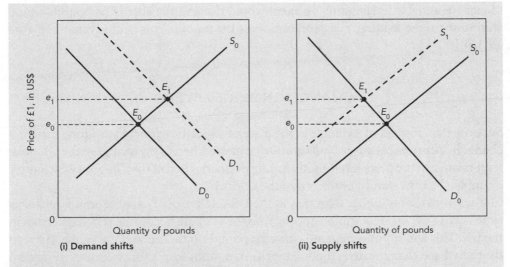

Figure 19.3. Changes in exchange rates

An increase in the demand for pounds or a decrease in the supply will cause the pound to appreciate; a decrease in the demand or an increase in supply will cause it to depreciate. The initial demand and supply curves, D_0 and S_0, are shown as solid lines. Equilibrium is at E_0 with an exchange rate of e_0. An increase in the demand for pounds, as shown by a rightward shift in the demand curve from D_0 to D_1 in part (i), or a decrease in the supply of pounds, as shown by a leftward shift in the supply curve from S_0 to S_1 in part (ii), will cause the pound to appreciate. In both parts the new equilibrium is at E_1, and the appreciation is shown by the rise in the exchange rate from e_0 to e_1.

A decrease in the demand for pounds, as shown by a leftward shift in the demand curve from D_1 to D_0 in part (i), or an increase in the supply of pounds, as shown by a rightward shift in the supply curve from S_1 to S_0 in part (ii), will cause the pound to depreciate. The equilibrium shifts from E_1 to E_0, and the depreciation is shown by the fall in the exchange rate from e_1 to e_0 in both parts.

will be demanded; that is, the demand curve for pounds will shift to the left, and the pound will depreciate. This too is illustrated in Figure 19.3(i), by a reverse of the previous shift.

A RISE IN THE FOREIGN PRICE OF IMPORTS

Suppose that the dollar price of US-produced videos increases sharply. Suppose also that UK consumers have an elastic demand for US videos since they can easily switch to UK substitutes. In this case they will spend fewer dollars for US videos than they did before. Hence they supply fewer pounds to the foreign exchange market. The supply curve of pounds shifts to the left, and the pound will appreciate. If the demand for US videos were inelastic, spending on them would rise and the supply of pounds would shift to the right, leading to a depreciation of the pound. This is illustrated in Figure 19.3(ii).

CHANGES IN PRICE LEVELS

Suppose that, instead of a change in the price of a specific exported product, there is a change in *all* prices because of inflation. What matters here is the change in the UK price level *relative* to the price levels of its trading partners. (Recall that, in our two-country example, the USA stands for the rest of the world.)

If UK inflation is higher than that in the USA, UK exports are becoming relatively expensive in US markets while imports from the USA are becoming relatively cheap in the UK. This will shift the demand curve for pounds to the left and the supply curve to the right. Each change causes the dollar price of pounds to fall, that is, causes the pound to depreciate.

If the price level of one country is rising relative to that of another country, the equilibrium value of its currency will be falling relative to that of the other country.

Indeed, the price level and the exchange rate are both measures of a currency's value. The price level is the value of a currency measured against a typical basket of goods, while the exchange rate values a currency against other currencies. So domestic inflation and currency depreciation are both indicators of the same phenomenon—the falling value of the domestic currency.

CAPITAL MOVEMENTS

Major capital flows can exert a strong influence on exchange rates, especially since the size of capital flows (in the modern globalized financial system) can swamp trade payments on any particular day. An increased desire by UK residents to invest in US assets will shift the supply curve for pounds to the right, and the pound will depreciate. This is illustrated in Figure 19.3(ii).

A significant movement of investment funds has the effect of appreciating the currency of the capital-importing country and depreciating the currency of the capital-exporting country.

This statement is true for all capital movements—short term or long term. Because the motives that lead to large capital movements are likely to be different in the short and long terms, however, it is worth considering each separately.

Short-term capital movements

A major motive for short-term capital flows is a change in interest rates. International traders hold transactions balances just as domestic traders do. These balances are usually lent out on a short-term basis rather than being left in a non-interest-bearing deposit. Naturally, the holders of these balances will tend to lend them, *other things being equal* (*especially exchange rate expectations*), in those markets where interest rates are highest. Thus, if one major country's short-term rate of interest rises above the rates in most other countries, there will tend to be an inflow of short-term capital into that country (or, at least, of deposits in major financial centres denominated in that country's currency) in an effort to take advantage of the high rate, and this will tend to appreciate the currency. If these short-term interest rates should fall, there will most likely be a sudden shift away from that country as a location for short-term funds, and its currency will tend to depreciate.

A second motive for short-term capital movements is speculation about a country's exchange rate. If foreigners expect the pound to appreciate, they will rush to buy assets denominated in pounds; if they expect the pound to depreciate, they will be reluctant to buy or to hold UK financial assets.

Long-term capital movements

Long-term capital movements are largely influenced by long-term expectations about another country's profit opportunities and the long-run value of its currency. A US firm would be more willing to purchase a UK firm if it expected that the profits in pounds would buy more dollars in future years than the profits from investment in a US factory. This could happen if the UK business earned greater profits than the US alternative, with exchange rates remaining unchanged. It could also happen if the profits were the same but the US firm expected the pound to appreciate relative to the dollar.

STRUCTURAL CHANGES

An economy can undergo structural changes that alter the equilibrium exchange rate. 'Structural change' is an all-purpose term for a change in technology, the invention of new products, or anything else that affects the pattern of real production. For example, when a country's products do not improve in quality as rapidly as those of some other countries, that country's consumers' demand (at fixed prices) shifts slowly away from its own products and toward those of its foreign competitors. This causes a slow depreciation in the first country's currency, because the demand for its currency is shifting slowly leftwards, as illustrated in Figure 19.3(i).

An important example of a structural change in recent UK history was the discovery of oil and gas in the North Sea. This reduced UK demand for imported oil, leading to a reduced supply of sterling in the foreign exchange market and an appreciation of sterling. (See the discussion pertaining to Figure 19.4 below.)

The behaviour of exchange rates

The degree of exchange rate variability experienced since the early 1970s is generally thought to exceed that which can be explained by variations in the above determinants of exchange rates.

Why have exchange rates been so volatile? This question remains at the centre of debate and controversy among researchers and policy commentators. In this section we provide only a cursory view of this and related questions about the behaviour of exchange rates.

First, we look at one measure of the value that the exchange rate would take on if it were subject to the influence of what might be called the underlying, or fundamental, market determinants. We can then compare this with the actual value of the exchange rate. Second, we provide one explanation for the divergence.

PURCHASING POWER PARITY

Purchasing power parity (PPP) theory holds that, over the long term, the average value of the exchange rate between two currencies depends on their relative purchasing power. The theory holds that a currency will tend to have the same purchasing power when it is spent in its home country as it would have if it were converted to foreign exchange and spent in the foreign country.

If, at existing values of relative price levels and the existing exchange rate, a currency has a higher purchasing power in its own country, it is said to be undervalued; there is incentive to sell foreign exchange and buy the domestic currency in order to take advantage of its higher purchasing power (that is, the fact that goods seem cheaper) in the domestic economy. This will put upward pressure on the domestic currency.

Similarly, if a currency has a lower purchasing power in its own country, it is said to be overvalued; there is incentive to sell the domestic currency and buy foreign exchange in order to take advantage of the higher purchasing power (cheaper goods) abroad. This will put downward pressure on the domestic currency.

The PPP exchange rate is determined by relative price levels in the two countries.

For example, assume that the UK price level rises by 20 per cent, while the US price level rises by only 5 per cent over the same period. The PPP value of the dollar then appreciates by approximately 15 per cent against sterling. This means that in the USA the prices of all goods (both US-produced and imported UK goods) would rise by 5 per cent, measured in dollars, while in the UK the prices of all goods (both UK-produced and imported US goods) would rise by 20 percent, measured in pounds sterling.

The PPP exchange rate adjusts so that the relative price of the two nations' goods

BOX 19.2.

Exchange rates and the quantity theory

A simple expression for the exchange rate can be derived from the quantity theory of money (as set out in Box 18.2) when there are two countries and an exchange rate that follows its PPP value.

Let the foreign country be denoted by an asterisk (*), so that it has an equation linking money, prices, income, and velocity:

$$M^*V^* = P^*Y^*. \tag{i}$$

Using values for home money supply, prices, velocity, and income we already had:

$$MV = PY. \tag{ii}$$

All we need to add is the relationship implied by PPP. This is that prices will be the same in both economies when converted at the current exchange rate:

$$PE = P^*, \tag{iii}$$

where P is the home country price level, P^* is the foreign country price level, and E is the exchange rate (number of units of foreign currency per pound sterling). Now all we do is rearrange (i) and (ii) as expressions for P and P^*, then substitute into (iii) and arrange as an expression for E. This gives:[†]

$$E = \frac{M^*}{M} \cdot \frac{Y}{Y^*} \cdot \frac{V^*}{V}. \tag{iv}$$

This is an important equation that gives us some new insights into the exchange rate. The first term is the ratio of the home and foreign money supplies. E falls in proportion to the home money supply and rises in proportion to the foreign money supply. This means that when the home money supply rises, the exchange rate depreciates in the same proportion. The logic of this has two steps. First, a rise in home money supply leads to a proportional increase in the home price level (for given levels of Y and V). Second, a rise in the home price level leads to a proportional depreciation of the home currency to preserve PPP.

The second term in (iv) has a very important implication. Domestic real GDP is positively related to E. This means that, other things being equal, a rise in domestic GDP leads to an appreciation of the home currency. The reason for this is that an increase in Y leads to an increased transactions demand for the home currency. As we have learned in this chapter, anything that increases demand for the home currency will tend to appreciate its exchange rate.

This simple model of exchange rates gives important insights but it is only a beginning. Many more complicated factors affecting interest rates and expectations can easily be incorporated by a more detailed specification of the determinants of V. However, the main elements of (iv) are recognizable in most of the empirical exchange rate models of the last two decades.

[†] The steps are as follows: (1) $P^* = M^*V^*/Y^*$ and $P = MV/Y$; (2) Substituting into (iii), $E(MV/Y) = M^*V^*/Y^*$; (3) Rearranging gives (iv).

(measured in the same currency) is unchanged, because the change in the relative values of two currencies compensates exactly for differences in national inflation rates.

If the actual exchange rate changes along with the PPP rate, the competitive positions of producers in the two countries will be unchanged. Firms that are located in countries with high inflation rates will still be able to sell their outputs on international markets, because the exchange rate adjusts to offset the effect of the rising domestic prices. An exchange rate that adjusts in line with the PPP exchange rate would also be referred to as a constant *real exchange rate*.[14] A simple model of the exchange rate implied by the quantity theory of money and PPP is set out in Box 19.2.

Figure 19.4 shows an index of the real exchange rate for the UK, the USA, and Germany. PPP requires that the real exchange rate should be constant in the long term. This is broadly true. Notice also, however, the large fluctuations around the PPP rate. The UK had a substantial rise in its real exchange rate in the late 1970s, associated with its emergence as an oil producer. This is shown on the chart by the high UK real exchange rate in 1980–1; and this led to a sharp loss of competitiveness of the non-oil sectors of the economy (especially manufacturing), causing a sharp decline in UK manufacturing output in the 1980–2 recession. The UK real exchange rate fell significantly between 1981 and 1986, and again in 1992 after departure from the ERM. The most dramatic swing in the 1980s, however, was in the US real exchange rate, which increased 50 per cent between 1980 and 1985, and then fell back to its 1980 level by 1987.

PPP governs exchange rate behaviour in the long term, but there can be significant deviations from PPP in the short to medium term.

Why have these wide fluctuations occurred? One of the most important reasons is associated with international differences in interest rates. Another related reason, responses to new information, is discussed in Box 19.3, along with a summary of the significance of exchange rate volatility for business.

EXCHANGE RATE OVERSHOOTING

Differences in interest rates between countries, arising from differences in monetary and fiscal policies as well as other factors, can trigger large capital flows as investors seek to place funds where returns are highest. These capital flows in turn will result in swings in the exchange rate between the two countries. Some economists argue that this is the fundamental reason for the wide fluctuations in exchange rates that have been observed.

---

[14] The real exchange rate is the inverse of competitiveness. A country whose goods were becoming relatively cheap in world markets would be said to be improving its competitiveness but to be having a falling real exchange rate, and vice versa. The real exchange rate is not an actual price of currency, it is an index number of the relative price of home and foreign goods.

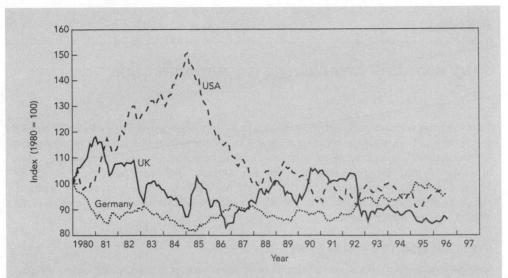

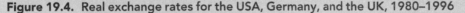

Figure 19.4. Real exchange rates for the USA, Germany, and the UK, 1980–1996

Deviations from PPP can be substantial in the short run, but over the long run exchange rates tend to converge to their PPP values. At the PPP exchange rate, the real exchange rate would be constant. The figure shows real exchange rates for three countries, calculated by adjusting actual exchange rate by an index of consumer prices, and set to a value of 100 in the first quarter of 1980.

The UK real exchange rate was already high compared to the early 1970s (not shown) in 1980, but it continued to rise until early 1981. It then fell in stages. It rose again at the end of the 1980s but fell sharply after September 1992, when Britain left the ERM. The USA experienced a dramatic appreciation of its real exchange rate from 1980 to 1985, after which time it fell back; in the middle of 1996, the US real exchange rate was roughly the same as in 1980. The real exchange rate of Germany fell in the early 1980s, but then cycled about a fairly constant level.

All of these figures are broadly consistent with the view that PPP holds in the long term. It is clear, however, that deviations from PPP can be sustained over lengthy periods—the US real exchange rate took nearly a decade to return to its long run level.

Source: Datastream (IMF data series).

To illustrate, suppose that an exogenous change in monetary policy causes UK interest rates to rise 4 percentage points above those in New York. The interest rate differential will lead to a capital inflow into the UK. UK and foreign investors alike will sell assets denominated in US dollars and buy UK assets that earn higher interest. These capital inflows will lead to an increased demand for pounds on the foreign exchange market as investors exchange dollars for pounds to buy UK assets. The increased demand will in turn lead to an appreciation of sterling.

A relative rise in domestic interest rates will cause a capital inflow and an appreciation of the home currency.

BOX 19.3.

Why exchange rate changes are unpredictable

In this chapter we have outlined many of the factors that influence exchange rates. The point of this box is that, despite knowing a lot about exchange rates, it is virtually impossible to forecast exchange rate changes with any degree of accuracy. Indeed, there is a great deal of evidence that exchange rate changes are random. The accompanying chart shows monthly changes in pound/dollar exchange rate for 1985–96. There is no obvious systematic pattern in these changes. First, we explain why this is so and, second, we set out the implications of this for business.

Exchange rates respond to news

Foreign exchange markets are rather different from markets in consumer goods. The vast bulk of trading takes place between the professional foreign exchange dealers of banks. They do not meet the people they are trading with face to face; rather, they do their transactions over the telephone, and the other party to the deal could be anywhere in the world.

Deals done by the professional dealers are all on a large scale, typically involving sums no smaller than £1 million and often very much larger. Each dealer tends to specialise in deals between a small number of currencies, say, the pound and Deutschmark. But the dealers in all currencies for each bank sit close together, in a dealing room, so that they can hear what is going on in other markets. When a big news event breaks, anywhere in the world, this will be shouted out to all dealers in the room simultaneously.

Each dealer is also faced with several TV screens and many buttons that will connect him or her very quickly by telephone to other dealers. Speed of transaction can be very important if you are dealing with large volumes of money in a market that is continuously changing the prices quoted. Latest price quotes from around the world appear on the screens. However, contracts are agreed over the telephone (and nowadays are recorded in case of disagreement) and the paperwork follows within two days.

Because exchange rates are closely related to expectations and to interest rates, the foreign exchange dealers have to keep an eye on all major news events affecting the economic environment. Since all the players in the foreign exchange markets are professionals, they are all well informed, not just about what has happened but also about forecasts of what is likely to happen. Accordingly, the exchange rate, at any point in time, reflects not just history but also current expectations of what is going to happen in future.

As soon as some future event comes to be expected it will be reflected in the current exchange rate. Events expected to happen soon will usually be given more weight than distant events. The only component in today's news that will cause the exchange rate to change is what was not expected to happen. The unforecastable component of news can be thought of as a random error. It is random in the sense that it has no detectable pattern to it and it is unrelated to the information available before it happened.

Some events are clearly unforecastable, like an earthquake in Japan or a head of state having a heart attack. Others are the production of economic statistics for which forecasts have generally been published. In the latter case, it is the deviations of announced figures from their forecast value that, if large, tend to move exchange rates.

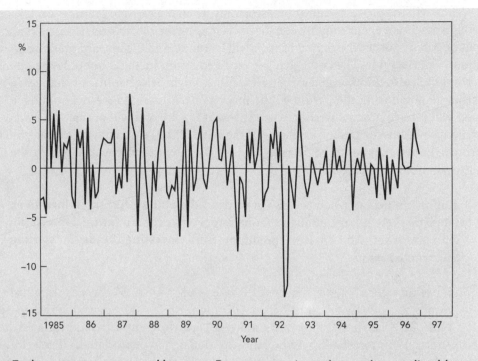

Exchange rates are moved by news. Because news is random and unpredictable, exchange rates will tend to move in a random way.

Some people, observing the volatility of exchange rates, conclude that foreign exchange markets are inefficient. However, with well-informed professional players who have forward-looking expectations, new information is rapidly and efficiently transmitted into prices. Volatility of exchange rates, therefore, reflects the volatility of relevant events around the world.

Implications for business

The unpredictability of exchange rate changes has important implications for business, especially for international business, where profits will be directly affected by exchange rate changes. There are two key points to notice.

First, businesses should take account of the risk involved in volatile and rapidly changing exchange rates. Risk is a fact of business life, but it is important to know what the range of possible outcomes is in making business decisions. Buying exchange rate forecasts is usually a waste of money. Acting upon an assumption about what a particular exchange rate is going to be is extremely dangerous. Many businesses have folded as a result of faulty exchange rate assumptions.

Second, where the profitability of a particular deal is dependent upon exchange rate outcomes, a business should look to find ways of hedging the exchange rate risk—via forward markets, options, or appropriate funding strategies.

Exchange rate changes are near random and, therefore, unpredictable, so businesses should be looking to hedge exchange rate risk wherever possible.

Sources: Data for the chart are from Datastream.

Macroeconomic policy

When will the process stop? It will stop only when the expected returns on UK and foreign assets are again roughly equalized; as long as the return on UK assets is above that on foreign assets, the capital inflows will continue, and the upward pressure on the pound will continue. The key is that the expected return includes not only the interest earnings but also the expected gains or losses that might arise because of changes in the exchange rate during the period of the investment. A foreign investor holding a UK asset will receive pounds sterling when the asset is sold, and will at that time want to exchange pounds for foreign exchange. If the value of the pound has fallen, that will be a source of loss that has to be balanced against the interest income in assessing the net return on holding the asset.

> Equilibrium occurs when the rise in value of the pound sterling in foreign exchange markets is large enough that investors will expect a future depreciation that just offsets the interest premium from investing funds in sterling-denominated assets.

Suppose investors believe that the PPP rate is £1 = US$1.50, but, as they rush to buy pounds to take advantage of higher UK interest rates, they drive the rate to, say, £1 = US$1.75. (Because £1 now buys more dollars, the pound has appreciated, and because it takes more dollars to buy £1, the dollar has depreciated.) They do not believe this rate will be sustained and, instead, expect the pound to lose value in future periods. If foreign investors expect the pound to depreciate by 4 per cent per year, they will be indifferent between lending money in London and doing so in New York. The extra 4 per cent per year of interest that they earn in London is exactly offset by the 4 per cent that they expect to lose when they turn their money back into their own currency.

> A policy that raises domestic interest rates above world levels will cause the external value of the domestic currency to appreciate enough to create an expected future depreciation that will be sufficient to offset the interest differential.

While interest differentials persist, the exchange rate must deviate from its equilibrium or PPP value; this is often referred to as exchange rate *overshooting*, because, at the time interest rates are raised, the exchange rate will jump beyond its long-run equilibrium level. This is illustrated in Figure 19.5.

The argument that a rise in domestic interest rates will cause an appreciation of the home currency requires an important proviso. The interest rate rise has to occur with all other factors—especially long-run inflation expectations—held constant. If, for example, it was a rise in expectations of future inflation that triggered off events, the story would be quite different. In this case, the interest rate rise would be responding to these expectations and to the consequent expectation of a long-run *depreciation* in the home currency. Now the change in the exchange rate would depend on the size of the interest rate rise relative to the size of the expected long-run depreciation. In short, we

Figure 19.5. Exchange rate overshooting

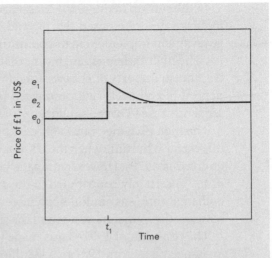

The adjustment of exchange rates to policy changes often involves overshooting the long-run equilibrium. The figure illustrates how the exchange rate may move over time after the Bank of England tightens monetary policy by raising short-term interest rates. The tighter monetary policy will lower the domestic price level (relative to what it would otherwise have been) and will appreciate the nominal exchange rate, leaving the real exchange rate unchanged in the long run. However, higher interest rates will make the exchange rate jump (appreciate) to a point from which it will be expected to depreciate. The expected rate of depreciation will be just equal to the interest differential between home and foreign interest rates, assuming that domestic and foreign rates were equal to start with. The initial exchange rate is e_0. At time t_1, the Bank of England raises domestic interest rates and the exchange rate appreciates to e_1. Over time, it then depreciates back towards the new long-run equilibrium level of e_2. If the economy starts and finishes in full equilibrium, the appreciation from e_0 to e_2 will be proportional to the reduction in the price level caused by the tighter monetary policy and there will be no change in the real exchange rate. However, at e_1 there has been an appreciation of the real exchange rate, so the domestic economy has suffered a temporary loss in competitiveness.

need to be careful when applying economic analysis that works *holding other things constant* to a world where many things are changing simultaneously.

Implications of overshooting

One policy implication of exchange rate theory is that a central bank that is seeking to use its monetary policy to attain its domestic policy targets may have to put up with large fluctuations in the exchange rate. Indeed, overshooting of the exchange rate in response to interest rate changes may be one of the most important elements of the monetary transmission mechanism.

In the case of a tightening of monetary policy that raises interest rates, the overshooting (appreciation) of the pound beyond its PPP rate would put export- and import-competing industries under temporary but severe pressure from foreign competition, because UK goods would become expensive relative to imported goods. The resulting fall in demand for UK goods would open up a recessionary gap, thus providing a further mechanism by which the restrictive monetary policy was transmitted to the rest of the economy.

The last two recessions in the UK both illustrate this mechanism at work. Both were associated with tight monetary policy and an overvalued exchange rate, although, since there were world-wide recessions at roughly the same time, domestic factors cannot be the whole story.

Macroeconomic policy

In the run-up to the 1980–2 recession, the pound had appreciated strongly. In 1979, interest rates were raised sharply and the pound appreciated further, as the Thatcher government implemented its commitment to control inflation by tight monetary policy. The high exchange rate meant that domestic producers became very uncompetitive, and so imports of cheaper foreign goods rose. Between late 1979 and early 1981, domestic manufacturing output fell by nearly 20 per cent and unemployment subsequently rose to over 3 million.

The high exchange rate cannot be blamed on tight monetary policy alone, because this was also the time when the UK was emerging as an oil producer (and the price of oil doubled in 1979). However, monetary policy (especially the sharp rise in interest rates in 1979) certainly contributed to the overshooting of sterling, and the extremely high exchange rate was undoubtedly a central element in the transmission mechanism between the monetary sector and the real economy.

The recession of 1991–3 was made worse by an attempt to maintain an overvalued exchange rate. From 1981 to 1988 the economy had seen a sustained recovery, but by 1988 inflationary pressures had built up. The government tightened monetary policy in the autumn of 1988 by raising interest rates. Higher interest rates created a higher foreign exchange value of the pound than would otherwise have happened. Then, in October 1990, the pound was pegged in the ERM. The onset of recession and fall of inflation, which was evident from 1991, would normally have permitted a reduction in interest rates (and subsequent decline in the foreign exchange value of sterling), but ERM membership prevented this. This was because of the need to keep interest rates consistent with those of other ERM members, notably Germany. In September 1992 sterling was forced to leave the ERM by speculative pressure that caused reserve losses (as illustrated in Figure 19.2). This permitted a sharp fall in UK interest rates and was associated with a fall in the exchange rate. (Sterling fell from nearly $2.00 per pound in the summer of 1992 to around $1.50 after September, and stayed around that level for the next couple of years.) The fall in interest rates and the exchange rate led fairly quickly to economic recovery by the spring of 1993.

What we have learned so far in this chapter is that the exchange rate is an essential element of the transmission mechanism that turns monetary policy shocks into real shocks in an open economy under flexible exchange rates. In the remainder of this chapter we briefly review the significance of the exchange rate regime for monetary and fiscal policies in a world of highly mobile financial capital.

The exchange rate regime and macroeconomic policy

We have already seen (in Box 18.3) that the openness of an economy affects the way in which macroeconomic policy works. Now that we have studied exchange rates we can draw together the most important implications of different exchange rate regimes for macroeconomic policy. In the model that we developed in Chapters 14–18 we implicitly assumed that we were dealing with an economy that had a fixed exchange rate and one subject to a limited degree of international capital mobility. In the last couple of decades, however, financial capital has become highly mobile, as country after country has abolished capital controls. Indeed, it is now common to talk about the *globalization* of the financial system. Accordingly, we first discuss the significance of integrated international financial markets, then we summarize how this financial integration affects monetary and fiscal policy choices.

Mobile financial capital

Recall that, when we talk about capital flows in the context of the balance of payments, we are not talking about imports and exports of capital goods; rather, we are talking about international flows of borrowing and lending, or trade in assets and liabilities, such as shares and bonds, or lending by banks in one country to customers in another.

Capital flows matter for two reasons. First, as we saw in Chapter 18, actual net capital flows must equal (with opposite sign) actual net exports. This relationship is true by definition so it must always hold. It is important to realize, however, that the economic causation between net exports and capital flows is not unidirectional. Changes affecting capital flows will have implications for net exports (possibly via the exchange rate), just as shifts affecting net exports will have implications for the capital account.

The second reason capital flows matter for the macro model is that they influence the domestic interest rate and therefore affect the transmission mechanism. If domestic residents are free to borrow and lend internationally, and foreign residents are free to borrow and lend in this country, they will borrow where the interest rate is lowest and lend where it is highest. Mobile capital tends to drive the domestic interest rate towards the level in world markets. In effect, the domestic economy is a price taker in world markets. The price involved here is the interest rate on loans and deposits.

We say more about how this affects domestic interest rates shortly, but the key point is that, in an open economy with mobile financial capital, we cannot analyse the determination of the domestic interest rate using domestic demand and supply factors alone. Changes in the domestic interest rate brought about by domestic shocks or policy changes will generate reactions through capital flows and net exports, which will inevitably complicate the picture.

The significance of mobile capital for the economy varies with the exchange rate regime. For simplicity, we consider only the two extreme regimes of rigidly fixed exchange rates and perfect floating. In the first, domestic interest rates will be set at world levels; in the latter there is considerable freedom for domestic interest rates to differ from world levels, but such differences have significant effects on the exchange rate. Let us see why this is so.

INTEREST RATES UNDER FIXED EXCHANGE RATES

'Fixed exchange rates' means that the market value of two currencies is tied together within a narrow range (see Figure 19.2). For the purposes of the present discussion we assume that the currencies are fixed together so closely that the exchange rate can be considered as a single number, such as $1.50 = £1. We also assume that everybody expects that this fixed exchange rate will be maintained indefinitely, so market particip-ants expect no future changes in currency values.

If two currencies are pegged rigidly together, with no expectation that the exchange rate can change, then risk-free interest rates, such as those on short-term Treasury bills, will be identical in both currencies. This must be true because, if it were not true, lenders would sell the assets with the lower yield and buy the assets with the higher yield. This process of *interest arbitrage* will only stop when both rates are identical. Of course, if there were capital controls that prevented investors moving their funds from one currency to another, this would not happen. This is why globalization of finance is significant; in modern markets most countries' residents are free to move funds to wherever they wish.

> **Perfect capital mobility under a fixed exchange rate regime means that domestic and foreign interest rates on risk-free assets must be identical.**

INTEREST RATES WITH FLOATING EXCHANGE RATES

Under floating exchange rates (with perfect capital mobility) it is still true that investors will want to move funds to where they yield the greatest expected return, and borrowers will want to borrow where the expected interest cost is lowest. However, with variable exchange rates there is an additional complication—exchange rates can change, so comparing interest rates in different currencies is more complicated.

Suppose that the interest rate on a dollar-denominated asset is 5 per cent and on a sterling-denominated asset it is 8 per cent (both riskless). Under what circumstances would an investor be indifferent between holding one or other of these two assets? Clearly, if exchange rates were expected to stay constant, investors would all move their funds into the sterling-denominated assets, so either interest rates or exchange rates (or both) cannot be in equilibrium (because as investors move their funds this will affect asset prices and exchange rates). However, if investors expect sterling to depreciate against the dollar by 3 per cent per annum, then they would expect to get the same return on each asset and would be indifferent between the two.

This means that, under floating exchange rates, there is no reason why there should be equality of interest rates. However, it must be true for an equilibrium of asset holding that the difference between any two interest rates is equal to the expected rate of change of the exchange rate. (The currency with the higher interest rate must be expected to depreciate at an annual rate equal to the annual interest differential.) This proposition, which is known as *uncovered interest parity*,[15] is an important part of the theory of exchange rate overshooting discussed above.

> Under floating exchange rates (and perfect capital mobility) the interest differential between two currencies is equal (in equilibrium) to the expected rate of change in the exchange rate.

We now discuss how these relationships affect monetary and fiscal policy.

Monetary policy and the exchange rate regime

In Chapter 18 we set out what we called the transmission mechanism for policy changes originating in the monetary sector. A change in monetary policy was presumed to take effect via a change in the money supply leading to a change of interest rates. (In many countries, the policymakers actually change interest rates first, and this then leads to a money supply change; but this does not change the principles involved.) Interest rate changes then lead to changes in investment, which are represented in our macro model by a change in aggregate demand. This shift in *AD* then works through the economy via changes in GDP and the price level (as illustrated in Figure 18.9). Let us now see how the exchange rate regime changes this story.

FIXED EXCHANGE RATE

Under a fixed exchange rate, with perfect capital mobility, the domestic interest rate cannot deviate from the rate in the rest of the world, because, if it does, it will generate massive inflows or outflows of capital. Under fixed exchange rates, massive desired capital inflows or outflows will force a reversal of the monetary policy change.

Suppose, for example, that the UK monetary authorities decide to relax domestic monetary policy, starting from a position of equilibrium (at potential GDP) with domestic interest rates at the world level. Suppose the authorities increase the money supply. Domestic residents will find that they have excess money balances and they will attempt to buy more domestic bonds, thus driving their price up and the interest rate down. Investors will then note that the interest rate on domestic bonds is now below that on foreign bonds, and they will attempt to switch their holdings from domestic bonds to foreign bonds in order to get the now higher foreign interest yield. In the process they will sell sterling and buy foreign exchange, thereby putting downward

---

[15] 'Uncovered' means that the exchange risk is not hedged, or *covered*, in the forward market. When exchange rate risk is hedged this leads to *covered interest parity*, which holds more or less exactly. This latter relationship means that the forward premium on a currency is equal to the interest differential.

pressure on the exchange rate of sterling. However, the authorities are pegging the exchange rate, so they have to buy up all the excess supply of sterling at the pegged exchange rate. Indeed, they will have to buy up enough sterling so that they take all that is offered. In effect, they will have to buy back so much sterling that the money supply falls back to where it started, the domestic interest rate is back to its original position, and there is no excess supply of sterling in the foreign exchange market. In other words, the monetary policy change has had to be reversed. Any change in monetary policy under this environment would have the same effect—that is, no effect at all.

> **Monetary policy for a single country under fixed exchange rates, with perfect capital mobility, is powerless to have any effect over the economy.**

This would also be the position with UK monetary policy if the UK were to become a member of the proposed EU single currency system. Monetary policy would be determined by the European Central Bank rather than by the UK monetary authorities. None of this says that monetary forces are unimportant, merely that one small country in the global system is unable to set monetary conditions on its own—it is a price taker in world money markets.

FLOATING EXCHANGE RATE

Under floating exchange rates the situation is quite different, because the monetary authorities are not obliged to buy back any excess of domestic money via the foreign exchange market. They do have freedom to change the domestic money supply and the domestic interest rate. A relaxation of monetary policy will increase the money supply and lower domestic interest rates, and a tightening of monetary policy will lower the domestic money supply and raise the domestic interest rate.

However, the domestic monetary authorities cannot influence world interest rates, and the uncovered interest parity condition set out above will generally hold. Investment funds will only be in equilibrium when expected returns are equalized between currency denominations. This means that, when there is a monetary policy change, the exchange rate will jump to a position from which it is expected to appreciate or depreciate at a rate given by the interest differential. Let us see how this affects the transmission mechanism.

Suppose again that we start with the economy in equilibrium at potential GDP with given price level and equality between domestic and foreign interest rates. The domestic authorities now relax domestic monetary policy, increasing the money supply and lowering the domestic interest rate. What happens to the rest of the economy?

Domestic interest rates have fallen, so it might look as though investment should rise. This may happen, but the impact is limited by the fact that the uncovered interest parity condition must still hold. This means that, since world interest rates are unchanged, most investors will not perceive that there has been a fall in the real cost of capital. There is, however, likely to be some increase in cash flow for consumers with mortgages as they find their repayments falling, so there will be some effect of lower interest rates on consumers' expenditure. This will increase domestic aggregate demand.

The exchange rate will also have to change. This is the most important channel of transmission of monetary forces. As domestic interest rates fall there will be a tendency for capital to flow out of the country. However, as holders sell sterling they drive down the exchange rate. We know that when the economy has fully adjusted to the higher money supply it will have a higher price level, so it must also have a lower exchange rate for PPP to hold. However, given that the domestic interest rate is now lower than foreign rates, uncovered interest parity requires that the domestic currency is expected to appreciate. How can it be that the domestic currency depreciates in the long term, but is *expected to appreciate* during the adjustment period? The answer is that it depreciates beyond its long-run equilibrium value and subsequently appreciates. This is the overshooting we described above (see Figure 19.5).

The existence of overshooting has important implications for the real economy. A monetary policy relaxation causes the real exchange rate to fall (because the nominal exchange rate falls before the domestic price level rises, thereby making domestic goods cheaper than foreign goods). This increases net exports, which is reflected in our model by a rightward shift of aggregate demand, and GDP and the price level then adjust as before to this shift. GDP and the price level both rise in the short term. This takes GDP above potential, so the *SRAS* curve starts to shift upwards. In the long run GDP returns to potential at a higher price level.

A tightening of monetary policy has the reverse effect. It leads the exchange rate to overshoot upwards. The real exchange rate rises, and domestic goods become expensive relative to foreign goods. Net exports fall and aggregate demand falls, creating a recessionary gap. If nothing else happens, the *SRAS* curve eventually shifts downwards and the economy returns to potential GDP at a lower price level, though it has been through a recession in the process.

Notice that during the transition to full equilibrium following a monetary policy change, there are predictable implications of the adjustments set out above for the balance of payments. When monetary policy is relaxed, the real exchange rate falls and net exports increase. This means that there is a current account surplus until PPP is restored; accordingly there must also be net capital outflows equal to the current account surplus. When monetary policy is tightened, the real exchange rate rises and net exports fall. This creates a current account deficit and a capital account surplus. Causation here does not run from current account to capital account, rather it is the financial markets that are determining where the exchange rate must go and this determines both the current and capital account reactions.

Monetary policy has powerful leverage over the economy under floating exchange rates and mobile capital, via its effect on the exchange rate. Induced real exchange rate changes shift the net export function.

One way to think about monetary policy choices is to note that the authorities can choose to set one of: the interest rate, the money stock, and the exchange rate. Whichever one of these they choose to set, they must then let the other two adjust to equate demand and supply in both the domestic money market and the foreign exchange market.

Fiscal policy and the exchange rate regime

Fiscal policy affects the real economy by one of two routes: first, a direct increase in final demand caused by a change of government spending or, second, a change in consumer spending brought about by a change in disposable income resulting from changes in net taxes. Both of these shift the *AD* curve and lead to the adjustment process illustrated in Figure 18.11. It is far from obvious why the impact of fiscal policy changes should be influenced by the exchange rate regime, but this is the case: under a fixed exchange rate, fiscal policy has a strong affect on GDP, while under floating exchange rates, fiscal policy has an impact that is muted by the reaction of the exchange rate.

FIXED EXCHANGE RATE

Suppose we start again with the economy in equilibrium, and the government decides to increase its expenditure. In Figure 18.11 we saw that this can be represented by a rightward shift of both the *IS* and *AD* curves. In part (i) of that figure it is clear that as the *IS* curve shifts right, with a given money supply (given *LM* curve), there is upward pressure on interest rates. This is because the increased output leads to an increase in transactions demand for money. Higher domestic interest rates attract capital inflows and this would tend to appreciate the exchange rate: demand for sterling has increased. However, in order to keep the exchange rate fixed, the monetary authorities have to sell sterling and buy foreign exchange in order to maintain the currency value (as in Figure 19.2). This sale of sterling releases new money into the domestic economy and increases the money supply. This increase in the money supply has to be sufficient to stop domestic interest rates rising, and it has the effect of shifting the *LM* curve to the right. This rightward shift of *LM* means that there is no rise in interest rates to choke off some of the multiplier effect. The *AD* curve shifts right by the full (open economy) multiplier (times the increase in government spending).

The adjustment process will now be as discussed in Figure 18.11. In the short term, GDP and the price level increase. Then, because GDP is above potential, the *SRAS* curve starts to shift upwards. Ultimately, the economy returns to potential GDP but at a higher price level. With a fixed exchange rate, this higher price level represents a loss of competitiveness, and the increase in government spending will have *crowded out* an equal amount of net exports; that is, net exports will fall by the same amount as government spending has risen. The economy will have a current account deficit and a capital account surplus (the economy is borrowing from the rest of the world).

> Under fixed exchange rates and perfect capital mobility, fiscal policy has a powerful influence over GDP in the short run, but the only long-run effect is to crowd out net exports.

Notice that this outcome differs from our discussion of fiscal policy in Chapter 18 mainly in the fact that, in the absence of perfect capital mobility, a fiscal policy expansion crowds out investment via a rise in interest rates. Here this interest rate rise is not possible, so it is the rise in domestic goods prices relative to foreign prices that reduces aggregate expenditure to its original level.

FLOATING EXCHANGE RATE

Suppose we again start with an increase in government spending, but now the exchange rate is floating: what difference does this make? As before, the increase in government spending shifts the *IS* curve to the right (as in Figure 18.11), and this puts upward pressure on domestic interest rates. Now, however, the interest rate does rise and this attracts inflows of financial capital, which in turn causes the exchange rate to appreciate. This rise in the exchange rate reduces competitiveness and causes net exports to fall. Hence, the effect on net exports is the same as under fixed rates but much more immediate. Price level changes may take a couple of years to respond to the increase in aggregate demand; the exchange rate increase can come within days.

The initial increase in government spending can be thought of as shifting the *AD* curve to the right, but the fall in net exports shifts it back to the left. Clearly, there is no long-term impact on GDP, but it is unlikely that there will be any short-term impact either, though this depends on the speed of reaction of net exports to an exchange rate appreciation.

> Under floating exchange rates and perfect capital mobility, fiscal policy changes rapidly crowd out net exports, via exchange rate changes, and have little impact on real GDP or the price level.

The mechanism just described is almost certainly an important part of the explanation of the appreciation of the real exchange rate of the USA between 1980 and 1985 shown in Figure 19.4. During this period, the US budget deficit was growing rapidly. This put upward pressure on domestic interest rates and caused massive capital inflows, which in turn led to an appreciation of the dollar and a current account deficit (fall in net exports). Thus, the mechanisms that we have just discussed are highly relevant to explaining events in the real-world economy.

Summary

1. International trade normally requires the exchange of the currency of one country for that of another. The exchange rate between two currencies is the amount of one currency that must be paid in order to obtain one unit of another currency.

2. Actual transactions among the firms, consumers, and governments of various countries are recorded in the balance of payments accounts. In these accounts any transaction that uses foreign exchange is recorded as a debit item, and any transaction that produces foreign exchange is recorded as a credit item. If all transactions are recorded, the sum of all credit items necessarily equals the sum of all debit items, because the foreign exchange that is bought must also have been sold.

3. Major categories in the balance of payments accounts are the trade, current, and capital accounts. When we talk about a balance of payments surplus or deficit, we are normally referring to the current account balance alone. A balance on current account must be matched by a balance on capital account of equal magnitude but opposite sign.

4. There is nothing inherently good or bad about deficits or surpluses on the current account. Persistent deficits or surpluses are unlikely to be sustained because they involve a build-up or run-down of a country's net foreign assets.

5. The demand for pounds arises from UK exports of goods and services, long-term and short-term capital flows into the UK, and the desire of foreign governments to use sterling assets as part of their reserves.

6. The supply of pounds to purchase foreign currencies arises from UK imports of goods and services, capital flows from the UK, and the desire of holders of sterling assets to decrease the size of their holdings.

7. The demand curve for pounds is negatively sloped and the supply curve of pounds is positively sloped when the quantities demanded and supplied are plotted against the price of pounds, measured in terms of a foreign currency.

8. When the central bank does not intervene in the foreign exchange market, there is a flexible, or floating, exchange rate. Under fixed exchange rates, the central bank intervenes in the foreign exchange market to keep the exchange rate within a specified range. To do this the central bank must hold sufficient stocks of foreign exchange reserves.

9. Under a flexible, or floating, exchange rate regime, the exchange rate is market-determined by supply and demand for the currency.

10. Fluctuations in exchange rates can be understood as fluctuations around a trend value that is determined by the purchasing power parity (PPP) rate. The PPP rate adjusts in response to differences in national inflation rates. Deviations from the PPP rate are related, among other things, to international differences in interest rates.

11. Monetary policy is powerless to affect the real economy under fixed exchange rates. With a floating exchange rate, monetary policy changes stimulate GDP mainly via effects of the exchange rate on net exports.

12. Fiscal policy has powerful short-run effects on GDP under fixed exchange rates; but has little effect under floating exchange rates because exchange rate changes cause net exports to change in the opposite direction. In both regimes, fiscal policy changes crowd out net exports in the long term.

Topics for review

- Balance of trade and balance of payments
- Current and capital account
- Mercantilist views on the balance of trade and volume of trade
- Foreign exchange and exchange rates
- Appreciation and depreciation
- Sources of the demand for and supply of foreign exchange
- Effects on exchange rates of capital flows, inflation, interest rates, and expectations about exchange rates
- Fixed and flexible exchange rates
- Adjustable pegs and managed floats
- Purchasing power parity
- Exchange rate overshooting
- Implications of exchange rate regimes for macroeconomic policy

Questions for discussion

1. What would be the effect on the UK balance of payments of each of the following: a rise in the value of US shares held in UK pension funds; more French people decide to vacation in the UK; a UK computer manufacturer gets a big order from Germany; a Japanese car manufacturer builds a new car plant on Tyneside?

Macroeconomic policy

2. Explain how a current account deficit could be consistent with a healthy economy.

3. What would be the effect on the sterling exchange rate of the following: a rise in US interest rates; a rise in German interest rates; a productivity improvement in UK industry; a bad harvest in UK agriculture; a new government launching an expansionary fiscal policy; expectations developing of higher domestic inflation?

4. Outline the steps that have to be taken in order to maintain a fixed exchange rate.

5. Explain why monetary policy has a different effect under fixed as opposed to floating exchange rates.

6. Trace out the impact of fiscal policy on GDP, net exports, and the price level, in the short and long run.

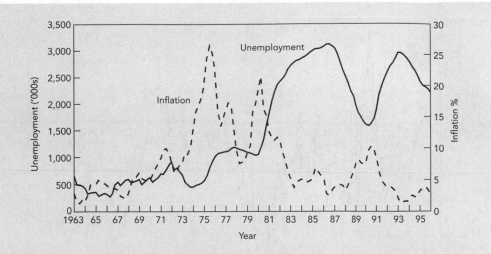

Figure 20.1. Inflation and unemployment in the UK, 1963–1996 (quarterly)

Inflation and unemployment are negatively related, but not perfectly so. Inflation and unemployment were both low in the 1960s, though inflation started to rise after the devaluation of sterling in 1967. Three major bursts of inflation are shown: 1972–5, 1979–81, and 1988–90. Unemployment trebled in the 1974–6 recession, from 500,000 to 1.5 million, and it doubled again as a result of the 1980–2 recession, from 1.5 million to over 3 million. By 1996, inflation was down to around 3 per cent, but unemployment was still about 2 million (though falling).

Sources: Datastream and Economic Trends.

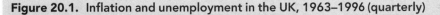

ever, a supply shock that shifts the *SRAS* curve upwards to the left (see Figure 16.12) is likely to raise inflation and unemployment simultaneously.

Figure 20.1 shows unemployment and inflation in the UK since 1963. The dominant pattern in the 1980s (and probably also in the 1960s) was of a clear inverse relationship between inflation and unemployment, suggesting that shocks to aggregate demand were the key drivers of the cycle. However, in the 1970s there were two clear shocks to aggregate supply, associated with major oil-price rises in 1973 and 1979; as predicted by the theory, these supply shocks led to rising unemployment at times of simultaneous high inflation—sometimes known as *stagflation*. Such dramatic shocks to aggregate supply as occurred in the 1970s are, fortunately, quite rare, so it is more likely that the dominant pattern over the business cycle will be the one shown in the 1980s and early 1990s of an inverse relationship between inflation and unemployment.

INDUSTRY CYCLES

Business cycles are important for most firms because almost all sectors of the economy are normally affected at the same time. Most sectors (or industries) tend to have an

clearly the case in the UK, where the investment goods sector is generally more volatile than manufacturing as a whole.

One of the reasons that some sectors are more volatile than others relates to the nature of the products involved. As we have seen from the food sector, people have to eat even when times are hard; however, they do not have to eat out, so the restaurant business is highly cyclical, while food manufacture and retailing is relatively stable.

Another source of volatility relates to durability. Some products are 'lumpy', in the sense that we buy them infrequently and consume their services over an extended period of time. Such products include the capital equipment purchased by firms (investment goods) and the durable goods purchased by consumers. Durable expenditure is highly volatile relative to non-durable expenditure. The reason for this is that purchases of durable goods (like cars, TVs, and hi-fi equipment) can be postponed when times are hard (as can the purchase of investment goods by firms, discussed in Chapter

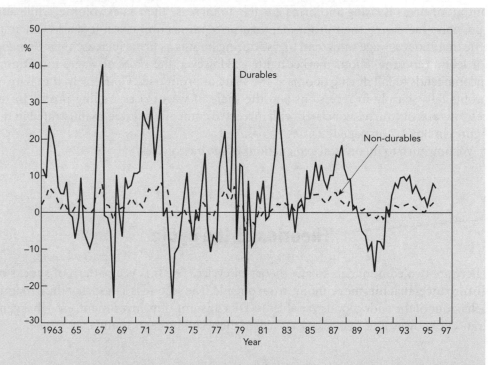

Figure 20.3. Growth rate of real consumers' expenditure on durable and non-durable goods, UK, 1963–1996

Expenditure on consumer durables shows much greater variability than expenditure on non-durables. This is because durable goods are lumpy and their purchase can be postponed when the economic environment is depressed or uncertain. Even in hard times, people continue to eat and consume basic services. When times improve, expenditure on basics does not rise dramatically but demand for 'big ticket' items shows a sharp pick-up.

Source: Datastream.

11). But when times look good, a high proportion of extra spending will go on these luxury items. Necessities, like food and shelter, will be purchased come what may. Thus, industrial sectors producing consumer durables will see much greater fluctuations in demand across the business cycle than sectors providing non-durable consumption goods. Figure 20.3 shows the growth rate of (real) consumer expenditure on both durables and non-durables; it clearly shows that expenditure on durables is volatile while expenditure on non-durables is much less so, even though, again, they both fall in recessions and rise during booms.

PROFITS AND WAGES

A final pattern relating to business cycles that is worthy of comment is that profits tend to be highly variable and pro-cyclical. This is because during booms the demand for the output of firms is rising and firms are able to increase their sales volume, while also (possibly) increasing their profit margins (price minus unit cost). It is also generally true that money-wage rates tend to rise during booms as firms increase their demand for labour and the labour market tightens. However, the *share* of wages in national income tends to fall during booms as the share of profit rises. Conversely, the share of profits falls sharply in recessions and the share of wages rises. Falling profits in recessions are, of course, associated with increased company failures, as illustrated in the figures in Box 1.2 on page 18.

We now turn to theoretical explanations of business cycles.

Theories of the cycle

There are two components to any theory of cycles. The first is a pattern of shocks or disturbances that hits the economy from outside. The second is a model of the dynamic behaviour of the endogenous variables (GDP, consumption, investment, etc.) that generate cycles over time. Let us look at each of these components in turn.

SYSTEMATIC OR RANDOM SHOCKS

One way in which cycles could be generated is if there were cycles in the exogenous shocks hitting the economy. In economies dominated by agriculture, cycles could be caused by weather patterns, over-planting followed by under-planting ('hog-cycles'), or perhaps even cycles in the incidence of crop diseases. In industrial economies, cycles could result from patterns of innovation (product cycles) or waves of productivity improvements. There are certainly, also, cycles in demand for exports from open economies resulting from cycles in the rest of the world (the correlation of cycles in different countries is shown in Figure 1.1 on page 16).

For a small open economy such as the UK, there are undoubtedly systematic movements in exogenous variables, notably world demand. None the less, most effort in the economic analysis of cycles has been directed towards how cycles can result from random external shocks (or discrete changes in exogenous variables) that then trigger some cyclical internal adjustment mechanism.

Most theories of this type rely on lags. Many empirical macro models that are designed to fit the data have quite long lags in their behavioural relations. For example, if a fall in the rate of interest makes a new investment programme profitable, it may take six months to plan it, three months to draw up contracts, six more months before spending builds up to its top rate, and another two years to complete the project.

A pioneering study by two US economists, Irma and M. A. Adelman, established that, if occasional random shifts in exogenous expenditures disturb a system of expenditure-determining equations all of which contain long lags, a cycle is generated. Here the disturbing influences are random or erratic, but the consequences are a cyclical path for the major endogenous macro variables, such as GDP and unemployment.

> **Each of the major components of aggregate expenditure has sometimes undergone shifts large enough to disturb the economic system significantly. The long lags in expenditure functions can then convert these shifts into cyclical oscillations in GDP.**

A recent line of theorizing has developed what are called equilibrium theories of the business cycle. (Some of these fall into the New Classical camp, but others are now in a group known as the *real business cycle* school; both are discussed below.) These rely on microeconomic models of markets that are always in equilibrium—a micro underpinning of cycle theory that has yet to gain general acceptance. None the less, they rely on the basic process used in the Keynesian empirical models where random shocks have systematic effects resulting from long lags that spread these effects out over time.

An even more recent line of research models the dynamic behaviour of the economy in complex non-linear systems of equations. These systems are known as *chaotic* (because they are related to a branch of mathematics known as *chaos theory*). What is interesting about them is that they can generate ongoing cycles without a need for external shocks of any kind. This line of enquiry is highly technical and in its infancy. We shall not discuss it further.

CYCLICAL ADJUSTMENT MECHANISMS

There may be many ways of formulating a dynamic model of the economy so that it generates cycles. Here we outline one simple mechanism that can generate cycles in response to discrete changes in exogenous variables. It is called the multiplier–accelerator mechanism. No one believes any longer that it provides *the* explanation of cycles, though it probably captures one major element of cyclical fluctuations. To understand it, we need to return to a discussion of the causes of variations in investment.

The accelerator theory of investment

In Chapter 18 above, we have investment changing in response to changes in interest rates. The **accelerator theory of investment** relies on another determinant of investment, which can only be formalized in a dynamic model. This theory relates investment to real GDP. The possibility of systematic fluctuations arises because the *level* of investment is related to *changes* in GDP.

The demand for machinery and factories is obviously derived from the demand for the goods that the capital equipment is designed to produce. If there is a demand that is expected to persist, and that cannot be met by increasing production with existing industrial capacity, then new plant and equipment will be needed.

Table 20.1. An illustration of the accelerator theory of investment

Year	Annual sales (£)	Change in sales (£)	Required stock of capital (£)[a]	Net investment increase in required capital stock (£)
(1)	(2)	(3)	(4)	(5)
1	10	0	50	0
2	10	0	50	0
3	11	1	55	5
4	13	2	65	10
5	16	3	80	15
6	19	3	95	15
7	22	3	110	15
8	24	2	120	10
9	25	1	125	5
10	25	0	125	0

With a fixed capital–output ratio, net investment occurs only when it is necessary to increase the stock of capital in order to change output. Assume that it takes £5 of capital to produce £1 of output per year. In years 1 and 2 there is no need for investment. In year 3 a rise in sales of £1 requires investment of £5 to provide the needed capital stock. In year 4 a further rise of £2 in sales requires an additional investment of £10 to provide the needed capital stock.

As columns (3) and (5) show, the amount of net investment is proportional to the *change* in sales. When the increase in sales tapers off in years 7–9, investment declines. When sales no longer increase in year 10, net investment falls to zero because the capital stock of year 9 is adequate to provide output for year 10's sales.

[a] Assuming a capital–output ratio of 5:1.

Investment expenditure occurs while the new capital equipment is being built and installed. If the desired stock of capital goods increases, there will be an investment boom while the new capital is being produced. But if nothing else changes, and even though business conditions continue to look rosy enough to justify the increased stock of capital, investment in new plant and equipment will cease once the larger capital stock is achieved.

This makes investment depend on changes in sales, and hence on changes in GDP, as illustrated in Table 20.1. The more formal derivation of the theory is outlined below.

Let there be a simple relationship between GDP (national output) and the amount of capital needed to produce it:

$$K = \alpha Y, \tag{1}$$

where K is the required capital stock. The coefficient α (the Greek letter alpha) is the capital–output ratio; $\alpha = K/Y$ and is also called the accelerator coefficient. Taking changes in (1), and noticing that investment is, by definition, the change in the capital stock, yields

$$I = \Delta K = \alpha \Delta Y. \tag{2}$$

This says that investment is some constant times the change in GDP. This is called the 'simple', or sometimes the 'naïve', accelerator. Figure 20.4 illustrates what happens to investment under the accelerator theory when GDP rises from one constant level to another.

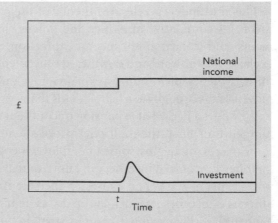

Figure 20.4. The accelerator and investment

When there is a change in the level of final output, there is a much bigger percentage change in the rate of investment. The figure illustrates the path over time of GDP and investment. We assume that GDP is constant but that at time t it jumps to a new higher level, and then continues at this level. Replacement investment carries on at some constant level while GDP is constant, but the increase in GDP requires a higher capital stock. This in turn requires a burst of *new investment*. Once this burst of new investment is over (shown as being spread out over time), the level of new investment returns to zero, so total investment is only at the level required for replacements. Hence, at the time that national output rose, a small percentage increase in GDP induced a large percentage increase in investment. However, even though GDP (hypothetically) stays at its new higher level, investment subsequently falls. In a full dynamic model, this fall in investment would induce a fall in GDP, causing the downturn in the cycle, as described in the text.

Macroeconomic policy

The main insight that the accelerator theory provides is its emphasis on the role of net investment as a *disequilibrium* phenomenon—something that occurs when the stock of capital goods differs from what firms and households would like it to be. This gives the accelerator its particular importance in connection with *fluctuations* in GDP. As we shall see, it can itself contribute to those fluctuations.

Taken literally, the accelerator posits a mechanical and rigid response of investment to changes in sales (and thus, aggregatively, to changes in GDP). It does so by assuming a proportional relationship between changes in GDP and changes in the desired capital stock, and by assuming a fixed capital–output ratio. Each assumption is to some degree questionable.

The accelerator alone does not give anything like a complete explanation of variations in investment in capital goods, and it should not be surprising that a simple accelerator theory provides a relatively poor overall explanation of changes in investment. Yet accelerator-like influences do exist, and they play a role in the cyclical variability of investment. Modern investment theories often include a flexible version of the accelerator, in which the coefficient α is a function of other variables such as interest rates.

Multiplier–accelerator interaction

The theory linking systematic fluctuations in GDP to systematic fluctuations in investment expenditure unites the accelerator theory just discussed with the version of Keynesian multiplier theory that sees the multiplier as a process working over time as successive rounds of induced expenditure build up in response to some initiating shock (see Box 14.2 on page 478).

This **multiplier–accelerator theory** of the cycle is divided into three steps. First, a theory of cumulative upswings and downswings explains why, once started, movements tend to carry on in the same direction. Second, a theory of floors and ceilings explains why upward and downward movements are eventually brought to a halt. And third, a theory of instability explains how, once a process of upward or downward movement is brought to a halt, it tends to reverse itself.

Why does a period of expansion or contraction, once begun, tend to develop its own momentum? First, the multiplier process tends to cause cumulative movements. As soon as a revival begins, some unemployed people find work again. These people, with their newly acquired income, can afford to make much-needed consumption expenditures. This new demand causes an increase in production and creates new jobs for others. As incomes rise, demand rises; as demand rises, incomes rise. Just the reverse happens in a downswing. Unemployment in one sector causes a fall in demand for the products of other sectors, which leads to a further fall in employment and a further fall in demand.

A second major factor is the accelerator theory. New investment is needed to expand existing productive capacity and to introduce new methods of production. When consumer demand is low and there is excess capacity, investment is likely to fall to a very low level; once demand starts to rise and entrepreneurs come to expect further rises, investment expenditure may rise very rapidly. Furthermore, when full employment of existing capacity is reached, new investment becomes one of the few ways available for firms to increase their output.

A third major explanation for cumulative movements is expectations. All production plans take time to fulfil. Current decisions to produce consumer goods and investment goods are very strongly influenced by business expectations. Such expectations can sometimes be volatile, and sometimes self-fulfilling. If enough people think, for example, that bond prices are going to rise, they will all buy bonds in anticipation of the price rise, and these purchases will themselves cause prices to rise. If, on the other hand, enough people think bond prices are going to fall, they will sell quickly at what they regard as a high price and thereby actually cause prices to fall. This is the phenomenon of *self-realizing expectations*. It applies to many parts of the economy. If enough managers think the future looks rosy and begin to invest in increasing capacity, this will create new employment and income in the capital-goods industries, and the resulting increase in demand will help to create the rosy conditions whose vision started the whole process. One cannot lay down simple rules about so complicated a psychological phenomenon as the formation of expectations, but there is a bandwagon effect. Once things begin to improve, people expect further improvements, and their actions, based on this expectation, help to cause further improvements. On the other hand, once things begin to worsen, people often expect further worsening, and their actions, based on this expectation, help to make things worse.

> **The multiplier–accelerator process, combined with changes in expectations that cause expenditure functions to shift, can explain the cumulative tendencies of recessions and recoveries.**

The next question that arises is: why do these upward and downward processes ever come to an end?

A very rapid expansion can continue for some time, but it cannot go on for ever because eventually the economy will run into bottlenecks (or ceilings) in terms of some resources. This will happen when firms cannot take on more workers without paying much higher wages to attract them from other firms. Inflation will pick up and either the government will put up interest rates or firms will cut investment in anticipation of a downturn. This expectation itself becomes self-fulfilling.

A rapid contraction, too, is eventually brought to an end. Firms can postpone investment and run down stocks, and consumers can put off buying new clothes and cars, but eventually confidence returns and a small pick-up in spending leads to a return to the upswing of the cycle, through the interaction of the multiplier and accelerator together.

Indeed, the accelerator can explain reversals of direction of expansions and contractions. We have seen that the accelerator makes the desired level of *new* (not replacement) investment depend upon the rate of change of GDP. If GDP is rising at a constant rate, then investment will be at a constant *level*. If there is a slackening in the speed at which output is rising, the level of investment will decline. This means that a *levelling off* in output at the top of a cycle may lead to a *decline* in the level of investment. The decline in investment at the upper turning point will cause a decline in the level of GDP. This will be intensified through the multiplier process.

The accelerator thus provides one theory of the upper turning-point.

What about the possible stabilization of output at a floor? Investment theory predicts that, sooner or later, an upturn will begin. If nothing else causes an expansion of business activity, there will eventually be a revival of replacement investment. As existing capital wears out, the capital stock will eventually fall to the level required to produce current output. At this stage new machines will be bought to replace those that are wearing out. The rise in the level of activity in the capital-goods industries will then cause, by way of the multiplier, a further rise in GDP. The economy has turned the corner. An expansion, once started, may trigger the sort of cumulative upward movement already discussed.

Controversies about the cause of cycles and the role of government

Many of the different schools of thought in economics have had their own approach to explaining business cycles; indeed, attempts to document and explain the cycle in activity predate modern macroeconomics. We concentrate here on the views of the major macro schools of thought, first outlined in the appendix to Chapter 18. It is of importance to note the contrasting views of the role of government in the business cycle. For Keynesians the instability that triggered cycles was in the private sector and it was for government to step in and stabilize the cycle. Other schools, however, see government as part of the problem; and extreme views see it as the major cause of instability.

THE MONETARIST APPROACH

Monetarists believe that the economy is inherently stable because private-sector expenditure functions are relatively stable and price adjustment will bring the economy back to potential GDP. In addition, they believe that shifts in the aggregate demand curve arise mainly from policy-induced changes in the money supply.[1]

---

[1] The view that fluctuations often have monetary causes is not new. The English economist R. G. Hawtrey (1879–1971), the Austrian Nobel Laureate F. A. von Hayek (1899–1991), and the Swedish economist Knut Wicksell (1851–1926) were prominent among those who have given monetary factors an important role in explaining the turning-points in cycles and/or the tendency for expansions and contractions, once begun, to become cumulative and self-reinforcing. Modern monetarists carry on this tradition.

The view that business cycles have mainly monetary causes relies partly on the evidence advanced by Milton Friedman and Anna Schwartz in their classic study *A Monetary History of the United States, 1867–1960*. They purported to have established a strong correlation between changes in the money supply and changes in economic activity. Major recessions have been associated with absolute declines in the money supply and minor recessions with the slowing of the rate of increase in the money supply below its long-term trend.

More recent work has shown that the Friedman–Schwartz relations are not as close, even in the USA, as these authors tried to show. Attempts to establish a similar close relation for the UK have not been successful. None the less, there is a broad association—even if it is a loose one—between changes in the money supply and changes in money GDP. When, for example, the latter rises rapidly during an inflation, the former rises as well.

The rough correlation between changes in the money supply and changes in the level of economic activity is generally accepted. But there is controversy over how this correlation is to be interpreted. Do changes in money supply cause changes in the level of aggregate demand and hence of business activity, or vice versa?

Friedman and Schwartz maintained that changes in the money supply cause changes in business activity. They argued, for example, that the severity of the Great Depression was the result of a major contraction in the money supply that shifted the aggregate demand curve far to the left.

According to monetarists, fluctuations in the money supply cause fluctuations in GDP.

This leads the monetarists to advocate a policy of stabilizing the growth of the money supply. In their view this would avoid policy-induced instability of the aggregate demand curve.

THE KEYNESIAN APPROACH

The traditional Keynesian explanation of cyclical fluctuations in the economy has two parts. First, it emphasizes variations in investment as a cause of business cycles and stresses the non-monetary causes of such variations, such as expectations, or as Keynes put it 'animal spirits'.[2]

Keynesians reject what they regard as the extreme monetarist view that only money matters in explaining cyclical fluctuations. Many Keynesians believe that both monetary and non-monetary forces are important in explaining cycles. Although they accept

---

[2] Like the monetarists, the Keynesians are modern advocates of views that have a long history. The great Austrian (and later American) economist Joseph Schumpeter (1883–1950) stressed such explanations early in the present century. Knut Wicksell and the German Arthur Spiethoff (1873–1957) both stressed this aspect of economic fluctuations before the emergence of the Keynesian school of thought.

serious monetary mismanagement as one potential source of economic fluctuations, they do not believe that it is the only, or even the major, source of such fluctuations. Thus, they deny the monetary interpretation of business-cycle history given by Friedman and Schwartz. They believe that most fluctuations in the aggregate demand curve are due to variations in the desire to spend on the part of the private sector and are not induced by government policy.

Keynesians also believe that the economy lacks strong natural corrective mechanisms that will always force it easily and quickly back to full employment (potential GDP). They believe that, while the price level rises fairly quickly to eliminate *inflationary* gaps, prices and wages fall only slowly in response to recessionary gaps. As a result, Keynesians believe that recessionary gaps can persist for long periods of time unless they are eliminated by an active stabilization policy.

The second part of the Keynesian view on cyclical fluctuations concerns the alleged correlation between changes in the money supply and changes in the level of economic activity. In so far as this correlation exists, the Keynesian explanation reverses the causality suggested by the monetarists. Keynesians argue that changes in the level of economic activity often cause changes in the money supply.

Certainly, Keynesians are on strong ground when there is a fixed exchange rate regime, because, as we saw in Chapter 19, the money stock is endogenously determined by demand under this regime. However, it is also true under floating exchange rates where monetary authorities operate monetary policy by pegging short-term interest rates, as in the UK. For a given interest rate, changes in GDP will cause changes in the money stock rather than vice versa.

> **According to Keynesians, fluctuations in GDP are often caused by fluctuations in autonomous expenditures. Further, they believe that fluctuations in GDP usually cause fluctuations in the money supply.**

Nevertheless, most Keynesians also agree that deliberate changes in monetary policy can cause GDP to change. However, notice that the monetarist approach makes the monetary authorities the main cause of cycles—hence the recommendation that they should be constrained to follow a rigid policy rule. For Keynesians, it is fluctuations in private-sector investment behaviour (and, perhaps, exports) that matter, and the authorities are the 'good guys' who can offset this privately generated instability. It is for this reason that Keynesians are generally interventionist and monetarists are non-interventionist.

A shift of emphasis within the Keynesian school has come about in recent years, associated with what is now called the *New Keynesian* school. Early Keynesians focused mainly on the use of aggregate demand (especially fiscal) policies to stabilize the cycle. New Keynesians would be happy to see GDP kept close to its potential level by whatever means possible, including monetary and fiscal policies, but they would also place stress on supply-side (labour-market) policies to eliminate persistent (equilibrium) unemployment.

THE NEW CLASSICAL APPROACH

The New Classical approach to explaining business cycles has something in common with the monetarists, in that the shock that sets off the cycle is a change in the money supply. However, what happens next in the New Classical story is quite different from traditional (monetarist or Keynesian) business cycle theory, because the New Classical school wanted a model in which markets were always in equilibrium. An alternative approach to modelling business cycles in 'equilibrium' models, which does not rely on monetary shocks, is discussed below.

The Lucas aggregate supply function

The key element in the New Classical approach is a particular specification of the aggregate supply function, which was formulated by US economist Robert Lucas.

In Chapter 16, where we first set out the *SRAS* curve, we assumed that in the short run output prices are variable (they can respond to changes in demand in the current period) while input prices (we shall concentrate here on wages) are fixed. In the long run, if output prices rise, wages get negotiated upwards to catch up with prices. This is what makes the *LRAS* curve vertical.

In the Lucas approach, wages are not just given on the basis of last period's equilibrium; rather, they are set at the beginning of the current period at the market-clearing level for *given expectations of what output prices in the current period will be*. In other words, they are set on the basis of forward-looking expectations of what the market outcome will be.

This may seem like a harmless modification of our original assumption, but it turns out to have fundamental implications. Figure 20.5 shows the implications for aggregate supply behaviour. The key point is that any shift in aggregate demand that is expected at the time wages are set, such as an announced (or anticipated) increase in the money supply, will lead the *SRAS* curve to shift up immediately. The economy will, therefore, experience an immediate increase in the price level and no increase in real GDP. Only an *unexpected* increase in *AD* will lead to an increase in GDP in the short run. Lucas assumed that this shock to *AD* would be an unexpected increase in the money supply.

> **Cycles in real economic activity, in the New Classical approach, are triggered only by unexpected increases in the money supply.**

We have already noted above that the New Classical economists assume that expectations are formed rationally. This means that the expectational errors that trigger cycles cannot be systematic. (If they were systematic, actors could learn from the pattern of mistakes and improve their forecasts.) It would be tempting to conclude from this that deviations from potential output must, therefore, be random—which is clearly contradicted by evidence. However, to avoid this erroneous implication, Lucas added a lagged adjustment process to his model. This meant that, once shocked, it behaved like

Figure 20.5. The Lucas aggregate supply curve

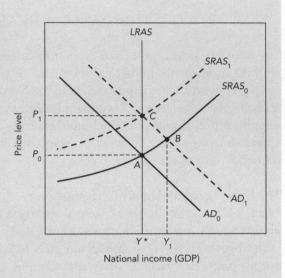

In the New Classical approach, a given *SRAS* curve applies only to un-expected shifts in *AD*. Suppose there is a shift in aggregate demand from AD_0 to AD_1. If the shift in aggregate demand is unexpected, the economy will move from the initial position at point *A* to point *B*, at the intersection of $SRAS_0$ and AD_1. This is the normal short-run outcome in the model we developed in earlier chapters. However, if the shift in *AD* is expected, agents will negotiate higher wages immediately on the basis of this expectation and the *SRAS* curve will shift up to $SRAS_1$. The price level will go straight from P_0 to P_1, and the economy will move from *A* to *C*, with no increase in GDP.

Policy ineffectiveness follows from the same analysis. Any predictable change in monetary or fiscal policy, causing a change in aggregate demand such as the shift in *AD* from AD_0 to AD_1, will lead to an immediate rise in prices from P_0 to P_1, and have no effect on real GDP (the economy goes direct from *A* to *C*). An unexpected policy change of the same magnitude, however, would take the economy from point *A* to point *B* in the short run, and to *C* only in the long run.

any of the other cycle models described above. Hence, it is difficult to distinguish this approach from others on the basis of observations of real-world cycles.

Policy invariance

A perhaps surprising implication of the New Classical approach is that changes in monetary or fiscal policy, which may be intended to influence economic activity by shifting the *AD* curve, will only have real effects if they are unexpected. For example, a stimulus to demand involving an announced increase in the money supply will create expectations of rising prices. These expectations will influence wage setting, so the *SRAS* curve will shift up immediately and prices will rise straight away with no temporary increase in output. This outcome is illustrated in Figure 20.5 by the fact that an anticipated money-supply increase shifts both *AD* to the right and *SRAS* to the left, the net effect being that the economy moves straight up the *LRAS* curve, the price level rising but real GDP remaining unchanged.

> According to the New Classical approach, only unanticipated policy changes lead to changes in real GDP. Systematic policy changes will be predictable and will have no real effects.

The proposition that only unexpected policy changes will have real effects is not widely accepted. One reason is that there is so much inertia in price- and wage-setting behaviour that very few contracts can be renegotiated as soon as a policy change is announced. Hence, the policymakers certainly have some leverage over real activity, even when they are making policy changes that are predictable.

A second reason is that the massive complexity of the economy makes it impossible for individual agents to know how some shock will affect their prices and quantities over any specified period of time. Leaving aside most of the complexities, let us just concentrate on the direct effects of an increase in the money supply. Say that the monetary authorities implement a 20 per cent increase in the money supply. If I anticipate the change by altering my prices and/or quantities tomorrow, will others wait, or will they also act tomorrow? If they do act, will they expect the same effect on prices as I do? Given the variety of contracts in the economy, what will be the time-sequence of all other reactions? The idea of everyone knowing the exact nature of some policy disturbance and solving the equations of the economy to determine the exact outcome of their acting to anticipate it seems far-fetched to many. After all, the great virtue of the price system is that it co-ordinates activity without the need for some far-seeing body of central planners to solve for equilibrium and set all prices and quantities.

However, the New Classical presumption that private agents have expectations of what policymakers are going to do and that this influences private behaviour is important. Without assuming omniscience, just reasonable approximate expectations, private anticipation of government action can affect the outcome of policies. This realization has had a fundamental impact on macroeconomic policy analysis. In both Keynesian and monetarist models, the government was exogenous to the model. However, in the New Classical framework the government and the private sector interact by trying to guess what the other is going to do. The conduct of policy becomes more like a 'game', where strategy and perception of the other players matter.

This change in perception of policy as interactive rather than exogenous has two important implications.

Policy credibility

If private agents are watching the government and trying to form expectations of its future behaviour, not only does it matter what the government does, but it also matters what agents think it will do in future. This means that a government needs more than just the correct current policies. It also needs to establish **credibility** that it will follow the correct policies in future.

Suppose, for example, that a government enters office with a commitment to control inflation. It introduces tight monetary and fiscal policies, which in due course succeed in bringing down inflation. Now, however, there is an election approaching, and the government would like to increase real GDP to improve its chances of re-election. It may be tempted to break its original commitment to anti-inflationary policies. However, private agents know that this incentive exists, so it matters to the outcome whether the private agents anticipate the government breaking its word or not. In other words, the government's credibility actually affects private behaviour. Of course, once the government has broken its commitments, it will be very hard to establish credibility again—at least, without a change in personnel.[3]

The Lucas critique

The assumption that private agents are forming expectations of government behaviour has important implications for how economic models can be used to predict the effects of changes in policy.

A great deal of effort over the last thirty years has gone into building empirical econometric macroeconomic models of the economy for forecasting purposes. Lucas pointed out that such models contain estimates of key behavioural parameters (such as the marginal propensity to consume) that were estimated from past data. These data were collected under particular policy regimes.

Any attempt to use such a model to predict the consequences of significant policy changes is likely to be erroneous. This is because the behaviour of private agents may change when the behaviour of policymakers changes, since they are interdependent in some areas.

One example might be the change of the underlying relationship between inflation and unemployment that occurred in the 1970s, as compared to the 1960s. This could be due to the fact that there was a fixed exchange rate regime until 1972. Once the regime changed to floating, much higher levels of inflation were permitted and very high unemployment resulted (partly) from attempts to control this high inflation.

Another example might be the failure of the government to understand (and the forecasters to forecast) the build-up of inflationary pressures in the economy in the late 1980s, following the financial innovations of the mid-1980s.

The Lucas critique suggests that there will be shifts in many private sector behaviour functions when there are significant changes in the policy regime. Hence, the effects of such regime changes will be impossible to forecast accurately using conventional models.

The New Classical approach to business cycles clearly supports a non-interventionist approach to macroeconomic policy. Governments can initiate shocks, but systematic attempts to stabilize cycles will be frustrated by their very predictability.

REAL BUSINESS CYCLES

Another group has also taken up the task of explaining business cycles in the context of equilibrium models of the economy. According to Professor Alan Stockman of the

---

[3] The fact that it may now be rational for the government to renege on its commitments was labelled *time inconsistency* by F. Kydland and E. Prescott.

University of Rochester, 'The purpose of real business cycle (RBC) theory is to explain aggregate fluctuations in business cycles without reference to monetary policy.'[4]

Real business cycle research has evolved from the New Classical attempt to explain cyclical fluctuations in the context of models in which equilibrium prevails at all times. In this sense, the models can be seen as an extension of the New Classical approach. The researchers' desire to model *equilibrium* outcomes reflects their belief that the channels through which monetary policy affects real outcomes in the traditional macro model are not clearly understood. The focus on *real* disturbances reflects their attempts to build a more convincing supply side to macro models.

The view of the business cycle found in RBC models is that fluctuations in real GDP are caused by fluctuations in the vertical *LRAS* curve. In contrast, the traditional theory of fluctuations is based on fluctuations in the *AD* curve.

The explanation of cyclical fluctuations that arises in RBC models is based on the role of supply (productivity) shocks originating from sources such as oil-price changes, technical progress, and changes in tastes.

In this view, output is always equal to potential GDP, but it is potential GDP itself that fluctuates.

Key propositions and criticisms

The RBC approach is controversial. The major claims in favour of it include:

1. It has been able to explain the recent behaviour of the US economy quite well statistically, while disavowing any role for aggregate demand fluctuations in the business cycle.

2. It suggests that an integrated approach to understanding cycles and growth may be appropriate, since both reflect forces that affect the *LRAS* curve. The distinction it makes is that some shocks are temporary (and thus have cyclical effects) and that some are permanent (and therefore affect the economy's growth).

3. It provides valuable insights into how shocks, regardless of their origin, spread over time to the different sectors of the economy. By abstracting from monetary issues, it is possible to address more details concerning technology and consumer choice, involving inter-temporal trade-offs between consumption, labour supply, and leisure.

4. It has focused on integrating the explanation of a number of facts that other approaches have ignored, such as seasonal and cyclical fluctuations, consumption varying less than output over the business cycle, and pro-cyclical movements of hours worked and of average labour productivity.

---

[4] Alan C. Stockman, 'Real business cycle theory: a guide, an evaluation, and new directions', *Federal Reserve Bank of Cleveland Monthly Review* 24(4) (1988), pp. 24–47.

Macroeconomic policy

Critics of the approach focus on some implausible results, express concern about its assumed underlying behaviour, and argue that the phenomena mentioned in point 4 have already been given satisfactory explanations. More importantly, they are sceptical about a model in which monetary issues are completely ignored. For example, they point out that RBC models are unable to provide insights into the correlation between money and output that is at the heart of the traditional macro model. Furthermore, RBC models are unable to provide insights into empirical regularities involving nominal variables, such as prices that apparently vary less than quantities and nominal prices that vary pro-cyclically. On top of this, any model of the cycle that *assumes* the absence of involuntary unemployment, even in deep recessions, is unlikely to achieve widespread acceptance.

Policy implications

Because the approach gives no role to aggregate demand in influencing business cycles, it provides no role for stabilization operating through monetary and fiscal policies. Indeed, the approach predicts that the use of such demand-management policies can be harmful.[5]

The basis for this prediction is the proposition in RBC models that cycles represent *efficient* responses to the shocks that are hitting the economy. Policymakers may mistakenly interpret cyclical fluctuations as deviations from full-employment equilibrium that are caused by fluctuations in aggregate demand. The policymakers may try to stabilize output and thereby distort the maximizing decisions made by consumers and firms. In turn, this distortion will cause the responses to the real shocks (as opposed to nominal, monetary shocks) to be inefficient.

Although only a minority of economists espouse these models as complete or even reasonable descriptions of the business cycle, and thus only a minority take seriously the strict implications for policy, many accept the view that real disturbances can play an important role in business cycles. It is, of course, highly controversial to argue that, whatever the cycles in the economy, they are an optimal response to shocks, upon which no policy actions can improve. Indeed, if this were the case, macroeconomics as a subject has no purpose, invented, as it was, to help policymakers cure recessions and alleviate unemployment.

THE POLITICAL BUSINESS CYCLE

As early as 1944, the Polish-born Keynesian economist Michal Kalecki (1899–1970) warned that once governments had learned to manipulate the economy, they might engineer an election-geared business cycle. In pre-election periods they would raise

---

[5] In reality, it is more of an assumption than a prediction because it is implicit in the assumption of continuous market clearing. This makes whatever happens to the economy, in response to real shocks, an optimal (equilibrium) adjustment with which policy changes can only interfere. This is not a result of analysis of actual policy, but it is a result of the assumption of equilibrium.

spending and cut taxes. The resulting expansionary demand shock would create high employment and good business conditions that would bring voters' support for the government. But the resulting inflationary gap would lead to a rising price level. So, after the election was won, the government would depress demand to remove the inflationary gap, also providing some slack for expansion before the next election.

This theory invokes the image of a vote-maximizing government, manipulating employment and GDP solely for electoral purposes. Few people believe that governments deliberately do this all the time, but the temptation to do it some of the time, particularly before close elections, may prove irresistible. In the UK electoral system, where the length of parliaments is flexible, it is also natural for the government to seek a general election at a time favourable to itself, within the maximum five-year horizon.

A naïve political business cycle, in which private agents never learn to anticipate that politicians are going to boost the economy before a general election, is impossible to justify in a world of rational expectations, or almost any theory of expectations in which actors learn. This is because there is no reason for voters to be fooled, certainly not repeatedly. Just as they form inflation expectations in relation to their wage-setting behaviour (in the Lucas aggregate supply curve, above), so they can use those same expectations to inform their voting behaviour, and punish a government that deliberately creates an inflationary gap, even though the full effects of the inflation may be to come. Credibility now matters, and probably always did.

However, a political cycle can follow from electoral considerations, even where expectations are rational, so long as the rival political parties have different policy agendas. The approach of an election, combined with a changing probability that a different party will come to power, influences expectations of what future policy will be and, thereby, changes behaviour even before the election has happened. This *partisanship* approach does not predict a simple pattern of pre-election boom and post-election slump (which is not supported by evidence anyway[6]). Rather, it merely says that expectations of electoral outcomes matter and they may cause shocks to the system at almost any time, via changes in the expectations of firms and consumers relating to the future.

STOP–GO

A policy-induced cycle may occur even in the absence of electoral considerations and partisan differences. Government and private agents need only be rather shortsighted. In this theory, when there is a recession and relatively stable prices, the public and the

---

6 There have been nine general elections in the UK between 1960 and 1997 (the two in 1974 are counted as one). Four of these took place in relative boom conditions but in three of these (1964, 1979, and 1997) the incumbent government was defeated. This leaves 1987 as the only clear case of a pre-election boom that was followed just over a year later by severe policy tightening. In 1983 and 1992, the government was returned to power despite recessions and high unemployment. In 1970 and 1974 (Feb.), governments called elections in recessions (1970 was the tail-end of a recession; 1974 was during the onset of recession) and lost. In 1966, there was a relative slowdown and a balance of payments crisis, but the incumbent government won.

government identify unemployment as the Number One economic problem. The government then engineers an expansionary demand shock. This, plus such natural cumulative forces as the multiplier and accelerator, expands the economy and cures unemployment. But, as GDP rises above its potential level, the price level begins to rise. At this point the unemployment problem is declared cured. Now inflation is seen as the nation's Number One economic problem and a contractionary policy shock is engineered. The natural cumulative forces again take over, reducing GDP to a recessionary level. The inflation subsides but unemployment rises, setting the stage once again for an expansionary shock to cure the unemployment problem.

Many commentators have criticized government policy in the past for causing fluctuations by shortsightedly pursuing expansion to cure unemployment (or achieve real growth), then contraction to cure inflation. This phenomenon has occurred often enough in the UK that it was given the name **stop–go policy,** or more simply just *stop–go.*

We have cast the stop–go cycle in its modern form of alternating concern over inflation and unemployment.[7] Historically, when the UK operated under a fixed exchange rate, the two competing policy goals were the balance of payments[8] and full employment. The balance of payments (net demand for sterling) could always be improved by depressing GDP and so reducing imports, which are positively related to GDP, but this would raise unemployment. The conflict encouraged policy swings, whereby income was depressed to remove a balance of payments deficit and then expanded to remove the heavy unemployment.

SUPPLY SHOCKS

Monetarist, Keynesian, and New Classical approaches to business cycle all assume that cycles are triggered by demand shocks—changes in the money supply, changes in autonomous investment, and money surprises. Only the real business cycle school, of the approaches we have discussed, emphasizes shocks coming from the supply side of the economy. Clearly, however, any shock that disturbs the equilibrium of the economy can generate a cyclical response so long as there is some lagged adjustment process within the economy.

The idea that supply shocks can cause cycles in real activity has a long pedigree in economics. In the nineteenth century, for example, serious credence was given to the theory that 'sun spots' triggered business cycles on earth. The logic was that changes in the intensity of the sun's rays, associated with the observation of spots on the sun,

---

7 It might be argued that unemployment was abandoned as a target by the 1980s Conservative government. However, the 1985–8 boom (the Lawson Boom), fuelled by tax cuts and rapid money-supply increases, followed by a sharp raising of interest rates and tax increases, is the most dramatic go–stop cycle of all.

8 In this case what mattered was not the current account but the current plus capital account, which are not necessarily equal at a fixed exchange rate. The authorities had to meet the net demand or supply of foreign exchange out of reserves, as explained in Figure 19.2.

affected the quality of the harvest on earth. Variations in harvest would provide a shock to the real incomes of farmers, and variations in food prices would affect real wages in other sectors. Such shocks could take several seasons to work through the system.

Notice also, as is clear from part (ii) of Figure 17.7, on pages 560–1, that the two most extreme cycles in economic activity in this century were associated with the First and Second World Wars. The impact of a war on the economy is complex, but it has both demand- and supply-shock elements. There were also lesser shocks to the world economy caused by the Korean War in the early 1950s and the Vietnam War of the late 1960s and early 1970s.

In the recent past, the most important supply shocks have been changes in energy prices associated with the 1973 and 1979 OPEC oil-price rises. The fact that all major countries were affected by these energy-price shocks simultaneously did much to ensure that the 1974–5 and 1980–2 recessions were world-wide phenomena that could not be explained by domestic demand shocks alone. The economic cycle in Germany (and perhaps much of Europe) has also been affected by the fall of the Berlin wall in 1989 and the massive costs of reconstruction that followed (this is both a demand and a supply shock).

It is now widely agreed that supply shocks and demand shocks can both be import-ant, that most of the factors we have discussed can contribute to cycles, but that no two economic cycles are ever quite the same. This means that explanations based upon a single key causal factor will never be adequate for every case. The long-term trend in real GDP is upwards, but, despite over half a century of macroeconomic analysis of stabilization policy, cycles about the trend appear to be endemic. Policymakers, in principle, have the tools to reduce fluctuations in the economy, but, in practice, they frequently make things worse.

Macroeconomics: the unfulfilled promise

In the 1950s and 1960s, it was widely believed that the business cycle had been abolished. Many economists thought that the newly invented tools of macroeconomic stabiliza-tion policy meant that recessions could be avoided. Indeed, the 1950s and 1960s were a period of relative stability. Unemployment and inflation were both low, and, although there were cycles in activity (see Figure 20.1), these cycles did not involve any major fall in output, only variations in positive growth rates.

In contrast, since the early 1970s there have been three recessions during which out-put fell (1974–5, 1980–1 and 1991–2). We have already seen, in Figure 20.1, the impact of these recent recessions on unemployment.

What is the reason for this change in experience since the early 1970s? Is it the aban-donment of Keynesian counter-cyclical stabilization policy by governments and the accompanying abandonment of the commitment to 'full employment'? Or is it some other change in the environment?

Macroeconomic policy

Economists cannot give definitive answers to these questions, but they can dismiss the simple argument that stabilization policy worked in the 1950s and 1960s and was responsible for the relative stability of that period.

From the Second World War until 1972, the UK operated under a fixed exchange rate regime. This meant that there was virtually no discretion in the operation of monetary policy (though exchange controls gave limited monetary independence) and fiscal policy was heavily constrained by recurrent balance of payments crises (reserve losses). These occurred whenever there was a tendency for domestic demand to expand too fast (relative to domestic output). Certainly, there were 'stop–go' cycles in fiscal-policy stance, but the evidence supports the view that fiscal policy, on balance, was mildly *destabilizing* in the 1950s and 1960s.

This is important because it suggests that the stability of the 1950s and 1960s was not the result of active stabilization policies at all. Rather it was the result of the absence of major exogenous shocks. The world economy was growing stably with low inflation. There were no major demand or supply shocks coming from the international economy. Neither were there any real exchange rate shocks (until the 1967 devaluation) coming from swings in the nominal exchange rate.

The first major demand shock came in the late 1960s and early 1970s, and resulted from US expenditures on the war in Vietnam. This created inflationary gaps in many countries simultaneously in the early 1970s. On top of this, in the UK, was added the positive demand shock resulting from the expansionary monetary and fiscal policies associated with the Barber boom of 1971–3. The first oil shock compounded the subsequent recession, which would have occurred anyway once monetary policy had been tightened.

The recession of 1980–2 was also affected by exogenous energy shocks, combined with an internal (and world-wide) cycle and compounded by mis-timed policy interventions. In contrast, the most recent cycle, leading to the 1990–2 recession, was not affected significantly by energy shocks, but it was made worse by the government's aggregate demand policies. These permitted an increase in aggregate demand in 1987–8, when there was already an inflationary gap, and reduced aggregate demand in 1990–2, when the economy was already in recession.

Thus, it is reasonable to conclude that a contribution to the greater amplitude of business cycles since 1970 has come from the demand and supply shocks that have affected the world economy, especially the two energy-price shocks (which affected all industrial countries simultaneously). However, there is undoubtedly a contribution from inappropriate domestic aggregate demand policies. These have certainly not been what any Keynesian would have recommended, but neither have they been monetarist. Monetarists recommend stable monetary growth across the cycle (and generally support a balanced budget on average over the cycle). Keynesians recommend counter-cyclical fiscal (and perhaps) monetary policy. No school of thought, so far as we are aware, recommends pro-cyclical aggregate demand policies (as were clearly evident during the Barber and Lawson booms).

Could it be that governments always get it wrong? The difference between the 1950s and 1960s and the floating era may be that in the earlier period governments just had less room for discretionary policy (because of the fixed exchange rate and the balance of payments constraint). With floating rates they were free to make much bigger mistakes. The optimistic outcome is that policymakers will learn from past mistakes, and, at least, not add fuel to the inflationary fire next time around. So, in the absence of major external shocks, the next cycle may be less severe than the last.

Notice, however, that when most major countries experience a similar cycle (as shown in Figure 1.1 on page 16) the explanation probably lies not in any single country but in world-wide economic forces. Globalization of the world economy has tied most economies closer together and there is little that any one government can do in the face of a shift of world aggregate demand. Realistically, therefore, the business cycle is here to stay and business people are going to have to learn to live with it.

Summary

1. Output in different sectors tends to move together over the business cycle.

2. Output of investment goods tends to fluctuate more than that of consumer goods and services. Demand for durable goods fluctuates more than that for non-durables.

3. Profits are strongly pro-cyclical, but the share of wages in national income is mildly counter-cyclical.

4. Cycles in the economy may result from random exogenous shocks or from discrete changes in exogenous variables combined with dynamic interaction of the multiplier and the accelerator (or many other possible lagged adjustment mechanisms).

5. Monetarists think that the dominant cause of business cycles is changes in the money supply. Many Keynesians think that it is swings in autonomous expenditures (investment and exports).

6. The New Classical school emphasizes that only unexpected shifts in aggregate demand will have real effects. Real business cycle theorists assume that supply-side shocks trigger the cycle in a market-clearing model.

7. Systematic aggregate demand policies cannot affect real GDP in the New Classical model.

8. Policy credibility is important once it is perceived that private agents' behaviour is influenced by their expectations of the government's future policy actions.

9. Both demand and supply shocks can trigger cycles but no two cycles are ever exactly the same.

10. Macroeconomics was invented in order to give governments the tools to control business cycles. However, most now believe that monetary and fiscal polices have only a modest role in the stabilization of the business cycle. The business cycle is a global phenomenon that most governments cannot influence.

Topics for review

- Cyclical behaviour of sectors
- Durable and non-durable expenditures
- The share of profits and wages
- The accelerator
- Multiplier–accelerator interaction
- Lucas aggregate supply curve
- Money surprises
- Policy invariance
- Credibility
- The political business cycle

Questions for discussion

1. Rank the following products in terms of their expected volatility (of demand) over the business cycle, and discuss the reasons for your ranking: take-away pizzas; cars; holidays on the Costa Brava; popular music CDs; visits to the cinema; dishwashers; shoes; champagne; haircuts; cans of baked beans; jeans.

2. Explain why capital and durable goods industries exhibit greater volatility than those producing non-durable consumer goods.

3. Outline how the interaction of the accelerator and multiplier mechanisms can generate cycles in the economy.

4. Why do monetarists recommend policy rules while Keynesians advocate discretion for policymakers?

5. Are there any important differences between 'equilibrium' and 'disequilibrium' approaches to the business cycle?

6. Macroeconomics was invented to show how governments could stabilize the economy. However, many commentators take the view that government macro policies have made the cycle worse. Assess the proposition that governments should not attempt counter-cyclical macro policies.

GLOSSARY

absolute advantage The advantage that one region is said to have over another in the production of some commodity when an equal quantity of resources can produce more of that commodity in the first region than in the second.

absolute price The price of a good or service expressed in monetary units. Also called a money price.

accelerator theory of investment The theory that the level of investment depends on the rate of change of national output.

actual consumption The consumption of the flow of services that is provided by the commodities that consumers buy.

actual expenditure See *realized expenditure*.

adaptive expectations The expectation of a future variable formed on the basis of an adjustment that is some proportion of the error in expectations made last period. The error is the difference between what was expected last period and what actually happened.

AD curve See *aggregate demand curve*.

added value The difference between total revenue and total costs, where the latter include costs of capital. This is another term for *economic profit* or pure profit.

adjustable peg system A system with these two characteristics: (1) the exchange rate is pegged at a publicly announced par value; (2) the exchange rate is adjusted from time to time in the face of fundamental disequilibria.

administered price A price that is set by the decisions of individual firms rather than by impersonal market forces.

adverse selection The tendency for people most at risk to insure, while people least at risk do not, so that the insurers get an unrepresentative sample of clients within any one fee category.

agents Decision makers, including consumers, workers, firms, and government bodies.

aggregate demand (AD) The total desired purchases of all the nation's buyers of final output.

aggregate demand curve A curve that plots all combinations of the price level and GDP that yield equilibrium in the goods and the asset markets—i.e. that yield *IS–LM* equilibrium.

aggregate demand shock A shift in the *aggregate demand curve* resulting from an autonomous change in exogenous expenditures or the money supply (or equivalently, a policy-induced change in interest rates).

aggregate desired expenditure (AE) Total amount of purchases of currently produced goods and services that all spending units in the economy wish to make.

aggregate production function The technical relationship that expresses the maximum national output that can be produced with each combination of capital, labour, and other resource inputs. See also *production function*.

aggregate supply (AS) The total desired output of all the nation's producers.

aggregate supply curve A curve relating the economy's total desired output, Y, to the price level, P.

aggregate supply shock A shift in the *aggregate supply curve* resulting from an exogenous change in input prices or from technical change (exogenous or endogenous). The most common example is the oil-price shocks of the 1970s.

allocative efficiency Situation that occurs when resources cannot be reallocated to produce a different bundle of goods that would allow someone to be better off while no one is made worse off.

appreciation When a change in the free-market exchange rate raises the value of one currency relative to others.

arbitrage Trading activity based on buying where a product is cheap and selling where it has a higher price (from the French word 'arbitrer': to referee or arbitrate). Arbitrage activity helps to bring prices closer in different sections of the market. The term 'arbitrageurs' (often shortened to 'arbs') has been erroneously applied in the USA to traders who have attempted to profit from inside information or to *speculate*.

asymmetric information A situation in which some economic agents have more information than others. The two most common examples in economics are: (1) in labour markets, where workers have more (or different) information about their own characteristics than do firms (employers), and (2) in the theory of the firm, where there is a separation of ownership (shareholders) from control (managers). In the latter case see also *principal–agent problem*.

automatic fiscal stabilizers Stabilizers that arise because the value of some tax revenues and benefits changes with the level of economic activity. For example, income tax revenue rises as personal incomes rise, corporation tax rises with company profits, and unemployment benefit falls as employment increases.

autonomous variable See *exogenous variable.*

average fixed cost (*AFC*) Total fixed cost divided by the number of units produced.

average product (*AP*) Total output divided by the number of units of the variable input used in its production.

average propensity to consume (*APC*) Total consumption expenditure divided by total income, *C*/*Y*.

average propensity to import Total imports divided by total income, *IM*/*Y*.

average propensity to save (*APS*) Total saving divided by total income, *S*/*Y*.

average propensity to tax Total tax revenue divided by total national income, *T*/*Y*.

average revenue (*AR*) Total revenue divided by the number of units sold.

average total cost (*ATC*) Total cost of producing any given output divided by the number of units produced, i.e. the cost per unit.

average variable cost (*AVC*) Total variable cost divided by the number of units produced. Also called unit cost.

balanced budget A situation in which current revenue is exactly equal to current expenditure.

balanced-budget multiplier Equals the change in equilibrium GDP divided by the balanced-budget change in government expenditure that brought it about.

balance of payments accounts A summary of the records of a country's transactions that involve payment or receipts of foreign exchange.

balance of trade The difference between imports and exports of goods.

bank notes Paper currency originally issued as a receipt for deposits of gold or silver. Later created by banks on a fractional reserve basis. Now almost universally issued by *central banks.*

barriers to entry Anything that prevents new firms from entering an industry that is earning profits.

barter The trading of goods directly for other goods.

base period See *base year.*

base rate The interest rate quoted by UK banks as the reference rate for much of their loan business. For example, a company may be given a loan at 'base plus 2%'. The base rate changes periodically when the monetary authorities signal that they wish money-market rates in general to change. The equivalent term used by US banks is prime rate.

base year A year, or other point in time, chosen for comparison purposes in order to express or compute index numbers. Also called base period.

bill A tradable security, usually with an initial maturity of up to six months, that pays no explicit interest and so trades at a discount to its maturity value. See also *Treasury bill* and *bills of exchange.*

bills of exchange Written orders to pay a sum of money to another party at a future date, usually in exchange for delivery of goods. Widely used in the finance of international trade because they enable exporters to receive finance (minus a discount) as soon as the goods are shipped, while the importer does not pay until the goods have been received. Bills of exchange that have been 'accepted', or guaranteed, by a good name in the City of London become prime bank bills.

black market A market in which goods are sold illegally at prices that violate the legal restrictions on prices.

bond In economic theory, any evidence of a debt carrying a legal obligation to pay interest and repay the principal at some future time.

boom Period of high output and high employment. See also *depression.*

bounded rationality Decisions taken on the basis of incomplete information that involve doing the best that is attainable in the circumstances.

break-even price The price at which a firm is just able to cover all of its costs, including the opportunity cost of capital.

Bretton Woods system The fixed exchange rate regime introduced after the Second World War. It broke down in the early 1970s when several major countries floated their exchange rates. (For the UK this happened in 1972.) So called because it was the outcome of an agreement reached in 1944 in a town called Bretton Woods in the US state of New Hampshire.

broad money A money stock measure that includes interest-bearing savings deposits as well as current accounts and cash. The standard UK measure of broad money today is *M4.*

budget surplus (deficit) The excess (shortfall) of current revenue over (below) current expenditure, usually with reference to the government.

building societies Financial institutions taking savings deposits and making loans (mortgages) for house purchases. The recent trend has been for them to diversify and become more like banks. Originally they were more like clubs that would disband once all the members had a house. Modern societies are 'permanent'. They are the British

Glossary

equivalent of US savings and loan institutions, also referred to as thrifts.

built-in stabilizer Anything that reduces the economy's cyclical fluctuations and that is activated without a conscious government decision. See also *automatic fiscal stabilizers*.

business cycles Fluctuations in the general level of activity in an economy that affect many sectors at roughly the same time, though not necessarily to the same extent. In recent times, the period from the peak of one cycle to the peak of the next has varied in the range of five to ten years. Used to be known as trade cycles.

buyout When a group of investors buys up a controlling interest in a firm.

capacity The output that corresponds to the minimum short-run *average total cost*.

capital account Record of international transactions related to movement of long- and short-run capital.

capital consumption allowance An estimate of the amount by which the capital stock is depleted through its contribution to current production. Also called *depreciation*.

capital deepening Increasing the ratio of capital to labour.

capital goods All the man-made aids to further production, such as tools, machinery, and factories, that are used in the process of making other goods and services rather than consumed for their own sake.

capital inflow Arises when overseas residents buy assets in the domestic economy or domestic residents sell claims on foreign assets.

capital–labour ratio The ratio of the amount of capital to the amount of labour used to produce any given output.

capital markets Bond and equity markets in which companies and governments sell securities to finance their long-term needs.

capital outflow Arises when overseas residents sell assets in the domestic economy or domestic residents buy foreign assets.

capital–output ratio The number of units of capital required to produce each unit of output. Most commonly appears in macroeconomics in the *accelerator theory of investment*.

capital stock The total quantity of capital.

capital widening Increasing the quantity of capital without changing the proportions in which the factors of production are used.

cartel A group of firms that agree to act as if they were a single unit.

cash base See *high-powered money*.

central authorities See *government*.

central bank A bank that acts as banker to the commercial banking system and often to the government as well. In the modern world, usually a government-owned and -operated institution that controls the banking system and is the sole money-issuing authority.

centrally planned economy See *command economy*.

CEO Chief executive officer or managing director.

certificate of deposit (CD) A tradable IOU (debt instrument) issued by a bank in exchange for a deposit of money, repayable with interest at a specific date.

ceteris paribus 'Other things being equal', as when all but one of the independent variables are held constant in order to study the influence of the remaining independent variable on the dependent variables.

change in demand A *shift* in the whole demand curve, i.e. a change in the amount that will be bought at *each* price.

change in the quantity demanded An increase or decrease in the specific quantity bought at a specified price, represented by a movement along a demand curve.

chaos theory Branch of mathematics in which non-linear equation systems can generate data series that have no pattern detectable by traditional means.

circular flow of income The flow of expenditures on output and factor services between domestic (as opposed to foreign) firms and domestic households.

classical dichotomy The concept in *classical economics* that monetary forces could influence the general price level but had no effect on real activity. Related to the concept of *neutrality of money*.

classical economics Usually refers to the body of thought on economics that had built up in the hundred years or so before the 1930s; often associated (probably incorrectly) with the notion that government policy cannot influence the level of economic activity. It is contrasted with *Keynesian economics*, which tried to break down the *classical dichotomy*.

clearing banks The UK name for the *commercial banks* that were members of the London Clearing Banks Association, which organized the clearing of cheques for member banks.

clearing house A place where interbank debts are settled.

closed economy An economy that does not engage in international trade.

closed shop Firm in which only union members can be employed. Closed shops may be either 'pre-entry' or 'post-entry', where the worker must join the union on becoming employed.

collective consumption goods See *public goods*.

command economy An economy in which the decisions of the central authorities (as distinct from households and firms) exert the major influence over the allocation of resources and the distribution of income. See also *free-market economy*.

commercial banks Banks that take deposits from the general public and make loans. In the USA, commercial banking has been legally separated from *investment banking*, but in many other countries banks have both commercial banking and investment banking operations in the same entity, sometimes referred to as universal banking.

commercial bills See *bills of exchange*.

commercial paper Short-term interest-bearing debt instruments issued by companies.

commercial policy The government's policy towards international trade, investment, and related matters.

commodities In the world of commerce, a term that usually refers to basic goods, such as wheat and iron ore, that are produced by the primary sector of the economy. Sometimes also used by economists to refer to all goods and services. See also *products*.

common market An agreement among a group of countries to have free trade and free movement of labour and goods among themselves and a common set of barriers to trade with other countries.

common property resource A resource that is owned by no one and may be used by anyone.

comparative advantage Ability of one nation (or region or individual) to produce a commodity at a lower opportunity cost in terms of other products forgone than another nation.

comparative statics Short for 'comparative-static equilibrium analysis'; studying the effect of some change by comparing the positions of static equilibrium before and after the change is introduced.

competition policy Policies designed to prohibit the acquisition and exercise of monopoly power by business firms. Also called anti-monopoly policy.

competitive devaluations When several countries devalue their currencies in an attempt to gain a competitive advantage over each other.

complements Two goods for which the quantity demanded of one is negatively related to the price of the other.

concentration ratio The fraction of total market sales (or some other measure of market occupancy) controlled by a specific number of the industry's largest firms, four-firm and eight-firm concentration ratios being most frequently used.

conglomerate merger When firms selling quite unrelated products merge. Also called a lateral merger.

constant returns Situation that occurs when a firm's output increases exactly as fast as its inputs increase.

consumer Anyone who consumes goods or services to satisfy his or her wants.

consumers' surplus The difference between the total value consumers place on all units consumed of a commodity and the payment they must make to purchase that amount of the commodity.

consumption The act of using goods and services to satisfy wants.

consumption expenditure The amount that individuals spend on purchasing goods and services for consumption. See also *saving*.

consumption function The relationship between personal planned consumption expenditure and all of the forces that determine it, especially disposable income.

contestable market A market is perfectly contestable if there are no sunk costs of entry or exit, so that potential entry may hold the profits of existing firms to low levels—zero in the case of perfect contestability.

convertibles Usually refers to *bonds* that carry an option to convert the debt into the issuing company's *equity* at a specified price and within a specified period of time. The option to buy equity, if stripped from the bond and traded separately, is called a *warrant*.

co-operative solution Situation where existing firms co-operate to maximize their joint profits.

cost minimization An implication of profit maximization that the firm will choose the method that produces specific output at the lowest attainable cost.

creative destruction Schumpeter's theory that high profits and wages earned by monopolistic or oligopolistic firms and unions are the spur for others to invent cheaper or better substitute products and techniques that allow them to gain some of these profits.

credibility Extent to which actors in the private sector of the economy believe that the government will carry out the policy it promises in the future. Credibility is important in policy analyses in macro models that assume *rational expectations*, since expectations of future policy action influence current behaviour.

cross-elasticity of demand The responsiveness of demand for one commodity to changes in the price of another, defined as the percentage change in quantity demanded of one commodity divided by the percentage change in the price of another commodity.

crowding-out effect The lowering of interest-sensitive expenditure because a rise in GDP causes a rise in the interest rate. It explains the difference between the values of the interest-constant and the interest-sensitive multipliers.

current account Account recording all international transactions in goods and services.

customs union A group of countries that agree to have free trade among themselves and a common set of barriers against imports from the rest of the world.

cyclical fluctuations Periodic (auto-correlated) oscillations of any economic time-series around its trend.

cyclically adjusted deficit (CAD) An estimate of expenditures minus revenues, not as they actually are, but as they would be if potential GDP had been achieved (i.e. if there was neither an inflationary nor a recessionary gap). Also called full-employment deficit or high-employment deficit.

cyclically balanced budget Budget that is balanced over the period of one cycle.

cyclical unemployment See *demand-deficient unemployment*.

DCF See *discounted cash flow*.

debt instruments Any written documents that record the terms of a debt, often providing legal proof of the conditions under which the principal and interest will be paid.

decision lag The time it takes to assess a situation and decide what corrective action should be taken.

decreasing returns A situation in which output increases less than proportionately to inputs as the scale of production increases.

deficit Shortfall of current revenue below current expenditure.

deflation A decrease in the general price level.

demand Entire relationship between the quantity of a commodity that buyers wish to purchase per period of time and the price of that commodity, other things being equal.

demand curve A graphical relation showing the quantity of some commodity that households would like to buy at each possible price.

demand-deficient unemployment Unemployment that occurs because aggregate desired expenditure is insufficient to purchase all of the output of a fully employed labour force. Also called cyclical unemployment.

demand for money The amount of wealth everyone in the economy wishes to hold in the form of money balances.

demand function A functional relation between quantity demanded and all of the variables that influence it.

demand management Policies that seek to shift the aggregate demand curve by shifting either the *IS* curve (fiscal policy) or the *LM* curve (monetary policy).

demand schedule A numerical tabulation that shows the quantities that are demanded at selected prices.

depreciation (1) The loss in value of an asset over a period of time due to physical wear and tear and obsolescence. (2) A fall in the free-market value of domestic currency in terms of foreign currencies. See also *capital consumption allowance*.

depression A prolonged period of very low economic activity with very high unemployment and excess capacity. See also *boom*.

derived demand The demand for an input into production that results from the demand for the products it is used to make.

desired expenditure See *planned expenditure*.

developed countries Usually refers to the rich industrial countries of North America and Western Europe, Japan, and Australasia.

developing countries Not *developed countries*. See *less developed countries*.

differentiated product A product that is produced in several varieties, or brands, all of which are sufficiently similar to distinguish them, as a group, from other products (e.g. cars).

direct investment See *foreign direct investment*.

direct taxes Taxes levied on persons that can vary with the status of the taxpayer.

dirty float See *managed float*.

discounted cash flow (DCF) Calculation of the present value of cash flows in different periods.

discount rate The difference between the current price of a bill and its maturity value expressed as an annualized interest rate.

discouraged worker Someone of working age who has withdrawn permanently from the labour force because of the poor prospects of employment.

discretion Policy made by judgemental methods rather than by following rigid rules. Used especially in the context of the old debate between *monetarism* and *Keynesian economics* in which monetarists called for a money growth rule and Keynesians recommended policy discretion.

diseconomies of scale See *decreasing returns*.

disembodied technical change A technical change that is the result of changes in the organization of production that are not embodied in specific capital goods, e.g. improved management techniques.

disequilibrium A state of imbalance between opposing forces so that there are forces leading to change.

disposable income The after-tax income that consumers have to spend or to save.

distribution of income The division of national income among various groups.

division of labour The breaking-up of a production process into a series of repetitive tasks, each done by a different worker.

double counting In national income accounting, adding up the total outputs of all the sectors in the economy so that the value of intermediate goods is counted in the sector that produces them *and* every time they are purchased as an input by another sector.

duopoly An industry containing exactly two firms.

economic growth The positive trend in the nation's total output over the long term.

economic models A term used in several related ways: sometimes as a synonym for theory, sometimes for a specific quantification of a general theory, sometimes for the application of a general theory to a specific context, and sometimes for an abstraction designed to illustrate some point but not meant as a full theory on its own.

economic profits or losses The difference between the revenues received from the sale of output and the opportunity cost of the inputs used to make the output. Negative economic profits are economic losses. Also called pure profits or pure losses, or simply profits or losses.

economic rent Excess that a factor of production is paid above what is needed to keep it in its present use.

economies of scale See *increasing returns*.

economies of scope Economies achieved by a firm that is large enough to engage efficiently in multi-product production and associated large-scale distribution, advertising, and purchasing. In a strict sense, it means that producing many goods together enables each to be produced at lower average cost.

economy Any specified collection of interrelated marketed and non-marketed productive activities.

ECU The European Currency Unit. Invented in 1979 with the establishment of the *EMS*, it is valued as a weighted basket of EMS member currencies and will eventually be replaced by the Euro.

effective exchange rate Index number of the value of a country's currency relative to a weighted basket of other currencies. Whereas an *exchange rate* measures the rate of exchange of a currency for another currency, changes in the effective exchange rate indicate movements in a single currency's value against other currencies in general.

efficiency wage A wage rate above the market-clearing level that enables employers to attract and keep the best workers as well as providing the

employees with an incentive to perform (i.e. not get sacked). It helps to explain why wage rates do not adjust to clear labour markets.

elastic Describes the situation where the percentage change in quantity is greater than the percentage change in price (elasticity greater than 1).

elasticity of demand See *price elasticity of demand*.

elasticity of supply See *price elasticity of supply*.

embodied technical change A technical change that is the result of changes in the form of particular capital goods.

employed Status of those persons working for others and paid a wage or salary.

EMS The European Monetary System, established in 1979 to limit the fluctuations between member countries' exchange rates.

endogenous variable Variable that is explained within a theory. Also called an induced variable.

entrepreneur One who innovates, i.e. one who takes risks by introducing both new products and new ways of making products.

entry barrier Any natural barrier to the entry of new firms into an industry, such as a large minimum efficient scale for firms, or any firm-created barrier, such as a patent.

envelope Any curve that encloses, by being tangent to, a series of other curves. In particular, the envelope cost curve is the *LRAC* curve, which encloses the *SRAC* curves by being tangent to each without cutting any of them.

equation of exchange $MV = PT$, where M is the money stock, V is the velocity of circulation, P is the average price of transactions, and T is the number of transactions. As usually defined, it is an identity that says that the value of money spent is equal to the value of goods and services sold. However, with additional assumptions it provides a basis for the *quantity theory of money*.

equilibrium A state of balance between opposing forces so that there is no tendency to change.

equilibrium employment (or unemployment) The level of employment (or unemployment) that is achieved when GDP is at its potential level. Traditionally referred to as full employment.

equilibrium price The price at which quantity demanded equals quantity supplied.

equilibrium quantity The amount that is bought and sold at the equilibrium price.

equities Certificates indicating part ownership of a joint-stock company.

ERM The Exchange Rate Mechanism of the *EMS*.

EU The European Union, formerly known as the European Community (EC).

eurobonds Typically, dollar-denominated bonds issued outside the USA; in general usage, any bonds issued in the international money markets outside the country whose currency is involved. They are very important financial instruments in *globalized* financial markets.

eurodollar market A market in wholesale bank deposits and loans that grew rapidly in the 1960s and 1970s. The bulk of the business was denominated in dollars and it was done outside the control of US banking regulations.

ex ante expenditure See *planned expenditure.*

excess capacity theorem Theorem stating that each firm in a monopolistically competitive industry is producing at less than its capacity output, and thus at higher than minimum average cost.

excess demand The amount by which quantity demanded exceeds quantity supplied at some price; negative *excess supply.*

excess supply The amount by which quantity supplied exceeds quantity demanded at some price; negative *excess demand.*

exchange rate The rate at which two national currencies exchange for each other. It is often expressed as the amount of domestic currency needed to buy one unit of foreign currency.

execution lag The time it takes to initiate corrective policies and for their full influence to be felt.

exhaustive expenditures Government's purchases of currently produced goods and services. Also called government direct expenditure.

exogenous variable A variable that influences other variables within a theory but is itself determined by factors outside the theory. Also called an autonomous variable.

expenditure See *planned expenditure.*

explicit collusion When firms explicitly agree to co-operate rather than compete. See also *tacit collusion.*

ex post expenditure See *realized expenditure.*

external balance When the value of the balance of payments is equal to some target level.

external economies Economies of scale that arise from sources outside of the firm.

externalities Costs (or benefits) of a transaction or activity that are incurred (or received) by someone in society but not felt directly by the parties to the transaction or instigators of the activity. Examples include the costs of pollution caused by factories and the impact on non-smokers of being in the same room as a smoker.

extrapolative expectations Expectation formation based upon the assumption that a past trend will continue into the future. The simplest form of extrapolation would be the assumption that next period's value of a variable will be the same as this period's.

factor markets Markets where factor services (inputs) are bought and sold.

factor services The services of *factors of production*: land, labour, and capital.

factors of production Resources used to produce goods and services, frequently divided into the basic categories of land, labour, and capital. Sometimes entrepreneurship is included in the category of labour.

fiat money Inconvertible paper money that is issued by government order (or fiat).

final products The outputs of the economy after eliminating all double counting.

financial capital The funds used to finance a firm, including both equity capital and debt. Also called money capital.

financial innovation Innovation that occurs when new products are introduced into the financial system, or when existing suppliers behave in new ways. Changes are often a complex interaction of regulatory changes, changing technology, and competitive pressures.

financial intermediaries Financial institutions that stand between those who deposit money and those who borrow it.

fine-tuning The attempt to maintain GDP at, or near, its full-employment level by means of frequent changes in fiscal and/or monetary policy.

firm An independent business unit that organizes production of goods and services that it sells to other firms, to consumers, or to the government.

fiscal policy Attempts to influence the aggregate demand curve by altering government expenditure and/or government revenues, thus shifting the *IS* and *AD* curves.

fixed-capital formation See *fixed investment.*

fixed cost A cost that does not change with output. Also called overhead cost, unavoidable cost, or indirect cost.

fixed exchange rate Exchange rate that is held within a narrow band around a pre-announced par value by intervention of the country's central bank in the foreign exchange market.

fixed factors Inputs of which the amount available in the short run is fixed.

fixed investment Investment in plant and equipment.

floating exchange rate Exchange rate that is left free to be determined on the foreign exchange market by the forces of demand and supply.

floating interest rate One that moves continuously in line with current market conditions.

flow variable See *stock variable.*

foreign direct investment (FDI) Investment by non-residents in the form of a takeover or capital investment in a domestic branch, plant, or subsidiary corporation in which the investor has voting control. See also *portfolio investment.*

foreign exchange Foreign currencies and claims to them in such forms as bank deposits, cheques, and promissory notes payable in the currency.

foreign exchange market The market where foreign exchange is traded—at a price that is expressed by the *exchange rate.*

free-market economy An economy in which the spending and production decisions of individuals and firms (as distinct from the central authorities) exert the major influence over the allocation of resources. See also *command economy.*

free-rider problem The problem that arises because people have a self-interest in not revealing the strength of their own preferences for a public good in the hope that others will pay for it.

free trade An absence of any form of government interference with the free flow of international trade.

free-trade area An agreement between two or more countries to abolish tariffs on all, or most, of the trade among themselves, while each remains free to set its own tariffs against other countries.

full-capacity output The highest output at which minimum costs can be obtained.

full-cost pricing Refers to the situation where, instead of equating marginal revenue with marginal cost, firms set prices equal to average cost at normal capacity output plus a conventional mark-up.

full-employment output See *potential output.*

function Loosely, an expression of a relationship between two or more variables. Precisely, Y is a function of the variables $X_1, \ldots, X_n$ if, with every set of values of the variables $X_1, \ldots, X_n$, there is associated a unique value of the variable Y.

gains from trade Advantages realized as a result of specialization made possible by trade.

game theory See *theory of games.*

GDP See *gross domestic product.*

GDP gap See *output gap.*

general price level The average level of the prices of all goods and services produced in the economy. Usually just called the price level.

Giffen good A good with a positively sloped demand curve.

gilt-edged securities UK government bonds; so called because they are considered to carry lower risk than private-sector debt.

given period Any particular period that is being compared with a base period.

globalization The process by which most economies round the world have become more interdependent. The term is applied especially to the increased integration of financial markets that has

occurred over the last three decades as a result of reducing regulatory barriers to international financial flows.

GNP See *gross national product.*

gold exchange standard A monetary system in which US currency was directly convertible into gold, and other countries' currencies were indirectly convertible into the gold-backed US dollar at a fixed rate.

gold standard Currency standard whereby a country's money is convertible into gold.

goods Tangible products, such as cars or shoes.

goods markets Markets where goods and services are bought and sold.

government In economics, all public agencies, government bodies, and other organizations that belong to, or owe their existence to, the government. Sometimes (more accurately) called the central authorities.

government direct expenditures See *exhaustive expenditures.*

government failure Where the government achieves less than the benefits it could achieve through perfectly efficient action.

gross domestic product (GDP) The value of total output actually produced in the whole economy over some period, usually a year (although quarterly data are also available).

gross investment The total value of all investment goods produced in the economy during a stated period of time.

gross national product (GNP) Total final output (or value added) over which domestic residents have a claim, whether production is located at home or abroad. Equal to GDP plus net property income earned from abroad.

gross return on capital The market value of output minus all non-capital costs, split into depreciation, pure return, risk premium, and pure profit; typically expressed as a percentage of the capital stock.

gross-tuning Use of monetary and fiscal policies to attempt to correct only large deviations from potential GDP. It is contrasted with *fine-tuning,* which aims to adjust aggregate demand frequently in order to keep GDP close to its potential level at all times.

high-employment deficit An estimate of expenditures minus tax revenues, not as they actually are, but as they would be if potential GDP had been achieved (i.e. if there was neither an inflationary nor a recessionary gap). Also called full-employment or cyclically adjusted deficit.

high-employment national income (output) See *potential output.*

Glossary

high-powered money The monetary magnitude that is under the direct control of the central bank. It is composed of cash in the hands of the public, bank reserves of currency, and clearing balances held by the commercial banks with the Bank of England. Measured by *M0*.

hog cycles A term used to characterize cycles of over- and under-production because of time-lags in the production process. For example, high prices for pork today lead many farmers to start breeding pigs; when the pigs mature there will be an increased supply of pork, which will drive down its price; so fewer farmers will breed pigs and the price will rise again, starting the cycle over again.

homogeneous product A product is homogeneous when, in the eyes of purchasers, every unit is identical to every other unit.

horizontal merger Union or *merger* of firms at the same stage of production in the same industry.

household All the people who live under one roof and who take, or are subject to others taking for them, joint financial decisions.

human capital The capitalized value of productive investments in persons. Usually refers to value derived from expenditures on education, training, and health improvements.

hyperinflation Episodes of very rapid inflation.

hysteresis The lagging of effects behind their causes. In economics, the term has come to relate to persistence or irreversibility of effects. An example is the difficulty of returning the long-term unemployed back to work because their skills have deteriorated. It also implies path dependency, which means that the ultimate equilibrium is not independent of how the economy gets there (i.e. it is not unique).

identification problem The problem of how to estimate both demand and supply curves from observed market data on prices and quantities actually traded.

implicit contracts Transactions, especially hiring workers, in which not everything expected from both parties is explicitly written down.

imputed costs The costs of using inputs into production already owned by the firm, measured by the earnings they could have received in their best alternative employment.

incentive compatibility Where the interaction of agents is such that their personal incentives lead them to act in such a way that an overall optimum outcome is achieved.

incidence In tax theory, where the burden of a tax finally falls.

income effect Effect on quantity demanded of a change in real income, relative prices held constant.

income-elastic Describes the situation where the percentage change in quantity demanded exceeds the percentage change in income that brought it about.

income elasticity of demand The responsiveness of quantity demanded to a change in income. Defined as the percentage change in quantity demanded divided by the percentage change in income.

income-inelastic Describes the situation where the percentage change in quantity demanded is smaller than the percentage change in income.

incomes policies Government intervention in the setting of factor rewards across broad sectors of the economy. They can take many forms, from the government's setting of voluntary guidelines for wage and price increases, to consultation on wage and price increases, to consultation on wage and price norms between unions, management, and government, to compulsory controls on wages, prices, and profits.

increasing returns A situation in which output increases more than in proportion to inputs as the scale of a firm's production increases. A firm in this situation, with fixed factor prices, is a decreasing-cost firm.

incremental costs Increase in costs associated with a small but discrete change in output.

incremental ratio When Y is a function of X, the incremental ratio is the change in Y divided by the change in X that brought it about, $\Delta Y/\Delta X$. The limit of this ratio as ΔX approaches 0 is the derivative of Y with respect to X, dY/dX.

incremental revenues The increase in revenue that results from a small but discrete increase in output.

indexation When a contract, for wages, pensions, or repayment of debt, is specified in real terms. Any specified money payment would be increased to compensate for actual inflation. More generally, the term applies to any contingent contract tied to an index number.

index of retail prices See *retail price index*.

indicators Variables that policymakers monitor for the information they yield about the state of the economy.

indirect tax A tax levied on a transaction rather than on a person or company. For example, VAT on restaurant meals is indirect because it is tied to the restaurant bill.

induced Anything that is determined within a theory or economic model; the opposite of autonomous or exogenous. Also called endogenous.

induced expenditure Any expenditure flow that is related to national income (GDP) or to any other variable explained by a theory.

694

industry A group of firms that sell a well-defined product or closely related set of products.

inelastic (demand) Describes the situation where the percentage change in quantity (demanded) is less than the percentage change in price that brought it about (elasticity is less than 1 in absolute terms).

inferior good A commodity with a negative income elasticity; i.e. its demand diminishes when income increases.

inflation An increase in the general price level.

inflation-adjusted surplus (deficit) The *budget surplus (deficit)* when the *inflation tax* is incorporated.

inflationary gap A negative output gap, i.e. actual GDP exceeds *potential output* (GDP).

inflationary shock Any autonomous shift in aggregate demand or aggregate supply that causes the price level to rise.

inflation tax The implicit revenue to the government that accrues from the fall in real value of its outstanding debt resulting from inflation.

influence costs Costs associated with workers playing internal politics in order to gain personal advancement. Influence costs are generally borne by the firm in the form of lost output and reduced profit.

infrastructure The basic facilities (particularly transportation and communication systems) on which commerce depends.

injection An increase in spending on the output of the domestic economy that arises from outside the economic model, such as an increase in export demand.

inputs The materials and factor services used in the process of production.

inside assets Assets that are the liability of other agents in the same sector or economy so that they net out for the sector or economy as a whole.

insider–outsider model An analysis of labour markets that gives more influence over market outcomes to those in employment (usually via trade union representation) than to the unemployed.

instruments The variables that policymakers can control directly. (In econometrics, instruments are proxy variables used in regression equations because of their desirable statistical properties—usually independence from the equation error.)

interest The amount each year paid on a loan, usually expressed as a percentage (e.g. 5%) or as a ratio (e.g. 0.05) of the principal loan.

intermediate products All goods and services used as inputs into a further stage of production.

internal economies Economies of scale that arise from sources within the firm.

internalizing an externality Doing something that makes an *externality* enter into the firm's own calculations of its private costs and benefits.

internal labour market An employment system within an organization in which individuals have a career path within the organization and senior posts are generally filled by internal promotions.

internal rate of return (IRR) The discount rate that makes the *net present value* of the returns on a specific investment project equal to zero. It is a measure of the yield on an investment project.

invention The discovery of something new, such as a new production technique or a new product.

inventories See *stocks*.

investment The act of producing or purchasing goods that are not for immediate consumption but will be used in production in the future.

investment banks The US term for banks that specialize in corporate finance, especially trading and underwriting securities. The UK term for the same kind of institution is *merchant bank*.

investment demand function A negative relationship between the quantity of investment per period and the interest rate, holding other things constant.

investment expenditure Expenditure on capital goods.

investment goods Goods produced not for present consumption, i.e. capital goods, inventories, and residential housing.

invisibles Services, typically in the balance of payments, that involve international payments that are unrelated to physical goods trade or assets, such as insurance, banking, and tourist expenditures.

involuntary unemployment When a person is willing to accept a job at the going wage rate but cannot find such a job.

IRR See *internal rate of return*.

IS curve The locus of combinations of the interest rate and the level of real GDP for which desired aggregate expenditure equals actual GDP. So called because, in a closed economy with no government, it also reflects the combinations of the interest rate and GDP for which investment equals saving, $I = S$. In general, it reflects a point for which injections equal withdrawals.

IS/LM model A diagrammatic representation of a model of aggregate demand determination based upon the locus of equilibrium points in the aggregate expenditure sector (*IS*) and the monetary sector (*LM*). It is incomplete as a model of GDP determination because it does not include an aggregate supply curve.

joint-stock company A firm regarded in law as having an identity of its own. Its owners hold shares with limited liability for the company's

Glossary

minimum efficient scale (MES) The smallest level of output at which long-run average cost is at a minimum; the smallest output required to achieve the economies of scale in production and/or distribution.

mixed economy An economy in which some decisions about the allocation of resources are made by firms and households and some by the central authorities.

mobile capital Financial capital that is free to move to the market where expected returns are the highest.

monetarism The doctrine that monetary magnitudes exert powerful influences in the economy and that control of these magnitudes is a potent means of affecting the country's macroeconomic behaviour, especially its inflation rate.

monetary equilibrium A situation in which there is no excess demand for or supply of money.

monetary policy Policy that works through shifting aggregate demand by altering the supplies of monetary aggregates or the short-term rate of interest (or possibly by fixing the exchange rate).

monetary transmission mechanism The mechanism that turns a monetary shock into a real expenditure change and thus links the monetary and the real sides of the economy.

money Any generally accepted medium of exchange, i.e. anything that will be widely accepted in exchange for goods and services.

money demand function Functional relationship that determines the demand to hold money balances, such as: the demand for real money balance depends on real GDP and the interest rate.

money income Income measured in terms of current money values.

money market The market in which banks, companies, and the public sector invest or finance their short-term financial surpluses or deficits. It is contrasted with *capital markets* (bonds and equities), in which long-term financing is achieved.

money multiplier The ratio of the money stock (by any definition broader than *M0*) to the monetary base (*high-powered money*).

money national product See *nominal GDP*.

money price See *absolute price*.

money rate of interest The amount of interest paid on a loan in money terms.

money stock See *supply of money*.

money supply See *supply of money*.

monopolist A single seller in any market.

monopolistic competition A market structure in which there are many sellers and freedom of entry but in which each firm sells a product somewhat differentiated from the others, giving it some control over its price.

monopoly A market structure that exists when an industry is in the hands of a single producer.

monopsonist A sole purchaser of a product.

moral hazard Risk that arises from people taking actions that increase social costs because they are insured against private loss. The term applies more generally to any change in behaviour that results from opportunism arising after a contractual arrangement has been undertaken, such as an employee who decides to take it easy after having obtained a long-term employment contract.

multi-divisional form of business organization (M-form) Business structure based on combining functions, such as production, marketing, and sales, into groups focusing on specific products. Each division is a cost centre and has its own operational manager.

multinational enterprises (MNEs) See *transnational corporations*.

multiplier The ratio of the change in GDP to the change in autonomous expenditure that brought it about.

multiplier–accelerator theory The explanation of business cycles that is based on the interaction of the *multiplier* and the accelerator.

NAIRU The amount of unemployment that exists when GDP is at its potential level and that, if maintained, will result in a stable rate of inflation.

Nash equilibrium In the case of firms, an equilibrium that results when each firm in an industry is currently doing the best it can given the current behaviour of the other firms in the industry.

national debt The central government's debt.

national income In general, the value of the nation's total output, and the income generated by the production of that output, measured in this book by GDP.

national product A generic term for the nation's total net output (value added), which is measured more specifically by GNP or GDP.

natural monopoly An industry whose market demand is sufficient to allow only one firm to produce at its minimum efficient scale.

natural rate of unemployment The level of unemployment in a competitive economy that corresponds to potential GDP and that is associated with stable inflation. For most purposes it is equivalent to the *NAIRU*, but the latter applies to imperfectly competitive economies as well.

natural scale A scale in which equal absolutes are represented by equal distances.

near money Anything that fulfils the store-of-value function and is readily convertible into a medium of exchange, but that is *not* itself a medium of exchange.

negatively related Refers to a relationship where an increase in one variable is associated with a decrease in another.

net domestic product *Gross domestic product* minus an allowance for *depreciation* (or *capital consumption*).

net exports Total exports minus total imports ($X - IM$).

net investment Gross investment minus replacement investment. New capital that represents net additions to the capital stock.

net present value (*NPV*) The discounted value today of the difference between revenues and costs over some succession of future periods. When a project's *NPV* is used as an investment criterion, a firm should undertake the project if its net present value is positive.

net taxes Total tax receipts net of *transfer payments*.

network effects Economies of scale that increase the usefulness of a product the more others use it. The telephone, for example, is more useful for each of us the more other people are connected.

neutrality of money Hypothesis that the level of real GDP is independent of the level of money stock.

New Classical theory A theory that the economy behaves as if it were perfectly competitive with all markets always clearing; where deviations from full employment can occur only if people make mistakes and where, given rational expectations, these mistakes will not be systematic.

New Keynesian economics A recent research agenda that has focused on explaining why prices do not adjust to clear markets, especially the labour market. It differs from the traditional Keynesian approach in its concern for *equilibrium unemployment* as well as *demand-deficient* (or cyclical) *unemployment*.

newly industrialized countries (NICs) Formerly underdeveloped countries that have become major industrial exporters in recent times. Sometimes called newly industrialized economies (NIEs).

nominal GDP Total net output (value added) valued at current money prices.

nominal interest rate Actual interest rate in money terms. It is contrasted with the *real rate of interest*, which is the nominal interest rate minus the inflation rate (or expected inflation rate).

nominal money supply The money supply measured in monetary units, not adjusted for changes in the price level.

non-cooperative equilibrium An equilibrium reached when firms calculate their own best policy without considering competitors' reactions.

non-market sector That portion of an economy in which producers must cover their costs from some source other than sales revenue.

non-renewable or exhaustible resources Any productive resource that is available as a fixed stock that cannot be replaced once it is used, such as oil.

non-strategic Behaviour that takes no account of the reactions of others, as when a firm acts in *perfect* or *monopolistic competition*.

normal-capacity output The level of output that the firm expects to maintain on average.

normal good A commodity whose demand increases when income increases.

NPV See *net present value*.

NX Symbol used in the macroeconomics sections of this book for net exports, which are exports minus imports.

OECD Organization for Economic Co-operation and Development. A Paris-based economics research institute and policy forum supported by the major industrial countries.

official financing Refers to items that represent international transactions involving the monetary authorities of the country whose balance of payments is being recorded.

oligopoly An industry that contains only a few firms.

open economy An economy that engages in international trade.

open-market operations Sales or purchases of securities by the central bank aimed at influencing monetary conditions.

opportunity cost The cost of using resources for a certain purpose, measured by the benefit given up by not using them in their best alternative use.

options Financial instruments that give the buyer the right but not the obligation to buy (call options) or sell (put options) an underlying asset at a specific price within a period of time.

output gap The difference between actual output and potential output ($Y^* - Y$); positive output gaps are called *recessionary gaps*, negative output gaps are called *inflationary gaps*.

outputs The goods and services that result from the process of production.

outside assets Assets held by a sector or economy that are liabilities of agents in another sector or economy.

overshooting Occurs when the impact effect of a shock takes a variable beyond its ultimate equilibrium level. Most widely applied to the exchange rate. A characteristic of a wide class of exchange rate models under rational expectations is that when monetary policy is, say, tightened the exchange rate initially appreciates to a point from which it will depreciate towards its long-run equilibrium level.

Glossary

Pareto-efficiency See *Pareto-optimality*.

Pareto-optimality A situation in which it is impossible, by reallocating production or consumption activities, to make at least one person better off without making anyone worse off. Also called Pareto-efficiency.

partisanship Influences on economic policy (or on expected economic policy) deriving from the differences in priority and constituency of political parties. It is an important component in some modern theories of the *political business cycle*.

partnership An enterprise with two or more joint owners, each of whom is personally responsible for all of the partnership's debts.

paternalism The belief that the individual is not the best judge of his or her own self-interest; someone else knows better.

path dependence Non-uniqueness of equilibrium resulting from the possibility that what happens in one period affects the stock of physical and human capital for a long time subsequently. Sometimes referred to as *hysteresis*.

payback period The time it takes to recoup the cost of an investment.

per capita economic growth The growth of per capita GDP or GNP (national income per person).

perfect capital mobility Arises when there are no artificial barriers to the movement of financial capital and investors regard domestic and foreign securities (riskless) as perfect substitutes.

perfect competition A market structure in which all firms in an industry are price takers and in which there is freedom of entry into, and exit from, the industry.

permanent income The maximum amount that a person can consume per year into the indefinite future without reducing his or her wealth.

permanent-income theory A theory that relates actual consumption to *permanent income*.

perpetuity Bond that pays a fixed sum of money each year for ever and has no redemption date. Sometimes called a consol.

personal disposable income (*PDI*) The gross income of the personal sector less all direct taxes and national insurance contributions.

per-unit tax See *specific tax*.

Phillips curve Relates the percentage change of money wages (measured as an annual rate) to the level of unemployment (measured as the percentage of the labour force unemployed).

physical capital Machinery and buildings that are desired as an input into the productive process.

planned expenditure What people intend to spend.

policy invariance A proposition associated with the *New Classical school*. It states that systematic changes in monetary and fiscal policy cannot affect real GDP. The conditions required for this to be true are not generally thought to hold.

political business cycles Cycles in the economy resulting from the political goals of incumbent (or partially incumbent) politicians. The simplest form of these is the deliberate pre-election boom, though modern theories are more subtle.

poll tax A tax that takes the same lump sum from everyone.

portfolio balance See *portfolio equilibrium*.

portfolio disequilibrium Situation that exists when wealth holders have too many of some assets and too few of others in their current portfolios.

portfolio equilibrium Situation that exists when wealth holders have the desired proportions of assets in their portfolios. Also called portfolio balance.

portfolio form of business organization (P-form) Companies structured as a collection of many subsidiary companies. Each subsidiary is a separate legal entity, though subsidiaries are often wholly owned by the main company.

portfolio investment Investment in bonds and other debt instruments that does not imply ownership, or in minority holdings of shares that do not establish legal control.

positively related Refers to the relationship where an increase in one variable is associated with an increase in the other.

potential output (GDP), Y^* The level of output at which there is a balance between inflationary and deflationary forces, and at which there is also no *demand-deficient unemployment* (the economy is at the *NAIRU*) and the existing capital stock is being run at its normal rate of utilization.

precautionary balances The amount of money people wish to hold because of uncertainty about the exact timing of receipts and payments.

predatory pricing The policy of setting prices at a level that will drive some competitors out of business, usually with the intention of raising prices once competition has been eliminated.

present value The value now of a sum to be received in the future. Also called discounted present value.

price controls Anything that influences prices by laws, rather than by market forces.

price differentiation (or discrimination) Situation arising when firms sell different units of their output at different prices for reasons not associated with cost. See also *segmentation*.

price elasticity of demand The percentage change in quantity demanded divided by the percentage change in price that brought it about. Often called elasticity of demand.

price elasticity of supply The percentage change in quantity supplied divided by the percentage change in price that brought it about. Often called elasticity of supply.

price index A statistical measure of the average level of some group of prices relative to some base period.

price level See *general price level*.

price makers Firms that administer their prices. See *administered price*.

price system An economic system in which prices play a key role in determining the allocation of resources and the distribution of the national product.

price taker A firm that can alter its rate of production and sales within any feasible range without having any effect on the price of the product it sells.

prime rate US terminology for *base rate*.

principal The amount of a loan; or the individual (or firm) who takes ownership of a transaction.

principal–agent problem The problem of resource allocation that arises because contracts that will induce agents to act in their principal's best interests are generally impossible to write or too costly to monitor; as when managers of firms do not do what their shareholders would wish them to do.

principle of substitution The idea that methods of production will change if relative prices of inputs change, with relatively more of the cheaper input and relatively less of the more expensive input being used.

principle of value additivity Companies are valued as the sum of their parts. There is no additional value generated by diversity of businesses, since investors can achieve optimal portfolio diversification for themselves.

private cost The value of the best alternative use of the resources used in production as measured by the *producer*.

private sector That part of the economy in which the organizations that produce goods and services are owned by private agents such as households and firms.

pro-cyclical Positively co-related with the *business cycle* in GDP.

producer Any agent that makes goods or services.

producers' surplus Total revenue minus total cost. The market value that the firm creates by producing goods, net of the cost of inputs currently used to create those goods.

production The act of making goods and services.

production function A functional relation showing the maximum output that can be produced by each and every combination of inputs.

production-possibility boundary A curve that shows the alternative maximum combinations that can be attained if all available productive resources are used; it is the boundary between attainable and unattainable output combinations.

productive efficiency Production of any output at the lowest attainable cost for that level of output.

productivity Output per unit of input employed.

products General term referring to all goods and services. Sometimes also referred to as *commodities*.

profit (1) In ordinary usage, the difference between the value of outputs and the value of inputs. (2) In microeconomics, the difference between revenues received from the sale of goods and the value of inputs, which includes the opportunity cost of capital. Also called *pure profit* or *economic profit*. (3) In macroeconomics, the component of GDP at factor cost in addition to income from employment, rent, and self-employment income; this is essentially the part of national income other than rent accruing to the ownership of incorporated businesses.

profit-maximizing output The level of output that maximizes a firm's profits. Sometimes also called the optimal output.

progressive tax A tax that takes a larger percentage of people's income the larger their income is. See also *regressive tax*.

protectionism Any departure from free trade designed to give some protection to domestic industries from foreign competition.

proxy An order from a stockholder that passes the right to vote to a nominee, usually an existing member of the board of a firm.

PSBR See *public sector borrowing requirement*.

public corporation A body established to run a nationalized industry. It is owned by the state but is usually under the direction of a more or less independent, state-appointed board.

public goods Goods and services that, once produced, can be consumed by everyone in the society whether they pay for them or not. Also called collective consumption goods.

public sector That portion of the economy in which production is owned and operated by the government or by bodies created by it, such as nationalized industries.

public sector borrowing requirement (PSBR) The combined excess of expenditure over revenue of the central government, the local authorities, and public corporations, minus asset sales.

public-sector debt The outstanding debt of central government, local authorities, and public corporations.

purchasing power of money The amount of goods and services that can be purchased with a given amount of money.

purchasing power parity (PPP) exchange rate The exchange rate between two currencies that equates their purchasing powers and hence adjusts for relative inflation rates.

purchasing power parity theory Theory that the equilibrium exchange rate between two national currencies will be the one that equates their purchasing powers, that is, makes prices the same in each country when converted at the current exchange rate.

pure profit Any excess of a firm's revenue over all opportunity costs, including those of capital. Also called *economic profit*.

pure rate of interest See *pure return on capital*.

pure return on capital The amount that capital can earn in a riskless investment. Also called the pure rate of interest.

quantity actually bought and sold The amount of a commodity that consumers and firms actually succeed in purchasing and selling.

quantity demanded The amount of a commodity that consumers wish to purchase in some time-period at a particular price.

quantity supplied The amount of a commodity that firms offer for sale in some time-period at a particular price.

quantity theory of money Theory predicting that the price level and the quantity of money vary in exact proportion to each other—i.e. changing M by X% changes P by X%.

quasi-rent Factor payments that are *economic rent* in the short run and *transfer earnings* in the long run.

ratchet effect Problem of wage incentives that arises when production targets are raised in response to increased productivity. Workers may be discouraged by the fact that their effort this period has led to higher targets next period.

rational expectations The theory that people understand how the economy works and learn quickly from their mistakes, so that, while random errors may be made, systematic and persistent errors are not made.

ratio scale See *logarithmic scale*.

reaction curve Curve showing one firm's profit-maximizing output for each given quantity sold by its competitor.

real business cycles Approach to the explanation of business cycles that uses dynamic equilibrium market-clearing models and relies on productivity shocks as a trigger. In such models, all cycles are an optimal response to the real shock and there are no deviations from potential GDP: rather, it is the full equilibrium value of GDP that fluctuates over time.

real capital Physical assets that include factories, machinery, and stocks of material and finished goods. Also called *physical capital*.

real exchange rate Index of the relative prices of domestic and foreign goods.

real GDP See *real national product*.

real income The purchasing power of money income.

realized expenditure What people actually succeed in spending.

reallocation of resources Some change in the uses to which the economy's resources are put.

real money supply The money supply measured in purchasing-power units, M/P.

real national product Total output valued at base-year prices.

real product wage The proportion of the sale value of each unit that is accounted for by labour costs (including the pre-tax nominal wage rate, benefits, and the firm's national insurance contributions).

real rate of interest The money rate of interest minus the inflation rate; expresses the real return on a loan.

real wage The money wage deflated by a price index to measure the wage's purchasing power.

recession A sustained drop in the level of economic activity.

recessionary gap A positive output gap, when actual GDP falls short of potential GDP.

redemption date The time at which the principal of a loan is to be paid.

regressive tax A tax that takes a smaller percentage of people's incomes the larger their income is. See also *progressive tax*.

relational contracts Contracts in which what is expected by both sides is not written out in detail but develops as an ongoing relationship.

relative price Any price expressed as a ratio of another price.

renewable resources Productive resources that can be replaced as they are used up, as with physical capital; distinguished from non-renewable resources, which are available in a fixed stock that can be depleted but not replaced.

rental price The cost per period of hiring something such as a machine or a building.

replacement investment Investment that replaces capital as it wears out. If it is equal to *depreciation*, or *capital consumption*, it does not increase the capital stock.

replacement ratio Benefits received by those out of work as a proportion of the wage of those in employment.

resource allocation The allocation of the economy's scarce resources among alternative uses.

resource-based theory of the firm See *knowledge-based theory of the firm.*

retail price index (RPI) An index of the general price level based upon the consumption pattern of typical consumers.

risk premium The return on capital that is necessary to compensate owners of capital for the risk associated with a specific investment; usually expressed as a premium over the risk-free rate of interest.

satisficing Refers to the target of achieving a satisfactory level of profit rather than the very highest level achievable.

saving Income received by consumers that they do not spend on the output of firms through *consumption expenditure.*

segmentation Used in this book to refer to the ability of a monopolist to charge different prices for the same product to different customers or market segments. The term is used more generally in business studies to apply also to the different quality requirements of different customer groups.

seignorage The revenue that accrues to the issuer of money.

self-employed Those people who work for themselves.

sellers' preferences Allocation of commodity in excess demand by the decision of suppliers.

services Intangible products, such as haircuts, banking, and medical services.

shares See *equities.*

shifting The passing of tax incidence from the person who initially pays it to someone else.

short run In microeconomics, the period of time over which some inputs, such as capital, are fixed. In macroeconomics, the period during which the price level is still adjusting to some shock and GDP can deviate from its potential level.

short-run aggregate supply (*SRAS*) curve The total amount that will be produced and offered for sale at each price level on the assumption that all input prices are fixed.

short-run equilibrium Generally, equilibrium subject to some inputs or prices being held constant over the time-period being considered; while in the long run these will be allowed to adjust.

short-run supply curve A curve showing the relation between quantity supplied and price when one or more input is fixed; under perfect competition an industry supply curve is the horizontal sum of marginal cost curves (above the level of average variable costs) of all firms in an industry at a point in time, but excluding any responses of newly entering firms.

shut-down price The price that is equal to a firm's average variable cost, below which it will produce no output.

signalling The use of arbitrary characteristics (especially of potential employees) to give a measure of unobservable qualities.

simple multiplier Usually applies to the value of the *multiplier* in the aggregate expenditure system before any account is taken of the feedback from the monetary sector and from aggregate supply.

single proprietorship An enterprise with one owner who is personally responsible for everything that is done. More commonly called a *sole trader.*

slump A period of low output and low employment.

social cost Private costs plus *externalities.* The true cost to society as a whole of an activity in terms of the other potential outputs forgone.

sole trader Non-incorporated business operated by a single owner. Modern UK terminology for a *single proprietorship.*

specialization of labour The organization of production by which individual workers specialize in the production of certain goods or services.

specific tax A tax expressed as so much per unit, independent of its price. Also called a per-unit tax.

speculation Taking a financial position that will yield profits if prices move in a particular direction in the future but will yield losses if they move the other way.

speculative motive The motive that leads agents to hold money in reaction to the risks inherent in a fluctuating price of bonds, or because bond prices are expected to move in a particular direction (down). More generally, it refers to the asset motive for holding money.

***SRAS* curve** See *short-run aggregate supply curve.*

stabilization policy The attempt to reduce fluctuations in GDP, employment, and the price level by stabilizing GDP at or close to its potential level.

stagflation The simultaneous occurrence of a recession (with its accompanying high unemployment) and inflation.

stock See *equities.*

stockbuilding The process of building *stocks.*

stocks Accumulation of inputs and outputs held by firms to facilitate a smooth flow of production in spite of variations in delivery of inputs and sales of outputs. Sometimes called inventories.

stock variable A variable that does not have a time dimension. It is contrasted with a flow variable.

stop–go policy Swings of policy stance between expansion to cure unemployment and contraction to cure inflation.

strategic Behaviour that takes into account the actual or anticipated reactions of others to one's own actions, as when a firm makes decisions that take account of rival firms' expected reactions in oligopolistic markets.

structural unemployment Unemployment that exists because of a mismatch between the characteristics of the unemployed and the characteristics of the available jobs in terms of region, occupation, or industry.

substitutes Two goods are substitutes if the quantity demanded of one is *positively related* to the price of the other.

substitution effect The change in quantity demanded of a good resulting from a change in the commodity's relative price, eliminating the effect of the price change on real income.

sunk costs Costs that once incurred can never be recovered. Once such costs have been incurred they should not influence future allocation decisions since they do not affect incremental (marginal) costs in the future.

supply The whole relation between the quantity supplied of some commodity and its own price.

supply curve The graphical representation of the relation between the quantity of some product that firms wish to make and sell per period of time and the price of that product, *ceteris paribus*.

supply function A functional relation between the quantity supplied and all the variables that influence it.

supply of effort The total number of hours people in the labour force are willing to work. Also called supply of labour.

supply of labour See *supply of effort*.

supply of money The total amount of money available in the entire economy. Also called the money supply or the money stock.

supply schedule A numerical tabulation showing the quantity supplied at a number of alternative prices.

supply-side policies Policies that seek to shift either the short-run or the long-run aggregate supply curve.

supply shocks A shift in any aggregate supply curve caused by an exogenous change in input prices or technology.

surprise aggregate supply curve See *Lucas aggregate supply curve*.

tacit collusion Refers to a situation in which a small group of firms that recognize the influence each has on the others acts without any explicit agreement to achieve the co-operative equilibrium. See also *explicit collusion*.

takeover When one firm buys another firm.

targets The variables in the economy that the policymakers wish to influence. Typical policy tar-

gets might be attached to inflation, unemployment, and real growth.

tariffs Taxes designed to raise the price of imported goods.

tax wedge The difference between what employers pay out for each employee and the amount of that money that ends up in the employee's pocket.

tender offer An offer to buy directly, for a limited period of time, some or all of the outstanding stock of a corporation from its shareholders at a specified price per share, in an attempt to gain control of the corporation. Also called a takeover bid.

term The amount of time between a bond's issue date and its redemption date.

terms of trade The ratio of the average price of a country's exports to the average price of its imports.

theory of games The theory that studies rational decision making in situations in which one must anticipate the reactions of one's competitors to the moves one makes.

third-party effects See *externalities*.

time inconsistency The problem that arises in rational-expectation models when policymakers have an incentive to abandon their commitments at a later time. The existence of this incentive is generally understood by private-sector agents and it may influence their current behaviour.

total cost (*TC*) The total of all costs of producing a firm's output, usually divided into *fixed* and *variable costs*.

total final expenditure The total expenditure required to purchase all the goods and services that are produced domestically when these are valued at market prices.

total fixed costs The total of a firm's costs that do not vary in the short run.

total product (*TP*) Total amount produced by a firm during some time-period.

total revenue (*TR*) The total amount of revenue that the firm receives from the sale of its output.

total variable costs The total of a firm's costs that do vary in the short run.

tournaments Labour markets within an organization in which employees compete with others at the same level to achieve promotion. Pay attaches to jobs, but workers are motivated by the potential for promotion.

tradables Goods and services that enter into international trade.

trade bills See *bills of exchange*.

trade cycles See *business cycles*.

trade or craft union An organization of workers with a common set of skills, no matter where, or for whom, they work.

trade-weighted exchange rate The average of the exchange rates between a particular country's currency and those of each of its major trading partners, with each rate being weighted by the amount of trade with the country in question. Also called *effective exchange rate.*

transfer earnings The amount that a factor must earn in its present use to prevent it from moving (i.e. transferring) to another use.

transfer payments Payments not made in return for any contribution to current output, such as unemployment benefits.

transmission mechanism See *monetary transmission mechanism.*

transnational corporations (TNCs) Firms that have operations in more than one country. Also called multinational enterprises (MNEs).

Treasury bill A promise to repay a stated amount at some specified date between 90 days and 1 year from the date of issue, issued by the Treasury at a discount to redemption value.

underdeveloped countries See *less developed countries.*

unemployment The percentage of the workforce out of work but seeking employment. In UK statistics, must also be registered and claiming benefit.

unitary form of business organization (U-form) Structure in which the CEO co-ordinates the activity of functional departments.

unit cost See *average variable cost.*

unit elasticity An elasticity with a numerical measure of 1, indicating that the percentage change in quantity is equal to the percentage change in price (so that total expenditure remains constant).

utility The satisfaction that a consumer receives from the consumption of goods and services.

value added The value of a firm's output minus the value of the inputs that it purchases from other firms.

value of money See *purchasing power of money.*

variable Any well-defined item, such as the price of a commodity or its quantity, that can take on various specific values.

variable cost A cost that varies directly with changes in output. Also called direct cost or avoidable cost.

variable factors Inputs whose amount can be varied in the short run.

velocity of circulation The number of times an average unit of money is used in transactions within a specific period. Defined as the ratio of nominal GDP to the money stock.

vertical merger Union or *merger* of firms at different stages of production.

very long run Period of time in which the technological possibilities open to a firm are subject to change.

vicious circle of poverty Describes the situation existing when a country has little capital per head and so is poor; because it is poor, it can devote few resources to creating new capital rather than producing goods for consumption; because little new capital can be produced, capital per head remains low, and the country remains poor.

visibles Goods, i.e. things such as cars, pulpwood, aluminium, coffee, and iron ore, that we can see when they cross international borders.

visible trade Trade in physical products. Also called merchandise trade.

voluntary unemployment Unemployment that occurs when there is a job available but the unemployed person is not willing to accept it at the existing wage rate.

wage-cost-push inflation An increase in the price level owing to increases in money wages that are not associated with excess demand for labour.

wage–price spiral The process set up by a sequence of wage-cost pushes that shifts the $SRAS$ curve to the left and monetary accommodation that shifts the AD curve to the right.

warrant The option component of a convertible bond. When separated from the bond, it is a call option on a company's equity.

winner's curse The observation that the winner of a takeover bid often pays too much for the target. The winner is the highest bidder and thus all other bidders and the previous owners of the assets placed a lower value on them. Applies also to any competitive tendering process.

withdrawals Income received by either firms or households that is not passed on by buying domestic output; the main withdrawals are saving, imports, and taxes. Also called leakages.

working population The total of the employed, the self-employed, and the unemployed, i.e. those who have a job plus those who are looking for work.

X-inefficiency Failure to use resources efficiently within the firm so that firms are producing above their relevant cost curves and the economy is inside its production-possibility boundary.

yield curve A graph plotting the yield on securities of different maturities against the term to maturity.

INDEX

Notes: Students can find brief definitions of the headings in **bold** type in the Glossary on pages 686–705. Page references to boxes are also in **bold** type. Page references in *italics* indicate figures or tables, but these are only given when the figure or table appears on a different page from the main discussion in the text.

Abbey National Building Society
  580–1
absenteeism 323
absolute advantage 23–5
absolute price 71
accelerator theory of investment
  666–70
acceptance houses 126n.
accountancy firms 122
acquisition, *see* mergers; takeovers
actual aggregate expenditure (*AE*)
  454–5
AD, see aggregate demand
adaptive expectations 618n.
added value 138
Adelman, I. and M. A. 665
adjustable peg system 633, 634–6
adjustment mechanism:
  and cyclical fluctuations 560–1,
    570–1, 665–70
  and demand shocks 550, 551–3,
    552, 559
administered price 245, 248
advantage:
  absolute 23–5
  comparative 22–5, **23–5**, *170*,
    176–7, 625, **626**
adverse selection 292–3, 327
advertising 239, 246, 261–2
AE, see aggregate expenditure
agents 46, 60; *see also* principal–agent
  problem
aggregate demand (*AD*) 510–20,
  525–32, 588–602, 603–5, 670–1
  and government expenditure
    500–2, 562–4
  and increasing GDP 557, *558*
  interaction with aggregate supply
    525–6
  and interest rates 592–4
  IS–LM curves derivation 594–602
  and Keynesian revolution 501, **528**
  and monetary equilibrium 588–93
  and money supply and demand
    592–3, *595*, 603–5, 670–1
  and price level 514–20, 525–6,
    555–6, 603–10
  see also aggregate demand shock
aggregate demand curve 514–20,
  527–32, 544–9, 564–7
  and *AE* curve 514–17, *518–19*
  and multiplier 519–20, 602

and output gap 544–9
  for pounds 630–1, 636
  shape of **516**, 517, 603
  shifts and movements 514, 518,
    519–20, 527–32, 564–7
aggregate demand shock 518, 531–5,
    545–56, 668–76
  anticipated **552**
  and business cycles **559**, 560–2,
    660–1, 668–9, 670–6, 682
  contractionary 550–4
  expansionary 549–50, **559**
  and GDP 527–9, 532–5, 550
  inflation and *548*, 549–50, **552**,
    660–1
  long-run effects of 549–56
  price level and 527–9, 532–5, 550
  SRAS curve and 527–9, 531–5,
    550–4, **552**
  and unit labour costs 545–9, 550,
    551–4
aggregate expenditure (*AE*) 454–76,
  492–7, 499–506, 510–13, 592–3
  actual 454–5
  autonomous and induced 455, 459,
    466, 477, 485
  changes in 499–506
  desired 454–73, 492–7
  function 466–8, 474–6, 494–7
  and interest rates 592–3
  and national income 466–8
  planned 454–5, 499–505
  and price level 510–13
  see also national expenditure
aggregate expenditure curve 470–1,
  474–6, 510–17, 531, 533–5
  and *AD* curve 514–17, *518–19*
  45° line 470–1, 485
  and multiplier *530*, 531
  shifts 474–6, 510–13, 514, 533–5
aggregate output, *see* national product
aggregates and aggregation 412
  across industries 451–2
  monetary **580–1**, 590
  see also aggregate demand; aggregate
    expenditure; aggregate supply
aggregate supply (*AS*) 520–6
  asymmetric response to change
    533, 547–9
  and increasing GDP 557–8
  interaction with aggregate demand
    525–6

and long-run equilibrium 555–6
  and price level 520–6
  see also aggregate supply shock
aggregate supply curve 521–6
  Lucas theory of 673–6, 679
  for pounds 632
  shifts in 524–5
  see also long-run aggregate supply
    curve (*LRAS*); short-run
    aggregate supply curve (*SRAS*)
aggregate supply shock 524–5, 527,
    535–6
  and business cycles 660–1, 676–8,
    680–1
  and GDP 527, 535–6
  and inflation 535, 536, 660–1
  input prices as 524
  in oil industry 173, 176, 536, 681
  and unemployment 660–1
air transport 225, **232–3**, 246–7, 264
alcohol and brewing industry 260,
    306–8
Allied Colloids PLC 394
Allied Lyons (now Allied Domecq)
    PLC **260**, 306
allocation of resources, *see* resource
    allocation
allocative efficiency 280, 282–6, 298–9
AP, see average product
APC, see average propensity to
    consume
Apple Macintosh 168
appreciation 492, 628, 638, 639
  and monetary policy **596–7**, 642–8
AR, see average revenue
arbitrage, interest 650
AS, see aggregate supply (*AS*)
assembly lines **169**
assets:
  financial 576–9
  inside or outside 511
asymmetric information 288, 292–3
  labour market 324, 327–8, 330–1,
    341
ATC, see average total cost
Austrian school 616–17
automatic fiscal stabilizers 567–8
autonomous expenditure 455, 459,
    466, 477, 519–20
  government expenditure as part
    502
AVC, see average variable cost

average cost 152–5, **156–7**
average cost pricing 298–9
average fixed cost (*AFC*) 152, 153–4
average product (*AP*) 146–51
average propensity to consume (*APC*) 459, 460
average propensity to save 462
average revenue (*AR*) 191–3
   under monopoly 215–17
average total cost (*ATC*) 152, 153–4
   under monopoly 2*20*
   under perfect competition 204–6
average variable cost (*AVC*) 152, 153–5, 185–6
   shape of curves 155, **156**
   under monopoly 218
   under perfect competition 194, *198*, 205–6

balanced budget 486–7, 504–5, 568
balance of payments accounts 620–7, 636
   capital account 621, 622–3, 624
   current account 621–2, 624, 625–7
   surplus or deficit 625–7
balance of trade 626
balances, money, *see* money balances
Banking Act (1979) 225
Bank of England, in foreign exchange market 629, 632–3, 634–6
banks and banking 12, 225
   central banks 634–6
Barber boom 682
barriers to entry 222–6, **224–5**, 259–65, 288–9
   imperfect competition 247, 249, 259–65, 288–9
   licensing as 225
   monopolistic 11, 222–6
   patent laws as 223–5, **224–5**
   technological 223
   see also entry and exit
Baumol, W. J. 263
Bentham, Jeremy 47n.
bills 126
BMW 623
Böhm-Bawerk, E. 616n.
bonds 126–7, 576–9
   government 356, **359**, 487n., 510–11
   and interest rates 126–7, 356, **359**, 576–9, **596–7**
   yield to maturity 365
booms 15, **414–15**, 448, 547–8, 553, 682
bounded rationality 129–30, 324–5
brand proliferation 259–61, **260**, 262
   see also differentiated product
break-even price 202
Bretton Woods system 634
British Airways PLC **232–3**
British Gas PLC 305
British Rail **233**
brownfield investment 623
budget balance, *see* balanced budget
budget deficit 417, 487

budget surplus 487–8, 567–8
business confidence 465
business cycles 15–17, 413–15, **414–15**, **559**, 560–71, 659–85
   characteristics 660–4
   and company liquidation **18–19**, 414–15, 664
   cyclical adjustment mechanisms 560–1, 570–1, 665–70
   and demand shocks **559**, 560–2, 660–1, 668–9, 670–6, 682
   globalized 683
   in industry sectors 661–4
   inflation and unemployment in 660–1, 681
   long-wave 659–60
   and macroeconomic policy 16–17, 450, 562–71, 670–6, 678–81; fiscal 16, 562–71, 672; monetary 670–2, 673–6
   profits and wages in 664
   return of 681–3
   and supply shocks 660–1, 676–8, 680–1
business cycle theories 664–70
   chaotic 665
   equilibrium 665, 673–8
   Keynesian 671–2, 681, 682
   Lucas theory of 673–6, 679
   monetarist 670–1, 682
   multiplier–accelerator 666–70
   New Classical 617, 665, 673–6
   political 678–9
   real business cycle (RBC) 617, 665, 676–8, 680
   stop–go government policies 679–80
   systematic or random shocks 664–5
buyouts 399, 404

call options 364
capacity 154, 156
   defined 155
   excess 236, 237–8, 453
   under-utilized 151, 155, 157, 533
   in very long run 204–5
capital:
   cost of 357
   depreciation 134–5, 425, 432
   as factor of production 132
   financial 9–10, 123–7, 346
   formation 425, 465
   income from, *see* returns
   mobile, *see* capital flows
   new 199
   old or obsolete 204–7
   opportunity cost of 134, 198–9, 348, 356–7
   physical 9–10, 123, 346–70
   real 9–10, 123
   weighted average cost of 357
   see also human capital; investment
capital account, balance of payments 621, 622–3, 624
capital consumption allowance 425

capital flows 37–9, 623, 629–30, 638–9, 643–55
   and exchange rates 638–9
   globalization 37–9
   and interest rates **596–7**, 643–8
   and net exports 649
   perfect capital mobility 649–55
capital goods 9–10, 345–6, 368–70, 424–5
   see also physical capital
capital–labour ratio 156–7, 160
Capital Liberalization Directive, EU 39
capital stock 425
Carroll, L. 71
cartels 255
cash flow:
   discounted 353–6
   and lease-or-buy decisions 368–70
   net 355, 364–5, 366–7
central authorities, *see* government
central banks 634–6
Central Electricity Generating Board (CEGB) **167–8**
central planning, *see* command economies
CEOs, *see* chief executive officers
ceteris paribus, use in economics 49
Chamberlin, E. 235, 239
Chandler, Jr., A. D. 250
Channel Tunnel 72–7, 101, 267–8, 272–3, **274–5**
chaos theory of business cycles 665
charities 123
cheating 253, 255, 258
chief executive officers (CEOs) 381, 382, 383–4
   pay 339, **340**
circular flow of income and expenditure 421–2, 423, **472**, 480, 498–9
closed economy model of national income 453, 454–80
coal industry **108–9**, 362
Coase, R. 128, 391
collective consumption goods 288, 291–2
collusion 255, 303–4
command economies 6–9, **7–8**, 128–9, 279
commercial bills 126
common property resources 290–1
comparative advantage 22–5, **23–5**, 625, **626**
   and technical change **170,** 176–7
competition:
   competitive fringe 248
   competitive markets 69
   non-price 246
   very-long-run 258–9, 266–7
   see also imperfect competition; monopolistic competition; oligopoly; perfect competition
competition policy 296–308
   monopoly control 297–300
   to strengthen competition 303–8

competitiveness, international 412, 491–2, 642
complementary goods 55–6, 101
compound interest **352**
computer chips industry 77–81, 85
concentration 10–12, 171–2, 249, 250, 394
see also mergers
congestion, road 78–9
conglomerates 14, 395–9, **396–7**
constant costs **156–7**, 163
constant prices 435
constant returns 163
consumer goods 6, 663–4
consumer price index (CPI) 412
consumers and **consumption** 20, 36, 46, 47
changes in 57, 510–12
disposable income 434, 456–63, 493–4
saving function 461–2
see also individuals
consumers' surplus 228–30, 284
consumption expenditure 89, 424, 456–63, 510–13, 663–4
consumption function 456–61, 510–13
and 45° line 460–1
Keynesian 457, 458, 462
and price level 510–13
propensity to consume 459, 460–1, 494, *495*, 500, 504
and wealth 462–3, 511–12
contact lens market **306–8**
contestable markets 263–5
contractionary shocks 550–4
contracts 324–35
co-operation, oligopolistic 250–1, 255–8
co-ordination:
command economy failure of 7–8
of suppliers 393
within firms 379–80, **392–3**
core competencies 25
corporate control 14–15, 250, 399–404
see also mergers; takeovers
cost curves:
long-run 161–4, 172–3
monopolistic 215
shape 155, **156**, 161–2, 163–4
shifts in 172–3
short-run 152–8, 172–3
and size of firm 163–4
cost minimization 158–60, 391–5
costs:
average 152–5, **156–7**; *see also* average total cost; average variable cost
constant **156–7**, 163
of entry 249, 263–5
factor 133–5, 430–1
of firms 133–5, 142–79
fixed 137, 152, 162
imputed 133–4
increasing 162–3
incremental 152, **188–9**
influence 339
inputs 132–5
long-run 158–73
long-run average 161–4, **168**, 203–4, 237, 246–7
marginal, *see* marginal cost
one-time 165–6
opportunity, *see* opportunity cost
and output 61, 142–77, 521
private 289–90
product development 166, 246–7, 249, 262
production 61, 132–5, 193–4
set-up 223, 261–2
short-run 151–8, 172–3, 193–4, 195–6, 215
short-run average total 203–4
short-run marginal 152, 153–5, 203
social 289–90
sunk 135, 263–4, 346, 361–4
total 152, 153–4; *see also* average total cost
transaction 128–9
unit 152, 521–2, **533**
unit labour 545–9, 550, 551–4
variable 137, 144, 146–58, **157**; *see also* average variable cost
CPS Chemicals 394
creative destruction 226–7, 266–7
credibility 675–6
credit cards 583n.
cross-elasticity of demand 101
cross-subsidization 301
crowding-out effect 556n., *608*, 610, 655
currency:
appreciation and depreciation 596–7, 628, 638, 639, 642–8
reserves 630, 634, 635–6
single European 596, 652
see also demand for money; foreign exchange market; supply of money
current account, balance of payments 621–2, 624, 625–7
cyclical adjustment mechanisms 560–1, 570–1, 665–70
cyclical fluctuations 30, 500–1, **559**, 560–2, 660–1, 664–81
employment 30, 660–1, 681
in GDP **559**, 560–2, 664–81
inflation 660–1, 681
stabilization 500–1, 553
see also business cycles
Cyert, R. M. and March, J. G. 379–80

deadweight loss 448–9
debentures 127
debt:
firm's 126–7
Public Sector Borrowing Requirement 487
term 126
see also budget deficit
debt instruments 126–7

decision lag 569
decision taking:
consensual **337**
in the firm 119–20, 158
and incrementalism **188–9**
on investment 346, 352–73
and risk 134, 356–7, 360–1
wait-and-see approach 360–1, 363, **364–5**
declining industries 206–7, **362**
decreasing returns 163, 164
deficit:
balance of payments 625–7
budget 417, 487
see also debt
deflation, demand-shock 550–1
deflator, implicit 435–8, **436–7**
delayering 35, **392–3**
demand 46–59
in action 72–81, **73**
and changes in taste 57
for complementary goods 55–6, 101
derived 314–19
determinants of 48–9, 52–3
environmental variables 56
excess 67
factor, *see* derived demand
final 420
as flow 48
and income 52–3, 54, 56, **96**, 99–101
for inferior goods 56, **105**
input 314–24
for labour 314–19
laws of 69–71
measurement of 104–9
nature of 47–8
and price 49–59, 67–72
and substitute goods 55, 74–5, 95–6, 101
see also aggregate demand (*AD*); demand and supply; elasticity of demand
demand and supply 69–81
in action 72–81, **73**, **78–9**, 84–5
in foreign exchange market 633–4, 636–7
of labour 316–24
'laws of' 69–71, **73**
measurement 104–9
demand curves:
of firm 316–18
horizontal 183, 191, 193
identification problem 106–9
individual 50–1
industry 183, 318–19
for labour 316–19, 321–2
long-run 97–9
market 51–2, 53–4
and market structure 183
movements along and shifts in 54–9
negative 87, 234, 236, 237, 286–7
in perfect competition 183
short-run 97–9
slope 85, 87, 91–3
and supply curves 67–9

under monopoly 215–22
demand failure 454
demand for money 580–8, 592–3
  demand for money function 588
  foreign exchange 628–31, 636–8
  interest rates and 584–5, *587*, 588, *591*
  precautionary 583–4
  price level and 585–7, 588
  speculative 584–5
  and transmission mechanism 592–3
  and wealth 576, 584–5
demand function 48–9
demand management 501
demand schedules:
  individual 50, 51
  market 51, *53, 66*
demergers 396–7
depreciation:
  capital 134–5, 425, 432, **596–7**, 642–8
  currency 628, 638, 639
depression 413–14, 464
deregulation 302–3
derived demand 314–19; *see also* factors of production; inputs
destocking 424
devaluation 492, 635–6
differentiated product 113, 231, 237–9, 244–6
  under oligopoly 248, 249, 259–61
  and vertical integration 395
  see also brand proliferation
diminishing average productivity 147
diminishing returns, law of 143, 148–51, 155, 348
direct taxes 431
discounted cash flow (*DCF*) 353–6
discounting:
  bills 126
  present value 349, 353–6, 368–70
discount rates 126, 356–7
  nominal 358
  real 358
diseconomies of scale 163, 164
disequilibrium 68–9; *see also* equilibrium
disposable income 434, 456–63
  and consumption expenditure 456–63
  and income taxes 493–4
distribution of income 294–5
  and demand 52–3, 56
  equitable or efficient 294–5
  redistribution 294
dividends 125
divisibility of fixed inputs **156–7**
division of labour 166, **169**, 248
double counting 419–21
downstream integration 389
duopoly 251
durables and non-durable goods 663–4

Early Keynesians 613–14

earnings, *see* income; pay; wages
economic bads 441
economic efficiency 158, 279–88
  and takeovers 400–4
economic growth 16, 301, 560
  and GDP 557, 559–62
  and inflation 416–17
  and stabilization policies 570–1
economic models 4, 447
  GDP with changing price level 509–36
  GDP in closed economy without government 453–80
  GDP in open economy with government 485–507
economic policy, *see* fiscal policy; macroeconomic policy; monetary policy; stabilization policy
economic profit, *see* profits
economic rent 200–1, 429
economics:
  defined 5, 28–9
  of the firm 9–10
  of organizations 12–14
economic systems:
  command 6–9
  market 5–6
economies of scale 162, 163–7, **167–8**
  and allocative efficiency 287–8
  and business integration 388–90
  in electricity industry **167–8**
  in imperfect competition 246–7, 248–9
  see also increasing returns
economies of scope 164–5, 249, 388–90
efficiency 279–88
  allocative 280, 282–6, 298–9
  and distribution of income 294–5
  economic 158, 279–88, 400–4
  engineering **283**
  government policies for 296–7
  monopolistic inefficiency 286, *287*, 288–9
  oligopolistic 287–8
  Pareto 280
  in perfect competition 285–6
  productive 280–2, **283**, 285, 286
  of scale 261–2, 287–8
  technical 158, **283**
  X-inefficiency **283**
  see also resource allocation
efficiency wage 327–31, 338, 553
elasticity of demand 86–101, **96**, 184
  in action 109–13
  cross- 101
  income 99–101, **105**
  price, *see* price elasticity of demand
  unit 88, 89
elasticity of supply 101–4
electricity industry 145, **167–8, 306–8**, 353–6
employment 12–13, 29–30, 34–6, 313–44, **337**
  contracts and performance monitoring 324–35

  cyclical 30, 660–1, 681
  income from 429
  internal labour market 335–42
  Japanese arrangements **337**
  lifetime **337**
  and living standards 29–30
  long-term relationships 336–8
  and market-clearing wage 321–2
  primary and secondary sectors 335–6
  structural changes 34–6
  UK 29–30, *35*
  see also labour; unemployment; working population
endogenous change 173–7, **174–5**
Engel, E. and Engel curves 100–1
engineering:
  engineering efficiency **283**
  new materials **174–5**
entry and exit:
  cost of 249, 263–5
  in imperfect competition 222–6, 247
  profits as signals 198–202, 222, 226, 235, 259–65
  under monopolistic competition 236
  under perfect competition 190, 198–202, 206
  see also barriers to entry; economies of scale
environment 8, 441
equilibrium:
  co-operative 251
  exchange rate 439
  imperfect competition 251–4
  long-run 198–204, 222–7
  macroeconomic 525–6
  market 68–9
  monetary 588–94, 599–600
  monopolistic 218–22
  Nash 252–3, **256–7**
  non-cooperative 251–4, 269–72
  in perfect competition 193–204
  self-policing 252–3
  short-run **188**, 193–8, 203–4, 218–22
  zero-profit 199, 202
  see also disequilibrium
equilibrium employment 321
equilibrium GDP 468–71, 476–80, 485, 492–507, 510–36
  and 45° line 470–1, 485
  and aggregate expenditure 499–507
  in closed economy without government 468–71
  determining 468–71, 496–7
  and exchange rates 651–5
  and fiscal policy 500–5
  and government expenditure 502–3
  income–expenditure approach 468–71, 492–7, 505–6
  IS–LM curves 594–602
  long-run 555–6, 557–62
  and multiplier 476–80, **478**, 499–500

equilibrium GDP (*cont.*)
  and net exports 500
  in open economy with government
    492–9
  and paradox of thrift 564–7, **566–7**
  and price level 510–36, 555–6,
    603–10
  saving–investment approach
    470–1, **472**, 497–9
  short-run 525–6, 557–62
  and tax rates 503–4
equilibrium price 66, 67, 68–70
  in perfect competition 196–7
equilibrium quantity 68–9
equilibrium theories of business cycles
  665, 673–8
equities 123–5; *see also* capital
ERM, *see* Exchange Rate Mechanism
eurobonds 127
European Union (EU):
  competition policies 304–5
  single currency 596, 652
  see also Exchange Rate Mechanism
Eurotunnel PLC 76–7
evolutionary theory of firm 380–1
excess capacity 236, 237–8, 453
excess demand and supply 67–8
Exchange Equalization Account 629
Exchange Rate Mechanism (ERM)
  634, *643*, 648
exchange rates 628, 632–55
  adjustable peg system 633, 634–6
  behaviour of 640–8
  and business cycles 672, 676, 682
  and capital flows 638–9
  changes in 636–9
  and competitiveness 491–2, 642
  determination of 628–9, 632–48
  equilibrium 439
  expectations 639, **644–5**
  and fiscal policy 654–5
  fixed 633, 634–6, 650, 651–2, 654–5,
    672, 676
  floating 418, **596–7**, 633–4, 650–1,
    652–4, 655, 672, 676
  and inflation 638
  and interest rates **596–7**, 643–8
  and monetary policy 418, **596–7**,
    642–8, 651–4, 672
  and net export function 649, 653
  overshooting 642–8, 651
  pegged 633, 634–6
  and purchasing power parity (PPP)
    439, 492n., 640–2, **641**
  and quantity theory of money **641**
  real 642, *643*
  and recession 647–8
  and transmission mechanism
    596–7, 648
  volatility 640, **644–5**
  see also foreign exchange market
execution lag 569
exit, *see* entry and exit
expansionary shocks 549–50, **559**
expectations:
  adaptive 618n.

and business cycles 669, 673–6
exchange rate 639, **644–5**
expected returns 348
extrapolative 618n.
and inflation **552**
interest rates **359**
and investment 465
Keynesian theory of 671
rational 616–18, 673–4, 679
self-realizing 669
expenditure, *see* aggregate expenditure; autonomous expenditure;
  consumption expenditure; government expenditure; investment
  expenditure; national expenditure
exports:
  as autonomous expenditure 489,
    490, 500
  and demand for pounds 629
  as injection in circular flow of
    income 498
  in National Income Accounts
    427–8
  net 427–8, 488–92, 500
  net export function 488–92, 500,
    512–13
  prices and exchange rates 636–7
  see also international trade
externalities 288, 289–90
extrapolative expectations 618n.

factor cost 132–5, 430–1
factors of production 17–20, 132–5
  economic rent **200–1**, 429–31
  see also capital; derived demand;
    inputs; labour; land
failure:
  command economies 7–8, 279
  demand 454
  market 6, 279, 288–93
fallacy of composition **516**
falling-cost industries 298, 299
fat cats **340**
FDI, *see* foreign direct investment
final demand 420
final goods and services 420
finance, company 123–7
financial assets, *see* assets
financial capital 10, 123–7, 346
financial markets, globalization 649
  see also foreign exchange market
financial regulation 225
Financial Services Act (1986) 225
fine-tuning 569
firm, theory of 9–10, 119, 127–30,
  131–2
  evolutionary 380–1
  knowledge-based or resources-
    based 128–9, 377–8
  modelling 142–3
  neoclassical 129–30
  transaction cost 128–9
firms 9–10, 60–5, 119–41, 142–79,
  180–209, 352–73
  as agents 60
  as command economy 6–9, 128–9

control and ownership 122, 125,
  130, 326
costs 133–5, 151–8
decision taking 10, 119–20, 158,
  188–9
economics of 9–10, 12–14
effect of business cycles **18–19**,
  414–15, 661–4
financing 9–10, 123–7
forms of 120–3, **120–1**
human resources 342, 373
in imperfect markets 11–12, 183,
  214–39, 242–77
labour demand and supply 316–24
liquidation of **18–19**, 414–15, 664
in long run 145, 158–73, **188–9**,
  193, 198–204, 222–7
marginal and intramarginal 202–3
market for corporate control 14–15,
  250, 399–404
market or non-market sector 123
market structure 181–3
monopolistic 11, 183, 214–34
in monopolistic competition 214,
  234–9
number in UK 122
oligopolistic 11–12, 139, 214, 227,
  247–76
as organizations 378–88
output 146–77
over- or undervalued 398–9, **402–3**,
  403
in perfect competition 10–11,
  180–207
in short run 144–5, 146–58, **188**,
  193–4
size of 163–4, 166, 248–50, **392–3**
subsidiaries 384–8
supply function 61
in very long run 145, 173–7, **189**,
  193, 204–7
see also integration; investment
  appraisal; non-profit
  maximization; organizational
  structure; profit maximization
fiscal policy 417, 484, 500–5, 562–71,
  607–10
  and budget deficit or surplus 417,
    487, 567–8
  and business cycles 16, 562–71,
    672
  compared with monetary 595,
    603–4, 607–10
  discretionary 562, 568–70, 683
  effect of change 607–10
  and equilibrium GDP 500–5
  and exchange rates 654–5
  expansionary 607–10
  fine-tuning 569
  gross-tuning 569–70
  and inflationary gaps 564, *565*, *608*,
    609
  Keynesian 614, 672
  lags in 569
  long-run effect *608*, 609–10
  pro-cyclical 568

and recessionary gaps 563, 564
short-run effect 607–9
stabilization 500–1, 563–71
and taxation 503–4, 562, 564
fishing industry 290–1
fixed-capital formation 425, 465
fixed cost 137, 152, 162
fixed exchange rates 633, 634–6, 650,
651–2, 654–5, 672, 676
fixed factors 144, 156–7
flexible exchange rates, *see* floating
exchange rates
flexible manufacturing 166–8,
169–70, 177, 267
flexible wages 551–3
floating exchange rates 418, **596–7**,
633–4, 650–1, 652–4, 655, 672,
676
floating rate notes (FRNs) 126–7
flows:
capital, *see* capital flows
cash 353–6, 364–5, 366–7, 368–70
circular flow of income and
expenditure 421–2, 423, 498–9
from use of physical capital 347
global investment 37–9
production 143
fluctuations, *see* cyclical fluctuations
focus 25, 399
food production 662–4
Fordism 166, 169
foreign competition 412
foreign direct investment (FDI) 37–9,
124, 623
foreign exchange market 596–7,
627–39, **644–5**
and capital flows 638–9
demand and supply 633–4, 636–8
and interest rates **596–7**
role of Bank of England 629, 632–3,
634–6
unpredictability **644–5**
see also exchange rates
foreign exchange reserves 630, 634,
635–6
foreign income 490
free goods 78
free-market economies 6
Friedman, M. 457, 614, 671, 672
full-employment income 447
future returns 348, 349–52, 358–60,
369–70
future value (*FV*) **352**

game theory 251–4, **256–7**, 273–6
gaps, *see* inflationary gap; output gap;
recessionary gap
Garton Ash, T. 8
GDP, *see* equilibrium GDP; gross
domestic product
GDP gap, *see* output gap
General Agreement on Tariffs and
Trade (GATT) 37
General Motors 381
Glaxo Wellcome PLC 11, **120–1,** 171,
223, 384–5, 400–2

globalization 36–9, 683
financial 649
investment flows 37–9
labour market 37
of production **125,** 394
GNP, *see* gross national product
goods 20
capital 9–10, 345–6, 368–70, 424–5
complementary 55–6, 101
durables and non-durable 663–4
final 420
free 78
inferior 56, **105**
intermediate 420
investment 424–5, 662–3
merit 295
public 288, 291–2
substitute 55, 74–5, 95–6, 101
government, role in model of national
economy 451, 453–4
government bonds 356, **359**, 487n.,
510–11
government budget:
balanced 486–7, 504–5, 568
deficit 417, 487
Public Sector Borrowing
Requirement 487
surplus 487–8, 567–8
government expenditure 425–7,
485–6, 498–9, 502–3
and aggregate demand 562–4
effect on GDP 502–3, 562
and exchange rates 654–5
exclusion of transfer payments 426,
485–6
on goods and services 425–7,
485–6
and inflationary gap 555–6
as injection in circular flow of
income 498–9
government intervention 278–9,
288–308, 562–71, 670–6, 678–81
and business cycles 16–17, 450,
562–71, 670–6, 678–81
case for 288–96
in declining industries 207, **362**
in foreign exchange markets 632–3
in market failure 279, 288–93
or market mechanism 278–9,
288–308, **552,** 553, 672
in market structure 296–308
reducing 279, 302–3
scepticism about 301–2
government policy, *see* competition
policy; fiscal policy;
macroeconomic policy; monetary
policy; stabilization policy
government revenue 486–8, 567–8
gross capital formation 425
gross domestic product (GDP) 20,
421–34, 453–80, 485–507,
509–36
actual and potential 447–9, 544–9,
554–6
and aggregate expenditure 466–8,
494–5

at factor cost 430–1
at market prices 431–2, 438
changes in 473–80, 666–8
cyclical fluctuations **559,** 560–2,
664–81
and demand for money 582–3,
584–5, **587,** 588
demand-determined **528**
and demand shocks 527–9, 532–5,
550
expenditure-based 422, 423–9
GDP gap 447–9, 544–9
and government expenditure
502–3, 562
and growth 557, 559–62
income-based 422, 429–32
increasing 557–8
international comparisons 438–40,
442
and investment expenditure 666–8,
669–70
measurement of 432–4, 435–8,
436–7
models of, *see* economic models
omissions from 440–2
and price level 510–36, 555–6
and supply shocks 527, 535–6
see also equilibrium GDP; national
income
gross national product (GNP) 432–4
gross-tuning 569–70
growth, *see* economic growth

Hanson PLC 14, **396–7,** 398–9
Harrod, Sir R. **362**
Hayek, F. A. von 7, 13, 616n.
Hicks, Sir J. 594
horizontal differentiation 244
horizontal integration 14, 389–90
hostile takeovers 400, 404
households, as agents 46; *see also*
consumers and consumption
housing 370, 425, 429, 464–5
human capital and resources 342,
371–3

IBM 168
ICI PLC 14
identification problem 106–9
illegal activities 440
imperfect competition 11–12, 183,
213–41, 242–77
barriers to entry 247, 249, 259–65,
288–9
differentiated product 113, 231,
237–9, 244–6, 259–61
and economies of scale 246–7,
248–9
equilibrium 251–4
key features 243–7
non-price competition 246
prices 213–14, 245–6, 248
see also monopolistic competition;
monopoly; oligopoly
implicit contracts 325
implicit deflator 435–8, **436–7**

Index

implicit price 348
imports 427, 489–90, 498, 500
  marginal propensity to import 499, 500
  prices and exchange rates 637–8
  see also international trade
imputed costs 133–4
incentive compatibility 379
incentives 322–3, 326–7, 330–5, 340, 379
  and disincentives 322–3
  incentive pay 322–3, 330, 331–4, 340
  for managers 13, 326–7
  misplaced in command economies 7–8
  and performance monitoring 332–3, 334–5
  perverse 333–4
income:
  in circular flow 498–9
  and demand 52–3, 54, 56, 96, 99–101
  foreign 490
  lifetime 342
  in national accounting 429–32
  net property 433
  permanent 457, 462–3
  personal 434, 456–63
  see also equilibrium GDP; gross domestic product (GDP); national income; wages
income distribution, *see* distribution of income
income effect 320–1, 322–3, 329–30
income elasticity of demand 99–101, 105
income–expenditure model of national income 468–71, 492–7, 505–6
income tax 323, 493–4, 498
increasing costs 162–3
increasing returns 162, 165–72
incremental costs 152, 188–9
incrementalism 188–9
incremental product 148
incremental revenue 184–5, 188–9, 191
index-linked government bonds 359
indirect taxes 431
individuals:
  as agents 46
  demand 46–59
  personal investment decisions 371–3
  protection for 295
  see also consumers and consumption; households
induced expenditure 455, 459
industry 183
  declining 206–7, 362
  demand curves 183, 318–19
  demand for labour 318–19
  falling-cost 298, 299
  rising-cost 298, 299
  supply curves 194–6, *197*

industry standards 168–71
inefficiency, *see* efficiency
inelastic demand 88, 89–90
inequality 294–5
inferior goods 56, 105
inflation 412, 416–17, 491–2, 660–1, 676, 679–80
  and business cycles 660–1, 681
  demand-shock 5*48*, 549–50, 552, 660–1
  economic growth and 416–17
  and exchange rates 638
  and expectations 552
  and interest rates 358–60, 359, 416–17
  and international competitiveness 491–2
  and prices 71–2, 491–2
  stagflation 535, 536
  and supply shocks 535, 536, 660–1
  treatment in investment appraisal 357–60
  unemployment and 660–1, 676, 679–80
  and wage contracts 546n.
  see also price level; purchasing power
inflationary gap 448, 544, 549–50, 555–6, 672
  and fiscal policy 564, 565, 608, 609
  and government expenditure 555–6
  and increase in aggregate demand 557
  and monetary policy 605–7
  and unit labour costs 545–9, 550
influence costs 339
information asymmetry 288, 292–3
  in labour markets 324, 327–8, 330–1, 341
information lag 569
information technology (IT) 392–3
injections, circular flow of income 498–9
innovation 36
  and 'creative destruction' 226–7, 266–7
  and market structure 287, 300, 301
  technical 392–3
  see also technical change
input prices 64, 151–2, 172–3, 176–7
  and output gap 544–9
  as supply shock 524
inputs 20, 132, 143–5, 160–1, 314–24
  costs 132–5
  demand 314–24
  derived demand 314–19
  fixed 144, 156–7
  lumpy 345
  mix 159–60
  and outputs 143–5
  and principle of substitution 160–1
  variable 144
  see also capital; costs; derived demand; factors of production; labour; land
inside assets 511

insurance:
  and asymmetric information 293, 327
  and perverse incentives 333–4
integration 388–99
  conglomerate 14, 395–9, 396–7
  horizontal 14, 389–90
  vertical 14, 390–5
interdependence, technological 390–1
interest:
  compound 352
  on debt 126–7
interest rates 418, 576–9, 588–602, 596–7
  and aggregate expenditure 592–3
  and demand for money 584–5, *587*, 588, *591*
  determination of 588–90
  discount rate 126
  equilibrium *591*
  exchange rates and capital flows 596–7, 642–8
  expected 359
  and government bonds 356, 359
  and inflation 358–60, 359, 416–17
  and investment 353–6, 464–5, 592–4, 598–9
  and IS–LM curves 598–602
  and market price 578–9
  and monetary policy 16–17, 418, 590–2
  and money supply 590–2, 593–4
  nominal 358–60, 359
  present value and 349–52, 353–6, 576–7
  real 358–60, 359, 464–5
  in transmission mechanism 592–4, 595–8, 596–7
intermediate goods and services 420
intermediate products 132
internal labour market 335–42
internal rate of return (*IRR*) 354, 364–6
international prices 491–2, 638, 640–2
international trade 485
  and comparative advantage 25, 625, 626
  and foreign exchange transactions 627–8
  growth of service inputs 35
  see also balance of payments accounts; exchange rates; exports; imports; open economies
intervention, *see* government intervention
intramarginal firms 202–3
investment 13, 345–76
  accelerator theory of 666–8, 669–70
  crowding out 556n., *608*, 610
  foreign 37–9, 124, 623
  global flows 37–9
  gross and net 425
  long-run policies 300
  and money supply 592–3
  options 364–5
  returns, *see* returns

saving–investment model of
  equilibrium GDP 470–1, **472,**
  497–9
see also capital; capital flows; interest
  rates; monetary transmission
  mechanism
investment appraisal 346, 352–73
  flexibility allowance 360
  in human capital 371–3
  internal rate of return (*IRR*)
    approach 364–6
  net present value (*NPV*) approach
    353–6, 358–60, 365–6, 371–3,
    398–9
  option pricing theory 361–3, **364–5**
  options **364–5**
  payback period criterion 354, 366–7
  personal 371–3
  in practice 367–8
  risk allowance 134, 356–7, 360–1
  and sunk costs 361–4
  treatment of inflation 357–60
  and value additivity 398
  wait-and-see approach 360–1, 363,
    364–5
  weighted average cost of capital 357
investment demand function 593, 598
investment expenditure 353–6,
  424–5, 463–6, 592–4, 598–9,
  666–8
  autonomous 466
  and changes in GDP 666–8
  and interest rates 353–6, 464–5,
    592–4, 598–9
investment flows 37–9
investment goods 424–5, 662–3
invisibles account 622–3
IS curve 598–9, 613–15
IS–LM model 594–602, 603–9,
  613–15

Japan:
  employment arrangements **337**
  lean production **169–70, 393**
Java programming language 168, 171
jobs, *see* employment
joint-stock companies 122
joint ventures **124,** 387–8
'just-in-time' methods **170,** 266, **393,**
  424

Kaldor, N. 238–9
Kalecki, M. 678–9
Kay, J. 138
Keynes, J. M. 457, **528,** 584
Keynesian economics 457, 501, **528,**
  613–14, 617–18, 671–2
  aggregate demand 501, **528**
  and business cycles 671–2, 681, 682
  consumption function 457, 458,
    462–3
  early Keynesians 613–14
  expectations (animal spirits) theory
    671
  fiscal policy 614, 672
  interventionist 562, 571, 672

and Keynesian revolution 501, **528**
  multiplier theory 668
  New Keynesians 617–18, 672
  SRAS curve **528,** 613–14
knowledge:
  and increasing returns 171–2
  knowledge-based theory of firm
    128–9, 377–8
Kondratieff cycles 660

labour 132, 144, 146–58, 314–24,
  545–9
  capital–labour ratio **156–7,** 160
  demand for 314–19, 321–2, 543;
    and output gap 545–9
  hours worked 320–1
  rental or purchase price of **347**
  specialization and division of 22–5,
    166, **169, 170,** 248
  substitutability 159–60
  supply of effort 319–24, **322–3**
  unit labour costs 545–9
  as variable cost 144, 146–58, 545–9
  see also employment; factors of
    production; human capital;
    productivity; unemployment;
    wages; working population
labour markets:
  globalization 37
  heterogeneity in 12–13
  internal 335–42
  signalling 330–1
labour productivity, *see* productivity
lags:
  and business cycles **559,** 665
  fiscal policy 569
Laidler, D. 616
land 132
large-scale production 166–8
law of diminishing returns 143,
  148–51, 155, 348
leakages, circular flow of income **472,**
  480, 498–9
lean production 166–8, **169–70, 393**
learning:
  by doing 25
  curves 25, 171
  and internal labour markets 336–8
  see also innovation; knowledge
leasing capital goods 368–70
leisure 320–1, **322–3**
licensing, as entry barrier 225
licensing arrangements **124**
life-cycle theory of consumption 457
lifetime employment **337**
lifetime income 342
limited liability companies 121–2
limited partnerships 121–2
liquidation, company **18–19,** 414–15,
  664
liquidity preference theory 590
living standards 29–34, 150, 416,
  438–40
  international comparisons 438–40,
    442
  and technological change 176

LM curve 599–600, 613–15
loans, to firms 126–7
long run 145, 158
  firms in 158–73, 222–7
  macroeconomic 452–3
  profit maximization **188–9,** 193
  see also very long run
long-run aggregate supply (*LRAS*)
  curve 521, 554–6, 557–62
long-run average cost (*LRAC*) curve
  161–4, **168,** 203–4, 237, 246–7
long-run cost 158–73
long-run decision making 158
long-run demand curves 97–9
long-run equilibrium 198–204,
  222–7, 236
long-run output 158–73
long-run returns 162–3
long-run supply curves 196; *see also*
  long-run aggregate supply curve
losses, as signal 202
lotteries 225
LRAC, see long-run average cost curve
LRAS, see long-run aggregate supply
  curve
Lucas aggregate supply theory 616,
  673–6, 679
lumpy consumption expenditure 663
lumpy inputs 345

M0 (monetary base) **580–1,** 590
M2 **580–1**
M3 **580–1**
M4 (broad money) **580–1**
M-form structure of business organization 381, 383–4
macroeconomic equilibrium 525–6
macroeconomic policy 418–19, 562,
  648–55, 672
  credibility 675–6
  stop–go 679–80
  targets and instruments 418–19
  unexpected 674–5
  see also fiscal policy; government
    intervention; monetary policy;
    stabilization policy
macroeconomics 5, 412–42, 446–81
  assumptions 450–4
  defined 412
  evolution 450
  and growth 560
  time-scale 452–3
  see also schools of macroeconomic
    thought
Major, John **566–7**
managed float 633
management buyouts 399
managers:
  incentives 13, 326–7
  and principal–agent theory 293,
    325–7
  skills 398–9
manufacturing:
  flexible 166–8, **169–70,** 177, 267
  lean production 166–8, **169–70, 393**
  mass production 166, **169**

Index

March, J. G., *see* Cyert, R. M. and March, J. G.
marginal cost (*MC*) 152, 153–5, 180–1, 185–9, 286–7
  and allocative efficiency 284–5, 286
  equal to marginal revenue 180–1, 185–9, 203, 286–7
  and profit maximization 185, *186*
  short-run 152, 153–5
  under monopoly 218–22
marginal cost pricing 298, 299, 300
marginal firms 202–3
marginal physical product (*MPP*) 315–16, 348
marginal product (*MP*) 146–51
marginal propensity not to spend 467–8, 480, 496
marginal propensity to consume (*MPC*) 459, 460, 494, *495*, 500, 504
marginal propensity to import 499, 500
marginal propensity to save (*MPS*) 461, 462, 498
marginal propensity to spend:
  and aggregate expenditure 467–8, 495, 496–7
  and multiplier **478,** 479–80, 499–500, 504, 568
marginal revenue (*MR*) 180–1, 184–9, 191–3, 203, 286–7
  equal to marginal cost 180–1, 185–9, 203, 286–7
  relationship with price ·192, 286–7
  and segmentation 233–4
  under monopoly 215–19, 233–4
marginal revenue product (*MRP*) 315–18
  of capital 348
  and seniority 341–2
market, concept of 66
market clearing, New Classical school 616–17, 673–5
market clearing wage 321–2
market economies 6
market entry and exit, *see* barriers to entry; entry and exit
market equilibrium 68–9
market externalities, *see* externalities
market failure 6, 279, 288–93, 391–5
market for corporate control 14–15, 250, 399–404
market mechanism 182
  or government intervention 278–9, 288–308, **552,** 553, 672
  and privatization 303
  and resource allocation 265–6
  and social goals 293–6
market power:
  monopolistic 288–9
  oligopolistic 247, 265–6
market price 65–72
  of financial assets 577–9
  GDP at 431–2, 438
  and interest rates 578–9

markets 5–6, 9
  competitive 69
  contestable 263–5
  corporate control 14–15, 250, 399–404
  foreign exchange **596–7,** 627–39, **644–5**
  graphical analysis of 67–9
  housing 464–5
  labour 12–13, 37, 330–1, 335–42
market share 258
market structure 10–12, 181–3
  and profit maximization 180–209
  see also imperfect competition; monopolistic competition; monopoly; oligopoly; perfect competition
Marshall, A. 329
mass production 166, **169**
'materials revolution' **174–5**
maturity date 126
maximization, *see* non-profit maximization; profit maximization
MBA, appraisal of investment in 371–3
MC, see marginal cost
measurement:
  of demand and supply 104–9
  of elasticity 86–95, **94**
  national income 432–4, 435–8
  national product 419–21, **420,** 432–4
  of opportunity cost 133–5
Menger, C. 616n.
mercantilism 625, **626**
merchandise account 621–2
mergers 14–15, 305–8, **306–8,** 399, 404
  conglomerate 397–8
  and demergers **396–7**
  see also corporate control; integration; takeovers
merit goods 295
microeconomic policy, *see* competition policy
microeconomics 5, 412
microelectronics 77–81, 84–5
minimization of cost 158–60, 391–5
minimum efficient scale 261, 262, 287–8, 298n.
mining (coal) industry **108–9,** 362
MMC, *see* Monopolies and Mergers Commission
mobile capital 649–54
models, *see* economic models
Modigliani, F. 457
monetarism 614–16, 670–1, 682
monetary aggregates **580–1**
monetary equilibrium 588–94, 599–600
monetary policy 590–2, **596–7,** 599–610, 642–8, 651–4, 670–2, 674–5
  and business cycles 670–2, 674–5
  compared with fiscal 595, 607–10

effect of changes 603–7, 610
  and exchange rates 418, **596–7,** 642–8, 651–4, 672
  and inflationary gaps 605–7
  and interest rates 16–17, 418, 590–2, **596–7**
  and *IS–LM* curves 599–602
  long-run effect 605–7
  in open economy **596–7**
  short-run effect 603–5
  and single European currency 596, 652
  see also supply of money
monetary shocks 591, 592–4, 603–7
monetary transmission mechanism 592–3, 595–8, **596–7,** 603–4, 648
money 575–610
  demand, *see* demand for money
  opportunity cost of 582
  quantity theory of **586,** 587, 607, **641**
  real and nominal 585–7, 601–2
  supply, *see* supply of money
  time value of 356
  velocity of circulation **586**
money balances 580–7
  precautionary 583–4
  real and nominal 585–7
  speculative 584–5
  transactions 582–3
money demand function 588
money price 71
monitoring, performance 325–7, 334–5, 382–4, 385, 388
Monopolies and Mergers Commission (MMC) 304, 305–8, **306–8**
monopolistic competition 11–12, 214, 234–9, 287; *see also* imperfect competition
monopolistic practices 288, 296–7
monopoly 11, 183, 214–34, 297–300
  barriers to entry 11, 222–6
  costs 215, 218–22
  and 'creative destruction' 226–7
  demand curves 215–22
  direct control of 297–300
  equilibrium 218–27
  firms in 214–34
  government intervention 297–300, 304–8
  inefficiency under 286, *287,* 288–9
  market power 288–9
  multi-plant 221–2
  multi-price 227–34
  natural 223, 297–300
  no supply curve for 220–1
  pricing 215–17, 227–34, 298–300
  profits 218–22
  revenue 215–18
  single-price 214–27, 234
  and vertical integration 394–5
  in very long run 300
moral hazard 292–3, 553
mortgages 464–5
motor industry 391–4
movements, *see* shifts and movements

MP, see marginal product
MPC, see marginal propensity to consume
MPP, see marginal physical product
MRP, see marginal revenue product
multi-divisional form (M-form) of business organization 381, 383–4
multinational enterprises (MNEs), *see* transnational corporations
multiple regression analysis 104–6
multiplier 476–80, **478**, 499–500, 529–32, 666–70
and *AD* curve 519–20, 602, 604–5
and *AE* curve 5*30*, 531
balanced-budget 505
and changes in government expenditure 502–3
and marginal propensity to spend **478**, 479–80, 499–500, 504, 568
and *SRAS* curve 529–32
and tax rates 504, 568
multiplier–accelerator theory of business cycles 666–70

Nash equilibrium 252–3, **256–7**
national debt, *see* budget deficit; Public Sector Borrowing Requirement (PSBR)
national defence 291–2
national expenditure 423–9, 454–68
composition 424–8
total 428–9
see also aggregate expenditure; consumption expenditure; government expenditure; investment expenditure; net exports
National Health Service 123
national income 421–42, 446–81
circular flow of 421–2, 423, 498–9
determination of 446–81
equilibrium, *see* equilibrium GDP
factor and non-factor payments 429–32
hydraulic analogy **472**
National Income Accounts 421–34
per capita 438–40
potential, *see* potential GDP
see also gross domestic product (GDP)
nationalization 301–2
National Lottery 225
national product 20, 412, 419–44, 446–81
measurement 419–21, **420**, 432–4
natural monopoly 223, 297–300
neighbourhood effects 289
Nelson, R. R. and Winter, S. G. 380
neoclassical economics, theory of the firm 129–30
neo-mercantilism **626**
net cash flow 355, 364–5, 366–7
net domestic product 432
net export function 488–92, 500, 512–13, 649, 653

net exports 427–8, 488–92, 500, 649
autonomous or induced 489–90, 500
net present value (*NPV*):
and decision to lease or buy 368–70
in investment appraisal 353–6, 358–60, 365–6, 371–3, 398–9
treatment of inflation 358–60
see also present value (*PV*)
net property income 433
New Classical theory 616–18, 665, 673–6
New Keynesian economics 617–18, 672
newspaper industry 109–13, 267, 268–72, **270–1**
nominal demand for money 585–7
nominal discount rate 358
nominal interest rate 358–60, **359**
nominal wages 522–3
non-cooperative equilibrium 251–4, 269–72
non-excludable public goods 291–2
non-market sector 123
non-price competition 246
non-profit maximization 64–5, 130
and evolutionary theory 380–1
maximization of present value 380
satisficing behaviour 130, 379
utility 47
non-rivalrous public goods 291–2
non-tariff barriers (NTBs) **125**
normal profits 137–8
North, D. 128
North Sea oil and gas 639
NPV, see net present value (*NPV*)

obsolete capital 204–7
Office of Fair Trading (OFT) 304, 305
OFGAS 205
oil industry:
OPEC 255
supply shocks 173, 176, 536, 681
oligopoly 11–12, 139, 214, 227, 247–76, 301–3
and allocative efficiency 287–8
barriers to entry 247, 249, 259–65
case studies 267–75, **270–1, 274–5**
and 'creative destruction' 266–7
differentiated product 244–6, 248, 249, 259–60
innovation in 287, 301
market power 247
profit maximization 139, 250–4, 266
profits 250, 259–65, 266
public control of 301–3
size of firms 248–50
strategic behaviour 247–8, 249, 250–65, **256–7**
see also game theory; imperfect competition
one-time costs 165–6
one-time games 256–7
OPEC, *see* Organization of Petroleum Exporting Countries

open economies 485–507
transmission mechanism **596–7**, 648
opportunity cost 21–2, 27, 133–5
and calculation of profits 136–8
of financial capital 134, 198–9, 356–7, 371–2
of money 582
of physical capital 348
optimality, Pareto **257**, 280
optimum output 186–9, 193–4
see also non-profit maximization; profit maximization
option pricing theory 361–3, **364–5**
options, call or put **364**
organizational structure 13–14, 120–3, 128, **131–2**, 378–99
co-ordination and 379–80, **392–3**
delayering 35, **392–3**
of firms 120–3, **120–1**
flattened **392–3**
and information technology **392–3**
multi-divisional form (M-form) 381, 383–4
portfolio form (P-form) 381, 384–8, **386–7**
and size of firms **392–3**
unitary form (U-form) 381–3
Organization of Petroleum Exporting Countries (OPEC) 255
organizations 12–14, 377–406
business integration 388–99
firms as 378–88
output:
and allocative efficiency 282–5
and costs 61, 142–77, 521
and input 143–5
long-run 158–73
national, *see* national product
optimum 186–9, 193–4
per capita *32*
and prices 521–2
short-run 146–51
and value added **420**
zero 185, 187
output gap 447–9, 544–9
outside assets 511
outsourcing 35, **393**
overshooting 642–8, 651, 653
ownership of firms 122, 125, 130, 326
nationalization 301–2
privatization **168**, 302–3, 308
public 297–8

P-form structure of business organization 381, 384–8, **386–7**
Panzar, J. C. 263
Pareto-optimality 257, 280
participation, labour force 320
partnerships 121, 122
passing off 225
patent laws 223–5, **224–5**
paternalism 295
pay:
incentive **322–3**, 330, 331–4
internal labour market 336–8

Index

pay (*cont.*):
 performance-related 332–3
 and promotion 336–8
 of senior and chief executives 339,
  340
 for superstars **328–9**
 see also wages
payback period 354, 366–7
payoff matrix 251–2, **254**
peaks in business cycles **414–15**
pegging, exchange rate 633, 634–6
pensions 412, 486
perfect capital mobility 649–55
perfect competition 10–11, 73,
  189–207
 assumptions 189–90
 demand curves 183, 190–3
 economic efficiency in 285–6
 entry and exit 190, 198–203
 in long run 198–204
 new capital 199
 prices and price taking 190, 192–3,
  196–7, 199–202
 profits and profit maximization
  184–8, 192–206
 revenue 190–3
 in short run 193–8, 203–4
 supply curves 194–6
 in very long run 204–7
performance monitoring 325–7
 and incentives 332–3, 334–5
 and organizational structure 382–4,
  385, 388
 ratchet effect 335
permanent-income theory 457, 462–3
perpetuities 577
personal disposable income 434,
  456–63, 493–4
perverse incentives 333–4
physical capital 9–10, 123, 346–70
 appraisal of investment in 346,
  352–73
 durability of 346–8
 leasing or buying 368–70
 marginal revenue product 348
 opportunity costs 348
 present value of future returns
  349–52
 see also capital goods
piece work 332
planned expenditure 454–5, 499–505
policies, *see* competition policy; fiscal
  policy; macroeconomic policy;
  monetary policy; stabilization
  policy
political business cycles 678–9
pollution 8, 441
population, and supply of labour 319
portfolio equilibrium 590
portfolio form (P-form) structure of
  business organization 381,
  384–8, **386–7**
portfolio investment 623
potential output (GDP) 447–9,
  544–9, 554–6
 long-run 554–6

 short-run 544–9
PPP, *see* purchasing power parity
precautionary balances 583–4
predatory pricing 113, 262–3, **307–8**
present value (*PV*) **347**, 349–56,
  358–60, 365–70, 576–8
 and decision to lease or buy 368–70
 discounting 349, 353–6, 368–70,
  576
 of firm 60
 of future returns 348, 349–52,
  358–60, 369–70, 576–8
 and inflation 358–60
 and interest rates 349–52, 353–6,
  576–7
 in investment appraisal 353–6,
  358–60, 365–6, 398–9
 of single future payment 349–50,
  576–7
 of stream of future payments
  350–1, 577–8
price differentiation, *see* segmentation
price elasticity of demand 86–99, **105**
 determinants of 95–9
 long- and short-run 97–9
 measurement of 86–95, **94**
 in newspaper industry 109–13, 269
 and segmentation **232–3**
 and slope of demand curve 85, 87,
  91–3
 under monopoly 217, 218–19
price elasticity of supply 101–4
price level 412, 510–36, 543–74,
  602–10
 and aggregate demand 514–20,
  525–6, 555–6
 and aggregate expenditure 510–14
 and aggregate supply 520–6
 changes in 510–36, 544–9, 602–10,
  638
 and consumption function 510–13
 and demand for money 585–7, 588
 and demand shocks 527–9, 532–5,
  550
 and equilibrium GDP 510–36,
  555–6, 603
 and exchange rates 638
 and GDP 453, 510–36, 543–62,
  602–10
 and inflation 71–2
 and multiplier 529–32
 and net export function 512–13
 and supply shocks 527, 535–6
 variable 509–10
 and wealth 510–12, 555
 see also inflation
price makers 245, 522
prices:
 absolute 71
 administered 245, 248
 break-even 202
 constant 435
 costs of changing 245–6
 and demand 49–59, 67–72
 entry-attracting 199–200
 equal to marginal revenue 192

 equilibrium 66, 67, 68–70, 196–7
 exit-inducing 200–2
 implicit 348
 input, *see* input prices
 international comparisons 491–2,
  638, 640–2
 labour, *see* wages
 and marginal cost 284–5, 286
 market 65–72, 431–2, 438, 577–9; of
  financial assets 577–9
 money 71
 oil 173, 176, 536
 and output 521–2
 relative 71
 rental or purchase **347**, 348
 short-run stability 245–6
 shut-down 185–6
 and supply 61–5
price system 8, 65–72
price takers 190, 192–3, 319, 521–2
pricing:
 average cost 298–9
 in imperfect competition 213–14,
  245–6, 248
 marginal cost 298, 299, 300
 monopoly 215–17, 227–34,
  298–300
 option 361–3, **364–5**
 predatory 113, 262–3, **307–8**
 road **78–9**
 under perfect competition 196–7,
  199–202
primary sector employment 335–6
principal–agent problem 130, 293,
  325–7
 incentives to overcome 326–7, **340**,
  379
 and internal labour market 338
principle of substitution 160–1
principle of value additivity 398
prisoner's dilemma 253, **254**, **257**
private costs 289–90
private limited companies 122
privatization **168**, 302–3, 308
producers 20, 60
product:
 average 146–51
 differentiated, *see* differentiated
  product
 homogeneous 189
 incremental 148
 innovation 36
 intermediate 132
 marginal 146–51
 marginal physical 315–16
 marginal revenue 315–18
 total 146–8
product design 170
product development costs 166,
  246–7, 249, 262
production:
 craft methods **169**
 flexible manufacturing 166–8,
  169–70, 177, 267
 as flow 143
 globalization of **125**, 394

'just-in-time' methods **170**, 266, **393**, 424
large-scale 166–8
lean 166–8, **169–70**, **393**
mass 166, **169**
see also output
production costs 61, 132–5
short-run 193–4
production function 143–5, 161, 172
and technical change 176–7
production-possibility boundary 25–8, 281–4
productive efficiency 280–2, **283**, 285, 286
productivity 31–4
diminishing average 147
and shifts in *SRAS* curve 525, 550
in UK (1920–95) 31–2
and wages 546–9, 550, 551–3
profit and loss account 136–7
profit maximization 60, 129–30, **131–2**, 158–60, 180–209
and derived demand 314–15
long-run **188–9**, 193
marginal cost and marginal revenue 180–1, 185–9
and market structure 180–209
and present value of firm 60
rules for 185–9
and segmentation 227–34
short-run **188**, 192–3
under monopoly 218–31
under oligopoly 139, 250–4, 266
under perfect competition 184–8, 192–206
see also non-profit maximization
profits 133, 136–9
added value as 138
and business cycles 664
cyclical 664
definitions of 136–8
economic and accounting 136–7
long-run **188–9**, 193
and market entry 198–202, 222, 226, 235, 259–65
maximization, *see* profit maximization
monopolistic 219–20
and National Income Accounts 430
normal and supernormal 137–8
oligopolistic 250, 259–65, 266
opportunity cost and calculation of 136–8
in perfect competition 197–8
pure 137
and segmentation 228–31
short-run 197–8
as signals 139, 198–202, 222, 226, 235, 259–65
and takeovers 402–3
undistributed 125
zero-profit equilibrium 199, 202
promotion 336–8, 341–2
propensities:
not to spend 467–8, 480, 496

to consume 459, 460, 494, *495*, 500, 504
to import 499, 500
to save 461–2, 498
to spend 467–8, 479–80, 495, 496–7, 500, 504
PSBR, *see* Public Sector Borrowing Requirement
public corporations 122
public goods 288, 291–2
public limited companies 122
public ownership:
natural monopolies 297–8
see also nationalization
Public Sector Borrowing Requirement (PSBR) 487
purchase price:
of labour **347**
of physical capital 348
purchasing power parity (PPP) 439, 492n., 640–2, *641*
see also exchange rates
pure profits 137
put options 364
PV, see present value

quality control 7
quantity theory of money 586, 587, 607
and exchange rates **641**

random shocks:
and business cycles 664–5
and exchange rates **644–5**
ratchet effect 335
rational expectations 616–18, 673–4, 679
real business cycle (RBC) theory 617, 665, 676–8, 680
real discount rate 358
real exchange rate 642, *643*
real money balances 585–7
real rate of interest 358–60, *359*, 464–5
real wages 522–3
recession 15, 412, 562
and demand for labour 543, 661, 681
and exchange rates 647–8
and investment expenditure 464
and paradox of thrift 565–7, **566–7**
and wages 547–9, 553
recessionary gap 448, 544, 545–9, 559–60, 672
and fiscal policy *563*, 564
and unit labour costs 545–9
recovery, economic **414–15**
redemption date 126–7
redistribution of income 294; *see also* distribution of income
regression analysis 104–6
regulation:
of competition 223–5, 296–7, 301–2
and deregulation 302–3
financial 225
of market entry 225

and regulatory capture 301–2
of vertical integration 395
Reid, G. C. 163–4
relational contracts 324–5
relative prices 71
rent:
economic **200–1**, 429
imputed 429
rental periods 346–7
rental price 347, 348
repeated games **257**
replacement investment 425
research and development (R&D) 165–6, 171
reservation wages 327–8
reserve currency 630
residential investment 425, 464–5; *see also* housing
resource allocation 17–28, 139, 279–88, 298–9
and market mechanism 265–6
profits as signals 139, 199
see also efficiency; resources
resource-based theory of the firm 128–9, 377–8
resources 17–20
common property 290–1
restrictive practices 288, 296–7, 304–5
Restrictive Practices Court (RPC) 304
Retail Price Index (RPI) 412
returns:
on capital 134
constant 163
decreasing 163, 164
from takeovers 400–3
future 348
increasing 162, 165–72
internal rate of return (*IRR*) 354, 364–6
law of diminishing 143, 148–51, 155
long-run 162–3
and risk 134, 356–7
revenue:
government 486–8, 567–8
incremental 184–5, **188–9**, 190–3, 215–18
in perfectly competitive firms 190–3
under monopoly 215–18
see also marginal revenue
revenue curves 185
reward structures 13
Ricardo, D. **200–1**
rising-cost industries 298, 299
risk:
aversion to 584
CEOs as risk takers 340
diversification 385–6, 398
exchange rate 645
and return on investment 134, 356–7, 360–1
risk premium 134, 356–7
road transport:
bus services **306–8**
and public goods 292
road pricing **78–9**

Index

Robbins, Lord L. 616n.
robotics 166
RPC, *see* Restrictive Practices Court
RPI, *see* Retail Price Index

Sangster, A. 367–8
Sargent, T. 616
satisfaction maximization 47
satisficing 130, 379
saving 456, 461–2, 470–1, **472**, 497–9
   propensity to save 461–2, 498
   saving–investment model of
     national income 470–1, **472**,
     497–9
   and thrift paradox 564–7, **566–7**
   and wealth 511–12
saving function 461–2
scale:
   decreasing returns to 163, 164
   increasing returns to 162, 165–72
   minimum efficient 261, 262, 287–8,
     298n.
   see also economies of scale
scarcity 20–1, 27
schools of macroeconomic thought
   613–18
   Austrian 616–17
   early Keynesian 613–14
   modern Keynesian 615–16
   monetarist 614–16, 670–1, 682
   New Classical 616–18, 665, 673–6
   New Keynesian 617–18, 672
   see also Keynesian economics
Schumpeter, J. 226–7, 266–7, 671n.
Schwartz, A. 671, 672
secondary sector employment 335–6
Securities and Investment Board (SIB)
   225
segmentation 227–34, **232–3**
self-employment 429
semiconductor industry 77–81
senior and chief executives 339, **340**
seniority 341–2
services 6, 20
   employment in 34–6
   for final consumption 36, 420
set-up costs 223, 261–2
sex composition, labour force 320
shareholders:
   returns from takeovers 400–3
   separation of ownership and control
     130, 326
shares 123–5
   effect of takeovers on 400–2
shifts and movements:
   aggregate demand curve 514, 518,
     519–20, 527–32, 564–7
   aggregate expenditure curve 474–6,
     510–13, 514, 533–5
   aggregate supply curve 524–5, 550,
     552, 557–8, 560–2
   demand curves 54–9
   supply curve 63–5
shocks:
   demand, *see* aggregate demand
     shock

exogenous 664–5
monetary 591, 592–3, 603–7
random 664–5
supply, *see* aggregate supply shock
short run 144–5, 146–58
   macroeconomic 452
   output optimization 193–4
   profitability 197–8
short-run aggregate supply (*SRAS*)
   curve 521–6
   changes in money supply 603–7
   cyclical fluctuations and 560–2
   demand shocks and 527–9, 531–5,
     550–4, **552**
   Keynesian **528**, 613–14
   and multiplier 529–32
   and output gap 544–9
   and price level 521–6
   shape of 521–3, 532–5
   shifts and movements in 524–5,
     550, **552**, 557–8, 560–2
   supply shocks and 527, 535–6
short-run average total cost (*SRATC*)
   curve 203–4
short-run costs 151–8
   and perfect competition 193–4,
     195–6
   relationship with long-run cost
     172–3
   under monopoly 215
short-run demand curves 97–9
short-run equilibrium 188
   under monopolistic competition
     235–6
   under monopoly 218–21
   under perfect competition 193–8,
     203–4
short-run marginal cost (*SRMC*) 152,
   153–5, 203
short-run output 146–51
short-run profit maximization 188,
   192–3
short-run supply curves:
   absent under monopoly 220–1
   of firm 194–6
   of industry 195–6, *197*
   see also short-run aggregate supply
     curve (*SRAS*)
shut-down price 185–6
SIB, *see* Securities and Investment
   Board
signalling, labour market 327, 330–1
signals:
   losses as 202
   profits as 139, 198–202, 222, 226,
     235, 259–65
   quantity sold as 245
   wage rates as 327, 330–1
single European currency 596, 652
single proprietorships, *see* sole traders
size of firms:
   oligopolistic 248–50
   and organizational structure **392–3**
   and shape of cost curves 163–4
   and use of specialized technology
     166

skills, management 398–9
slack, organizational 379
Sloan, Jr., A. P. 381
slumps 414–15, 547–8
Smith, Adam **169**, 248
social costs 289–90
social obligations 295–6
sole traders 120–1, 122
South West Water PLC 305
specialization of labour 22–5, 166,
   170
speculation 639
speculative demand for money
   584–5
Spietoff, A. 671n.
SRAS, see short-run aggregate supply
   curve
SRATC, see short-run average total
   cost curve
SRMC, see short-run marginal cost
stabilization policy 500–1, 553,
   562–71, 670–6, 678–81, 682
   or automatic stabilizers 567–8
   and business cycles 16–17, 450,
     562–71, 670–6, 678–81
   and economic growth 570–1
   and exchange rates 418, **596–7**,
     642–8, 651–4, 672
   see also fiscal policy; government
     intervention; monetary policy
stagflation 535, 536
stakeholders 130, 379–80
standards:
   industry 168–71
   of living, *see* living standards
sterling:
   demand for pounds 628–31, 636–7
   as reserve currency 630
   supply of pounds 628, 631–2
sticky wages 553
Stockman, A. 676–7
stocks 347, 424
   capital 425
   and just-in-time production **170**,
     266, 424
   stockbuilding 424, 464
stocks and shares, *see* shares
stop–go government policy 679–80
strategic behaviour 247–8, 249,
   250–65
   competitive 251–4, 258–9
   co-operative 250–1, 255–8
   and equilibrium concepts 252–3,
     256–7
   strategies **256–7**
structural change 639
subsidiary firms 384–8, 391–3
subsidies:
   cross 301
   in National Income Accounts 431
substitutes and substitution:
   demand 55, 74–5
   in elasticity of demand 95–6, 101
   principle of 160–1
substitution effect 320–1, **322–3**,
   329–30

sunk costs 135, 263–4, 346, 361–4
 of entry 263–4
 future 361–4
 and investment appraisal 346,
  361–4
 past 135, 361
sun spot theory of business cycles
  680–1
supernormal profits 137–8
superstars, economics of **328–9**
suppliers:
 co-ordination of 393
 long-term relationships **174–5**,
  392–3
supply 60–5
 in action 72–81, **73**
 elasticity of 101–4
 excess 68
 'laws' of supply and demand 69–71,
  70
 see also aggregate supply (*AS*);
  demand and supply
supply curves 62–3
 absent under monopoly 220–1
 coal **108–9**
 and demand curves 67–9
 effect of new entrants 199
 identification problem 106–9
 and input prices 64, 524
 of labour 320–1, **322–3**
 long-run 196
 shifts and movements in 63–5
 short-run 194–6, *197*, 220–1
 slope of 102–3
 and technical change 65
 see also aggregate supply curve; long-
  run aggregate supply curve
  (*LRAS*); short-run aggregate
  supply curve (*SRAS*)
supply function 61
supply of effort 319–24, **322–3**
supply of money 579, 590–3, 670–1,
  673–6
 and aggregate demand 592–4, *595*,
  670–1
 and business cycles 670–1, 673–6
 changes in 592–4, **596–7**, 603–7
 and interest rates 590–2, 593–4
 and investment 592–4
 and money multiplier
 of pounds 628, 631–2
 see also monetary policy
supply schedule 61–2, 63, 66
supply-side policies 672
surplus:
 balance of payments 625–7
 budget 487–8
 consumer 228–30, 284

tacit collusion 255
takeovers 14–15, 399–404
 effects of 400–4
 hostile 400, 404
 returns to shareholders 400–3
 winner's curse **402–3**
 see also integration; mergers

taste, consumer 57
taxation:
 direct taxes 431
 disincentive effects 323
 and fiscal policy 503–4, 562, 564
 government revenue from 486, 487,
  567–8
 income tax 323, 493–4, 498
 indirect taxes 431
 and National Income Accounts 431,
  486, 487–8
 value added tax (VAT) 431
Tax Exempt Special Savings Accounts
  (TESSAs) **566–7**
tax rates 487–8, 503–4, 518
 and multiplier 504, 568
tax wedge 431, 568
TC, see total cost
technical change:
 endogenous 173–7, **174–5**
 and job structure 34–6
 and organizational structure 392–3
 and supply curves 65
 in very long run 173–7, **189**, 204–6,
  300
 see also innovation; knowledge
technical efficiency 158, **283**
technological interdependence 390–1
technology, and returns to scale
  166–71
telecommunications industry 300
television industry 225, **306–8**
tender offers 400
term of debt 126
TFC, see total fixed cost
theory of games 251–4, **256–7**, 273–6
third-party effects 289
thrift, paradox of 564–7, **566–7**
time:
 as dimension of investment
  decisions 346–8
 individual rate of preference 373
 'just-in-time' methods **170**, 266,
  393, 424
 lifetime employment **337**
 lifetime income 342
 present and future of physical capital
  346–7
 time-scale in macroeconomics
  452–3
 time value of money 356
 see also present value
The Times elasticity of demand
  109–13, 268–9
Tirole, J. 394n.
TNCs, *see* transnational corporations
Tobin, J. 584, 616
Tomkins PLC 14, 396–7, 398
total cost (*TC*) 152, 153–4
total fixed cost (*TFC*) 152, 153–4
total product (*TP*) 146–8
total revenue (*TR*) 184–5, 191–3
 under monopoly 216–18
total variable cost (*TVC*) 152, 153–4
tournaments 338–41
Toyota 393, 623

TP, see total product
trade:
 balance of **626**
 deficit and surplus 625–7
 volume of **626**
 see also international trade
trade account 621–2
trade cycles, *see* business cycles
trade marks **225**
transaction costs 128–9
transactions demand for money
  582–3, 609
transfer payments 426, 570–1
transmission mechanism, *see* monetary transmission mechanism
transnational corporations (TNCs)
  37, 123, **124–5**
transport:
 air **232–3**, 246–7
 bus services **306–8**
 cross-Channel journeys 72–6,
  267–8, 272–3, **274–5**
 road pricing **78–9**
troughs in business cycles **414–15**
TVC, see total variable cost

U-form structure of business
  organization 381–3
UK Atomic Energy Authority 205
uncertainty:
 in input market 393–4
 and investment 348, 365
uncovered interest parity 651
underground activity 440–1
undistributed profits 125
unemployment 412, 417, 448–9,
  660–1
 cyclical 30, 660–1, 681
 deadweight loss from 448–9
 and inflation 660–1, 676, 679–80
 New Keynesian theories of 617–18
 and output gap 549
 and paradox of thrift 565–6
 and supply shocks 660–1
 supply-side policies 672
 see also employment; labour;
  working population
unemployment benefits 486
unitary form (U-form) **of business
  organization** 381–3
unit costs 152, 521–2, **533**
unit elasticity of demand 88, 89
unit labour costs 545–9, 550, 551–4
upstream integration 389
user cost, *see* opportunity cost
utility maximization 47
utilization, capacity 151, 155, **157**,
  533
 normal rate of 448, 544

value:
 future 352
 present, *see* present value
value added 419–21, **420**
value added tax (VAT) 431
value additivity principle 398

Index

variable costs 137, 152–5, **157**
  labour as 144, 146–58
variable factors 144
velocity of circulation of money 586
vertical differentiation 244
vertical integration 14, 390–5
  and technological interdependence
    390–1
very long run 145, 173–7, 204–7
  competition 258–9, 266–7
  monopoly 300
  profit maximization **189,** 193
  reaction to oil supply shocks 176
  and technical change 173–7, **189,**
    204–6, 300
visible account 621–2
volume of trade **626**
von Mises, L. 616n.

wage rates 315–22
  cyclical 664
  income and substitution effects
    320–1, **322–3,** 329–30
  market clearing 321–2
  and output gap 545–9

signalling effect 327, 330–1
wages:
  contracts 324–5, 546n.
  efficiency 327–31, 338, 553
  flexible or inflexible 551–3
  incentive pay **322–3,** 330, 331–4,
    340
  and inflation 546n.
  nominal 522–3
  and output gap 545–9
  and productivity 546–9, 550, 551–3
  real 522–3
  rental or purchase price 347
  reservation 327–8
  sticky 553
  of superstars **328–9**
  in UK (1940–95) 32–3
  see also labour; pay
wait-and-see investment policies
  360–1, 363, **364–5**
Wallace, N. 616
war, and cyclical fluctuations 562, 681
wealth:
  and consumption function 463
  and demand for money 576, 584–5

effect of price level changes 510–12
  and saving 511–12
weighted average cost of capital
  (*WACC*) 357
Wicksell, K. 671n.
Williamson, O. 128, 383n.
Willig, R. D. 263
winner's curse 402–3
Winter, S. G., *see* Nelson, R. R. and
  Winter, S. G.
work-in-progress 424
working population 320
  UK (1900–95) 29–30
  women in 320
work–leisure choice 320–1, **322–3**
World Trade Organization (WTO) 37

X-inefficiency 283

yields 365–6

Zantac 11, 171, 223
Zeneca PLC 14
zero output 185, 187
zero-profit equilibrium 199, 202

CHAPTER 20

Government Policy and the Business Cycle

Characteristics of business cycles	660		Policy invariance	674
Inflation and unemployment	660		Policy credibility	675
Industry cycles	661		The Lucas critique	676
Profits and wages	664		Real business cycles	676
			Key propositions and criticisms	677
Theories of the cycle	664		Policy implications	678
Systematic or random shocks	664		The political business cycle	678
Cyclical adjustment mechanisms	665		Stop–go	679
The accelerator theory of investment	666		Supply shocks	680
Multiplier–accelerator interaction	668			
			Macroeconomics: the unfulfilled promise	681
Controversies about the cause of cycles				
and the role of government	670		**Summary**	683
The monetarist approach	670			
The Keynesian approach	671		**Topics for review**	684
The New Classical approach	673			
The Lucas aggregate supply function	673		**Questions for discussion**	684

THE macroeconomic model that we built up in the previous chapters helps us to explain the determinants of the price level and deviations of GDP from potential. Here we extend our study of the behaviour of the economy a step further by taking a closer look at the cyclical nature of fluctuations in activity and the role of government in these cycles. Understanding the cycle in the economy is of vital importance for business, as we pointed out in Chapter 1, because sustainable businesses have to ride out recessions as well as take advantage of booms. Not without reason is the cycle in the economy now known as the 'business cycle'.

Business cycles have been observed for almost as long as recorded history. The Old Testament, for example, talks about a pattern in which seven good years are followed by seven lean years. In more recent times, the cyclical nature of economic activity has been equally apparent, and scholars have long tried to establish regularities in the data.

Some have tried to make a case for the existence of a *long-wave* cycle, with a duration